Estimation of the Expected Market Risk Premium for Corporate Valuations

Schriften zur quantitativen Wirtschaftswissenschaft

Herausgegeben von Gunter Löffler,
Frank Richter und Paul Wentges

Band 4

PETER LANG
Frankfurt am Main · Berlin · Bern · Bruxelles · New York · Oxford · Wien

Hannes Gsell

Estimation of the Expected Market Risk Premium for Corporate Valuations

Methodologies and Empirical Evidence for Equity Markets in Key Countries

PETER LANG
Internationaler Verlag der Wissenschaften

Bibliographic Information published by the Deutsche Nationalbibliothek
The Deutsche Nationalbibliothek lists this publication in the Deutsche Nationalbibliografie; detailed bibliographic data is available in the internet at http://dnb.d-nb.de.

Zugl.: Ulm, Univ., Diss., 2010

Umschlaggestaltung und Lichtbildwerk:
Olaf Glöckler, Atelier Platen, Friedberg

D 289
ISSN 1869-277X
ISBN 978-3-631-61401-3

www.peterlang.de

Preface

Although discounted-cash-flow models have been applied in practice and research earlier to extract implied valuation parameters like discount rates or long-term growth rates, the publication by Claus/Thomas (2001) in the Journal of Finance represents a milestone. It was (or still is) not uncommon to use a market risk premium of around 5 to 6% in order to determine the cost of capital for valuation purposes. This range has some support based on empirical observations of average historical rates of return of stock market indices relative to proxies for risk-free rates. "Equity premia as low as three percent" was the question raised by Claus/Thomas, which they support by their analyses on the basis of a model, that incorporates analysts' earnings expectations, certain terminal value assumptions, and observed market prices. The impact on the results of common valuation models is material: Assuming for the purpose of illustration a risk-free rate of 4%, then the value of one Euro in perpetuity is 10.53 Euros if the risk premium is 5.5% or 14.29 Euros if it is only 3%—a difference of some 35%.

In the years afterwards, a broad variety of models have been developed and applied. The instant work by Hannes Gsell includes the vast majority of such models, properly defines them in terms of methodology and practical application. Furthermore, those models are applied within a comprehensive empirical study including equity markets in Canada, France, Germany, Japan, U.K., and U.S.A. for the period from 1989 to 2006 and for Germany even until 2009. He provides ample evidence that the variation in the market risk premium is higher than the difference between 5.5% and 3% suggests. The capital market conditions and expectations as a whole, including but not limited to interest rates, are relevant when determining market risk premia, and it is possible that these fluctuate between zero and 10%. Of course, this has huge implications for practical valuations. But, as Hannes Gsell rightfully points out, there are no good reasons to use current interest rates in combination with risk premia based on historical averages to determine discount rates for expected cash flows. In the German valuation practice the "Stichtagsprinzip" is widely accepted with regards to the risk-free rate, and it should be as well for the market risk premium.

This monograph is an excellent summary of implied cost-of-capital methods and it contains insightful empirical analyses. I recommend it to everyone who deals with business valuation.

Frank Richter
Ulm, October 2010

Preliminary Remarks and Acknowledgements

This piece of research was accepted as doctoral thesis by the faculty of mathematics and economics at Ulm University in 2010. Given my professional background in investment banking, conducting research in the area of corporate valuation was a natural choice. The dissertation is focused on the estimation of the expected market risk premium (MRP) for corporate valuations and provides a comprehensive conceptual review of currently available estimation methodologies as well as a large-scale empirical study for six key global equity markets. While this book is based on a rigorous academic analysis, the estimation of the expected MRP for corporate valuations is a very practical issue. Today, academic researchers as well as practitioners predominantly infer the expected MRP from historical averages. This thesis, however, argues for the adoption of expected MRP estimates implied by valuation models, market prices, and analysts' estimates reflecting the capital market conditions at the valuation date according to the "Stichtagsprinzip". The empirical analyses provided in this book demonstrate the volatility of the expected MRP over time (in particular throughout the recent financial crisis) which underlines the importance of expected MRP estimates for specific valuation dates. Despite certain limitations, implied expected MRP estimates appear preferable to historical averages and should become more frequently used by valuation practitioners.

Several people have contributed to the success of this research project and I am very grateful for their support.

Firstly, I want to thank my academic advisor Prof. Dr. Frank Richter for guiding me towards this very interesting subject and for the ongoing discussions which have provided me with very helpful suggestions to structure the dissertation. I am particularly thankful for his patience given the delays due to my professional obligations. His support was truly invaluable.

Secondly, I would like to thank Prof. Dr. Kai-Uwe Marten for acting as co-referee of my thesis and Prof. Dr. Leo Brecht as chairman of the doctoral committee.

Thirdly, I would like to thank current and former colleagues at the German office of Goldman Sachs for supporting my doctoral project and granting me the required freedom to successfully complete this project. In particular, I would like to express my sincere gratitude to Dorothee Blessing, Dr. Wolfgang Fink, and Dr. Marcus Schenck.

Fourthly, I am indebted to Udo Kießlich and Prof. Dr. Leo Schuster for reviewing my manuscript. In addition, I want to thank current and former colleagues at the Institute of Strategic Management and Finance (Ulm University) for their support.

Lastly, this dissertation would not have been possible without the tremendous encouragement and love of my parents, my grandparents, and Salima. You supported me at all times despite the constraints for our family life. To all of you I would like to dedicate this book.

Hannes Gsell
Seebruck/Frankfurt, December 2010

Contents

List of Exhibits[1]

[1] Note that exhibits without a source are based on own calculations by the author.

List of Tables[2]

[2] Note that tables without a source are based on own calculations by the author.

List of Abbreviations

ACF	autocorrelation function
adj.	adjusted
AG	Aktiengesellschaft
agg	aggregation
AGM	annual general meeting
AMEX	American Stock Exchange
arith.	arithmetic
avg.	average
CAC	cotation assistée en continu
CAD	Canadian-Dollar
CAGR	compounded annual growth rate
CAP	earnings capitalization model
CAPM	capital asset pricing model
CDAX	Composite Deutscher Aktienindex
CFO	chief financial officer
coeff.	coefficient
Comp.	composite
conv.	convergence
CRSP	Center for Research in Security Prices of the University of Chicago
DAX	Deutscher Aktienindex
DCF	discounted cash flow
DIV	dividend discount and dividend growth model
div.	dividend
DJ	Dow Jones
DPS	dividends per share
DS	Datastream
EBI(DA)AT	earnings before interest (and depreciation/amortization) after taxes
EBIT(DA)	earnings before interest and taxes (and depreciation/amortization)

ed.	edition
ed(s).	editor(s)
EFP	explicit forecast period
e.g.	exempli gratia
EPS	earnings per share
et al.	et alii
etc.	et cetera
EUR	Euro
ew	equal-weighted
excl.	excluding
exp.	expected
FAUB	Fachausschuss für Unternehmensbewertung und Betriebswirtschaft
FAZ	Frankfurter Allgemeine Zeitung
ff.	and the following pages
fn.	footnote
FTSE	Financial Times and the London Stock Exchange
GAAP	Generally Accepted Accounting Principles
GBP	Great Britain Pound
GDP	gross domestic product
geo.	geometric
govt.	government
GTIS	Global Treasury Information System
hist.	historical
HPS	Hotelling-Pabst-statistic
IAS	International Accounting Standards
IBES (I/B/E/S)	Institutional Brokers' Estimate System
IDW	Institut der Wirtschaftsprüfer
i.e.	id est
IFRS	International Financial Reporting Standards
i.i.d.	independent and identically distributed
Inc.	Incorporated
incl.	including

ind.	industry
IPO	initial public offering
IRR	internal rate of return
JKM	Jacquier/Kane/Marcus estimator
JPY	Japanese-Yen
LBO	leveraged buyout
LID	linear information dynamics
lt.	long-term
LTG	long-term growth
LTM	last twelve months
MLE	maximum likelihood estimator
MPEG	modified PEG
MRP	market risk premium
MSCI	Morgan Stanley Capital International
MSE	mean squared error
MV	market value
n.	number
NA	not available
NAp	not applicable
Nasdaq	National Association of Securities Dealers Automated Quotations
nn.	numbers
nom.	nominal
NOSH	number of shares outstanding
NPV	net present value
NSS	Nelson/Siegel/Svensson model
NV	naamloze vennootschap
NYSE	New York Stock Exchange
OLS	ordinary-least-squares
OTC	over-the-counter
p.	page
PB (P/B)	price-to-book ratio
PE (P/E)	price earnings ratio

PEG	price-earnings-to-growth ratio
perp.	perpetual
PGR	perpetual growth rate
pp.	pages
reg.	regression
REX(P)	Deutscher Rentenindex (Performance)
RI	residual income/earnings
RIV	residual income/residual earnings model
S&P	Standard & Poor's
SEC	Securities and Exchange Commission
s.o.p.	see original publication
st. dev.	standard deviation
Strips	separate trading of registered interest and principal securities
T-bill/bond	treasury bill/bond
TOPIX	Tokyo Stock Price Index
TSE	Tokyo Stock Exchange
TSX	Toronto Stock Exchange
TV	terminal value
UK	United Kingdom
US	United States
USD	US-Dollar
US-GAAP	United States Generally Accepted Accounting Principles
Vol.	volume
vw	value-weighted
WMR	WM/Reuters
WS	Worldscope
YRS	years

List of Symbols

$\sim$	symbol for random variables
$-$	symbol for mean
$\wedge$	symbol for estimated parameter from sample, realization of random variable
$\lvert\bullet\rvert$	modulus
#	number
α,β	linear regression coefficients
β	beta factor
$\beta_{0,1,2,3}$	coefficients in NSS-model
δ	dividend yield
ε	error term
ζ	distribution difference
η	convergence factor
θ	payout ratio
μ	true mean of a distribution
π	inflation rate
ρ	correlation coefficient
σ^2	variance
σ	standard deviation
$\tau_{(c,d,\, i,\, cg)}$	(corporate, dividend, interest, and capital gain) tax rate
$\tau_{1,2}$	converge parameter in NSS-model
∞	infinite
a,b,c,h,o,w	multi-purpose parameters
A	arithmetic mean
agr	agr term of CAP model
B	book value
C	cash flow
$\operatorname{cov}[\bullet;\bullet]$	covariance
d	days, difference

D	dividend
Dur	duration (Macaulay)
E	earnings
E^c	cum-dividend earnings
$E[\bullet]$	unconditional expected value
$E_s[\bullet]$	conditional expected value at s
exp	Euler's number
f	free float factor
f	dividend payment frequency
F	face value
g	growth rate
G	geometric mean, compounded growth rate
H_0	null hypothesis
i,j,J	index parameters
k	cost of capital, investment horizon
K	chaining factor
l	parameter vector
ln	natural logarithm
log	logarithm
m	multiple, months
M	index for market portfolio
n	number of shares outstanding, number of observations, index for nominal
p	p-value, index for perpetuity
P	price/equity value
r	return, continuous return, index for real Note: The differentiation between upper/lower-case letters for discrete/continuous returns is only used when both definitions appear in the same context. Otherwise, a lower case letter is generally used to denote returns.
R	discrete return, rank
$R[\bullet]$	rank
(adj.) R^2	(adjusted) R-squared
r^b	return on book equity

r_{cg}	capital gain
r^e	cost of equity
r^f	risk-free rate
r^p	market risk premium (MRP)
r^s	risk surcharge
r_τ	after personal tax return
$r_{t,t+1} / r_{t,T}$	forward rate (one-period return)/spot rate
$r_{u,l}$	unlevered, levered return
$r_{uc,c}$	unconditional, conditional return
r_{YTM}	yield-to-maturity
s,t,u	time index parameters
S	compounded return estimator
$se[\bullet]$	standard error
$std[\bullet]$	standard deviation
t	t-statistic
T	end of time period (number of observations), Wilcoxon test parameter
$T_{(d, i, cg)}$	(dividend, interest, and capital gain) tax factor
U	index for uniform, unbiased
v	variance ratio
$V^{(E,D)}$	value (equity, debt)
$var[\bullet]$	variance
y	year, parameter in general valuation model
Z	Z-value

1 Introduction

1.1 Relevance and problem formulation

The market risk premium (MRP) is a core element of financial economics and a key parameter for evaluating the performance of equity markets worldwide. It represents the difference between the rate of return on the market portfolio of stocks and the risk-free rate[3]. This definition can be further substantiated by specifying whether the MRP is determined from a historical (ex-post MRP) or forward-looking (ex-ante/expected MRP) perspective[4]. While only ex-post MRPs are directly observable from market data, most financial decisions require an estimate of the expected MRP. E.g., individual investors and asset managers take the expected MRP into consideration when deciding which fraction of their portfolio to invest in equity, bonds, or other assets[5]. Competition authorities trying to set an appropriate level for allowed returns in a regulated industry also need the expected MRP as an essential input parameter[6]. Furthermore, the expected MRP has a fundamental role in determining a firm's cost of capital for capital budgeting decisions and corporate valuations[7] applied by managers, controllers, investment bankers, or auditors. From a corporate law perspective, it is relevant for auditors, e.g., to determine the adequacy of valuations for squeeze-outs or statutory mergers[8].

Until today, expectations of the MRP have been predominantly[9] derived by assuming that the unconditional average of realized (ex-post) MRPs over the longest possible

---

3 See, e.g., Cornell, B. (1999), p. 18, Mehra, R./Prescott, E. (2003), p. 891, Cochrane, J. (2005), pp. 8-9, Copeland, T./Weston, F./Shastri, K. (2005), p. 171, Ross, S./Westerfield, R./Jaffe, J. (2008), p. 267, Goetzmann, W./Ibbotson, R. (2006), p. 3, Richter, F. (2006a), p. 4, Mehra, R./Prescott, E. (2008), p. 2, and Brealey, R./Myers, S./Allen, F. (2008), p. 175.

4 See Cornell, B. (1999), p. 19.

5 See Cornell, B. (1999), p. 1.

6 See Cooper, I. (1996), p. 158. See also Maddox, F./Pippert, D./Sullivan, R. (1995). See also Bundesnetzagentur (2008), pp. 14-17 and Frontier Economics (2008) for an example of using the MRP to determine allowed returns in the regulated utilities sector.

7 See, e.g., Cornell, B. (1999), p. 1, Welch, I. (2000), p. 501, Arnott, R./Ryan, R. (2001), p. 61, Fama, E./French, K. (2002), p. 637, Drobetz, W. (2000), p. 366, Drobetz, W. (2003a), p. 4, Jacquier, E./Kane, A./Marcus, A. (2005), p. 38, and Goetzmann, W./Ibbotson, R. (2006), pp. 7-8.

8 See, e.g., Marten, K.-U./Müller, S. (2005), p. 977 and Marten, K.-U./Quick, R./Ruhnke, K. (2007), pp. 663-669.

9 See, e.g., Brennan, M. (1997), p. 82, Welch, I. (2000), p. 503, Claus, J./Thomas, J. (2001), p. 1629, Gebhardt, W./Lee, C./Swaminathan, B. (2001), p. 136, Fama, E./French, K. (2002), p. 637, Brennan, M. (2003), p. 185, Stehle, R. (2004), p. 910, Goetzmann, W./Ibbotson, R. (2006), p. 4, and Wagner, W./Saur, G./Willershausen, T. (2008), p. 739. See also Elton, E. (1999), p. 1199. Goetzmann, W./Ibbotson, R. (2008), pp. 517-523 provide a history on the measurement of the ex-post MRP.

historical period is the appropriate estimate for the expected MRP. While not specifically recommending this approach, many leading textbooks provide ex-post MRP averages as a reference point for the expected MRP[10]. This approach implicitly requires the expected MRP to be stationary and independent from the market environment[11]. The issue associated particularly with the latter assumption becomes evident when analyzing the capital markets development during the recent financial crisis. Can it be true that the expected MRP used by investors was constant at the historical average of ~6%[12] and thereby independent from the market price level during the period January 2007 and September 2009 while the monthly price-dividend ratio for the German market index CDAX fluctuated between 20x and 52x[13]? Intuitively one would assume that declining market valuations were at least partially driven by an increased expected MRP due to higher risk aversion of investors. The continued usage of historical averages is also surprising since a "cut-off date approach" is by now widely agreed for the determination of the risk-free rate while previously used historical averages are rejected[14]. Consequently, there is substantial criticism regarding ex-post MRP averages in the academic literature[15].

---

[10] See, e.g., Damodaran, A. (2001), pp. 160-164, Spremann, K. (2004), pp. 157-162, Copeland, T./Weston, F./Shastri, K. (2005), p. 173, Koller, T./Goedhart, M./Wessels, D. (2005), pp. 298-303, Ballwieser, W. (2007), pp. 95-99, Brealey, R./Myers, S./Allen, F. (2008), pp. 176-179, Ross, S./Westerfield, R./Jaffe, J. (2008), pp. 267-268, Drukarczyk, J./Schüler, A. (2009), pp. 221-224, and Kruschwitz, L. (2009), p. 388.

[11] See Richter, F. (2005), p. 130 and Richter, F. (2006a), p. 12.

[12] Arithmetic average pre-tax MRPs of the CDAX between 1955 and 2006 based on data provided by Stehle, R. (2004) with updates available at: http://lehre.wiwi.hu-berlin.de/Professuren/bwl/bb/aktien/DatenReihen.

[13] Based on the longest available data set provided by Datastream (code: CDAXGEZ(DY)).

[14] See Gebhardt, G./Daske, H. (2005), p. 650, Knoll, L. (2006), p. 525, Obermaier, R. (2006), p. 472, Kruschwitz, L./Löffler, A. (2008), pp. 805-806, Obermaier, R. (2008), pp. 493-494, and Drukarczyk, J./Schüler, A. (2009), pp. 209-210. See also Richter, F. (2005), p. 129. In the German literature this approach is referred to as "Stichtagsprinzip"; see Matschke, M. (1979), pp. 216ff., Hetzel, H. (1988), pp. 725-728, Moxter, A. (1983), p. 172, Baetge, J./Krause, C. (1994), p. 450, Schwetzler, B. (1996), pp. 1090-1091, and Obermaier, R. (2005), p. 4.

[15] See Cornell, B. (1999), p. 101, Elton, E. (1999), pp. 1199-1200, Claus, J./Thomas, J. (2001), p. 1630, Gebhardt, W./Lee, C./Swaminathan, B. (2001), p. 136, Gode, D./Mohanram, P. (2003), p. 399, Richter, F. (2005), p. 127, Daske, H./Gebhardt, G./Klein, S. (2006), pp. 3-4, Richter, F. (2006a), p. 29, Ballwieser, W. (2007), pp. 96-99, Reese, R. (2007), p. 1, Easton, P. (2009), pp. 307-308, and Hachmeister, D./Wiese, J. (2009), pp. 58-59.

Against this background, continuously growing conceptual as well as empirical research has recently been published in the German and Anglo-American academic literature[16] with a focus on ex-ante models allowing the direct estimation of expected returns and MRPs based on the internal rate of return (IRR) equating the current market capitalization with the present value of cash flows implied by analysts' forecasts and a terminal value[17]. The IRR method allows estimating the expected MRP not only unconditionally assuming independent ex-ante MRPs but also conditional on the market price level at a specific point in time[18]. As to be shown, unlike the unconditional ex-post average, the unconditional average of ex-ante MRPs has the advantage that it is not distorted by a potential non-stationarity of expected returns[19]. The ability to calculate a conditional expected MRP is a further advantage of the ex-ante model since empirical evidence indicates that expected returns and

---

[16] For early research focussing on the dividend discount model to estimate expected returns/MRPs see, e.g., Malkiel, B. (1979), Brigham, E./Shome, D./Vinson, S. (1985), Harris, R./Marston, F. (1992, 2001), Gordon, J./Gordon, M. (1997), Khorana, A./Moyer, C./Patel, A. (1997), and Cornell, B. (1999). For more recent research using residual income and earnings capitalization models to measure the magnitude of expected returns/MRPs, see Claus, J./Thomas, J. (2001), Gebhardt, W./Lee, C./Swaminathan, B. (2001), Easton, P. et al. (2002), Easton, P. (2004), Koch, J. (2005), Reese, R. (2005, 2007), Daske, H./Gebhardt, G./Klein, S. (2006), Desrosiers, S./Lemaire, N./L'Her, J.-F. (2007), and Easton, P./Sommers, G. (2007). Beyond the determination of the magnitude of expected returns and MRPs, residual income and earnings capitalization models were also used for four other categories of empirical studies: (1) Evaluation of expected return/MRP estimates regarding their association with risk factors in the cross-section or regarding their predictive power; see Gebhardt, W./Lee, C./Swaminathan, B. (2001), Gode, D./Mohanram, P. (2003), Cheng, F./Jorgensen, B./Yoo, Y. (2004), Botosan, C./Plumlee, M. (2005), Easton, P./Monahan, S. (2005), Guay, W./Kothari, S./Shu, S. (2005), Reese, R. (2005, 2007), Schröder, D. (2007), and Esterer, F./Schröder, D. (2007a,b). (2) Asset pricing studies; see Brav, A./Lehavy, R./Michaely, R. (2005), Pastor, L./Sinha, M./Swaminathan, B. (2008), and Lee, C./Ng, D./Swaminathan, B. (2009). (3) Investigation of conceptual as well as empirical aspects of expected return/MRP estimates; see Ballwieser, W. (2005), Daske, H./Wiesenbach, K. (2005), Daske, H./Gebhardt, G. (2006), Dausend, F./Schmitt, D. (2006a), Easton, P. (2006), Richter, F. (2006a), Krotter, S. (2007), Wallmeier, M. (2007), Easton, P. (2009), Huges, J./Liu, J./Liu, J. (2009), and Lambert, R. (2009). (4) Analysis of the relation between firm characteristics or regime changes (mainly accounting related) and cost of capital; see Botosan, C. (1997), Botosan, C./Plumlee, M. (2002), Hribar, P./Jenkins, N. (2004), Dhaliwal, D. et al. (2005), Daske, H. (2006), Hail, L./Leuz, C. (2006), Dhaliwal, D./Krull, L./Li, O. (2007), Daske, H. et al. (2008), and Hail, L./Leuz, C. (2009). For a similar classification of this research, see Huges, J./Liu, J./Liu, J. (2009), pp. 247-248. For references in selected textbooks, see Damodaran, A. (2001), pp. 171-175, Koller, T./Goedhart, M./Wessels, D. (2005), pp. 304-305, Richter, F. (2005), pp. 126-127, Ballwieser, W. (2007), pp. 100-102, and Drukarczyk, J./Schüler, A. (2009), p. 220. See also Hachmeister, D./Wiese, J. (2009), p. 59 for a recent evaluation in the German auditors journal.

[17] See Ballwieser, W. (2005), p. 322 and Richter, F. (2006a), p. 13.

[18] See Richter, F. (2005), p. 128. See also Harris, R./Marston, F. (1992), p. 68.

[19] See Cornell, B. (1999), p. 101, Elton, E. (1999), pp. 1205-1206, Richter, F. (2005), p. 130, and Easton, P. (2009), pp. 309-311.

MRPs are dependent on the current market price level[20]. It will however be discussed that the prerequisites required to infer expected returns and thereby MRPs from IRRs are inconsistent with a dependent return distribution[21]. Despite the apparent fundamental differences between the usage of ex-post and ex-ante MRPs, both concepts provide constant estimates of the expected MRP going forward[22]. While conditional expected MRP estimates from the IRR method fluctuate for different points in time, the single estimate for a specific date provides a constant expected MRP going forward similar to an infinite spot rate for bond yields.

A further set of research can be summarized under the return decomposition framework that separates the return estimate to calculate the expected MRP into its components dividend yield, dividend growth, and change in price-dividend ratio[23]. This method can be used to derive unconditional expected MRP estimates both from ex-post as well as ex-ante data. Under this framework, Richter (2006a) presented a simple model to determine a conditional and time-variable expected MRP based on an assumed convergence of the price-dividend ratio[24]. Exhibit 1 classifies these approaches according to the dimensions timing of input data and dependence of MRPs[25].

---

[20] See Richter, F. (2006a), pp. 12-13.

[21] See Richter, F. (2006a), p. 18. See also Huges, J./Liu, J./Liu, J. (2009), pp. 247 and 254 and Lambert, R. (2009), pp. 260-261 and 264.

[22] See Richter, F. (2005), p. 122, Richter, F. (2006a), p. 18, and Pastor, L./Sinha, M./Swaminathan, B. (2008), p. 2864.

[23] See, e.g., Blanchard, O. (1993), Arnott, R./Ryan, R. (2001), Arnott, R./Bernstein, P. (2001), Fama, E./French, K. (2002), Ibbotson, R./Chen, P. (2003), Richter, F. (2005, 2006a), and Dimson, E./Marsh, P./Staunton, M. (2008). For references in leading text books, see Spremann, K. (2004), pp. 162-165, Copeland, T./Weston, F./Shastri, K. (2005), pp. 173-174, Koller, T./Goedhart, M./Wessels, D. (2005), p. 305, Brealey, R./Myers, S./Allen, F. (2008), pp. 179-180, and Drukarczyk, J./Schüler, A. (2009), p. 220.

[24] See also Blanchard, O. (1993) for a model estimating conditional expected MRP estimates.

[25] The academic literature also proposes to use expert surveys to determine the expected MRP based on opinions of key members in the financial community (e.g., economists, analysts, CFOs, etc.). This approach is not discussed within this study since it may provide a heuristic consensus view but does not represent a fundamental methodology to develop expected MRP estimates. See Welch, I. (2000), Welch, I. (2001), and Graham, J./Harvey, C. (2008) for examples of expert surveys. Appendix 1 summarizes the findings of Graham, J./Harvey, C. (2008).

Exhibit 1 Classification of estimation methods for the expected MRP[26]

	Historical (ex-post) data	**Forward-looking (ex-ante) data**
Independent expected MRP (unconditional estimate)	• Average of ex-post MRPs *(<u>constant</u> exp. MRP estimate)* • Average of decomposition-based adj. ex-post MRPs *(<u>constant</u> exp. MRP estimate)*	• Average of IRR-based ex-ante MRPs *(<u>constant</u> exp. MRP estimate)* • Average of decomposition-based ex-ante MRPs *(<u>constant</u> exp. MRP estimate)*
Dependent expected MRP (conditional estimate)	• Econometric (regression) models – not covered in this study	• IRR-based ex-ante MRP at the estimation date *(<u>constant</u> exp. MRP estimate)* • Decomposition-based ex-ante MRP at the estimation date *(<u>time-variable</u> exp. MRP estimate)*

The existing research on methodologies to estimate the expected MRP discusses various conceptual issues as well as provides empirical evidence for a large number of countries. However, most studies exclusively focus on one of the three mentioned methodologies (historical averages, IRR-based estimates, or decomposition-based estimates) and neglect important interdependences. An exception is the work of Reese (2007) who provides a comprehensive review of conceptual issues relating to the expected MRP estimation from ex-post data and the application of different equity valuation models (dividend discount model, residual income model, and earnings capitalization model)[27] including risk-free rate specifications for the IRR approach. He also discusses the issues of different estimates when used as input parameter for corporate valuations based on risk-adjusted discount rates under the CAPM. Reese provides empirical evidence on the expected MRP using the IRR method for the German market until 2004. This dissertation has a similar research approach as

---

[26] See Goyal, A./Welch, I. (2003), p. 640 for a similar classification of ex-post data approaches. For selected articles on return/MRP prediction using econometric models (regression of historical MRPs on lagged dividend yields and other independent variables), see, e.g., Goyal, A./Welch, I. (2003), Gode, D./Mohanram, P. (2003), Boudoukh, J./Richardson, M./Whitelaw, R. (2008), Campbell, J./Thompson, S. (2008), Cochrane, J. (2008), Goyal, A./Welch, I. (2008), and Lettau, M./Nieuwerburgh, S. (2008). Other examples for forecasting expected returns using regression models include Cochrane, J. (1997), pp. 9-11, Brennan, M. (1997), pp. 83-88, Wallmeier, M. (1997), Ang, A./Liu, J. (2004), Lewellen, J. (2004), Richter, F. (2005), pp. 132-137, and Cochrane, J. (2005), pp. 404-410. For summaries, see Koller, T./Goedhart, M./Wessels, D. (2005), pp. 303-304, Campbell, J./Thompson, S. (2008), pp. 1509-1510, and Goyal, A./Welch, I. (2008), pp. 1501-1503.

[27] See also Easton, P. (2009) for a conceptual review of all three equity valuation models.

Reese by focusing on conceptual and empirical problems but refines and extends his work in various aspects. Several of the conceptual extensions compared to Reese are based on Richter (2006a), in particular with respect to assumptions underlying each estimation approach and price level dependent expected MRP estimates.

- Reese's work on the conceptual foundations of each methodology is revisited in particular with respect to the assumption of deterministic expected returns when estimated as the IRR of the multi-period valuation formula. In addition, the valuation model specifications for the IRR approach are refined regarding discounting periods and terminal value concepts (e.g., alternative perpetual growth estimates and multiples). Finally, the discovered issue of negative expected MRP estimates is further investigated[28].
- Beyond the scope of Reese, this thesis puts particular focus on time-conditional expected MRP estimates given the evidence that expected returns and MRPs are potentially not independent over time. For this purpose, expected MRP estimates from the IRR approach are tested for correlation with relative-price measures. Furthermore, the overview of estimation methodologies is conceptually as well as empirically extended by the return decomposition approach since it allows to make the impact of price level changes on realized MRPs transparent and can also be used as a tool to derive time-variable expected MRP estimates. In addition, the important question is discussed whether unconditional or conditional expected MRP estimates based on the "cut-off date principle" should be used for valuation purposes.
- The empirical data set used for the estimation of expected MRPs is extended with respect to both the geographical reach and the analysis period. While Reese provides estimates only for the German market between 1989 and 2004, this dissertation determines and compares expected MRPs for six global equity

---

[28] This issue was also identified by Daske, H./Gebhardt, G./Klein, S. (2006), p. 15 and Reese, R. (2007), pp. 107-10. See also Richter, F. (2006a), p. 25. Reese mentions that the periods of negative conditional expected MRPs coincide with a high risk-free rate level without going into further detail.

markets including Germany from 1989 to 2006[29]. For the German market, an extended series of IRR-based expected MRP estimates is provided until September 2009 to investigate the impact of the recent financial crisis.

Exhibit 2 summarizes the research approach of this dissertation.

Exhibit 2 Research approach of this thesis

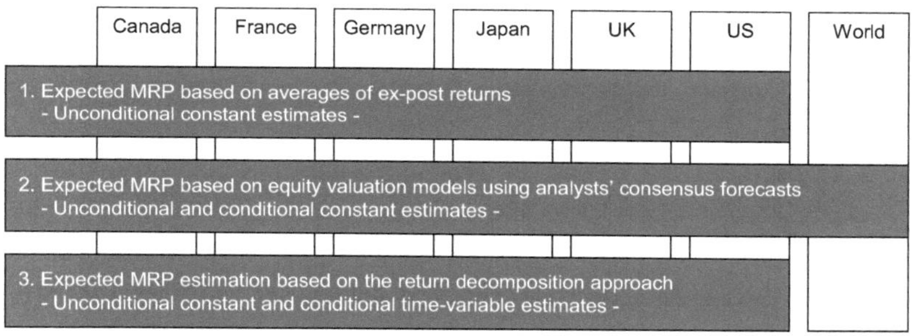

Note: A "world" index is approximated by the aggregation of the six sample countries for the IRR-based method.

Certain aspects related to the subject of this dissertation are intentionally excluded. Since the empirical focus of this study is to analyze solely the magnitude of the expected MRP, the data set is aggregated for each local market. The aggregation method has the advantage of replicating the characteristics of the market portfolio as close as possible but does not allow for cross-sectional analyses at the firm or industry level. Furthermore, this study is only focused on the analysis of market-based estimates of the expected MRP but not on analyzing whether the thereby derived estimates are consistent with expected MRPs derived from fundamental economic consumption models which determine the "theoretical" expected MRP based on the risk aversion of an representative investor and the correlation between market returns and changes in consumption[30]. Therefore, the debate on the

---

29 The starting point of the analysis period in 1989 is set due to the insufficient availability of IBES analyst forecasts before this date. The chosen country sample Germany, Canada, France, Japan, United Kingdom (UK), and United States (US) is identical to the selection by Claus/Thomas (2001), Chen/Jorgensen/Yoo (2004) (except for Australia), Pastor/Sinha/Swaminathan (2008), and Lee/Ng/Swaminathan (2009) (both except for Italy) to ensure comparability with existing research and represents with one exception (Italy) the G7 countries. Two other recent studies by Hail/Leuz (2006) and Desrosiers/Lemaire/L'Her (2007) cover up to 40 countries in their samples. However, Hail/Leuz only provide expected returns averages of different models and Desrosiers/Lemaire/L'Her's data and estimation quality is not transparent.

30 See Cornell, B. (1999), pp. 137-141. See also Cochrane, J. (2005), pp. 3-22 for the fundamentals of consumption-based asset pricing theory.

discovered difference between theoretically derived and market-implied estimates of the expected MRP—the equity premium puzzle—is not discussed herein[31]. Finally, this study does not focus on the question whether a local or global market expected MRP should be used when applying the CAPM as well as further implications from international asset pricing models[32].

1.2 Structure of the thesis

Against this background, the dissertation is organized into seven chapters to address all relevant aspects of the defined scope. Chapter 2 starts with a presentation of required concepts for the ex-post as well as ex-ante MRP analysis including statistical properties of returns/MRPs, the valuation concepts to derive expected MRP estimates using the IRR method, and the impact of selected influence factors on the expected MRP. In Chapter 3, the equity and bond indices used for the expected MRP estimation are described with respect to composition and performance throughout the analysis period. This provides the basis for the expected MRP determination based on the three introduced concepts in Chapters 4, 5, and 6. Chapter 4 covers expected MRP estimates based on realized return averages. After summarizing and comparing the results of long-term studies on historical averages, key measurement issues are discussed such as averaging methodology, measurement period, and survivorship bias. Chapter 5 starts with a review of the key valuation models used to determine IRR-based expected MRP estimates. This is followed by a demonstration of their equivalence. Before the results are discussed and compared across countries, the sample data is presented together with specific methodological considerations. This chapter also includes a summary of previous research on cross-sectional and time-series analyses using expected MRP estimates from the IRR-based method in order to determine their association with risk factors. Thereafter, the focus is shifted

---

31 See Mehra, R./Prescott, E. (1985) for the seminal article on the equity premium puzzle. See also Cornell, B. (1999), pp. 126-157 for a qualitative and Mehra, R./Prescott, E. (2003) or Mehra, R./Prescott, E. (2008) for a rigorous summary of the debate.

32 For key research on international asset pricing models and tests, see, e.g., Solnik, B. (1974a,b,c,d and 1977), Grauer, F./Litzenberger, R./Stehle, R. (1976), Stehle, R. (1977), Sercu, P. (1980), Stulz, R. (1981, 1992, and 1995a,b), Adler, M./Dumas, B. (1983), Harvey, C. (1991, 1995, and 2000), Chan, K./Karolyi, G./Stulz, R. (1992), Ferson, W./Harvey, C. (1993 and 1994), Dumas, B./Solnik, B. (1995), Stulz, R./Wasserfallen, W. (1995), Erb, C./Harvey, C./Viskanta, T. (1996), De Santis, G./Gerard, B. (1998), Griffin, J. (2002), Karolyi, G./Stulz, R. (2003), Zhang, X. (2006), Solnik, B./McLeavey, D. (2008), and Lee, C./Ng, D./Swaminathan, B. (2009). See also the summary by Copeland, T./Weston, F./Shastri, K. (2005), pp. 844-856.

on the key topic of price level dependence of the conditional expected MRP estimates and its implications for valuations. The findings are also discussed in context of an empirical analysis of conditional expected MRP estimates during the recent financial crisis. In Chapter 6, the return decomposition approach is presented with its specifications in order to derive unconditional and constant as well as conditional and time-variable expected MRP estimates. The discussion of results is preceded by a review of previous research using this framework. Finally, Chapter 7 provides a summary of key theses from this dissertation.

2 Conceptual preparations

This section provides the foundations for the general concepts used throughout the analysis. After the definition of the MRP, basic concepts for return calculations and time-series analyses are introduced which provide the basis for evaluating expected MRP estimates based on realized MRP averages. Thereafter, the valuation concept using risk-adjusted discount rates is introduced as a foundation of the IRR-based approach and as a key application of expected MRPs in corporate valuations. The remainder of this chapter deals with specific factors influencing the measurement of realized or expected MRPs such as the risk-free rate, currencies, inflation, and personal taxes.

2.1 Definition and calculation of the MRP

The MRP is defined as the difference between the return on the market portfolio of common stock and the return on the risk-free asset which is typically represented by a government security[33].

In formal terms, the MRP $\tilde{R}_t^p$ for year t can be calculated either as the geometric[34] or arithmetic[35] difference between the uncertain stock return $\tilde{R}_t$ and the risk-free rate R_t^f which is assumed to be deterministic. Similarly, the expected MRP $E_s\left[\tilde{R}_t^p\right]$ can be derived conditional on the information available at time s[36]:

F 2-1 Overview of calculation methodologies for the MRP

	MRP	Expected MRP
Geometric difference	$\tilde{R}_t^p = \frac{1+\tilde{R}_t}{1+R_t^f} - 1$	$E_s\left[\tilde{R}_t^p\right] = \frac{1+E_s\left[\tilde{R}_t\right]}{1+R_t^f} - 1$
Arithmetic difference	$\tilde{R}_t^p = \tilde{R}_t - R_t^f$	$E_s\left[\tilde{R}_t^p\right] = E_s\left[\tilde{R}_t\right] - R_t^f$

---

33 See, e.g., Campbell, J./Lo, A./MacKinlay, C. (1997), pp. 12-13, Cornell, B. (1999), p. 18, Tsay, R. (2005), pp. 5-6, Mehra, R./Prescott, E. (2003), p. 891, Goetzmann, W./Ibbotson, R. (2006), p. 3, Richter, F. (2006a), p. 4, and Mehra, R./Prescott, E. (2008), p. 2.

34 See, e.g., Ibbotson, R./Sinquefield, R. (1976), p. 35, Dimson, E./Marsh, P./Staunton, M. (2002), pp. 163-164, Ibbotson, R./Chen, P. (2003), p. 89, Koller, T./Goedhart, M./Wessels, D. (2005), p. 299, and Goetzman, W./Ibbotson, R. (2006), p. 16. See also Section 2.2.1 for a derivation of this expression.

35 See, e.g., Ibbotson, R./Sinquefield, R. (1976), p. 35, Campbell, J./Lo, A./MacKinlay, C. (1997), pp. 12-13, and Tsay, R. (2005), pp. 5-6.

36 See also Richter, F. (2006a), p. 4 for a definition of the expected MRP using a deterministic risk-free rate.

In academic textbooks and studies, both calculation methods are applied. However, the arithmetic difference method appears to dominate in the calculations of the MRP particularly due to its simplicity or due to the assumption of log-returns. Given the low magnitude of returns, differences between both calculation methods are small[37].

A related point of interest is the denomination of the MRP. Based on the geometric calculation approach the MRP is a ratio. Therefore, it does not have any denomination and lacks a numeraire in terms of currency. It is assumed that this property applies also to the arithmetically calculated MRP. This allows the comparison of MRPs across different countries even if the underlying data for stock returns and risk-free rates are denominated in the respective local currencies.[38]

For the calculations within this dissertation, the arithmetic calculation method is used to calculate the MRP in order to be consistent with similar recent studies[39].

2.2 Basics of asset return calculations

After defining the MRP, this section provides basic concepts related to return calculations and properties.

2.2.1 Return calculations

Denoting P_t as the certain price of an asset at time t, the simple discrete return $\tilde{R}_{t,t+1}$ for holding the asset from time t to $t+1$ can be defined as follows, if it is assumed that the asset is not returning any cash flows to the asset holder such as dividends or interest[40]:

F 2-2 $$1+\tilde{R}_{t,t+1} = \frac{\tilde{P}_{t+1}}{P_t}$$

---

[37] See Ibbotson, R./Sinquefield, R. (1976), p. 37 and fn. 19 and Dimson, E./Marsh, P./Staunton, M. (2002), p. 164.

[38] See Claus, J./Thomas, J. (2001), p. 1647 and Dimson, E./Marsh, P./Staunton, M. (2002), p. 164.

[39] See, e.g., Claus, J./Thomas, J. (2001), Gebhardt, W./Lee, C./Swaminathan, B. (2001), Easton, P. et al. (2002), Gode, D./Mohanram, P. (2003), Daske, H./Gebhardt, G./Klein, S. (2006), or Reese, R. (2007).

[40] See Campbell, J./Lo, A./MacKinlay, C. (1997), p. 9 and Tsay, R. (2005), p. 3. Also similar to Cochrane, J. (2005), p. 8.

Returns are not unitless but defined with respect to a certain time period[41]. In a multi-period scenario, holding the asset for k periods between t and $t+k$ yields a k-period simple return[42]

F 2-3
$$\begin{aligned} 1+\tilde{R}_{t,t+k} &= \frac{\tilde{P}_{t+k}}{P_t} = \frac{\tilde{P}_{t+1}}{P_t}\frac{\tilde{P}_{t+2}}{\tilde{P}_{t+1}}\cdots\frac{\tilde{P}_{t+k}}{\tilde{P}_{t+k-1}} = \left(1+\tilde{R}_{t+1}\right)\left(1+\tilde{R}_{t+2}\right)\cdots\left(1+\tilde{R}_{t+k}\right) \\ 1+\tilde{R}_{t,t+k} &= \prod_{u=1}^{k}\left(1+\tilde{R}_{t+u}\right) \end{aligned}$$

which is simply the product of the k one-period simple gross returns. These multi-period returns are also referred to as compound returns.

Up to this point, discrete compounding was used with returns being compounded m times per return horizon (i.e., one time)[43]:

F 2-4
$$1+\tilde{R}_{t,t+1} = \left(1+\frac{\tilde{R}_{t+1}}{m}\right)^{m}$$

If m converges to infinity, we move from discrete to continuous compounding. The relationship between discrete $\tilde{R}$ and continuous $\tilde{r}$ returns can be expressed as follows[44]:

F 2-5
$$\begin{aligned} \tilde{r}_{t,t+1} &= \ln\left(1+\tilde{R}_{t,t+1}\right) = \ln\frac{\tilde{P}_{t+1}}{P_t} = \ln\left(\tilde{P}_{t+1}\right)-\ln\left(P_t\right) \\ 1+\tilde{R}_{t,t+1} &= \exp\left(\tilde{r}_{t,t+1}\right) \end{aligned}$$

Using relationship F 2-5 and neglecting the time index, one can derive the expression for the MRP based on the geometric difference used in Section 2.1:

F 2-6
$$\tilde{R}^{p} = \exp\left(\tilde{r}^{p}\right)-1 = \exp\left(\tilde{r}-r^{f}\right)-1 = \exp\left(\ln\left(\frac{1+\tilde{R}}{1+R^{f}}\right)\right)-1 = \frac{1+\tilde{R}}{1+R^{f}}-1$$

In a multi-period scenario with continuous returns, F 2-5 can be rewritten as:

F 2-7
$$\begin{aligned} \tilde{r}_{t,t+k} &= \ln\left(1+\tilde{R}_{t,t+k}\right) = \ln\left[\left(1+\tilde{R}_{t+1}\right)\left(1+\tilde{R}_{t+2}\right)+\ldots+\left(1+\tilde{R}_{t+k}\right)\right] \\ \prod_{u=1}^{k}\left(1+\tilde{R}_{t+u}\right) &= \prod_{u=1}^{k}\exp\left(\tilde{r}_{t+u}\right) = \exp\left(\sum_{u=1}^{k}\tilde{r}_{t+u}\right) \end{aligned}$$

---

41 See Campbell, J./Lo, A./MacKinlay, C. (1997), p. 10.

42 See Campbell, J./Lo, A./MacKinlay, C. (1997), pp. 9-10 and Tsay, R. (2005), p. 3.

43 See Copeland, T./Weston, F./Shastri, J. (2005), p. 890 and Tsay, R. (2005), p. 4.

44 See Campbell, J./Lo, A./MacKinlay, C. (1997), p. 11, Spremann, K. (2002), p. 486, and Tsay, R. (2005), p. 4.

For assets which make periodic cash payments such as dividends or interest, the previous expressions for discrete and continuous returns have to be modified. The numerator of the simple discrete return formula now also includes the cash flow $\tilde{C}_{t+1}$ (e.g., dividend or interest) in addition to the future price $\tilde{P}_{t+1}$[45]:

F 2-8 $$1+\tilde{R}_{t,t+1} = \frac{\tilde{C}_{t+1}+\tilde{P}_{t+1}}{P_t}$$

The corresponding continuous expression is as follows:

F 2-9 $$\tilde{r}_{t,t+1} = \ln\left(\frac{\tilde{C}_{t+1}+\tilde{P}_{t+1}}{P_t}\right) = \ln\left(\tilde{C}_{t+1}+\tilde{P}_{t+1}\right) - \ln\left(P_t\right)$$

It is typically assumed that the standard return horizon equals one year. Multi-period returns are therefore often annualized to make investments with different time horizons comparable. The following expression provides the annualized single-period discrete return which is also referred to as the geometric mean return G_R[46]:

F 2-10 $$G_R = \left[\prod_{u=1}^{k}\left(1+\tilde{R}_{t+u}\right)\right]^{\frac{1}{k}} - 1$$

An approximation of the annualized single-period discrete return can be derived using a first-order Taylor expansion which is also called arithmetic mean A_R[47]:

F 2-11 $$A_R = \frac{1}{k}\sum_{u=1}^{k}\tilde{R}_{t+u}$$

Since only two numbers are sufficient to calculate the geometric mean for discrete returns over a certain time period—the beginning and ending value—the geometric annualized return is independent from the return development during the intermediate period. In contrast, the arithmetic mean takes all intermediate values into account and therefore captures return fluctuations over time. Therefore, it is always larger than the geometric mean[48]. An approximation is that the arithmetic mean will exceed the geometric mean by one-half of the variance of annual returns.

---

[45] See Campbell, J./Lo, A./MacKinlay, C. (1997), p. 12, Spremann, K. (2002), p. 476, Tsay, R. (2005), p. 5, and Mills, T./Markellos, R. (2008), p. 5.

[46] See Campbell, J./Lo, A./MacKinlay, C. (1997), p. 10. See also Spremann, K. (2002), pp. 477-478.

[47] See Campbell, J./Lo, A./MacKinlay, C. (1997), p. 10.

[48] Only in the unlikely case that the annual returns are identical over the entire analyzed time period, the arithmetic mean will be the same as the geometric mean; see also Cornell, B. (1999), p. 38 and Missiakoulis, S./Vasiliou, D./Eriotis, N. (2008), p. 5.

This approximation is reasonably accurate, if $1+\tilde{R}$ have a distribution that is close to lognormal[49]. It can also be shown that the arithmetic mean of continuous returns A_r is equal to the natural logarithm of one plus the geometric mean of discrete returns G_R. F 2-12 shows this relationship[50]:

F 2-12
$$\begin{aligned} 1+G_R &= \left[\prod_{u=1}^{k}\left(1+\tilde{R}_{t+u}\right)\right]^{\frac{1}{k}} = \left[\prod_{u=1}^{k}\exp\left(\ln\left(1+\tilde{R}_{t+u}\right)\right)\right]^{\frac{1}{k}} \\ &= \left[\prod_{u=1}^{k}\exp\left(\tilde{r}_{t+u}\right)\right]^{\frac{1}{k}} = \left[\exp\left(\sum_{u=1}^{k}\tilde{r}_{t+u}\right)\right]^{\frac{1}{k}} = \exp\left(\frac{1}{k}\sum_{u=1}^{k}\tilde{r}_{t+u}\right) = \exp\left(A_r\right) \\ \ln\left(1+G_R\right) &= A_r = \frac{1}{k}\sum_{u=1}^{k}\tilde{r}_{t+u} \end{aligned}$$

The difference between the arithmetic and geometric average for the determination of the expected MRP will be discussed in-depth in Section 4.3.1.

2.2.2 Selected marginal return distributions

Several statistical distributions are frequently used to describe the marginal (unconditional) distribution of random asset returns[51]. Within this study, the focus is on the normal and lognormal distributions which are briefly reviewed in the following. One of the most common approaches in analyses of asset returns is to assume the temporally independent, identically distributed (i.i.d.) normal model[52]. This model implies that returns are assumed to be independent over time, i.e., no serial correlation, identically distributed over time, and follow a normal distribution with a constant mean and variance[53]. Despite its appeal, the normal distribution for discrete returns suffers from conceptual as well as empirical issues. Firstly, it is inconsistent with the limited liability concept of most financial assets which implies that the lower bound for the return is -1 or -100%. Secondly, if single-period returns are normal, then the multi-period returns are not normally distributed. Thirdly, empirical analyses

---

49 See, e.g., Dimson, E./Marsh, P./Staunton, M. (2002), p. 182, Mehra, R./Prescott, E. (2003), p. 891, Richter, F. (2005), p. 129, Mehra, R./Prescott, E. (2008), p. 3, and Missiakoulis, S./Vasiliou, D./Eriotis, N. (2008), pp. 4-5. See also Levy, H./Gunthorpe, D. (1993).

50 See also Jacquier, E./Kane, A./Marcus, A. (2003), p. 47, Tsay, R. (2005), p. 17, and Reese, R. (2007), p. 35.

51 See Tsay, R. (2005), p. 14.

52 See Campbell, J./Lo, A./MacKinlay, C. (1997), p. 15 and Tsay, R. (2005), p. 14 for the remainder of this paragraph.

53 As to be seen in a later section, the implication of a constant mean and variance over time is consistent with the concept of weak stationarity.

of historical returns show a positive excess kurtosis compared to the normal distribution[54].

An alternative to the normal model is the assumption of i.i.d. normal continuous or log-returns[55]. This approach implies consequently that discrete returns are distributed i.i.d. lognormal[56]. Then the expected discrete return $E\left[\tilde{R}\right] = \mu_R$ can be expressed as the exponential function of the continuous mean return μ_r plus one half of the continuous return variance $\text{var}\left[\tilde{r}\right]$ [57]

F 2-13 $$1+E\left[\tilde{R}\right]=1+\mu_R=\exp\left(\mu_r+\frac{\text{var}\left[\tilde{r}\right]}{2}\right)$$

and the associated variance of the simple discrete return is as follows:

F 2-14 $$\text{var}\left[\tilde{R}\right]=\exp\left(2\mu_r+\text{var}\left[\tilde{r}\right]\right)\left[\exp\left(\text{var}\left[\tilde{r}\right]\right)-1\right]$$

Assuming log-returns to be normally distributed has the advantage of a lower bound for discrete returns of -1 while no restriction is on the continuous return due to relation presented in F 2-5[58]. Empirically, the issue of a missing positive excess kurtosis remains also for a normal distribution of log-returns[59].

2.2.3 Basic properties for historical return series

Beyond the marginal distribution, further concepts are required to describe the stochastic return process which is the sequence of random returns indexed by time[60]. The successive development of asset returns and the associated question of return predictability based on historical data is an intensively debated topic in the field of

---

54 See also Tsay, R. (2005), pp. 17-19.

55 See Campbell, J./Lo, A./MacKinlay, C. (1997), pp. 15-16 and Tsay, R. (2005), pp. 14-15 for the remainder of this paragraph.

56 Precisely one plus the simple discrete return is lognormally distributed; see Campbell, J./Lo, A./MacKinlay, C. (1997), p. 15.

57 See Campbell, J./Lo, A./MacKinlay, C. (1997), p. 15, Spremann, K. (2002), p. 486, and Tsay, R. (2005), p. 14. See also Elton, E./Gruber, M. (1974), pp. 485-486 and Jacquier, E./Kane, A./Marcus, A. (2003), p. 47.

58 See Campbell, J./Lo, A./MacKinlay, C. (1997), p. 15 and Tsay, R. (2005), p. 14. See also Jacquier, E./Kane, A./Marcus, A. (2003), p. 53, fn. 5 and Drobetz, W. (2003b), p. 4.

59 See also Tsay, R. (2005), pp. 17-19.

60 See Gujarati, D./Porter, D. (2009), p. 740, Greene, W. (2008), p. 630, and Wooldrige, J. (2009), p. 340 for the definition of general stochastic processes.

financial economics[61]. Any discussion is centered on the efficient market hypothesis stating that a market is called efficient if all available information is fully reflected in asset prices[62]. While the degree of efficiency is related to the definition of the available information set[63], the consequence of informationally efficient markets is that price changes must be unforcastable assuming that current prices reflect the expectations and information of all investors[64]. This would imply that returns follow the stochastic process of a martingale or random walk and the assumption of i.i.d. returns is correct. Without discussing the formal properties of the various random walk versions and the associated testing procedures[65], it can be concluded that the empirical evidence on the basis of historical return series—which can also be regarded as realizations of a stochastic process—does not support the proposition of returns following random walks[66]. This implies that the assumption of i.i.d. return distributions—as in the previous section—may not be appropriate, since returns are potentially dependent over time. Dependence of returns is often also assumed to be an indicator of dependence among MRPs implying returns and risk-free rates to be independent[67].

As discussed in the introduction, the assumption on dependence of MRPs over time is crucial in determining the appropriate methodology to estimate the expected MRP. E.g., using unconditional averages of realized MRPs to estimate the expected MRP requires independent MRP distributions. In case MRPs are dependent, econometric time-series models could be used for estimation[68]. The potential dependence is related to serial correlation (autocorrelation) between MRPs or correlation with other variables such as relative price measures (e.g., the price-dividend ratio). Another concept that is important in order to assess the capability of historical MRPs to provide useful information for forecasts of the expected MRP is stationarity. The

---

[61] See Campbell, J./Lo, A./MacKinlay, C. (1997), pp. 24-25 and 27.

[62] See Fama, E. (1970b, 1991, 1998). See also the works of Samuelson, P. (1965) and Malkiel, B. (1992). For a contemporary summary review of the efficient markets hypothesis, see Pesaran, H. (2006).

[63] See Fama, E. (1970b) and Roberts, H. (1967).

[64] See Campbell, J./Lo, A./MacKinlay, C. (1997), p. 20 and Cochrane, J. (2005), pp. 389-391.

[65] See, e.g., Campbell, J./Lo, A./MacKinlay, C. (1997), pp. 27-80 for a review of random walk properties, empirical tests, and evidence.

[66] See the summaries of Campbell, J./Lo, A./MacKinlay, C. (1997), pp. 65-80 and Cochrane, J. (2005), pp. 389-391. For early evidence see also Mandelbrot, B. (1963).

[67] See Damodaran, A. (2002), pp. 161-162 and Richter, F. (2006a), pp. 12-13.

[68] See Tsay, R. (2005), pp. 24 and 32-96 for an overview of approaches using serial correlation such as autoregressive and moving-average models.

following sections provide a discussion of relevant issues regarding serial correlation or autocorrelation, dependence on relative prices, and stationarity of returns.

2.2.3.1 Autocorrelation

Autocorrelation, i.e., the correlation between two occurrences of a return series ordered in time[69], is of key importance in defining the return process[70]. For the efficient markets hypothesis to hold, implying that stock prices follow at least the weakest form of a random walk, returns must not be serially correlated for all lags and horizons[71]. For the purposes of this study, autocorrelation between returns is of key importance primarily due to the implications for the appropriate averaging methodology for historical returns and the derivation of the multi-period valuation formula required for the IRR method.

There is extensive empirical literature on serial correlation in particular in the US due to its importance for testing the efficient markets hypothesis. Main tests for serial correlation of returns include the coefficient of autocorrelation at various lags and horizons[72] and the variance ratio[73]. Despite the quantity of literature, there are ambiguous results for the autocorrelation of returns. Early empirical studies on stochastic dependence of serial returns in the context of market efficiency tests focus on short horizons (daily or weekly returns) providing only weak evidence of negative autocorrelation[74]. Fama/French (1988a)[75] use long-horizon return regressions and found negative and significant first-order coefficients for time horizons beyond one year. However, since the first-order autocorrelations for increasing return horizons

---

69 See Gujarati, D./Porter, D. (2009), p. 413.

70 Note that autocorrelation implies dependence but the argument cannot be inverted since dependence could also be related to correlation with another variable.

71 See Campbell, J./Lo, A./MacKinlay, C. (1997), p. 44.

72 A test to identify violations of zero autocorrelations in both directions and at all lags is the Portmanteau statistic (Q-statistic by Pierce-Box and Ljung-Box statistic) using the sum of squared autocorrelation coefficients; see Campbell, J./Lo, A./MacKinlay, C. (1997), p. 47 and Tsay, R. (2005), pp. 25-29.

73 See Campbell, J./Lo, A./MacKinlay, C. (1997), pp. 48-55, Cochrane, J. (2005), p. 411, and Drobetz, W. (2003b), pp. 13-14. The variance ratio is actually only an indirect test for serial correlation. As a random walk test, it can be also viewed as a test for serial correlation. For uncorrelated returns, the variance ratio (defined as $\text{var}\left[\tilde{R}_{t,t+k}\right]/k\ \text{var}\left[\tilde{R}_{t+1}\right]$) is equal to one under the null hypothesis since the variance of random walk increments needs to develop as a linear function of the time interval (implying non-stationarity). A variance ratio above (below) one implies positive (negative) autocorrelation or mean aversion (reversion); see, e.g., Poterba, J./Summers, L. (1988), p. 30 or Cochrane, J. (2005), p. 411.

74 See Fama, E. (1970b).

75 See Fama, E./French, K. (1988a), pp. 253-264.

appear to follow a U-shaped path, the authors conclude that eventually a random-walk component dominates the development of stock prices[76]. In a further study, Porteba/Summers (1988) [77] analyze mean-reversion through the variance-ratio test. In their analysis, the authors found variance ratios above one indicating positive serial correlation/mean aversion over short periods and variance ratios below one indicating negative serial correlation/mean-reversion for longer return intervals—the latter results hold true for all six countries analyzed within this study[78]. Other studies using similar approaches also find indications for serial correlation of returns[79].

However, more recent empirical evidence is not consistent with the previous results, in particular when different testing methodologies and data sets are applied. Campbell/Lo/MacKinlay (1997) report significant positive autocorrelation coefficients for daily, weekly, and monthly returns from 1962 to 1994 of equally- and value-weighted CRSP indices[80]. The authors also analyze variance ratios for the same period and find that the identified autocorrelations can only be confirmed with significant variance ratios above one for the equally weighted index[81]. Cochrane (2005) presents evidence that long-run regressions support negative autocorrelation only for two to four year horizons which disappears by ten years. However, his long-run variance ratio is clearly below one supporting mean reversion. Other studies providing conflicting evidence for the support of the mean-reversion hypothesis are discussed by Jorion (2003) in addition to further non-supportive evidence[82]. The data sets of both Dimson/Marsh/Staunton (2006) as well as Morningstar Inc. (2007c) show no significant autocorrelation coefficients[83]. In case of Dimson/Marsh/Staunton that also includes the analyzed equity markets outside the US (only two of the 17 analyzed markets had significant serial correlation coefficients at the 95% confidence level). The Morningstar Inc. evidence specifically for the US MRP from 1926 to 2006

---

[76] See Fama, E./French, K. (1988a), pp. 253 and 265-266.

[77] See Poterba, J./Summers, L. (1988).

[78] See Poterba, J./Summers, L. (1988), pp. 40-41 and 53.

[79] See, e.g., Lo, A./MacKinlay, C. (1988) (positive autocorrelations for weekly returns based on the variance ratio test). See also Finnerty, J./Leistikow, D. (1993, 1994) and Ibbotson, R./Lummer, S. (1994).

[80] See Campbell, J./Lo, A./MacKinlay, C. (1997), pp. 66-68.

[81] Tsay shows for CRSP data from 1926 to 1997 that the monthly value-weighted index returns have significant Ljung-Box statistics indicating serial correlation; see Tsay, R. (2005), pp. 28-29.

[82] See Jorion, P. (2003), pp. 8-9 and 23-25 with reference to Richardson, M./Stock, J. (1989) and Kim, M./Nelson, C./Startz, R. (1991).

[83] See Dimson, E./Marsh, P./Staunton, M. (2006), pp. 11-15 and Morningstar Inc. (2007c), pp. 80-82.

shows a first-order autocorrelation coefficient of close to zero implying randomness of the MRP development[84].

The authors of the Morningstar Inc. valuation yearbook conclude that there is some contradiction among academics on the topic of mean reversion and that the existing evidence is not conclusive enough to support it[85]. The various views on a potential autocorrelation of returns are also evidenced by the Welch survey among financial economists. When asked whether they agree with zero return autocorrelations agreeing and disagreeing answers are approximately equal[86].

2.2.3.2 Dependence on relative prices

With weak evidence for dependence of returns due to serial correlation, one may conclude that there is only a limited forecastability of returns supporting the efficient markets hypothesis. Despite weak serial correlation, there is stronger empirical evidence that returns are predictable due to dependence on relative prices such as the price-dividend ratio[87]. Studies find that any price divisor including dividends can explain a certain portion of expected return variation[88]. Still, there are also concerns expressed that the return predictability is spurious[89].

In a widely recognized article on the accuracy of the CAPM using cross-sectional data for 2,267 stocks during July 1963 to December 1990, Fama/French (1992) showed that the average monthly regression coefficient between realized returns and the log book-to-market ratio is significantly positive with a value of 0.5 and a t-value of 5.71[90]. In their study, the regression between stock returns and the book-to-market ratio is actually the strongest model to explain return variations. These results were confirmed for the German stock market by Wallmeier (1997) running monthly regressions of the excess returns on price level factors such as earnings-price ratio, cash flow-price ratio, and book-to-market ratio between July 1967 and June 1994. Again, the price level factors have the coefficients with the highest significance levels.

---

84 See Morningstar Inc. (2007c), p. 81.

85 See Morningstar Inc. (2007c), p. 80.

86 See Welch, I. (2000), pp. 523-524. See also generally on this topic Cochrane, J. (2005), pp. 411-415 and Wagner et al. (2006), p. 1018.

87 See Cochrane, J. (2005), pp. 410 and 414 and Campbell, J./Thompson, S. (2008), p. 1509.

88 See Cochrane, J. (2005), p. 392.

89 See Campbell, J./Thompson, S. (2008), p. 1510, Cochrane, J. (2008), p. 1534, and Lettau, M./Nieuwerburgh, S. (2008), p. 1608.

90 See, e.g., Fama, E./French, K. (1992), p. 439 and 441. See also Copeland, T./Weston, F./Shastri, K. (2005), p. 169 and Richter, F. (2005), pp. 111-112.

Specifically, Wallmeier calculates the highest and most significant univariate coefficient for the cash flow-price ratio with lower but similar results for the book-to-market ratio and earnings-price ratio[91].

For the dividend yield, Fama/French showed already in 1988 that the non-lagged dividend yield can explain 21% (19%) of the nominal variation in future returns at a four year horizon of value (equal)-weighted portfolios of NYSE stocks between 1941 and 1986 despite only low coefficients of determination for shorter return horizons[92]. In a similar analysis, Campbell/Lo/MacKinlay (1997) found a coefficient of determination in the amount of 26% for 48 months return horizons using CRSP data between 1927 and 1994[93]. Cochrane (2005) also confirms these results and found an even higher R-squared over a five year horizon using updated data between 1947 and 1996[94]. However, for one-year returns, Cochrane (2008) finds a lower r-squared of 5.8% with an only marginally significant slope coefficient using CRSP data for the period 1926 to 2004[95]. Despite only little predictability over shorter horizons due to the persistence of the dividend yield, large coefficients of determination can be achieved in regression analysis over longer horizons[96].

Similarly to the positive relation between expected returns and dividend yields, it is also investigated whether dividend yields are a predictor of the expected MRP. This would essentially imply that the risk-free rate and the dividend yield are independent. Goyal/Welch (2003) provide evidence that regressing the ex-post MRP on the dividend yield results in a significant coefficient at conventional levels for US market data between 1926 and 1990. The results of Cochrane (2008) using the MRP are similar to the aforementioned analysis for returns with a marginally significant slope coefficient and a R-squared of 7.4%[97].

---

91 See Wallmeier, M. (1997), pp. 278-279.

92 See Fama, E./French, F. (1988b), pp. 12-13. The R^2 increases to 57% (42%) for value (equal)-weighted portfolios using a shorter data set from 1957 to 1986.

93 See Campbell, J./Lo, A./MacKinlay, C. (1997), pp. 168-269. Similarly to Fama/French (1988b). Their R^2 using a shorter data set from 1952 to 1994 with 42% is also higher at the 48 months return horizon.

94 See Cochrane, J. (2005), p. 392.

95 See Cochrane, J. (2008), pp. 1533-1534.

96 See Cochrane, J. (2005), pp. 392-294. See also Lettau, M./Ludvigson, S. (2001).

97 See Cochrane, J. (2008), pp. 1533-1534.

Further evidence of negative relation between relative prices and returns/MRPs supports the price level dependence of returns[98]. Still, several authors suggest that the regression coefficients are upward biased due to the persistence of predictor variables such as the dividend yield[99]. As a result of this bias the statistical significance of previous results is questioned. Recognizing the deficiencies of regression coefficients, Cochrane (2008) still argues in favor of return predictability: "[S]ince the dividend yield is stationary, one of dividend growth or price growth must be forecastable to bring the dividend yield back following a shock. (...) A null hypothesis in which returns are not forecastable must also specify that dividend growth is forecastable, and the statistical evaluation of that null must also confront the lack of dividend-growth forecastability in the data"[100]. Cochrane later adds: "'Failing to reject the null' does not mean that we wholeheartedly accept the i.i.d. worldview"[101].

Besides the significance level of slope coefficients, another aspect of return/MRP predictability is the out-of-sample performance of models. Goyal/Welch (2003) confirm the good in-sample fit of regressing returns on the price-dividend ratio but also show that the unconditional average ex-post MRP has a better out-of-sample estimation performance than estimated expected MRPs from dividend yield based regression models[102]. The poor performance of the dividend yield as well as a large variety of other variables in predicting the MRP is confirmed by Goyal/Welch (2008)

---

[98] See Litzenberger, R./Ramaswamy, K. (1979), Rozeff, M. (1984), Shiller, R. (1984), pp. 488-491, Campbell, J./Shiller, R. (1988a,b), and Richter, F. (2005), pp. 114-115. See also the summaries by Fama, E. (1991), pp. 1577-1599, Brennan, M. (1997), p. 82, Cochrane, J. (1997), p. 8, Campbell, J./Lo, A./MacKinlay, C. (1997), p. 267, Wallmeier, M. (1997), pp. 229-230, Fama, E./French, K. (2002), p. 640, Cochrane, J. (2005), pp. 391-395, Richter, F. (2005), pp. 106-107, and Siegel, J. (2008), p. 145. Concerning methodological issues, see Hodrick, R. (1992) and Goetzmann, W./Jorion, P. (1993, 1995). See also Fama, E./French, K. (1989) who find that variability of expected returns is also driven by the business cycle.

[99] See primarily Goetzmann, W./Jorion, P. (1993), Nelson, C./Kim, M. (1993), and Stambaugh, R. (1999). See also the contributions of Cavangh, C./Elliott, G./Stock, J. (1995), Kothari, S./Shanken, J. (1997), Lewellen, J. (2004), Torous, W./Volkanov, R./Yan, S. (2004), Campbell, J./Yogo, M. (2006), Jansson, M./Moreira, M. (2006), Polk, C./Thompson, S./Vuolteenaho, T. (2006), Ang, A./Bekaert, G. (2007), and Boudoukh, J./Richardson, M./Whitelaw, R. (2008). For summaries, see Campbell, J./Thompson, S. (2008), p. 1510, Cochrane, J. (2008), p. 1534 incl. fn. 2, and Lettau, M./Nieuwerburgh, S. (2008), pp. 1608-1609.

[100] Cochrane, J. (2008), p. 1535.

[101] Cochrane, J. (2008), p. 1538.

[102] See Goyal, A./Welch, I. (2003), pp. 643-644 and 650-651. The authors differentiate between price-dividend ratio and dividend yield as independent variable. The price-dividend ratio outperforms the dividend yield in terms of forecasting accuracy. See also Wooldridge, J. (2008), pp. 651-652 for the difference between in-sample and out-of-sample criteria to decide on the suitability of forecasting models.

for a more recent data set until 2005. For the period 1975 to 2005, no model had a superior out-of-sample performance compared to the prevailing historical mean MRP and only few models had satisfying in-sample accuracy[103].

The Goyal/Welch results are challenged by Campbell/Thompson (2008). Despite finding a similarly week out-of-sample performance for typical linear regressions using monthly data until 2005 (e.g., for regressions on the price-dividend ratio), Campbell/Thompson show how to improve the out-of-sample performance compared to the historical average by imposing restrictions on the sign of the slope coefficient and the sign of the MRP forecast which results in an improved out-of-sample performance so that the price-dividend ratio is superior to historical averages. For annual regressions, the out-of-sample performance of several valuation ratios is superior to historical average even excluding restrictions[104]. Still, the authors confirm the Goyal/Welch finding of a lower MRP predictability for a more recent analysis period from 1980 to 2005. During this period the dividend-price ratio has underperformed the historical average with respect to its out-of-sample performance which the authors explain by the increased popularity of share repurchases in recent years. In contrast, other relative price measures such as the earnings-price ratio were superior after imposing restrictions[105]. Finally, it should be noted that the out-of-sample prediction performance is not a test for predictability but rather an indicator of the limited practical usefulness of return/MRP forecasts[106].

In summary, the empirical evidence for dependence of returns/MRPs on the market price level and thereby its predictability is less unanimously supported by the recent literature than during the last century. Still, the dependence of expected returns and MRPs on relative prices is not refuted[107] and will be an important property used in later parts of this study.

2.2.3.3 Stationarity

In addition to the potential dependence of the expected MRP on relative prices, it is also important to discuss the concept of stationarity which closer describes the process movement over time.

---

[103] See Goyal, A./Welch, I. (2008), pp. 1503-1504.
[104] See Campbell, J./Thompson, S. (2008), pp. 1511-1517.
[105] See Campbell, J./Thompson, S. (2008), pp. 1521-1522.
[106] See Cochrane, J. (2008), pp. 1538 and 1566.
[107] See most prominently Cochrane, J. (2008).

Stationarity of a time series is critical for drawing inferences about the future from historical data. In its strong form, a process is strongly stationary if the joint probability distribution of any set of observations in a sequence is the same regardless of the origin in the time series[108]. This implies that all random variables in the process are identically distributed, but no restriction is put on the correlation between variables apart from correlation being constant across all time periods[109]. For most empirical applications weak or covariance stationarity of a time series is sufficient[110] which is defined as follows assuming a finite second moment (variance) for the time series[111]: "[A] stochastic process is said to be [weakly or covariance] stationary if its mean and variance are constant over time and the value of the covariance between the two time periods depends only on the distance or gap or lag between the two time periods and not the actual time at which the covariance is computed" [112]. This definition implies that a stochastic process is weakly or covariance stationary, if its mean, variance, and covariance are time invariant and its variance is finite[113].

From the definition above, it should become immediately obvious why stationarity is critical for forecasting stochastic variables such as the expected MRP. If the historical MRP series were non-stationary, e.g., with a time-variable mean, each period is rather an episode than a period of values which can be generalized also for the future. A stationary time series, however, will tend to revert to its mean (mean reversion[114]) and fluctuates with an approximately constant amplitude around this mean[115]. Therefore, stationary time series do not have a trend so that meaningful

---

[108] See Greene, W. (2008), p. 636. See also Tsay, R. (2005), p. 25.

[109] See Wooldridge, J. (2008), p. 378. The lag-one correlation between terms of a sequence can actually take any value from minus one to one. As to be seen shortly, the development of the autocorrelation function with increasing lags is decisive whether a process is stationary or not.

[110] See Gujarati, D./Porter, D. (2009), p. 740 and Greene, W. (2008), p. 636. Note that a normal weakly stationary process is also strictly stationary; see Gujarati, D./Porter, D. (2009), p. 740, fn. 6 and Tsay, R. (2005), p. 25.

[111] See Tsay, R. (2005), p. 25 and Wooldridge, J. (2008), p. 378.

[112] Gujarati, D./Porter, D. (2009), p. 740. See also Tsay, R. (2005), p. 25, Mills, T./Markellos, R. (2008), pp. 10-12, Greene, W. (2008), p. 636, and Wooldridge, J. (2008), pp. 378-379.

[113] See Greene, W. (2008), p. 719.

[114] The term mean reversion should be treated with care since it is often used to imply stationarity as well as negative serial correlation. However, a mean-reverting stationary process can have any first-order autocorrelation and negative serial correlation may only relate to longer horizons. E.g., stationary return processes were found to have negative serial correlation for long-term return horizons; see, e.g., Fama, E./French, K. (1988), p. 249 who show for a return process that the autocorrelation coefficient converges to -0.5 as the return horizon increases to infinity.

[115] See Gujarati, D./Porter, D. (2009), p. 741 and Tsay, R. (2005), p. 25.

averages can be taken but are not required to be constant[116]. A typical example for a stationary process is the purely random white noise process whose variables are i.i.d. normal[117]. In contrast, random walk processes are generally non-stationary even if they have a time-invariant mean since the constant variance condition is violated[118]. The concept of stationarity should not be confused with the concept of weak dependence between random variables in a time series. However, weak dependence is typically assumed in addition to stationarity[119] so that the correlations within a covariance stationary sequence can be characterized as follows: A covariance stationary process is weakly dependent if the correlation between two terms of the sequence goes to zero sufficiently quickly as the lags between the terms increase[120]. Therefore, weakly stationary processes which are said to be weakly dependent are asymptotically uncorrelated with the lagged coefficients of autocorrelation converging to zero with increasing lags[121]. The decline of autocorrelations is either by geometric progression, if the lag one correlation is positive, or alternating in sign, if it is negative[122].

The stationarity of a time series can be tested through testing the coefficients of autocorrelation at different lags (autocorrelation function – ACF)—e.g., in a correlogram—or dividing the data set into subsamples in order to check for

---

[116] See Cochrane, J. (2005), pp. 8-9.

[117] See Gujarati, D./Porter, D. (2009), p. 741 and Greene, W. (2008), p. 716.

[118] See Campbell, J./Lo, A./MacKinlay, C. (1997), p. 32, Gujarati, D./Porter, D. (2009), p. 742, and Greene, W. (2008), pp. 739-740. If the random walk model includes a drift parameter, the process also breaches the constant mean condition in addition to having a non-constant variance.

[119] This property is also referred to as ergodicity which is required in addition to stationarity to ensure predictability based on a time series. Based on asymptotic independence, the ergodic theorem states that if time series are stationary and ergodic, then mean and variance will converge towards the true mean and variance of the population. As a consequence, the "autocovariances must decline sufficiently rapidly with increasing lags"; see Greene, W. (2008), pp. 637-638 and 728.

[120] See Wooldridge, J. (2008), p. 379 and Greene, W. (2008), pp. 633-634 for a prove of this property based on an autoregressive process of order one with independent and identically distributed disturbances and the stability condition that the modulus of the correlation coefficient between two adjacent terms in the sequence is smaller than one. The stability condition is required to maintain a finite variance which is required for stationarity.

[121] See Wooldridge, J. (2008), p. 379.

[122] See Greene, W. (2008), p. 634.

consistent results across the subsamples[123]. More formal procedures include unit root tests[124] such as the Dickey-Fuller or augmented Dickey-Fuller test.

In summary, stationarity of historical MRPs is vital to make any inferences about the future MRP development. Stationarity most importantly implies a constant mean to avoid any trends in the data series and a constant as well as finite variance which insures fluctuations around the constant mean with identical amplitudes. In order to be stationary, the autocorrelation at the first lag is irrelevant but needs to converge quickly to zero at higher lags.

2.3 Expected MRP and valuation under uncertainty

This section reviews forward-looking valuation models under uncertainty in order to discuss the required assumptions for deriving expected MRPs using the IRR method as well as to show the specifications of expected MRP estimates, disregarding how determined, when applied for valuation purposes.

Generally, two schools of thought have developed over time on how to incorporate the uncertainty about expected cash flows in valuation analyses[125]: Firstly, the uncertain cash flow streams are transformed into certainty equivalents that are discounted at the risk-free rate (certainty equivalent method). Secondly, the expected values of the uncertain cash flows are discounted using risk-adjusted expected returns (risk-adjusted discount rate method) which is the predominant method among practitioners[126]. Both approaches require concepts to operationalize the risk adjustment to the expected cash flows or the discount rate. The academic literature

---

[123] See Tsay, R. (2005), p. 25.

[124] As discussed in fn. 120, a stability condition is required for an autoregressive process of the order one to be stationary. The stability condition is violated if the lag-one coefficient is equal to one which implies that the process has a unit root. Unit root testing describes a significance test to determine if the autocorrelation coefficient is one; see Gujarati, D./Porter, D. (2009), pp. 744 and 754-760.

[125] See, e.g., Moxter, A. (1983), pp. 155-156, Schwetzler, B. (2000), pp. 469-470, Grinblatt, M./Titman, S. (2002), pp. 371-373, Spremann, K. (2002), pp. 316-317, Brennan, M. (2003), pp. 170-171, Rapp, M. (2004), pp. 1-2, Copeland, T./Weston, F./Shastri, K. (2005), pp. 156-157, Hachmeister, D. (2006), pp. 144-146, Laitenberger, J. (2006), p. 83, Ballwieser, W. (2007), p. 65, Rosarius, S. (2007), pp. 58-59, Brealey, R./Myers, S./Allen, F. (2008), pp. 250-252, Drukarczyk, J./Schüler, A. (2009), pp. 39-41, and Hachmeister, D./Wiese, J. (2009), p. 58.

[126] See Spremann, K. (2002), p. 317, Brennan, M. (2003), p. 169, Rapp, M. (2004), p. 2, Spremann, K. (2004), p. 255, Hachmeister, D. (2006), p. 143, Laitenberger, J. (2006), p. 83, Rosarius, S. (2007), p. 59, Brealey, R./Myers, S./Allen, F. (2008), pp. 250-252, and Hachmeister, D./Wiese, J. (2009), p. 58.

mainly discusses two alternative concepts[127]: the Bernoulli theory based on the individual utility functions of the decision maker[128] and market-based approaches. The latter can be subdivided into (1) the implied cost of capital which infers expected returns from replication assets with identical or proportionate cash flow forecasts and an observable market price[129], (2) equilibrium market models such as the CAPM under which expected returns are a function of systematic risk[130], and (3) the risk-neutral valuation approach under which the subjective probabilities used to calculate the expected values of cash flows are replaced by risk-neutral probabilities inferred from security prices, state-contingent cash flows and the risk-free rate[131].

The following section focuses on the implied cost of capital concept to estimate risk-adjusted discount rates since the IRR method used to determine the expected MRP is based on this framework. Thereafter, selected aspects of the CAPM are discussed in order to establish concepts that are relevant when expected MRP estimates are used as input parameter for the CAPM formula when determining risk-adjusted discount rates for multi-period valuations.

2.3.1 Risk-adjusted discount rates based on implied cost of capital

Risk-adjusted discount rates based on the implied cost of capital method are determined as the IRR equating the present value of the infinite stream of expected cash flows and the current market value. The key concept of this procedure is the

---

[127] See, e.g., Wiese, J. (2006a), p. 13 and Rosarius, S. (2007), p. 59. See also Bamberg, G./Dorfleitner, G./Krapp, M. (2004), pp. 102-103, Rapp, M. (2004), p. 1, Rapp, M. (2006), p. 775, and Hachmeister, D./Wiese, J. (2009), p. 58.

[128] For a summary overview, see Schneeweiß, H. (1963), pp. 203-212. See also Bamberg, G./Dorfleitner, G./Krapp, M. (2006), Ballwieser, W. (2007), pp. 65-78, and Kruschwitz, L. (2009), pp. 301-312. For the fundamentals, see Neumann, J./Morgenstern, O. (1967), pp. 24-29 and 642-657. In the German literature also referred to as "Individualistischer Ansatz" according to Drukarczyk, J./Schüler, A. (2009), p. 55. See also Schwetzler, B. (2000), p. 469 and Rosarius, S. (2007), p. 59.

[129] See Gebhardt, W./Lee, C./Swaminathan, B. (2001), p. 135, Daske, H./Gebhardt, G./Klein, S. (2006), p. 3, and Reese, R. (2007), p. 62. The implied cost of capital method is also referred to "DCF-method" (see Gordon, M. (1974), Siegel, J. (1985), pp. 46-47, Grinblatt, M./Titman, S. (2002), pp. 388-391, and Brennan, M. (2003), pp. 185-187) or "ex-ante approach" (see Ballwieser, W. (2005), p. 322, Reese, R. (2007), p. 1, and Ballwieser, W. (2007), p. 100).

[130] See Brennan, M. (2003), p. 170. In the German literature also referred to as "marktorientierter Ansatz" according to Drukarczyk, J./Schüler, A. (2009), pp. 55ff. and Rosarius, S. (2007), p. 59 or "objektivierter Ansatz" according to Wiese, J. (2006a), p. 13.

[131] For the fundamentals, see Ross, S. (1978), pp. 453-474, Cox, J./Ross, S./Rubinstein, M. (1979), pp. 229-263, and Harrison, M./Kreps, D. (1979), pp. 388-399. See also Richter, F. (2001), pp. 182-183, Richter, F. (2002c), pp. 137-138, Kelleners, A. (2004), pp. 48ff., Richter, F. (2005), pp. 18-22, Wiese, J. (2006), pp. 47-49, and Rapp, M. (2006), pp. 775-776.

infinite cash flow valuation formula. It can be derived by assuming that the conditional expected one-period return $E_t\left[\tilde{r}_{t,t+1}\right]$ is defined as the sum of the conditional expected cash flow $E_t\left[\tilde{C}_{t+1}\right]$ and future value $E_t\left[\tilde{V}_{t+1}\right]$ in t divided by the value $\tilde{V}_t$ minus one[132]:

F 2-15 $$E_t\left[\tilde{r}_{t,t+1}\right]=\frac{E_t\left[\tilde{C}_{t+1}+\tilde{V}_{t+1}\right]}{\tilde{V}_t}-1$$

Solving recursively for $\tilde{V}_t$, the one-period valuation formula can be written as follows[133]

F 2-16 $$\tilde{V}_t=\frac{E_t\left[\tilde{C}_{t+1}+\tilde{V}_{t+1}\right]}{1+E_t\left[\tilde{r}_{t,t+1}\right]}=\frac{E_t\left[\tilde{C}_{t+1}+\tilde{V}_{t+1}\right]}{1+\tilde{k}_{t,t+1}}$$

and the expected one-period return $E_t\left[\tilde{r}_{t,t+1}\right]$ represents the risk-adjusted discount rate or cost of capital $\tilde{k}_{t,t+1}$[134]. For the infinite valuation formula, it is often assumed that the expected return (and thereby the cost of capital) is deterministic $E_t\left[\tilde{r}_{t,t+1}\right]=k_{t,t+1}$[135]. Under this condition, the infinite valuation formula can be derived by repeatedly substituting out future prices, using the law of iterated expectations, and assuming transversality[136]:

F 2-17 $$V_s=\sum_{t=s+1}^{\infty}\frac{E_s\left[\tilde{C}_t\right]}{\prod_{u=s}^{t-1}\left(1+k_{u,u+1}\right)}$$

---

[132] See Rapp, M. (2004), p. 9, Kruschwitz, L./Löffler, A. (2005), pp. 22-23, Richter, F. (2005), p. 7, Laitenberger, J. (2006), p. 83, Laitenberger, J./Löffler, A. (2006), p. 291 (the latter two exculding expectations), and Rapp, M. (2006), p. 780. See also Shiller, R. (1981), p. 424.

[133] See Campbell, J./Lo, A./MacKinlay, C. (1997), p. 254, Richter, F. (2005), pp. 8 and 12, Kruschwitz, L./Löffler, A. (2005), p. 25, and Laitenberger, J. (2006), p. 84. For a different cost of capital concept using yields, see Spremann, K. (2004), pp. 109-122 and Kruschwitz, L./Löffler, A. (2005), pp. 5-6.

[134] See Kruschwitz, L./Löffler, A. (2005), pp. 22-25 and Laitenberger, J.(2006), p. 83.

[135] See Fama, E. (1996), p. 418, Rapp, M. (2004), p. 1, Kruschwitz, L./Löffler, A. (2005), pp. 23-24, Laitenberger, J. (2006), p. 81, Laitenberger, J./Löffler, A. (2006), p. 292.

[136] See Rapp, M. (2004), p. 2, Kruschwitz, L./Löffler, A. (2005), p. 25, Laitenberger, J. (2006), pp. 83 and 85, Laitenberger, J./Löffler, A. (2006), p. 292, and Rapp, M. (2006), p. 779.

The typical textbook valuation formula immediately follows if the cost of capital is a constant $k_{u,u+1} = k$ and s is the present[137]:

F 2-18 $$V_s = \sum_{t=s+1}^{\infty} \frac{E_s\left[\tilde{C}_t\right]}{(1+k)^{t-s}}$$

Therefore, if the cost of capital is non-stochastic or even a constant number, it is equal to the expected one-period return [138]. Relaxing the assumption of a deterministic expected return, Laitenberger (2006) shows that F 2-17 can only be derived if for all periods s,t [139]:

F 2-19 $$\text{cov}_s\left[\tilde{V}_{t+1}, E_{t+1}\left[\tilde{r}_{t+1,t+2}\right]\right] = 0$$

When the covariance term is not zero, the cost of capital used in F 2-17 is not equal to the expected one-period return but needs to be modified[140]:

F 2-20 $$k_{u,u+1} = E_s\left[\tilde{r}_{u,u+1}\right] + \frac{\text{cov}_s\left[\tilde{V}_u, E_u\left[\tilde{r}_{u,u+1}\right]\right]}{E_s\left[\tilde{V}_u\right]}$$

F 2-19 is satisfied by assuming that the conditional expected return $E_u\left[\tilde{r}_{u,u+1}\right]$ is a deterministic number[141] which is the case when returns are serially uncorrelated[142]. Assuming in addition that the return distributions are identical over time (i.i.d. return distribution) is sufficient to justify a constant cost of capital due to constant unconditional expected returns $E_s\left[\tilde{r}_{u,u+1}\right]$ [143]. Under these conditions, the IRR that equates F 2-18 is equivalent to the expected return.

Finally note that if the expected cash flow in F 2-18 is defined according to the amount attributable to equity holders, the cost of capital is also referred to as cost of equity which will be denoted as r^e [144]. This concept will be applied in Chapter 5.

---

[137] See Shiller, R. (1981), pp. 421 and 424, Ohlson, J. (1995), p. 666, Campbell, J./Lo, A./MacKinlay, C. (1997), pp. 254-256, Kruschwitz, L./Löffler, A. (2005), p. 26, and Richter, F. (2005), pp. 13 and 17. For a version using continuous expected returns, see Huges, J./Liu, J./Liu, J. (2009), pp. 249 and 252.

[138] See Hughes, J./Liu, J./Liu, J. (2009), p. 252. See also already Samuelson, P. (1965).

[139] See Laitenberger, J. (2006), pp. 84-85.

[140] See Laitenberger, J. (2006), p. 85.

[141] See Laitenberger, J. (2006), p. 85. See also Richter, F. (2006a), p. 31.

[142] See Richter, F. (2006a), p. 31. See also Richter, F. (2005), pp. 15-16.

[143] See Richter, F. (2005), p. 13 and Richter, F. (2006a), p. 31.

[144] See Kruschwitz, L./Löffler, A. (2005), pp. 66-67 and Richter, F. (2005), p. 40.

Risk-adjusted discount rates can now be determined as constant expected return of appropriate benchmark assets using the IRR method. This approach is one of the oldest concepts to estimate expected returns[145] and, when rigorously applied, is closely related to the theoretical concept of tracking portfolios[146], which is also referred to as replication[147] or duplication[148]. It is based on the principle that the market price of one or a combination of financials assets which perfectly tracks the uncertain cash flow of the asset to be valued should be equivalent to value of the asset itself[149]. Perfect tracking thereby means that the cash flows are identical at each point in time and in each possible state[150] which implies identical distributions over time.

It is assumed that only one benchmark asset i replicates the payoff of the valuation object j by having an identical distribution of cash flows for all t. It can then be shown that the implied cost of capital of benchmark asset i is the correct risk-adjusted discount rate to determine the value of asset j[151]:

F 2-21 $$\mathrm{P}_{\mathrm{i,s}} = \sum_{\mathrm{t=s+1}}^{\infty} \frac{E_{\mathrm{s}}\left[\tilde{\mathrm{C}}_{\mathrm{i,t}}\right]}{\left(1+\mathrm{k}_{\mathrm{i}}\right)^{\mathrm{t-s}}} = \sum_{\mathrm{t=s+1}}^{\infty} \frac{E_{\mathrm{s}}\left[\tilde{\mathrm{C}}_{\mathrm{j,t}}\right]}{\left(1+\mathrm{k}_{\mathrm{i}}\right)^{\mathrm{t-s}}} = \mathrm{V}_{\mathrm{j,s}} \quad \text{with } E_{s}\left[\tilde{\mathrm{C}}_{\mathrm{j,t}}\right] = E_{s}\left[\tilde{\mathrm{C}}_{\mathrm{i,t}}\right] \text{ for all t}$$

The restrictive assumption of perfect tracking can be relaxed if there is a linear relationship between the value of j and i. Then proportionate cash flows of j and i are sufficient[152]:

F 2-22 $$\mathrm{cP}_{\mathrm{i,s}} = \mathrm{c}\sum_{\mathrm{t=s+1}}^{\infty} \frac{E_{\mathrm{s}}\left[\tilde{\mathrm{C}}_{\mathrm{i,t}}\right]}{\left(1+\mathrm{k}_{\mathrm{i}}\right)^{\mathrm{t-s}}} = \sum_{\mathrm{t=s+1}}^{\infty} \frac{E_{\mathrm{s}}\left[\tilde{\mathrm{C}}_{\mathrm{j,t}}\right]}{\left(1+\mathrm{k}_{\mathrm{i}}\right)^{\mathrm{t-s}}} = \mathrm{V}_{\mathrm{j,s}} \quad \text{with } E_{s}\left[\tilde{\mathrm{C}}_{\mathrm{j,t}}\right] = \mathrm{c}E_{s}\left[\tilde{\mathrm{C}}_{\mathrm{i,t}}\right] \text{ for all t}$$

As a side comment, it should be noted that the valuation of uncertain cash flow streams by estimating the expected return from an replication asset appears unnecessarily complex since the same result can be achieved by applying a simple

---

145 See already Gordon, M./Shapiro, E. (1956), p. 106.
146 See Grinblatt, M./Titman, S. (2002), p. 373 and Hachmeister, D. (2006), p. 144.
147 See, e.g., Spremann, K. (2002), pp. 321ff. and Spremann, K. (2004), pp. 104ff.
148 See, e.g., Bamberg, G./Dorfleitner, G./Krapp, M. (2006), pp. 109-113, Richter, F. (2005), pp. 23-33 and Rapp, M. (2006), p. 775. Duplication is primarily used with respect to the risk-neutral valuation framework.
149 See Grinblatt, M./Titman, S. (2002), p. 373 and Spremann, K. (2004), p. 104. See also Richter, F. (2003), pp. 317-318.
150 See Richter, F. (2003), p. 314.
151 Similar to Spremann, K. (2004), p. 111.
152 See Richter, F. (2003), p. 315 and Richter, F. (2005), pp. 17 and 121.

cash flow multiple of the tracking asset if the condition is met that cash flows and values have a linear relationship[153]:

F 2-23

$$V_{j,s} = cP_{i,s} = \frac{E_s\left[\tilde{C}_{j,s+1}\right]}{E_s\left[\tilde{C}_{i,s+1}\right]} P_{i,s} = m_{i,s+1} E_s\left[\tilde{C}_{j,s+1}\right]$$

$$\text{with } c = \frac{E_s\left[\tilde{C}_{j,s+1}\right]}{E_s\left[\tilde{C}_{i,s+1}\right]} \text{ and } m_{i,s+1} = \frac{P_{i,s}}{E_s\left[\tilde{C}_{i,s+1}\right]}$$

For the estimation of the expected MRP using the IRR concept, it is assumed that $E_s\left[\tilde{C}_{M,t}\right]$ represents the aggregated expected cash flow at s and $P_{M,s}$ the aggregated market value of all assets traded on the stock market. Then, F 2-18 can be rewritten as[154]

F 2-24 $$-P_{M,s} + \sum_{t=s+1}^{\infty} \frac{E_s\left[\tilde{C}_{M,t}\right]}{\left(1+IRR\right)^{t-s}} = 0$$

where IRR represents the expected constant market return $E_s\left[\tilde{r}_M\right]$ if the previous assumption of an i.i.d. return distribution is applied implying deterministic conditional and constant unconditional expected returns. Deducting the deterministic risk-free rate from $E_s\left[\tilde{r}_M\right]$ leads consequently to the expected MRP[155]. A detailed discussion of the conceptual specifications of the risk-free rate for the IRR method is provided in 2.3.2 and 2.4.

2.3.2 Risk-adjusted discount rates based on the CAPM

Instead of estimating risk-adjusted expected returns directly from alternative assets through perfect replication, an asset pricing model can be used. This is of particular importance when no appropriate alternative assets are available for perfect replication[156]. The most widely used asset pricing model to estimate risk-adjusted expected returns from market parameters is the capital asset pricing model (CAPM) published almost simultaneously by Sharpe (1964), Lintner (1965) and Mossin (1966) in the 1960s based on the earlier innovations in portfolio theory developed by

---

[153] See Richter, F. (2006a), p. 17. See also Richter, F. (2003), pp. 315-316.
[154] See Richter, F. (2005), p. 18.
[155] See Richter, F. (2006), pp. 18 and 31.
[156] See Grinblatt, M./Titman, S. (2002), pp. 373-374 and Richter, F. (2003), p. 322.

Markowitz (1952) [157] regarding risk reduction through diversification and the separation theorem of Tobin (1958). Under a very restrictive set of assumptions[158], the CAPM provides the single-period return which a risk-averse and utility maximizing investor with a mean-variance optimized portfolio would expect from an investment in a risky asset with asset returns assumed to be normally distributed. In equilibrium, the expected return based on the CAPM can be expressed according to the following well known formula:

F 2-25

$$\begin{aligned} E\left[\tilde{r}_j\right] &= r^f + \frac{\operatorname{cov}\left[\tilde{r}_j;\tilde{r}_M\right]}{\operatorname{var}\left[\tilde{r}_M\right]}\left(E\left[\tilde{r}_M\right]-r^f\right) \\ &= r^f + \beta_j\left(E\left[\tilde{r}_M\right]-r^f\right) \\ &= r^f + \beta_j E\left[\tilde{r}^p\right] \\ &= r^f + E\left[\tilde{r}_j^s\right] \end{aligned}$$

with:

$E\left[\tilde{r}_j\right]$ = expected return of asset j

r^f = risk-free rate

$\operatorname{cov}\left[\tilde{r}_j;\tilde{r}_M\right]$ = covariance of expected returns on market and asset j

$\operatorname{var}\left[\tilde{r}_M\right]$ = variance of the expected market return

$E\left[\tilde{r}_M\right]$ = expected market return

β_j = beta factor of asset j

$E\left[\tilde{r}^p\right]$ = expected MRP

$E\left[\tilde{r}_j^s\right]$ = expected risk surcharge for asset j

The expected return according to the CAPM equals the risk-free rate plus a risk-surcharge consisting of the beta factor (quantity of risk) multiplied with the expected MRP of the market portfolio (price of risk).

---

[157] See Ballwieser, W. (2005), p. 321.

[158] See Sharpe, W. (1964), pp. 427-433, Lintner, J. (1965), pp. 15-16, Mossin, J. (1966), pp. 769-775, and Treynor, J. (1961), pp. 15-21. See also for contemporary summaries Richter, F. (1999), p. 57, Copeland, T./Weston, F./Shastri, K. (2005), pp. 147-148, Ballwieser, W. (2007), pp. 94-95, Rosarius, S. (2007), p. 61, Bodie, Z./Kane, A./Marcus, A. (2009), p. 280, and Kruschwitz, L. (2009), p. 369.

For interpretation purposes, it is convenient to express the beta factor using the correlation coefficient ρ_{jM}[159]:

$$\textbf{F 2-26}\quad \beta_j = \frac{\text{cov}[\tilde{r}_j;\tilde{r}_M]}{\text{var}[\tilde{r}_M]} = \frac{\rho_{jM}\,\text{std}[\tilde{r}_j]\text{std}[\tilde{r}_M]}{\text{var}[\tilde{r}_M]} = \frac{\rho_{jM}\,\text{std}[\tilde{r}_j]}{\text{std}[\tilde{r}_M]}$$

This expression demonstrates that the beta factor measures the relative risk of asset j in relation to the market portfolio[160]. However, relative risk is not determined based on the ratio of both standard deviations alone but by also reflecting the correlation between asset j and the market portfolio. Thereby only systematic risk is compensated whereas asset specific or idiosyncratic risk is assumed to be fully diversifiable[161]. When the CAPM formula is applied to the entire market, the beta factor is one since the covariance between the returns of the market portfolio equal its variance[162]:

$$\textbf{F 2-27}\quad \beta_M = \frac{\text{cov}[\tilde{r}_M;\tilde{r}_M]}{\text{var}[\tilde{r}_M]} = \frac{\text{var}[\tilde{r}_M]}{\text{var}[\tilde{r}_M]} = 1$$

This analytically confirms that the risk surcharge of the market portfolio is equal to the expected MRP. Generally, the MRP required by the CAPM formula is based on a forward-looking expected value. This comes back to the issue raised in the introduction that using historical data is generally not in compliance with the CAPM. However, the usage of ex-post MRPs is consistent with the CAPM, if the average of ex-post MRPs is equal to the expected MRP, i.e., when MRPs follow an i.i.d. normal process and parameter uncertainty is ignored. This topic will be discussed in Section 4.3.1.

The CAPM can also be derived by replicating cash flow distributions with tracking portfolios that consist of a certain allocation between the market portfolio and riskless assets[163]. When the tracking portfolio replicates the cash flows imperfectly—i.e., with regards to its standard deviation—its value is still equal to the valuation object if

---

[159] See, e.g., Spremann, K. (2004), p. 134 and Richter, F. (2005), p. 33.

[160] See Drukarczyk, J./Schüler, A. (2009), pp. 56-57 and Kruschwitz, L. (2009), pp. 372-373.

[161] See, e.g., Spremann, K. (2004), pp. 133-135, Copeland, T./Weston, F./Shastri, K. (2005), p. 152, and Ballwieser, W. (2007), pp. 94-95.

[162] See Copeland, T./Weston, F./Shastri, K. (2005), p. 152 and Drukarczyk, J./Schüler, A. (2009), p. 57.

[163] See Spremann, K. (2002), pp. 321-327, Grinblatt, M./Titman, S. (2002), pp. 374-379, Bamberg, G./Dorfleitner, G./Krapp, M. (2004), pp. 112-113, Richter, F. (2005), pp. 28-33, Hachmeister, D. (2006), pp. 144-146, and Richter, F. (2007b), pp. 7-8.

the tracking error represents no systematic risk. Compliant with a key principle of the CAPM, it is assumed that the tracking error can be fully diversified implying a zero net present value[164]. It is therefore only required that an asset and its tracking portfolio have the same expected value and the same amount of systematic risk measured by the beta factor in order to determine the expected return. The beta factor also represents the share of the tracking portfolio invested in the market portfolio[165].

Despite its appeal as closed theoretical concept and the ease of implementation in practical applications, the empirical analyses of the CAPM have shown unsatisfactory results regarding its ability to explain return differences[166].

Since the CAPM is a one-period model[167], the application of CAPM-based discount rates for valuing uncertain multi-period cash flows requires further restrictions. Fama (1977) has developed the conditions under which the one-period CAPM can be repeatedly used to value uncertain cash flows over multiple periods[168]. Firstly, uncertainty about market values is defined as the reassessment through time of the underlying probability distribution of cash flows. Secondly, uncertainty about the risk-adjusted discount rate is inadmissible[169]. Therefore, the parameters risk-free rate, market price of risk $\left(E\left[\tilde{r}_{M,t}\right]-r_t^f\right)/\mathrm{var}\left[\tilde{r}_{M,t}\right]$, and the covariance term $\mathrm{cov}\left[\tilde{r}_{j,t};\tilde{r}_{M,t}\right]$ must evolve deterministically over time in order to ensure pricing in compliance with the

---

[164] See Grinblatt, M./Titman, S. (2002), p. 375 and Richter, F. (2006), pp. 30-31.

[165] See Grinblatt, M./Titman, S. (2002), p. 375, Richter, F. (2003), p. 312, fn. 7, Richter, F. (2005), p. 40, and Hachmeister, D. (2006), pp. 145-146.

[166] See, e.g., Copeland, T./Weston, F./Shastri, K. (2005), pp. 164-171, Fama, E./French, K. (2004), pp. 30-44, Campbell, J./Lo, A./MacKinlay, C. (1997), pp. 211-218, and Hachmeister, D. (2000), pp. 187-189 for summaries of empirical studies for the US and German capital market.

[167] See, e.g., Copeland, T./Weston, F./Shastri, K. (2005), p. 156 and Ballwieser, W. (2007), p. 94.

[168] On the issue of CAPM-based risk-adjusted discount rates in context for multi-period valuations, see also Fama, E. (1996), pp. 424-426, Brennan, M. (1997), pp. 82-83, Schwetzler, B. (2000), pp. 475-480 associated with Kürsten, W. (2002) and Schwetzler, B. (2002), Röder, K./Müller, S. (2001), Brennan, M. (2003), pp. 175-180, Bamberg, G./Dorfleitner, G./Krapp, M. (2004), pp. 114-115, Stehle, R. (2004), pp. 912-913, Hachmeister, D. (2006), pp. 147-148, Laitenberger, J. (2006), pp. 83-86, Wiese, J. (2006a), pp. 36-41, Wiese, J. (2006b), pp. 243-244, Ballwieser, W. (2007), p. 81, Reese, R./Wiese, J. (2007), pp. 47-48, Rosarius, S. (2007), p. 63, Drukarczyk, J./Schüler, A. (2009), pp. 68-72, or Hachmeister, D./Wiese, J. (2009), p. 58.

[169] See Fama, E. (1977), pp. 7-14.

CAPM[170]. However, the fact that these parameters must be known when applying the CAPM in a multi-period setting does not mean that they necessarily need to be constant over time[171]. In summary, consistency with the CAPM requires risk-adjusted discount rates to evolve deterministically in a multi-period context and the reassessment of expected cash flows is the only source of risk.

The final topic discussed in this section relates to inconsistencies arising when combining time-variable risk-free rates with constant MRPs. As a starting point, the most general version of the multi-period valuation formula for infinite expected cash flow streams using CAPM-based one-period risk-adjusted discount rates can be expressed as follows[172]:

F 2-28 $$V_{j,s} = \sum_{t=s+1}^{\infty} \frac{E_s\left[\tilde{C}_{j,t}\right]}{\prod_{u=s}^{t-1}\left(1 + r^f_{u,u+1} + \beta_{j,u,u+1} r^p_{u,u+1}\right)} = \sum_{t=s+1}^{\infty} \frac{E_s\left[\tilde{C}_{j,t}\right]}{\prod_{u=s}^{t-1}\left(1 + r^f_{u,u+1} + r^s_{j,u,u+1}\right)}$$

In F 2-28, the present value of an uncertain cash flow stream is determined by using a deterministic but time-variable one-period discount rate consistent with the CAPM[173]. The components of the risk-adjusted discount rate such as the risk-free rate, the beta factor, and the MRP can be time-variant but must follow a known path over time (therefore $E\left[\tilde{r}^p\right] = r^p$). This implies that each individual future cash flow can be discounted using parameters with equivalent maturity. One should note that the risk-free rates used in F 2-28 are based on forward rates beyond the first period which can be recursively determined from the observable spot rates along the term

---

[170] This non-stochastic property of market parameters is required since the multi-period CAPM pricing process only holds if relationships at t between uncertainty about the returns realized and uncertainty about the characteristics of the portfolio opportunity set represented by the joint distribution of security returns one period ahead are ruled out; see Fama, E. (1970a), pp. 168-169 and Fama, E./MacBeth, J. (1974), p. 49. Therefore, stochastic variations in the risk-free rate or the market price of risk would breach this restriction and investors would be incentivized to use their portfolio decision at $t-1$ to hedge against such uncertainties leading to a pricing process inconsistent with the CAPM; see Merton, R. (1973), pp. 875-880, Long (1974), and Wallmeier, M. (1997), p. 87.

[171] See Fama, E. (1977), p. 19.

[172] Similar to, e.g., Fama, E. (1977), pp. 14 and 19, Wiese, J. (2006b), p. 244, or Reese, R./Wiese, J. (2007), p. 47. Also similar to Laitenberger, J. (2006), p. 83, Laitenberger, J./Löffler, A. (2006), p. 292 and Rapp, M. (2006), p. 779. An alternative derivation of this expression can be found in Brennan, M. (1997), p. 83; see also Richter, F. (1999), pp. 66-67.

[173] See Brennan, M. (1997), p. 81.

structure curve[174]. It should also be noted that when expressing F 2-28 with spot time-variable risk-free rates and risk surcharges as

F 2-29 $$V_{j,s} = \sum_{t=s+1}^{\infty} \frac{E_s\left[\tilde{C}_{j,t}\right]}{\left(1 + r_{s,t}^{f} + r_{j,s,t}^{s}\right)^{t-s}}$$

the valuation result differs from F 2-28 since the implied discount rates are different due to $\left(1 + r_{s,s+1}^{f} + r_{s,s+1}^{s}\right)\left(1 + r_{s+1,s+2}^{f} + r_{s+1,s+2}^{s}\right)\ldots\left(1 + r_{T-1,T}^{f} + r_{T-1,T}^{s}\right) \neq \left(1 + r_{s,T}^{f} + r_{s,T}^{s}\right)^{T}$. In Table 75 illustrative discount rates for the forward and spot rate models are provided showing the small but obvious difference over longer horizons.

In order to operationalize the parameters of F 2-28 for empirical applications, further assumptions are frequently taken regarding the development of the risk-free rate and the risk surcharge. A first derivative continues to use a term-structure based risk-free rate but assumes a constant risk surcharge which implies a constant beta factor and MRP[175]. In the absence of practical models to determine the term structure of the MRP, practitioners regard this simplification as necessary[176]. The valuation formula can then be expressed as follows[177]:

F 2-30 $$V_{j,s} = \sum_{t=s+1}^{\infty} \frac{E_s\left[\tilde{C}_{j,t}\right]}{\prod_{u=s}^{t-1}\left(1 + r_{u,u+1}^{f} + \beta_j r^{p}\right)} = \sum_{t=s+1}^{\infty} \frac{E_s\left[\tilde{C}_{j,t}\right]}{\prod_{u=s}^{t-1}\left(1 + r_{u,u+1}^{f} + r_j^{s}\right)}$$

Operationalizing the infinite sum, F 2-30 is typically modified to reflect a period with explicit year-by-year cash flow and discount rate forecasts and a terminal period which assumes the underlying asset to be in a steady state with constant and

---

[174] See Reese, R. (2007), p. 25 and Obermaier, R. (2008), p. 505. The requirement to use forward rates is also driven by the fact that the CAPM is originally a single-period model which does not foresee any multi-period rates such as spot rates for $t > 1$; see Reese, R. (2007), pp. 25-26. The relationship between spot rates and forward rates can be expressed as follows $(1 + r_{s,T}^{f})^{T} = (1 + r_{s,s+1}^{f})(1 + r_{s+1,s+2}^{f})\ldots(1 + r_{T-1,T}^{f})$; see Copeland, T./Weston, F./Shastri, K. (2005), pp. 260-261, Fabozzi, F. (2005), pp. 148-151, and Ilmanan, A. (2005), pp. 160-163.

[175] This implies constant covariance risk and constant market price of risk; see Drukarczyk, J./Schüler, A. (2009), pp. 68-72.

[176] See Jonas, M./Wieland-Blöse, H./Schiffarth, S. (2005), pp. 651-652.

[177] See, e.g., Claus, J./Thomas, J. (2001), p. 1636 or Reese, R. (2007), p. 25.

deterministic cash flow growth[178]. With $r^f_{s,T+1} + r^s_j > g_j$, F 2-30 can then be rewritten as follows[179]:

F 2-31

$$V_{j,s} = \sum_{t=s+1}^{\infty} \frac{E_s\left[\tilde{C}_{j,t}\right]}{\prod_{u=s}^{t-1}\left(1 + r^f_{u,u+1} + r^s_j\right)}$$
$$= \sum_{t=s+1}^{T} \frac{E_s\left[\tilde{C}_{j,t}\right]}{\prod_{u=s}^{t-1}\left(1 + r^f_{u,u+1} + r^s_j\right)} + \frac{E_s\left[\tilde{C}_{j,T}\right]\left(1+g_j\right)}{\left(r^f_{s,T+1} + r^s_j - g_j\right) \prod_{u=s}^{T-1}\left(1 + r^f_{u,u+1} + r^s_j\right)}$$

Since the terminal value concept is only introduced at this stage to show certain analytical relationships, the technical specifications will be discussed in Section 5.1. One should note that the usage of time-variable risk-free rates with a constant risk surcharge is criticized[180]. In a further step of simplification, the forward risk-free rates are replaced by spot rates of equivalent maturity compared to the respective cash flow[181]:

F 2-32

$$V_{j,s} = \sum_{t=s+1}^{\infty} \frac{E_s\left[\tilde{C}_{j,t}\right]}{\left(1 + r^f_{s,t} + \beta_j r^p_M\right)^{t-s}} = \sum_{t=s+1}^{\infty} \frac{E_s\left[\tilde{C}_{j,t}\right]}{\left(1 + r^f_{s,t} + r^s_j\right)^{t-s}}$$
$$= \sum_{t=s+1}^{T} \frac{E_s\left[\tilde{C}_{j,t}\right]}{\left(1 + r^f_{s,t} + r^s_j\right)^{t-s}} + \frac{E_s\left[\tilde{C}_{j,T}\right]\left(1+g_j\right)}{\left(r^f_{s,T+1} + r^s_j - g_j\right)\left(1 + r^f_{s,T} + r^s_j\right)^{T-s}}$$

Even if consistently applied[182], the valuation result of equations F 2-30 and F 2-32 using the same risk surcharge differs since $\left(1 + r^f_{s,s+1} + r^s\right)\left(1 + r^f_{s+1,s+2} + r^s\right) \neq \left(1 + r^f_{s,s+2} + r^s\right)^2$ unless the term structure of the risk-free rate is flat or the risk surcharge is zero[183]. Therefore, F 2-32 is not consistent with the starting equation F 2-28. Already at this

---

[178] See Campbell, J./Lo, A./MacKinlay, C. (1997), p. 256.

[179] See on the conceptual considerations of multi-stage models, e.g., Damodaran, A. (2002), pp. 329-331, Koller, T./Goedhart, M./Wessels, D. (2005), p. 271, or Lobe, S. (2005), pp. 8 and 65-104 for a detailed summary of terminal value considerations. A similar formula is applied by Claus, J./Thomas, J. (2001), p. 1363. Note that due to the assumption of a constant discount rate for the terminal value period, the perpetual risk-free rate becomes a spot rate since forward and spot rates are equal for flat term structures.

[180] See Richter, F. (2002a), p. 357, fn. 62.

[181] See Reese, R. (2007), p. 25 and Reese, R./Wiese, J. (2007), pp. 46-47. See also Ballwieser, W. (1988), pp. 805-809 and Brennan, M. (2003), pp. 175-178 for the necessary conditions of this version.

[182] Using the approach to determine the forward rate as presented in fn. 174.

[183] See Reese, R. (2007), p. 25 and Reese, R./Wiese, J. (2007), p. 47.

point, the issue of combining variable risk-free rates with a constant MRPs could be raised but will be discussed at a later stage.

From this point, it is only a minor step to assume an entirely constant risk-adjusted discount rate over time including a risk-free rate with a flat term structure[184]:

F 2-33
$$\begin{aligned} V_{j,s} &= \sum_{t=s+1}^{\infty} \frac{E_s\left[\tilde{C}_{j,t}\right]}{\left(1+r^f+\beta_j r_M^p\right)^{t-s}} = \sum_{t=s+1}^{\infty} \frac{E_s\left[\tilde{C}_{j,t}\right]}{\left(1+r^f+r_j^s\right)^{t-s}} \\ &= \sum_{t=s+1}^{T} \frac{E_s\left[\tilde{C}_{j,t}\right]}{\left(1+r^f+r_j^s\right)^{t-s}} + \frac{E_s\left[\tilde{C}_{j,t}\right]\left(1+g_j\right)}{\left(r^f+r_j^s-g_j\right)\left(1+r^f+r_j^s\right)^{T-s}} \end{aligned}$$

This version is the common valuation formula among practitioners and is consistent with F 2-28 unlike F 2-32 since $\left(1+r_{s,s+1}^f+r^s\right)\left(1+r_{s+1,s+2}^f+r^s\right)=\left(1+r_{s,s+2}^f+r^s\right)^2$ with $r_{s,s+1}^f=r_{s+1,s+2}^f=r_{s,s+2}^f$[185]. Assuming a constant risk-adjusted discount rate implies that the portfolio opportunities of investors through the risk-free rate and the market price of risk as well as the degree of association between the reassessed firm and market cash flows through $\text{cov}\left[\tilde{r}_j;\tilde{r}_M\right]$ are the same each period. Regarding the covariance term, "[o]ne might argue that the reassessment risk $\text{cov}\left[\tilde{r}_j;\tilde{r}_M\right]$ is inherent in the type of production activity that will generate the cash flow $\tilde{C}_t$ and in the types of activities that generate the cash flows of other firms. Since the types of production activities represented in the market may not change that much over reasonable periods, the presumption that $\text{cov}\left[\tilde{r}_j;\tilde{r}_M\right]$ is the same for each period t may not be unreasonable"[186].

As shown in this section, the repeated usage of the CAPM in multi-period valuation models is related to strict limitations on the uncertainty of input parameters. Further restrictions of valuation models are dependent on the assumed development of the risk-free rate throughout the valuation period. The next section investigates the correct definition of the risk-free rate, addresses the question which valuation model should be used in empirical studies, and discusses implications for the expected MRP estimation.

---

[184] Similar to, e.g., Fama, E. (1977), p. 20, Richter, F. (1999), p. 67, Stehle, R. (2004), p. 913, Wiese, J. (2006a), p. 38, Reese, R./Wiese, J. (2007), p. 47 or Ballwieser, W. (2007), pp. 80-81. For the general conditions associated with this simplified valuation formula, see also Ballwieser, W. (1988), pp. 805-809, Brennan, M. (1997), p. 83, and Richter, F. (1999), p. 67.

[185] See also Reese, R./Wiese, J. (2007), p. 47.

[186] Fama, E. (1977), p. 16. Note that the symbols are adjusted to the format of this study.

2.4 Expected MRP and the risk-free rate

As a core input parameter to determine realized and expected MRPs, the determination of the appropriate risk-free rate is of key importance. Risk-free assets are required to be free of default and reinvestment risk[187] and perfectly price-indexed to guarantee the return also in real terms[188]. In addition, the risk-free asset may not have any currency or maturity risk[189]. The return on the risk-free asset (risk-free rate) has also the property of a beta of 0 implying no covariance with the market portfolio[190]. For empirical purposes, government securities are typically used as risk-free assets[191].

With respect to the appropriate maturity of the risk-free rate, empirical studies typically use short-term government bills or long-term government bonds as risk-free assets and show MRPs for both definitions[192]. Treasury bills are viewed as the closest benchmark for a risk-less security due to their short maturities. Long-term treasury bonds are more exposed to price fluctuations due to changing interest rates driven by factors such as central bank policy or expected inflation[193]. Still, when using expected MRPs to determine risk-adjusted discount rates for valuation purposes, it is often argued that long-term governments bonds should be used as risk-free asset in order to match the maturity of long-term cash flow streams[194]. Furthermore, it is argued that the correct choice between the short-term and long-term risk-free rate is less important than the consistent use of the respective rate in the expected return estimation[195]. However, this statement does not imply that the expected return is the

---

[187] See Damodaran, A. (2002), pp. 154-155.

[188] See Bodie, Z./Kane, A./Marcus, A. (2009), p. 167. The authors note that the risk of unpredictable changes in the real interest rate remains.

[189] See Ballwieser, W. (2007), p. 83 and Hachmeister, D./Wiese, J. (2009), p. 55.

[190] See Copeland, T./Weston, F./Shastri, K. (2005), p. 152 or Koller, T./Goedhart, M./Wessels, D. (2005), p. 296, fn. 5.

[191] See Reese, R./Wiese, J. (2007), p. 39, Kruschwitz, L./Löffler, A. (2008), p. 805, and Hachmeister, D./Wiese, J. (2009), p. 55. See also Moxter, A. (1983), p. 146 and Wilhelm, J./Brüning, L. (1992), pp. 272-273 who call such securities "quasi" risk-less.

[192] See, e.g., Koller, T./Goedhart, M./Wessels, D. (2005), pp. 296-297, Ballwieser, W. (2007), p. 83, and Drukarczyk, J./Schüler, A. (2009), p. 209.

[193] See Jonas, M./Wieland-Blöse, H./Schiffarth, S. (2005), pp. 651-652 and Morningstar Inc. (2007c), pp. 76-77.

[194] See Damodaran, A. (2002), p. 161, Stehle, R./Hausladen, J. (2004), p. 934, Koller, T./Goedhart, M./Wessels, D. (2005), p. 296, and Morningstar Inc. (2007c), p. 75.

[195] E.g., using the CAPM to infer the expected cost of equity requires the usage of an expected MRP which is based on the same risk-free rate definition as the risk-free rate itself; see Damodaran, A. (2002), pp. 155 and 161 and Koller, T./Goedhart, M./Wessels, D. (2005), pp. 296-297.

same for different consistently used risk-free rates[196]. In order to provide more substance to these rather general statements[197], the issue needs to be discussed in a more systematic manner.

In order to identify the correct maturity definition of the risk-free rate when determining the expected MRP, the specifications of risk-free rates in valuation models are discussed first. Thereafter, the implications for the appropriate maturity of the risk-free rate to be used in calculations of the ex-post and ex-ante MRPs are deduced.

2.4.1 Concepts of risk-free rate specifications in valuation models

There appears agreement in the German literature that the risk-free rate should be determined based on the instantaneous yield level at the valuation date ("cut-off date principle" or "Stichtagsprinzip") in order to adequately reflect the realizable opportunity return of the risk-free asset at the time of the investment evaluation[198]. In addition, the maturity of the individual cash flow forecasts should match the maturity of the risk-free rate used in the discount rate for the relevant period. It is suggested to use the market yield curve of spot rates or the implied one-year forward rates to determine maturity-equivalent risk-free rates[199].

Returning to the conceptual considerations on the usage of adjusted discount rates for multi-period valuations[200], it should be noted that using risk-free spot rates with maturities over one year is inconsistent with the one-period assumption of the CAPM[201]. As shown by F 2-28, when applying the one-period CAPM repeatedly to discount cash flows over multiple periods, non-constant one-period discount rates

---

[196] It should be noted that this statement is only true, if the beta factor equals one.

[197] See also Richter, F. (2002a), pp. 357-358 and Obermaier, R. (2008), p. 505.

[198] See Gebhardt, G./Daske, H. (2005), p. 650, Knoll, L. (2006), p. 525, Obermaier, R. (2006), p. 472, Kruschwitz, L./Löffler, A. (2008), pp. 805-806, Obermaier, R. (2008), pp. 493-494, and Drukarczyk, J./Schüler, A. (2009), pp. 209-210. See also for a discussion of the "Stichtagsprinzip" Matschke, M. (1979), pp. 216ff., Hetzel, H. (1988), pp. 725-728, Moxter, A. (1983), p. 172, Baetge, J./Krause, C. (1994), p. 450, Schwetzler, B. (1996), pp. 1090-1091, and Obermaier, R. (2005), p. 4.

[199] See, e.g., Schwetzler, B. (1996), pp. 1081-1101, Copeland, T./Weston, F./Shastri, K. (2005), p. 264, Gebhardt, G./Daske, H. (2005), pp. 653-655, Jonas, M./Wieland-Blöse, H./Schiffarth, S. (2005), p. 647, Koller, T./Goedhart, M./Wessels, D. (2005), p. 297, Richter, F. (2005), p. 122, Knoll, L. (2006), p. 525, Obermaier, R. (2006), p. 472, Ballwieser, W. (2007), p. 83, Drukarczyk, J./Schüler, A. (2009), pp. 209-213, Reese, R. (2007), pp. 5-7, Kruschwitz, L./Löffler, A. (2008), p. 806, Obermaier, R. (2008), p. 493, Lampenius, N./Obermaier, R./Schüler, A. (2008), p. 246, and Hachmeister, D./Wiese, J. (2009), p. 55.

[200] See Section 2.3.2.

[201] See Brennan, M. (2003), p. 179 and fn. 26 and Brealey, R./Myers, S./Allen, F. (2008), p. 245. See also Reese, R. (2007), p. 57.

are multiplied over time[202]. Strictly following this conceptual prerequisite, compliance with the CAPM would require the determination of one-period discount rates based on the expected MRP relative to a one-year forward risk-free rate implied by the current spot rate curve[203]. Furthermore, when using the yield curve of spot rates to recursively calculate the implied one-period forward rates, the estimates are affected by the maturity spread typically included in the yield curve[204]. According to the liquidity theory, one-period forward rates therefore not only reflect expectations about the future interest rate but also include a liquidity premium in order to compensate risk-averse investors for the price risk associated with holding longer-term maturities[205]. In order to eliminate this bias, it is suggested to estimate the liquidity premium and deduct it from the forward rate[206].

Disregarding whether the limitations of the CAPM are taken into account, using maturity-equivalent risk-free rates requires the parameterization of the term structure curve which will be discussed in the following.

2.4.1.1 Variable risk-free rate approaches

The most simplistic approach to determine the risk-free rate behavior over different maturities is to use the current yield-to-maturity[207] of government bonds which

---

[202] See Reese, R. (2007), p. 57.

[203] See Brennan, M. (2003), p. 179, fn. 26.

[204] See Fabozzi, F. (2005), p. 137.

[205] See, e.g., Fabozzi, F. (2005), p. 155 and Copeland, T./Weston, F./Shastri, K. (2005), pp. 262-264. For a summary of other theories of the forward rate development, see Fabozzi, F. (2005), pp. 151-156.

[206] Similar to the approach by Brealey, R./Myers, S./Allen, F. (2008), p. 245 who, however, adjust spot rates in contrast to forward rates. Brealey/Myers/Allen suggest to use spot rates on long-term bonds and deduct the historical average term premium between the spot rates of bills and long-term bonds in order to derive a proxy for the future one-period risk-free rate excluding the liquidity premium. See also Cornell, B./Hirshleifer, J./James, E. (1997), pp. 13-14.

[207] The yield-to-maturity (hereafter simply referred to as yield) r_{YTM} of coupon as well as zero-coupon bonds equates the present value of (coupon and) face payment(s) and the current market price of the bond according to the following formula; see, e.g., Copeland, T./Weston, F./Shastri, K. (2005), pp. 259-260:

$$V_s = \sum_{t=s+1}^{T} C_t / (1 + r_{YTM})^{t-s} + F_T / (1 + r_{YTM})^{T-s} \text{ (coupon bond)}$$

$$= F_T / (1 + r_{YTM})^{T-s} \text{ (zero-coupon bond)}$$

Note that the yield to maturity is equal to the interest yield if the face value equals the current price of the bond. If the bond price is higher (lower) than the face value, the interest yield is higher (lower) than the redemption yield since it does not include the capital gain component when held to maturity.

typically include coupon payments[208]. However, coupon bonds have shorter effective maturities—also referred to as Macaulay duration[209]—since coupon payments occur before the maturity of the face value repayment. Therefore, zero-coupon bonds or zero-bonds[210] are used since all payments associated with this type of security are made at the true maturity date[211]. The separate trading of interest and principal claims of coupon bonds as so-called Strips[212] facilitates this approach. However, since the trading liquidity of Strips is substantially lower compared to coupon bonds[213], it appears more precise to use recursive methods[214] to derive implied zero-bond rates indirectly from coupon bonds[215]. A further suggestion to use swap rates[216]—particularly due to the available long maturities of up to 50 years—is also rejected in the literature since swap rates include counterparty risk which would need to be quantified and then deducted from the swap rate in order to derive the risk-free rate[217].

In summary, it was discussed that implied zero-bond yields based on government bonds including coupons are the basis for developing the term structure of the risk-less rate. However, two issues still remain: Firstly, yields are only available for selected maturities with gaps existing particularly in the long-term spectrum. Secondly, there are no yields observable beyond a 30 year maturity in most

---

208 See Obermaier, R. (2008), p. 494.

209 See, e.g., Fabozzi, F./Buetow, G./Johnson, R. (2005), p. 205, Bodie, Z./Kane, A./Marcus, A. (2009), p. 516, and Brealey, R./Myers, S./Allen, F. (2008), pp. 64-65.

210 See, e.g., Fabozzi, F./Flemming, M. (2005), p. 241 and Bodie, Z./Kane, A./Marcus, A. (2009), pp. 465-466.

211 See Jonas, M./Wieland-Blöse, H./Schiffarth, S. (2005), p. 647, Obermaier, R. (2006), p. 473, Reese, R. (2007), pp. 7-8, Reese, R./Wiese, J. (2007), p. 40, Kruschwitz, L./Löffler, A. (2008), p. 806, Obermaier, R. (2008), p. 494, and Drukarczyk, J./Schüler, A. (2009), pp. 211-213.

212 “Strips” means Separate Trading of Registered Interest and Principal Securities; see Fabozzi, F./Flemming, M. (2005), pp. 241-242.

213 See Reese, R. (2007), pp. 7-8, Reese, R./Wiese, J. (2007), p. 40, and Ballwieser, W. (2007), p. 84. See also Deutsche Bundesbank (1997), p. 63 for Germany and Grinblatt, M./Longstaff, F. (2000), pp. 1422-1425 and 1432-1435 for the US.

214 This approach is called bootstrapping; see, e.g., Gruber, W./Overbeck, L. (1998), pp. 59-73, Fabozzi, F. (2005), pp. 142-145, Gebhardt, G./Daske, H. (2005), pp. 651-653 incl. fn. 9 and 13, or Obermaier, R. (2008), pp. 494-495.

215 See Kruschwitz, L./Löffler, A. (2008), p. 806.

216 For a review of swap rate determination, see Fabozzi, F./Mann, S./Choudhry, M. (2005), pp. 1261-1266.

217 See Gebhardt, G./Daske, H. (2005), p. 650, Reese, R. (2007), p. 15, and Reese, R./Wiese, J. (2007), p. 43.

countries[218] which would be required for valuing an infinite cash flow stream. Therefore, it is required to discuss concepts that allow a continuous estimation of yields for all maturities including an estimation of the infinite yield.

In the German academic literature it is widely accepted to model the term structure of the risk-free rate based on the approach developed by Nelson/Siegel (1987)[219] and extended by Svensson (1994)—from here on referred to as NSS-model—which allows normal, inverse, U- or S-shaped curves[220]. Based on these models, the functional relationship between yield and maturity can be expressed based on the parameter vector $l=(\beta_0,\beta_1,\beta_2,\beta_3,\tau_1,\tau_2)$[221] which needs to be estimated[222]:

F 2-34

$$\begin{aligned} r_{s,t}^{f}(l) &= \beta_0 \\ &+\beta_1 \frac{1-\exp(-t/\tau_1)}{t/\tau_1} \\ &+\beta_2 \left(\frac{1-\exp(-t/\tau_1)}{t/\tau_1} - \exp(-t/\tau_1) \right) \\ &+\beta_3 \left(\frac{1-\exp(-t/\tau_2)}{t/\tau_2} - \exp(-t/\tau_2) \right) \end{aligned}$$

For $t \to \infty$ the risk-free rate converges to β_0 with τ_1 and τ_2 determining the speed of

218 An exception is France, where 50-year government bonds are issued. Still, the issue of no observable yields to infinity remains.

219 See Nelson, C./Siegel, A. (1987), pp. 473-489.

220 See Jonas, M./Wieland-Blöse, H./Schiffarth, S. (2005), pp. 647-648, Wagner, W. et al. (2006), p. 1015, Obermaier, R. (2006), pp. 473-474, Reese, R. (2007), pp. 8-14, Reese, R./Wiese, J. (2007), pp. 40-43, Ballwieser, W. (2007), pp. 83-86, Obermaier, R. (2008), pp. 494-496, Lampenius, N./Obermaier, R./Schüler, A. (2008), pp. 246-247, Drukarczyk, J./Schüler, A. (2009), pp. 211-213, and Hachmeister, D./Wiese, J. (2009), p. 55. The approach is also used by several European central banks such as the European Central Bank and the German Bundesbank; see Bank for International Settlements (2005), pp. xi-xii and Deutsche Bundesbank (1997), pp. 61-66. However, the US, the UK, and Japan use Smoothing Spline-Models; see Obermaier, R. (2008), fn. 22 and Reese, R. (2007), pp. 8-9 for a discussion of Spline models.

221 Monthly or even daily estimations for the parameters are made available, e.g., by Deutsche Bundesbank for the period since 1979 (http://www.bundesbank.de/statistik/statistik_zeitreihen.php?lang=de&open=zinsen&func=list&tr=www_s300_it03a) and by the European Central Bank for the period since 2006 (http://www.ecb.int/stats/money/yc/html/index.en.html).

222 Note that $r_{s,t}^{f}$ is a continuous return in the NSS-model. For a discussion of the estimation procedure, see Reese, R. (2007), pp. 9-11, Reese, R./Wiese, J. (2007), p. 41, and Hachmeister, D./Wiese, J. (2009), p. 55.

convergence[223] implying a close to constant level to infinity[224]. The yields estimated by the NSS-model are continuous spot rates so that discrete spot rates for usage within risk-adjusted discount rates need to be converted before application[225]. Despite the advantage of deriving spot rates for any maturity along the estimated term structure curve based on the NSS-model, the estimated spot rates may differ from the true available market-based spot rates. This underlines that the estimation of spot rates for any maturity comes at the price of differences to the available market rates[226].

Despite having established a framework to estimate a continuous term structure curve for the risk-free rate which also provides a proxy for the yield development to infinity, the determination of the appropriate "perpetual risk-free rate" needs to be discussed further when F 2-31 is used including the typical terminal value with a constant cash flow growth and a constant discount rate. The literature discusses various approaches to determine the perpetual risk-free rate. A first suggestion foresees the usage of a historical average of the risk-free rate for the longest available maturity. Historical averages have been widely used by practitioners[227] and were also supported in the academic literature[228]. The majority of authors, however, dismisses the historical approach and refers to the potential sources of bias when using historical averages such as averaging methodology, averaging period, inconsistency with the longest observable rate, and non-transferability of historical

---

[223] See Reese, R. (2007), p. 9 and Obermaier, R. (2008), p. 496.

[224] See Sack, B. (2000), p. 20 for the observation that this contradicts with observable long-term yields of Strips. However, this observations does not reflect a potential distortion of the Strips' yields due to their low trading liquidity; see Reese, R./Wiese, J. (2007), p. 43.

[225] See 2.2.1 for the formula to convert continuous rates into discrete rates. Note however, that the parameters provided by Deutsche Bundesbank directly yield discrete rates due to a differing estimation approach compared to Svensson; see Reese, R./Wiese, J. (2008), p. 42 and Obermaier, R. (2008), p. 496.

[226] See Knoll, L. (2006), pp. 526-527. Knoll estimates a permanent overstatement through the NSS method of 12 to 56 basis points based on a sample of stripped 30-year bonds from 2002 to 2005.

[227] It should be noted that until 2004 the German auditors association explicitly referred to the usage of historical averages for the determination of the perpetual risk-free rate in their valuation principals; IDW (2000), p. 837, n. 121.

[228] See Widmann, B./Schieszl, S./Jeromin, A. (2003), p. 802.

capital market conditions for the future[229]—in particular when yields have a potentially non-stationary mean. Therefore, the long-term market expectations provided by the long end of term structure curve[230] should be the basis for the perpetual risk-less rate[231].

When entirely relying on current market data, a first concept assumes a flat long-term yield curve and proposes to use the longest observable zero-bond yield as perpetual risk-free rate[232]. This approach is widely accepted[233] and appears plausible given the empirically observable convergence towards a flattened yield curve to infinity[234]. Another concept suggests using the β_0 parameter of the NSS-model as perpetual growth rate since it represents the value to which the term structure curve converges until infinity[235]. However, it is stressed that β_0 is not estimated to provide a proxy for the perpetual yield but in combination with the other parameters of the NSS-model that approximate the yield curve with least deviations. Therefore, it is possible that an almost identical yield curve can be modeled with other values for the estimated parameters showing the limited validity of β_0 as indicator of the infinite yield level[236]. Even the founding fathers for the NSS-model admit that the accuracy of the model within the shorter maturity bands does not necessarily imply the same level of

---

229 See Schwetzler, B. (1996), pp. 1081-1011, Knoll, L./Deininger, C. (2004), p. 373, Gebhardt, G./Daske, H. (2005), pp. 654-655, Jonas, M./Wieland-Blöse, H./Schiffarth, S. (2005), p. 653 (see also p. 649 for an illustration of observed distortions from the usage of an historical average), Reese, R. (2007), p. 5, Reese, R./Wiese, J. (2007), p. 38, Ballwieser, W. (2007), p. 87, Obermaier, R. (2008), p. 497, and Drukarczyk, J./Schüler, A. (2009), pp. 210-211. See also Lampenius, N./Obermaier, R./Schüler, A. (2008) for a study on valuation distortions mainly resulting from the usage of historical based yield assumptions in official valuation reports.

230 See Gebhardt, G./Daske, H. (2005), p. 650 and Obermaier, R. (2008), p. 497. Both articles stress that for the purposes of valuation, the current yield expectation of the alternative benchmark asset are to be used disregarding its current level. Another argument suggests using a convergence process to a historical mean yield when current mean levels are abnormally high (low); see Richter, F. (2002a), p. 358.

231 Some authors suggest a three-months averaging of current yields in order to smoothen the underlying volatility; see Jonas, M./Wieland-Blöse, H./Schiffarth, S. (2005), p. 652. Given the efficiency of the bond markets, this argument does not appear plausible and is not consistent with a strictly market-based risk-free rate derivation; see Knoll, L. (2006), p. 527, Obermaier, R. (2006), p. 475, Reese, R. (2007), p. 17, and Ballwieser, W. (2007), p. 86.

232 See Schwetzler, B. (1996), pp. 1081-1011 and Gebhardt, G./Daske, H. (2005), p. 654.

233 See Richter, F. (2002a), p. 358, Gebhardt, G./Daske, H. (2005), p. 654, Reese, R. (2007), p. 20, Reese, R./Wiese, J. (2007), p. 45, and Hachmeister, D./Wiese, J. (2009), p. 56.

234 See Obermaier, R. (2008), p. 499.

235 See Obermaier, R. (2006), p. 476, Reese, R. (2007), pp. 16-17, Reese, R./Wiese, J. (2007), pp. 43-44 (both Reese articles mention the problems of the NSS-model to estimate inverse yield curves for longer maturities), and Obermaier, R. (2008), pp. 499-500.

236 See Obermaier, R. (2006), p. 475 and Hachmeister, D./Wiese, J. (2009), p. 56.

accuracy for longer maturity levels[237]. This issue is also exemplified by the considerable volatility of β_0 estimates over time including several substantial outliers[238].

A similar approach, assuming a flat long-term yield curve with a converging risk-free rate is the linear regression based on an Ornstein/Uhlenbeck process[239]. The convergence is thereby estimated according to the following regression equation:

F 2-35 $r_{s,t}^f - r_{s,t-1}^f = \hat{\alpha} + \hat{\beta} r_{s,t-1}^f + \hat{\varepsilon}$

After estimating the regression parameters from the observable zero-bond yields, the infinite yield level can be calculated as follows:

F 2-36 $r_{s,\infty}^f = -\frac{\hat{\alpha}}{\hat{\beta}}$

Disregarding the debate on the validity of the regression approach in context of the one-period CAPM[240], it needs to be highlighted that this method only leads to plausible results for normal (e.g., non-inverse or linear) curves and should therefore not be used when the empirical term structure curve takes abnormal shapes[241].

Therefore, consistently plausible results for the perpetual risk-free rate are only provided by assuming a flat term structure for the long-term based on the longest observable zero-bond yield due to the various issues associated with using historical yields, the β_0 implied by the NSS-model, or $r_{s,\infty}^f$ from the regression approach[242].

---

[237] See Nelson, C./Siegel, A. (1987), p. 487.

[238] See Jonas, M./Wieland-Blöse, H./Schiffarth, S. (2005), p. 650 and Obermaier, R. (2008), p. 503.

[239] See Obermaier, R. (2006), pp. 476-477, Obermaier, R. (2008), pp. 500-502, and Hachmeister, D./Wiese, J. (2009), p. 56. See also Dixit, A./Pindyck, R. (1993), pp. 74-78 and Richter, F. (2002a), pp. 109-111. For a detailed discussion of the underlying Ornstein/Uhlenbeck process, see Vasicek, O. (1977).

[240] See Reese, R./Wiese, J. (2007), pp. 44-45, Obermaier, R. (2008), pp. 500-501, and Hachmeister, D./Wiese, J. (2009), p. 57 for a discussion of using stochastic yields to determine the risk-free rate while the multi-period version of the CAPM requires it to be deterministic. Obermaier rightfully stresses that the input data can be regarded as deterministic so that there is no consistency issue.

[241] See Obermaier, R. (2008), pp. 501-502 and Hachmeister, D./Wiese, J. (2009), p. 57.

[242] See Reese, R. (2007), p. 20, Reese, R./Wiese, J. (2007), p. 45, Ballwieser, W. (2007), p. 85, Obermaier, R. (2008), pp. 503-504, Drukarczyk, J./Schüler, A. (2009), p. 211, and Hachmeister, D./Wiese, J. (2009), p. 56. This approach is also recommended by the valuation council (FAUB) of the German auditors association (IDW); see IDW (2008b), p. 491.

2.4.1.2 Uniform risk-free rate approaches

Several authors in the German literature propose to determine an implied uniform risk-free rate to simplify the application of valuation formulas[243]. In the modified approach by Reese/Wiese (2007), the implied uniform rate r_U^f is calculated under the simplifying assumption that cash flows grow at a constant rate so that F 2-30 can be rewritten as[244]:

F 2-37 $$V_s = \sum_{t=s+1}^{\infty} \frac{C_s(1+g)^t}{\prod_{u=s}^{t-1}\left(1+r_{u,u+1}^f+r^s\right)} = \frac{C_s(1+g)}{r_U^f+r^s-g}$$

Now the initial cash flow cancels out and the equation can be solved for the implied uniform risk-free rate:

F 2-38 $$r_U^f = \frac{(1+g)}{\sum_{t=s+1}^{\infty} \frac{(1+g)^t}{\prod_{u=s}^{t-1}\left(1+r_{u,u+1}^f+r^s\right)}} + g - r^s$$

Similarly, the expression based on F 2-32 is as follows[245]:

F 2-39 $$r_U^f = \frac{(1+g)}{\sum_{t=s+1}^{\infty} \frac{(1+g)^t}{\left(1+r_{s,t}^f+r^s\right)^t}} + g - r^s$$

Assuming that estimates of the risk-free spot and forward rate are available until infinity, Reese/Wiese analyze the derivation of the implied uniform rate by using a constant expected MRP estimate based on historical averages and running the summation term for a large enough number of periods so that the error of neglecting the period to infinity becomes negligible[246]. Despite its appeal, this approach is to be criticized due to the simplified expected cash flow process driven by a uniform

---

[243] See Jonas, M./Wieland-Blöse, H./Schiffarth, S. (2005), pp. 648 and 652 or Wagner, W. et al. (2006), pp. 1015-1016.

[244] See Reese, R. (2007), pp. 25-26 and Reese, R./Wiese, J. (2007), pp. 46-47. See also Knoll, L./Deininger, C. (2004), pp. 371ff. for an alternative calculation method for the implied uniform riskless rate using the duration concept.

[245] See Reese, R. (2007), pp. 25-26, Reese, R./Wiese, J. (2007), pp. 46-47, and Obermaier, R. (2008), p. 498. See also Hachmeister, D./Wiese, J. (2009), p. 56 for a similar expression.

[246] See also Reese, R. (2007), pp. 26-27 and Reese, R./Wiese, J. (2007), pp. 48-49. These authors use 1000 periods. See also different approaches by Jonas, M./Wieland-Blöse, H./Schiffarth, S. (2005), p. 648 (250 periods) and Obermaier, R. (2008), p. 498 (up to 1,500 periods). Both authors do not include a risk surcharge term in their calculations.

expected growth rate[247] and the identified limit quality of risk-free rate estimates beyond the last observable maturity[248].

2.4.2 Reality on risk-free rate specifications in valuation models

In summary, using forward risk-free rates implied by the term structure of spot rates at the valuation date and assuming a flat perpetual risk-free rate based on the longest reliable maturity is the most accurate definition of the risk-free rate in applied valuation models. In combination with a constant expected MRP, this argumentation would support the application of F 2-31. However, due to the complexity in derivation and implementation, the risk-free rate is often assumed to be flat for empirical and practical applications as in F 2-33 and equal to the long-term bond rate[249]. Damodaran (2002) provides this reasoning: "A purist's view of the risk-free rate would then require different risk-free rates for each period, and different expected returns. As a practical compromise, however, it is worth noting that the present value effect of using year-specific risk-free rates tends to be small for most well-behaved term structures"[250]. With respect to the appropriate long-term maturity, Koller/Goedhart/Wessels suggest: "For U.S.-based corporate valuation, the common proxy is the 10-year-government bond (longer-dated bonds such as the 30-year treasury might match the cash flow stream better, but their illiquidity can cause stale prices and yield premiums)"[251]. This view is also shared among several other authors of the German[252] as well as US[253] valuation literature while the preference for 10-

---

[247] See Gebhardt, G./Daske, H. (2005), p. 655, Knoll, L. (2006), p. 528, Obermaier, R. (2006), pp. 477-478, and Obermaier, R. (2008), pp. 498-499.

[248] See Hachmeister, D./Wiese, J. (2009), p. 56.

[249] See Cornell, B./Hirshleifer, J./James, E. (1997), p. 13 and Jonas, M./Wieland-Blöse, H./Schiffarth, S. (2005), pp. 651-652. See also Damodaran, A. (2002), p. 155 and Copeland, T./Weston, F./Shastri, K. (2005), p. 526. Key Anglo-American textbooks on valuation also recommend the application of a constant risk-free rate valuation model; see, e.g., Damodaran, A. (2002), p. 161, Koller, T./Goedhart, M./Wessels, D. (2005), p. 296, Copeland, T./Weston, F./Shastri, K. (2005), p. 526, Ross, S./Westerfield, R./Jaffe, J. (2008), p. 495, and Brealey, R./Myers, S./Allen, F. (2008), p. 245.

[250] Damodaran, A. (2002), p. 155. Well-behaved term structures are assumed to be normal upward sloping yield curves with long-term rates being 2-3% higher compared to short-term rates.

[251] Koller, T./Goedhart, M./Wessels, D. (2005), p. 296. See also Morningstar Inc. (2007c), p. 75.

[252] See, e.g., Gebhardt, G./Daske, H. (2005), p. 653 and Widmann, B./Schieszl, S./Jeromin, A. (2003), p. 801.

[253] See, e.g., Copeland, T./Weston, F./Shastri, K. (2005), p. 259 and Koller, T./Goedhart, M./Wessels, D. (2005), p. 296. See also the survey of Bruner at al. (1998) which finds for a sample of 27 leading US corporations that 33% use 10-year treasuries as risk-free rate and another 33% treasuries with 10 to 30-year maturities; see Bruner et al. (1998), p. 17.

year maturities is stronger in the US compared to Germany[254]. Ultimately, previous studies in this field require the usage of 10-year maturities in order to deliver comparable results[255].

2.4.3 General risk-free rate specifications for this study

Based on the discussion in the previous section, the risk-free rate maturities used in this study for the calculation of ex-ante as well as ex-post expected MRP estimates need to be defined. The guiding principle is consistency with the predominant empirical and practical valuation model F 2-33. Consistency thereby means that the risk-free rate used in the valuation model must have the identical maturity as the risk-free rate used to determine the expected MRP. In order to underline the importance of this aspect, the following example illustrates the bias resulting from inconsistent maturities[256].

It shall be assumed that the expected MRP estimate relative to 10-year government bond spot rates is equal to 5.00% while the expected return is flat as presented in Table 1. If this expected MRP is used in a valuation framework using variable risk-free rates (i.e., F 2-32) instead of constant spot risk-free rates (i.e., F 2-33) and assuming a typical upward sloping term structure curve due to impact of the liquidity premium, the usage of a constant expected MRP would ceteris paribus lead to an understatement of the expected returns for the periods $t < 10$. As shown in Table 1, the expected return for period 1 would then equal 8.00% instead of 9.80% using constant average rates for the expected MRP and the 10-year spot risk-free rate.

---

254 E.g., Ballwieser, W. (2007), p. 87 favors 30-year maturities. See also the discussion in Wenger, E. (2003), pp. 480-484 and Schmitt, D./Dausend, F. (2006), pp. 233-236.

255 See Sections 5.1.3, 5.2.4, and 5.3.3.

256 This issue of consistency is particularly highlighted because the recent German literature (see, e.g., Gebhardt, G./Daske, H. (2005), Reese, R. (2007), or Reese, R./Wiese, J. (2007)) which advocates the usage of variable risk-free rates fails to explicitly state that this requires either a term structure for the MRP or at least the usage of a constant expected MRP calculated on an average maturity risk-free rate, i.e., using variable risk-free rates for the IRR-based approach or a historical average risk-free rate of all available maturities when calculating unconditional ex-post MRPs; see, e.g., Stehle, R. (2004), pp. 920-921 who uses the REXP-based rate which is based on a portfolio of all German government bonds with a maturity > 1 year. See also Obermaier, R. (2008), p. 505.

Table 1 Impact of inconsistent risk-free rate maturities on the expected MRP

	r^f	r	r^p	r^p		r	r
	(1)	(2)	(2) - (1)	(3)		(3) + (1)	10y (3) + (1)
Maturity	Current spot rate	Const. expected return	Expected MRP based on variable spot rate	Expected MRP based on const. 10y spot rate	beta	Variable spot r^f + const. expected r^p	Const. spot r^f + const. expected r^p
1	3.00%	9.80%	6.80%	5.00%	1	8.00%	9.80%
2	3.30%	9.80%	6.50%	5.00%	1	8.30%	9.80%
3	3.58%	9.80%	6.23%	5.00%	1	8.58%	9.80%
4	3.83%	9.80%	5.98%	5.00%	1	8.83%	9.80%
5	4.05%	9.80%	5.75%	5.00%	1	9.05%	9.80%
6	4.25%	9.80%	5.55%	5.00%	1	9.25%	9.80%
7	4.43%	9.80%	5.38%	5.00%	1	9.43%	9.80%
8	4.58%	9.80%	5.23%	5.00%	1	9.58%	9.80%
9	4.70%	9.80%	5.10%	5.00%	1	9.70%	9.80%
10	**4.80%**	**9.80%**	**5.00%**	**5.00%**	**1**	**9.80%**	**9.80%**

Note: All figures are only for illustrative purposes.

This example shows the impact of using a constant expected MRP estimate in combination with a variable risk-free rate. An almost opposite case can also occur when, e.g., the expected MRP is estimated based on the IRR approach using a valuation model with variable risk-free rates. Then, the expected MRP is measured relative to an average maturity creating another bias when applied in a valuation model using a constant risk-free rate. These examples illustrate that the potential advantage of using variable risk-free rates creates other sources of bias.

Therefore, the dominance of constant risk-free rate valuation models based on 10-year government bond rates is accepted and consistent estimates for the expected MRP both using ex-post as well as ex-ante data for this maturity are provided[257].

2.4.4 Return components of the ex-post risk-free rate

A final topic related to the risk-free rate is the definition of the correct return calculation methodology when choosing long-term bonds rates as risk-free rate for ex-post MRP calculations. Generally, the ex-post total return of assets comprises two

---

[257] There is, however, also empirical evidence that this issue of consistency is of minor magnitude for IRR-based expected MRP estimates. Claus/Thomas (2001) came to the conclusion that the difference in results of applying F 2-31 compared to F 2-33 is negligible based on estimates for the US. "While the (...) equity premium estimates (...) derived from non-flat risk-free rates are in concept more accurate than those derived by subtracting 10-year risk-free rates from the flat k (...) the numbers reported (...) are very similar (...). We only consider equation (5) [flat risk-free rate model] estimates hereafter because (a) the magnitudes of the discount rates and their relation to risk-free rates are more transparent for the risk premium estimates based on constant risk-free rates, and (b) forward one-year rates for different maturities are not available for the other five markets"; Claus, J./Thomas, J. (2001), p. 1641.

key individual components[258]: the income return[259] and the capital appreciation (gain) return. The one-period total return expression for the risk-less asset can therefore be expressed as follows:

$$\text{F 2-40} \quad \tilde{r}_t \text{ (total return)} = \frac{\tilde{C}_t}{\tilde{P}_{t-1}} \text{(income return)} + \frac{\tilde{P}_t - \tilde{P}_{t-1}}{\tilde{P}_{t-1}} \text{(capital appreciation return)}$$

The issue is now whether to include the income return only or the capital gain as well. As shown by Table 2, there are is no common approach used within empirical studies on the ex-post MRP.

Table 2 Overview of risk-free rate definitions of selected authors of historical MRP studies

Authors	Approach	Reasoning
Arnott/Bernstein (2002)[260]	• Income return only	• Capital appreciation return zero in expectation
Dimson/Marsh/Staunton (2002)[261]	• Total return	• Equal treatment of equity and bond returns
Ibbotson/Cheng (2003)[262]	• Income return only	• No particular reasoning provided
Stehle (2004)[263]	• Total return	• No particular reasoning provided
Morningstar Inc. (2007c)[264]	• Income return only	• Capital appreciation return not risk-less
Siegel (2008)[265]	• Total return	• No particular reasoning provided

Whereas there is agreement that the income return should be part of the risk-less rate to compute the realized MRP, there are differing views on including the capital appreciation return[266]. The widely used valuation yearbook of Morningstar Inc. (formerly Ibbotson Associates) argues that the risk-less rate used to estimate the expected MRP should only include the income return since the capital appreciation

---

258 Morningstar Inc. mentions the reinvestment return as a third component that refers to the return originating from reinvesting the investment income from a prior period; see Morningstar Inc. (2007c), p. 76. However, this return component is a conceptual necessity required for compounding over multi-periods and thus irrelevant for the above discussion.
259 Income return is also referred to as interest yield.
260 See Arnott, R./Bernstein, P. (2002), p. 75.
261 See Dimson, E./Marsh, P./Staunton, M. (2002), p. 171.
262 See Ibbotson, R./Cheng, P. (2003), p. 89.
263 See Stehle, R. (2004), p. 920.
264 See Morningstar Inc. (2007c), pp. 76-77.
265 See Siegel, J. (2008), pp. 15 and 17.
266 Note that the issue of including the capital appreciation return only applies if bonds are chosen as benchmark. In case of bills, the income returns equals the total return; see Richter, F. (2005), p. 101.

return is not truly risk-less[267]. More precisely, the capital appreciation return is uncertain since it is driven by unexpected changes in the market bond yields that lead to according price changes. Therefore, the income return is a better estimate of the risk-free rate since investors earn the income return when holding a bond to maturity without any capital loss[268]. In contrast, Dimson/Marsh/Staunton use the total return on bonds to determine their historical MRPs. They argue that changes in the price level of bonds also affect equity prices and should therefore be consistently treated within both components of the realized MRP[269]. Still, the authors acknowledge that including the capital appreciation return for bonds may lead to confusing results if only short periods are analyzed which were subject to severe changes in the price level of bonds due to a reassessment of expectations (e.g., in expected inflation). Despite the differing points of view, the ultimate impact of using different risk-less return definitions is almost negligible over long historical return series[270]. According the Morningstar Inc., the US arithmetic average capital appreciation return from 1926 to 2006 equals 0.3%—an indication for the insignificant difference between income return and total return[271]. The herein used historical MRP calculations follow the concept of Morningstar Inc. and include only the income return component.

For approaches to estimate the ex-ante expected MRP, this issue does not apply since the current yield-to-maturity is the correct forward-looking rate.

2.5 Expected MRP and currencies

Another important conceptual aspect is the consistent usage of currency denominations. Any estimate of the expected MRP requires a precise definition of the underlying market. Herein, markets are defined by country which requires a consistent approach regarding the currency denomination of returns. Disregarding whether expected MRPs are determined using ex-post or ex-ante data, there are two generic methods to solve the currency issue. One approach requires that all input parameters for the MRP determination are denominated in the local currency

---

267 See Morningstar Inc. (2007c), pp. 76-77. See also Arnott, R./Bernstein, P. (2002), p. 75 and Stehle, R./Hausladen, J. (2004), pp. 935-936.

268 See Morningstar Inc. (2007c), p. 77.

269 See Dimson, E./Marsh, P./Staunton, M. (2002), p. 171.

270 See Stehle, R./Hausladen, J. (2004), p. 936.

271 See Morningstar Inc. (2007b), p. 4.

including a risk-free rate representative of the local portfolio of government bonds[272]. Secondly, all input parameters may be converted into the currency of one reference market using the appropriate forward exchange rates[273]. This approach consequently requires the unique usage of the risk-free rate representative of the reference market.[274]

For this study, the first method is applied since the availability of forward rates is limited so that currency conversions may not lead to fully consistent results. Finally note that the thereby calculated expected MRPs are still comparable since the MRP has no currency denomination as discussed in Section 2.1[275].

2.6 Expected MRP and inflation

There are factors that reduce the gross level of returns such as, e.g., inflation or personal taxes resulting in a lower net level available for consumption[276]. In this context, the question arises how inflation and personal taxes influence the expected MRP? The focus is first put on the relationship between inflation and the expected MRP while the impact of personal taxation is discussed in the next section.

Stock as well as bond returns can generally be calculated in nominal or real terms with the difference being related to the price level change of consumer goods. Real returns are therefore adjusted for the effect of expected inflation and indicate the true purchasing power of returns[277]. In contrast to nominal returns, which can be determined on the basis of currently observed market prices, real returns cannot be observed with the exception of yields for inflation-indexed bonds. A relationship that links nominal and real returns is the so-called Fisher effect[278]. It assumes that the ex-ante real rate of return is entirely determined through equilibrium on the product market and investor time preferences[279]. This means that ex-ante real returns are assumed to be independent from the expected inflation rate implying no change in capital productivity as a consequence of expected price level changes[280]. Under

---

[272] See, e.g., Claus, J./Thomas, J. (2001), p. 1647.

[273] See, e.g., Desrosiers, S./Lemaire, N./L'Her, J.-F. (2007), pp. 78-79.

[274] See Damodaraon, A. (2002), p. 156, Copeland, T./Weston, F./Shastri, K. (2005), p. 849, and Koller, T./Goedhart, M./Wessels, D. (2005), p. 591.

[275] See also Claus, J./Thomas, J. (2001), p. 1647.

[276] See Poddig, T./Dichtl, H./Petersmeier, K. (2008), p. 120.

[277] See Varian, H. (2006), pp. 190-191 and Mankiw, G. (2007), pp. 91-92 and 94.

[278] See Fisher, I. (1930), pp. 41-44.

[279] See Cooray, A. (2003), p. 135.

[280] See Mankiw, G. (2007), pp. 91-94 and Poddig, T./Dichtl, H./Petersmeier, K. (2008), p. 120.

these conditions the nominal return can be expressed as the sum of ex-ante (ex-post) real return and expected (ex-post) inflation rate. This relationship states that a change in the expected inflation rate leads to a one-to-one adjustment in the nominal rate due to the independence of the ex-ante real rate[281].

Formally, the ex-ante Fisher relationship can be expressed again in a geometric and arithmetic form[282]:

F 2-41 $$\begin{aligned} 1+\mathrm{R}_t^n &= (1+\mathrm{R}_t^r)(1+E[\tilde{\pi}_t]) \\ \mathrm{R}_t^n &= \mathrm{R}_t^r + E[\tilde{\pi}_t] + \mathrm{R}_t^r E[\tilde{\pi}_t] \end{aligned}$$ **geometric relationship**

F 2-42 $\mathrm{r}_t^n = \mathrm{r}_t^r + E[\tilde{\pi}_t]$ **arithmetic relationship**

with:

$\mathrm{R}_t^n / \mathrm{r}_t^n$ = discrete/continuous nominal return

$\mathrm{R}_t^r / \mathrm{r}_t^r$ = discrete/continuous real return

$E[\tilde{\pi}_t]$ = expected inflation rate

For discrete returns, the geometric version is applicable[283]. It includes the loss in purchasing power of both initial capital and intra-period proceeds in the term $\mathrm{R}_t^r E[\tilde{\pi}_t]$ [284]. The cross product term $\mathrm{R}_t^r E[\tilde{\pi}_t]$ is often ignored due to its negligible magnitude so that the arithmetic version [285] applies which is, however, only appropriate for continuous returns. Based on the Fisher relation, real returns can be calculated either directly by deducting expected inflation from nominal returns or indirectly using deflated input parameters such as prices—an alternative approach observed in empirical studies[286].

Using the Fisher relationship, the impact of inflation on the expected MRP can be analyzed. As illustrated by F 2-43, the expected MRP remains unchanged whether it is calculated in nominal or real terms[287] provided that the arithmetic or geometric

---

[281] See Wong, K.-F./Wu, H.-J. (2003), p. 917.

[282] See Varian, H. (2006), p. 191, Mankiw, G. (2007), pp. 91 and 94, and Blanchard, O. (2009), pp. 321-322 and 621. See also Moxter, A. (1983), pp. 189-190.

[283] See also the derivation of the geometric difference for the MRP in Section 2.2.1.

[284] See Poddig, T./Dichtl, H./Petersmeier, K. (2008), p. 121.

[285] See Varian, H. (2006), p. 191.

[286] See, e.g., Fama, E./French, K. (2002).

[287] See Dimson, E./Marsh, P./Staunton, M. (2002), p. 164 and Copeland, T./Weston, F./Shastri, K. (2005), p. 173.

calculation approach is consistently used and the Fisher effect holds for stock as well as bond returns.

F 2-43 Nominal and real expected MRP for consistent calculations

Arithmetic approach	Geometric approach[288]
$E[\tilde{r}_{n,t}] = E[\tilde{r}_{r,t}] + E[\tilde{\pi}_t]$ less $r^f_{n,t} = r^f_{r,t} + E[\tilde{\pi}_t]$ equals $E[\tilde{r}^p_{n,t}] = E[\tilde{r}_{n,t}] - r^f_{t,r} = E[\tilde{r}^p_{r,t}]$	$1+E[\tilde{R}_{n,t}] = \frac{1+E[\tilde{R}_{r,t}]}{1+E[\tilde{\pi}_t]}$ divided by $1+R^f_{n,t} = \frac{1+R^f_{r,t}}{1+E[\tilde{\pi}_t]}$ equals $1+E[\tilde{R}^p_{t,n}] = \frac{1+E[\tilde{R}_{r,t}]}{1+R^f_{r,t}} = 1+E[\tilde{R}^p_{r,t}]$

However, if both approaches are inconsistently combined, the expected MRP does not remain unaffected. The case of mixing arithmetic MRP calculation with the geometric the Fisher effect for discrete returns is not just a hypothetical case. E.g., it occurs in the standard valuation formula with a constant risk-adjusted discount factor (constant risk-free rate and MRP) and a constant perpetual growth rate is applied[289]. In order to achieve identical valuation results when using real and nominal input parameters[290], the following relationship for the real and nominal MRP needs to be considered assuming the geometric Fisher effect to hold and the inflation rate to be constant[291]:

F 2-44
$$V^r_{M,t} = \frac{E_t\left[\tilde{C}^r_{M,t+1}\right]}{r^f_r + r^p_r - g^r_M} = \frac{E_t\left[\tilde{C}^n_{M,t+1}\right]}{r^f_n + r^p_n - g^n_M} = V^n_{M,t}$$
$$\text{with } r^p_n = r^p_r\left(1+\pi\right)$$

The validity of the Fisher relationship for stock and bond returns has been the topic of numerous empirical investigations with inconsistent results particularly due to

---

288 Assuming returns and inflation to be independent.

289 Similar to F 2-33 when applied to an entire market and with a constant perpetual growth rate from period one onwards. If applied to individual assets, one would need to additionally assume a beta factor of one.

290 See Moxter, A. (1983), pp. 190-192 who demonstrates the equivalence under the certainty equivalent method when consistent input data is used.

291 See Appendix 2 for a derivation of this relationship.

different time horizons of returns and specifications of the utilized proxy for the expected inflation rate[292].

Against the fundamental relation between inflation and return according to Fisher and the intuition that stocks should be a hedge against inflation as they are claims against real assets, several studies focusing on US data sets and short-term stock returns with a horizon of one year or less found negative correlations between ex-ante (ex-post) nominal returns and expected (ex-post) inflation[293]. Following research tried to explain the contradictory result with tax non-neutralities[294], money illusion of investors[295], and a negative correlation between inflation and real economic activity[296]. In contrast, using long-term instead of short-term returns leads to a positive relation between ex-ante as well as ex-post inflation and stock returns[297] supporting the Fisher effect also in an international context[298]. With regards to bond returns, the support of the Fisher relation is similarly mixed in US empirical studies. In particular, the postulated one-to-one relationship between nominal interest rates and inflation cannot be confirmed[299].

Even if the general validity of the Fisher relationship remains questionable, based on existing empirical evidence, the demonstrated irrelevance of inflation for the MRP calculation still holds if expected inflation impacts stock and bond returns in the same magnitude so that its influence cancels out. Sharpe (2002) provides empirical evidence for the US market during the period 1983 and 1998 that the MRP is unrelated to the expected inflation rate. This finding suggests that the effect of expected inflation on long-term equity returns is similar to the effect on long-term bond returns[300].

2.7 Expected MRP and personal taxes

Another factor that reduces the gross level of returns is personal taxation. Personal taxes on all kinds of investor income such as dividends, interest, or realized capital

[292] See Boudoukh, J./Richardson, M. (1993), p. 1346 and Sharpe, S. (2002), pp. 632-634 for a review of studies on the relation between inflation and stock returns. See Cooray, A. (2003), pp. 136-143 for a summary of studies regarding the relationship between inflation and interest rates.

[293] See, e.g., Lintner, J. (1975), Bodie, Z. (1976), or Fama, E./Schwert, W. (1977).

[294] See Feldstein, M. (1980).

[295] See Modigliani, F./Cohn, R. (1979).

[296] See Fama, E. (1981), Geske, R./Roll, R. (1983), and Kaul, G. (1987).

[297] See Boudoukh, J./Richardson, M. (1993).

[298] See Wong, K.-F./Wu, H.-J. (2003).

[299] See Cooray, A. (2003), pp. 146-147.

[300] See Sharpe, S. (2002), pp. 644-646.

gains are in so far important as they influence the net return earned on the personal investor level. The already raised question of how personal taxes affect the expected MRP and thereby asset prices is intensively debated in the literature[301].

In the German literature it is widely accepted that for the purposes of valuation, the effect of personal taxes should be recognized since their existence is not value neutral from the investor perspective[302]. This is contradictory to the fact that many leading American textbooks exclude personal taxation from their suggested valuation models, however, without providing reasons[303]. Still, the issues arising when incorporating the impact of personal taxes in valuations are also recognized in Germany[304]. In order to more systematically analyze the impact of personal taxes on the expected MRP, risk-adjusted discount rates and valuation results, the focus is again first put on the implied cost of capital method and thereafter on the CAPM[305].

2.7.1 Risk-adjusted discount rates based on the implied cost of capital method

It is assumed that the existence of personal taxes affects observable market prices. Under such circumstances, risk-adjusted discount rates can be determined with the same IRR methodology as described in Section 2.3.1 using proportionate or even

---

301 See Jonas, M./Löffler, A./Wiese, J. (2004), p. 898, Richter, F. (2002a), pp. 332-337, Richter, F. (2004), p. 20, Hower, S. (2008), p. 2, and Kruschwitz, L./Löffler, A. (2008), p. 808. See also for a summary article on the impact of investor taxation on asset prices Shackelford, D./Shevlin, T. (2001), pp. 350-359. Fama, E./French, K. (1998), pp. 835-837 conclude that the impact of taxes is weak.

302 See Moxter, A. (1983), pp. 177-180, Leuthier, R. (1988b), pp. 158-160, Ballwieser, W. (1995), p. 36, Richter, F. (2002a), pp. 327-330, Baetge, J./Niemeyer, K./Kümmel, J. (2005), pp. 315-316, Ballwieser, W. (2007), pp. 102-104, Ballwieser, W./Kruschwitz, L./Löffler, A. (2007), pp. 765-766, Dausend, F./Schmitt, D. (2007), p. 288, Wiese, J. (2007a), p. 368, Heintzen, M./Kruschwitz, L./Löffler, A./Maiterth, R. (2008), pp. 276-277, Kruschwitz, L./Löffler, A. (2008), pp. 808-809, and Hachmeister, D./Wiese, J. (2009), pp. 60-61.

303 See, e.g., Damodaran, A. (2002), Copeland, T./Weston, F./Shastri, K. (2005), Koller, T./Goedhart, M./Wessels, D. (2005), Ross, S./Westerfield, R./Jaffe, J. (2008), and Brealey, R./Myers, S./Allen, F. (2008). See also the comments by Richter, F. (2004), p. 21 and Stehle, R. (2004), p. 914 who assumes that the ignorance of US authors is related to the similar taxation of interest, dividends, and capital gains.

304 See Schneider, D. (1992), pp. 246-250, Richter, F. (2003), and Richter, F. (2007a) on the "Steuerparadoxon" which refers to unintuitive effects of personal taxation on valuations in cases where the asset and the return of the replication asset used for discounting are not equivalently affected by personal taxation; Richter, F. (2007a), p. 6.

305 For a review of other approaches to reflect personal taxes in the cost of equity and the associated prerequisites, see Richter, F. (2002a), pp. 332-337 and Richter, F. (2004), pp. 21-22.

perfectly replicated cash flows. However, three different risk-adjusted discount rates can be calculated[306]:

F 2-45 $$-P_{i,s}^{\tau} + \sum_{t=s+1}^{\infty} \frac{E_s\left[\tilde{C}_{i,t}\right](1-\tau)}{(1+IRR_1)^{t-s}} = 0$$

F 2-46 $$-P_{i,s}^{\tau} + \sum_{t=s+1}^{\infty} \frac{E_s\left[\tilde{C}_{i,t}\right]}{(1+IRR_2)^{t-s}} = 0$$

F 2-47 $$-P_{i,s} + \sum_{t=s+1}^{\infty} \frac{E_s\left[\tilde{C}_{i,t}\right]}{(1+IRR_3)^{t-s}} = 0$$

with:

$P_{i,s}^{\tau}$ = observable markt price of asset i affected by personal taxes

$P_{i,s}$ = hypothetical market price of asset i unaffected by personal taxes

$E_s\left[\tilde{C}_{i,t}\right]$ = expected cash flow pre personal taxes of asset i in t conditional on the information at s

τ = personal tax rate

IRR_1 = expected return derived from post-tax expected cash flows and affected market prices

IRR_2 = expected return derived from pre-tax expected cash flows and affected market prices

IRR_3 = expected return derived from pre-tax expected cash flows and unaffected market prices

Under formulas F 2-45 and F 2-46 risk-adjusted discount rates can be derived that lead to identical valuation results disregarding whether the expected cash flows in the numerator is reduced by personal taxes or not[307]. This result is convenient since it implies that the no knowledge of the marginal tax rate of the asset and replication asset is required in order to achieve the same valuation result as with personal tax adjusted expected cash flows[308]. Still, the approach requires both assets to be affected by the same tax regime. F 2-47 cannot be implemented in practice since market prices unaffected by personal taxes are not observable[309].

In summary, if perfect or proportional replication assets are available for the estimation of expected returns, then personal taxes are irrelevant for valuations with IRR-based risk-adjusted discount rates[310].

---

[306] See Richter, F. (2003), p. 312.

[307] See Richter, F. (2003), p. 312.

[308] See Richter, F. (2003), p. 311 and Richter, F. (2007a), p. 10.

[309] See Richter, F. (2003), p. 312.

[310] See Richter, F. (2003), p. 327 and Richter, F. (2007b), p. 13.

2.7.2 Risk-adjusted discount rates based on the Tax-CAPM

In the absence of appropriate replication assets to infer risk-adjusted discount rates reflecting the impact of personal taxes on asset prices, again a capital market model is required[311]. Whereas the pre-personal tax (pre-tax) expected returns can be inferred from the already discussed CAPM, an estimate for post-personal tax (post-tax) expected returns including a tax-adjusted expected MRP is less readily available. An analytical model for the expected return required by investors in an environment where different personal taxes on dividends, interest, and realized capital gains exist is the so-called Tax-CAPM initially presented by Brennan (1970)[312]—an extension of the standard CAPM. In a one-period setting with deterministic dividend yields[313] an equilibrium can be characterized that reflects personal taxes[314]. Assuming equal taxation of dividend and interest income, the classic version of the Tax-CAPM can be expressed as follows[315]:

F 2-48 $$E\left[\tilde{r}_j\right]=r^f+\beta_j\left(E\left[\tilde{r}_M\right]-r^f-\left(\delta_M-r^f\right)T\right)+\left(\delta_j-r^f\right)T$$

with:

$E\left[\tilde{r}_j\right]$ = expected return of asset j

r^f = risk-free rate

β_j = beta factor of asset j

$E\left[\tilde{r}_M\right]$ = expected return on the market portfolio

δ_M = dividend yield on the market portfolio

T = tax factor

δ_j = dividend yield of asset j

---

311 See Richter, F. (2007a), p. 12.

312 See Brennan, M. (1970), pp. 420-423.

313 See Brennan, M. (1970), p. 420, Long, J. (1977), p. 27, and Litzenberger, R./Ramaswamy, K. (1979), p. 166.

314 See Jonas, M./Löffler, A./Wiese, J. (2004), p. 900 and Wiese, J. (2007a), p. 370. Note that the prices which ultimately determine the expected returns in equilibrium are always influenced by the tax regime. This implies that CAPM-based expected returns pre personal taxes are still influenced by personal taxes through the tax-affected asset prices; see Jonas, M./Löffler, A./Wiese, J. (2004), pp. 902-903.

315 See Brennan, M. (1970), p. 423, Litzenberger, R./Ramaswamy, K. (1979), p. 172, and Wiese, J. (2006c), p. 11. The Brennan version assumes equal taxation of dividends and interest but different capital gains taxation.

A more general version with different personal tax rates on dividends, interest, and realized capital gains was formulated by Jonas/Löffler/Wiese (2004)[316] splitting the expected return into expected capital gain $E\left[\tilde{r}_{cg}\right]$ and dividend yield δ:

F 2-49 $$E\left[\tilde{r}_{j,cg}\right]T_{cg}+\delta_j T_d = r^f T_i + \beta_j\left(E\left[\tilde{r}_{M,cg}\right]T_{cg}+\delta_M T_d - r^f T_i\right)$$

The tax factors T_d, T_i, and T_{cg} are not weighted averages of the individual average taxes on dividends, interest, and capital gains but ratios of investors' marginal tax rates on dividends, interest, and capital gains weighted according to the marginal rate of substitution between expected return and variance of return—all unobservable[317]. Interestingly, the calculation of the beta factor is unchanged compared to the standard CAPM while the expected MRP differs substantially[318]. Assuming identical personal tax rates for all individual investors solves the problem of individual and unobservable marginal tax rates and utility functions of investors[319]. With this specification, the tax factors in the Tax-CAPM equation can be expressed as ratios of uniform tax rates for dividends, interest, and capital gains:

F 2-50 $$T_d = \frac{1-\tau_d}{\left(1-\tau_{cg}\right)^2}\quad,\quad T_i = \frac{1-\tau_i}{\left(1-\tau_{cg}\right)^2},\ T_{cg} = \frac{1}{1-\tau_{cg}}$$

Ultimately, the operationalized Tax-CAPM for single-periods can be expressed as follows[320]:

F 2-51 $$E\left[\tilde{r}_{j,cg}\right]\left(1-\tau_{cg}\right)+\delta_j\left(1-\tau_d\right)=r^f\left(1-\tau_i\right)+\beta_j\left(E\left[\tilde{r}_{M,cg}\right]\left(1-\tau_{cg}\right)+\delta_M\left(1-\tau_d\right)-r^f\left(1-\tau_i\right)\right)$$

---

[316] For a detailed derivation of this expression see Jonas, W./Löffler, A./Wiese, J. (2004), pp. 905-906. See also Wiese, J. (2006c), pp. 7-19. See Hower, S. (2008), pp. 99-101 and 124-126 for a summary of issues around the Brennan and the Jonas/Löffler/Wiese version of the Tax-CAPM.

[317] See Jonas, M./Löffler, A./Wiese, J. (2004), pp. 905-906. See also Brennan, M. (1970), p. 422 and Litzenberger, R./Ramaswamy, K. (1979), p. 173.

[318] See Wiese, J. (2007a), p. 370.

[319] See Jonas, M./Löffler, A./Wiese, J. (2004), p. 904.

[320] See Jonas, M./Löffler, A./Wiese, J. (2004), p. 906 and Wiese, J. (2007a), p. 369. See also Richter, F. (2003), pp. 322-323 and Hower, S. (2008), pp. 117-118. For a derivation of Tax-CAPM formulas for various tax regimes using the replication method, see Richter, F. (2005), pp. 53-54 and Richter, F. (2007b), pp. 9-20. Unfortunately, there are very few empirical investigations available regarding the validity of the Tax-CAPM. Apart from providing references, this topic will not be further discussed within this study. For Germany there are only rather simplistic empirical analyses available. See Hower, S. (2008), pp. 171-224 who shows for a rather short analysis period between 2001 and 2006 that the difference of the coefficient of determination for explaining ex-post returns with the standard CAPM and the Tax-CAPM expected return period is minimal. See also Dausend, F./Schmitt, D. (2006b), pp. 157-161 who use a similar approach for the Tax-CAPM only but find a higher coefficient of determination.

with:

$E\left[\tilde{r}_{j,cg}\right]$ = expected capital gain of asset j

δ_j = dividend yield of asset j

r^f = risk-free rate

β_j = beta factor of asset j

$E\left[\tilde{r}_{M,cg}\right]$ = expected return on the market portfolio

δ_M = dividend yield on the market portfolio

$\tau_{d,i,cg}$ = tax rate on dividends, interest, or capital gains

For the special case that all three tax rates are equal—e.g., as implemented in Germany from 2009 onwards under the "Abgeltungssteuer" assuming annual taxation of capital gains[321]—F 2-51 can be further simplified[322]:

F 2-52
$$\begin{aligned}&\left(E\left[\tilde{r}_{j,cg}\right]+\delta_j\right)(1-\tau)=\left(r^f+\beta_j\left(E\left[\tilde{r}_{M,cg}\right]+\delta_M-r^f\right)\right)(1-\tau)\\&E\left[\tilde{r}_j\right](1-\tau)=\left(r^f+\beta_j\left(E\left[\tilde{r}_M\right]-r^f\right)\right)(1-\tau)\end{aligned}$$

F 2-52 shows for equal tax rates that the post-tax expected return can simply be calculated by taxing the entire expected return expression. Another interesting implication is the irrelevance of distribution policy on the post-tax expected return[323].

Returning to the general case, the Tax-CAPM expected MRP $E\left[\tilde{r}_\tau^p\right]$ compares to the standard CAPM expected MRP $E\left[\tilde{r}^p\right]$ as follows:

F 2-53
$$\begin{aligned}E\left[\tilde{r}_\tau^p\right]&=E\left[\tilde{r}_{M,cg}\right](1-\tau_{cg})+\delta_M(1-\tau_d)-r^f(1-\tau_i)\\&=E\left[\tilde{r}_{M,cg}\right]+\delta_m-r^f-E\left[\tilde{r}_{M,cg}\right]\tau_{cg}-\delta_M\tau_d+r^f\tau_i\\&=E\left[\tilde{r}^p\right]-E\left[\tilde{r}_{M,cg}\right]\tau_{cg}-\delta_M\tau_d+r^f\tau_i\\\text{with } E\left[\tilde{r}^p\right]&=E\left[\tilde{r}_M\right]-r^f=E\left[\tilde{r}_{M,cg}\right]+\delta_M-r^f\end{aligned}$$

This relationship implies that the after-tax expected MRP equals to pre-tax expected MRP if:

---

321 See, e.g., Dausend, F./Schmitt, D. (2007), pp. 287-288, Zeidler, G./Schöninger, S./Tschöpel, A. (2008), p. 278, and Hachmeister, D./Wiese, J. (2009), p. 61.

322 See Wiese, J. (2007a), p. 370, Dausend, F./Schmitt, D. (2007), pp. 291-292 (note that Dausend/Schmitt fail to assume that this relation is only correct in a single-period context), Richter, F. (2007a), p. 7, and Zeidler, G./Schöninger, S./Tschöpel, A. (2008), p. 282.

323 See Wiese, J. (2006b), p. 245 and Wiese, J. (2007a), p. 370.

F 2-54
$$-E\left[\tilde{r}_{M,cg}\right]\tau_{cg} - \delta_M \tau_d + r^f \tau_i = 0$$
$$E\left[\tilde{r}_{M,cg}\right]\tau_{cg} + \delta_M \tau_d = r^f \tau_i$$

F 2-54 shows that the expected MRPs are equal if the absolute tax impact on capital gain return and dividend yield in sum is equal to the absolute tax impact on the risk-free rate. If all tax rates are equal, the post-tax expected MRP is equal to the taxed pre-tax expected MRP:

F 2-55
$$E\left[\tilde{r}^p\right] = E\left[\tilde{r}_M\right] - r^f$$
$$E\left[\tilde{r}^p_\tau\right] = E\left[\tilde{r}_{M,cg}\right](1-\tau) + \delta_M(1-\tau) - r^f(1-\tau)$$
$$= \left(E\left[\tilde{r}_{M,cg}\right] + \delta_M - r^f\right)(1-\tau)$$
$$= E\left[\tilde{r}^p\right](1-\tau)$$

In a multi-period context[324], the derivation of the Tax-CAPM is more complicated in particular due to the timing and frequency of realizing capital gains. Applying the single-period Tax-CAPM on an annual basis would imply for all investors to realize their capital gains on a yearly basis[325] which may be inconsistent with their actual investment behavior. The Tax-CAPM would therefore overestimate the tax impact since the time value effect of deferring the capital gains would not be captured[326]. A simplified approach to solve the frequency issue of realizing capital gains would be to introduce a differing effective capital gains tax rate $\overline{\tau}_{cg} < \tau$ which is the average risk preference weighted rate of all investors[327]. Under the new German regime (2009) with $\tau_i = \tau_d = \tau$, the Tax-CAPM version of Brennan (1970) [328] would then be applicable which is does not imply a irrelevance of distribution policy as shown in F 2-56[329]:

---

[324] Several assumptions for the application of the one-period model in a multi-period context have already been discussed in Section 2.3.2. See for a further discussion also Wiese, J. (2006b), pp. 242-248.

[325] For other tax models using instantaneous taxations see Sick, G. (1990), p. 1433, Richter, F. (2002b), section 3, Samuelson, P. (1964), Dirrigl, H. (1988), and Löffler, A./Schneider, D. (2002).

[326] See Wiese, J. (2006b), p. 243 and Wiese, J. (2007a), p. 370.

[327] See Wiese, J. (2007a), p. 370. See also Richter, F. (2007a), pp. 10-12 for alternative approaches to incorporate capital gains taxes in the Tax-CAPM.

[328] See Brennan, M. (1970), p. 423.

[329] See Wiese, J. (2007a), p. 370 and Hachmeister, D./Wiese, J. (2009), p. 61.

F 2-56
$$E\left[\tilde{r}_{j,cg}\right]\left(1-\overline{\tau}_{cg}\right)+\delta_j\left(1-\tau\right)=r^f\left(1-\tau\right)+\beta_j\left(E\left[\tilde{r}_{M,cg}\right]\left(1-\overline{\tau}_{cg}\right)+\delta_M\left(1-\tau\right)-r^f\left(1-\tau\right)\right)$$
$$\text{with}\quad E\left[\tilde{r}_{j/M,cg}\right]=E\left[\tilde{r}_{j/M}\right]-\delta_{j/M}$$
$$E\left[\tilde{r}_j\right]\left(1-\overline{\tau}_{cg}\right)-\delta_j\left(\tau-\overline{\tau}_{cg}\right)=r^f\left(1-\tau\right)+\beta_j\left(E\left[\tilde{r}_M\right]\left(1-\overline{\tau}_{cg}\right)-\delta_M\left(\tau-\overline{\tau}_{cg}\right)-r^f\left(1-\tau\right)\right)$$

Under this framework the relationship between pre- and post-tax expected MRP is as follows:

F 2-57
$$\begin{aligned}E\left[\tilde{r}_\tau^p\right]&=E\left[\tilde{r}_{M,cg}\right]\left(1-\overline{\tau}_{cg}\right)+\delta_M\left(1-\tau\right)-r^f\left(1-\tau\right)\\&=E\left[\tilde{r}^p\right]-E\left[\tilde{r}_{M,cg}\right]\overline{\tau}_{cg}-\left(\delta_M-r^f\right)\tau\end{aligned}$$

Determining $\overline{\tau}_{cg}$ is problematic as it requires the information on each individual investor's holding[330] periods and the general asset performance. For an individual investor, it is suggested to calculate the effective annually applied capital gains tax rate when an investor holds an asset for T periods and the asset price grows at g [331]:

F 2-58 $$P\left(1+g\left(1-\tau_{cg}\right)\right)^T=P\left(1+\left(1-\tau\right)\left(\left(1+g\right)^T-1\right)\right)$$

Solving for τ_{cg} shows that the effective capital gains tax rate decreases with increasing holding period length and asset price growth[332]:

F 2-59 $$\tau_{cg}=1-\frac{\left(1+\left(1-\tau\right)\left(\left(1+g\right)^T-1\right)\right)^{1/T}-1}{g}$$

How to transform this individual tax rate into $\overline{\tau}_{cg}$ remains open which will most likely only be possible by assuming uniform holding periods and price growth rates for all investors[333].

Another core issue with using the single-period Tax-CAPM in a multi-period setting is related to the deterministic dividend yield assumption which would imply deterministic

---

330 See Hachmeister, D./Wiese, J. (2009), p. 61.

331 See Wiese, J. (2007a), p. 370.

332 See Auerbach, A. (1983), p. 919 and Wiese, J. (2007a), p. 371. See also Wagner, W./Saur, G./Willershausen, T. (2008), p. 736 and Zeidler, G./Schöninger, S./Tschöpel, A. (2008), pp. 280-282.

333 See Wagner, W./Saur, G./Willershausen, T. (2008), p. 736, fn. 34, Zeidler, G./Schöninger, S./Tschöpel, A. (2008), p. 281, and Hachmeister, D./Wiese, J. (2009), p. 61 for a summary of empirical investigations of effective capital gains tax rates. See also Kruschwitz, L./Löffler, A. (2008), p. 810 for a critical view on fixing existing Tax-CAPM formulas by inferring holding periods. Therefore, see Richter, F. (2007b) for a new approach to reflect holding periods in valuation equations after personal taxes.

capital gains and thereby a risk-less development of share prices[334]. In a multi-period application, the dividend yield, however, needs to be stochastic and the only consistent solution would be to assume that dividends and capital gains are taxed identically so that the dividend yield becomes irrelevant since Tax-CAPM versions allowing for a stochastic dividend yield appear too complex for applications[335]. Despite the new German tax regime (2009) with identical rates for dividends and capital gains, the equivalence only exists in a multi-period framework when capital gains are realized annually as discussed above. The multi-period application of the Tax-CAPM also requires deterministic uniform tax rates[336].

A final remark relates to the fictitious nature of the Tax-CAPM. Key elements such as the expected market return or the market dividend yield are defined as pre-tax parameters which are neither historically nor forward-looking observable in a market environment affected by personal taxes[337].

2.7.3 Irrelevance of personal taxation under the Tax-CAPM

After introducing the Tax-CAPM as a theoretical concept to estimate expected after-tax returns and establishing a relation between the pre-tax and post-tax expected MRP, the focus is shifted on the question under which conditions personal taxes are irrelevant in valuations using the Tax-CAPM. Generally, this is the case when numerator and denominator of the valuation equation[338] or, stated differently, when valuation object and the benchmark asset to derive the cost of capital are identically affected by personal taxation[339].

A prominent case of personal tax irrelevance in valuations occurs when the numerator is based on economic income—i.e., cash flow (here dividends D) plus capital gain—and assuming all tax rates on dividends, interest and capital gains to be

[334] See Jonas, M./Löffler, A./Wiese, J. (2004), p. 904, fn. 15 and Wiese, J. (2006b), pp. 245-248.

[335] See Jonas, M./Löffler, A./Wiese, J. (2004), p. 904, Wiese, J. (2006b), pp. 245-248, and Wiese, J. (2007a), p. 371. For the derivation and discussion of a Tax-CAPM version with stochastic dividend yields, see Mai, J. (2006), pp. 1234-1242. See also Wiese, J. (2007b), pp. 9-10 and 22-26.

[336] See Wiese, J. (2006b), p. 247.

[337] See Richter, F. (2003), pp. 323 and 326-328.

[338] See Knoll, L./Rasinger, W./Wala, T. (2006), p. 2 and Hachmeister, D./Wiese, J. (2009), p. 61. See also the Richter, F. (2004), pp. 21 and 31-32.

[339] See Richter, F. (2005), p. 51 and Richter, F. (2007a), pp. 7-8 and 12. See also Ballwieser, W. (2007), pp. 102-103 for a simplified summary of irrelevance conditions.

equal $\tau_d = \tau_i = \tau_{cg} = \tau$[340]. This is equivalent to assume that the holding period is one year under the new German tax regime. Analytically, the irrelevance can be shown as follows[341]:

F 2-60
$$\begin{aligned} V_{j,s} &= \frac{D_{j,s}(1+g_j)(1-\tau) - E_s\left[\tau\left(\tilde{V}_{j,s+1} - V_{j,s}\right) + \tilde{V}_{j,s+1}\right]}{1 + r^f(1-\tau) + \beta_j\left(\delta_M(1-\tau) + r_{M,cg}(1-\tau) - r^f(1-\tau)\right)} \\ &= D_{j,s}\frac{1+g_j}{r^f + \beta_j\left(\delta_M + r_{M,cg} - r^f\right) - g_j} = D_{j,s}\frac{1+g_j}{r-g_j} \end{aligned}$$

$$\text{with } E_s\left[\tilde{V}_{j,s+1}\right] = V_{j,s}(1+g_j)$$

Alternatively, it could be assumed that the holding period is infinite so that the impact of taxing the ultimate capital gain can be neglected. Then only the cash flow of the asset is taxed in the numerator and equal treatment of the expected benchmark return requires also no taxation of capital gains $r_{M,cg}(1-\tau) = r_{M,cg}$[342]. If additionally $\beta_j r_{M,cg} = g_j$[343], e.g., by assuming that the growth rates of the valuation object and the market portfolio are equal $r_{M,cg} = g_j$ which also implies $\beta_j = 1$[344], personal tax irrelevance can be derived as follows[345]:

F 2-61
$$\begin{aligned} V_{j,s} &= \frac{D_{j,s}(1+g_j)(1-\tau)}{r^f(1-\tau) + \beta_j\left(\delta_M(1-\tau) + r_{M,cg} - r^f(1-\tau)\right) - g_j} \\ &= \frac{D_{j,s}(1+g_j)(1-\tau)}{r^f(1-\tau)(1-\beta_j) + \beta_j\delta_M(1-\tau) + \beta_j r_{M,cg} - g_j} \\ &= D_{j,s}\frac{1+g_j}{r^f(1-\beta_j) + \beta_j\delta_M} \end{aligned}$$

The irrelevance of personal taxation under the condition that the valuation object and the expected benchmark return used as discount rate are equally taxed is also

---

340 See Samuelson, P. (1964), p. 605, Dirrigl, H. (1988), p. 299, Leuthier, R. (1988a), p. 515, Richter, F. (2004), pp. 30-31, Richter, F. (2005), pp. 50-51, and Richter, F. (2007b), pp. 9-10.

341 See Richter, F. (2007a), p. 7.

342 See Richter, F. (2007a), p. 6.

343 See Richter, F. (2007a), p. 6.

344 See Richter, F. (2004), p. 31. See also Richter, F. (2007a), p. 5 and Richter, F. (2007b), p. 13 for a replication argument.

345 See Richter, F. (2007a), pp. 5-7 with changes in notation. See also Richter, F. (1999), p. 65, Ollmann, M./Richter, F. (1999), p. 172, Richter, F. (2003), p. 323, Richter, F. (2004), p. 31, Richter, F. (2005), p. 54, Richter, F. (2006b), p. 104, and Richter, F. (2007b), pp. 3 and 11.

recognized by the IDW for terminal value purposes[346]. Before the introduction of capital gains taxes in Germany, irrelevance was assumed for terminal value calculations when the post-tax return equals $r_{j,\tau} = r_j - \delta_j \tau$, the perpetual growth rates equals $g_j = r_j\left(1-\theta_j\right)$, and the payout ratio of the asset equals the payout ratio of the replication asset $\theta_i = \theta_j = \delta_j / r_j$ [347]:

F 2-62
$$\begin{aligned}V_{j,s} &= \frac{E_s\left[\tilde{D}_{j,s+1}\right]\left(1-\tau_d\right)}{r_{j,\tau}-g} = \frac{E_s\left[\tilde{D}_{j,s+1}\right]\left(1-\tau_d\right)}{r_j-\delta_j\tau_d-g_j} = \frac{E_s\left[\tilde{D}_{j,s+1}\right]\left(1-\tau_d\right)}{r_j-\delta_j\tau_d-r_j\left(1-\theta_j\right)}\\ &= \frac{E_s\left[\tilde{D}_{j,s+1}\right]\left(1-\tau_d\right)}{r_j-\delta_j\tau_d-r_j+\delta_j} = \frac{E_s\left[\tilde{D}_{j,s+1}\right]\left(1-\tau_d\right)}{\delta_j\left(1-\tau_d\right)} = \frac{E_s\left[\tilde{E}_{j,s+1}\right]\theta_j\left(1-\tau_d\right)}{r_j\theta_j\left(1-\tau_d\right)} = \frac{E_s\left[\tilde{E}_{j,s+1}\right]}{r_j}\end{aligned}$$

Including taxation of capital gains, the abovementioned assumptions are no more sufficient to establish personal tax irrelevance for terminal valuation calculations. Still, authors close to the IDW appear willing to maintain no differentiation between pre and post personal tax valuation for terminal value purposes. This obviously requires a further assumption to maintain equivalent taxation of the valuation object and the alternative asset from which the discount rate is inferred. While the equivalence of payout ratios was sufficient excluding capital gains taxation, an equivalent frequency of realizing capital gains (or an identical effective capital gains tax rate) is now additionally assumed to maintain personal tax irrelevance[348]. This implies that future dividends resulting from cash flow growth due to returns on retained earnings are assumed to be taxed by the capital gains tax rate rather than the dividend tax rate. This simplification of reality is frequently justified by the ability of firms to use share repurchases which would trigger capital gains taxes[349].

The above discussion has shown that personal taxation is irrelevant for valuations under the Tax-CAPM if the valuation object and the benchmark asset from which the

---

[346] See Wagner, W. et al. (2004), p. 897, IDW (2005), pp. 1308-1309, nn. 45-47 and 53, and Ballwieser, W. (2007), p. 82.

[347] See Wagner, W. et al. (2004), p. 897, Wiese, J. (2007a), p. 372, and Hachmeister, D./Wiese, J. (2009), p. 62.

[348] See also Wiese, J. (2007), p. 373. See also Ballwieser, W. (2007), p. 82 and Hachmeister, D./Wiese, J. (2009), p. 62.

[349] See Wiese, J. (2007a), p. 374, Zeidler, G./Schöninger, S./Tschöpel, A. (2008), pp. 278-280, and Hachmeister, D./Wiese, J. (2009), p. 62. Wiese alternatively mentions that irrelevance can be also achieved by assuming payout ratios of one which eliminates the issue of different taxation of future dividend growth from retained earnings; see Wiese, J. (2007a), p. 373.

discount rate is inferred are equally taxed. As long as equally taxed benchmark assets are available, personal taxes can be neglected for valuation purposes.[350]

2.7.4 Implications for the expected MRP estimation

Following the preceding discussion on the impact of personal taxation on risk-adjusted discount rates and asset prices, the questions needs to be answered whether IRR-based estimates of the expected MRP should be determined on a pre- or post-tax basis[351]. The answer is based on practical considerations when using risk-adjusted discount rates for the valuation of assets in a market environment that is affected by personal taxation. As presented in Section 2.7.1, post-tax F 2-45[352] and pre-tax F 2-46 expected market returns can be estimated using the tax affected market prices. This dissertation focuses only on pre-tax expected returns and MRPs[353] for the following reasons:

- Firstly, personal taxes are only relevant for valuation purposes when a benchmark asset that is equally taxed as the valuation object is not available. This is likely one reason why many valuation analyses by practitioners exclude personal taxes. While capital markets professionals such as corporate finance managers, investment bankers, or research analysts typically neglect personal taxation in valuations, only the German auditors association IDW[354] requires personal taxes

---

350 See Richter, F. (2007a), pp. 12-13.

351 The option to use historical post personal tax MRPs is already excluded upfront since changing tax regimes over time do not allow for the application of historical averages; see Richter, F. (2003), pp. 325 and 327-328 and Ballwieser, W./Kruschwitz, L./Löffler, A. (2007), p. 769.

352 Precedent estimations of the expected MRP after personal taxes are only available for Germany. Stehle, R. (2004), pp. 914-921 provides an approach to estimate the expected MRP post personal taxes based on historical data. For a direct ex-ante estimation of the post personal tax expected MRPs under the old German tax regime ("Halbeinkünfteverfahren") see Dausend, F./Schmitt, D. (2006a) and Reese, R. (2007), pp. 124-127. Dausend/Schmitt use an post personal tax residual income model based on Harris/Kemsley (1999) and Dausend/Lenz (2006) and estimate the expected MRP for the period 2002 to 2006 on the rather small sample of DAX and MDAX firms. Reese (2007) uses a simple dividend discount model with constant perpetual growth and retention adjustment to estimate the expected MRP between 2002 and 2004 for the aggregated CDAX. The retention adjustment is consistent with Wagner et al. (2006), p. 1026.

353 However, note that the impact of personal taxes dependent on the regime in each country cannot be fully eliminated as discussed in fn. 314.

354 See IDW (2008a), pp. 74-75, nn. 43-47. See also Jonas, M./Löffler, A./Wiese, J. (2004), p. 899, Richter, F. (2004), p. 21, Wagner, W. et al. (2006), p. 1006, and Wagner, W./Saur, G./Willershausen, T. (2008), p. 731.

to be reflected[355]. Still, even the IDW assumed neutrality of personal taxes for perpetuity based terminal value calculations[356].

- Secondly, calculating and comparing returns and MRPs after personal taxation in global capital markets creates additional issues. Even when solving the problem of varying tax rates by investor type—e.g., private vs. institutional—by assuming a uniform rate as above, the question remains which tax regime to use when determining the uniform rate since investors in, e.g., the German market could have their tax domicile relevant for personal taxation in each country worldwide[357]. Since the taxation of dividends, interest income, and capital gains varies strongly from country to country the after-tax expected German market return and MRP is different for each foreign investor. This implementation issue may also explain why capital markets related valuations are primarily performed on a pre-tax basis[358].
- Thirdly, when studying MRPs for equity markets in different countries, comparability cannot be achieved, and is rather distorted, by calculating post-tax rates using the domestic income tax regime of each market. Since the comparison of MRPs in the selected countries worldwide is one of the research goals of this dissertation, focusing on pre-tax MRPs is inevitable. This approach is also consistent with similar studies on the expected MRP and therefore allows for comparability of results[359].

However, it should be noted, that when neglecting a personal tax adjustment in the numerator of F 2-45 for the estimation of the expected MRP using the IRR method, the required market prices remain affected by personal taxation implying that its influence cannot be entirely eliminated.

2.8 Conclusions

The analysis of ex-post MRPs as well as the application of valuation formulas to derive ex-ante expected MRPs require a certain set of assumptions on distributional

---

[355] See Richter, F. (2007a), p. 1.

[356] See Wagner, W. et al. (2004), p. 897, IDW (2005), pp. 1308-1309, nn. 45-47 and 53, and Ballwieser, W. (2007), p. 82. See also Hachmeister, D./Wiese, J. (2009), p. 62 for a recent view under capital gains taxation.

[357] See also Ollmann, M./Richter, F. (1999), pp. 173-176.

[358] Richter, F. (2007a), p. 1.

[359] See, e.g., Claus, J./Thomas, J. (2001), Gebhardt, W./Lee, C./Swaminathan, B. (2001), Easton, P. et al. (2002), Gode, D./Mohanram, P. (2003), Daske, H./Gebhardt, G./Klein, S. (2006), Reese, R. (2007), Pastor, L./Sinha, M./Swaminathan, B. (2008), and Lee, C./Ng, D./Swaminathan, B. (2009).

as well as time-series properties of random returns. In addition, further specifications are required in particular regarding the risk-free rate.

- For the estimation of the expected MRP, returns are often assumed to be i.i.d. normal. In this case, the return process has the attractive properties of independence and stationarity. While there is weak evidence that returns are serially correlated over time, stronger evidence exists on the dependence of returns and MRPs on relative price measures such as the price-dividend ratio. These findings support at least partially the predictability of returns/MRPs which underlines the importance of conditional estimates.
- The IRR-based method to estimate the expected MRP relies on cash flow valuation models with risk-adjusted discount rates. When risk-adjusted discount rates are determined as IRR, they are equal to the expected return when returns have an i.i.d. distribution implying deterministic conditional and constant unconditional expected returns. The expected MRP can then be determined as the difference between the expected market return and the deterministic risk-free rate whereby the expected market return is based on the constant IRR that equates the net present value of the infinite stream of expected market cash flows with the current market value of all traded assets. A capital market model, such as the CAPM, is not required to hold for the estimation of the expected MRP using the IRR method.
- When the estimated MRP is used as an input parameter to determine CAPM-based risk-adjusted discount rates, the repeated application of such rates in multi-period valuations is associated with strict conditions. Uncertainty may only exist about the reassessment of expected cash flows which consequently implies that all components of the expected return, including the expected MRP, are required to be deterministic. Compliance with the CAPM further requires valuation formulas with variable one-period (forward) discount rates.
- Despite the inconsistency with the CAPM and the availability of variable forward risk-free rates implied by observable term structures of spot rates (neglecting the issue of liquidity premia), valuation models applied in empirical studies and practical applications predominantly use constant risk-free rates based on spot rates of 10-year government bonds.
- Consistency in the risk-free rate maturity for the expected MRP determination as well as for the expected return calculation for valuations is a key prerequisite to prevent valuation errors. In order to provide consistent estimates of the expected

MRP for standard valuation models with constant risk-free rates, it was decided to use the 10-year government bond rate as risk-free rate for all MRP calculations within this study. The same approach was utilized by almost all studies on forward-looking estimates of the expected MRP. Finally, it was discussed that for the estimation of expected MRPs based on historical averages, the historical risk-free rates should only include the income return component.

- Determining expected MRPs from valuation models for various countries requires the consistent denomination of input parameters in the local currency. Therefore, the used risk-free rate needs to be based on the same currency as the expected cash flow forecasts. Since the expected MRP does not have a currency denomination, estimates for different countries are comparable.
- Based on the Fisher effect, a relationship can be developed between the nominal and real expected MRP. The nominal and real expected MRP should be identical if the calculation methods are consistent. However, inconsistencies occur frequently, e.g., in standard valuation formulas. Empirical evidence on the validity of the Fisher effect is inconclusive.
- Personal taxation is only relevant for valuation purposes when no benchmark asset is available to derive the expected return that is equally affected by personal taxes as the valuation object itself. Further considering the globalization of shareholder structures, it is not surprising that pre-tax valuation models are largely used by practitioners. Against this background and in order to maintain comparability between the expected MRP estimates across countries, it was decided to estimate pre-tax expected MRPs within this study. However, due to the reflection in market prices, the impact of personal taxation cannot be fully eliminated.

Based on this set of theoretical concepts and underlying assumptions, the expected MRP estimates are determined in this study. Before the three basic estimation methodologies are presented, the next chapter provides a detailed description of utilized indices and summarizes the general market performance during the analysis period.

3 Description and performance of country indices

Disregarding based on which methodology the expected MRP is estimated, the reference index used as sample to approximate the market portfolio in the respective countries needs to be defined and described with respect the its constituents and calculation specifications (e.g., weighting). In order to approximate the country market portfolio, it is necessary to choose the broadest available reference index covering a maximum portion of the market capitalization of the true market portfolio[360]. Such indices are commonly referred to as "all-share indices" and are available for all major markets from different index providers.

All required data for historical analyses can be derived from aggregate index parameters such as total return, price return, or dividend yield. In contrast, the forward-looking data can largely only be collected by cumulating individual data points like earnings or dividends forecasts for all index constituent. Using a common index as a starting point ensures the maximum degree of data comparability but inconsistencies in the number of included firms cannot be avoided due to the limited completeness of individual data sets[361].

For the expected MRP calculation, it is also required to specify the government bond index used to determine the risk-free rate either as interest or redemption yield dependent on the methodology. With the exception of Germany, this analysis relies on the Datastream local government bond benchmark indices with a 10-year maturity. For Germany, a particular 10-year maturity index provided by Deutsche Börse AG is used in order to be consistent with previous research on the expected MRP in Germany[362].

This chapter provides a description of the specifications of the utilized all-share equity and bond indices for each analyzed country with a special focus on their composition and the calculation method of historical returns. The depth of discussion may vary across indices according to the level of public information on the index methodologies. In order to facilitate the interpretation of the later derived expected MRP estimates, this chapter also discusses the performance of key market parameters during the analysis period. The discussion of performance development

---

[360] See, e.g., Dimson, E./Marsh, P./Staunton, M. (2008), p. 8.

[361] As to be seen at a later point, the number of firms in the respective country samples for historical and forward-looking data sets differs since the availability of IBES forecast data is limited (i.e., not all index constituents are covered).

[362] See Daske, H./Gebhardt, G./Klein, S. (2006), p. 13 and Reese, R. (2007), p. 97.

is mainly centered on the qualitative analysis of three main groups of variables: economic indicators such as nominal/real GDP growth and inflation, total returns of equity and bond indices, and relative performance measures for equity and bond markets such as dividend yield and redemption yield. Note that all shown indices are denominated in the local currency.

3.1 Germany

Recent empirical analyses of the capital market development in Germany usually use the CDAX as the all-share index to represent the market portfolio and the REX as reference for the government bond market[363]. Both indices are provided by Deutsche Börse AG.

3.1.1 Description of the equity index – CDAX

The CDAX index includes all German stocks admitted to the Prime Standard and General Standard[364] segments both from classic and technology sectors as shown in Exhibit 3. Therefore, the index reflects the performance of the entire German equity market[365].

Exhibit 3 Overview of the German indices structure by Deutsche Börse AG

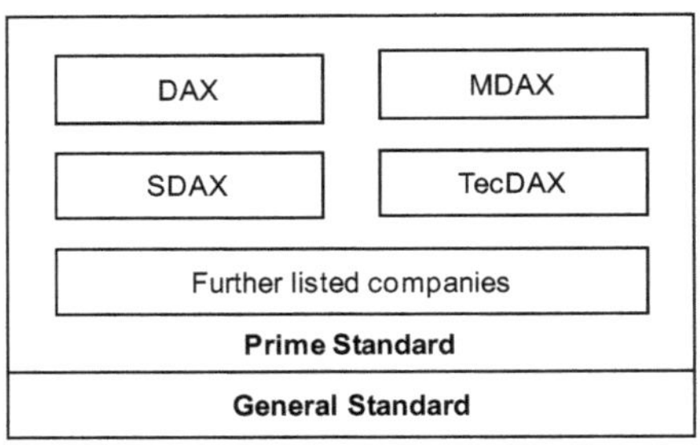

Source: Deutsche Börse (2007a), p. 7.

---

[363] See, e.g., Stehle, R. (2004), Daske, H./Gebhardt, G./Klein, S. (2006), and Reese, R. (2007).
[364] General Standard is the segment with the minimum legal requirements for listings and is regulated by the EU. In addition to the requirements of General Standard, Prime Standard companies must comply with international transparency standards; see Deutsche Börse AG (2003), p. 7.
[365] See Deutsche Börse AG (2007a), p. 9.

Deutsche Börse AG calculates the CDAX index value according to the following formula[366]:

$$\textbf{F 3-1} \quad \text{Index value}_t = \frac{\sum_{j=1}^{J} P_{j,t} n_{j,T} f_{j,T} c_{j,t}}{\sum_{j=1}^{J} P_{j,0} n_{j,0}} K_T * \text{Base}$$

with:

t = time of index calculation
T = time of last chaining factor calculation
j = individual constituent stock
J = last constituent stock of the index
$P_{j,t}$ = share price of stock j at t
$n_{j,T}$ = number of shares outstanding of stock j at T
$f_{j,T}$ = free float factor of stock j at T
$c_{j,t}$ = adjustment factor for stock j at t
K_T = chaining factor at T
Base = in case of CDAX 100

All indices of Deutsche Börse AG including the CDAX are based (start value = 100) on the reference date as of 30 December 1987. Formula F 3-1 shows that the index value is calculated as the ratio of the current free float adjusted market capitalization of the markets constituents and the base date market capitalization multiplied by a chaining factor and the base value[367]. Thereby the CDAX index is value-weighted, whereby the weighting of any individual stock is proportionate to its free-float adjusted share in the overall index capitalization. The weights are based solely on the free-float portion of the issued share capital including all classes of shares. In order to reflect changes in the firms issued capital such as capital increases, capital reductions, nominal value changes and share splits, subscription rights, or spin-offs an adjustment factor is necessary[368]. The adjustment factor is also used to reflect dividends and other distributions if the total return version of the index is calculated

[366] See Deutsche Börse AG (2007a), p. 24. A detailed review of the index formula for the other analyzed indices is neglected as the general calculation procedure is similar and differences primarily relate to the inclusion of adjustments in the numerator (e.g., CDAX) or the denominator (e.g., S&P/TSX Composite, FTSE All-Share, TOPIX).
[367] See Deutsche Börse AG (2007a), p. 24.
[368] See Deutsche Börse AG (2007a), pp. 29-37.

assuming that all proceeds are reinvested in the index portfolio. Furthermore, a chaining factor K_T [369] is required due to continuous changes in the index composition resulting from new listings, mergers & acquisitions, and deletions[370]. During each quarterly chaining process, the number of shares included in the issued share capital as well as the free-float factor is updated[371]. The index performance itself is provided both as a price and a total return index.

Exhibit 4 shows the approximated composition of the CDAX according to the value-weights of industry sectors[372]. Despite a declining share over time, the German equity market is dominated by the financial institutions sector followed by industrials and consumer goods. Noteworthy is the strong increase of the telecommunication and technology sectors primarily at the expense of financials and basic materials. The average Herfindahl index[373]—as an indicator of industry concentration—for the German market is 16.6%.

---

[369] See Deutsche Börse AG (2007a), pp. 37-38 for a detailed description of the chaining procedure.

[370] New listings in the Prime Standard or General Standard segments of the Frankfurt Stock Exchange are included in the all share indices (e.g., CDAX) on the day after first trading. Deletions from the index are effected after the close of trading on the last quoted day. Merged companies are deleted from the index immediately after their delisting. In mergers where the new shares do not constitute the continued quotation of one of the incumbent companies, they are included in the index as an entirely new issue; see Deutsche Börse (2007a), p. 16.

[371] See Deutsche Börse (2007a), p. 10.

[372] The definition of industry sectors is based on the categorization of Datastream. Note that only firms are included for which also IBES estimates are available. Therefore, the composition does not fully reflect the official index composition.

[373] The Herfindahl index (also called Herfindahl Hirshmann Index – HHI) is defined as the sum of squared (value-weighted) market shares of all firms in an industry. For the usage in this study, the HHI is applied to entire industries since not the concentration within one industry but within the entire market is of relevance; see Roll, R. (1992), p. 8.

Exhibit 4 CDAX index composition by key industry sectors

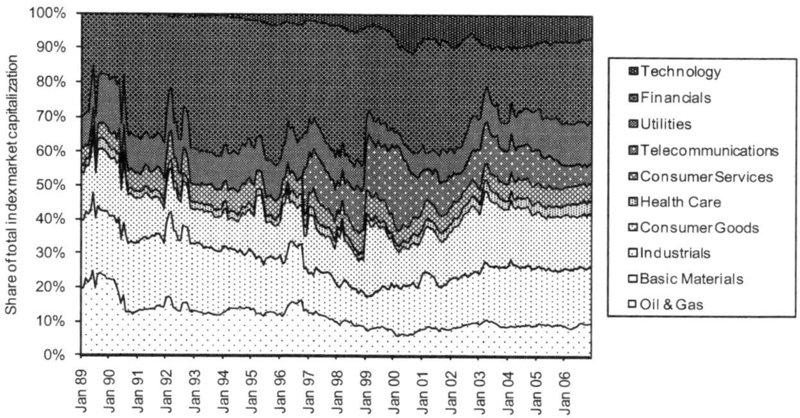

Source: Industry codes based on Datastream (code: ICBIC).

3.1.2 Description of the government bond index – REX

As an indicator for the German government bond market, the REX index comprises 30 national, synthetic bonds with fixed maturities between one and ten years and a fixed coupon. Using prices from the Frankfurt Stock Exchange the index includes all Federal Government Bonds ("Bundesanleihen"), Federal Debt Obligations ("Bundesobligationen") and Treasury Notes ("Schatzanweisungen") issued by the Federal Republic of Germany, the German Unity Fund, and the former Treuhandanstalt privatization agency. All bonds carry a fixed coupon and have between 0.5 and 10.5 years in residual maturity. The prices of these bonds are used for the pricing of the relevant synthetic bonds. REX indices are calculated and distributed once a day. Based on these synthetic bonds the overall index, ten maturity sub-indices, and three coupon-class subindices are determined. For the purposes of this study, the 10-year maturity sub-index is selected.[374]

---

[374] See Deutsche Börse AG (2007b), p. 17.

3.1.3 Performance during the analysis period

Exhibit 5 documents the economic development of Germany during the analysis period. It was mainly impacted by the reunification in the early 1990s and two short recession periods with negative real GDP growth in 1993 and between 2002 and 2003. During the entire analysis period, the nominal GDP growth had an average of 4.2% (2.4% excluding the years prior to 1993 due to the impact of reunification). The lagged correlation between GDP growth and the inflation rate becomes clearly obvious in Exhibit 5. Following a period of high GDP growth after the German reunification, the inflation rate declined from its peak level of 6.3% in 1992 to a low point of 0.2% in 1999. From 2000 onwards, the inflation rate followed a mean reverting path around the 1.5% level.

Exhibit 5 Development of German ex-post GDP growth and inflation rate[375]

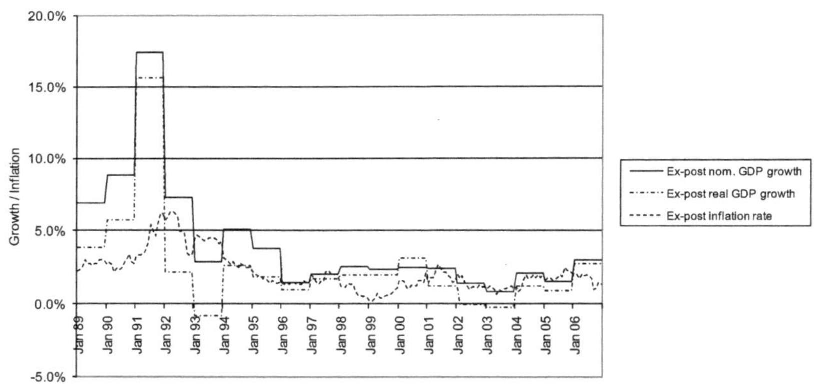

Source: Datastream (codes: BDGDPL.., BDRGDP.., BDCP7500F).

In this economic environment, the CDAX total return index increased 386% from 1989 until its peak in 2000 at the top the so-called millennium bubble as shown in Exhibit 6[376]. After a substantial decline of the index by 65% between 2001 and 2003, the market almost reached the year 2000 index level by end of 2006. The

[375] Annual year-over-previous year GDP growth rate and annual month-over-previous month inflation rate.

[376] See Shiller, R. (2001), pp. 5-6.

development of the REX (10 YRS) index is much less volatile. From 1989, it rose continuously throughout the entire analysis period by a total of 234%.

Exhibit 6 Total return performance of CDAX and REX 10-year sub-index

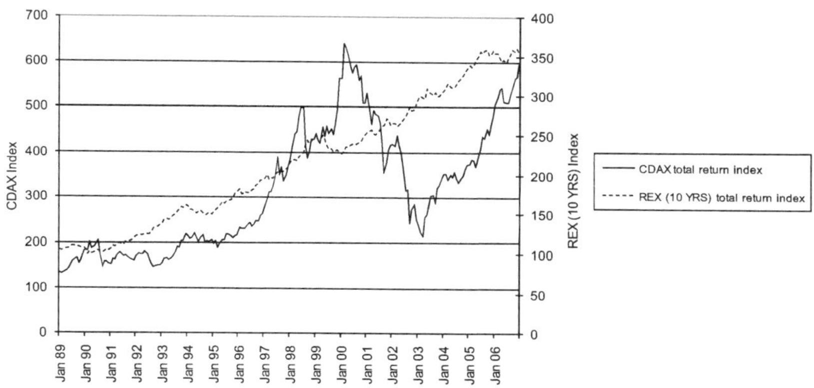

Source: Datastream (codes: CDAXGEN(RI), REXA10Y(TR)).

As shown in Exhibit 7, the continuous rise of the REX (10 YRS) total return index is associated with a steady decline in the redemption yield. Using the ex-post inflation rate as a proxy for the expected inflation rate, a key influence factor of the nominal redemption yield, the graphical analysis indicates that the declining redemption yield is at least partially driven by lower expected inflation. In contrast, the CDAX-based dividend yield shows a stationary development around the 2% level.

Exhibit 7 Development of CDAX dividend yield and 10-year REX sub-index redemption yield

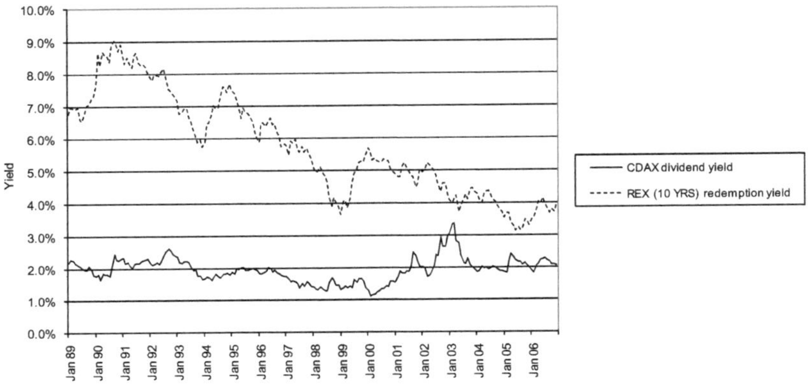

Source: Datastream (codes: CDAXGEZ(DY), REXA10Y(RY)).

The index increase between 1997 and 2001 and decrease between 2001 and 2003 is negatively correlated with the dividend yield. Table 3 shows the Pearson/Spearman correlation coefficients[377] between realized one-period return and end-of-period dividend yield as well as between realized returns for holding periods of one, five, and ten years and the beginning-of-period dividend yield[378]. The end-of-period correlation coefficients are significantly negative confirming the graphical result. Furthermore, the beginning-of-period coefficients are positive and significant for a five year holding period. This is supporting evidence of dependence between expected returns and dividend yields—an issue that will be extensively discussed in later parts of this study[379].

[377] See Section 4.2.2 for a discussion.

[378] Similar to Richter, F. (2005), p. 115.

[379] The relationship between dividend yield and expected return is investigated in detail in Section 6.3 of this study (see in particular F 6-10).

Table 3 Correlation between realized returns and the dividend yield – CDAX

Holding period	k=1	k=5	k=10
Pearson $[D_{t-1}/P_{t-1};r_{t,t+k}]$	0.3049	0.6339	0.3282
p-value	(0.2186)	(0.0149)	(0.3886)
Pearson $[D_t/P_t;r_{t,t+k}]$	-0.6647		
p-value	(0.0026)		
Spearman $[D_{t-1}/P_{t-1};r_{t,t+k}]$	0.2903	0.6601	0.2929
p-value	(0.2426)	(0.0102)	(0.4444)
Spearman $[D_t/P_t;r_{t,t+k}]$	-0.5795		
p-value	(0.0102)		

Note: P-values with a significance level of at least 5% are highlighted in grey.

3.2 Canada

The most comprehensive Canadian equity market index with sufficient data availability is the TSX/S&P Composite index provided by Standard & Poor's. The Canadian government bond market is measured—as all following markets—by the Datastream benchmark 10-year government bond index. The specifications of this index are identical across all other countries and therefore only discussed in this section.

3.2.1 Description of the equity index – S&P/TSX Composite

The S&P/TSX Composite is the principal broad market measure and headline index for the Canadian equity market. The index comprises common stock and income trust units. The constituents of the S&P/TSX Composite are also members of either the S&P/TSX equity indices (the S&P/TSX Equity, the S&P/TSX Equity MidCap, or the S&P/TSX Equity SmallCap) or the series of indices including income trusts (S&P/TSX Income Trust, the S&P/TSX 60, the S&P/TSX MidCap, or the S&P/TSX SmallCap), or both. The Canadian index structure is illustrated by Exhibit 8.[380]

[380] See Standard & Poor's (2006), p. 1.

Exhibit 8 Overview of the Canadian indices structure by Standard & Poor's

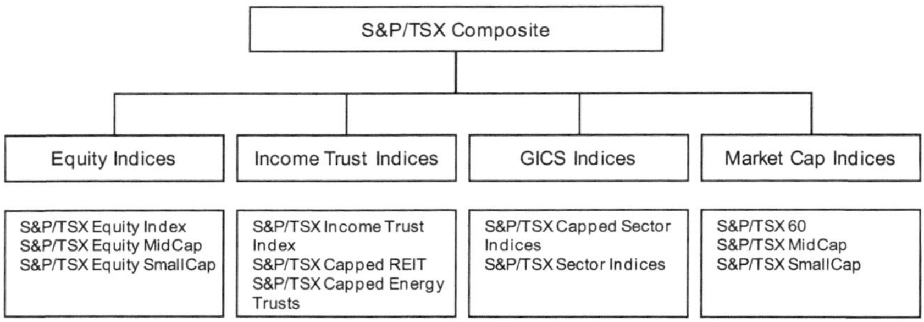

Source: Standard & Poor's (2006), p. 3.

Additions to the S&P/TSX Composite are generally only made as part of the quarterly review process. Deletions from the index are executed at the first practical date following the index committee's determination that a corporate action has been successful.[381]

Eligibility factors for inclusion in the S&P/TSX Composite index include criteria regarding market capitalization, liquidity, domicile of the issuer, and certain other restrictions[382].

The S&P/TSX Composite is value-weighted according to the free-float of the respective issue and chained in order to guarantee continuity in index values due to additions and deletions to the index, rights issues, share buybacks and issuances, and spin-offs[383]. A total return index[384] is calculated for the S&P/TSX Composite as well as a price index.

The approximated composition of the S&P/TSX Composite according to the value-weights of industry sectors is shown in Exhibit 9[385]. Not surprisingly, the Canadian equity market is dominated by the financial and oil & gas sectors due to its large number of trusts and its geographical characteristics. The importance of the

---

[381] See Standard & Poor's (2006), pp. 5 and 8.

[382] See Standard & Poor's (2006), pp. 5-6 for a comprehensive review of the eligibility criteria.

[383] See Standard & Poor's (2006), p. 9.

[384] The total return calculation includes, in addition to the price return, stock dividends paid in kind, stock dividends paid with securities, rights distributions, and cash distributions less than 4% of the underlying stock price; see Standard & Poor's (2006), p. 14.

[385] The definition of industry sectors is based on the categorization of Datastream. Note that only firms are included for which also IBES estimates are available. Therefore, the composition does not fully reflect the official index composition.

telecommunication and technology sectors quickly shrunk following the turn of the millennium transferring lost weight to the oil & gas sector. The average Herfindahl index for the Canadian market of 26.9% is the highest in the sample due to the dominance of only two sectors.

Exhibit 9 S&P/TSX Composite index composition by key industry sectors

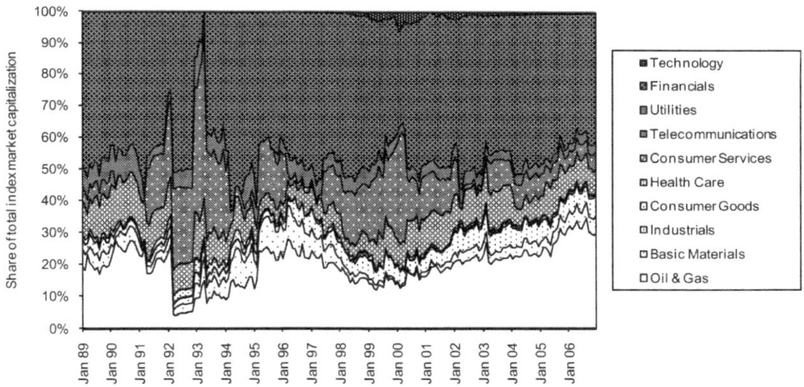

Source: Industry codes based on Datastream (code: ICBIC).

3.2.2 Description of the government bond index – Datastream benchmark index

All herein used Datastream benchmark government bond indices are based on single bonds. The particular bond selected is the most representative bond available for the given maturity band at each point in time. Furthermore, benchmark bonds are selected with further consideration given to liquidity, issue size, and coupon. Generally, the chosen benchmark is the latest issue within the given maturity band.[386]

---

[386] Based on information provided by Datastream on 10 October 2007. This description of the utilized benchmark government bond index provided by Datastream applies to all markets except Germany.

3.2.3 Performance during the analysis period

In the early 1990s, the Canadian economic development is characterized by a recession period with a declining real GDP in 1991 as illustrated by Exhibit 10. Subsequently, real and nominal GDP growth is continuously positive reaching peak levels in 2000. Following the 2001 terrorist attacks in the US, real GDP growth remained relatively stable at a lower level compared to the preceding high growth years. On average, the nominal GDP growth rate was 4.9% during the analysis period. As a consequence of the 1991 recession, the inflation rate declined substantially turning even negative throughout 1994. After a rise in line with positive GDP growth, the inflation rate fluctuated around the two percent level until the end of the analysis period.

Exhibit 10 Development of Canadian ex-post GDP growth and inflation rate

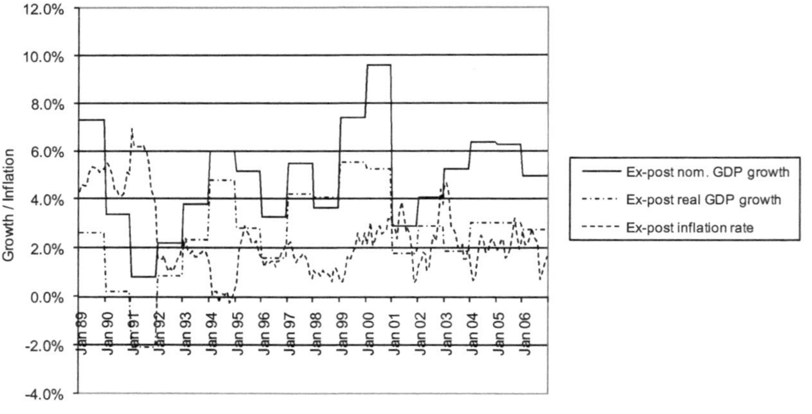

Source: Datastream (codes: CNGDPL.., CNRGDP.., CNOCP009F).

Against this economic background, the S&P/TSX Composite index rose continuously—with the exception of a short interruption in 1998—to a preliminary peak in 2000 (+346%) as shown in Exhibit 11. After the following bear market period leading to a 43% decline of the index value until the end of 2002, the index regained 127% leading to a record level at the end of the analysis period. The Datastream 10-year government bond index for Canada shows a much more consistent growth throughout the entire analysis period of in total 383%.

Exhibit 11 Total return performance of S&P/TSX Composite and Datastream 10-year Canadian government bond benchmark index

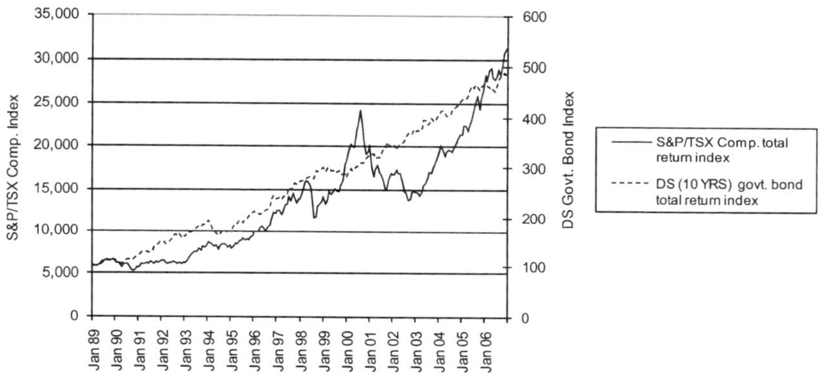

Source: Datastream (codes: TTOCOMP(RI), BMCN10Y(RI)).

This almost monotonic rise coincides with an opposite development of the respective redemption yield which in the early 1990 reflects the decline in inflation. Exhibit 12 further shows that the S&P/TSX Composite dividend yield also declined steadily until the peak level of equity valuations in 2000 indicating non-stationarity during this period. In the following period however, the dividend yield showed tendencies of mean reversion.

Exhibit 12 Development of S&P/TSX Composite dividend yield and Datastream 10-year Canadian government bond benchmark index redemption yield

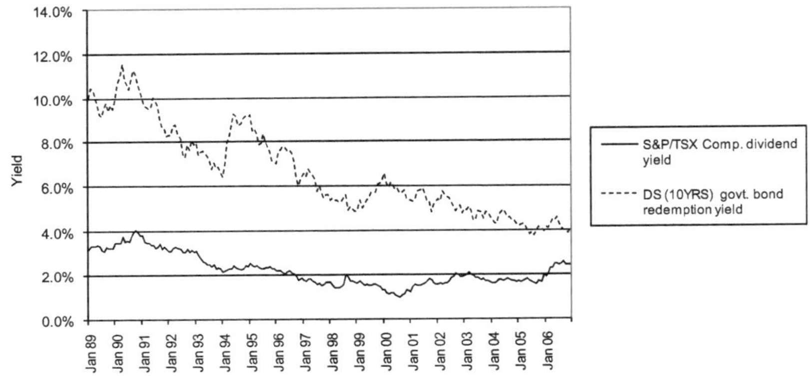

Source: Datastream (codes: TTOCOMP(DY), BMCN10Y(RY)).

Table 4 demonstrates again the negative correlation between one-year realized returns and the end-of-period dividend yield. However, the coefficients are weaker compared to Germany. When using the beginning-of-period dividend yield, the correlation coefficients increase with the holding period. While there is almost no correlation with one-year returns, the coefficients increase to 0.49/0.42 for a ten-year holding period but remain insignificant.

Table 4 Correlation between realized returns and the dividend yield – S&P/TSX Composite

Holding period	k=1	k=5	k=10
Pearson $[D_{t-1}/P_{t-1};r_{t,t+k}]$	0.0698	0.3729	0.4928
p-value	(0.7832)	(0.1891)	(0.1777)
Pearson $[D_t/P_t;r_{t,t+k}]$	-0.2498		
p-value	(0.3175)		
Spearman $[D_{t-1}/P_{t-1};r_{t,t+k}]$	0.2024	0.4154	0.4167
p-value	(0.4206)	(0.1397)	(0.2646)
Spearman $[D_t/P_t;r_{t,t+k}]$	-0.1497		
p-value	(0.5532)		

3.3 France

The analysis of the French capital market is complicated by the limited availability of all-share index data. Therefore, it is necessary to base the analysis on a narrower index.

3.3.1 Description of the equity index – CAC AllShares/40

The CAC AllShares index includes all stocks listed on the Paris market with annual velocity [387] of more than 5% disregarding any restrictions for the market capitalization[388]. It is the broadest index of the French market and encompasses all other indices as illustrated by Exhibit 13.

Exhibit 13 Overview of the French indices structure by Euronext NV

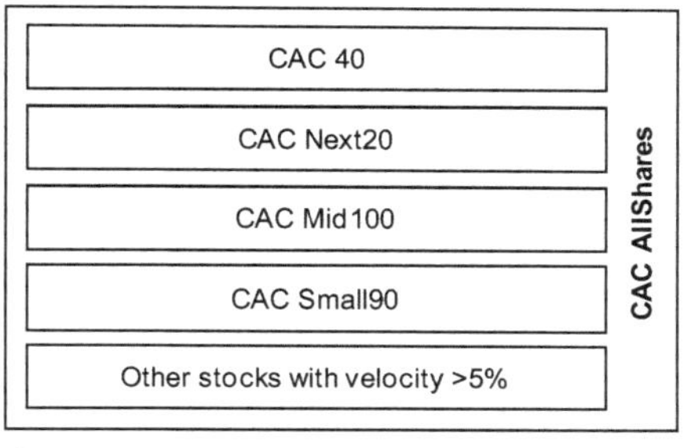

Source: Euronext NV (2005), p. 5.

Unfortunately, data for the CAC AllShares is only available from 2005 onwards. The only index for which a sufficient data set is available is the CAC 40 index which is weighted by free-float market capitalizations. Eligible are the most liquid French and foreign stocks out of the 100 largest market capitalizations listed on Euronext in Paris[389]. The general review of eligibility for the CAC 40 constituents is conducted quarterly[390].

---

[387] In this context, velocity is the ratio of trading volume to the total number of shares outstanding.
[388] See Euronext NV (2005), p. 5.
[389] See Euronext NV (2005), p. 11.
[390] See Euronext NV (2005), p. 7.

Exhibit 14 shows the approximated composition of the CAC 40 by industry sectors[391]. The index is comparatively balanced with the sectors consumer goods, consumer services, and financials having on average the largest weights. Again, the declining share of the telecommunication and technology sectors post 2000 is captured by natural resources. The low average Herfindahl index for the French market of 15.1% reflects the balanced composition of the CAC 40.

Exhibit 14 CAC 40 index composition by key industry sectors

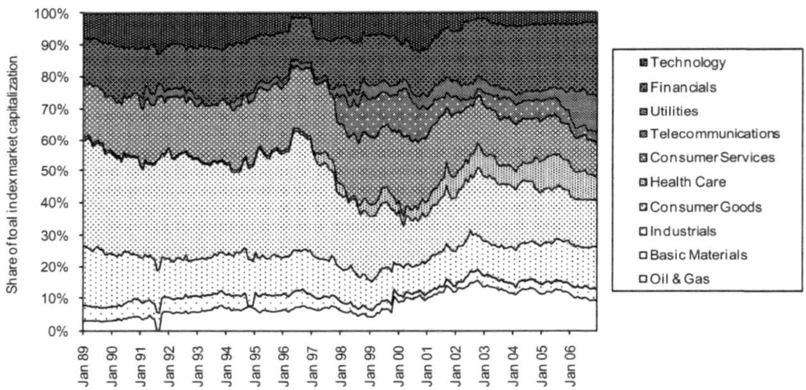

Source: Industry codes based on Datastream (code: ICBIC).

3.3.2 Performance during the analysis period

Like Canada, France witnessed a recession period in the early 1990s, however, not until 1993 as illustrated by Exhibit 15. Thereafter, the French economy showed a familiar development with steadily rising nominal and real GDP growth until 2001 and stable growth at a lower level in the period until 2006 leading to an average nominal GDP growth rate over the analysis period of 3.8%. In accordance with the economic downturn in the early 1990s, the inflation rate continually declined but even continued on its downward track reaching almost zero by the end of 1998. After a rapid rise during the boom period of 2000, the French inflation rate fluctuated around the two percent level until 2006.

[391] The definition of industry sectors is based on the categorization of Datastream. Note that only firms are included for which also IBES estimates are available. Therefore, the composition does not fully reflect the official index composition.

Exhibit 15 Development of French ex-post GDP growth and inflation rate

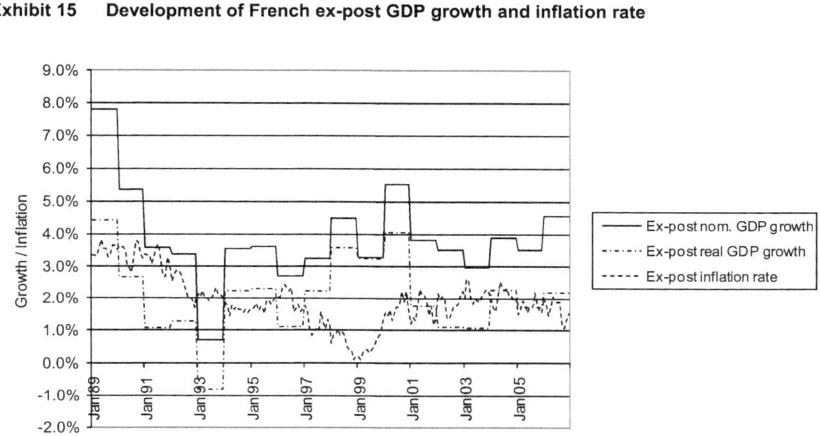

Source: Datastream (codes: FRGDPL.., FRRGDP.., FRI64...F).

Exhibit 16 illustrates that the economic development had little impact on the French equity markets until 1995. Throughout that period the total return index of the CAC 40 rose only slowly by 48%. The typical peak pattern—to be observed in almost all analyzed markets—around the millennium started to unfold not until 1996 with a substantial rise in the index by 296% reaching its climax in 2000. Following the period market corrections between 2001 and 2003 (-59%), the CAC 40 had almost entirely regained its losses by the end of 2006. The associated dividend yield—as illustrated by Exhibit 17—showed a mean reverting development throughout the analysis period with a phase of particular low dividend yield levels coinciding with the stock market peak between 1998 and 2003. Interestingly enough, the renewed rise of the CAC 40 until the end of 2006 did not result in a lower level of dividend yields.

Exhibit 16 Total return performance of CAC AllShares/40 and Datastream 10-year French government bond benchmark index

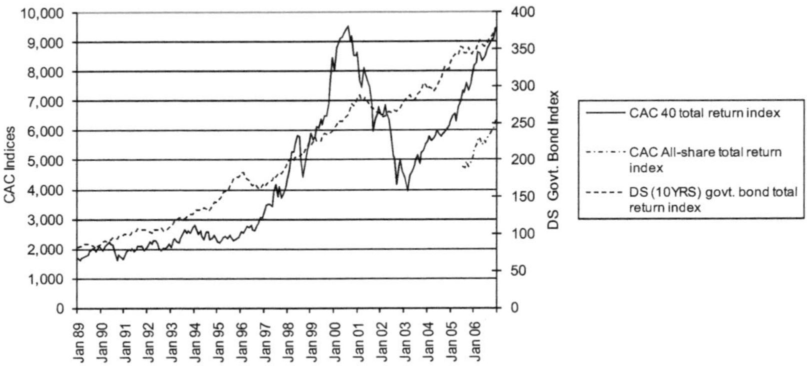

Source: Datastream (codes: FRCAC40(RI), FRCACAS(RI), BMFR10Y(RI)).

The potential dividend yield dependence of returns is again demonstrated by negative correlation coefficients for one-period returns and the end-of-period dividend yield. Furthermore, returns of a five-year holding have significant positive coefficients with the beginning-of-period dividend yield as shown in Table 5.

Table 5 Correlation between realized returns and the dividend yield – CAC 40

Holding period	k=1	k=5	k=10
Pearson $[D_{t-1}/P_{t-1};r_{t,t+k}]$	0.3795	0.6455	0.2482
p-value	(0.1203)	(0.0126)	(0.5196)
Pearson $[D_t/P_t;r_{t,t+k}]$	-0.3306		
p-value	(0.1803)		
Spearman $[D_{t-1}/P_{t-1};r_{t,t+k}]$	0.2406	0.7129	0.0833
p-value	(0.3362)	(0.0042)	(0.8312)
Spearman $[D_t/P_t;r_{t,t+k}]$	-0.3738		
p-value	(0.1265)		

Note: P-values with a significance level of at least 5% are highlighted in grey.

Returning to Exhibit 16, the total return index of the French Datastream 10-year government bond index rose almost monotonic during the analysis period by 304%. This development is consistent with the continuous decline of the respective redemption yield as illustrated by Exhibit 17. Comparing the redemption yield development to the evolution of the inflation rate indicates correlations in particular until the inflation rate low in 1999.

Exhibit 17 Development of CAC 40 dividend yield and Datastream 10-year French government bond benchmark index redemption yield

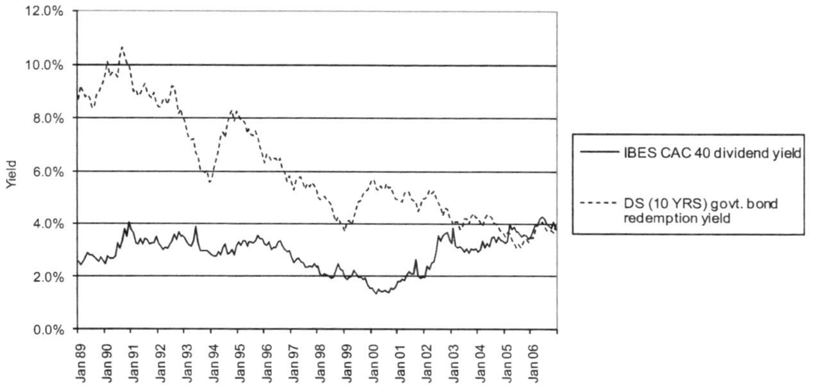

Source: Datastream (codes: @:FRCAC40(ADVYLD), BMFR10Y(RY)).

3.4 Japan

In 1969, Tokyo Stock Exchange Inc. (TSE) introduced the TOPIX (Tokyo Stock Price Index) as a composite index of all domestic common stocks listed on the TSE First Section in order to provide investors with a comprehensive measure of the general development of the Japanese equity market.

3.4.1 Description of the equity index – TOPIX

The TOPIX index is the broadest measure of the Japanese equity market only neglecting minor stocks of the TSE Second Section and the emerging companies market “Mothers”[392]. It is the aggregate of the constituents of TOPIX Core 30, TOPIX Core 70, TOPIX Mid 400, TOPIX Small, and certain other stocks as illustrated by Exhibit 18.

---

[392] For a detailed list of eligibility requirements, see Tokyo Stock Exchange Inc. (2007), pp. 24-25 for first and second section and p. 27 for “Mothers”. First and second section are mainly divided by the factors size and liquidity.

Exhibit 18 Overview of the Japanese indices structure by Tokyo Stock Exchange Inc.

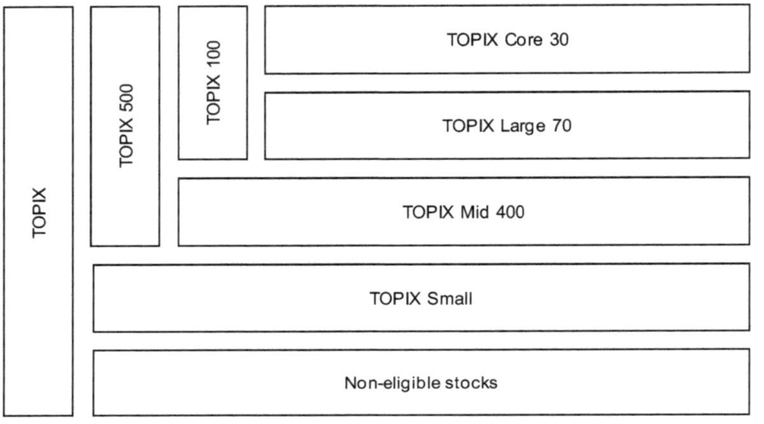

Source: Tokyo Stock Exchange Inc. (2007), p. 21.

Based on 1 April 1998 at a value of 1,000[393], TOPIX is a value-weighted index with a free-float adjustment introduced at the end of October 2005[394]. It is provided as total return as well as price return index. In order to accurately reflect changes in the market structure due to, e.g., delistings, new issues, or mergers & acquisitions activity, the constituents list of the TOPIX is reviewed in January (additions and deletions) and July (additions only)[395].

As shown by Exhibit 16, the approximated composition of the TOPIX according the value-weights of industry sectors is concentrated in particular until 1997[396]. On average, the consumer goods and industrials sector make up more than 50% of the index market capitalization. As a consequence of high concentration, the average Herfindahl index for the Japanese market is 18.9%.

---

393 See Tokyo Stock Exchange Inc. (2007), p. 21.

394 See Tokyo Stock Exchange Inc. (2007), p. 17.

395 See Tokyo Stock Exchange Inc. (2007), p. 21.

396 The definition of industry sectors is based on the categorization of Datastream. Note that only firms are included for which also IBES estimates are available. Therefore, the composition does not fully reflect the official index composition.

Exhibit 19 TOPIX index composition by key industry sectors

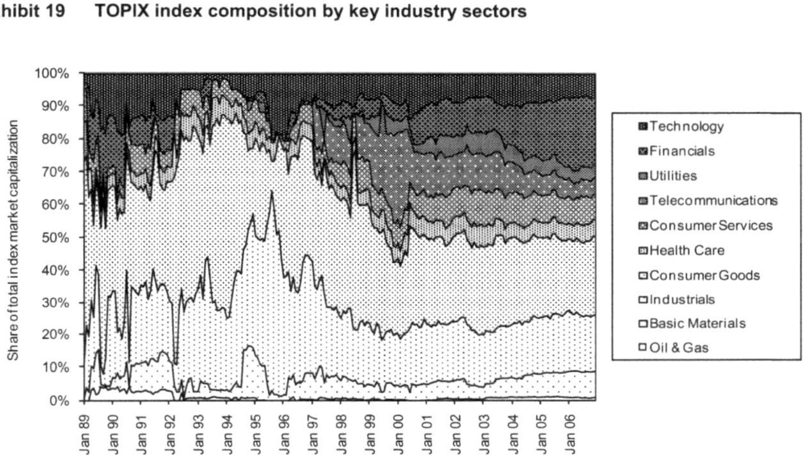

Source: Industry codes based on Datastream (code: ICBIC).

3.4.2 Performance during the analysis period

The development of the Japanese economy certainly stands apart from the other analyzed countries due to its lengthy recession experience including periods of deflation. As Exhibit 20 shows, the substantial GDP growth was interrupted by 1992 with real GDP growth approaching zero and the inflation rate turning into negative numbers soon thereafter. After a short recovery between 1994 and 1997, Japan slipped again into recession in 1998 and remained in a difficult economic situation until 2003. The average nominal GDP growth is therefore comparatively low at 1.7%. Throughout this period, deflation dominated with real GDP growth continuously surpassing nominal figures. It took until 2004, before nominal GDP growth rates returned to permanent positive figures.

Exhibit 20 Development of Japanese ex-post GDP growth and inflation rate

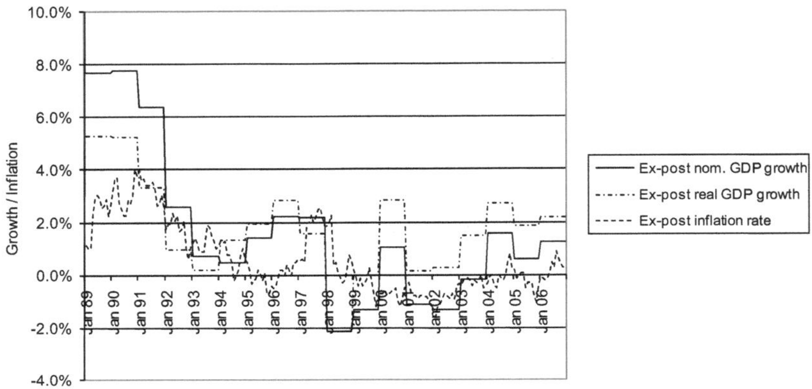

Source: Datastream (codes: JPGDPL.., JPRGDP.., JPOCP009F).

In this economic environment, the Japanese equity market behaved unlike the standard pattern of the other analyzed markets as shown in Exhibit 21. After declining from its peak level in the early 1990s, the TOPIX total return index fluctuated around a side-wards trend throughout the remainder of the analysis period with a total period return of -17%. The standard peak pattern around the millennium can only be observed at a smaller magnitude compared to other markets. However, in line with the other markets, the TOPIX regained substantially since 2003 (+122%). Exhibit 22 illustrates that the associated dividend yield development of the TOPIX showed an increasing trend over time indicating non-stationarity during this period.

Exhibit 21 Total return performance of TOPIX and Datastream 10-year Japanese government bond benchmark index

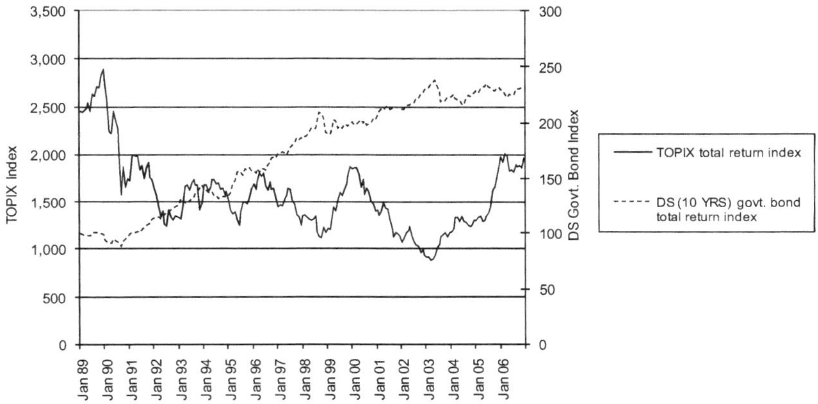

Source: Datastream (codes: TOKYOSE(RI), BMJP10Y(RI)).

Table 6 shows that while the negative correlation between end-of-period dividend yields and one-year returns is low, the coefficients for various return horizons and the beginning-of-period dividend yields are consistently high, already for a one-year holding period.

Table 6 Correlation between realized returns and the dividend yield – TOPIX

Holding period	k=1	k=5	k=10
Pearson $[D_{t-1}/P_{t-1};r_{t,t+k}]$	0.5813	0.5598	0.4538
p-value	(0.0114)	(0.0374)	(0.2198)
Pearson $[D_t/P_t;r_{t,t+k}]$	-0.3028		
p-value	(0.2219)		
Spearman $[D_{t-1}/P_{t-1};r_{t,t+k}]$	0.6369	0.5055	0.3766
p-value	(0.0046)	(0.0652)	(0.3178)
Spearman $[D_t/P_t;r_{t,t+k}]$	-0.2028		
p-value	(0.4196)		

Note: P-values with a significance level of at least 5% are highlighted in grey.

In contrast, the government bond index shows a familiar continuous rise during the investigation period even though at a lower magnitude. Accordingly, the redemption yield continuously declines to comparatively low levels illustrating the influence of deflation.

Exhibit 22 Development of TOPIX dividend yield and Datastream 10-year Japanese government bond benchmark index redemption yield

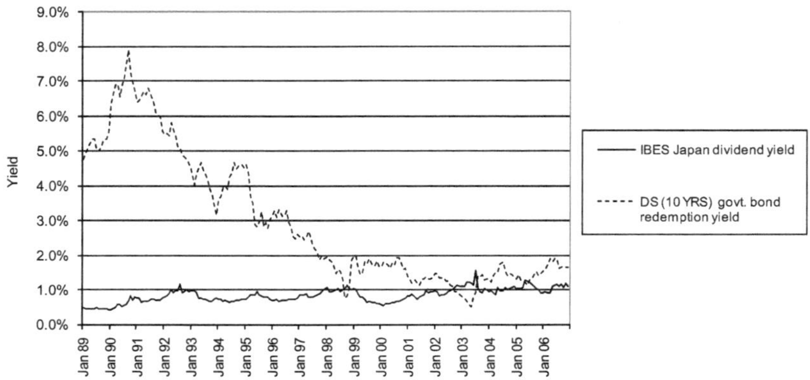

Source: Datastream (codes: @:JPIBES(ADVYLD), BMJP10Y(RY)).

3.5 United Kingdom

The widest equity index covering approximately 98%[397] of the UK equity market is the FTSE All-Share provided by FTSE International Limited.

3.5.1 Description of the equity index – FTSE All-Share

The FTSE All-Share index is the aggregation of the FTSE 100, FTSE 250 (together forming the FTSE 350), and FTSE Small Cap indices[398].

Exhibit 23 Overview of the UK indices structure by FTSE

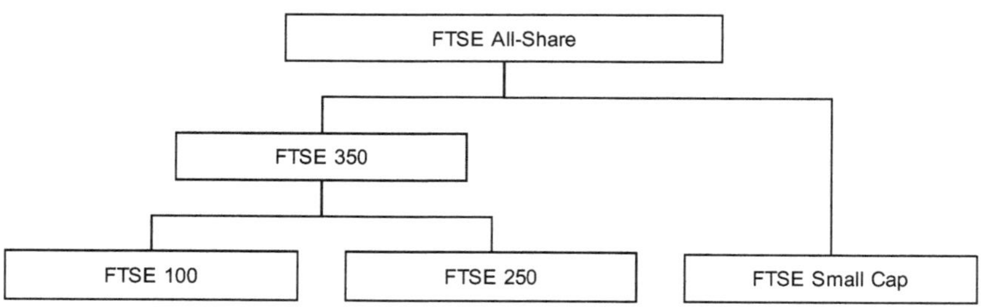

Source: FTSE International Limited (2007a), p. 17.

---

[397] See FTSE International Limited (2007a), p. 17.
[398] See FTSE International Limited (2007a), p. 17.

The FTSE All-Share is designed to represent at least 98% of the full market capitalization, i.e. before the application of any investability weightings, of all UK companies qualifying as eligible for inclusion in the index[399]. All companies with a full listing on the London Stock Exchange are eligible for inclusion in the FTSE All-Share index. Issuers must further comply with a range for criteria such as nationality and liquidity[400].

The FTSE All-Share is a value-weighted index with the weights of each firm being proportionate to its market value contribution adjusted for free-float restrictions and cross-holdings[401]. The index is published for total and price return[402].

Deletions from the index following delisting, a successful takeover bid, or a committee ruling are executed on a quarterly basis. Additions to the index from new issues are either made under the early entry rule after the first day of trading if the firm qualifies for the FTSE 100 (100 largest UK firms by market capitalization) or normally in course of the quarterly review process if the firm qualifies for the FTSE All-Share index[403].

Exhibit 24 presents the approximated composition of the FTSE All-Share index according the value-weights of industry sectors[404]. While generally balanced, the index is dominated by the consumer service and financial sector with the former (latter) decreasing (increasing) over time. Due to its balanced composition, the average Herfindahl index for the UK market is comparatively low at 15.5%.

---

[399] See FTSE International Limited (2007b), p. 16.

[400] See FTSE International Limited (2007b), pp. 8-12 for a complete description of the eligibility criteria.

[401] See FTSE International Limited (2007b), pp. 9-10.

[402] See FTSE International Limited (2005), pp. 11-12. The reference also provides details on the calculation method to incorporate dividend payments.

[403] See FTSE International Limited (2007b), pp. 20-21.

[404] The definition of industry sectors is based on the categorization of Datastream. Note that only firms are included for which also IBES estimates are available. Therefore, the composition does not fully reflect the official index composition.

Exhibit 24 FTSE All-Share index composition by key industry sectors

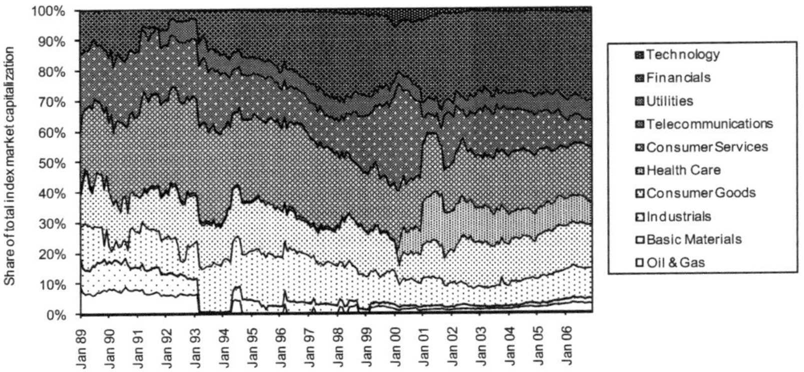

Source: Industry codes based on Datastream (code: ICBIC).

3.5.2 Performance during the analysis period

After a recession at the beginning of the 1990s, the British economy showed a comparatively stable phase of real and nominal GDP growth until the end of the analysis period. Average nominal GDP growth over the analysis period was at 5.6%. Similarly, the inflation rate declined sharply following the negative real GDP growth in 1991 and fluctuated around the familiar two percent level since then. Exhibit 25 illustrates the evolution of key indicators of the British economy.

Exhibit 25 Development of UK ex-post GDP growth and inflation rate

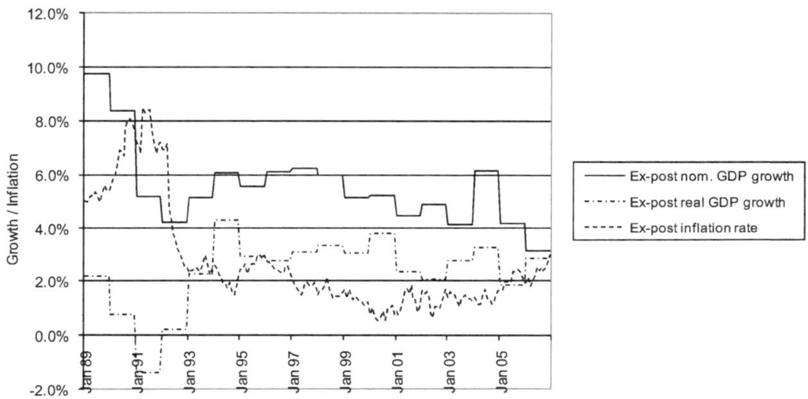

Source: Datastream (codes: UKGDPL.., UKRGDP.E, UKOCP009F).

In the stable economic environment, the British equity market behaved much alike the other Western countries in this analysis with a peak around the millennium and further substantial growth following the market downturn until 2003. Exhibit 26 shows, however, that the rise of 449% to the millennium peak level started already a few years earlier compared to its European counterparts Germany or France. Following a 43% decline, the FTSE All-Share index surpassed the 2000 peak already at the end of 2005. In parallel to the increase of the FTSE All-Share total return index in the 1990s, Exhibit 27 shows that its associated dividend yield declined from almost up to six percent in 1990 down to almost two percent during the millennium peak. After an intermediate rise as a consequence of the market downturn, the dividend yield remained stable at around three percent. This dividend yield development may indicate non-stationarity throughout the analysis period.

Exhibit 26 Total return performance of FTSE All-Share and Datastream 10-year UK government bond benchmark index

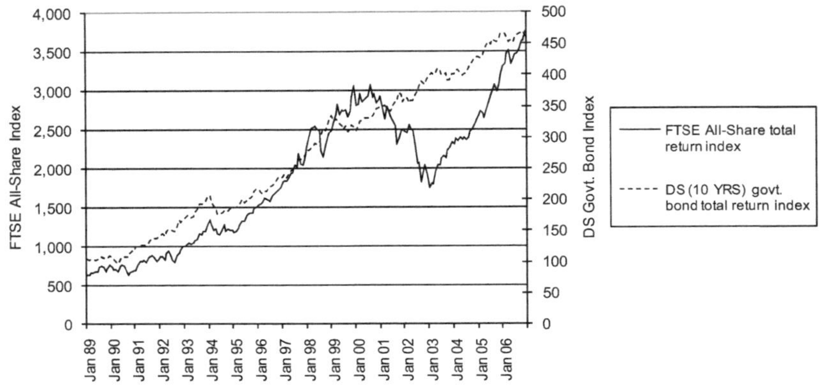

Source: Datastream (codes: FTALLSH(RI), BMUK10Y(RI)).

While there is almost no correlation between the end-of-period dividend yield and the one-period return as shown in Table 7, the five and ten year holding period return are significantly correlated with the beginning-of-period dividend yield. This indicates dependence between expected returns and the dividend yield also for the UK market.

Table 7 Correlation between realized returns and the dividend yield – FTSE All-Share

Holding period	k=1	k=5	k=10
Pearson $[D_{t-1}/P_{t-1};r_{t,t+k}]$	0.5154	0.8033	0.7425
p-value	(0.0286)	(0.0005)	(0.0220)
Pearson $[D_t/P_t;r_{t,t+k}]$	-0.0091		
p-value	(0.9713)		
Spearman $[D_{t-1}/P_{t-1};r_{t,t+k}]$	0.4530	0.8374	0.7167
p-value	(0.0590)	(0.0002)	(0.0298)
Spearman $[D_t/P_t;r_{t,t+k}]$	0.0588		
p-value	(0.8167)		

Note: P-values with a significance level of at least 5% are highlighted in grey.

The Datastream 10-year British government bond total return index shows a familiar development with a close to monotonic rise during the entire investigation period of in total 361%. The associated redemption yield declined in parallel almost six percent until 1999 with a lower rate of decline thereafter.

Exhibit 27 Development of FTSE All-Share dividend yield and Datastream 10-year UK government bond benchmark index redemption yield

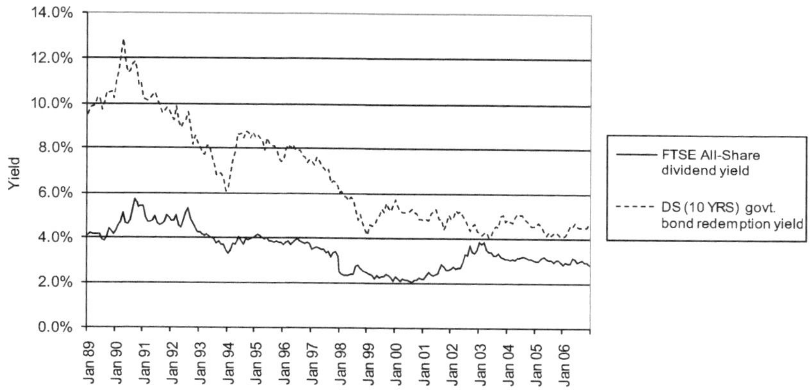

Source: Datastream (codes: FTALLSH(DY), BMUK10Y(RY)).

3.6 United States

Unlike the other countries with only one prime provider for the local all-share index, there are three firms providing broad-market indices in the United States: Standard & Poor's offers the S&P Total Market index, DowJones Indexes/Wilshire Associates supply the Wilshire 5000 Composite index, and Russell Investment Group provides the Russell 3000 index. All index providers claim that their all-share indices cover almost entirely the US market capitalization with differences primarily relating to the number of included micro-cap companies. For this study, all analysis are based on the Russell 3000 index since it has the only complete series of total return data in Datastream for the entire analysis period. [405]

3.6.1 Description of the equity index – Russell 3000

The Russell 3000 index consists of the 3,000 largest US companies based on total market capitalization. The index thereby covers approximately 98% of the investable US equity market[406]. Exhibit 28 illustrates the range of indices aggregated in the Russell 3000.

---

[405] See Dow Jones & Co Inc./Whilshire Associates Inc. (2007), p. 1, Standard & Poor's (2007), p. 4, and Russell Investment Group (2006), p. 1.

[406] See Russell Investment Group (2006), p. 2. See also Siegel, J. (2008), p. 45.

Exhibit 28 Overview of the US indices structure by Russell Investment Group

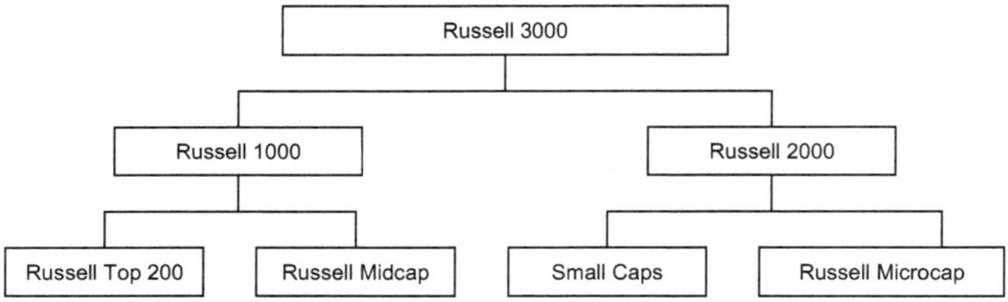

Source: Russell Investment Group (2006), p. 1.

Criteria for the inclusion of securities in the Russell 3000 include US incorporation[407], trading on a major US exchange, a minimum trading price of USD 1.00 at the review date, company structure requirements, and share type[408] requirements[409]. Stocks eligible for index inclusion are weighted by their free-float adjusted market capitalization[410]. The base date for the Russell 3000 is 31 December 1986 at an index value of 140[411].

The Russell 3000 is completely rebuilt during the annual reconstitution process occurring in June of each year[412]. However, following corporate actions such as delisting, bankruptcy, mergers and acquisitions, or similar activities, the respective stock will be excluded from the index as soon as the corporate action is complete with no new company being added as replacement. The only additions between reconstitution dates are made following spin-offs and initial public offerings (quarterly review). Changes in the number of shares outstanding due to buybacks, secondary offerings, merger activity with a non-index member, and other changes are updated at the end of the month if the cumulative change to shares outstanding is greater

---

[407] In addition, firms incorporated in the following countries may also qualify of index inclusion if either their headquarter or their primary exchange is in the United States: Bahamas, Belize, Bermuda, British Virgin Islands, Cayman Islands, Channel Islands, Cook Islands, Gibraltar, Isle of Man, Liberia, Marshall Islands, Netherlands Antilles, and Panama.

[408] Preferred and convertible preferred stock, redeemable shares, participating preferred stock, warrants and rights, and trust receipts are not eligible.

[409] See Russell Investment Group (2007), pp. 7-8.

[410] See Russell Investment Group (2007), p. 12.

[411] See Russell Investment Group (2007), p. 23.

[412] See Russell Investment Group (2007), p. 6.

than 5%[413]. For the total return calculations, dividend payments include also special distributions unless they exceed 10% of the aggregate share price.[414]

As shown in Exhibit 29[415], the approximated composition of the Russell 3000 according the value-weights of industry sectors is most balanced among all countries in the sample with an average Herfindahl index of only 12.1%[416]. The composition over time is primarily driven by the technology sector which temporarily represented more than 30% of the US market but declined post the 2000 peak.

Exhibit 29 Russell 3000 index composition by key industry sectors

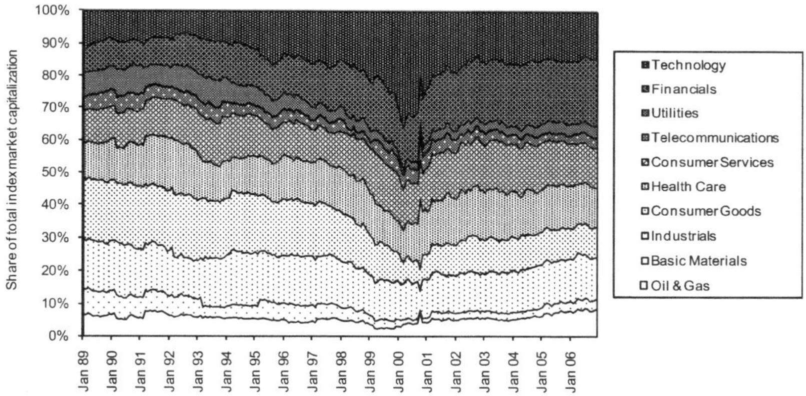

Source: Industry codes based on Datastream (code: ICBIC).

3.6.2 Performance during the analysis period

Despite a recession in 1991, the US economy recovered rapidly and showed the largest real and nominal GDP growth of the investigated countries until the terrorist attacks of 11 September 2001. After a two year recovery period, the strong positive GDP growth was reestablished until the end of the analysis period resulting in an average nominal GDP growth rate of 5.4%. Following the recession period, the US inflation rate declined until 1998 from over six percent in 1990 to below two percent in

---

[413] See Russell Investment Group (2007), pp. 16-20.

[414] See Russell Investment Group (2007), p. 20.

[415] Siegel, J. (2008), p. 53.

[416] The definition of industry sectors is based on the categorization of Datastream. Note that only firms are included for which also IBES estimates are available. Therefore, the composition does not fully reflect the official index composition.

1998. Thereafter, fluctuations in a larger corridor between one and four percent marked the inflation rate development during the end of the high GDP growth period and the subsequent turmoil with ultimate recovery.

Exhibit 30 Development of US ex-post GDP growth and inflation rate

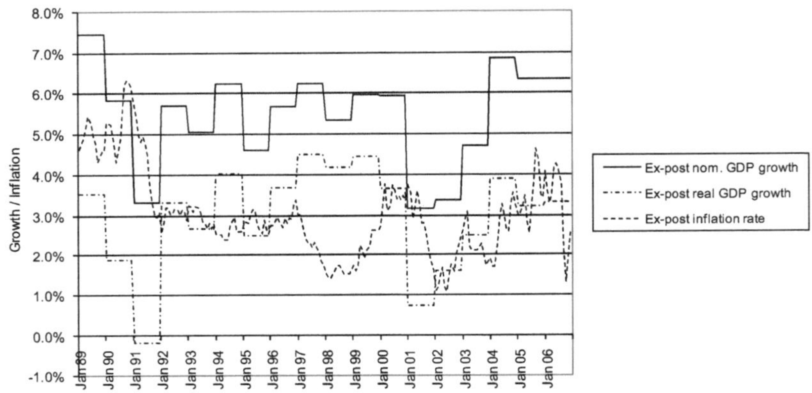

Source: Datastream (codes: USGDPL.., USRGDP.., USOCP009F).

Despite the comparatively larger GDP growth, the US equity market developed directionally similar to the other Western countries in this analysis. This includes a rise of 601% in the Russell 3000 total return index up to the peak in 2000, a downturn by 44% until 2002, and a recovery of 95% throughout the remainder of the analysis period as illustrated by Exhibit 31. The associated dividend yield of the Russell 3000 declined around three percent between the early 1990s and the end of the millennium peak representing strong indications for non-stationarity during this period. Thereafter, Exhibit 32 shows that the dividend yield remained stable at a level of two percent. This shift in the dividend yield was already identified by many researchers and will be discussed in detail later in this study[417].

---

[417] See, e.g., Fama, E./French, K. (2002), pp. 651-652 or Goyal, A./Welch, I. (2003), pp. 641-642.

Exhibit 31 Total return performance of Russell 3000 and Datastream 10-year US government bond benchmark index

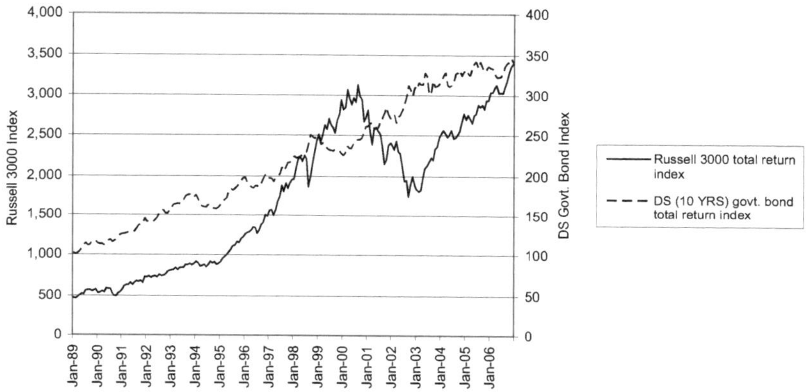

Source: Datastream (codes: FRUSS3L(RI), BMUS10Y(RI)).

Table 8 shows that similarly to the UK, there is almost no correlation between the end-of-period dividend yield and the one-period realized return. However, there are highly significant correlation coefficients for the five and ten year holding period returns compared to the beginning-of-period dividend yield. This relationship was identified for almost all countries including the US.

Table 8 Correlation between realized returns and the dividend yield – Russell 3000

Holding period	k=1	k=5	k=10
Pearson $[D_{t-1}/P_{t-1};r_{t,t+k}]$	0.3926	0.7132	0.9075
p-value	(0.1071)	(0.0042)	(0.0007)
Pearson $[D_t/P_t;r_{t,t+k}]$	0.0068		
p-value	(0.9786)		
Spearman $[D_{t-1}/P_{t-1};r_{t,t+k}]$	0.4448	0.6440	0.9000
p-value	(0.0644)	(0.0129)	(0.0009)
Spearman $[D_t/P_t;r_{t,t+k}]$	0.0258		
p-value	(0.9191)		

Note: P-values with a significance level of at least 5% are highlighted in grey.

Similar to the other countries in the sample, the US Datastream 10-year government bond index steadily rose during the investigation period of in total 242%. At the same time, the associated redemption yield declined more than four percent between 1989 and 2006.

Exhibit 32 Development of Russell 3000 dividend yield and Datastream 10-year US government bond benchmark index redemption yield

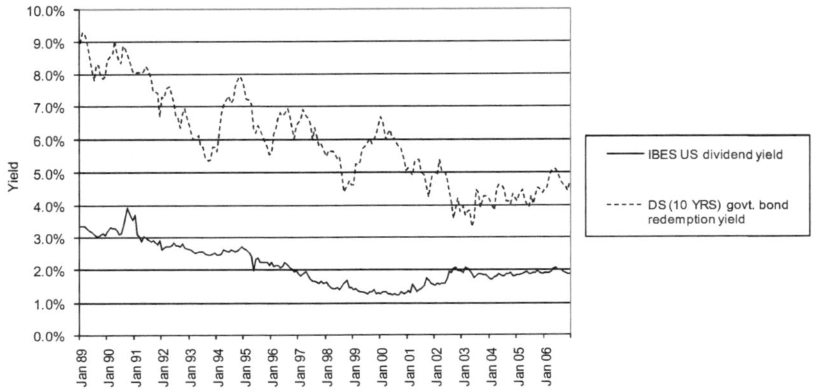

Source: Datastream (codes: @:USIBES(ADVYLD), BMUS10Y(RY)).

3.7 Selected limitations in cross-country comparisons

The comparison of expected MRPs across all previously described markets is subject to the assumption that all markets have similar characteristics regarding factors that influence the expected MRP[418]. However, for selected factors substantial differences can be observed across the countries in the sample of this study.

A primary issue is the impact of accounting differences due to inconsistencies in local GAAPs. Since the conservatism of accounting systems influences the long-term growth rate used in valuation models, GAAP differences may impact IRR-based expected MRP estimates.[419]

Another important structural difference is related to the industry structure of the market. Roll (1992) shows that substantial parts of differences in stock return levels among countries can be explained through industry composition and exchange rates[420]. Among Roll's other findings using daily stock return data between 1988 and 1991 is that market return volatility is positively related to the Herfindahl index on industry weights. Furthermore, correlation between countries can be explained by a

[418] See, e.g., Wallmeier, M. (1997), pp. 137-154 for a comprehensive summary of factors which are used to estimate expected returns.

[419] See Hail, L./Leuz, C. (2006), p. 492.

[420] See Roll, R. (1992), pp. 15-31.

similar industry structures[421]. The relevance of industry composition for the level of country returns implies that the industry structure also affects the magnitude of the expected MRP. Exhibit 33 illustrates the differences in industry composition across the sample countries and shows that the average Herfindahl index over the analysis period ranges from 12.1% in the US to 26.9% in Canada.

Exhibit 33 Comparison of approximated industry compositions based on market capitalization

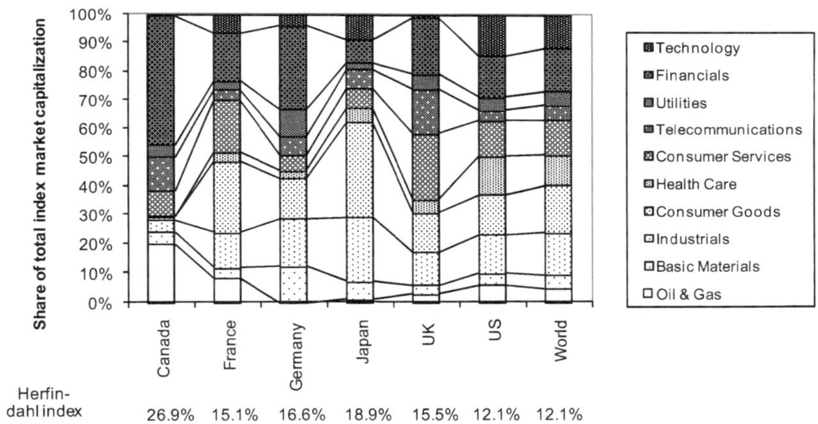

Source: Datastream (avg. over analysis period).

Expected MRP estimates are further influenced by financial leverage. As shown by Modigliani/Miller for perfect capital markets[422], the levered cost of equity is equal to the cost of equity of an entirely equity financed firm plus a premium to compensate for the financial risk of leverage expressed as the debt-to-equity ratio times the spread between the unlevered cost of equity and the cost of debt adjusted for the impact of corporate taxes (the impact of personal taxes is intentionally excluded)[423]:

F 3-2 $r_l^e = r_u^e + (1-\tau_c)(r_u^e - r^f)\frac{V^D}{V^E}$

---

[421] See Roll, R. (1992), pp. 5-10 and 31-37.

[422] See Copeland, T./Weston, F./Shastri, K. (2005), p. 559 for a summary of conditions.

[423] See Modigliani, F./Miller, M. (1958), p. 271 for the first published version excluding corporate taxes and Modigliani, F./Miller, M. (1963), p. 439 for the version including corporate taxes. See also Copeland, T./Weston, F./Shastri, K. (2005), pp. 567-569 and Ballwieser, W. (2007), pp. 99-100.

This suggests that a country with a higher leverage level should have higher expected returns and consequently a higher expected MRP. As shown by Exhibit 34, the debt-equity-ratio varies substantially among the countries in the sample providing further evidence for the limited comparability of expected MRP levels between countries.

Exhibit 34 Comparison of leverage levels across analyzed markets (excl. financial firms)

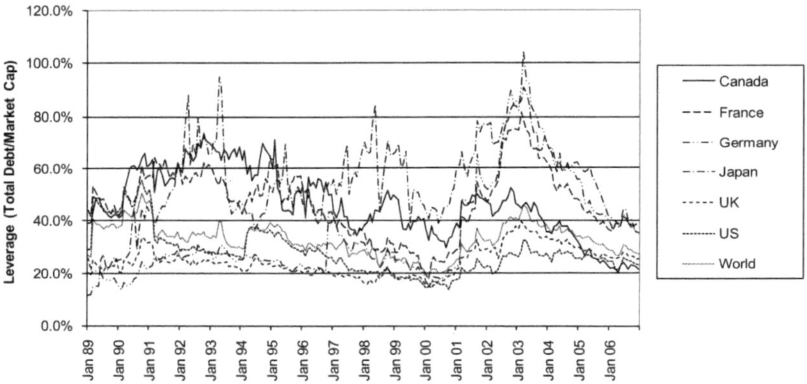

Source: Worldscope, IBES, Datastream.

Finally, Table 9 summarizes the mean values of capital market indicators during the analysis period. For the volatility in annual total returns, differences occur in particular among the Anglo-American countries and the European/Asian countries. The remaining parameters for relative price and interest levels show similar values for the Western countries with Japan standing apart primarily due to the low interest environment in Japan throughout large parts of the analysis period.

Table 9 Summary of key capital market indicators

	Mean parameters (1989-2006)					
	St. dev. ex-post returns	Payout ratio	Dividend yield	P/E_{+1} ratio	Redemption yield	Ex-post inflation rate
Canada	15.26%	37.41%	2.33%	14.4x	6.68%	2.41%
France	24.62%	32.19%	3.16%	17.4x	6.07%	1.96%
Germany	23.57%	39.17%	2.02%	19.4x	5.74%	2.22%
Japan	25.18%	25.77%	0.87%	32.1x	2.99%	0.65%
UK	16.17%	44.77%	3.73%	15.0x	6.83%	2.71%
US	16.97%	32.15%	2.34%	18.2x	5.99%	3.01%

This selection of factors influencing the expected MRP level can only provide an indication for potential differences across the sample. The sample size of only six countries does not allow for the usage of more sophisticated econometric models to identify which factors significantly explain differences.

3.8 Conclusions

Disregarding whether the expected MRP is determined based on ex-post or ex-ante data, the appropriate definition of equity and bond indices is essential for the quality of the estimate. In particular, the construction of the equity index requires the broadest possible market coverage in order to replicate a market portfolio as required by the CAPM as close as possible. Still, comparability across countries is limited not only by differences in capital market indicators but also due to the composition of the real economy.

- While the index calculation methodologies are broadly similar across all countries, there is a substantial difference in the approximated industry composition limiting the comparability of market returns across countries. As a consequence, the Herfindahl index varies between 12.1% for the most balanced market (US) and 26.9% for the most fragmented market (Canada).
- Apart from Japan, all sample countries had a similar economic environment during the analysis period. Average GDP growth of Canada, the UK, and the US was around five percent, with the continental European countries performing one to two percent below. Inflation rates declined consistently over the analysis period to an average level of around two percent for many countries. The exception is Japan with long periods of recession and deflation.
- The pattern of the equity market performance is very again similar across countries with the exception of Japan. Typically, the total return indices reached their first peak at the turn of the millennium and returned to their peak levels at the end of 2006 after falling around 45% to 65% between 2000 and 2003. In contrast, the Japanese market had a negative performance over the entire analysis period.
- The analysis has shown first indications of a dividend yield dependence of expected returns due to the positive correlation between beginning-of-period dividend yields and realized returns in particular with holding periods of five to ten years. Furthermore, there are indications of a non-stationary dividend yield

development in Canada, the UK, and the US due to a decline over the analysis period.

- All government bond indices rose almost continuously during the analysis period which coincides with a consistent decline in redemption yields. Graphical analyses indicate that this development appears at least partially driven by falling inflation rates.
- Finally, the comparison of selected factors influencing returns and MRPs shows differences across the sample countries particularly regarding leverage, market volatility, and the already identified industry composition. These factors need to be taken into considerations when the time-series results for the expected MRP are compared among countries.

4 Expected MRP estimation based on averages of ex-post returns

As already discussed, calculating the expected MRP based on unconditional averages of historical MRPs is the predominant method[424]. Generally, this approach assumes a stationary development of the expected MRP over time implying that the degree of risk aversion and the quantity of systematic risk of market portfolios remain unchanged[425]. Under these conditions, historical capital market conditions can be applied for the future[426]. Furthermore, using unconditional historical averages as expected values assumes MRP distributions to be independent over time implying no correlation and predictability[427]. Even under this rigorous set of assumptions, the unbiasedness of the sample estimator for the true mean of historical MRPs is a further issue to be considered[428]. Ultimately, the expected MRP estimates from this methodology are constant over time[429].

Despite several issues associated with the abovementioned assumptions, numerous studies [430] continuously measure the historical MRP, but the results are often inconsistent due to diverging assumptions and methodologies. The methodological differences are related to one are more of the following key issues:

- Averaging methodology: Arithmetic vs. geometric mean
- Measurement period: Long vs. short periods
- Sample selection: Survivorship bias
- Definition of risk-free rate: Total return vs. cash return[431]

In order to discuss all aspects related to the estimation of the expected MRP from realized MRP averages, this chapter is organized into three major sections. The first section provides a brief review of key studies on historical MRP averages followed by

---

[424] See, e.g., Brennan, M. (1997), p. 82, Elton, E. (1999), p. 1199, Welch, I. (2000), p. 503, Claus, J./Thomas, J. (2001), p. 1629, Gebhardt, W./Lee, C./Swaminathan, B. (2001), p. 136, Fama, E./French, K. (2002), p. 637, Brennan, M. (2003), p. 185, Stehle, R. (2004), p. 910, Richter, F. (2005), pp. 128-129, Goetzmann, W./Ibbotson, R. (2006), p. 4, Kruschwitz, L./Löffler, A. (2008), pp. 806-807, and Wagner, W./Saur, G./Willershausen, T. (2008), p. 739.

[425] See Blume, M. (1974), p. 634, Cooper, I. (1996), p. 159, Damodaran, A. (2002), pp. 160 and 163, Spremann, K. (2004), p. 159, Goetzmann, W./Ibbotson, R. (2006), p. 8, Daske, H./Gebhardt, G. (2006), p. 534, Morningstar Inc. (2007c), pp. 91-92, Reese, R. (2007), pp. 30 and 60, and Breuer, W./Fucks, D./Mark, K. (2009), p. 1.

[426] See Ballwieser, W. (2002), p. 739 and Kruschwitz, L./Löffler, A. (2008), p. 807.

[427] See, e.g., Cooper, I. (1996), pp. 163-164, Brennan, M. (1997), p. 82, Brennan, M. (2003), p. 183, and Breuer, W./Fucks, D./Mark, K. (2009), p. 1.

[428] See Jacquier, E./Kane, A./Marcus, A. (2003), p. 46.

[429] See Brennan, M. (2003), p. 188.

[430] See Section 4.1.

[431] This issue was already discussed in Section 2.4.4.

a statistical comparison across the analyzed countries. Thereafter, a detailed discussion is provided for each identified issue with a particular focus on the averaging methodology.

4.1 Discussion of results

In Section 2.2.3, the basic concepts to analyze historical MRP series were reviewed. It was argued that in order to transform historical unconditional MRP averages into expected values, the MRP must be stationary and independent over time. Despite contradicting empirical evidence in particular on the assumed independence over time, numerous studies are available measuring the averages of long horizon MRP data. Table 10 (Germany only) and Table 11[432] provide a detailed overview of the key studies on the ex-post MRP for all six countries discussed within this study and a world sample. The overview tables also include information on the specifications of the computation with respect to utilized indices, MRP calculation method, risk-free reference asset and return measure, as well as averaging period. Despite the comparatively short analysis period of this study when analyzing historical returns, the averages are provided for comparison purposes with the other utilized methods to derive the expected MRP.

The comprehensive summary for the German market shows that the arithmetic average MRP relative to government bonds for the Germany market range between 4.48% and 8.35% dependent on the denomination and survey period. The spread of geometric averages is similar but as expected at lower levels (1.20% and 5.28%) since it disregards to the volatility over time. The large difference in results is particularly related to studies measuring the MRP since the post world war II period and before. Using data from Stehle (2004), Reese shows that for various starting points between 1948 and 1961 the arithmetic (geometric) average MRP for the period until 2006 differs by almost 8% (6%) and questions the inclusion of the immediate post war period[433]. While the precise definition of the measurement period appears an arbitrary exercise[434], authors close to the German auditor association

---

[432] Despite being irrelevant for the remainder of this study, MRPs relative to bills are also provided for completeness reasons.

[433] See Reese, R. (2007), p. 33. See also Stehle, R./Hartmond, A. (1991), pp. 380-381 and Stehle, R./Huber, R./Maier, J. (1996), pp. 300-301.

[434] See also the remark by Stehle, R./Hartmond, A. (1991), p. 380.

(IDW) frequently refer to the data series from Stehle[435] starting in 1955[436]. Still, provided the data quality is sufficient[437], the assumption of independent MRPs over time implies to use to longest available measurement period which is also discussed in Section 4.3.2.

For Canada, France, Japan, and the UK, the longest available historical MRP series are provided by Dimson/Marsh/Staunton (2008). While the arithmetic (geometric) averages for Canada, France, and the UK are within a range between 5.29% and 6.03%, the mean MRP estimate for Japan is substantially higher at 9.98% based on the Dimson/Marsh/Staunton data. The longest historical MRP series are available for the US with a maximum measurement period of up to 205 years. An obvious pattern in the decline in historical averages with longer historical measurement periods. While Dimson/Marsh/Staunton provide an arithmetic average of 6.49% for data starting in 1900, the Siegel series from 1802 onwards provides an arithmetic average of only 4.6% in nominal terms. The estimate from the data series by Shiller starting in 1871 falls in between this range. Finally, the arithmetic average of the global historical MRP estimate by Dimson/Marsh/Staunton for a sample of 17 countries is 5.15%.

In summary, historical MRP averages differ substantially across studies particularly due to their sensitivity to the measurement period. When using the consistent data series from Dimson/Marsh/Staunton (1900-2005), the arithmetic average relative to bonds for all countries in the sample falls within a range of 5.29% to 9.98% with Germany and Japan having the highest estimates associated with the highest volatility measured as standard deviation.

---

[435] See Stehle, R. (2004).

[436] See, e.g., Wagner, W. et al. (2006), pp. 1016-1019 or Wagner, W./Saur, G./Willershausen, T. (2008), p. 739.

[437] Stehle, R./Hartmond, A. (1991), p. 381, fn. 23a argue that the data quality starting in 1954 increased due to refined and extended calculations of the Federal Statistical Office.

Table 10 Overview of key studies on the historical MRP across countries (I)[438]

Authors	Denom-ination	Equity index	MRP calculation	T-bill index	T-bond index	T-bond return measure	Period	Hist. MRP relative to bills: Arith. Mean	Geo. Mean	Std. dev.	Std. error	Hist. MRP relative to bonds: Arith. Mean	Geo. Mean	Std. dev.	Std. error
Germany															
Conen/Väth (1993)	Nominal	(5)	Simple difference	-	(6)	Total/income return	1876-1992	-	-	-	-	6.75%	-	-	-
	Real	(5)	Simple difference	-	(6)	Total/income return	1876-1992	-	-	-	-	6.59%	-	-	-
Bimberg (1993)	Nominal	(7)	Simple difference	(8)	(9)	Total return	1954-1992	8.65%	5.37%	28.12%	4.75%	7.32%	4.42%	26.38%	4.46%
	Real	(7)	Simple difference	(8)	(9)	Total return	1954-1988	8.55%	5.42%	27.48%	4.65%	7.23%	4.45%	25.80%	4.36%
Baetge/Krause (1994)	NA	FAZ-Index	Simple difference	-	NA	Income return only	1967-1991	-	-	-	-	-	2.65%	-	-
Gielen (1994)	Nominal	(10)	Simple difference	-	NA	NA	1960-1993	-	-	-	-	-	1.20%	-	-
Morawietz (1994)	Nominal	(11)	Simple difference	(12)	(13)	Total return	1870-1992	6.66%	4.35%	23.60%	2.13%	5.33%	3.05%	-	-
Steiner/Uhlir (2001)	Nominal	(14)	Simple difference	(15)	(16)	Total return	1953-1988	9.8%	-	27.7%	4.62%	6.5%	-	-	-
	Real	(14)	Simple difference	(15)	(16)	Total return	1953-1988	9.8%	-	-	-	6.5%	-	-	-
Mehra/Prescott (2003)	Real	NA	Simple difference	NA	NA	NA	1978-1997	6.6%	-	-	-	-	-	-	-
Stehle (2004) (1) with updates (2)	Nominal	CDAX	Simple difference	-	REXP	Total return	1955-2006	-	-	-	-	6.10%	3.22%	24.87%	3.45%
	Nominal	DAX	Simple difference	-	REXP	Total return	1955-2006	-	-	-	-	6.55%	3.26%	26.59%	3.69%
Richter (2005)	Nominal	DAX (17)	Simple difference	NA	> 8 years	NA	1954-2002	6.21%	-	-	-	4.48%	-	-	-
Morningstar Inc. (2007a) (3)	Nominal	MSCI country index	Simple difference	30 days	> 3 years	Income return only	1970-2006	s.o.p	-	-	-	s.o.p	-	-	-
Dimson/Marsh/Staunton (2008) (4)	Real	(18)	Geometric difference	(19)	(20)	Total return	1900-2005	9.07%	3.83%	33.49%	3.28%	8.35%	5.28%	27.41%	2.69%
Gsell (2010)	Nominal	CDAX	Simple difference	-	10 years	Income return only	1989-2006	-	-	-	-	5.52%	2.68%	23.98%	5.65%

Note: All historical MRPs are presented before personal taxes. Where no annual data is available, the geometric mean MRP is approximated by the simple difference between the geometric means of stock and bond/bill index returns. Std. dev. and std. error recalculated where not provided. "s.o.p." means see original publication.

(1) For other return series of Stehle, see Appendix 5.

(2) See http://www.wiwi.hu-berlin.de/Professuren/bwl/bb/ as of 10 October 2007.

(3) See Morningstar Inc. (2007a), pp. 4-10 for a detailed description of the utilized data.

(4) See Dimson, E./Marsh, P./Staunton, M. (2008), p. 509 for a detailed description of the utilized data. Data set excludes 1922-1923.

(5) Equity indices: 1875-1913 "Institut für Konjunkturforschung" index, 1914-1943 "Statistisches Reichsamt" index, 1948-1950 Federal Statistical Office Germany index, 1951-1970 FAZ index, 1971-1992 MSCI Germany index.

(6) Bond indices: approximation of German national bank data until 1941, 1948-1966 index of government, national railway, and national post bonds, 1967-1992 REX.

(7) Equity index: Federal Statistical Office Germany index (value-weighted price index including 90% of stocks traded on the Frankfurt Stock Exchange excl. preferred shares).

(8) Bill index: German national bank data for average unweighted monthly money market instruments.

(9) Bond index: Government bonds with a minimum repayment period of 8 years (all nominal values).

(10) Equity index: Federal Statistical Office Germany index.

(11) Equity indices: 1870-1913 "Institut für Konjunkturforschung" data, 1924-1943 Federal Statistical Office Germany data, 1950-1992 Federal Statistical Office Germany data.

(12) Bill index: 1870-1913 "Institut für Konjunkturforschung" data, 1924-1941 "Statistisches Reichsamt" data, 1950-1992 German national bank data.

(13) Bond index: 1870-1913 "Institut für Konjunkturforschung" data, 1924-1941 "Statistisches Reichsamt" data, 1950-1992 German national bank data.

(14) Equity indices: 1953-1984 Federal Statistical Office Germany index, 1984-1988 FAZ index.

(15) Bill index: 1953-1978 bills of government, national railway and national post with a 6-months maturity, 1979-1988 3-months money market instruments.

(16) Bond returns based on bond prices from the German Statistical Yearbook and secondary market returns.

(17) 1954-1972 Bimberg data, 1973-1988 average from Bimberg data and Datastream data, 1989-2002 datastream data.

(18) Equity indices: 1900-13 Donner index (Gielen), 1914-1918 Gielen OTC index, 1919-1924 and 1948-1953 Federal Statistical Office Germany index, 1924-1948 various unspecified data, 1954-1992 Stehle/Huber/Maier index, 1993-2000 CDAX.

(19) Bill index: until 1945 private bills, assumption of 2% between 1946-1950 and 3% 1951-1953, treasury bills 1954.

(20) Bond index: 1900-1923 German 3% perpetuals, 1924-1935 mortgage bonds, 1936-1967 various unspecified sources, 1968-2000 REX.

Source: Conen, R./Väth, H. (1993), pp. 643-644, Bimberg, L. (1993), pp. 131, 180-209, and add-in page with updated figures, Baetge, J./Krauss, C. (1994), pp. 452-453, Gielen, G. (1994), p. 85 (using a 7% risk-less rate according to Ballwieser, W. (2007), p. 97), Morawietz, M. (1994), pp. 114, 136, 142, 202-205, and 209-210, Steiner, R./Uhlir, H. (2001), pp. 162-166, Mehra, R./Prescott, E. (2003), p. 895, Stehle, R. (2004), pp. 922-927, Richter, F. (2005), p. 101, Morningstar Inc. (2007a), pp. 11-114, and Dimson, E./Marsh, P./Staunton, M. (2008), p. 488.

[438] See Stehle, R. (1999), p. 19, Daske, H./Gebhardt, G. (2006), p. 533, Wagner, W. et al. (2006), pp. 1027-1028, Ballwieser, W. (2007), p. 97, Reese, R. (2007), p. 31, and Drukarczyk, J./Schüler, A. (2009), p. 222 for similar summary tables on the German MRP.

Table 11 Overview of key studies on the historical MRP across countries (II)

Authors	Denom-ination	Equity index	MRP calculation	T-bill index	T-bond index	T-bond return measure	Period	Hist. MRP relative to bills: Arith. Mean	Geo. Mean	Std. dev.	Std. error	Hist. MRP relative to bonds: Arith. Mean	Geo. Mean	Std. dev.	Std. error
Canada															
Morningstar Inc. (2007a) (1)	Nominal	MSCI country index	Simple difference	30 days	≥ 10 years	Income return only	1970-2006	s.o.p	-	-	-	s.o.p	-	-	-
Dimson/Marsh/Staunton (2008) (2)	Real	Various linked indices	Geometric difference	NA	NA	Total return	1900-2005	5.88%	4.54%	16.71%	1.62%	5.67%	4.15%	17.95%	1.74%
Gsell (2010)	Nominal	S&P/TSX Composite	Simple difference	-	10 years	Income return only	1989-2006	-	-	-	-	4.51%	3.33%	15.78%	3.72%
France															
Mehra/Prescott (2003)	Real	NA	Simple difference	NA	NA	NA	1973-1998	6.3%	-	-	-	-	-	-	-
Morningstar Inc. (2007a) (1)	Nominal	MSCI country index	Simple difference	30 days	> 5 years	Income return only	1970-2006	s.o.p	-	-	-	s.o.p	-	-	-
Dimson/Marsh/Staunton (2008) (2)	Real	Various linked indices	Geometric difference	NA	NA	Total return	1900-2005	9.27%	6.79%	24.19%	2.35%	6.03%	3.86%	22.29%	2.16%
Gsell (2010)	Nominal	CAC 40	Simple difference	-	10 years	Income return only	1989-2006	-	-	-	-	6.73%	4.08%	24.93%	5.88%
Japan															
Mehra/Prescott (2003)	Real	NA	Simple difference	NA	NA	NA	1970-1999	3.3%	-	-	-	-	-	-	-
Morningstar Inc. (2007a) (1)	Nominal	MSCI country index	Simple difference	30 days	all bonds	Income return only	1970-2006	s.o.p	-	-	-	s.o.p	-	-	-
Dimson/Marsh/Staunton (2008) (2)	Real	Various linked indices	Geometric difference	NA	NA	Total return	1900-2005	9.84%	6.67%	27.82%	2.70%	9.98%	5.91%	33.06%	3.21%
Gsell (2010)	Nominal	TOPIX	Simple difference	-	10 years	Income return only	1989-2006	-	-	-	-	-1.17%	-4.20%	25.63%	6.04%
UK															
Mehra/Prescott (2003)	Real	NA	Simple difference	NA	NA	NA	1947-1999	4.6%	-	-	-	-	-	-	-
Morningstar Inc. (2007a) (1)	Nominal	MSCI country index	Simple difference	30 days	20 years	Income return only	1970-2006	s.o.p	-	-	-	s.o.p	-	-	-
Dimson/Marsh/Staunton (2008) (2)	Real	Various linked indices	Geometric difference	NA	NA	Total return	1900-2005	6.14%	4.43%	19.84%	1.93%	5.29%	4.06%	16.60%	1.61%
Gsell (2010)	Nominal	FTSE All-share	Simple difference	-	10 years	Income return only	1989-2006	-	-	-	-	5.30%	4.05%	15.91%	3.75%
US															
Shiller (2005) (3) with updates (4)	Nominal	S&P 500 (Composite)	Simple difference	1 year	10 years	Income return only	1871-2006	5.72%	4.02%	18.17%	1.56%	5.77%	4.25%	17.69%	1.52%
	Real	S&P 500 (Composite)	Simple difference	1 year	10 years	Income return only	1871-2006	5.38%	3.77%	18.07%	1.55%	5.53%	4.02%	17.47%	1.50%
Morningstar Inc. (2007b,c) (5)	Nominal	(6)	Simple difference	30 days	20 years	Income return only	1926-2006	s.o.p	-	-	-	s.o.p	-	-	-
	Nominal	(7)	Simple difference	30 days	20 years	Income return only	1926-2006	s.o.p	-	-	-	s.o.p	-	-	-
Dimson/Marsh/Staunton (2008) (2)	Real	Various linked indices	Geometric difference	NA	NA	Total return	1900-2005	7.41%	5.51%	19.64%	1.91%	6.49%	4.52%	20.16%	1.96%
Mehra/Prescott (2008)	Real	NA	Simple difference	NA	NA	NA	1889-2005	6.36%	-	-	-	-	-	-	-
	Real	NA	Simple difference	NA	NA	NA	1946-2005	7.48%	-	-	-	-	-	-	-
Siegel (2008)	Nominal	NA	Simple difference	NA	NA	NA	1802-2006	5.4%	4.0%	-	-	4.6%	3.3%	-	-
	Real	NA	Simple difference	NA	NA	NA	1802-2006	5.4%	4.0%	-	-	4.5%	3.3%	-	-
Gsell (2010)	Nominal	Russell 3000	Simple difference	-	10 years	Income return only	1989-2006	-	-	-	-	7.40%	6.08%	16.84%	3.97%
World															
Dimson/Marsh/Staunton (2008) (2)	Real	Various linked indices	Geometric difference	NA	NA	Total return	1900-2005	6.07%	4.74%	16.65%	1.62%	5.15%	4.04%	14.96%	1.45%

Note: All historical MRPs are presented before personal taxes. Where no annual data is available, the geometric mean MRP is approximated by the simple difference between the geometric means of stock and bond/bill index returns. Std. dev. and std. error recalculated where not provided. "s.o.p." means see original publication.

(1) See Morningstar Inc. (2007a), pp. 4-10 for a detailed description of the utilized data.
(2) See Dimson, E./Marsh, P./Staunton, M. (2008), pp. 507-514 for a detailed description of the utilized data.
(3) See Shiller, R. (1993), pp. 439-446 for a detailed discussion of the underlying data series.
(4) See http://www.econ.yale.edu/~shiller/ as of 17 October 2007. Bill data only available until 2004.
(5) See Morningstar Inc. (2007b), p. 2 and Morningstar Inc. (2007c), pp. 26 and 72-75 for a detailed description of the utilized data. Morningstar Inc. return series were initiated through the research of Ibbotson, R./Sinquefield, R. (1976).
(6) S&P 90 (1926-1956), S&P 500 (1957-2006).
(7) Value-weighted NYSE Composite Index.

Source: Mehra, R./Prescott, E. (2003), pp. 895-896, Shiller, R. (2005), pp. 3-5 (see also Shiller, R. (1993), pp. 439-446), Morningstar Inc. (2007a), pp. 11-114, Morningstar Inc. (2007b), pp. 4-11, Morningstar Inc. (2007c), p. 72, Dimson, E./Marsh, P./Staunton, M. (2008), p. 488, Mehra, R./Prescott, E. (2008), pp. 7-8, and Siegel, J. (2008), pp. 13, 15 (see also Siegel, J. (1992)).

4.2 Comparison of historical MRPs between countries

While the short measurement period of this study is inferior to the long-horizon studies in order to determine the unconditional average MRP, it can be used to analyze the MRP equivalence and correlation across the countries in the sample.

4.2.1 Comparison of unconditional averages

Standard statistical procedures for comparing means of two dependent samples are applied in order to test the hypothesis that two country MRP means $\overline{r}_a^p$ and $\overline{r}_b^p$ are identical. The annual MRP sample for country a is dependent of the MRP sample of country b, since each annual MRP observation of country a can be related to one specific annual MRP observation of country b, i.e., the MRP of the same year within the analysis period[439]. This dependence of the samples requires the usages of particular matched-pair tests[440]. Furthermore, assumptions are required with respect to the underlying distribution of the MRP realizations. The parametric standard paired t-test requires the realized MRP samples to be normally distributed[441]. Under this scenario, a t-statistic is calculated according to the following formula

F 4-1 $$t = \frac{\overline{d} - \left(\overline{r}_a^p - \overline{r}_b^p\right)}{\hat{\sigma}_d}\sqrt{n}$$

with $\overline{d}$ equal to the average difference of paired MRP observations, $\hat{\sigma}_d$ being the estimated standard deviation of the sample differences, and $n-1$ degrees of freedom. When testing for identical sample means, the null hypothesis can now be formulated as follows: $H_0 : \overline{r}_a^p - \overline{r}_b^p = 0$. The null hypothesis of identical average MRPs is rejected if the determined t-value is above the critical value according to the chosen significance level $|t| > t_{1-\alpha/2}$.[442]

Since the true distribution of the MRP for each local market is not precisely known, it appears plausible to also use a non-parametric mean comparison test which does not require an assumption on the MRP distribution. In case of dependent samples, the Wilcoxon matched-pairs signed rank test is the appropriate approach to

---

[439] See Hartung, J./Elpelt, B./Klösener, K.-H. (2009), p. 533. Note that despite two samples are dependent, the individual observations within each sample are still assumed to be independent.
[440] See Hartung, J./Elpelt, B./Klösener, K.-H. (2009), p. 534.
[441] See Hartung, J./Elpelt, B./Klösener, K.-H. (2009), p. 534.
[442] See Hartung, J./Elpelt, B./Klösener, K.-H. (2009), pp. 536-537.

determine whether two sample means are identical[443]. In contrast to the paired t-test, the Wilcoxon matched-pairs signed rank test determines the identity of two sample means according to the ranked differences of each matched pair[444]. For large samples ($n > 15$) the Wilcoxon test statistic is approximately normally distributed and is calculated as follows[445]:

F 4-2

$$Z = \frac{T^+ - \overline{T}}{\hat{\sigma}_T} = \frac{T - \frac{n(n+1)}{4}}{\sqrt{\frac{n(n+1)(2n+1)}{24}}}$$

$$T^+ = \sum_{j=1}^{n} c_j * R_j \quad \text{with } c_i = \begin{cases} 1, \text{ if } R_j > 0 \\ 0, \text{ if } R_j < 0 \end{cases}$$

Intuitively, this procedure tests through rank numbers R_j whether the differences are symmetrically distributed so that the median of the difference distribution ζ is equal to 0. The null hypothesis for a test on identical means can therefore formulated as $H_0 : \zeta = 0$ and is rejected if $|Z| > Z_{1-\alpha/2}$.[446]

Both tests on the identity of sample means are now applied to the realized MRP series derived in this study. Table 12 shows the results for the historical mean MRP comparison across the analyzed six countries. It becomes obvious that the t-/Z-values for comparison of all possible combinations and both test procedures are not significant at a confidence level of 95% so that the null hypothesis of equal means is not rejected in all cases. However, it should be noted that the low magnitude of t-/Z-values is primarily driven by the high underlying standard errors.

---

443 See Hartung, J./Elpelt, B./Klösener, K.-H. (2009), pp. 539-541.

444 When ties occur between certain ranks, the average rank value is applied. However, this requires the usage of a test statistic different from the herein presented; see Hartung, J./Elpelt, B./Klösener, K.-H. (2009), p. 541.

445 See Hartung, J./Elpelt, B./Klösener, K.-H. (2009), pp. 540-541.

446 See Hartung, J./Elpelt, B./Klösener, K.-H. (2009), pp. 541-543.

Table 12 Mean comparison tests on the historical MRP 1989-2006 between countries

Hist. MRP 1989-2006 - Paired t-test (t-value)/Wilcoxon matched-paired singed rank test (Z-value)

	Canada	France	Germany	Japan	UK	US
Canada	0.0000	-0.2830	-0.1520	1.3720	-0.2400	-0.7190
(p-value)		(0.7771)	(0.8789)	(0.1701)	(0.8107)	(0.4724)
France	-0.6806	0.0000	0.2400	1.3720	0.1090	-0.4140
(p-value)	(0.5053)		(0.8107)	(0.1701)	(0.9133)	(0.6791)
Germany	-0.3238	0.4373	0.0000	1.1980	0.5440	-0.3270
(p-value)	(0.7500)	(0.6674)		(0.2311)	(0.5862)	(0.7439)
Japan	1.3768	1.6048	1.2987	0.0000	-1.2410	-1.5460
(p-value)	(0.1864)	(0.1270)	(0.2114)		(0.2145)	(0.1221)
UK	-0.3391	0.4914	0.0748	-1.3191	0.0000	-0.9800
(p-value)	(0.7387)	(0.6294)	(0.9412)	(0.2046)		(0.3271)
USA	-0.8411	-0.1753	-0.4752	-1.4628	-0.9568	0.0000
(p-value)	(0.4119)	(0.8629)	(0.6407)	(0.1618)	(0.3521)	

Note: Paired t-test t-value (Wilcoxon matched-pairs singed rank test Z-value) is below (above) the diagonal. P-values with a significance level of at least 5% are highlighted in grey.

4.2.2 Comparison of cross-country correlation

Another topic of interest is the relation of the annual MRP development among countries, i.e., the correlation of the conditional ex-post MRP behavior over time. As for the mean comparison, standard parametric and non-parametric statistical measures of correlation are applied.

Firstly, if the individual MRP observations within a country sample are assumed to be normally distributed, the Pearson correlation coefficient ρ_{Pearson} is the appropriate metric to measure linear relationships. It is calculated as follows using the realized observations of the MRP for country a and b[447]:

F 4-3 $$\rho_{\text{Pearson}} = \frac{\sum_{j=1}^{n}\left(\hat{r}_{a,j}^{P} - \overline{r}_{a}^{P}\right)\left(\hat{r}_{b,j}^{P} - \overline{r}_{b}^{P}\right)}{\sqrt{\sum_{j=1}^{n}\left(\hat{r}_{a,j}^{P} - \overline{r}_{a}^{P}\right)^{2}\sum_{j=1}^{n}\left(\hat{r}_{b,j}^{P} - \overline{r}_{b}^{P}\right)^{2}}}$$

The coefficient takes values between -1 (perfect negative correlation) and +1 (perfect positive correlation). No correlation between two MRP series is implied by a coefficient of zero. Under the normal distribution case, a t-test can be applied to determine whether two MRP series are statistically related. The relevant t-statistic is calculated as follows:

F 4-4 $$t = \frac{\rho_{\text{Pearson}}\sqrt{n-2}}{\sqrt{1-\rho_{\text{Pearson}}^{2}}}$$

---

447 See Hartung, J./Elpelt, B./Klösener, K.-H. (2009), p. 546.

Based on this test statistic, the null hypothesis of no correlation between two MRP series can be formulated $H_0 : \rho_{Pearson} = 0$ and is rejected if $|t| > t_{1-\alpha/2}$.[448]

Secondly, if no assumption is being made about the underlying distribution of the MRP observations, the non-parametric correlation coefficient developed by Spearman $\rho_{Spearman}$ can be used. This coefficient determines a possible relation according to rank values R and is therefore also called rank correlation coefficient[449]:

F 4-5 $$\rho_{Spearman} = \frac{\sum_{j=1}^{n}\left(R\left[\hat{r}_{a,j}^{p}\right]-\bar{R}\left[\hat{r}_{a}^{p}\right]\right)\left(R\left[\hat{r}_{b,j}^{p}\right]-\bar{R}\left[\hat{r}_{b}^{p}\right]\right)}{\sqrt{\sum_{j=1}^{n}\left(R\left[\hat{r}_{a,j}^{p}\right]-\bar{R}\left[\hat{r}_{a}^{p}\right]\right)^{2}\sum_{j=1}^{n}\left(R\left[\hat{r}_{b,j}^{p}\right]-\bar{R}\left[\hat{r}_{b}^{p}\right]\right)^{2}}}$$

Similar to the Pearson metric, the Spearman correlation coefficient lies between -1 and +1. Significance tests with respect to no correlation between two MRP series are based on the so-called Hotelling-Pabst-statistic (HPS):

F 4-6 $$HPS = \sum_{j=1}^{n}\left(R\left[r_{a,j}^{p}\right]-R\left[r_{b,j}^{p}\right]\right)^{2}$$

The null hypothesis of no correlation between two MRP series is $H_0 : \rho_{Spearman} = 0$ and can be rejected if $HPS < HPS_{\alpha/2}$ or $HPS > HPS_{1-\alpha/2}$.[450]

Applying both correlation coefficients to the historical MRP series within the analysis period from 1989 to 2006 leads to the results shown in Table 60. Except for the relation between Japan and the US, all correlation coefficients for both parametric and non-parametric measures are significantly positively correlated since the null hypotheses are rejected for a confidence level of 95% in all cases.

---

448 See Hartung, J./Elpelt, B./Klösener, K.-H. (2009), pp. 73-78 and 546-548.

449 See Hartung, J./Elpelt, B./Klösener, K.-H. (2009), p. 554.

450 See Hartung, J./Elpelt, B./Klösener, K.-H. (2009), pp. 79-80 and 553-556.

Table 13 Correlation coefficients for the historical MRP 1989-2006 between countries

	Historical MRP 1989-2006 - Pearson's/Spearman's correlation coefficient					
	Canada	France	Germany	Japan	UK	US
Canada	1.0000	0.7234	0.8535	0.7337	0.7998	0.5088
(p-value)		(0.0007)	(0.0000)	(0.0005)	(0.0001)	(0.0311)
France	0.8167	1.0000	0.8204	0.4923	0.7317	0.5459
(p-value)	(0.0000)		(0.0000)	(0.0380)	(0.0006)	(0.0191)
Germany	0.8593	0.8769	1.0000	0.6326	0.8844	0.6223
(p-value)	(0.0000)	(0.0000)		(0.0048)	(0.0000)	(0.0058)
Japan	0.7409	0.6393	0.6139	1.0000	0.6409	0.3602
(p-value)	(0.0004)	(0.0043)	(0.0067)		(0.0042)	(0.1421)
UK	0.8075	0.8674	0.8806	0.5852	1.0000	0.6182
(p-value)	(0.0001)	(0.0000)	(0.0000)	(0.0107)		(0.0063)
USA	0.6039	0.7210	0.7152	0.3744	0.8400	1.0000
(p-value)	(0.0080)	(0.0007)	(0.0008)	(0.1259)	(0.0000)	

Note: Pearson's (Spearman's) correlation coefficient is below (above) the diagonal. P-values with a significance level of at least 5% are highlighted in grey.

4.3 Issues of historical MRP averages

As evidenced by the results shown in Section 4.1, several issues are associated with analyzing historical MRPs. Therefore, the purpose of this section is to provide a systematic discussion of each individual issue.

4.3.1 Averaging methodology

Each scholar estimating the expected MRP from realized MRPs of a certain index portfolio has to address the question which averaging method to use for calculating the mean historical MRP[451]. Despite the significance of this question, leading financial textbooks provide differing recommendations on whether to use the arithmetic mean, the geometric mean, or a combination of both as documented in Table 14[452]. These inconsistent recommendations appear largely driven by different assumptions on the distribution and autocorrelation of MRPs. Furthermore, convenience in implementation may lead authors to neglect potential sources of estimation bias.

[451] See Brennan, M. (2003), pp. 169-170 and Mehra, R./Prescott, E. (2008), p. 2.

[452] In addition, other authors such as Baetge/Krause discuss the difference between the arithmetic and geometric mean but completely neglect the discussion which one to use for valuation purposes; see Baetge, J./Krause, C. (1994), pp. 450-453. Welch even writes that it is unclear whether the arithmetic or geometric mean is appropriate when using it for capital budgeting decisions based on the CAPM. Interestingly enough, he continues his survey focusing on arithmetic means without any further justification; see Welch, I. (2000), p. 503.

Table 14 Overview of recommended averaging methodologies by leading German and American textbooks

Authors	Recommended approach	Comments
Ballwieser (2007)[453] and Drukarczyk/ Schüler (2009)[454] refer to Stehle (2004)[455]	• Arithmetic avg. for valuation • Geometric avg. or weighted unbiased avg. for long-term compounding applications	• Assumes independent and identically distributed returns • Weighted unbiased estimators according to the work of Blume (1974) for compounding and Cooper (1996) for discounting • Ballwieser raises doubts about the general validity of Stehle's argumentation since German returns do not appear to be stochastically independent
Brealey/Myers/Allen (2008)[456]	• Arithmetic avg.	• Assume independent and identically distributed returns (implied by used example) with a known mean • Arithmetic avg. provides the correct opportunity cost of capital that equals present value and discounted expected payoff • Impact of survivorship bias and a decreasing dividend yield addressed
Copeland/Weston/ Shastri (2005)[457]	• Arithmetic avg.	• Assume independent and identically distributed returns (implied by used example) with no parameter uncertainty • Probability weighted returns of all branches provide ex ante expected return • Geometric avg. appropriate for historical performance analysis
Damodaran (2002)[458]	• Geometric avg.	• Assumes negative autocorrelation of returns • Postulates argument that the aim to determine long-term expected returns supports the use of geometric avg. • Favors longest possible time horizon to minimize standard errors despite a potential change in investor risk aversion

[453] See Ballwieser, W. (2007), pp. 95-99.
[454] See Drukarczyk, J./Schüler, A. (2009), pp. 218-224.
[455] See Stehle, R. (2004), pp. 910-911 and 918-919.
[456] See Brealey, R./Myers, S./Allen, F. (2008), pp. 175-180.
[457] See Copeland, T./Weston, F./Shastri, K. (2005), pp. 171-172.
[458] See Damodaran, A. (2002), pp. 160-163.

Authors	Recommended approach	Comments
Koller/Goedhart/ Wessels (2005)[459]	• Arithmetic avg. in one-period context • Two possibilities in multi-period context • (1) Arithmetic avg. of multi-period holding returns rather than compound single-period averages • (2) Weighted unbiased estimator	• Assume independent and identically distributed returns and negative autocorrelation of returns • Source of bias in multi-period context due to estimation error and negative autocorrelation in returns • Weighted unbiased estimator according to Blume (1974)[460] • Recommended historical MRP for US: 5.5% (1-2% deduction for survivor bias)
Levy/Sarnat (1994)[461]	• Geometric avg.	• No further reasoning provided
Morningstar Inc. (2007c)[462] (formerly Ibbotson Associates)	• Arithmetic avg.	• Assume independent and identically distributed returns (implied by used example) with a known mean
Ross/Westerfield/Jaffe (2008)[463]	• Arithmetic avg.	• No reasoning is provided

459 See Koller, T./Goedhart, M./Wessels, D. (2005), pp. 299-302.

460 Koller/Goedhart/Wessels only mention the weighted unbiased Blume (1974) estimator which—as to be shown shortly—is only appropriate for compounding of cash flows and neglect the valuation-related weighted unbiased Cooper (1996) estimator for application in discount rates.

461 See Levy, H./Sarnat, M. (1994), p. 495.

462 See Morningstar Inc. (2007c), pp. 77-79.

463 See Ross, S./Westerfield, R./Jaffe, J. (2008), pp. 267-268.

In order to approach the issue of the appropriate averaging method more systematically, it is initially assumed that the distribution of observed returns is the true distribution of returns ruling out any uncertainty about distribution parameters such as mean or standard deviation. After discussing this scenario, the findings are reviewed assuming that realized returns are only a sample out of the true return distribution. In this more complex but relevant case, the distribution parameters are uncertain and estimation errors occur.[464]

4.3.1.1 Distribution parameter certainty

In addition to the assumption that the distribution of realized returns represents the entire population, it is usually assumed that returns are independent and identically distributed—frequently also referred to as i.i.d. returns. This implies that the underlying process is strictly stationary over time with a constant expected rate of return. The validity of the assumptions particularly with respect to a potential serial correlation of returns is discussed at a later point.

For simplicity, the following statistical arguments on averaging methodologies are primarily based on returns and not on the MRP itself since they are essentially the same[465]. One may also regard this approach as the additional assumption of a deterministic risk-free rate[466].

In such an environment, the choice between the arithmetic and geometric mean as a proxy for the expected return used to infer the expected MRP is widely agreed[467]. Richter describes their intuitive difference as follows[468]: "The geometric mean is calculated along a path (a time series, depicted as 'horizontal average') of realized rates of returns, whereas the arithmetic mean [...] is the average of all possible future

---

[464] See Cooper, I. (1996), p. 160, Stehle, R. (2004), p. 919, Reese, R. (2007), p. 36, and Drukarcyzk, J./Schüler, A. (2009), p. 223.

[465] See Cooper, I. (1996), p. 160, fn. 2. Cooper argues that including a time-varying risk-free rate would complicate the reasoning without changing the ultimate question regarding arithmetic or geometric averaging of past data.

[466] See Richter, F. (2006a), p. 6 who also assumes a deterministic risk-free rate for his analysis.

[467] See Blume, M. (1974), pp. 634-635, Kritzman, M. (1994), p. 13, Cooper, I. (1996), p. 159, Fama, E. (1996), p. 417, Damodaran, A. (2002), p. 161, Dimson, E./Marsh, P./Staunton, M. (2002), p. 182, Brennan, M. (2003), pp. 183-184, Mehra, R./Prescott, E. (2003), p. 891, Stehle, R. (2004), pp. 918-919, Copeland, T./Weston, F./Shastri, K. (2005), pp. 171-172, Koller, T./Goedhart, M./Wessels, D. (2005), p. 301, Morningstar Inc. (2007c), pp. 77-79, Reese, R. (2007), pp. 36-37, Brealey, R./Myers, S./Allen, F. (2008), pp. 175-176, Mehra, R./Prescott, E. (2008), pp. 2-3, Missiakoulis, S./Vasiliou, D./Eriotis, N. (2008), p. 6, and Drukarczyk, J./Schüler, A. (2009), p. 223.

[468] See also Cornell, B. (1999), p. 39 and Drobetz, W. (2003a), p. 7 for similar statements.

rates of return in one point in time ('vertical average'). [The geometric mean] [...] tells you what the average rate of return has been in the past, and [the arithmetic mean] [...] tells you what you can expect on average in the future, e.g., next year"[469]. To understand in more depth why the arithmetic average is the appropriate unbiased estimate of the expected return, the argument is developed formally and complemented by an example.

Starting point for the formal argument is again the multi-period valuation formula derived in Section 2.3.1. Assuming that the periodical cash flows are zero and $\text{cov}_t\left[\tilde{V}_{t+1}, E_{t+1}\left[\tilde{R}_{t+2}\right]\right]=0$, the prospective expected value of an asset conditional on the information at time t can be written for a finite period as follows[470]:

F 4-7
$$\begin{aligned} E_t\left[\tilde{V}_{t+k}\right] &= V_t\, E_t\left[\left(1+\tilde{R}_{t+1}\right)\left(1+\tilde{R}_{t+2}\right)\ldots\left(1+\tilde{R}_{t+k}\right)\right] \\ &= V_t\left(1+E_t\left[\tilde{R}_{t+1}\right]\right)\left(1+E_t\left[\tilde{R}_{t+2}\right]\right)\ldots\left(1+E_t\left[\tilde{R}_{t+k}\right]\right) \end{aligned}$$

If the unconditional expected return is constant over time so that $E_t\left[\tilde{R}_{t+u}\right]=E_t\left[\tilde{R}\right]$ for $u=1,2,\ldots,k$, F 4-7 reduces to

F 4-8 $$E_t\left[\tilde{V}_{t+k}\right]=V_t\left(1+E_t\left[\tilde{R}\right]\right)^k$$

which shows that the expected one-period return is the correct rate that relates the current value to its expected future value[471]. Therefore, if returns are assumed to be i.i.d. in order to satisfy $\text{cov}_t\left[\tilde{V}_{t+1}, E_{t+1}\left[\tilde{R}_{t+2}\right]\right]=0$ and if each occurrence has the same probability, then the unconditional expected return is constant over time and equal to the arithmetic mean of the return distribution $E_t\left[\tilde{R}\right]=A$[472]. Under these conditions, the arithmetic mean is the correct rate for compounding and discounting purposes:

F 4-9 $$E_t\left[\tilde{V}_{t+k}\right]=V_t\left(1+E_t\left[\tilde{R}\right]\right)^k=V_t\left(1+A\right)^k$$

---

[469] Richter, F. (2006a), p. 6. See also Copeland, T./Weston, F./Shastri, K. (2005), p. 172 and Missiakoulis, S./Vasiliou, D./Eriotis, N. (2008), p. 5.

[470] Similar to Fama, E. (1996), p. 417, Stehle, R. (2004), pp. 918-919, and Breuer, W./Fucks, D./Mark, K. (2009), pp. 4-5 who, however, not explicitly mention the covariance condition.

[471] See Fama, E. (1996), p. 417, Stehle, R. (2004), p. 919, and Breuer, W./Fucks, D./Mark, K. (2009), pp. 4-5.

[472] See also Reese, R. (2007), p. 37 who, however, only refers to independent returns.

F 4-10 $V_t = \frac{E_t\left[\tilde{V}_{t+k}\right]}{(1+A)^k}$

Since the geometric mean is usually[473] smaller than the arithmetic mean, using the geometric mean for discounting would overestimate the current value[474]:

F 4-11 $V_t = \frac{E_t\left[\tilde{V}_{t+k}\right]}{(1+A)^k} < \frac{E_t\left[\tilde{V}_{t+k}\right]}{(1+G)^k}$

The following example illustrates the formal finding for a binomial return distribution of i.i.d. returns and shows the difference between the arithmetic and geometric mean[475]. From one period to another, the i.i.d. rates of return are assumed to be 30% and -10% which are equally likely. Exhibit 35 shows the development of an initial investment amount of EUR 1.00 based on a binomial model with four periods. The expected return of 10% is equal to the arithmetic mean $E_t\left[\tilde{R}\right] = A = (30\% - 10\%)/2 = 10\%$ while the geometric mean is lower at $G = \sqrt{(1+30\%)(1-10\%)} - 1 \approx 8.17\%$. When determining the present value of the expected payoff in $t = 4$, only a discount rate equal to the arithmetic mean leads to the initial investment:

$$V_0 = \frac{E_0\left[\tilde{V}_4\right]}{(1+A)^4} = \frac{1.4641}{(1+0.1000)^4} = 1.0000$$

As already formally derived, using the lower geometric mean of 8.17% would not lead to the initial investment:

$$V_0 = \frac{E_0\left[\tilde{V}_4\right]}{(1+G)^4} = \frac{1.4641}{(1+0.0817)^4} \approx 1.0695$$ [476]

---

[473] Both means are only equal when all observed returns used for averaging have the same value.

[474] See Fama, E. (1996), p. 417 and Stehle, R. (2004), pp. 918-919.

[475] Similar example as Richter, F. (2006a), pp. 6-8. See also Copeland, T./Weston, F./Shastri, K. (2005), pp. 171-172, Koller, T./Goedhart, M./Wessels, D. (2005), p. 301, Morningstar Inc. (2007c), pp. 77-79, Reese, R. (2007), pp. 36-37, and Brealey, R./Myers, S./Allen, F. (2008), pp. 175-176.

[476] Results calculated using unrounded input variables.

Exhibit 35 Development of the initial investment in the binomial example

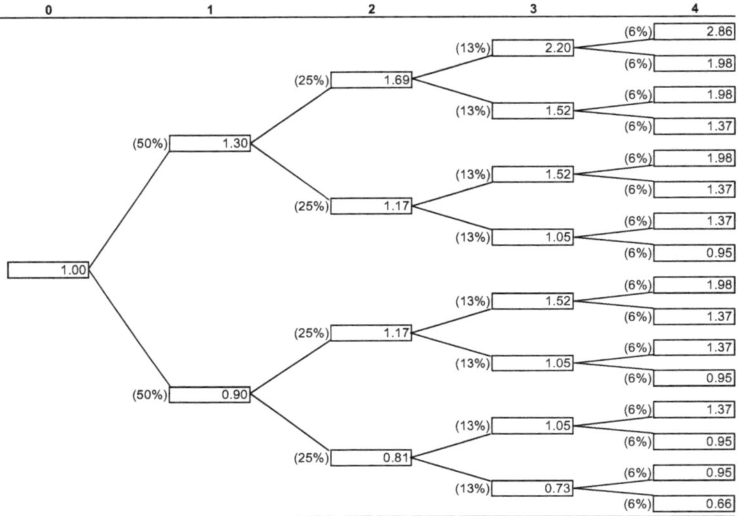

t	0	1	2	3	4
$E[V_t]$		1.1000	1.2100	1.3310	1.4641
$E[r]$		10.00%	10.00%	10.00%	10.00%
Median $[V_t]$		1.1000	1.1700	1.2870	1.3689

Note: Values in parantheses show the probability of the respective payoff.

This example clearly shows that when the parameters of the return distribution are known and returns are i.i.d. with equal probabilities, the arithmetic mean is the appropriate unbiased estimate of the expected return to be applied for calculating the expected MRP which can then be used for discounting or compounding of cash flows[477].

An interesting observation is concerning the impact of i.i.d. returns on the distribution of future values. Exhibit 35 shows that for investment horizons greater than one period, the expected value of the distribution of future payoffs exceeds the median. This implies that distributions of future payoff with more than one period are no more symmetrical, but skewed to the right (to the top in Exhibit 35). Therefore, the probability to realize the expected future payoff is lower than 50%. The level of skewness increases with the length of the investment horizon.[478]

---

[477] See also Jacquier, E./Kane, A./Alan, M. (2003), p. 46.

[478] See Fama, E. (1996), pp. 416 and 419-426 (Fama assumes normally distributed returns), Drobetz, W. (2003a), pp. 8-9, Hachmeister, D. (2006), p. 148, and Reese, R. (2007), p. 37.

As already shown in Table 14, some authors reject the assumption of independent returns based on empirical evidence that returns are negative serially correlated. Revisiting the above example and assuming the extreme case of perfect negative serial correlation—each positive return is followed by a negative return—only two paths are possible which both yield an expected future payoff of EUR 1.37. Now the appropriate average that equates the discounted expected future payoff with the initial investment is the geometric mean[479].

$$V_0 = \frac{E_0\left[\tilde{V}_4\right]}{(1+G)^4} = \frac{1.3689}{(1+0.0817)^4} = 1.0000$$ [480]

This demonstrates that the ultimate choice between the arithmetic and geometric mean is strongly influenced by the assumption on autocorrelation between returns.

4.3.1.2 Distribution parameter uncertainty – i.i.d. normal returns

Despite returning to the assumption of a strictly stationary process with independent and identically distributed returns, now the more realistic scenario is discussed under which the observed historical returns represent only a sample out of the true distribution. This implies that any calculated average of realized returns is only an estimate of the true mean and subject to estimation error[481]. The uncertain returns $\tilde{R}_t$ can therefore be described as follows[482]:

F 4-12 $\tilde{R}_t = \mu + \tilde{\varepsilon}_t$

where $E\left[\tilde{R}\right] = \mu$ is the true mean of the return distribution and $\tilde{\varepsilon}_t$ is a random variable being independently and normally distributed with a mean of zero and a standard deviation identical to that of $\tilde{R}_t$. The arithmetic mean now becomes itself a normally distributed random variable $\tilde{A}$ and can be expressed including the estimation error which is dependent on the sample size T[483]:

[479] See Mehra, R./Prescott, E. (2003), pp. 891-892 and Reese, R. (2007), p. 40.

[480] Results calculated using unrounded input variables.

[481] See Richter, F. (2006a), pp. 6-7 and Breuer, W./Fucks, D./Mark, K. (2009), pp. 5-6.

[482] See Blume, M. (1974), pp. 634-635. See also Indro, D./Lee, W. (1997), pp. 82-83 for a similar argument using a different notation.

[483] See Blume, M. (1974), p. 635. See also Reese, R. (2007), p. 41.

F 4-13
$$\tilde{A} = \frac{1}{T}\sum_{t=1}^{T}\tilde{R}_t = \mu + \frac{1}{T}\sum_{t=1}^{T}\tilde{\varepsilon}_t = \mu + \tilde{h}$$
$$\text{with } \tilde{h} = \frac{1}{T}\sum_{t=1}^{T}\tilde{\varepsilon}_t$$

As an average of independent and normally distributed random variables, $\tilde{h}$ is another normal variate with an expected value of zero and a variance equal to[484]:

F 4-14 $$\operatorname{var}[h] = \frac{1}{T^2}\operatorname{var}\left[\sum_{t=1}^{T}\tilde{R}_t\right] = \frac{1}{T}\operatorname{var}\left[\tilde{R}\right]$$

which approaches zero as T approaches infinity. The estimator $\tilde{A}$ is now said to be unbiased if its expected value is equal to the true mean $E\left[\tilde{A}\right] = \mu$[485]. Due to the fact that $E\left[\tilde{h}\right] = 0$ the expected value of the estimated arithmetic mean equals the true mean of the return distribution and $\tilde{A}$ is therefore an unbiased estimator[486].

The derivation of an unbiased estimator is more complex in a multi-period context[487], e.g., when the estimator is used for compounding over $k > 1$ periods or generally for discounting purposes[488]. Applying expectations to F 4-13, compounding over k periods, and applying the aforementioned criterion for an unbiased estimator yields the following relationships[489]:

F 4-15 $$(1+\mu)^k = \left(E\left[1+\tilde{A}\right]\right)^k \begin{cases} = E\left[\left(1+\tilde{A}\right)^k\right] = E\left[\left(1+\mu+\tilde{h}\right)^k\right] & \text{for } k = 1 \\ < E\left[\left(1+\tilde{A}\right)^k\right] = E\left[\left(1+\mu+\tilde{h}\right)^k\right] & \text{for } k > 1 \end{cases}$$

F 4-15 shows that due to Jensen inequality[490] the expected compounded arithmetic mean estimator is only equal to the compounded true mean and thereby unbiased if $k = 1$. This is due to the fact that $\left(1+\mu+\tilde{h}\right)^k$ is a strictly convex function for $k > 1$.

---

484 See Richter, F. (2006a), p. 7. See also Poddig, T./Dichtl, H./Petersmeier, K. (2008), p. 86-87 for the statistical fundamentals.

485 See Greene, W. (2008), p. 1028 and Wooldridge, J. (2008), pp. 750-752.

486 See also Brennan, M. (2003), p. 183, Richter, F. (2006a), p. 7, Missiakoulis, S./Vasiliou, D./Eriotis, N. (2008), p. 6, and Breuer, W./Fucks, D./Mark, K. (2009), p. 6.

487 See Fama, E./French, K. (1999), p. 1943.

488 See also Breuer, W./Fucks, D./Mark, K. (2009), pp. 6-8.

489 Similar to Blume, M. (1974), p. 635 and Reese, R. (2007), p. 43. See also Indro, D./Lee, W. (1997), pp. 82-83 and Jacquier, E./Kane, A./Marcus, A. (2005), p. 40.

490 See Greene, W. (2008), p. 991 and Hartung, J./Elpelt, B./Klösener, K.-H. (2009), pp. 113 and 1020.

Consequently, the expected compounded arithmetic mean estimator contains an upward bias for $k > 1$ which increases with the number of compounding periods.
The same approach can be used to analyze a potential bias of the geometric mean in a multi-period setting. Using the standard definition of the geometric mean, inserting F 4-12 with the estimation error, and rearranging yields[491]:

F 4-16
$$1+\tilde{G} = \left[\prod_{t=1}^{T}\left(1+\tilde{R}_t\right)\right]^{1/T} = \left[\prod_{t=1}^{T}\left(1+\mu+\tilde{\varepsilon}_t\right)\right]^{1/T} = \left(\left(1+\mu\right)^T + \tilde{o}\right)^{1/T}$$
$$\text{with } \tilde{o} = \prod_{t=1}^{T}\left(1+\mu+\tilde{\varepsilon}_t\right) - \left(1+\mu\right)^T$$

Additionally, it is assumed that every $\left(1+\tilde{R}_t\right)$ exceeds zero[492], at least one $\tilde{\varepsilon}_t$ is nonzero, and the expected value of $\tilde{o}$ is equal to zero. Applying expectations to F 4-16, compounding over k periods, and applying the aforementioned criterion for an unbiased estimator yields the following relationships[493]:

F 4-17
$$\left(1+\mu\right)^k = \left(E\left[1+\tilde{G}\right]\right)^k \begin{cases} > E\left[\left(1+\tilde{G}\right)^k\right] = E\left[\left(\left(1+\mu\right)^T + \tilde{o}\right)^{k/T}\right] & \text{for } k < T \\ = E\left[\left(1+\tilde{G}\right)^k\right] = E\left[\left(\left(1+\mu\right)^T + \tilde{o}\right)^{k/T}\right] & \text{for } k = T \\ < E\left[\left(1+\tilde{G}\right)^k\right] = E\left[\left(\left(1+\mu\right)^T + \tilde{o}\right)^{k/T}\right] & \text{for } k > T \end{cases}$$

F 4-17 shows that the expected geometric mean estimator is an unbiased estimate of the true mean if the number of observations equals the number of compounding periods. However, for k less (larger) than T, $E\left[\left(1+\tilde{G}\right)^k\right]$ is downward (upward) biased since a positive number raised to the k/T power is a concave (convex) function and Jensen inequality applies. In summary, Blume shows that for $k > 1$ and $k < T$ the arithmetic mean estimate is upward biased and the geometric mean estimate is downward biased implying that an unbiased estimator within this range is a combination of both mean estimates.
Against this background, Blume has developed different methods to obtain an approximately unbiased estimate of the mean to be applied as expected return for

---

[491] See Blume, M. (1974), p. 635.
[492] This may be seen as a conflict with the normal distribution but Blume shows that the normal assumption is still valid for typical return distributions; see Blume, M. (1974), p. 635.
[493] Similar to Blume, M. (1974), p. 635 and Reese, R. (2007), p. 44.

multi-period compounding purposes. His preferred and most widely cited[494] approach is a weighted unbiased estimator which includes the arithmetic as well as geometric mean estimate[495]:

F 4-18
$$\text{Blume} = a\left(1+\tilde{A}\right)^{k} + (1-a)\left(1+\tilde{G}\right)^{k}$$
$$\text{with} \quad a = \frac{T-k}{T-1}$$

F 4-18 incorporates the property that for $k=1$ the arithmetic mean estimate and for $k=T$ the geometric mean estimate are unbiased estimators. Therefore, the weighting factor a takes the value of one for $k=1$ and zero for $k=T$.

On the basis of Blume's analysis, Cooper has investigated the properties of the arithmetic and geometric mean estimate when applied in the discount rate to value multi-period cash flows[496]. In this case, both the arithmetic as well as the geometric mean based multi-period discount factor are upward biased estimators since positive numbers to the $-k$ or $-k/T$ power are strictly convex functions. Using Jensen inequality yields therefore[497]:

F 4-19 $$(1+\mu)^{-k} = \left(E\left[1+\tilde{A}\right]\right)^{-k} < E\left[\left(1+\tilde{A}\right)^{-k}\right] = E\left[\left(1+\mu+\tilde{h}\right)^{-k}\right]$$

F 4-20 $$(1+\mu)^{-k} = \left(E\left[1+\tilde{G}\right]\right)^{-k} < E\left[\left(1+\tilde{G}\right)^{-k}\right] = E\left[\left((1+\mu)^{T}+\tilde{o}\right)^{-k/T}\right]$$

These relationships imply that the one-period estimates of the arithmetic and geometric mean are downward biased in relation to the correct discount rate. Furthermore, as the geometric mean is always smaller than the arithmetic mean it is consistently more biased compared to the latter[498].

For the purposes of discounting, Cooper has therefore developed an approximately unbiased weighted estimator[499]:

---

494 See, e.g., Cooper, I. (1996), p. 161, Indro, D./Lee, W. (1997), p. 84, Stehle, R. (2004), p. 919, Koller, T./Goedhart, M./Wessels, D. (2005), p. 302, and Richter, F. (2006a), pp. 11-12.

495 See Blume, M. (1974), pp. 636-637.

496 See also the summary by Brennan, M. (2003), p. 184 and Butler, J./Schachter, B. (1989) for a general discussion of estimation risk related to discount rates.

497 See Cooper, I. (1996), p. 160 for the next paragraph. See also Reese, R. (2007), pp. 44-46.

498 See Cooper, I. (1996), p. 160.

499 See Cooper, I. (1996), p. 161.

$$\text{F 4-21} \quad \begin{aligned} &\text{Cooper} = b\left(1+\tilde{A}\right)^{-k} + \left(1-b\right)\left(1+\tilde{G}\right)^{-k} \\ &\text{with} \quad b = \frac{T+k}{T-1} \end{aligned}$$

Cooper's weighting factor b differs from Blume's weighting factor since it always puts a positive weight greater than one on the multi-period arithmetic mean estimate and a negative weight on the multi-period geometric mean estimate. Therefore, the approximately unbiased discount factor no more lies in-between both mean estimates for $k > 1$ and $k < T$ but always below the purely arithmetic estimator. Furthermore, for $k = T$ the Cooper estimator is approximately $\text{Cooper} = 2\left(1+\tilde{A}\right)^{-k} - \left(1+\tilde{G}\right)^{-k}$ while the Blume estimator is solely based on the geometric mean[500].

The directional bias of the arithmetic and geometric mean estimate, its increase over longer horizons, as well as the ability to reduce the bias through adjusted estimators based on a weighted average of the arithmetic and geometric mean is confirmed by statistical return simulations[501]. However, Blume's as well as Cooper's estimator reach negative and thereby non-meaningful levels for long-term compounding/discounting periods[502]. This problem is caused by the Taylor series approximation utilized to obtain the respective weighted unbiased estimators[503]. A demonstration of the bias directions and the imprecision for longer horizons using return simulations is provided in Appendix 3.

4.3.1.3 Distribution parameter uncertainty – i.i.d. normal log-returns

The issue of whether the arithmetic or geometric mean of a historical series provides an unbiased estimator is similar when log-returns are assumed to be distributed i.i.d. normal. As discussed in Section 2.2.2, this implies that the simple discrete returns are lognormally distributed[504]. In this case, the conclusion remains the same that with known mean and variance, the arithmetic average is the correct unbiased

---

[500] See Cooper, I. (1996), p. 161.
[501] See Blume, M. (1974), pp. 637-638, Indro, D./Lee, W. (1997), pp. 84-89, and Breuer, W./Fucks, D./Mark, K. (2009), pp. 8-10.
[502] See also Richter, F. (2006a), p. 12 and Reese, R. (2007), pp. 55-56.
[503] See Richter, F. (2006a), p. 12.
[504] See Jacquier, E./Kane, A./Marcus, A. (2003), p. 46.

estimator[505]. However, when including a sampling error, only a combination of both averages will generally provide an unbiased estimator as to be seen from the following discussion[506]. The reason for the bias is again the nonlinear function of the return estimator when compounded over more than one period. Even if the errors are symmetrical, the effects on the mean estimate are asymmetrical and lead to return distributions that are skewed to the right[507]. While it was only possible to derive approximate analytical formulas for the unbiased discrete estimator using the Blume/Cooper approach[508], it possible to develop closed form solutions for normally distributed continuous returns[509]. It is further possible to relax the assumptions of independent returns to a certain degree[510].

Relying on the prerequisites discussed in Section 4.3.1.1, the pricing equations under the continuous return format shall be defined as follows for compounding[511]

F 4-22 $E_t\left[\tilde{V}_{t+k}\right] = V_t\left(1+E_t\left[\tilde{R}\right]\right)^k = V_t\left(1+\mu_R\right)^k = V_t\exp\left[\left(\mu_r + \frac{1}{2}\operatorname{var}\left[\tilde{r}\right]\right)k\right]$

and discounting[512]:

F 4-23 $V_t = \frac{E_t\left[\tilde{V}_{t+k}\right]}{\left(1+E_t\left[\tilde{R}\right]\right)^k} = \frac{E_t\left[\tilde{V}_{t+k}\right]}{\left(1+\mu_R\right)^k} = E_t\left[\tilde{V}_{t+k}\right]\exp\left[\left(\mu_r + \frac{1}{2}\operatorname{var}\left[\tilde{r}\right]\right)(-k)\right]$

One can now define the maximum likelihood estimator (MLE)[513] of the true mean as[514]:

F 4-24 $\tilde{A}_r = \frac{1}{T}\sum_{t=1}^{T}\ln\left(1+\tilde{R}_t\right) = \mu_r + \frac{\operatorname{std}\left[\tilde{r}\right]}{T}\sum_{t=1}^{T}\tilde{\varepsilon}_t$

---

505 See Jacquier, E./Kane, A./Marcus, A. (2003), p. 47.
506 See Jacquier, E./Kane, A./Marcus, A. (2003), p. 40.
507 See Jacquier, E./Kane, A./Marcus, A. (2003), p. 47.
508 See Jacquier, E./Kane, A./Marcus, A. (2005), p. 40.
509 Jacquier, E./Kane, A./Marcus, A. (2005), p. 41 and Reese, R. (2007), p. 47.
510 See Cooper, I. (1996), p. 161 and Reese, R. (2007), p. 47.
511 See Jacquier, E./Kane, A./Marcus, A. (2005), pp. 40-41 and Reese, R. (2007), p. 47.
512 See Reese, R. (2007), p. 47 and Cooper, I. (1996), p. 161 for the continuous discount factor.
513 See Gujarati, D./Porter, D. (2009), p. 825 and Greene, W. (2008), p. 72.
514 See Jacquier, E./Kane, A./Marcus, A. (2005), p. 41 and Reese, R. (2007), p. 48.

Assuming that the standard error of the mean estimate is $\mathrm{std}[\tilde{r}]/\sqrt{T}$ and $\omega \sim N(0,1)$, the above expression can be rewritten as [515]:

F 4-25 $\tilde{A}_r = \mu_r + \omega \frac{\mathrm{std}[\tilde{r}]}{\sqrt{T}}$

Inserting $\tilde{A}_r$ into F 4-22 leads to the multi-period return estimator based on the arithmetic mean $\hat{S}_A = \exp\left[\left(\tilde{A}_r + \mathrm{var}[\tilde{r}]/2\right)k\right]$ [516] which can be rewritten as follows using F 4-25[517]:

F 4-26

$$\hat{S}_A = \exp\left[\left(\tilde{A}_r + \frac{\mathrm{var}[\tilde{r}]}{2}\right)k\right] = \exp\left[\left(\mu_r + \omega\frac{\mathrm{std}[\tilde{r}]}{\sqrt{T}} + \frac{\mathrm{var}[\tilde{r}]}{2}\right)k\right]$$
$$= \exp\left[\left(\mu_r + \frac{\mathrm{var}[\tilde{r}]}{2}\right)k\right]\exp\left[\left(\omega\frac{\mathrm{std}[\tilde{r}]}{\sqrt{T}}\right)k\right]$$

Taking expectations on both sides of the equation, one can analytically show that the arithmetic multi-period estimator is always upward biased[518]:

F 4-27 $E\left[\hat{S}_A\right] = (1+\mu_R)^k E\left\{\exp\left[\left(\omega\frac{\mathrm{std}[\tilde{r}]}{\sqrt{T}}\right)k\right]\right\} = (1+\mu_R)^k \exp\left(\frac{\mathrm{var}[\tilde{r}]}{2}\frac{k^2}{T}\right)$

On the basis of F 4-27, it is now possible to derive an unbiased estimator $\hat{S}_U$ of the arithmetic cumulative return by deducting the bias term[519]:

F 4-28 $\hat{S}_U = \hat{S}_A \exp\left(-\frac{\mathrm{var}[\tilde{r}]}{2}\frac{k^2}{T}\right)$

Similarly, the bias of using the geometric mean as basis for the multi-period return estimator can be developed. Therefore, recall from F 2-12 that the arithmetic mean of

---

515 See Jacquier, E./Kane, A./Marcus, A. (2003), p. 47 and Jacquier, E./Kane, A./Marcus, A. (2005), p. 41.

516 See Jacquier, E./Kane, A./Marcus, A. (2005), p. 42 and Reese, R. (2007), p. 48.

517 See Jacquier, E./Kane, A./Marcus, A. (2005), p. 41 and Reese, R. (2007), p. 48.

518 See Jacquier, E./Kane, A./Marcus, A. (2003), pp. 48-49, Jacquier, E./Kane, A./Marcus, A. (2005), p. 42, and Reese, R. (2007), p. 48. See also Cooper, I. (1996), p. 162.

519 See Jacquier, E./Kane, A./Marcus, A. (2003), p. 49, Jacquier, E./Kane, A./Marcus, A. (2005), p. 43, and Reese, R. (2007), p. 49. See also Cooper, I. (1996), p. 162.

the continuous returns is equal to the geometric mean of the discrete returns. From here, the following expression can be established[520]:

F 4-29
$$\begin{aligned}\hat{S}_G &= \exp\left[\left(\tilde{A}_r\right)k\right] \\ &= \exp\left[\left(\mu_r + \omega\frac{\text{std}[\tilde{r}]}{\sqrt{T}}\right)k\right] \\ &= \exp\left[\left(\mu_r + \frac{\text{var}[\tilde{r}]}{2}\right)k\right]\exp\left[\left(\omega\frac{\text{std}[\tilde{r}]}{\sqrt{T}} - \frac{\text{var}[\tilde{r}]}{2}\right)k\right]\end{aligned}$$

Taking expectations allows again the separation of the bias included in the estimator $\hat{S}_G$. It becomes obvious that compounding over multi-periods leads only to an unbiased result if the holding period equals the number of observations in the sample[521]:

F 4-30
$$\begin{aligned}E\left[\hat{S}_G\right] &= \left(1+\mu_R\right)^k E\left\{\exp\left[\left(\omega\frac{\text{std}[\tilde{r}]}{\sqrt{T}} - \frac{\text{var}[\tilde{r}]}{2}\right)k\right]\right\} \\ &= \left(1+\mu_R\right)^k \exp\left[\frac{\text{var}[\tilde{r}]}{2}\left(\frac{k}{T}-1\right)k\right]\begin{cases} < \left(1+\mu_R\right)^k & \text{for } k<T \\ = \left(1+\mu_R\right)^k & \text{for } k=T \\ > \left(1+\mu_R\right)^k & \text{for } k>T \end{cases}\end{aligned}$$

Also for this case, an unbiased estimator $\hat{S}_U$ for the cumulative returns can be derived using the geometric mean[522]:

F 4-31 $$\hat{S}_U = \hat{S}_G \exp\left[-\frac{\text{var}[\tilde{r}]}{2}\left(\frac{k}{T}-1\right)k\right]$$

Ultimately, the unbiased cumulative return estimator can also be expressed as a linear combination of the arithmetic average and geometric average mean[523]:

---

520 See Jacquier, E./Kane, A./Marcus, A. (2005), p. 42 and Reese, R. (2007), p. 49.

521 See Jacquier, E./Kane, A./Marcus, A. (2005), p. 43 and Reese, R. (2007), p. 49. Note that there is no reason to limit the number of observations in the sample to the compounding period in order to derive an unbiased estimator. Including the maximum number of sample observations is vital to increase the precision of the estimate.

522 See Cooper, I. (1996), p. 162. See also Reese, R. (2007), p. 49.

523 See Jacquier, E./Kane, A./Marcus, A. (2003), p. 49, Jacquier, E./Kane, A./Marcus, A. (2005), p. 43, and Reese, R. (2007), p. 50. When deriving the MSE (mean squared error; see, e.g., Greene, W. (2008), pp. 1028-1030) which also minimizes the variance of the estimator, the weighting factor changes to $c = \left(1 - 3H/T\right)$; see Jacquier, E./Kane, A./Marcus, A. (2005), p. 44 and Reese, R. (2007), pp. 50-51.

F 4-32
$$\begin{aligned} JKM &= \exp\left\{\left[c\left(\tilde{A}_r + \frac{var[\tilde{r}]}{2}\right) + (1-c)\tilde{A}_r\right]k\right\} \\ &= \exp\left[\left(\tilde{A}_r + \frac{var[\tilde{r}]}{2}\right)k\right]^c \exp\left[\left(\tilde{A}_r\right)k\right]^{(1-c)} \\ &= \left(\hat{S}_A\right)^c \left(\hat{S}_G\right)^{1-c} \\ \text{with } c &= \left(1 - \frac{k}{T}\right) \end{aligned}$$

The unbiased compounded return estimator is therefore always below the arithmetic mean which is only negligible if the compounding period is very short. For longer investment horizons the weight on the geometric mean increases. If $k > T$, the weight on the arithmetic (geometric) mean is negative (above one) resulting in an unbiased return estimator below both of them[524]. Note that this unbiased estimator resembles to the estimator for normally distributed discrete returns, however, provides a closed and not approximated solution[525].
The above discussion so far provides unbiased estimators for compounding cases. In order to apply the unbiased estimators in F 4-28, F 4-31, and F 4-32 for discounting purposes, k needs to be simply replaced by $-k$. This also implies a change in the weighting factor $c = (1 + k/T)$ [526].

In summary, the maximum likelihood estimator—i.e., the sample arithmetic mean—is biased when the holding period k is large compared to the number of sample observations T. When log-returns are assumed to be normally distributed, a closed form solution can be derived for the unbiased estimator[527]. It can be shown that also for long horizons the unbiased estimators for lognormal returns take plausible values compared to the non-meaningful values from the Taylor approximation for normal returns. Again a return simulation is provided in Appendix 4 to demonstrate the direction of the bias and the long horizon precision of the estimators.
In order to allow a certain degree of serial correlation among returns, Cooper (1996) proposes an amended version of an unbiased estimator for lognormal discrete

---

524 See Jacquier, E./Kane, A./Marcus, A. (2003), p. 49.
525 See Reese, R. (2007), p. 50.
526 Similar to Cooper, I. (1996), pp. 161-162. See also Reese, R. (2007), p. 50.
527 See Jacquier, E./Kane, A./Marcus, A. (2005), p. 40.

returns[528]. It is assumed that only multi-period returns for certain intervals are serially uncorrelated[529] allowing for autocorrelation between period-by-period returns. Cooper calls this setting 'transient disequilibrium' which provides the basis for changes in the return distribution variance over the horizon. The expression for the unbiased estimator with independent n-period returns is then as follows[530]:

F 4-33 $$\hat{S}_U = \hat{S}_G \exp\left[-\frac{1}{2}\frac{\operatorname{var}[\tilde{r}_n]}{n}\left(\frac{k}{T}-1\right)k\right]$$

Rearranging to introduce the variance ratio[531] as indicator of stochastic dependence yields:

F 4-34 $$\hat{S}_U = \hat{S}_G \exp\left[-\frac{v\operatorname{var}[\tilde{r}]}{2}\left(\frac{k}{T}-1\right)k\right] \text{ with } v = \frac{\operatorname{var}[\tilde{r}_n]}{n\operatorname{var}[\tilde{r}]}$$

For a variance ratio of one implying stochastic independence, the results are identical to the previous presentation for independent returns. It becomes obvious that positive (negative) autocorrelation implied by variance ratios above (below) one decrease (increase) the correction term compared to F 4-31. Consistent with the case of a certain return path with perfect negative autocorrelation, the geometric mean is the unbiased estimator for a variance ratio of zero.

4.3.2 Measurement period

Apart from the averaging methodology, the results in Section 4.1 show that the estimate of the expected MRP depends on to the chosen measurement period. While there are some arguments in favor for shortened or selected periods, the assumption of independent MRPs consequently requires to include all observations—also including extraordinary values[532]. A further argument for the longest possible measurement period relates to the accuracy of the average return estimator. The accuracy of $\tilde{A}$ is limited due to the substantial impact of its standard error which is equal to its standard deviation divided by the square root of the number of

---

[528] See Cooper, I. (1996), pp. 164-165. See also Reese, R. (2007), pp. 53-54.

[529] Note that this does not imply that returns are generally independent each period. It rather means that returns for certain intervals (i.e., 5-year returns) are stochastically independent.

[530] See Cooper, I. (1996), p. 164. See also Reese, R. (2007), p. 53.

[531] See also fn. 73.

[532] Any limitation of the spectrum of MRP observations violates the assumption of independent MRPs. See also Morningstar Inc. (2007c), pp. 82-83 and Kruschwitz, L./Löffler, A. (2008), p. 807.

observations $se\left[\tilde{A}\right]=std\left[\tilde{R}\right]/\sqrt{T}$ [533]. Note that the precision of the mean estimate cannot be increased by using shorter measurement intervals such as daily or monthly returns[534]. Table 15 provides an example[535] on the precision of the arithmetic mean estimate of the expected MRP using the historical data on the German MRP from Dimson/Marsh/Staunton[536].

Table 15 Accuracy of arithmetic mean MRP estimates at various standard error levels

Assumptions	
$\hat{A}_{R^P}$	8.35%
$std\left[\hat{R}^P\right]$	27.41%
T	106

Standard error sensitivity

		Standard deviation of MRP realizations				
		15.00%	20.00%	27.41%	30.00%	35.00%
Number of observations (T)	25	3.00%	4.00%	5.48%	6.00%	7.00%
	50	2.12%	2.83%	3.88%	4.24%	4.95%
	75	1.73%	2.31%	3.17%	3.46%	4.04%
	106	1.46%	1.94%	2.66%	2.91%	3.40%
	150	1.22%	1.63%	2.24%	2.45%	2.86%
	200	1.06%	1.41%	1.94%	2.12%	2.47%
	250	0.95%	1.26%	1.73%	1.90%	2.21%

Confidence intervals of standard error and arith. mean (st. dev.=27.41%; T=50)

Confidence level		Standard error range		Arith. mean range	
68.3%	$\pm1\sigma$	-3.88%	3.88%	4.47%	12.23%
95.4%	$\pm2\sigma$	-7.75%	7.75%	0.60%	16.10%
99.7%	$\pm3\sigma$	-11.63%	11.63%	-3.28%	19.98%

Confidence intervals of standard error and arith. mean (st. dev.=27.41%; T=250)

Confidence level		Standard error range		Arith. mean range	
68.3%	$\pm1\sigma$	-1.73%	1.73%	6.62%	10.08%
95.4%	$\pm2\sigma$	-3.47%	3.47%	4.88%	11.82%
99.7%	$\pm3\sigma$	-5.20%	5.20%	3.15%	13.55%

533 See Wooldridge, J. (2008), pp. 752-753. See also Blume (1974), p. 635.

534 See Spremann, K. (2004), p. 162, Jacquier, E./Kane, A./Marcus, A. (2005), p. 41, and Richter, F. (2005), p. 128, fn. 98.

535 See Cornell, B. (1999), p. 44, Welch, I. (2000), p. 505, Dimson, E./Marsh, P./Staunton, M. (2002), pp. 182-183, Drobetz, W. (2003a), p. 11, Richter, F. (2005), p. 128, Richter, F. (2006a), p. 11, and Reese, R. (2007), p. 42 for similar examples.

536 See Dimson, E./Marsh, P./Staunton, M. (2006), p. 18 (historical MRP relative to bonds).

Under the assumption of a normally distributed estimator, the intervals for the arithmetic mean are presented at various confidence levels. It becomes obvious that in order to be, e.g., 99.7% certain that the true arithmetic mean falls within certain boundaries, such an interval would range from -3.28% to 19.98%. The width of this range already indicates the imprecision underlying the arithmetic mean estimates from historical returns. Therefore, it appears plausible to use to longest possible time-period when relying on historical returns to infer the expected MRP in order to decrease the impact of the standard error[537]. Still, even if up to 250 years of historical returns were available, the confidence interval for 99.7% certainty would still range from 3.15% to 13.55% based on German data. Such findings lead Cornell to the frustrated conclusion that "historical averages of the risk premium (...) are at best rough estimates of the appropriate risk premium to use going forward. Even if it is assumed that the future is like the past, the estimates are so imprecise that it is not clear what the risk premium has truly been in the past"[538]. Still, it appears advisable to use the longest available series of historical MRPs when expected MRP estimates are calculated based on unconditional historical averages.

4.3.3 Survivorship bias

Another issue when inferring the expected MRP from historical data is related to the so-called survivorship bias. In contrast to France, Germany, or Japan, certain global equity markets—in particular the Canadian, UK, and US market—have witnessed a strong continuous performance uninterrupted by complete market breakdowns as a consequence of wars, political turmoil, hyperinflation, or similar events[539]. Despite providing the most complete data set on returns, the US market may for this reason not be a good reference point as to what should be expected in the future. Furthermore, survival bias may also impact the results on the potential mean reversion property of returns.[540]

---

[537] See Dimson, E./Marsh, P./Staunton, M. (2006), pp. 16 and 19.

[538] Cornell, B. (1999), p. 45. See also Richter, F. (2005), p. 129.

[539] Exchanges in both the UK and the US were only shut for a period during World War I. In general, there were around 36 exchanges operating at the beginning of the twentieth century with more than half of them suffering from at least one trading interruption; see Brown, S./Goetzmann, W./Ross, S. (1995), p. 855. See also Dimson, E./Marsh, P./Staunton, M. (2008), pp. 477-478 for a discussion of trading interruptions worldwide.

[540] See Brown, S./Goetzmann, W./Ross, S. (1995), pp. 853-856, Jorion, P./Goetzmann, W. (1999), p. 956, and Cornell, B. (1999), p. 60.

The concept of survival bias was theoretically developed by Brown/Goetzmann/Ross (1995) and empirically tested through the works of, e.g., Jorion/Goetzmann (1999) and Dimson/Marsh/Staunton (2002, 2008). The analysis of Brown/Goetzmann/Ross is based on a survival conditioned return process. Their model defines a critical level for stock prices and assumes the market to collapse if the prices fall below this level. It is then shown, that excluding ex-post all return paths that fall below the critical stock price level leads to an overestimation of the true unconditional return expectation [541]. On this basis, the authors develop the following ex-post [542] relationship between the unconditional return (ex-ante) $\tilde{r}_{uc}$ and the return $\tilde{r}_{c}$ conditional (ex-post) on the probability of not falling below the critical level a [543]:

F 4-35 $$\tilde{r}_{c} = \tilde{r}_{uc} + \frac{2\tilde{r}_{uc}(1-a)}{a}$$

This relationship shows that the conditional return is primarily driven by the survival probability. At 100% certainty of not falling below the critical market collapse level, the conditional return equals the unconditional return since there is no uncertainty about a potential market failure. As the probability of market collapse increases, the survival bias leads to a higher conditional return resulting in an upward biased historical MRP. This implies high conditional returns for emerging markets with a substantial probability of failure. For the US, the authors parameterize their model and derive a theoretical difference between the unconditional and conditional MRP of approximately 4.0% at a risk-free rate of 4.0%, and unconditional MRP of also 4.0%, and a market survival probability of 80%.[544]

The concept of survival bias also implies that the volatility of returns conditional on market survival is lower as in general. Thus, standard volatility measures such as standard deviation for returns and standard errors of means may be understated in case of survival bias. For a similar reason, markets having survived show evidence of mean reversion. Permanent recovery from downturns without collapsing leads to higher mean reversion in survived markets[545]. "If the equity market survives, then we find that average return in the beginning is higher than average return near the end of

---

[541] See Drobetz, W. (2003a), p. 14.
[542] See Jorion, P./Goetzmann, W. (1999), p. 954.
[543] See Brown, S./Goetzmann, W./Ross, S. (1995), pp. 856-861 for a detailed derivation of the expression.
[544] See Brown, S./Goetzmann, W./Ross, S. (1995), pp. 861-862 and Cornell, B. (1999), pp. 61-62.
[545] See Cornell, B. (1999), p. 62.

the time period. For this reason, statistical measures of long-term dependence are typically biased towards the rejection of a random walk"[546].

The empirical analysis by Jorion/Goetzmann investigates real returns of 39 countries for data series going back until 1921 when available[547]. The authors do not measure the MRP in the herein defined form as the difference between the total return on a portfolio of stocks and the risk-free rate but use the real capital appreciation (i.e., nominal capital return less inflation excluding the income return component) as a proxy. Despite this limitation required by missing dividend data in many analyzed countries, the authors claim that the results allow for inferences on a potential survival bias[548]. Dimson/Marsh/Staunton object that view by arguing that the contribution of dividends to total returns has a similar magnitude as the MRP itself[549]. Jorion/Goetzmann report that the geometric average of the US real capital return is the highest in the sample at 4.32% with the average of all 39 countries at approximately 0.75%. This large differential is considered as unusual and potentially attributed to survival bias—the magnitude appears in line with the theoretical findings of Brown/Goetzmann/Ross. Given the observed levels of volatility, the differential is not driven by a higher risk level in the US. The results also show that the other surviving countries Canada and the UK show higher real returns as the non-surviving markets in France, Germany, and Japan.[550]

In addition to their cross-sectional analysis of 39 countries, Jorion/Goetzmann also construct two GDP weighted global indices based on their data set, one including only markets since their last interruption and the other including all available periods also prior to interruptions. Intuitively, one would assume that the difference between the average return of both indices is at least partially related to survivorship bias. In fact, the authors find that arithmetic and geometric real return averages of the global index including only survived markets are substantially above the index returns of all markets. This differential increases when the most highly weighted country—the US—is excluded from the index.[551]

---

[546] Brown, S./Goetzmann, W./Ross, S. (1995), p. 854.
[547] See also Goetzmann, W./Ibbotson, R. (2008), pp. 523-524.
[548] It is further shown for a more recent time period that the results also hold when the income return is included; see Jorion, P./Goetzmann, W. (1999), pp. 963-966.
[549] See Dimson, E./Marsh, P./Staunton, M. (2008), p. 475.
[550] See Jorion, P./Goetzmann, W. (1999), pp. 959-963.
[551] See Jorion, P./Goetzmann, W. (1999), pp. 971-978.

The more recent investigation of Dimson/Marsh/Staunton (2008) disagrees at least with the magnitude of a potential survivor bias and concludes that the concerns about such a bias are overstated[552]. Their analysis is based on a comprehensive global database of historical returns from 1900 to 2005 for 17 countries worldwide. In contrast to Jorion/Goetzmann, Dimson/Marsh/Staunton collected dividend data and therefore were able to calculate total equity returns. The authors use the geometric calculation method to derive the MRP[553]. Furthermore, the underlying risk-free rates for government bills and bonds are based on total returns. Their historical MRP results are derived by averaging over the entire time period from 1900 to 2005 with interruptions for the selected countries being bridged through approximations[554].

Dimson/Marsh/Staunton begin their argumentation on the level of survivorship bias in their data by comparing the arithmetic means of all countries in their sample. However, several countries had an up to 3.5% higher historical average MRP than the US. The authors continue to argue that comparisons of arithmetic means are of limited explanatory power since differences in volatility drive the absolute level of arithmetic means. Still, comparing geometric means leads to similar results despite controlling for volatility. While these findings may appear inconsistent with the Jorion/Goetzmann analysis, the differences can be explained through the applied methodology. The Jorion/Goetzmann findings on survival bias in US returns was derived using geometric mean real returns as reference metric whereas Dimson/Marsh/Staunton use geometric mean real MRPs. Based on real returns, the Dimson/Marsh/Staunton data would lead to the same conclusion on a potential survivorship bias of the US market. Due to the apparent similarity in real returns, the differing factor must be related to the performance of the risk-free reference assets used for calculating the real historical MRPs. Indeed, Dimson/Marsh/Staunton argue that higher average MRPs in certain countries are related to poor historical bill and bond returns.[555]

Dimson/Marsh/Staunton conclude that high returns of successful markets are mitigated by their correlation with above average bill and bond returns[556].

---

[552] See also Goetzmann, W./Ibbotson, R. (2008), pp. 523-524.

[553] See Section 2.1.

[554] Only for Germany the years 1922-1923 are omitted; see Dimson, E./Marsh, P./Staunton, M. (2008), p. 488.

[555] See Dimson, E./Marsh, P./Staunton, M. (2008), pp. 487-489.

[556] See also Mehra, R. (2003), p. 62.

"Consequently, the cross-sectional dispersion of equity premiums is narrower than the cross-sectional dispersion of equity returns. (...) We concluded above, therefore, that provided a very long run approach is taken, inferences from the United States do not appear to have given rise to very large overestimates of the historical world equity premium"[557]. According to the authors, a potential survivorship bias in the world MRP may much more likely be related to the omission of highly valued countries with no or unsatisfactory data coverage having suffered from complete market shut-downs such as Russia or China. However, it is claimed that the 17 countries in the sample cover approximately 90% of the market capitalization of the 33 existing exchanges by 1900 so that even the extreme assumption of a complete market breakdown in the remaining 10% would not change in the world average MRP substantially.[558]

4.4 Conclusions

The discussion of empirical results from estimating the expected MRP based on unconditional averages of ex-post MRPs focused on studies with the longest available measurement periods. The empirical results are non-uniform due to various measurement issues associated with using ex-post MRPs. Primarily, unconditional MRP averages relative to government bonds differ due to different averaging methodologies and measurement periods.

- Long-horizon studies on the German market provide arithmetic (geometric) average MRPs between 4.5% and 8.4% (1.2% and 5.3%).
- Long-horizon studies on the US market provide arithmetic (geometric) average MRPs between 4.5% and 7.1% (3.3% and 5.1%).
- Long-horizon studies on the remaining analyzed countries provide arithmetic (geometric) average MRPs between 4.0% and 10.0% (2.5% and 5.9%).
- The results demonstrate that the arithmetic average is generally larger than the geometric average due to the volatility during the measurement period.
- Analysis on the historical MRPs during 1989 and 2006 show no significant difference in the country mean estimates and significant parametric as well as non-parametric correlation coefficients among countries.

---

557 Dimson, E./Marsh, P./Staunton, M. (2008), pp. 490-492.

558 See Dimson, E./Marsh, P./Staunton, M. (2008), pp. 490-493.

The large discrepancy among various studies can be attributed to several issues in measuring historical return averages:

- The choice of the correct averaging methodology depends on certain assumptions regarding the MRP distribution. The arithmetic mean is the correct unbiased estimator when (log) return/MRP distributions are i.i.d. normal and if there is certainty about the return/MRP distribution parameters. Under parameter uncertainty, an unbiased estimator for compounding is provided by the arithmetic mean, if the horizon is only one period, or by the geometric mean, if the horizon equals the number of observations. In all other multi-period compounding scenarios or generally for discounting neither the arithmetic nor the geometric average are unbiased estimators of the true result. For compounding purposes, the arithmetic mean provides upward biased results while the geometric mean provides downward (upward) biased results for horizons shorter (longer) than the period for which observations are available. For discounting purposes, both means provide upward biased estimators and thereby downward biased discount rates which always have a stronger bias for the geometric mean. Unbiased estimators can be derived through a combination of both averages which have, however, only plausible values at long compounding/discounting horizons for i.i.d. normal log-returns/MRPs.
- The unbiasedness of the arithmetic mean under parameter certainty is based on the assumption of i.i.d. returns/MRPs which is challenged by empirical evidence. With perfect negative autocorrelation, the geometric average is an unbiased estimator.
- For practical purposes, the consideration of estimation errors for the expected MRP appears questionable since similar errors for other components of cost of capital or cash flows are typically not recognized. Furthermore, the application of the CAPM in a multi-period context requires the assumption of a deterministic cost of capital which is inconsistent with estimation errors[559].
- Based on the assumption of i.i.d. return and MRP distributions, the longest possible measurement period should be used in order to minimize the standard error of the mean estimator. Determining the correct measurement period is,

[559] See Reese, R. (2007), pp. 54-55. See also Section 2.3.2 for the discussion of allowable risk of CAPM parameters in a multi-period scenario.

however, also influenced by issues such as data quality, potentially non-recurring events, and permanent changes in the capital markets environment[560]. Still, any reason for adjusting the measurement period, apart from insufficient data quality, appears arbitrary so that using the longest available and unadjusted data series is advisable to comply with statistical rigor.

- Against earlier evidence on the existence of a survivorship bias for the selected markets with an uninterrupted capital markets history, recent empirical results suggests that the MRP is not affected particularly due to the similar impact of substantial market disruptions on the performance of stocks and the risk-free asset.

In addition to the previously mentioned empirical issues of historical return averages, there are also three important conceptual problems. Firstly, historical averages only allow for unconditional expected MRP estimates based on the assumed independence. However, the review in Section 2.2.3.2 showed that there is evidence for dependence of returns/MRPs which would require to conditionally estimate the expected MRP at the valuation date. This is not possible using historical averages[561]. Secondly, a potential dependence of returns/MRPs would imply a time-variable development of the expected MRP. In contrast, unconditional historical averages only provide a constant estimate over time. Thirdly, if the expected MRP is time-variable with potential periods of permanent non-stationarity implying no mean reversion, then the realized return is affected by a capital gain which is not recurring. This issue will be demonstrated in Table 71 of Chapter 6 after introducing the basic equity valuation models required to show the impact of changes in the expected MRP.

---

[560] See Brennan, M. (1997), p. 82 and Stehle, R. (2004), p. 921. E.g., Stehle argues to reduce the historical average MRP by 1.0% to 1.5% due to the better diversification capability of investors in more integrated international capital markets.

[561] See Richter, F. (2006a), pp. 12-13.

5 Expected MRP estimation based on equity valuation models using analysts' consensus forecasts

In contrast to estimating the expected MRP from historical averages, a new field of academic research has developed over recent years which analyzes direct observations of the expected MRP[562]. In this context, the expected MRP is derived as the IRR of a market-wide valuation formula equating the current market valuation and the present value of the infinite stream of future aggregated cash flows minus the risk-free rate. Despite potential bias, researchers rely on ex-ante analysts' consensus forecasts as input parameters for the valuation model. Its proponents argue that this new approach overcomes the backwards orientation of unconditional historical averages and provides a true forward-looking estimate of the expected MRP[563] that can be estimated both unconditional and conditional on the current market environment. Furthermore, such a forward-looking approach is free of many problems underlying the historical data method such as, e.g., potential non-stationarity or survival bias[564], but it has already been shown that restrictive assumptions—most prominently an i.i.d. return distribution—are required to use valuation formulas in a multi-period context[565]. In addition, this methodology provides, similarly to the historical average approach, constant unconditional and conditional expected MRP estimates over time[566] despite evidence for time-variable expected returns/MRPs[567].

In order to operationalize the general valuation formulas discussed in Section 2.3 for the estimation of the expected MRP, typical equity valuation models are used. Such

---

[562] See, e.g., Claus, J./Thomas, J. (2001), Gebhardt, W./Lee, C./Swaminathan, B. (2001), Easton, P. et al. (2002), Gode, D./Mohanram, P. (2003), Easton, P. (2004), Cheng, F./Jorgensen, B./Yoo, Y. (2004), Easton, P./Monahan, S. (2005), Botosan, C./Plumlee, M. (2005), Desrosiers, S./Lemaire, N./L'Her, J.-F. (2007), Pastor, L./Sinha, M./Swaminathan, B. (2008), Huges, J./Liu, J./Liu, J. (2009), and Lee, C./Ng, D./Swaminathan, B. (2009) for anglo-american articles. For German research see, e.g., Daske, H./Wiesenbach, K. (2005), Koch, J. (2005), Daske, H./Gebhardt, G./Klein, S. (2006), Daske, H./Gebhardt, G. (2006), Reese, R. (2005, 2007), Dausend, F./Schmitt, D. (2006a), Wallmeier, M. (2007), Schröder, D. (2007), and Esterer, F./Schröder, D. (2007a,b).

[563] See, e.g., Gode, D./Mohanram, P. (2003), p. 399, Daske, H./Gebhardt, G./Klein, S. (2006), p. 4, and Reese, R. (2007), p. 1.

[564] See Cornell, B. (1999), p. 101.

[565] See Section 2.3.

[566] See Brennan, M. (2003), p. 188, Richter, F. (2005), p. 122 and Richter, F. (2006a), p. 18.

[567] See Section 2.2.3.2.

equity valuation methods can be divided into direct and indirect approaches[568]. Indirect equity valuation—also referred to as the entity-method—firstly determines the value of the entire firm including equity and debt by discounting the infinite stream of expected free cash flows to equity and debt holders. The equity value is then derived by deducting the market value of debt and other interest-bearing items from the entity value. In contrast, direct equity valuation models only value the infinite stream of cash flows to shareholders (i.e., dividends) resulting in a direct estimate of the equity value. Direct equity valuation techniques can be divided into three basic methods: the dividend discount approach, the residual income approach, and the earnings capitalization approach[569]. Throughout this dissertation, the focus is exclusively on direct equity valuation approaches since available forecasts by analysts are only sufficient for direct equity valuations[570]. This is in-line with previous empirical investigations of the expected MRP using equity valuation methods.

The foundation of all direct equity valuation techniques is the dividend discount model which postulates that based on the no-arbitrage assumption the price of an asset (stock) is equal to the infinite stream of future cash flows (dividends) to the claim holder (shareholder). All other mentioned approaches are isomorphic derivatives of the dividend discount method and yield theoretically equivalent results. The equivalence in practical implementations for empirical purposes is a highly debated issue in the American accounting literature that culminated in a debate between Penman and Lundholm/O'Keefe regarding the usefulness of empirical research on the accuracy of equity valuation models and the claimed superiority of the residual income model[571]. Disregarding the different and apparently irreconcilable schools of thought, one can conclude that there is also a practical equivalence of the aforementioned equity valuation models. Despite this conclusion, several previously published studies on IRR-based expected MRPs are "randomly" using the entire range of equity valuation techniques without providing a general framework of when

---

[568] See Brealey, R./Myers, S./Allan, F. (2008), p. 538, Damodaran, A. (2002), pp. 382-385, Rapp, M. (2006), pp. 772-773, Drukarczyk, J./Schüler, A. (2009), pp. 125-131, Koller, T./Goedhart, M./Wessels, D. (2005), pp. 101-128, and Ross, S./Westerfield, R./Jaffe, J. (2008), pp. 488-495.

[569] See Penman/Sougiannis (1998), p. 346, Kothari, S. (2001), p. 173, Ohlson, J./Goa, Z. (2006), pp. 2-3, and Easton, P. (2009), pp. 260-270.

[570] For the entire analysis period, IBES does not provide estimates for capital expenditures and changes in net working capital which are required for the entity method.

[571] See Lundholm, R./O'Keefe, T. (2001a), Penman, S. (2001), and Lundholm, R./O'Keefe, T. (2001b).

there is equivalence among the models and when the resulting estimates of the expected MRP differ.

In order to overcome these deficiencies, this chapter is structured as follows. Firstly, the three direct equity valuation methods are sequentially derived—i.e., the dividend discount approach, the residual income approach, and the earnings capitalization approach. Furthermore, other model related aspects such as underlying assumptions, terminal value considerations, and variations in previous empirical studies are discussed. In the following, the debate on the practical equivalence of equity valuation models is summarized and the specific conditions under which all models yield equivalent results in empirical studies are identified. Based on these findings, the equity valuation models which will be applied in this dissertation are specified. Having concluded on the model-related aspects, the focus is shifted to the sample selection and data used for the ex-ante expected MRP estimation. This section will be followed by critical methodological considerations regarding the empirical usage of models and data. In the next section, the results for each country are presented individually. This includes a comparison with the results of previous studies on the forward-looking MRP. Despite the data structure of this study does not allow for cross-sectional analyses, the findings of previous research on risk factor correlation and forecast accuracy of the IRR-based method are reviewed. Thereafter, the topic of price level dependence of expected returns is addressed and exemplified for data during the recent financial crisis. Finally, the usage of expected MRPs estimates unconditional or conditional on the current market environment is evaluated for valuation purposes.

5.1 Dividend discount and dividend growth model (DIV)

The foundation of contemporary equity valuation models is the dividend discount model (DIV)[572]. In this section, the basic infinite model and its assumptions are discussed followed by a thorough evaluation of terminal value alternatives and a review of model versions in empirical research.

---

[572] See Ohlson, J. (1995), p. 663.

5.1.1 Basic model and assumptions

The concept of dividend discount valuation was first introduced by Williams (1938)[573]. In contemporary versions of the dividend discount model, the value of a stock V_s is derived as the present value of the infinite stream of expected dividends $E_s\left[\tilde{D}_t\right]$ [574] conditional on the information at s and discounted by the cost of equity r^e which is equal to the expected return if the conditional expected returns are deterministic and the unconditional expected returns are constant over time[575]:

F 5-1 $$V_s = \sum_{t=s+1}^{\infty} \frac{E_s\left[\tilde{D}_t\right]}{\left(1+r^e\right)^{t-s}}$$

Besides the prerequisites discussed in Section 2.3, assuming a constant cost of equity over time also requires a uniform leverage structure of the valuation object[576]. This basic form of the dividend discount model can be simplified for the special case of constant dividend growth until infinity[577]:

F 5-2 $$V_s = \frac{E_s\left[\tilde{D}_{s+1}\right]}{r^e - g_D} \Rightarrow r^e = \frac{E_s\left[\tilde{D}_{s+1}\right]}{V_s} + g_D$$

With constant perpetual dividend growth, F 5-2 can be derived by using an infinite geometric series and assuming $g_D < r^e$ [578]. Therefore, F 5-2 is only defined for $r^e > g_D$ [579] and as g_D approaches r^e the price converges to infinity[580]. A perpetual

---

573 See Williams, J. (1938), pp. 87-96.

574 Dividends are always assumed to be cash and net of cash capital contributions. The definition leads to the same result as the cash flow to equity approach; see Koller, T./Goedhart, M./Wessels, D. (2005), pp. 126-127. See also Ohlson, J. (1995), p. 666 and Koch, J. (2005), pp. 54-55.

575 See Campbell, J./Lo, A./MacKinlay, C. (1997), p. 255. See also, e.g., Shiller, R. (1984), p. 475, Ohlson, J. (1995), p. 666, Penman, S. (1997), p. 304, Frankel, R./Lee, C. (1998), p. 286, Brennan, M. (2003), p. 185, Ohlson, J. (2005), p. 326, Daske, H./Wiesenbach, K. (2005), p. 408, or Schröder, D. (2007), p. 586.

576 See, e.g., Koller, T./Goedhart, M./Wessels, D. (2005), p. 128, Brealey, R./Myers, S./Allan, F. (2008), p. 538, and Drukarczyk, J./Schüler, A. (2009), pp. 195-198.

577 See Campbell, J./Lo, A./MacKinlay, C. (1997), p. 256. See also the fundamental work excluding conditional expectations of Gordon, M./Shapiro, E. (1956), pp. 105-106 and Gordon, M. (1962) as well as other references such as Blanchard, O. (1993), pp. 80-81 and Hachmeister, D. (2000), pp. 156-157.

578 See Copeland, T./Weston, F./Shastri, K. (2005), pp. 887-888 for a detailed derivation.

579 Note that the price for $r^e < g_D$ is mathematically not negative as the valuation formula is not defined in this range; see Lobe, S. (2006), p. 12, fn. 45.

580 See, e.g., Brealey, R./Myers, S./Allan, F. (2008), p. 92.

dividend growth rate larger than the cost of equity is economically unreasonable to assume in the long-term[581]. Due to the work of Gordon/Shapiro (1956) and Gordon (1962), this one-stage constant growth form is often referred to as dividend growth model or Gordon growth model[582].

5.1.2 Terminal value considerations

In empirical research, one often finds a combination of the dividend discount and dividend growth model [583]. Such models—often referred to as multi-stage models—include a finite period of explicit dividend forecasts, optionally an interim convergence or fade period, and a terminal value period capturing the value of dividends beyond the finite horizon through a terminal perpetuity or multiple concept. The terminal perpetuity and terminal multiple approach are not fundamentally incompatible concepts but different approaches to measure the terminal value either through taking explicit assumptions on post horizon return and perpetual dividend growth (terminal perpetuity) or through using a parameter that consolidates the expectations on post horizon return and growth (terminal multiple).

In case of a terminal perpetuity approach, the basic two-stage formula can be expressed as follows[584]:

F 5-3 $$V_s = \sum_{t=s+1}^{T} \frac{E_s\left[\tilde{D}_t\right]}{\left(1+r^e\right)^{t-s}} + \frac{E_s\left[\tilde{D}_T\right]\left(1+g_D\right)}{\left(r^e-g_D\right)\left(1+r^e\right)^{T-s}}$$

Researchers have also developed more complex multi-stage models including periods of converging or non-linear dividend growth[585]. However, for the purposes of this study, the standard two-stage approach with an explicit forecast period and constant perpetual dividend growth is sufficient.

For empirical implementations, the precise estimate of the perpetual growth rate of dividends is of key importance but its determination is difficult since the perpetual growth rate is not directly observable in the market. Gordon/Shapiro substantiate the

---

[581] See Lobe, S. (2006), p. 12 and Brealey, R./Myers, S./Allan, F. (2008), p. 92.

[582] See Gordon, M./Shapiro, E. (1956), pp. 105-106 and Gordon, M. (1962).

[583] See the summary in Table 16.

[584] See, e.g., Damodaran, A. (2002), p. 329, Copeland, T./Weston, F./Shastri, K. (2005), p. 21, and Brealey, R./Myers, S./Allan, F. (2008), pp. 96-97.

[585] See Lobe, S. (2006), pp. 65-70 for a detailed discussion of non-linear growth models which are related to classical life-cycle models. See also Damodaran, A. (2002), pp. 337-342.

determination of dividend growth by deriving a formula for the theoretical dividend growth implied by the payout-ratio θ and return on book equity r^b for reinvestments[586] assuming no inflation[587]. Now, if the return on book equity for old and new investments is equal and constant, dividend growth can be expressed as $g_D = (1-\theta) r^b$ [588] and F 5-2 can be rewritten as[589]:

F 5-4 $$V_s = \frac{E_s\left[\tilde{E}_{s+1}\right]\theta}{r^e - (1-\theta) r^b} \text{ with } r^b = \text{const. and } r^e > (1-\theta) r^b$$

When expected dividends are expressed as expected earnings $E_s\left[\tilde{E}_{s+1}\right]$ times a constant payout-ratio it becomes obvious that growth in value can only be achieved if the return on book equity is above the cost of equity. Under the further assumption that the return on book equity equals the cost of equity, F 5-4 reduces to[590]:

F 5-5 $$V_s = \frac{E_s\left[\tilde{E}_{s+1}\right]}{r^e} \text{ with } r^e = r^b$$

The Gordon/Shapiro relationship formalizes the impact of the return on book equity and payout ratio on the dividend growth rate. It also limits the spectrum of plausible input assumptions. E.g., at a payout ratio of one the according earnings/dividends growth must be zero disregarding the return on book equity. The same result occurs when the return on book equity is zero.

Certain authors suggest that the Gordon/Shapiro expression for dividend growth excludes the impact of inflation[591]. It is argued that real dividend growth from retained

---

586 See Gordon, M./Shapiro, E. (1956), pp. 106-108.

587 See Wiese, J. (2007c), p. 4.

588 See Appendix 5 for the formal relationship between book value, earnings, and dividend growth.

589 See Spremann, K. (2002), pp. 226-228, Copeland, T./Weston, F./Shastri, K. (2005), pp. 502-503, Laitenberger, J./Tschöpel, A. (2003), p. 1361, Wiese, J. (2007a), p. 372, Wiese, J. (2007c), pp. 3-4, and Beyer, S. (2008) for the derivation of this expression (the latter three including personal taxes). See also Wagner, W. et al. (2006), pp. 1011 and 1025-1026. An example for the empirical application of this concept can be found in Brigham, E./Shome, D./Vinson, S. (1985), p. 37. Note that F 5-4 also demonstrates that the value of the asset is independent from the dividend policy; see Miller, M./Modigliance, F. (1961). It shows that the value maximization for an all-equity financed firm only depends on the differential between the expected return on book equity and the cost of equity. E.g., if both are equal, F 5-5 shows that the payout ratio is irrelevant; see Copeland, T./Weston, F./Shastri, K. (2005), p. 649 and Wiese, J. (2007c), p. 4.

590 Note that $r^e = r^b$ not necessarily implies a growth rate of zero but rather value neutral growth within $0 \le g < r^e$; see also Lee, C./Ng, D./Swaminathan, B. (2009), p. 313 and Wiese, J. (2007c), p. 3.

591 See Wiese, J. (2007c), p. 1 and Hachmeister, D./Wiese, J. (2009), p. 63.

earnings (organic growth) and inflation-based growth may co-exist. Bradley/Jarrell (2008) provide an extension of the Gordon/Shapiro including the inflation rate π[592]:

F 5-6 $g_D = (1-\theta) r^b + \theta\pi$

F 5-4 can then be rewritten as follows:

F 5-7 $V_s = \dfrac{E_s\left[\tilde{E}_{s+1}\right]\theta}{r^e - (1-\theta) r^b + \theta\pi}$

Assuming again that the return on book equity equals the cost of equity, F 5-7 reduces to:

F 5-8 $V_s = \dfrac{E_s\left[\tilde{E}_{s+1}\right]}{r^e - \pi}$ with $r^e = r^b$

These relationships imply that applications of the standard Gordon/Shapiro formula F 5-4 underestimate valuation results. However, they are based on the assumptions that firms can fully pass on inflation effects to their customers so that their own earnings increase by the inflation rate[593]. Furthermore, the general validity of the Bradley/Jarrell relationship and thereby the co-existence of organic and inflation-based growth has been disputed in the German literature[594]. The core issue relates to the recognition of inflation growth on replacement investments in future book values[595]. Given the controversy on the issue and the aim to maintain comparability to previous work, the relationship proposed by Bradley/Jarrell is not further used within this study.

Still, the assumptions required for the Gordon/Shapiro concept to determine the theoretical long-term dividend behavior are not without complications. Forecasting the infinite development of the return on book equity appears to be a similar challenge as forecasting the perpetual growth rate. In particular, the assumption of a

---

[592] See Bradley, M./Jarrell, G. (2008), pp. 67-68 for the derivation of this expression. See also Wiese, J. (2007c), pp. 4-8 and Hachmeister, D./Wiese, J. (2009), p. 63.

[593] See also Wiese, J. (2007c), p. 6 and Hachmeister, D./Wiese, J. (2009), pp. 63-64.

[594] See Hachmeister, D./Wiese, J. (2009), pp. 63-64 for summary of the arguments. For opposing views see Schwetzler, B. (2005), Schwetzler, B. (2007), Friedl, G./Schwetzler, B. (2009a), and Friedl, G./Schwetzler, B. (2009b).

[595] See Friedl, G./Schwetzler, B. (2009b), pp. 15-17 and Hachmeister, D./Wiese, J. (2009), pp. 63-64.

constant return on book equity above the required return on equity until infinity implies faster growth than the economy which is implausible in the long-term[596]. Therefore, most researchers use exogenous proxies for the long-term dividend growth rate. As the later presentation of previous research will show, such proxies include:

- g_D *equal to historical growth*[597]

  Due to its backward orientation, this concept is criticized as historical growth rates are not correlated with future growth rates and firm size effects[598]. In case of little correlation between growth rates over time, the unconditional historical average could be used but then growth rates would be required to be fully independent and stationary over time.

- g_D *equal to long-term earnings growth forecasted by analysts*[599]

  The validity of this assumption appears doubtful since analysts' forecasts may be overly optimistic[600]. In addition, the long-term IBES growth rate refers to one full business cycle with a three to five-year horizon which is not consistent with an infinite horizon[601].

- g_D *equal to ex-post or expected GDP growth rate*[602]

  This approach assumes that in the long-term individual firms growth should converge to the growth rate of the economy[603]. This concept is also often mentioned as the upper limit for the perpetual growth rate since no firm can grow faster than the economy until infinity[604].

---

596 See Damodaran, A. (2002), pp. 305 and 323, Copeland, T./Weston, F./Shastri, K. (2005), p. 503, and Koller, T./Goedhart, M./Wessels, D. (2005), p. 275.
597 See Damodaran, A. (2002), pp. 269-275.
598 See Damodaran, A. (2002), pp. 275-279.
599 See, e.g., Claus, J./Thomas, J. (2001), Harris, R./Marston, F. (1992 and 2001), or Malkiel, B. (1979). See also Damodaran, A. (2002), pp. 279-283.
600 See the summary of Claus, J./Thomas, J. (2001), p. 1634. See also Section 5.6.1.
601 See Thomson Financial (2008), p. 22.
602 See, e.g., Cornell, B. (1999) or Malkiel, B. (1979).
603 See also Copeland, T./Weston, F./Shastri, K. (2005), p. 503 and Koller, T./Goedhart, M./Wessels, D. (2005), p. 275.
604 See fn. 596.

- g_D *equal to the nominal risk-less rate*[605]

  Since the real risk-free rate is supposed to converge to the real growth rate of the economy, the nominal risk-free rate will approach nominal growth rate of the economy which was identified as upper limit for perpetual dividend growth[606].

- g_D *equal to ex-post or expected inflation rate*[607]

  Using this proxy basically assumes no fundamental post-horizon dividend growth from reinvestments but solely from price level increases.

An often neglected issue is that each of these perpetual growth proxies is associated with a specific assumption on the long-term payout ratio. E.g., when the perpetual dividend growth rate is set for a firm which used to have low payout ratios due to large reinvestments at returns above the cost of equity resulting in high dividend growth, one would need to adjust the historical payout ratio[608]. However, this may also imply that the assumed return on book equity of old and new investments of the firm may need to be adjusted. These difficulties may be an explanation of why many empirical studies use exogenous perpetual growth rates without adjusting the last observable payout ratio[609]. This issue appears most critical when a low proxy for the perpetual growth rate is chosen such as inflation which would actually imply zero fundamental growth and a payout ratio of one[610].

Due to the obvious difficulties in determining the appropriate perpetual growth rate of dividends, many financial practitioners prefer to rely on the terminal multiple approach while the popularity among academics is lower[611]. The intention of the following paragraphs is to discuss the usage of terminal multiples concept in practice and to demonstrate that, if correctly applied, the terminal multiple approach is identical to the terminal perpetuity concept since it also requires assumptions on the

---

605 See Damodaran, A. (2002), p. 306.

606 See Damodaran, A. (2002), pp. 275-279.

607 See, e.g., Desrosiers, S./Lemaire, N./L'Her, J.-F. (2007).

608 See Reese, R. (2007), pp. 125-126 for an example of adjusting the numerator to full distribution which is consistent with zero growth from reinvestments and capturing only inflation growth in the denominator.

609 See, e.g., Harris, R./Marston, F. (1992), pp. 64-65 or Claus, J./Thomas, J. (2001), pp. 1638 and 1641.

610 See, e.g., Desrosiers, S./Lemaire, N./L'Her, J.-F. (2007), p. 79 who use inflation-based growth but do not adjust the payout ratio.

611 An evidence may be the complete negligence of the multiple-based approach in the dissertation of Lobe (2006) on terminal value concepts for valuation. See also Koch, J. (2005), p. 36 and Ballwieser, W. (2007), pp. 203-204.

infinite development of dividend growth and payout ratio. Using observable spot multiples as terminal multiples is shown to be inappropriate. Thereby, certain myths on the qualities of the terminal multiple approach can hopefully be resolved.

Multiples are relations of market prices to certain financial reference parameters (flow or stock metrics) consolidating information such as expected return and growth[612]. Depending on the selected reference base, one can differentiate between entity value and equity value related multiples. As already discussed, this study focuses on direct equity valuation methods and therefore excludes entity value orientated multiples. Equity value multiples are characterized by the unique usage of shareholder related parameters with the market price in the numerator and reference metrics such as, e.g., earnings[613] (flow metric) or book value of equity (stock metric) in the denominator. A relation between the market price and dividends is more common in academic studies.[614]

Choosing, e.g., the one-year ahead spot PE ratio (m_s^{E+1}) for illustrative purposes, the multiple can formally be derived by rearranging F 5-3[615]:

$$P_s = \theta E_s \left[\sum_{t=s+1}^{T} \prod_{u=s+1}^{t} \frac{1+g_u^D}{1+r^e} + \prod_{u=s+1}^{T} \frac{1+g_u^D}{1+r^e} \frac{1+g_p^D}{r^e - g_p^D} \right]$$

F 5-9 $$m_s^E = \frac{P_s}{E_s} = \theta \left[\sum_{t=s+1}^{T} \prod_{u=s+1}^{t} \frac{1+g_u^D}{1+r^e} + \prod_{u=s+1}^{T} \frac{1+g_u^D}{1+r^e} \frac{1+g_p^D}{r^e - g_p^D} \right]$$

$$m_s^{E+1} = \frac{P_s}{E_s\left[\tilde{E}_{s+1}\right]} = \frac{\theta}{1+r^e} \left[1 + \sum_{t=s+2}^{T} \prod_{u=s+2}^{t} \frac{1+g_u^D}{1+r^e} + \prod_{u=s+2}^{T} \frac{1+g_u^D}{1+r^e} \frac{1+g_p^D}{r^e - g_p^D} \right]$$

The expression is less complex when assuming that dividend growth is constant over time so that the Gordon growth model can be used[616]:

---

612 For a detailed discussion of prerequisites for the usage of multiples, see Richter, F. (2005), pp. 65-73.

613 As a reference metric, either historical earnings or projected earnings may be used.

614 See Kelleners, A. (2004), pp. 146-147, Richter, F. (2005), pp. 81-83, and Damodaran, A. (2002), pp. 456-457.

615 Extended from Richter, F. (2005), p. 72. The subscript p refers to perpetuity parameters.

616 See Damodaran, A. (2002), p. 471 and Koch, J. (2005), p. 74. See also Fama, E./French, F. (1988b), p. 5 presenting a similar approach for the inverted price-dividend multiple (dividend yield).

$$P_s = \frac{E_s\left[\tilde{D}_{s+1}\right]}{r^e - g_D} = \frac{E_s\left[\tilde{E}_{s+1}\right]\theta}{r^e - g_D} = \frac{E_s\left(1+g_D\right)\theta}{r^e - g_D}$$

F 5-10 $$m_s^E = \frac{P_s}{E_s} = \frac{\left(1+g_D\right)\theta}{r^e - g_D} = \frac{\left(1+\left(1-\theta\right)r^b\right)\theta}{r^e - \left(1-\theta\right)r^b}$$

$$m_s^{E+1} = \frac{P_s}{E_s\left[\tilde{E}_{s+1}\right]} = \frac{\theta}{r^e - g_D} = \frac{\theta}{r^e - \left(1-\theta\right)r^b}$$

This illustrates that a multiple is primarily a consolidation of fundamental factors such as cost of equity and dividend growth and—in case of the PE ratio—additionally the payout ratio.

Formally, the multi-stage version of the DIV model using the terminal multiple approach can be stated as follows:

$$V_s = \sum_{t=s+1}^{T} \frac{E_s\left[\tilde{D}_t\right]}{\left(1+r^e\right)^{t-s}} + \frac{E_s\left[\tilde{V}_T\right]}{\left(1+r^e\right)^{T-s}}$$

F 5-11 with $E_s\left[\tilde{V}_T\right] = m_T^{E+1} E_s\left[\tilde{E}_{T+1}\right]$

$$V_s = \sum_{t=s+1}^{T} \frac{E_s\left[\tilde{D}_t\right]}{\left(1+r^e\right)^{t-s}} + \frac{E_s\left[\tilde{V}_T\right]}{\left(1+r^e\right)^{T-s}} = \sum_{t=s+1}^{T} \frac{E_s\left[\tilde{D}_t\right]}{\left(1+r^e\right)^{t-s}} + \frac{E_s\left[\tilde{E}_{T+1}\right]m_T^{E+1}}{\left(1+r^e\right)^{T-s}}$$

Whereas the terminal perpetuity approach requires an explicit assumption on the unobservable perpetual dividend growth, it is argued that the key advantage of the multiple approach is related to the observability of the multiple at the valuation date if the underlying asset is publicly traded. However, in order to apply the multiple at valuation date for a terminal value calculation, the observed ratio needs to be extrapolated from the valuation date to the terminal value period.[617]

The first and most common approach in practical applications of the terminal multiple concept is to assume that the spot multiple at the valuation date remains unchanged until the beginning of the terminal value period[618]. Among practitioners the equivalence between spot and forward multiples is also referred to as "entry = exit" case. The assumption implies that the multiple defining fundamentals such as primarily expected return and perpetual dividend growth remain unchanged until the terminal value period is reached. However, this approach is not without criticism. "Suppose we choose today's current industry average price-to-earnings (PE) ratio.

---

[617] See the similar criticism by Koller, T./Goedhart, M./Wessels, D. (2005), p. 286.
[618] See Damodaran, A. (2002), p. 304 and Koller, T./Goedhart, M./Wessels, D. (2005), p. 286.

This ratio reflects the economic prospects of the industry during the explicit forecast period as well as the continuing [terminal]-value. In maturing industries, however, prospects at the end of the explicit forecast period are likely to be very different from today's"[619]. Another example for rapid changes in multiples is related to firms in restructuring periods. Exceptionally low earnings levels lead to inflated multiples which cannot be the basis for a terminal value calculation. Furthermore, changes in the economic cycle may lead to substantial adjustments in the risk-free rate caused by the fiscal policy of central banks.

The difference between spot and forward multiples can also be analytically shown by deriving a formal relationship between both multiples. Based on F 5-9, the relationship between the spot m_s^{E+1} and forward PE$_{+1}$ ratio m_T^{E+1} can be established as follows[620]:

F 5-12

$$\begin{aligned} m_s^{E+1} &= \frac{\theta}{1+r^e}\left[1+\sum_{t=s+2}^{T}\prod_{u=s+2}^{t}\frac{1+g_u^D}{1+r^e}+\prod_{u=s+2}^{T}\frac{1+g_u^D}{1+r^e}\frac{1+g_p^D}{r^e-g_p^D}\right] \\ &= \frac{1}{1+r^e}\left[\theta+\theta\sum_{t=s+2}^{T}\prod_{u=s+2}^{t}\frac{1+g_u^D}{1+r^e}+\prod_{u=s+2}^{T}\frac{1+g_u^D}{1+r^e}\left(1+g_p^D\right)\frac{\theta}{r^e-g_p^D}\right] \\ &= \frac{1}{1+r^e}\left[\theta\left(1+\sum_{t=s+2}^{T}\prod_{u=s+2}^{t}\frac{1+g_u^D}{1+r^e}\right)+\prod_{u=s+2}^{T}\frac{1+g_u^D}{1+r^e}\left(1+g_p^D\right)m_T^{E+1}\right] \end{aligned}$$

F 5-12 shows that the value of the forward multiple is only driven by perpetual dividend growth while the spot multiple is also affected by the growth rates during the explicit forecast period. Spot and forward multiple are only equivalent if the growth rates during the explicit forecast period are equal to the constant perpetual growth rate. When taking into consideration that the growth rates during the explicit forecast period are typically higher than the perpetual growth level, the forward multiple should be lower than the spot multiple. The empirical results in Section 5.9 confirm that forward multiples are lower than spot multiples but despite the obvious shortcomings, the entry = exit assumption finds widespread application.

A second approach to extrapolate spot multiples assumes that spot multiples have converged to their unconditional historical mean until the end of the explicit forecast period. This concept is related to the empirical evidence presented in Section 2.2.3.2

---

[619] Koller, T./Goedhart, M./Wessels, D. (2005), p. 286. See also the concerns by Damodaran, A. (2002), pp. 304-305.

[620] The subscript p refers to perpetuity parameters.

that the price-dividend ratio is stationary and mean reverting[621]. Still, the potential mean reversion of spot multiples measured for the entire valuation period has only a secondary effect on the forward multiple development over the course of the forecast period. More important is the issue to quantify the impact of the exclusion of the explicit forecast period with typically higher growth rates on the forward multiple. Furthermore, the inclusion of mean reversion in the determination of the appropriate terminal multiple is related to another issue since the speed of convergence is unknown and empirical evidence—which will be discussed in Section 6.1.3—shows that the price-dividend ratio is very persistent implying a slow mean reversion process. Therefore, the unconditional average will mostly not have been reached at the end of the explicit forecast period of only five years. This introduces a further issue of the mean spot multiple methodology.

In summary, both frequently applied concepts to determine forward multiples—constant or historical average spot multiples—have serious deficiencies. The only possibility to derive a consistent forward multiple is the extrapolation of the parameters defining the forward multiple at the end of the explicit forecast period, i.e. cost of equity and perpetual dividend growth. Then the forward multiple can be calculated from these fundamentals. However, this procedure would then be equivalent to the terminal perpetuity concept and the usage of forward multiples is redundant. Still, results are provided for both terminal multiple concepts not because these methodologies are supported but because its users shall be made aware of their consequences[622].

A final alternative terminal value approach employed in empirical studies is the usage of direct analyst price forecasts at the end of the finite horizon[623]. The results of a study show that estimation errors are lower using analyst price forecasts than taking

---

621 See Damodaran, A. (2002), p. 477 for a remark on the general development of multiples over time. See also Koch, J. (2005), p. 75 who summarizes findings on the time variability of the P/E ratio due to permanent and transitory components in earnings with reference to Molodowsky, N. (1953), Nicholson, S. (1960) and Beaver, W./Morse, D. (1978). Note that such effects are only captured when a valuation model is assumed with non-constant expected growth rates in the short-term.

622 This is particularly dedicated to many bankers who justify the usage of spot multiples for terminal values by arguing that the market is more efficient than individual forecasts of fundamentals. It must be understood that spot and forward multiples are two different concepts which only provide equivalent results if expected return, growth, and payout ratio are constant over time.

623 See Penman, S. (2010), pp. 164-165.

arbitrary assumptions on perpetual growth rates or terminal multiples[624]. However, it should be stressed that analysts themselves need an approach to come up with their estimate which in return is based on either a perpetual growth rate assumption or a terminal multiple technique. Therefore, no estimates of the expected MRPs based on analyst price forecasts are provided but for each of the most widely used terminal value approaches.

5.1.3 Models used in empirical research

The dividend growth model has found rich application in first attempts to measure a forward-looking MRP estimate based on expected dividends and long-term growth rates provided by financial analysts. The key differentiating characteristics across the specific models used in empirical studies are (1) the length of the finite period of explicitly forecasted dividends and (2) the determination of the perpetual growth rate of dividends beyond the finite forecast horizon. Table 16 provides a summary of selected studies using the DIV model and their specification with regards to the basic model structure and the terminal value approach[625].

---

[624] See Courteau, L./Kao, J./Richardson, G. (2001).

[625] See also the summary by Brennan, M. (2003), pp. 185-186 and Ballwieser, W. (2005), pp. 326-328.

Table 16 Summary of empirical studies using the DIV model to infer the expected MRP

Authors	Basic model structure	Terminal value approach	Model specifications and relevant results
Malkiel (1979)	• (1) One-period dividend growth model • (2) Three-stage model: t+1 to t+5 dividend growth at the five-year earnings growth rate. Thereafter, convergence from the five-year earnings growth rate to long-term growth rate of the economy until t+20 followed by a terminal value	• (1) Constant growth rate based on the five-year earnings growth forecast of analysts • (2) Constant growth rate inferred by the long-term growth rate of the economy	• US market (1960-1977) • Average results for Dow Jones Industrial Average (averaging technique undefined) • Between 1960 and 1977 the risk premium fluctuates between 3% and up to 7% (using 10-year treasury rates as risk-free rate)
Brigham/ Shome/Vinson (1985)	• Two-stage model: Four explicit forecast periods plus terminal value period	• Perpetual growth rate approximated by theoretical earnings growth expressed as retention rate times return on book equity	• US market (1966-1984) • Estimates for DJ Electrics and DJ Industrials • Value-weighted averages • Annual estimation (1980-1984 quarterly) • Resulting risk premium not stable but fluctuating between 3.5% and 8.7% using 20-year bond rates
Harris/Marston (1992 and 2001)	• One-period dividend growth model	• Perpetual growth rate equal to the five-year earnings growth forecast of analysts	• US market (1982-1998) • Individual analysis with value-weighted average results for S&P 500 • Monthly estimation approach • Expected MRPs fluctuate between 5.18% and 9.17%
Gordon/ Gordon (1997)	• Various multi-stage models with different finite horizons • Analyst forecasts for future earnings and earnings growth rates (IBES) • Forecasted dividend and earnings are grown by the expected long-term earnings growth rate	• r^e assumed to equal r^b at the end of finite forecast period with the perpetual growth rate represented by retention rate times return on book equity	• US market – S&P 500 (1985-1991) • Quarterly estimation procedure • Avg. expected return range between 8.47% to 14.70% dependent on the length of the horizon before r^e equals r^b
Cornell (1999)	• Three-stage model: First five years dividends to grow at 5-year earnings growth. Between year t+5 and t+20 linear convergence to perpetual growth rate	• Perpetual growth rate equal to the nominal growth rate of the national economy	• US market (1996) • Value-weighted averages • Average expected return of 11.26% for dividend paying S&P 500 firms implying an expected MRP of 4.53% over bonds

Authors	Basic model structure	Terminal value approach	Model specifications and relevant results
Claus/Thomas (2001)	• One-period dividend growth model	• Perpetual growth equal to the five-year earnings growth forecast of analysts	• US market (1985-1998) • Annual estimation • Market aggregate value approach • Expected MRPs fluctuate between 4.71% and 9.15%
Botosan/ Plumlee (2002)	• Two-stage model: Five periods with explicit dividend forecasts followed by a terminal value	• Analyst price estimate for the end of the forecast period	• US market - NYSE/AMEX firms (1982-2000) • Value-weighted averages
Guay/Kothari/ Shu (2005)	• See Gordon/Gordon (1997)	• See Gordon/Gordon (1997)	• US market (1983-2004) • Estimation as of 10 June • Only expected return provided with an avg. of 10.1%
Botosan/ Plumlee (2005)	• (1) Two-stage model: Five periods with explicit dividend forecasts followed by a terminal value (See Botosan/Plumlee 2002) • (2) Five-period model with $\tilde{r}^b$ converging to r^e	• (1) See Botosan/Plumlee (2002) • (2) See Gordon/Gordon (1997)	• US-Market (1983-1993) • Risk-free rate based on 5-year treasury bonds • Estimates from third quarter (timing adjustment made[626] and foregone quarterly dividends reduced) • Average expected MRPs of (1) 6.4% and (2) 2.1%
Koch (2005)	• One-period dividend growth model	• Constant growth rate based on the five-year earnings growth forecast of analysts	• EUROSTOXX 50 plus 17 additional firms (1987-2002) • Estimation frequency and weighting-approach not specified • Risk-free rate based on one- and ten-year government bonds • Avg. expected MRP of 7.04% relative to ten-year government bonds

[626] The timing adjustment for discounting dividends reduces the discount year by the fraction of the year already past until the estimation date. Note that this assumes that all dividends are paid at the fiscal year-end which is not accurate for the following reason: Dividends are paid quarterly in the USA so that their duration is not a full-year.

Authors	Basic model structure	Terminal value approach	Model specifications and relevant results
Desrosiers/ Lemaire/L'Her (2007)	• No details on the specification of the dividend discount model structure	• Ex-post inflation rate as proxy for perpetual growth rate	• Expected MRP estimates for 19 countries (1988-2005) • Monthly estimation of monthly returns • US-Dollar hedged returns • No information regarding sample details and averaging method • Risk-free rate based on 91-day T-bills • Avg. annualized expected MRP of 4.9%
Lee/Ng/ Swaminathan (2007) and Pastor/Sinha/ Swaminathan (2008)	• Three-stage model: First three years based on IBES earnings growths. For the second period (t+4 to t+15), short-term IBES growth rates are assumed to converge exponentially to the long-run GDP growth rate (payout ratios also converge to the steady state level)	• See Gordon/Gordon (1997)	• Expected MRP estimates for the G-7 countries (1991-2000) • Monthly estimation • All returns US-Dollar denominated • Risk-free rate based on 10-year US government bonds • Results provided in the results section

5.2 Residual income model (RIV)

In addition to the DIV model, other equity valuation models have been developed which are based on forecasts of accrual accounting parameters such as earnings and book values. "These [parameters] are claimed to be 'more fundamental' attributes because, it is said, they relate to value generating activities within the firm rather than value-irrelevant distributions from the firm"[627]. As to be shown, such statements cannot be analytically supported since these models are all derivatives of the DIV model and yield equivalent results if consistently applied[628].

The first equity valuation method out of this category to be used for the expected MRP estimation is the residual income valuation (RIV) framework. Residual income—the terms residual income or residual earnings are used interchangeably—is an accrual "accounting-based performance measure defined by earnings minus a charge for the use of capital measured by beginning-of-period book value multiplied by the cost of capital"[629].

Again, the basic model structure is derived first and terminal value options as well as previous versions in empirical research are discussed thereafter.

5.2.1 Basic model and assumptions

The basic form of the RIV model and its equivalence to the DIV model based on the clean surplus accounting equation has long been known in the American[630] and German[631] academic literature[632]. A contemporary derivation that will also be the basis for further discussion was provided by Ohlson (2005) using the so-called "machinery for accounting-based valuations" which is purely mathematical and does

---

[627] Penman, S. (1997), p. 306.

[628] See Section 5.4. See also Reese, R. (2007), pp. 76-93.

[629] Ohlson, J. (1995), p. 662.

[630] See Preinreich, G. (1937, 1938), Edwards, E./Bell, P. (1961), Peasnell, K. (1982), Brief, R./Lawson, R. (1992), Ohlson, J. (1995), and Feltham, G./Ohlson, J. (1995).

[631] See Lücke, W. (1955), pp. 313-316. See also first reflections of Preinreich's work in Käfer, K. (1946), p. 79. See also Richter, F./Honold, D. (2000) and Richter, F. (2005), pp. 45-47.

[632] For a comprehensive review on previous work on the residual income model, see Reichert, J. (2007), pp. 7-57.

not require any references to economic or accounting concepts[633]. As a starting point, consider again the standard DIV model and the associated assumptions regarding the treatment of uncertainty:

F 5-1 $$V_s = \sum_{t=s+1}^{\infty} \frac{E_s\left[\tilde{D}_t\right]}{\left(1+r^e\right)^{t-s}}$$

Let $\left\{y_t\right\}_{t=s}^{\infty}$ be any sequence of numbers that satisfies the mild transversality condition $y_t/\left(1+r^e\right)^{t-s} \to 0$ as $t \to \infty$; then:

F 5-13 $$0 = y_s + \frac{y_{s+1} - \left(1+r^e\right)y_s}{\left(1+r^e\right)^{s+1}} + \frac{y_{s+2} - \left(1+r^e\right)y_{s+1}}{\left(1+r^e\right)^{s+2}} + \ldots$$

This equation holds because:

$$y_s + \sum_{t=s+1}^{\infty} \frac{y_t - \left(1+r^e\right)y_{t-1}}{\left(1+r^e\right)^{t-s}} = \frac{y_\infty}{\left(1+r^e\right)^{\infty}} = 0$$

Adding equations F 5-1 and F 5-13 yields

F 5-14 $$V_s = y_s + \sum_{t=s+1}^{\infty} \frac{E_s\left[\tilde{D}_t\right] + y_t - \left(1+r^e\right)y_{t-1}}{\left(1+r^e\right)^{t-s}}$$

which can be regarded as a universal valuation formula dependent on the specification of y_t.

Based on equation F 5-14 one can now derive the RIV model by putting y_t equal to the book value $\tilde{B}_t$ and assuming that the clean surplus accounting relation holds. The clean surplus relation assumes that all changes in book value must be either reflected in earnings or dividends and that dividends are declared and paid at the end of each period[634]. Under these conditions, the end of period book value $\tilde{B}_t$ can be

---

633 See Ohlson, J. (2005), pp. 330-331 and Ohlson, J./Jüttner-Nauroth, B. (2005), pp. 350-352 for the entire derivation. See also Botosan, C./Plumlee, M. (2005), p. 30, Brief, R./O'Hanlon, J./Peasnell, K. (2005), pp. 4-6, Ohlson, J./Goa, Z. (2006), pp. 9-10, and Easton, P. (2009), pp. 257-258. In the German literature this approach was adopted by Jüttner-Nauroth, B. (2006), pp. 133-134, Reese, R. (2007), pp. 64-65, and Ewert, R./Wagenhofer, A. (2008), p. 539.

634 See Ohlson, J. (1995), p. 666 and Feltham, G./Ohlson, J. (1995), p. 647. See also Ballwieser, W. (2005), pp. 324 and 330, Koch, J. (2005), p. 55, Ewert, R./Wagenhofer, A. (2008), pp. 537-538, Krotter, S. (2007), p. 693, and Reese, R. (2007), p. 65.

expressed as the beginning of period book value $\tilde{B}_{t-1}$ plus current period earnings $\tilde{E}_t$ and minus current period dividends $\tilde{D}_t$:

F 5-15 $\tilde{B}_t = \tilde{B}_{t-1} + \tilde{E}_t - \tilde{D}_t \Rightarrow \tilde{D}_t = \tilde{E}_t - \tilde{B}_t + \tilde{B}_{t-1}$

The clean surplus relation also implies that applying the RIV model still requires explicit forecasts of expected dividends.

Adding modified F 5-14 and F 5-15 provides the standard RIV model which expresses the value of an asset as the sum of its current book value plus the present value of the infinite stream of expected residual income:

F 5-16

$$\begin{aligned} V_s &= B_s + \sum_{t=s+1}^{\infty} \frac{E_s\left[\tilde{E}_t - \tilde{B}_t + \tilde{B}_{t-1} + \tilde{B}_t\right] - \left(1+r^e\right) E_s\left[\tilde{B}_{t-1}\right]}{\left(1+r^e\right)^{t-s}} \\ &= B_s + \sum_{t=s+1}^{\infty} \frac{E_s\left[\tilde{E}_t - r^e \tilde{B}_{t-1}\right]}{\left(1+r^e\right)^{t-s}} \end{aligned}$$

Replacing expected earnings by the expectation of current return on book equity $\tilde{r}_t^b$ times beginning of period book value $\tilde{B}_{t-1}$, F 5-16 can be rewritten as follows[635]:

5-17 $V_s = B_s + \sum_{t=s+1}^{\infty} \frac{E_s\left[\left(\tilde{r}_t^b - r^e\right)\tilde{B}_{t-1}\right]}{\left(1+r^e\right)^{t-s}}$ with $E_s\left[\tilde{E}_t\right] = E_s\left[\tilde{r}_t^b \tilde{B}_{t-1}\right]$

Although the derivation of the RIV model is solely based on algebra, the interpretation of expression F 5-16 is straightforward and intuitively appealing. It says that a firm's value is equal to its book value plus the present value of the infinite stream of anticipated residual earnings. Despite the utilization of accrual accounting measures, interestingly no further specifications regarding the accounting principles are required[636]. "As Peasnell (1982) notes, this formula is peculiar because one interprets it by referring to accounting concepts, yet the formula works regardless of the accounting principles that measure book values and earnings. Accounting constructs beyond the clean surplus restriction are irrelevant (...)"[637].

---

[635] For this expression with conditional expected values, it needs to be further assumed that all covariances between expected return on book equity and book value are zero. This can be achieved by assuming deterministic conditional expected returns on book equity; see Richter, F. (2006a), pp. 14-15. See also Wallmeier, M. (2007), p. 565.

[636] See Ohlson, J. (1995), pp. 665-667. See also Reese, R. (2007), p. 66.

[637] Ohlson, J. (1995), p. 667.

The RIV model can be utilized both from a per share as well as from an all-equity perspective. However, Ohlson (2005) identified additional assumptions that are required to validate the model under the two cases. The clean surplus relation in the per share case only holds if one were to assume a constant level of shares outstanding going forward or an issue price per share equal to the book value per share at that date[638]. In contrast, the all-equity perspective requires that issuing and buying shares are value-irrelevant transactions and that local GAAP measures capital contributions (distributions) correctly in terms of market values at the dates when the transactions occur.[639]

5.2.2 Terminal value considerations

In empirical studies, the RIV model is often transformed into a multi-stage version including an explicit forecast period, optionally a fade period during which the return on book equity converges to a target value, and a terminal value estimate[640]. As for the dividend discount model, one can generally estimate the value post the explicit forecast horizon through the terminal perpetuity or terminal multiple approach. Many considerations on the terminal value—which were discussed in Section 5.1.2—are similar to the DIV model. Therefore, only specific issues relating to the RIV model are discussed.

When deriving the infinite standard version of the RIV model, it was assumed that transversality applies so that $E_s\left[\tilde{B}_t\right]/\left(1+r^e\right)^{t-s}$ converges to zero until infinity. In the multi-stage version, the explicit forecast period is finite which implies that the term has not converged to zero yet. Therefore, F 5-16 can be rewritten as follows[641]:

---

638 In order to see the mentioned effect assume a firm which issues shares on 31 December with zero earnings and dividends. Then, the book value per share will increase if the issue price is larger than the book value per share before the transaction though the clean surplus relation suggests no change in book value per share.

639 See Ohlson, J. (2005), pp. 326-330. See also the review in Easton, P. (2009), pp. 267-268.

640 See, e.g., Claus, J./Thomas, J. (2001) for a multi-stage version with explicit forecast period and terminal value. See, e.g., Gebhardt, W./Lee, C./Swaminathan, B. (2001) or Daske, H./Gebhardt, G./Klein, S. (2006) for a multi-stage version including explicit forecast period, fade period, and terminal value.

641 See Brief, R./Lawson, R. (1992), p. 414, Brief, R. (1996), p. 4, and Penman, S. (2010), pp. 154-155. Notation adapted.

F 5-18

$$\begin{aligned} V_s &= B_s + \sum_{t=s+1}^{\infty} \frac{E_s\left[\tilde{E}_t - r^e \tilde{B}_{t-1}\right]}{\left(1+r^e\right)^{t-s}} = B_s + \sum_{t=s+1}^{T} \frac{E_s\left[\tilde{E}_t - r^e \tilde{B}_{t-1}\right]}{\left(1+r^e\right)^{t-s}} - \frac{E_s\left[\tilde{B}_T\right]}{\left(1+r^e\right)^{T-s}} + \frac{E_s\left[\tilde{V}_T\right]}{\left(1+r^e\right)^{T-s}} \\ &= B_s + \sum_{t=s+1}^{T} \frac{E_s\left[\tilde{E}_t - r^e \tilde{B}_{t-1}\right]}{\left(1+r^e\right)^{t-s}} + \frac{E_s\left[\tilde{V}_T - \tilde{B}_T\right]}{\left(1+r^e\right)^{T-s}} \end{aligned}$$

When introducing the terminal perpetuity, $E_s\left[\tilde{B}_T\right]/\left(1+r^e\right)^{T-s}$ cancels out and the expression takes the following form assuming constant perpetual growth of residual earnings[642]:

F 5-19

$$\begin{aligned} V_s &= B_s + \sum_{t=s+1}^{T} \frac{E_s\left[\tilde{E}_t - r^e \tilde{B}_{t-1}\right]}{\left(1+r^e\right)^{t-s}} - \frac{E_s\left[\tilde{B}_T\right]}{\left(1+r^e\right)^{T-s}} + \frac{E_s\left[\tilde{B}_T\right]}{\left(1+r^e\right)^{T-s}} + \frac{E_s\left[\tilde{E}_T - r^e \tilde{B}_{T-1}\right]\left(1+g_{RI}\right)}{\left(r^e - g_{RI}\right)\left(1+r^e\right)^{T-s}} \\ &= B_s + \sum_{t=s+1}^{T} \frac{E_s\left[\tilde{E}_t - r^e \tilde{B}_{t-1}\right]}{\left(1+r^e\right)^{t-s}} + \frac{E_s\left[\tilde{E}_T - r^e \tilde{B}_{T-1}\right]\left(1+g_{RI}\right)}{\left(r^e - g_{RI}\right)\left(1+r^e\right)^{T-s}} \end{aligned}$$

with $r^e > g_{RI}$

Determining the perpetual growth rate of residual income g_{RI} leads to similar issues as for the DIV model. In fact, researchers frequently use the same proxies for residual earnings growth such as the inflation rate or GDP growth[643]. This appears surprising since growth in residual earnings only equals dividend growth under one specific condition that will be discussed shortly. Under all other circumstances, residual income growth differs from dividend growth.

With reference to the Gordon/Shapiro substantiation of dividend growth[644], one can formally determine the growth rate of residual earnings as follows:

F 5-20

$$\begin{aligned} g_{RI,t} &= \frac{RI_{t+1}}{RI_t} - 1 = \frac{\left(r_{t+1}^b - r^e\right)B_t}{\left(r_t^b - r^e\right)B_{t-1}} - 1 \\ &= \frac{r_{t+1}^b - r^e}{r_t^b - r^e}\left[1 + \left(1-\theta_t\right)r_t^b\right] - 1 \text{ with } g_{B,t} = \left(1-\theta_t\right)r_t^b \end{aligned}$$

---

642 See, e.g., Claus, J./Thomas, J. (2001), p. 1636 or Wallmeier, M. (2007), p. 561. See also Penman, S. (2010), p. 163.

643 See the summary of previous research in Section 5.2.4.

644 See Section 5.1.1.

with:
RI = residual income
B = book value
r^b = return on book equity
θ = payout ratio
g_{RI} = residual income growth
g_B = book value growth

Assuming $r^b, \theta = \text{const.}$, it is obvious that residual earnings growth is equal to the growth rates of all other P&L and balance sheet parameters $g_{RI} = (1-\theta)r^b = g_B = g_E = g_D$. This state is also referred to as steady state and is more deeply discussed in Section 5.4.

Similarly to the DIV model, the RIV model also allows to analyze the long-term impact of the chosen residual earnings growth level on the implied return on book equity. Solving F 5-20 for the return on book equity gives the following expression[645]:

F 5-21 $$r_{t+1}^b = (r_t^b - r^e)\frac{1+g_{RI}}{1+(1-\theta_t)\ r_t^b} + r^e$$

This confirms again that r_t^b will be constant if $g_{RI} = (1-\theta)r^b$. More importantly, it shows that r_t^b will converge over time to r^e when $0 \le g_{RI} < (1-\theta)r^b$ and $\theta = \text{const.}$ For r_t^b to decline over time, earnings growth must be lower than previous year's growth in book value[646]. As illustrated by Exhibit 36 for an example with $r_0^b = 14\%$ and $r^e = 10\%$, the speed of r_t^b convergence to r^e increases the lower the assumed rate of residual earnings growth.

---

[645] A more complex analysis of the implications of a constant perpetual growth rate of residual earnings on a selection of financial parameters is provided by Olsson (2005) as presented in Appendix 6.

[646] The relationship for earnings growth equaling growth in book equity does not hold under this scenario (see Section 5.1.1 and Appendix 5).

$$g_{t+1}^E = \frac{E_{t+1}}{E_t} - 1 = \frac{RI_{t+1} + r^e B_t}{RI_t + r^e B_{t-1}} - 1 = \frac{RI_t(1+g_{t+1}^{RI}) + r^e B_{t-1}(1+g_t^B)}{RI_t + r^e B_{t-1}} - 1$$

with $g_{t+1}^{RI} = g_t^B = g = (1-\theta)r^b$

$$g_{t+1}^E = \frac{(1+g)(RI_t + r^e B_{t-1})}{RI_t + r^e B_{t-1}} - 1 = g$$

The above expression shows that only under steady state conditions earnings growth equals growth in book equity or residual earnings.

Exhibit 36 Development of the return on book equity at various growth levels of residual earnings

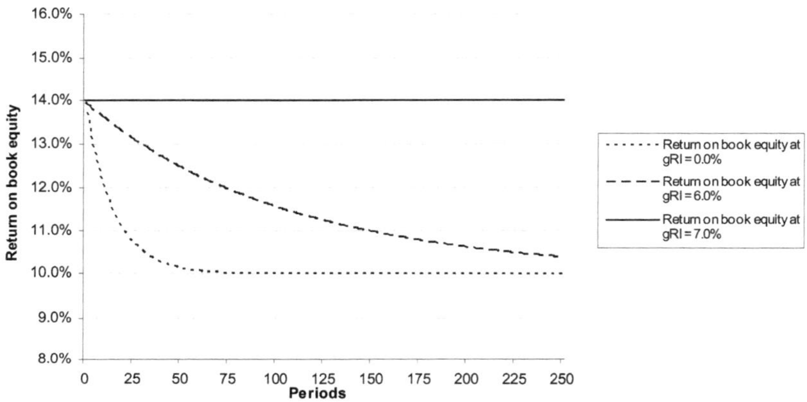

Intuitively, the popular scenario of zero residual earnings growth means that there are no new value creating projects of the firm with $r^b_{\text{new project}} > r^e$ so that r^b_t continuously approaches r^e [647]. Some researchers apply an even more conservative approach assuming that r^b_t equals r^e immediately as the terminal period is reached so that the terminal value reduces to expected book value at the beginning of the terminal period[648].

In addition to the perpetual growth concept, one can also apply the multiple-based terminal value calculation to the RIV model. With $E_s\left[\tilde{V}_T\right] = m_T^{E+1} E_s\left[\tilde{E}_{T+1}\right]$, F 5-18 can be rewritten as:

F 5-22 $$V_s = B_s + \sum_{t=s+1}^{T} \frac{E_s\left[\tilde{E}_t - r^e\tilde{B}_{t-1}\right]}{\left(1+r^e\right)^{t-s}} + \frac{E_s\left[\tilde{E}_{T+1} m_T^{E+1} - \tilde{B}_T\right]}{\left(1+r^e\right)^{T-s}}$$

Determining the value of the forward multiple required to apply F 5-22 is related to the same issues as discussed in Section 5.1.2 for the DIV model. Ultimately, in order to derive the forward multiple, one has to forecast the underlying parameters

[647] See, e.g., Gebhardt, W./Lee, C./Swaminathan, B. (2001) or Daske, H./Gebhardt, G./Klein, S. (2006). See also the remarks by Claus, J./Thomas, J. (2001), p. 1664.

[648] See also Richter, F. (2006a), pp. 14-15.

including the perpetual dividend growth which underlines that both concepts are essentially identical. This is obviously not the case, when current or average values of spot multiples are used in F 5-22. The consequences of this theoretically unfounded approach are shown in the results section.

5.2.3 Key issues in empirical model implementation

The practical implementation of the RIV model leaves the empirical researcher with the problem of forecasting not only future expected earnings but also future expected book values. This requires the application of the clean surplus relation which in return makes an assumption on future dividend levels necessary. Therefore, any application of the RIV model also requires explicit forecasts of expected dividends. In the aforementioned form, the RIV model consequently does not represent any improvement to the DIV model as argued by Dechow/Hutton/Sloan since it is not entirely independent from the distribution policy of the firm[649]. To finesse this problem, Ohlson[650] presented a linear model that frames the stochastic time-series behavior of residual earnings and non-accounting information which is often referred to as linear information dynamics (LID)[651]. According to his framework, residual earnings satisfy a modified autoregressive process which does not require any assumption on future dividend levels and is mainly driven by an information variable. However, the ability to implement this model in empirical research is limited due the issue of measuring the information variable and the persistence parameters[652]. Therefore, this study relies on the basic approach of forecasting future book values based on the clean surplus relation including a dividend policy assumption.

Further empirical issues of the RIV model are largely related to violations of the clean surplus assumption due to certain GAAP rules. While the clean surplus relation technically always holds when future book values are calculated as $\tilde{B}_t = \tilde{B}_{t-1} + \tilde{E}_t - \tilde{D}_t$, the estimates for earnings and dividends used in the application of the model may violate the true clean surplus relation when local accounting systems allow for value-relevant items to be charged directly to shareholders' equity without going through

[649] See Dechow, P./Hutton, A./Sloan, R. (1999), pp. 5-6.

[650] See Ohlson, J. (1995), pp. 667-669. See also Feltham, G./Ohlson, J. (1995).

[651] See Lee, C. (1999), p. 416.

[652] See O'Hanlon, J./Steele, A. (2000) for an example of applying the LID model to the estimation of the expected MRP in the UK.

the profit and loss account[653]. Empirical studies show that under IFRS and US-GAAP major "dirty surplus" items are related to profit neutral currency adjustments and the mark-to-market accounting for available-for-sale securities and cash flow hedges[654]. Such dirty surplus items can be further categorized into temporary, i.e. the violation is reversed at a later point in time, or permanent violations of clean surplus. Chen/Jorgensen/Yoo find that the ex-post deviation from the clean-surplus-relation measured as the difference between net income and comprehensive income is larger for France, Germany, and the UK compared to the remaining countries in the sample[655]. Still, any historical violations of the clean surplus relation—disregarding whether temporary or permanent—are generally irrelevant when using the RIV model with forecasted input parameters[656].

An exception was identified by Krotter (2007) relating to inconsistencies among input parameters due to historical clean surplus violations. More specifically, he refers to the usage of the target return of book equity for the convergence period and payout ratios based on historical data[657]. Krotter shows that when adjusting the normally value irrelevant starting book value in a RIV framework for dirty surplus adjustments and keeping the target return on book equity identical, the expected return differs in an illustrative single company example by approximately 0.7%. It should be obvious that the bias identified by Krotter is not related to a violation of the clean surplus relation going forward but related to the usage of a distorted historical parameter that affects value.[658]

Violations of the forward-looking or ex-ante clean surplus relationship are formally not possible since future book values are forecasted using this clean surplus relation. A bias only occurs when the estimated dividend stream is distorted due to an

---

[653] See Frankel, R./Lee, C. (1999), p. 10, Reese, R. (2007), pp. 89-91, and Krotter, S. (2007), p. 693. See also Ballwieser, W. (2005), p. 330.

[654] See Chen, F./Jorgensen, B./Yoo, Y. (2004), pp. 329-331 and Krotter, S. (2007), p. 697. See also Ordelheide, D. (1998), pp. 522-525, Schildbach, T. (1999), pp. 1819-1820, Lo, K./Lys, T. (2000), pp. 342-343, Deller, D. (2002), pp. 129-139, Zimmermann, J./Prokop, J. (2003), pp. 139-140, Prokop, J. (2003), pp. 162-167, Isidro, H./O'Hanlon, J./Young, S. (2004), pp. 390 and 396-397, Lachnit, L./Müller, S. (2005), pp. 1640-1642, and Reichert, J. (2007), pp. 144-151.

[655] See Chen, F./Jorgensen, B./Yoo, Y. (2004), p. 321.

[656] See Krotter, S. (2007), p. 708 and Reese, R. (2007), p. 90.

[657] This bias refers to the later discussed RIV model specifications of Gebhardt/Lee/Swaminathan (2001) and Daske/Gebhardt/Klein (2006). Other later used RIV model specifications are not affected by this bias since they do not include a convergence period to a target return on book equity.

[658] See Krotter, S. (2007), pp. 708-710. See also Reese, R. (2007), p. 90.

inconsistent treatment of expected violations, e.g., earnings are adjusted for P&L neutral direct effects to equity but payout ratios are not adjusted. Then the clean surplus relation would still hold but the valuation result would be biased for the RIV approach and all other valuation methodologies including the DIV model[659]. However, Frankel/Lee argue that the possibility for expected violations is low since "these adjustment items all serve to adjust the book value of an asset or a liability to its market value. Once an asset or liability has been marked-to-market, future market value adjustments are, by definition, mean zero in expectation"[660].

5.2.4 Models used in empirical research

The RIV model has been widely tested in particular regarding the debated superior accuracy in comparison to other valuation models. Furthermore, it has been the basis of several studies trying to explain stock market behavior using fundamental valuation techniques. Comparing the previously used model specifications with respect to explicit forecast period and terminal value is important for the model structure in this study. Therefore, Table 17 provides a summary of selected general studies implementing the RIV model followed by a detailed presentation of recent RIV model structures used to determine the expected MRP.

---

[659] See Reese, R. (2007), pp. 90-91. See also Chen, F./Jorgensen, B./Yoo, Y. (2004), p. 331.
[660] Frankel, R./Lee, C. (1999), p. 11.

Table 17 Summary of RIV model applications in empirical research (excluding MRP studies)

Authors	Basic model structure and inputs	Terminal value approach	Results of interest
Frankel/Lee (1998)	• Two- to three-stage RIV model with const. vs. varying $\tilde{r}^b$ • $\tilde{r}^b$ based on historical realizations and analysts' earnings forecasts • Historical dividend payout ratio	• Forecasted $\tilde{r}^b$ level with zero perpetual growth rate of residual income	• High correlation of RIV value with market valuations • Value (based on RIV model)/price ratio good predictor of long-term returns • Low portion of errors in IBES forecasts predictable
Penman/ Sougiannis (1998)	• RIV model separating financial and operating activities (Feltham/Ohlson[661]) • One to ten-period models • Ex-post data used to infer ex-ante valuation errors	• Two versions with zero and two (RIV) / four (DCF) percent terminal growth (lower growth for RIV compared to DCF due to an excessive $\tilde{r}^b$ growth)	• Valuation errors are lower using accrual accounting valuation models rather than cash flow or dividend discounting models • Accruals bring the future forward in time to facilitate finite horizon valuation
Frankel/Lee (1999)	• Two-stage RIV model • $\tilde{r}^b$ based on analysts' earnings forecasts • Dividend payout ratio based on the most recent historical year	• Forecasted $\tilde{r}^b$ level with no perpetual growth rate of residual income	• High correlation between fundamental RIV model valuations with cross-boarder stock prices
Lee/Myers/ Swaminathan (1999)	• 3-, 12-, 18-period RIV models based on analysts' earnings estimates • Last actual dividend payout ratio	• Convergence to industry target $\tilde{r}^b$ with zero perp. growth of residual earnings	• Value (based on RIV model)/price ratio has significant predictive power for future returns in contrast to traditional ratios
Abarbanell/ Bernard (2000)	• Two-stage RIV model (five periods) • Analysts' earnings and book value forecasts	• Forward PE multiple (entry=exit) times expected earnings less book value	• Hypothesis of overvaluation of near-term earnings cannot be clearly confirmed
Francis/Olsson/ Oswald (2000)	• Two-stage RIV model (five periods) • Analysts' earnings, dividends, and book value forecasts • Discount-period adjustment identical to Courteau/Kao/Richardson	• Two versions with zero and four percent (assumed to equal the inflation rate) terminal growth; however, due to similar conclusions focus on 4% case	• RIV model value estimates perform significantly better than dividend discount and free cash flow model value estimates[662]

---

[661] See Feltham, G./Ohlson, J. (1995).

[662] The authors make the following important point: "In theory, the models yield identical estimates of intrinsic values; in practice, they will differ if the forecasted attributes, growth rates, or discount rates are inconsistent"; Francis, J./Olsson, P./Oswald, D. (2000), p. 46. For example, inconsistencies arise if the attributes violate clean surplus, if discount rates violate the assumption of no arbitrage, unlimited borrowing, and lending at the rate of return, or if growth rates are not constant (i.e., the firm is not in steady state).

Authors	Basic model structure and inputs	Terminal value approach	Results of interest
Liu/Thomas (2000)	• Five-period RIV model • Expected earnings based on analysts' earnings forecasts • Dividend payout ratio based on the most recent historical year	• Intrinsically calculated future expected price-to-book ratio applied to the terminal year book value	• Extended model relating unexpected returns with unexpected earnings
Courteau/Kao/ Richardson (2001)	• Length of explicit forecast period undefined • Discount-period adjustment for the time of the year lapsed at estimation date[663] • Third-quarter analyst estimates (ValueLine)	• Three approaches: (1) Terminal price forecasts by analysts (2) No perpetual growth rate (3) Two percent perpetual growth without providing rationale	• RIV and DCF model are equivalent in finite horizon application when theoretical terminal value is used • Analyst price forecasts are more accurate in measuring terminal value than growth assumptions
Liu/Nissim/ Thomas (2002)	• (1) Frankel/Lee model (1998) • (2) Palepu/Healy/Bernard model (five-year model with a post horizon value of zero)[664] • (3) Gebhardt/Lee/Swaminathan (2001) • IBES forecasts	• See mentioned approaches	• Multiples outperform RIV values in explaining actual prices (due to measurement errors • Within RIV model approaches, (1) most accurate, (2) large pricing errors, (3) very large pricing errors
Ali/Hwang/ Trombley (2003)	• Two- to three-stage RIV models with const. vs. varying $\tilde{r}^b$ • $\tilde{r}^b$ based on historical realizations and analysts' earnings forecasts • Dividend payout ratio based on the most recent historical year	• Forecasted $\tilde{r}^b$ level with zero perpetual growth rate of residual income	• Validate value (based on RIV model)/price mispricing effect discovered by Frankel/Lee (1998) • Mispricing effect is largest around earnings announcement dates

663 Adjustment of the stub-period residual earnings according to the following formula:

$$\tilde{E}_{\left(1-\frac{d}{365}\right)} - \left[\left(1+r^e\right)^{\left(1-\frac{d}{365}\right)} - 1\right]\tilde{B}_{s+\frac{d}{365}}$$

This expression is based on clean surplus accounting and is therefore only valid under the assumption of dividends to be entirely paid at the fiscal year-end.

664 See Palepu, K./Healy, P./Bernard, V. (2000).

The summary table already indicates that there is a multitude of variations in the specific RIV model structures particularly with regards to the terminal value approach. In order to create the basis for the later comparison between the results of previous research work on the expected MRP and this study, the key characteristics of the predominant studies on the estimation of the expected MRP using RIV models are now described based on the categories model structure, terminal value approach, data, and averaging methodology[665]:

5.2.4.1 Claus/Thomas (2001)

Model structure	$P_s = B_s + \sum_{t=s+1}^{s+5} \frac{E_s\left[\tilde{E}_t - r^e\tilde{B}_{t-1}\right]}{\left(1+r^e\right)^{t-s}} + \frac{E_s\left[\tilde{E}_{s+5} - r^e\tilde{B}_{s+4}\right]\left(1+g_{RI}\right)}{\left(r^e - g_{RI}\right)\left(1+r^e\right)^5}$ • Explicit forecast period with residual income estimates for five future periods based on IBES consensus estimates and long-term growth rates • Expected returns are generally assumed to be flat in term structure. However, an alternative model is used that relaxes the assumption of flat risk-free rate. In this case, the forward risk-free rate develops according to the forward curve with the expected MRP being still flat:[666] $P_s = B_s + \sum_{t=s+1}^{s+5} \frac{E_s\left[\tilde{E}_t - \left(r_t^f + r^p\right)\tilde{B}_{t-1}\right]}{\left(1+r_t^f + r^p\right)^{t-s}} + \frac{E_s\left[\tilde{E}_{s+5} - \left(r_{s+5}^f + r^p\right)\tilde{B}_{s+4}\right]\left(1+g_{RI}\right)}{\left(r_{s+5}^f + r^p - g_{RI}\right)\left(1+r_{s+5}^f + r^p\right)^5}$
Terminal value approach	• Beyond the explicit forecast period, abnormal earnings are expected to constantly grow at the expected inflation rate. The expected inflation rate is derived based on the assumption that the real risk-free rate is approximately three percent[667]
Data	• US market • Period: 1985-1998 • Sample selection criteria: – Firms are included with at least two future periods of earnings forecasts, a five year earnings growth rate, share prices and shares outstanding – In addition, historical information such as last period book value, earnings and dividends

[665] For a review of selected models used in empirical studies, see also Ballwieser, W. (2005), pp. 326-328 and Easton, P. (2009), pp. 281-290.

[666] See also Daske, H./Gebhardt, G. (2006), p. 539 for a version of the Gebhardt/Lee/Swaminathan model using time-variable risk-free rates.

[667] The three percent estimate is justified by the observed yield of inflation-indexed government bonds issued in the US.

	– Where unavailable, explicit forecasts for the periods t+3 to t+5 are extrapolated using the five-year earnings growth rate • Estimation of r^e is conducted at one point during the year for the entire sample disregarding fiscal year-ends using[668]: – Last fiscal year-end book value – Forecasts collected as of 30-April – Share prices collected as of 31 December • Future book values are calculated based the clean surplus relation using IBES earnings' estimates and a historically determined constant payout ratio of 50% • Risk-free rate: 10-year treasury bond rate
Averaging methodology	• Market aggregate approach: Firm-level data are aggregated to generate market-level input parameters

5.2.4.2 Gebhardt/Lee/Swaminathan (2001)

Model structure	$P_s = B_s + \sum_{t=s+1}^{s+3} \frac{E_s\left[\tilde{E}_t - r^e \tilde{B}_{t-1}\right]}{\left(1+r^e\right)^{t-s}} + \sum_{t=s+4}^{s+11} \frac{E_s\left[\left(\tilde{r}_t^b - r^e\right)\tilde{B}_{t-1}\right]}{\left(1+r^e\right)^{t-s}} + \frac{E_s\left[\left(\tilde{r}_{s+12}^b - r^e\right)\tilde{B}_{s+11}\right]}{r^e\left(1+r^e\right)^{11}}$ • Explicit forecast period with residual income estimates for three future periods based on IBES consensus estimates and long-term growth rates • Convergence period starting after period t+3 assuming mean reversion of the t+3 $\tilde{r}_t^b$ to the median industry $\tilde{r}_t^b$. This is achieved by a simple linear interpolation between period t+3 and the target $\tilde{r}_t^b$ to be realized in period t+12
Terminal value approach	• From period t+12 onwards, the target level of $\tilde{r}^b$ is assumed to remain constant until infinity. "This does not imply that earnings or cash flows do not grow after period T [t+12], it rather assumes that any incremental economic profits (those from net new investments) after year T are zero. In other words, any growth in earnings or cash flow after year T is value neutral"[669]. As a result of this assumption, the $\tilde{r}_t^b$ continuously declines over time and asymptotically approaches the r^e • The target $\tilde{r}_t^b$ in period t+12 is calculated as the moving median of all firms in the same industry of the past 5-10 year (loss-making firms are excluded). The classification into 48 industries is adopted from Fama/French (1997)
Data	• US market • Period: 1979-1995

[668] For firms with a fiscal year-end other than December this creates a slight upward bias in the expected MRP estimate.
[669] Gebhardt, W./Lee, C./Swaminathan, B. (2001), p. 142.

	• Sample selection criteria: – Firms are included with at least two future periods earnings forecasts and a long-term EPS growth rate – CRSP stock price, trading volume and shares outstanding – Compustat book value and actual earnings/dividends • Estimation of r^e is calculated for each year on 30 June using: – 30 June stock price, earnings forecasts – Last fiscal year-end book value (synthetic book value based on clean surplus relation from earnings announcement until four months after fiscal year-end) • Future book values are calculated based the clean surplus relation using IBES earnings' estimates and the most recent historical payout ratio (share repurchases are excluded, range of payout ratio limited to 0 to 1, and negative earnings replaced by 6% times total assets) • Risk-free rate: 10-year treasury bond rate
Averaging methodology	• The expected MRP is calculated on a firm-level basis; a market-level expected MRP is computed as the equally weighted average of all individual expected MRPs

5.2.4.3 Easton/Taylor/Shroff/Sougiannis (2002)

In applying the terminal perpetuity approach according to the preceding discussions in Sections 5.1.2 and 5.2.2, researchers face to problem of having an equation with two unknown variables—perpetual growth rate of abnormal earnings and cost of equity. Both aforementioned approaches solve this issue by taking specific assumptions on the perpetual growth development of residual income. As an alternative, Easton et al. (2002) presented an approach that involves the simultaneous estimation of both the perpetual growth and return.

The authors apply the RIV model with certain modifications and express the current market valuation as a linear function of current book value and expected aggregate four-year cum-dividend earnings. Rearranging leads to a linear regression relation which is the basis for the estimation of perpetual growth and return. The derivation is based on a standard two-stage RIV model[670]:

[670] See also the summaries in Daske, H./Gebhardt, G./Klein, S. (2006), pp. 8-10 and Reese, R. (2007), pp. 69-72.

F 5-23 $P_s = B_s + \sum_{t=s+1}^{s+4} \frac{E_s\left[\tilde{E}_t - r^e\tilde{B}_{t-1}\right]}{\left(1+r^e\right)^{t-s}} + \sum_{t=s+5}^{\infty} \frac{E_s\left[\tilde{E}_t - r^e\tilde{B}_{t-1}\right]}{\left(1+r^e\right)^{t-s}}$

Expressing of all future book values $E_s\left[\tilde{B}_{s+1}\right], E_s\left[\tilde{B}_{s+2}\right], E_s\left[\tilde{B}_{s+3}\right]$ in the first summation as a function of expected earnings $E_s\left[\tilde{E}_{s+1}\right], E_s\left[\tilde{E}_{s+2}\right], E_s\left[\tilde{E}_{s+3}\right]$, expected dividends $E_s\left[\tilde{D}_{s+1}\right], E_s\left[\tilde{D}_{s+2}\right], E_s\left[\tilde{D}_{s+3}\right]$, and initial book value B_s yields the following term using the clean surplus relation[671]:

$$\sum_{t=s+1}^{s+4} \frac{E_s\left[\tilde{E}_t - r^e\tilde{B}_{t-1}\right]}{\left(1+r^e\right)^{t-s}}$$

F 5-24 $$= \frac{1}{\left(1+r^e\right)^4}\left\{\sum_{t=s+1}^{s+4} E_s\left[\tilde{E}_t\right] + \sum_{t=s+1}^{s+3}\left(\left(1+r^e\right)^{4-t} - 1\right)E_s\left[\tilde{D}_t\right] - \left(\left(1+r^e\right)^4 - 1\right)\tilde{B}_{t-1}\right\}$$

$$= \frac{1}{\left(1+r^e\right)^4}\left\{E_s\left[\tilde{E}_t^c\right] - \left(\left(1+r^e\right)^4 - 1\right)\tilde{B}_{t-1}\right\}$$

with $\sum_{t=s+1}^{s+4} E_s\left[\tilde{E}_t\right] + \sum_{t=s+1}^{s+3}\left(\left(1+r^e\right)^{4-t} - 1\right)E_s\left[\tilde{D}_t\right] = E_s\left[\tilde{E}_s^c\right]$

The final term represents the present value of the cumulative residual earnings for the next four-year period.

Reinserting in F 5-23 and treating the four-year residual income as a constant growth perpetuity yields:

F 5-25
$$P_s = B_s + \frac{E_s\left[\tilde{E}_s^c\right] - \left(\left(1+r^e\right)^4 - 1\right)B_s}{\left(1+r^e\right)^4 - \left(1+g_{RI}\right)^4}$$

$$= B_s + \frac{E_s\left[\tilde{E}_s^c\right] - (R-1)B_s}{R-G} \text{ with } R = \left(1+r^e\right)^4 \text{ and } G = \left(1+g_{RI}\right)^4$$

In order to develop the procedure to simultaneously forecast r^e and g_{RI}, one has to rearrange F 5-25 as follows to establish the basis for a linear regression analysis of the cross-section data[672]:

---

[671] Appendix 7 shows the derivation of the expression for a simplified two period example.

[672] For a similar regression approach excluding analysts' forecasts, see O'Hanlon, J./Steele, A. (2000). See also Easton, P. (2006), pp. 390-392, Easton, P./Sommers, G. (2007), p. 989, and Easton, P. (2009), p. 303.

$$\frac{E_s\left[\tilde{E}_t^c\right]}{B_s}=(G-1)+(R-G)\frac{P_s}{B_s}$$

F 5-26 with $\alpha = G-1$ and $\beta = R-G$

$$\frac{E_s\left[\tilde{E}_t^c\right]}{B_s}=\alpha+\beta\frac{P_s}{B_s}$$

Notice that this analysis is at the firm-level not at the market-level. Equation F 5-26 can therefore be written as the following linear relation for each firm j using estimated coefficients from the respective samples:

F 5-27 $$\frac{E_s\left[\tilde{E}_{j,t}^c\right]}{B_{j,s}}=\hat{\alpha}+\hat{\beta}\frac{P_{j,s}}{B_{j,s}}+\hat{\varepsilon}_j$$ [673]

"The linear relation between $E_s\left[\tilde{E}_{j,t}^c\right]/B_{j,s}$ and $P_{j,s}/B_{j,s}$ suggests that the average four-year expected rate of return $(R-1)$ and the average four-year growth in residual income $(G-1)$ may be estimated from the intercept and the slope coefficient from a linear regression of $E_s\left[\tilde{E}_{j,t}^c\right]/B_{j,s}$ on $P_{j,s}/B_{j,s}$ for any portfolio of $j=1,\ldots,J$. (...) The estimates of coefficients α and β are non-stochastic and may be regarded as the mean for the firm-specific coefficients" [674]. Therefore the cost of equity and perpetual growth resulting from the coefficients can be regarded as equally weighted averages of the sample. An advantage of the regression approach compared to the previous models is the possibility to measure the estimation accuracy through the standard errors of the coefficients[675].

The empirical proxy of $E_s\left[\tilde{E}_{j,t}^c\right]$ is obtained by using IBES earnings estimates and assuming dividends to remain at the historical level in absolute terms $E_s\left[\tilde{D}_t\right]=D_{t-1}$ [676].

---

[673] Easton et al. (2002) find that the error term of their sample is heteroskedastic which requires the usage of robust standard errors for significance tests of the estimators; see Easton et al. (2002), p. 663, fn. 11.

[674] Easton et al. (2002), pp. 662-663. Note that symbols are adapted to the standard format of this dissertation.

[675] See Wallmeier, M. (2007), p. 570.

[676] The two sources of error using these proxies are market expectations of earnings being different from the IBES estimates and expected dividends different from the historical level. Thus the independent variable (price-to-book ratio)—in contrast to the dependent variable—is free of error.

Other empirical specifications of the Easton et al. analysis are summarized in the following table:

Data	• US market • Period: 1981-1998 • Sample selection criteria: – Firms only with fiscal year-end December – Stock price and shares outstanding – Compustat book value and dividends – Firms are included with five future periods earnings forecasts or at least two future periods earnings forecasts plus a long-term growth rate • r^e and g_{RI} are calculated for each year as of 31 December using: – Prices, shares outstanding (Compustat) as of fiscal year-end 31-Dec – Synthetic book value as of 31 December based on book value $t-1$ and current year estimates of earnings and dividends according to the clean surplus relation – IBES estimates as of the third Thursday in December • Risk-free rate: 5-year treasury bond rate
Averaging methodology	• The resulting expected MRP based on the regression analysis using individual firm-level data can be viewed as an equally weighted expected MRP • Calculation of cum-dividend earnings requires cost of equity capital as input parameter resulting in a circularity problem. This issue is solved by an iterative procedure with a starting value of r^e equal to 12%

5.2.4.4 Daske/Gebhardt/Klein (2006)

Daske/Gebhardt/Klein basically apply the Gebhardt/Lee/Swaminathan and Easton et al. models except for one modification. As outlined before, all previous studies estimate the cost of equity for their expected MRP calculation only once a year at a specific predetermined date. In addition, there arises an issue from using input parameters at inconsistent points in time. Table 18 summarizes the date issue[677].

[677] See also Daske, H./Gebhardt, G./Klein, S. (2006), pp. 10-11.

Table 18 Dates of input parameters and estimates of key studies

Authors	Estimation date	Price date	Earnings estimate date	Book value date
Claus/Thomas[678]	• 30 April	• 31 December	• 30 April	• Actual 31 December
Gebhardt/Lee/ Swaminathan[679]	• 30 June	• 30 June	• 30 June	• Actual 31 December[680]
Easton et al.[681]	• 31 December	• 31 December	• Mid-December	• Synthetical 31 December[682]

Claus/Thomas use book values and market prices as of 31 December, whereas their IBES earnings estimates are based on the estimation date of 30 April. Though consistently using market prices and IBES estimates as of their 30 June estimation date, Gebhardt/Lee/Swaminathan include book values referring to 31 December. Only Easton et al. create a data set which consistently refers to the estimation date as of 31 December. In summary, the date matching issue of input variables is complex due to the at best quarterly announcement of financial statements and the additional time lag in their disclosure. A consistent usage of parameters relating to the very same date becomes at first sight only possible by synthetically calculating book values[683] for the required points in time as exemplified by Easton et al.

Daske/Gebhardt/Klein address these issues by (1) consistently using input variables that reflect the most currently available information at the estimation date including synthetical book values[684] and (2) by introducing a procedure that allows a daily

---

[678] See Claus, J./Thomas, J. (2001), p. 1639.

[679] See Gebhardt, W./Lee, C./Swaminathan, B. (2001), pp. 143-145.

[680] Actuals only used if 30 June is more than four months after fiscal year-end; otherwise synthetical book value based on clean surplus relation using previous year-end actual book value and expected earnings and dividends.

[681] See Easton, P. et al. (2002), p. 664.

[682] Synthetical book value based on the clean surplus relation using previous year-end actual book value and earnings as well as dividend forecasts as of December.

[683] Since book values are on average disclosed 2-3 months after the fiscal year-end, one can create forward book values using the expected earnings and dividends development based on the clean surplus relation.

[684] Virtual book values are required in the Daske/Gebhardt/Klein analysis for two reasons. Assume the implementation of the RIV model using their approach on 31 January for a firm or group of firms with 31 December fiscal year-end. Under normal circumstances on 31 January, the book value for the previous fiscal year is not published yet. Therefore, one has to firstly calculate the virtual book value for the previous fiscal year-end on 31 December using IBES forecasts and the clean surplus relation. Secondly, one has to again use the same approach to create a synthetical book value for the intra-fiscal year estimation date of 31 January. This approach allows for an individual company analysis and the inclusion of companies with different fiscal year-ends.

estimation which is being used to estimate the expected return on a monthly basis[685]. The daily estimation procedure requires some further explanations, particularly with respect to the systematic stock price development throughout the year.

As a base for their analysis, Daske/Gebhardt/Klein use an extended version of the standard RIV model to allow for a monthly estimation[686]. In short, their model is based on a daily synthetical book value as a starting point and a "stub-period" to capture the remaining unrealized part of the first future period[687]. The precise versions of the Gebhardt/Lee/Swaminathan and Easton et al. models in the daily format of Daske/Gebhardt/Klein are as follows:

- *Daske/Gebhardt/Klein version of Gebhardt/Lee/Swaminathan model[688]:*

F 5-28

$$P_{s+\frac{d}{365}} = E_s\left[\tilde{B}_{s+\frac{d}{365}}\right] + \frac{E_s\left[\tilde{E}_{s+1-\frac{d}{365}} - \left[\left(1+r^e\right)^{\left(1-\frac{d}{365}\right)} - 1\right]\tilde{B}_{s+\frac{d}{365}}\right]}{\left(1+r^e\right)^{\left(1-\frac{d}{365}\right)}} + \sum_{t=s+2}^{s+5} \frac{E_s\left[\tilde{E}_t - r^e \tilde{B}_{t-1}\right]}{\left(1+r^e\right)^{t-\left(s+\frac{d}{365}\right)}}$$

$$+\sum_{t=s+6}^{s+11} \frac{E_s\left[\left(\tilde{r}_t^b - r^e\right)\tilde{B}_{t-1}\right]}{\left(1+r^e\right)^{t-\left(s+\frac{d}{365}\right)}} + \frac{E_s\left[\left(\tilde{r}_{s+12}^b - r^e\right)\tilde{B}_{s+11}\right]}{r^e\left(1+r^e\right)^{\left(11-\frac{d}{365}\right)}}$$

$$\text{with } E_s\left[\tilde{B}_{s+\frac{d}{365}}\right] = E_s\left[B_s\left(1+\tilde{r}_{s+1}^b\right)^{\frac{d}{365}}\right]$$

- *Daske/Gebhardt/Klein version of Easton et al. model[689]:*

Constantly rolling the cum-dividend earnings forward to maintain a four year summation period with an adjusted initial book value allows for the monthly usage of the Easton et al. model in its standard format:

F 5-29

$$P_{s+\frac{d}{365}} = E_s\left[\tilde{B}_{s+\frac{d}{365}}\right] + \frac{E_s\left[\tilde{E}^c_{s+\frac{d}{365}} - \left[\left(1+r^e\right)^4 - 1\right]\tilde{B}_{s+\frac{d}{365}}\right]}{\left(1+r^e\right)^4 - \left(1+g_{RI}\right)^4}$$

---

[685] See Daske, H./Gebhardt, G./Klein, S. (2006), pp. 10-12.

[686] See also Easton, P. (2009), pp. 352-355.

[687] The Daske/Gebhardt/Klein approach is similar to adjustments in earlier RIV model-based studies by Francis/Olsson/Oswald (2000) and Courteau/Kao/Richardson (2001).

[688] See Daske, H./Gebhardt, G./Klein, S. (2006), p. 6 and Daske, H./Gebhardt, G. (2006), p. 537.

[689] See Daske, H./Gebhardt, G./Klein, S. (2006), p. 9.

with:

$$E_s\left[\tilde{E}^c_{s+\frac{d}{365}}\right]=E_s\left[\tilde{E}_{s+1-\frac{d}{365}}+\tilde{E}_{s+2}+\tilde{E}_{s+3}+\tilde{E}_{s+4}+\tilde{E}_{s+4+\frac{d}{365}}\right]+E_s\left[\tilde{D}_{s+1}\right]\left[\left(1+r^e\right)^{3+\frac{d}{365}}-1\right]$$
$$+E_s\left[\tilde{D}_{s+2}\right]\left[\left(1+r^e\right)^{2+\frac{d}{365}}-1\right]+E_s\left[\tilde{D}_{s+3}\right]\left[\left(1+r^e\right)^{1+\frac{d}{365}}-1\right]+E_s\left[\tilde{D}_{s+1}\right]\left[\left(1+r^e\right)^{\frac{d}{365}}-1\right]$$

$$E_s\left[\tilde{B}_{s+\frac{d}{365}}\right]=E_s\left[B_s\left(1+\tilde{r}^b_{s+1}\right)^{\frac{d}{365}}\right]$$

One problem of the Daske/Gebhardt/Klein approach needs to be addressed. Though their model captures the present value effect when calculating the expected return on a monthly basis, their reference period is the fiscal year instead of the dividend year due to the application of the clean surplus relation which assumes that dividends are directly paid at the fiscal year-end[690]. For a company with a 31 December year-end, this means that the model assumes that dividends are paid exactly on this particular day. However, for most countries dividends are paid multiple times throughout the year after the official corporate bodies (e.g., annual general meeting (AGM) or the board of directors) have voted on the dividend level. Therefore, there is a substantial time-lag between fiscal year-end and the dividend payment date[691]. This results in a slight upward bias in the estimated cost of equity from the true dividend payment date and to the fiscal year-end (theoretically underlying market price lower than implied by the discounting procedure of the model) and a slight downward bias during the rest of the year (opposite effect). Up to now, this issue appears not to be addressed in empirical studies[692]. The cumbersome implementation of the complex daily RIV model according to the Daske/Gebhardt/Klein specifications therefore appears of little value-added given the additional error potential through distorted present value effects.

5.2.4.5 Summary of selected other studies

Besides those RIV model variations presented in a very detailed manner, Table 19 summarizes additional studies using the RIV approach to determine the expected MRP. These studies use RIV models which are identical to the previously discussed version with only selected minor modifications.

---

690 See fn. 634.
691 See Section 5.7.2.
692 E.g., the survery of Easton (2009) does not address this issue.

Table 19 Summary of additional RIV model-based studies to estimate the expected MRP

Authors	RIV model structure and basic inputs	Terminal value approach	Further analysis specifications
Botosan/Plumlee (1997)	• Five-period model • Analyst forecasts for earnings and book values	• Price forecast based on long-term PE ratio	• Study on the impact of disclosure levels on cost of equity capital • US market • For 1991 only and limited sample (122 firms) • Prices as of 30 June • Fiscal year-end book value
Baginski/Wahlen (2003)	• Five-period model • IBES earnings forecasts • Dividend payout ratio equal to last historical year	• Terminal perpetuity with growth rate equal to risk-free rate minus 3 percent (Claus/Thomas approach)	• US market (1996-2004) • Restrictive sample selection procedure • Assume neutral value impact of share issues or repurchases • Prices as of 1-April • Risk-free rate equal to 10-year government bond rates • Averaging approach not specified
Gode/Mohanram (2003)	• Two RIV versions based on Gebhardt/ Lee/Swaminathan models and specifications • IBES estimates	• (1) Gebhardt/Lee/Swaminathan approach with target $\tilde{r}^b$ as previous 10-year moving median • (2) Previous industry median $\tilde{r}^b$ within the limits of the risk-free rate and 20%	• US market (1984-1998) • No details on averaging approach • Yearly 30 June estimation • Risk-free rate based on 10-year treasury bonds

Authors	RIV model structure and basic inputs	Terminal value approach	Further analysis specifications
Guay/Kothari/Shu (2005)	• Claus/Thomas and Gebhardt/Lee/Swaminathan model	• NA (see mentioned reference)	• US market (1983-2004) • Estimation as of 30 June
Botosan/Plumlee (2005)	• Gebhardt/Lee/ Swaminathan models and specifications • IBES estimates	• NA (see mentioned references)	• US-Market (1983-1993) • Risk-free rate based on 5-year treasury bonds • Estimates from third quarter (timing adjustment made[693] and foregone quarterly dividends reduced)
Easton/Monahan (2005)	• Claus/Thomas and Gebhardt/Lee/ Swaminathan models and specifications • IBES estimates	• NA (see mentioned references)	• US market (1981-1998) • Only December year-end firms • Equally weighted averages • 31 December estimation
Koch (2005)	• Gebhardt/Lee/ Swaminathan model and specifications • IBES estimates	• NA (see mentioned reference)	• EUROSTOXX 50 plus 17 additional firms (1987-2002) • Estimation frequency and weighting- approach not specified • Risk-free rate based on one- and ten-year government bonds
Reese (2005, 2007)	• Claus/Thomas and Gebhardt/Lee/Swaminathan models and specifications • IBES estimates	• NA (see mentioned references)	• German market - CDAX (1989-2004) • Monthly estimation (however, implementation not specified) • Equal and value-weighted results • Risk-free rate based on 10-year sub-index of REX
Desrosiers/Lemaire/L'Her (2007)	• Claus/Thomas model (only difference is the source of the terminal growth rate) • IBES estimates	• Last year inflation rate as proxy for perpetual growth rate (Datastream)	• Expected MRP estimates for 19 countries (1988-2005) • Monthly estimation • US-Dollar hedged returns • No information regarding sample details and averaging method
Lee/Ng/ Swaminathan (2007)	• Claus/Thomas model	• NA (see mentioned reference)	• Expected MRP estimates for the G-7 countries (1991-2000) • Monthly estimation • All returns US-Dollar denominated • Risk-free rate based on 10-year US government bonds

693 The timing adjustment for the discounting of dividends refers to reducing the discount year by the fraction of the year already past until the estimation date. Note that this assumes that all dividends are paid at the fiscal year-end which is not accurate for the following reason: Dividends are paid quarterly in the USA so that their duration is not a full-year.

As the preceding presentation of previous research approaches using the RIV model to estimate the expected MRP has shown, the key differences among the specific models are mainly related to the terminal value calculation.

5.3 Earnings capitalization models (CAP)

The reliance on the clean surplus relation is often viewed as a limitation of the RIV model[694]. Ohlson/Jüttner-Nauroth have therefore developed a valuation model that directly relates analysts' earnings forecasts to fundamental values without relying on book values which consequently does not require the clean surplus to be applied[695]. Additionally, their model has the advantage of being very parsimonious with respect to the required input variables. However, the Ohlson/Jüttner-Nauroth model is yet another algebraic modification of the DIV model and therefore delivers isomorphic results. From here onwards, this model and its derivatives are referred to as earnings capitalization (CAP) models.

5.3.1 Basic model and assumptions

The first steps in the mathematical derivation are identical to the RIV model[696]. Starting point is again equation F 5-14:

$$\textbf{F 5-14} \quad V_s = y_s + \sum_{t=s+1}^{\infty} \frac{E_s\left[\tilde{D}_t\right] + y_t - \left(1+r^e\right) y_{t-1}}{\left(1+r^e\right)^{t-s}}$$

Instead of introducing the clean surplus relation and book values, y_t is now replaced by capitalized one-year forward expected earnings $E_s\left[\tilde{E}_t\right]/r^e$. Including $E_s\left[\tilde{E}_t\right]/r^e$ and rearranging F 5-14 leads to[697]:

694 See, e.g., Gode, D./Mohanram, P. (2003), pp. 400 and 426, Ohlson, J./Jüttner-Nauroth, B. (2005), pp. 350, fn. 2 and 353, and Koch, J. (2005), p. 130.

695 See Ohlson, J./Jüttner-Nauroth, B. (2005). See also Easton, P. (2004). An earlier and similar approach was presented by Fairfield, P. (1994), pp. 23-25 which however includes book values.

696 See Ohlson, J./Jüttner-Nauroth, B. (2005), pp. 351-352 and Ohlson, J. (2005), pp. 331-332. For a different derivation see Easton, P. (2004), pp. 78-79. See also the summaries by Daske, H./Wiesenbach, K. (2005), pp. 409-411, Koch, J. (2005), pp. 129-131, Ohlson, J./Goa, Z. (2006), pp. 8-12, Reese, R. (2007), pp. 72-73, and Easton, P. (2009), p. 270.

697 See Appendix 8 for the derivation.

$$\mathrm{V_s} = \frac{E_s\left[\tilde{\mathrm{E}}_{s+1}\right]}{\mathrm{r^e}} + \sum_{t=s+1}^{\infty} \frac{E_s\left[\tilde{\mathrm{D}}_t\right] + \frac{E_s\left[\tilde{\mathrm{E}}_{t+1}\right]}{\mathrm{r^e}} - \left(1+\mathrm{r^e}\right)\frac{E_s\left[\tilde{\mathrm{E}}_t\right]}{\mathrm{r^e}}}{\left(1+\mathrm{r^e}\right)^{t-s}}$$

F 5-30
$$= \frac{E_s\left[\tilde{\mathrm{E}}_{s+1}\right]}{\mathrm{r^e}} + \sum_{t=s+1}^{\infty} \frac{E_s\left[\tilde{\mathrm{E}}_{t+1}\right] + \mathrm{r^e} E_s\left[\tilde{\mathrm{D}}_t\right] - \left(1+\mathrm{r^e}\right) E_s\left[\tilde{\mathrm{E}}_t\right]}{\mathrm{r^e}\left(1+\mathrm{r^e}\right)^{t-s}}$$

$$= \frac{E_s\left[\tilde{\mathrm{E}}_{s+1}\right]}{\mathrm{r^e}} + \sum_{t=s+1}^{\infty} \frac{E_s\left[\mathrm{agr}_t\right]}{\mathrm{r^e}\left(1+\mathrm{r^e}\right)^{t-s}}$$

with $E_s\left[\mathrm{agr}_t\right] = E_s\left[\tilde{\mathrm{E}}_{t+1}\right] + \mathrm{r^e} E_s\left[\tilde{\mathrm{D}}_t\right] - \left(1+\mathrm{r^e}\right) E_s\left[\tilde{\mathrm{E}}_t\right] = E_s\left[\tilde{\mathrm{E}}_{t+1} - \tilde{\mathrm{E}}_t\right] + \mathrm{r^e} E_s\left[\tilde{\mathrm{D}}_t - \tilde{\mathrm{E}}_t\right]$

This equity valuation approach is intuitively appealing since it starts from the capitalized one-year forward expected earnings. However, it remains to be discussed as how to interpret the valuation premium—or more explicitly the "agr term"—added to the capitalized one-year forward earnings. Generally, one can think of agr as an adjustment factor for the expected abnormal growth in earnings beyond period $t+1$. Therefore, the agr term "builds in Modigliani-Miller dividend irrelevance by correcting for earnings foregone due to dividend payouts (...). Thus, instead of $E_s\left[\tilde{\mathrm{E}}_{t+1} - \tilde{\mathrm{E}}_t\right]$, the OJ [Ohlson/Jüttner-Nauroth] model uses $E_s\left[\tilde{\mathrm{E}}_{t+1} - \tilde{\mathrm{E}}_t\right] + \mathrm{r^e} E_s\left[\tilde{\mathrm{D}}_t - \tilde{\mathrm{E}}_t\right]$; i.e., the abnormal change in earnings is defined to be the change in earnings in excess of the return on the net investment during the period $\mathrm{r^e} E_s\left[\tilde{\mathrm{D}}_t - \tilde{\mathrm{E}}_t\right]$"[698]. This implies that with full dividend payout ($\theta = 1$), the abnormal change in earnings is simply equal to earnings growth $E_s\left[\tilde{\mathrm{E}}_{t+1} - \tilde{\mathrm{E}}_t\right]$.

Finally, note that the alike the versatility of the RIV model, the capitalized earnings approach also holds for all accounting principles without any requirement that expected earnings are truthfully accounted[699].

5.3.2 Terminal value considerations

Similarly to the previous models, the standard CAP model can be transformed into a multi-staged version including either a perpetuity or multiple driven terminal value term for empirical applications. However, as exemplified by the next section,

---

[698] Gode, D./Mohanram, P. (2003), p. 402. Note that symbols are adapted to the standard format of this dissertation.

[699] See Ohlson, J./Jüttner-Nauroth, B. (2005), pp. 352-353.

researchers have primarily implemented this model in a single-stage version. Formally, the multi-stage version of the CAP model can be derived as follows:

F 5-31

$$V_s = \frac{E_s\left[\tilde{E}_{s+1}\right]}{r^e} + \sum_{t=s+1}^{\infty} \frac{E_s\left[agr_t\right]}{r^e\left(1+r^e\right)^{t-s}} = \frac{E_s\left[\tilde{E}_{s+1}\right]}{r^e} + \sum_{t=s+1}^{T} \frac{E_s\left[agr_t\right]}{r^e\left(1+r^e\right)^{t-s}} - \frac{E_s\left[\tilde{E}_T\right]}{r^e\left(1+r^e\right)^{T-s}} + \frac{E_s\left[\tilde{V}_T\right]}{\left(1+r^e\right)^{T-s}}$$

$$= \frac{E_s\left[\tilde{E}_{s+1}\right]}{r^e} + \sum_{t=s+1}^{T} \frac{E_s\left[agr_t\right]}{r^e\left(1+r^e\right)^{t-s}} + \frac{E_s\left[r^e\tilde{V}_T - \tilde{E}_T\right]}{r^e\left(1+r^e\right)^{T-s}}$$

Applying the terminal perpetuity approach, the following expression can be derived assuming constant perpetual growth rate of the agr term[700]:

F 5-32

$$V_s = \frac{E_s\left[\tilde{E}_{s+1}\right]}{r^e} + \sum_{t=s+1}^{T} \frac{E_s\left[agr_t\right]}{r^e\left(1+r^e\right)^{t-s}} - \frac{E_s\left[\tilde{E}_T\right]}{r^e\left(1+r^e\right)^{T-s}} + \frac{E_s\left[\tilde{E}_T\right]}{r^e\left(1+r^e\right)^{T-s}} + \frac{E_s\left[agr_T\right]\left(1+g_{agr}\right)}{r^e\left(r^e-g_{agr}\right)\left(1+r^e\right)^{T-s}}$$

$$= \frac{E_s\left[\tilde{E}_{s+1}\right]}{r^e} + \sum_{t=s+1}^{T} \frac{E_s\left[agr_t\right]}{r^e\left(1+r^e\right)^{t-s}} + \frac{E_s\left[agr_T\right]\left(1+g_{agr}\right)}{r^e\left(r^e-g_{agr}\right)\left(1+r^e\right)^{T-s}}$$

Regarding the determination of the perpetual growth rate for the agr term, the same considerations apply as discussed for the RIV model since $g_{agr} = g_{RI}$ in case residual earnings growth is constant[701]. Furthermore, the CAP model delivers a consistent result if the return on book equity equals the cost of equity[702].

In the multi-stage terminal multiple form, the CAP model can be stated as follows using $E_s\left[\tilde{V}_T\right] = m_T^{E+1}\tilde{E}_{T+1}$:

F 5-33

$$V_s = \frac{E_s\left[\tilde{E}_{s+1}\right]}{r^e} + \sum_{t=s+1}^{T} \frac{E_s\left[agr_t\right]}{r^e\left(1+r^e\right)^{t-s}} + \frac{E_s\left[r^e m_T^{E+1}\tilde{E}_{T+1} - \tilde{E}_T\right]}{r^e\left(1+r^e\right)^{T-s}}$$

With respect to determining the appropriate level of the utilized multiple, it is again referred to Section 5.1.2.

---

700 See Ohlson, J./Jüttner-Nauroth, B. (2005), p. 354 and Easton, P. (2004), p. 79 for a model with an immediate terminal perpetuity.

701 See Section 5.4.

702 Note that the CAP model is consistent with the finding in F 5-5 that—provided the return on book equity is equal to the cost of equity and the payout ratio is constant—the formula reduces to capitalized earnings.

5.3.3 Models used in empirical research

As in the previous section, the most relevant applications of the CAP model in empirical studies on the expected MRP are outlined first followed by a summary of other empirical work at the end of this section[703].

5.3.3.1 Gode/Mohanram (2003)

As part of a larger study, Gode/Mohanram use the CAP model to estimate expected returns. Their model can be derived by inverting the one-period version of expression F 5-32. After substitutions, the equation can be solved for r^e [704]:

F 5-34

$$r^e = \frac{1}{2}\left(g_{agr} + \frac{E_s\left[\tilde{D}_{s+1}\right]}{P_s}\right) + \sqrt{\left[\frac{1}{2}\left(g_{agr} + \frac{E_s\left[\tilde{D}_{s+1}\right]}{P_s}\right)\right]^2 + \frac{E_s\left[\tilde{E}_{s+1}\right]}{P_s}\left(\frac{E_s\left[\tilde{E}_{s+2} - \tilde{E}_{s+1}\right]}{E_s\left[\tilde{E}_{s+1}\right]} - g_{agr}\right)}$$

$$\text{with } a = \frac{1}{2}\left(g_{agr} + \frac{E_s\left[\tilde{D}_{s+1}\right]}{P_s}\right) \text{ and } g_{st} = \frac{E_s\left[\tilde{E}_{s+2} - \tilde{E}_{s+1}\right]}{E_s\left[\tilde{E}_{s+1}\right]}$$

$$r^e = a + \sqrt{a^2 + \frac{E_s\left[\tilde{E}_{s+1}\right]}{P_s}\left(g_{st} - g_{agr}\right)}$$

Based on this expression, Gode/Mohanram conduct their analysis. Further modifications and other specifications of their approach are summarized in the following table:

Model specifications	• Short-term growth determined as the average of the two-year growth rate and the long-term growth rate. Gode/Mohanram provide the following reasoning: "First, we do not want to throw away an important piece of data regarding the five-year growth expectations. Second, when eps2/eps1 is inordinately large because of artificially low eps1, such averaging provides more reasonable estimates of the short-term growth"[705]. $$g_{st} = \frac{E_s\left[\tilde{E}_{s+2} - \tilde{E}_{s+1}\right] / E_s\left[\tilde{E}_{s+1}\right] + g_{LTG}^{IBES}}{2}$$

[703] For a review of selected models used in empirical studies see also Easton, P. (2009), pp. 275-279 and 291-297.

[704] See also Ohlson, J./Jüttner-Nauroth, B. (2005), pp. 358-360.

[705] Gode, D./Mohanram, P. (2003), p. 408.

Terminal value	• Perpetual growth rate for abnormal earnings term equal to long-term growth assumption of Claus/Thomas
Data	• US market • Period: 1984-1998 • Sample selection criteria: – At least five analyst forecasts – Market cap at least USD 100m – Return data in CRSP and accounting data in Compustat available – EPS+1 and EPS+2 >0 – Long-term growth rate of IBES available • Future dividends based on the most recent historical payout ratio (share repurchases are excluded; range of payout ratio limited to 0 to 1, negative earnings replaced by 6% times total assets) • r^e is calculated for each year at the end of June using: – 30 June stock price and earnings forecasts • Risk-free rate: 10-year treasury bond rate
Averaging methodology	• Firm-level analysis - Averaging method undefined (appears to be equal-weighting)

5.3.3.2 Easton (2004)

Similarly to the RIV model, Easton developed an approach to circumvent the problem of determining an appropriate perpetual growth rate by establishing a linear regression model to simultaneously estimate expected return and perpetual growth. Starting with the standard CAP model, introducing the intercept α and slope coefficient β, and re-arranging yields a linear relationship between $E_s\left[\tilde{E}^c_{s+2}\right]/P_s$ and $E_s\left[\tilde{E}_{s+1}\right]/P_s$ [706]:

$$P_s = \frac{E_s\left[\tilde{E}_{s+1}\right]}{r^e} + \frac{E_s\left[\tilde{E}_{s+2} - \tilde{E}_{s+1}\right] - r^e E_s\left[\tilde{E}_{s+1} - \tilde{D}_{s+1}\right]}{r^e\left(r^e - g_{agr}\right)}$$

F 5-35 with $E_s\left[\tilde{E}^c_{s+2}\right] = E_s\left[\tilde{E}_{s+2}\right] + r^e E_s\left[\tilde{D}_{s+1}\right]$, $\alpha = r^e_{agr}\left(r^e_{agr} - g_{agr}\right)$ and $\beta = \left(1 + g_{agr}\right)$

$$\frac{E_s\left[\tilde{E}^c_{s+2}\right]}{P_s} = \alpha + \beta \frac{E_s\left[\tilde{E}_{s+1}\right]}{P_s}$$

[706] See Easton, P. (2004), pp. 81-82.

The expected return and perpetual abnormal growth can now be estimated based on the coefficients[707] from linearly regressing $E_s\left[\tilde{E}^c_{s+2}\right]/P_s$ on $E_s\left[\tilde{E}_{s+1}\right]/P_s$ for a portfolio of firms $j=1,\ldots,J$:

F 5-36 $$\frac{E_s\left[\tilde{E}^c_{j,s+2}\right]}{P_{j,s}}=\hat{\alpha}+\hat{\beta}\frac{E_s\left[\tilde{E}_{j,s+1}\right]}{P_{j,s}}+\hat{\varepsilon}_j$$

It again follows that estimates of r^e and g_{agr} implied by this regression are equally weighted averages of the underlying portfolio (i.e., the market portfolio).

In addition to the simultaneous estimation approach, Easton also determines the expected MRP based on three special cases of the standard CAP model. Firstly, consider the special case $g_{agr}=0$. This means that next period's abnormal growth in earnings provides the appropriate estimate of all future period's abnormal earnings growth and is therefore assumed to remain constant until infinity. Expression F 5-32 may now be rewritten in the following one-period form[708]:

F 5-37 $$P_s=\frac{E_s\left[\tilde{E}_{s+2}-\tilde{E}_{s+1}\right]+r^e_{MPEG}E_s\left[\tilde{D}_{s+1}\right]}{{r^e_{MPEG}}^2}$$

Expected earnings are constrained to $E_s\left[\tilde{E}_{s+2}\right]>E_s\left[\tilde{E}_{s+1}\right]>0$ so that the solution for F 5-37 has two real roots of which only one is meaningful and positive.

For the second special case, expected one-year forward dividends are assumed to be zero $E_s\left[\tilde{D}_{s+1}\right]=0$ in addition to the prior assumption $g_{agr}=0$. Now F 5-37 can be further simplified[709]

F 5-38 $$r^e_{PEG}=\sqrt{\frac{E_s\left[\tilde{E}_{s+2}-\tilde{E}_{s+1}\right]}{P_s}}=\sqrt{\frac{E_s\left[\tilde{E}_{s+2}-\tilde{E}_{s+1}\right]/E_s\left[\tilde{E}_{s+1}\right]}{PE}}=\sqrt{\frac{1}{PEG*100}}$$

---

707 Easton (2004) again finds that the error term is heteroskedastic requiring robust standard errors in order to test the significance of coefficients; see Easton, P. (2004), p. 82, fn. 21.

708 See Easton, P. (2004), p. 80.

709 See Easton, P. (2004), p. 81.

where the right-hand side represents the square root of the inverse of the PEG ratio[710] multiplied by 100.

In a third special case, the adjustment term for the future abnormal development in earnings growth is assumed to be zero ($E_s\left[\text{agr}_{s+1}\right]=0$). Now the cost of equity reduces to the one-year forward price/earnings ratio[711]:

F 5-39 $$r_{PE}^{e}=\frac{E_s\left[\tilde{E}_{s+1}\right]}{P_s}$$

Other empirical specifications of the Easton analysis are summarized in the following table:

Data	• US market • Period: 1981-1999 • Sample selection criteria: – Firms only with fiscal year-end December – Compustat stock price, shares outstanding, and dividends – IBES one-year forward earnings forecast and a three-year growth rate (used to calculate earnings t+2 and growth in PEG ratio) • r^e and g are calculated for each year as of 31-Dec using: – Prices, shares outstanding, and dividends as of fiscal year-end 31-Dec – Earnings estimates as of the third Thursday in December • Risk-free rate: 10-year treasury bond rate
Averaging methodology	• The resulting expected MRP based on the regression analysis using individual firm-level data can be viewed as an equally weighted market-level expected MRP • Expected MRP estimates for other methods are medians

5.3.3.3 Summary of selected other studies

The methodologies used in other studies using the CAP model to estimate the expected MRP are summarized in Table 20.

710 The PEG ratio is a widely utilized measure in the financial community to adjust the standard price/earnings ratio for growth. Formally, the PEG ratio is defined as follows:

$$\text{PEG}=\frac{\text{PE}}{E_s\left[\tilde{E}_{s+2}-\tilde{E}_{s+1}\right]/E_s\left[\tilde{E}_{s+1}\right]*100}$$

See, e.g., Damodaran, A. (2002), p. 462.

711 See Easton, P. (2004), p. 81.

Table 20 Summary of additional CAP model-based studies to estimate the expected MRP

Authors	CAP model structure and inputs	Terminal value approach	Further analysis specifications
Botosan/Plumlee (2005)	• Gode/Mohanram and Easton (PEG) model • IBES estimates	• See mentioned reference model	• US market (1983-1993) • Risk-free rate based on 5-year treasury bonds • Estimates from third quarter (timing adjustment made[712] and foregone quarterly dividends reduced)
Easton/Monahan (2005)	• Gode/Mohanram and all three Easton models	• See mentioned reference model	• US market (1981-1998) • Equally weighted results
Guay/Kothari/Shu (2005)	• Gode/Mohanram model	• See mentioned reference model	• US market (1983-2004) • Estimation frequency and weighting-approach not specified
Koch (2005)	• Easton (PEG) model and specifications • IBES estimates	• See mentioned reference model	• EUROSTOXX 50 plus 17 additional firms (1987-2002) • Estimation frequency and weighting-approach not specified • Risk-free rate based on one- and ten-year government bonds
Reese (2007)	• Gode/Mohanram and Easton (PEG) model and specifications • IBES estimates	• See mentioned reference model	• German market – CDAX (1989-2004) • Monthly estimation (however, implementation not specified) • Equal and value-weighted results • Risk-free rate based on 10-year sub-index of REX
Lee/Ng/ Swaminathan (2007)	• Gode/Mohanram and Easton-MPEG models	• See mentioned reference model	• Expected MRP estimates for the G-7 countries (1991-2000) • Monthly estimation • All returns US-Dollar denominated • Risk-free rate based on 10-year US government bonds

712 The timing adjustment for the discounting of dividends refers to reducing the discount year by the fraction of the year already past until the estimation date. Note that this assumes that all dividends are paid at the fiscal year-end which is not accurate for the following reason: Dividends are paid quarterly in the USA so that their duration is not a full-year.

5.4 Equivalence of equity valuation models in practical implementations

As already indicated in the introductory paragraph to this chapter, the equivalence of the aforementioned valuation methods in practical applications is debated[713]. In addition, various studies have been analyzing the accuracy of different valuation models in measuring market values, despite them being technically isomorphic[714]. In this section, it is shown that all three models are equivalent and deliver equivalent results in practical applications if the input data is consistent[715].

First, the formal preconditions for the equivalence of the DIV, RIV, and CAP model are reviewed. In order to derive the RIV and CAP model from the DIV model, certain assumptions were used that need to hold for the equivalence. While the validity of the clean surplus relation was only required for the RIV model[716], the mathematical derivation of both RIV and CAP model relies on an infinite sequence which requires estimation to infinity in order to maintain equivalence. This issue can be illustrated by adding F 5-2, the zero-sum expression, to the basic DIV model F 5-1 resulting in a general valuation equation. Any definition of y_t will result in an expression that is formally equivalent to the DIV model. However, recall that F 5-2 is only zero if $\{y_t\}_{t=s}^{\infty}$ is any sequence of numbers that satisfies the mild transversality condition $y_t/(1+r^e)^t \to 0$ as $t \to \infty$. Only under this condition, the general version of the valuation equation can be expressed as:

F 5-14 $$V_s = y_s + \sum_{t=s+1}^{\infty} \frac{E_s\left[\tilde{D}_t\right] + y_t - (1+r^e)\, y_{t-1}}{(1+r^e)^{t-s}}$$

If the sequence $\{y_t\}_{t=s}^{\infty}$ is only forecasted for a finite period, the equivalence of DIV, RIV, and CAP is not valid and F 5-14 must be rewritten as[717]:

F 5-40 $$V_s + \frac{y_T}{(1+r^e)^{T-s}} = y_s + \sum_{t=s+1}^{T} \frac{E_s\left[\tilde{D}_t\right] + y_t - (1+r^e)\, y_{t-1}}{(1+r^e)^{t-s}}$$

---

713 See Penman, S. (2001) and Lundhom, R./O'Keefe, T. (2001a,b).

714 See, e.g., Courteau, L./Kao, J./Richardson, G. (2001), Francis, J./Olsson, P./Oswald, D. (2000), Frankel, R./Lee, C. (1998), or Penman, S./Sougiannis, T. (1998).

715 See also Reese, R. (2007), pp. 77-89.

716 See also Lundhom, R./O'Keefe, T. (2001a), p. 332.

717 See, e.g., Brief, R./O'Hanlon, J./Peasnell, K. (2005), pp. 6-10 or Penman, S. (1998), p. 306.

This leads to the following modified relationship between the DIV model and the RIV/CAP models for a finite horizon analysis:

F 5-41

$$\sum_{t=s+1}^{T}\frac{E_s\left[\tilde{D}_t\right]}{(1+r^e)^{t-s}} = B_s + \sum_{t=s+1}^{T}\frac{E_s\left[\tilde{E}_t - r^e\tilde{B}_{t-1}\right]}{(1+r^e)^{t-s}} - \frac{E_s\left[\tilde{B}_T\right]}{(1+r^e)^{T-s}}$$
$$= \frac{E_s\left[\tilde{E}_{s+1}\right]}{r^e} + \sum_{t=s+1}^{T}\frac{E_s\left[agr_t\right]}{r^e(1+r^e)^{t-s}} - \frac{E_s\left[\tilde{E}_T\right]}{r^e(1+r^e)^{T-s}}$$

In order to establish isomorphic results among the three models, it is irrelevant whether this estimation to infinity is made in an explicit form or through the introduction of a terminal value estimate as shown in F 5-42:

F 5-42

$$V_s = \sum_{t=s+1}^{\infty}\frac{E_s\left[\tilde{D}_t\right]}{(1+r^e)^{t-s}} = \sum_{t=s+1}^{T}\frac{E_s\left[\tilde{D}_t\right]}{(1+r^e)^{t-s}} + \frac{E_s\left[\tilde{V}_T\right]}{(1+r^e)^{T-s}}$$
$$= B_s + \sum_{t=s+1}^{\infty}\frac{E_s\left[\tilde{E}_t - r^e\tilde{B}_{t-1}\right]}{(1+r^e)^{t-s}} = B_s + \sum_{t=s+1}^{T}\frac{E_s\left[\tilde{E}_t - r^e\tilde{B}_{t-1}\right]}{(1+r^e)^{t-s}} - \frac{E_s\left[\tilde{B}_T\right]}{(1+r^e)^{T-s}} + \frac{E_s\left[\tilde{V}_T\right]}{(1+r^e)^{T-s}}$$
$$= B_s + \sum_{t=s+1}^{T}\frac{E_s\left[\tilde{E}_t - r^e\tilde{B}_{t-1}\right]}{(1+r^e)^{t-s}} + \frac{E_s\left[\tilde{V}_T - \tilde{B}_T\right]}{(1+r^e)^{T-s}}$$
$$= \frac{E_s\left[\tilde{E}_{s+1}\right]}{r^e} + \sum_{t=s+1}^{\infty}\frac{E_s\left[agr_t\right]}{r^e(1+r^e)^{t-s}} = \frac{E_s\left[\tilde{E}_{s+1}\right]}{r^e} + \sum_{t=s+1}^{T}\frac{E_s\left[agr_t\right]}{r^e(1+r^e)^{t-s}} - \frac{E_s\left[\tilde{E}_T\right]}{r^e(1+r^e)^{T-s}} + \frac{E_s\left[\tilde{V}_T\right]}{(1+r^e)^{T-s}}$$
$$= \frac{E_s\left[\tilde{E}_{s+1}\right]}{r^e} + \sum_{t=s+1}^{T}\frac{E_s\left[agr_t\right]}{r^e(1+r^e)^{t-s}} + \frac{E_s\left[r^e\tilde{V}_T - \tilde{E}_T\right]}{r^e(1+r^e)^{T-s}}$$

In practical implementations the terminal value estimate $E_s\left[\tilde{V}_T\right]$ is usually determined either by a constant growth perpetuity or a terminal multiple.

In the terminal multiple case, the equivalence among the valuation models becomes directly obvious by replacing $E_s\left[\tilde{V}_T\right]$ with, e.g., the one-year forward price-earnings ratio multiplied with terminal-period expected earnings $E_s\left[\tilde{E}_{T+1}\right]m_T^{E+1}$.

If the terminal value is calculated as a perpetuity assuming constant perpetual growth of the respective valuation attribute—i.e., dividends, residual earnings, or abnormal growth terms (agr)—the discussion of the equivalence is more complex.

Firstly, the formal relationships are presented if a perpetuity is attached to the truncated finite horizon DIV, RIV, and CAP model[718]:

F 5-43
$$\frac{E_s\left[\tilde{D}_T\right](1+g_D)}{(r^e-g_D)(1+r^e)^{T-s}}=\frac{E_s\left[\tilde{B}_T\right]}{(1+r^e)^{T-s}}+\frac{E_s\left[\tilde{E}_T-r^e\tilde{B}_{T-1}\right](1+g_{RI})}{(r^e-g_{RI})(1+r^e)^{T-s}}$$
$$=\frac{E_s\left[\tilde{E}_T\right]}{r^e(1+r^e)^{T-s}}+\frac{E_s\left[agr_T\right](1+g_{agr})}{r^e(r^e-g_{agr})(1+r^e)^{T-s}}$$

The full equivalent valuation equations of the DIV, RIV, and CAP model using perpetuities then read as follows:

$$V_s=\sum_{t=s+1}^{T}\frac{E_s\left[\tilde{D}_t\right]}{(1+r^e)^{t-s}}+\frac{E_s\left[\tilde{D}_T\right](1+g_D)}{(r^e-g_D)(1+r^e)^{T-s}}$$
$$=B_s+\sum_{t=s+1}^{T}\frac{E_s\left[\tilde{E}_t-r^e\tilde{B}_{t-1}\right]}{(1+r^e)^{t-s}}-\frac{E_s\left[\tilde{B}_T\right]}{(1+r^e)^{T-s}}+\frac{E_s\left[\tilde{B}_T\right]}{(1+r^e)^{T-s}}+\frac{E_s\left[\tilde{E}_T-r^e\tilde{B}_{T-1}\right](1+g_{RI})}{(r^e-g_{RI})(1+r^e)^{T-s}}$$

F 5-44
$$=B_s+\sum_{t=s+1}^{T}\frac{E_s\left[\tilde{E}_t-r^e\tilde{B}_{t-1}\right]}{(1+r^e)^{t-s}}+\frac{E_s\left[\tilde{E}_T-r^e\tilde{B}_{T-1}\right](1+g_{RI})}{(r^e-g_{RI})(1+r^e)^{T-s}}$$
$$=\frac{E_s\left[\tilde{E}_{s+1}\right]}{r^e}+\sum_{t=s+1}^{T}\frac{E_s\left[agr_t\right]}{r^e(1+r^e)^{t-s}}-\frac{E_s\left[\tilde{E}_T\right]}{r^e(1+r^e)^{T-s}}+\frac{E_s\left[\tilde{E}_T\right]}{r^e(1+r^e)^{T-s}}+\frac{E_s\left[agr_T\right](1+g_{agr})}{r^e(r^e-g_{agr})(1+r^e)^{T-s}}$$
$$=\frac{E_s\left[\tilde{E}_{s+1}\right]}{r^e}+\sum_{t=s+1}^{T}\frac{E_s\left[agr_t\right]}{r^e(1+r^e)^{t-s}}+\frac{E_s\left[agr_T\right](1+g_{agr})}{r^e(r^e-g_{agr})(1+r^e)^{T-s}}$$

Secondly, notice an often neglected aspect. For F 5-13 to hold, the estimation must not only be made for an infinite period but also the post-horizontal growth of the respective definition of y_t —book value or earnings—must not be equal to or asymptote r^e[719]. Under a scenario, where the growth rate of y_t (g_y) is equal to r^e, the sum in F 5-13 is no more equal to zero[720]:

[718] See, e.g., Olsson, R. (2005), pp. 12-13.

[719] See Brief, R./O'Hanlon, J./Peasnell, K. (2005), pp. 4 and 8-9. The authors provide also an example of g_y asymptoting r^e. Compared to F 5-45, $y_\infty/(1+r^e)^\infty > y_0$ if g_y asymptotes r^e.

[720] Note that for the remainder of this section, expectation operators and random variable signs are intentionally neglected.

$$y_0 + \sum_{s=1}^{\infty} \frac{y_s - (1+r^e) y_{s-1}}{(1+r^e)^s} = \frac{y_\infty}{(1+r^e)^\infty} = 0$$

F 5-45 with $g_y = r^e$

$$y_0 + \sum_{s=1}^{\infty} \frac{(1+r^e) y_{s-1} - (1+r^e) y_{s-1}}{(1+r^e)^s} = \frac{y_\infty}{(1+r^e)^\infty} = y_0$$

The key question is now, under which conditions the growth rate of y_t for the RIV and CAP model equals or asymptotes r^e. It can be shown that y_t growth for the RIV and CAP model does not approach r^e if residual income growth[721] is constant below r^e [722] and the payout ratio is also constant in the range $0 < \theta \leq 1$ [723].

A special case within these boundaries is the steady state of a firm with all parameters performing homogeneous growth[724]. Given constant residual income growth, the steady state can be established if the constant payout ratio is calculated as follows[725]:

$$\frac{B_1}{B_0} = \frac{RI_1}{RI_0} = (1+g)$$

F 5-46 $$\frac{B_0 + E_1 - D_1}{B_0} = \frac{B_0 + E_1 - E_1\theta}{B_0} = (1+g)$$

$$\theta = \frac{E_t - (1+g) B_{t-1} + B_{t-1}}{E_t}$$

---

[721] The residual income perspective holds also true for the CAP model, since in case of constant growth in residual income the abnormal growth term (agr) of the CAP model grows at the identical constant rate (see Appendix 9). This guarantees that the growth of E_t / r^e or simplified E_t does not asymptote r^e and the same reasoning as for the RIV model can be applied.

[722] The restriction $g < r^e$ for the perpetuity usage as terminal value estimate has already been discussed in Section 5.1.1.

[723] See Brief, R./O'Hanlon, J./Peasnell, K. (2005), p. 12. Note that these assumptions are equivalent to the analysis of Olsson (2005) who provides formulas for the post-horizontal behavior of key parameters as presented in Appendix 6.
Note that in all other cases, at least theoretical equivalence among the models can still be created if the now non-zero $y_\infty / (1+r^e)^\infty$ term is incorporated in the valuation model.

[724] In this context, homogeneous growth means that all parameters relating to balance sheet and profit & loss statement are growing with the identical rate.

[725] Note that this approach to establish the steady state is similar to the concept proposed by Lundholm/O'Keefe; see Lundhom, R./O'Keefe, T. (2001a), p. 322.

Alternatively, if the payout ratio is fixed at its historical level, the constant growth rate of residual income to establish the steady state can be determined based on the following manner:

$$\frac{B_1}{B_0}=(1+g)$$

$$\frac{B_0+E_1-D_1}{B_0}=\frac{B_0+E_1(1-\theta)}{B_0}=(1+g)$$

$$(1+g)=\frac{B_0+((1+g)RI_0+r^eB_0)(1-\theta)}{B_0}$$

F 5-47 $$(1+g)=1+\frac{(1+g)RI_0+r^eB_0-(1+g)RI_0\theta-r^eB_0\theta}{B_0}$$

$$B_0g=(1+g)RI_0(1-\theta)+r^eB_0(1-\theta)$$

$$B_0g-RI_0(1-\theta)g-RI_0(1-\theta)=r^eB_0(1-\theta)$$

$$g(B_0-RI_0(1-\theta))=r^eB_0(1-\theta)+RI_0(1-\theta)$$

$$g=\frac{(1-\theta)(r^eB_0+RI_0)}{B_0-RI_0(1-\theta)}$$

Throughout this study, the growth rate of residual earnings is adjusted to establish the steady state, since it is more intuitive that a continuously rising growth rate of residual income at a constant payout ratio establishes at a certain level the steady state growth with a constant r^b compared to a sudden change in the payout ratio that also leads to a constant r^b disregarding the constant level of residual income growth. Table 21 summarizes the post-horizontal behavior of key parameters and the value equivalence of the DIV, RIV, and CAP model when a terminal perpetuity is used and residual income growth is within the defined boundaries[726].

---

[726] Based on the results by Brief, R./O'Hanlon, J./Peasnell, K. (2005), p. 12 and Olsson, R. (2005), pp. 5-13 (see Appendix 6). The results were verified using a tabulated procedure.

Table 21 Post-horizontal behavior and value equivalence of DIV, RIV, and CAP models using terminal perpetuities

	$g_{RI,agr} = 0 = \text{const.}$	$g_{RI,agr} = \text{steady state} = \text{const.}$	$-1 < g_{RI,agr} < 0$, $0 < g_{RI,agr} < r^e$ $g_{RI,agr} = \text{const.}$
$0 < \theta < 1$	Post-horizontal behavior: $r^b \rightarrow r^e$ $g_B \xrightarrow{\neq \text{const.}} (1-\theta) r^e$ $g_{E,D} \xrightarrow{= \text{const.}} (1-\theta) r^e$ Value equivalence: $P_s^{DIV} = P_s^{RIV} = P_s^{CAP}$	Post-horizontal behavior: $r^b \rightarrow \text{const.}$ $g_{B,E,D} \xrightarrow{= \text{const.}} (1-\theta) r^e$ Value equivalence: $P_s^{DIV} = P_s^{RIV} = P_s^{CAP}$	Post-horizontal behavior: $r^b \rightarrow r^e$ $g_{B,E,D} \xrightarrow{\neq \text{const.}} \max\left[(1-\theta) r^e ; g_{RI}\right]$ Value equivalence: $P_s^{DIV} \neq P_s^{RIV} = P_s^{CAP}$ due to non-constant growth of dividends
$\theta = 1$	Post-horizontal behavior: $r^b \rightarrow \text{const.}$ $g_{B,E,D} \xrightarrow{= \text{const.}} 0$ Value equivalence: $P_s^{DIV} = P_s^{RIV} = P_s^{CAP}$	Post-horizontal behavior: $r^b \rightarrow \text{const.}$ $g_{B,E,D} \xrightarrow{= \text{const.}} 0$ Value equivalence: $P_s^{DIV} = P_s^{RIV} = P_s^{CAP}$	Post-horizontal behavior: $r^b \rightarrow \infty$ $g_B \xrightarrow{= \text{const.}} 0$ $g_{E,D} \xrightarrow{\neq \text{const.}} g_{RI}$ Value equivalence: $P_s^{DIV} \neq P_s^{RIV} = P_s^{CAP}$ due to non-constant growth of dividends
$RI = 0$[727]	Post-horizontal behavior: $r^b \rightarrow \text{const.} = r^e$ $g_{B,E,D} \xrightarrow{= \text{const.}} (1-\theta) r^e$ Value equivalence: $P_s^{DIV} = P_s^{RIV} = P_s^{CAP}$	NA	NA

[727] It was already shown in the respective sections that $P_s^{DIV} = P_s^{RIV} = P_s^{CAP}$ since $E_{s+1}/r^e = B_s = E_{s+1}/r^e$ if $r^b = r^e$.

Table 21 shows that under two scenarios the equivalence among the valuation models using a terminal perpetuity is not holding due to the non-constant growth development of dividends which cannot be modeled through a terminal perpetuity. Under all other cases the included methods deliver isomorphic results.

In summary, the previous analysis showed that the DIV model delivers identical results compared to the RIV and CAP models if the models use an infinite horizon. While equivalence is already established when the infinite value is approximated through the terminal multiple approach, using a terminal perpetuity further requires that the post-horizontal growth of y_t—book value or earnings—must not be equal to or asymptote r^e. This is the case, when the constant perpetual residual income growth (equal to the perpetual growth of agr) is below r^e and the payout ratio is also constant in the range $0 < \theta \leq 1$. Finally, $g_{RI,agr}$ must be equal to zero[728] or in a steady state since otherwise the implied perpetual dividend growth is not constant and cannot be captured by the perpetuity concept.

A final conceptual aspect in this section refers to a commonly conducted mistake in the consistent practical implementation of the three models that consequently leads to differing results using terminal perpetuities even in the steady state [729]. Lundholm/O'Keefe call this mistake the "inconsistent forecast error" that occurs when the valuation attribute used as starting value in the terminal perpetuity is not consistent with the underlying financial statements of the forecast[730]. Dependent on the drivers of the forecasts—residual income growth and payout ratio in this discussion—D_{TV} may not be equal to $(1+g)D_{TV-1}$ as the dividend stream implied by the selected drivers behaves differently. To illustrate this issue, Table 22 provides a coherent financial statement forecast for the simplified case of steady state growth driven by residual income growth and the payout ratio[731].

---

[728] Note that Reese, R. (2007), p. 85 mistakenly argues that equivalence is only possible in the steady state case. This is not correct since equivalence can also be achieved if $g_{RI,agr} = 0$.

[729] Note that the same issue also applies to the case with $g_{RI,agr} = 0$.

[730] See Lundhom, R./O'Keefe, T. (2001a), p. 328. Note further that Lundholm/O'Keefe identify two further mistakes frequently committed in practical implementation of valuation models. The "missing cash flow error" is mainly related to violations of the already discussed clean surplus relation. Finally, the "incorrect discount error" only occurs in comparison to entity valuation models which are excluded from this study; see Lundhom, R./O'Keefe, T. (2001a), p. 316. See also the similar but less formal discussion in Reese, R. (2007), pp. 79-85.

[731] See Reese, R. (2007), p. 81 for a similar but non-abstract example.

Table 22 Coherent financial statement forecast during steady state growth

Case 1: Steady state from TV-2 onwards

	TV-2	TV-1	TV	TV+1
Residual income		RI_{TV-1}	$RI_{TV} =$ $(1+g)RI_{TV-1}$	$RI_{TV+1} =$ $(1+g)^2 RI_{TV-1}$
Payout ratio		θ	θ	θ
Earnings		$E_{TV-1} =$ $RI_{TV-1} + r^e B_{TV-2}$	$E_{TV} =$ $RI_{TV} + r^e B_{TV-1} =$ $(1+g)[RI_{TV-1} + r^e B_{TV-2}]$	$E_{TV+1} =$ $RI_{TV+1} + r^e B_{TV} =$ $(1+g)^2 [RI_{TV-1} + r^e B_{TV-2}]$
Dividends		$D_{TV-1} =$ $E_{TV-1}\theta =$ $(RI_{TV-1} + r^e B_{TV-2})\theta$	$D_{TV} =$ $E_{TV}\theta =$ $(1+g)[(RI_{TV-1} + r^e B_{TV-2})\theta]$	$D_{TV+1} =$ $E_{TV+1}\theta =$ $(1+g)^2[(RI_{TV-1} + r^e B_{TV-2})\theta]$
Book value of equity	B_{TV-2}	$B_{TV-1} =$ $B_{TV-2} + E_{TV-1} - D_{TV-1} =$ $B_{TV-2} + (RI_{TV-1} + r^e B_{TV-2})(1-\theta) =$ [732] $B_{TV-2}(1+g)$	$B_{TV} =$ $B_{TV-1} + E_{TV} - D_{TV} =$ $(1+g)^2 B_{TV-2}$	$B_{TV+1} =$ $B_{TV} + E_{TV+1} - D_{TV+1} =$ $(1+g)^3 B_{TV-2}$
Abnormal growth term (agr)		$agr_{TV-1} =$ $E_{TV} - E_{TV-1} + r^e(D_{TV-1} - E_{TV-1}) =$ [732] $RI_{TV-1}g$	$agr_{TV} =$ $E_{TV+1} - E_{TV} + r^e(D_{TV} - E_{TV}) =$ $(1+g)RI_{TV-1}g$	$agr_{TV+1} =$ $E_{TV+2} - E_{TV+1} + r^e(D_{TV+1} - E_{TV+1}) =$ $(1+g)^2 RI_{TV-1}g$

[732] See Appendix 9 for a derivation.

Case 2: Steady state from TV-1 onwards

	TV-2	TV-1	TV	TV+1
Residual Income		RI_{TV-1}	$RI_{TV} =$ $(1+g)\ RI_{TV-1}$	$RI_{TV+1} =$ $(1+g)^2 RI_{TV-1}$
Payout ratio		θ_{TV-1}	θ_{TV}	θ_{TV}
Earnings		$E_{TV-1} =$ $RI_{TV-1} + r^e B_{TV-2}$	$E_{TV} =$ $RI_{TV} + r^e B_{TV-1} =$ $(1+g) RI_{TV-1} + r^e B_{TV-1}$	$E_{TV+1} =$ $RI_{TV+1} + r^e B_{TV} =$ $(1+g)\left[(1+g) RI_{TV-1} + r^e B_{TV-1}\right]$
Dividends		$D_{TV-1} =$ $E_{TV-1}\theta_{TV-1} =$ $\left(RI_{TV-1} + r^e B_{TV-2}\right)\theta_{TV-1}$	$D_{TV} =$ $E_{TV}\theta_{TV} =$ $\left((1+g) RI_{TV-1} + r^e B_{TV-1}\right)\theta_{TV}$	$D_{TV+1} =$ $E_{TV+1}\theta_{TV} =$ $(1+g)\left[\left((1+g) RI_{TV-1} + r^e B_{TV-1}\right)\theta_{TV}\right]$
Book value of equity	B_{TV-2}	B_{TV-1}	$B_{TV} =$ $B_{TV-1} + E_{TV} - D_{TV} =$ [732] $(1+g) B_{TV-1}$	$B_{TV+1} =$ $B_{TV} + E_{TV+1} - D_{TV+1} =$ $(1+g)^2 B_{TV-1}$
Abnormal growth term (agr)		$agr_{TV-1} =$ $E_{TV} - E_{TV-1} + r^e\left(D_{TV-1} - E_{TV-1}\right) =$ [733] $RI_{TV-1} g$	$agr_{TV} =$ $E_{TV+1} - E_{TV} + r^e\left(D_{TV} - E_{TV}\right) =$ $(1+g) RI_{TV-1} g$	$agr_{TV+1} =$ $E_{TV+2} - E_{TV+1} + r^e\left(D_{TV+1} - E_{TV+1}\right) =$ $(1+g)^2 RI_{TV-1} g$

[733] See Appendix 9 for a derivation.

This formal analysis demonstrates that D_{TV} is only equal to $(1+g)D_{TV-1}=(1+g)\left[(RI_{TV-1}+r^eB_{TV-2})\theta\right]$ if steady state growth is already reached in TV-1. However, most implementations of a terminal perpetuity assume the steady state—or more generally the constant growth stage—to be reached with the beginning the terminal value period (TV). In this scenario, D_{TV} is equal to $((1+g)RI_{TV-1}+r^eB_{TV-1})\theta \neq (1+g)D_{TV-1}=(1+g)\left[(RI_{TV-1}+r^eB_{TV-2})\theta\right]$. Therefore, applying the frequently used starting value of $D_{TV}=(1+g)D_{TV-1}$ for the terminal perpetuity will lead to a systematic valuation difference between the DIV model and the RIV and CAP models. In order to establish equivalence among the valuation models D_{TV} needs to be calculated as $((1+g)RI_{TV-1}+r^eB_{TV-1})\theta$ which is the consistent value of D_{TV} implied by the other parameters[734]. Also note that the equivalence between RIV and CAP model cannot be impacted by the inconsistent forecast error, since the growth of residual earnings is under all defined states equal to the growth rate of agr. For the steady state case, Lundholm/O'Keefe conclude on this issue as follows: "Because the financial forecasts provide a unique expression of beliefs about what will happen in the future, all valuation models computed using these forecasts as inputs will be internally consistent and yield identical estimates"[735].

The exhaustive preceding discussion raises the question why different equity valuation techniques are used if they fundamentally deliver isomorphic results within technical boundaries. Lundholm/O'Keefe raise the same issue and thereby question the validity of research investigating the accuracy of different valuation techniques and in particular the potential superiority of the residual income model[736]. Penman strongly disagrees with this argument claiming that the truncation of the explicit forecast horizon due to bounded rationality provides the rationale for alternative valuation models to pure dividend discounting[737]. Acknowledging the technical

---

[734] See the example in Section 5.8 for an illustration of this case. See also Lundhom, R./O'Keefe, T. (2001a), pp. 328-330 and Reese, R. (2007), pp. 84-85 for other numerical examples.

[735] Lundhom, R./O'Keefe, T. (2001a), p. 328.

[736] See, e.g., Courteau, L./Kao, J./Richardson, G. (2001), Francis, J./Olsson, P./Oswald, D. (2000), Frankel, R./Lee, C. (1998), or Penman, S./Sougiannis, T. (1998).

[737] See Penman, S. (2001), p. 684.

correctness of the Lundholm/O'Keefe argument, Penman criticizes that it only holds under the steady state conditions[738] and for payout ratios greater than zero.

Besides the technical aspects of the debate, the core element of disagreement appears to be more fundamental. In order to categorize the apparently irreconcilable views of Penman and Lundholm/O'Keefe, Lobe introduces the concept of "exact vs. approximate" terminal values. Up to now, the discussion always presumed that there are precise expectations on the future financial development that find application in the finite explicit forecast period and—in a simplified form—in defining the input parameters for the terminal value approach. Leaving theoretical restrictions aside, under such circumstances, all equity valuation models must deliver equal results and we are in the world of exact terminal values which is the home of Lundholm/O'Keefe. However, in a practically not uncommon scenario, where there are—for whatever reason—no or only incomplete expectations on the future financial development beyond the finite horizon, the consistent determination of the valuation attribute for the terminal perpetuity underlying the dividend discount, residual income, and earnings capitalization model is not possible. Now, "[t]he practical issue is what accounting—cash accounting in discounted cash flow [including dividend discount models] or accrual accounting in so-called residual income models—best provides a base to which (...) a growth rate can be applied. If I forecast residual income for five years and then apply a 3 percent growth rate, for example, am I better served by that than by forecasting cash flows for five years and applying a growth rate?"[739]. Here, we are in the Penman world of approximate or ad-hoc terminal values where the superior equity valuation model as well as the terminal value inputs are selected on the basis of empirical evidence but by no precise theory.[740]

Based on the preceding discussion, the used equity valuation models are now specified together with the terminal value techniques used for the estimation of the expected MRP throughout this dissertation.

---

[738] The presented analysis showed that in fact equivalence can also be achieved if $g_{RI,agr} = 0$.

[739] Penman, S. (2001), p. 685.

[740] See Lobe, S. (2006), pp. 105 and 111-115. See also Lambert, R. (2009), p. 268.

5.5 Description of utilized models for estimating the expected MRP

As it was shown in the preceding section, the three mentioned equity valuation models deliver isomorphic results either if terminal multiples are used for the post-horizontal valuation or within certain restrictions when a constant growth perpetuity of the respective valuation attribute is applied as terminal value. The key limitations of the perpetuity case were identified to be a constant growth rate of residual income below r^e and a payout ratio also constant in the range $0 < \theta \leq 1$. Additionally, the consistent usage of one set of pro forma financial forecasts is required to eliminate a potential inconsistent forecast error. Remaining differences under this set of restrictions only occur when certain valuation attributes—e.g., dividends—follow a non-constant growth path and can therefore not be valued by a perpetuity. However, the theoretical value of an infinite explicit forecast period is still identical.

Based on these findings, results throughout this study are primarily calculated using the residual income valuation model with different terminal value scenarios of (1) a terminal perpetuity and (2) a terminal multiple. In order to proof the practical equivalence among the three equity valuation models, the following section will provide a calculation example which determines the expected MRP based on all three approaches and demonstrates identical results. Thereafter, all results are shown for the residual income model only. However, in order to establish comparability with previous studies using models with specific modifications to the standard model, results are also provided for non-residual income based models—e.g., for the CAP versions of Gode/Mohanram (2002) and Easton (2004).

Before presenting the variations of the residual income model with terminal perpetuity or multiple, one issue needs some further consideration. As the general research design of this analysis foresees a monthly estimation of expected returns, the annual model structure has to be modified to allow for intra-year implementation. The modification is critical, since—from a theoretical perspective—there is a systematic increase in stock prices throughout the dividend period due to the present value effect. The dividend period ranges from the ex-dividend date to the next dividend record date[741]. Due to the decreasing time-period to the next dividend payment date, the present value concept implies that the stock value—for illustrative purposes based on the DIV model—increases ceteris paribus[742] from the ex-dividend date to the next dividend record date one period later by the expected rate of return. On the following dividend ex-date the value of the stock is consequently expected to decline ceteris paribus by the value of the dividend payment. Formally, this can be shown as follows:

$$P_s^{\text{ex-dividend date}} = \frac{E_s\left[\tilde{D}_{s+1}\right]}{\left(1+r^e\right)} + \frac{E_s\left[\tilde{D}_{s+2}\right]}{\left(r^e - g_D\right)\left(1+r^e\right)}$$

F 5-48
$$P_{s+d}^{\text{intra dividend year}} = \left\{\frac{E_{s+d}\left[\tilde{D}_{s+1}\right]}{\left(1+r^e\right)} + \frac{E_{s+d}\left[\tilde{D}_{s+2}\right]}{\left(r^e - g_D\right)\left(1+r^e\right)}\right\}\left(1+r^e\right)^d$$

$$= \frac{E_{s+d}\left[\tilde{D}_{s+1}\right]}{\left(1+r^e\right)^{1-d}} + \frac{E_{s+d}\left[\tilde{D}_{s+2}\right]}{\left(r^e - g_D\right)\left(1+r^e\right)^{1-d}}$$

with d equal to the fraction of the period already past

F 5-49
$$P_{s+1}^{\text{dividend record date}} = E_{s+1}\left[\tilde{D}_{s+1}\right] + \frac{E_{s+1}\left[\tilde{D}_{s+2}\right]}{r^e - g_D}$$

$$P_{s+1}^{\text{ex-dividend date}} = \frac{E_{s+1}\left[\tilde{D}_{s+2}\right]}{r^e - g_D}$$

These relationships imply:

F 5-50
$$\tilde{P}_s^{\text{ex-dividend date}}\left(1+r^e\right) = \tilde{P}_{s+1}^{\text{dividend record date}}$$

$$\tilde{P}_{s+1}^{\text{ex-dividend date}} = \tilde{P}_{s+1}^{\text{dividend record date}} - E_{s+1}\left[\tilde{D}_{s+1}\right]$$

---

[741] Note that following the dividend declaration by the Board of Directors or following the approval by the AGM, a dividend record day is set which determines the list of stockholders entitled to receive the upcoming dividend payment. Until that day, the stock trades including the dividend entitlement for the period which is called cum-dividend. The day following the fixing of the dividend recipients list is called ex-dividend date because buyers of the stock from this date onwards are not entitled to receive the shortly upcoming dividend payment. Therefore the stock is said to trade ex-dividend; see Ross, S./Westerfield, R./Jaffe, J. (2008), pp. 511-512 and Brealey, R./Myers, S./Allen, F. (2008), pp. 444-445.

[742] The ceteris paribus condition implies that this particular result only holds true if expected dividends, growth, and return remain unchanged.

This discussion implies that s has to be defined as the sample ex-dividend date and that for the intra dividend period estimations an adjusted starting base for discounting $(s+d)$ has to be used to avoid a present value bias.

There are two important remarks necessary vis-à-vis the RIV approach presented by Daske/Gebhardt/Klein (2006). Firstly, the authors were the first to include the systematic intra-year movements of the stock price in the monthly estimation of the expected MRP. However, their empirically more complex approach using intra-year book values and a stub period[743] to adjust for the time past since the ex-dividend date is identical to the much simpler approach of trite compounding of full year values presented in this study[744]. Secondly, the issue of compounding future residual income to the appropriate point in time when market valuations are put into relation with the intrinsic value from the RIV model needs to be addressed. The appropriate starting point for all valuation considerations that by origin relate to the DIV model is the ex-dividend day and not the fiscal year-end as implied by the Daske/Gebhardt/Klein approach. Since this issue is mainly related to the data input structure of utilized databases, the reader is referred to the time-matching Section 5.7.3 for a more detailed discussion of problems related to setting the discounting reference date.

Including this modification, the standard residual income model with a five-period explicit forecast period and a terminal perpetuity is introduced:

F 5-51 $$P_{s+d}=\left\{B_s+\sum_{t=s+1}^{s+5}\frac{E_{s+d}\left[\tilde{E}_t-r^e\tilde{B}_{t-1}\right]}{\left(1+r^e\right)^{t-s}}+\frac{E_{s+d}\left[\tilde{E}_{s+5}-r^e\tilde{B}_{s+4}\right]\left(1+g_{RI}\right)}{\left(r^e-g_{RI}\right)\left(1+r^e\right)^5}\right\}\left(1+r^e\right)^d$$

As already discussed, the key challenge of the terminal perpetuity approach is to determine the appropriate perpetual growth rate. This study uses a selection of the approaches used in precedent research in a continuum ranging between two cases forming the upper and lower bounds for the expected MRP estimation. Table 23 provides a summary of the four general input assumptions for the terminal perpetuity.

---

[743] See Daske, H./Gebhardt, G./Klein, S. (2006), pp. 6-12.
[744] See Appendix 10. See also Easton, P. (2009), pp. 355-356 for a similar approach.

Table 23 Continuum of input assumptions for the terminal perpetuity case

	Lower bound			Upper bound
	1.1 $r_T^b = r^e$	**1.2** $g_{RI} = 0$	**1.3** $g_{RI} = \text{ex-post inflation}$ [745] with $0 < g_{RI} < g_{RI}^{\text{steady state}}$	**1.4** $g_{RI} = g_{RI}^{\text{steady state}}$
Description	• Firm has no more projects delivering returns above the cost of capital at the end of the finite forecast period	• All new projects of the firm do not contribute positive value so that r^b is approaching r^e	• For a finite period there are some new projects contributing positive value so that r^b is slower approaching r^e	• The firm is in a steady state with equal constant growth of all P&L and balance sheet items including a constant r^b
RIV terminal value formula[746]	$E_s\left[\tilde{V}_T\right] = E_s\left[\tilde{B}_T\right]$	$E_s\left[\tilde{V}_T\right] = E_s\left[\tilde{B}_T\right] + \frac{E_s\left[\tilde{E}_T - r^e\tilde{B}_{T-1}\right]}{r^e}$	$E_s\left[\tilde{V}_T\right] = E_s\left[\tilde{B}_T\right] + \frac{E_s\left[\tilde{E}_T - r^e\tilde{B}_{T-1}\right](1+g_{RI})}{(r^e - g_{RI})}$	$E_s\left[\tilde{V}_T\right] = E_s\left[\tilde{B}_T\right] + \frac{E_s\left[\tilde{E}_T - r^e\tilde{B}_{T-1}\right](1+g_{RI})}{(r^e - g_{RI})}$
Implied post-horizon r^b behavior[747]	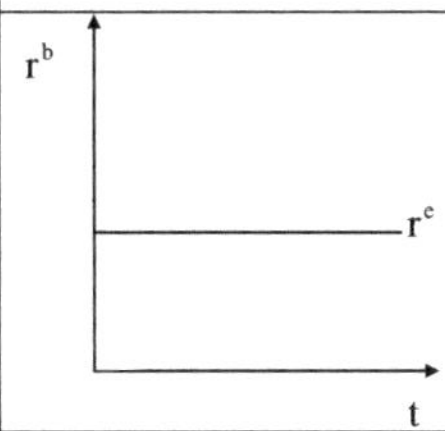	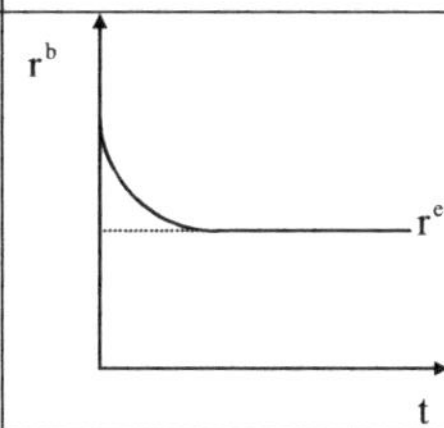	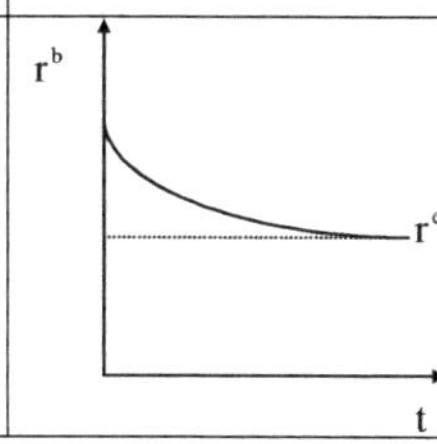	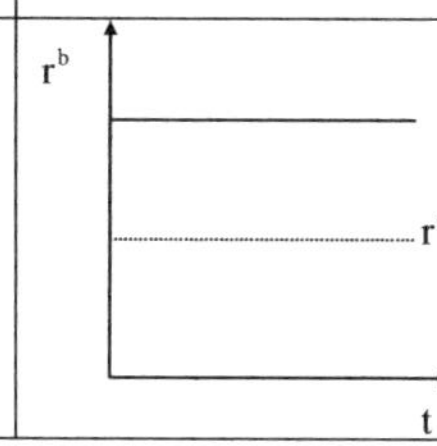

[745] Since direct expected inflation estimates from indexed bonds or swap markets are not available for all countries over the entire analysis period, the ex-post inflation rate implied by the cosumer price index until the estimation date is consistently used. See Section 5.14 for an analysis using swap market estimates.

[746] The here presented formulas neglect the intra-year discounting adjusting for simplicity purposes.

[747] The illustrative graphs assume a constant payout ratio.

As already mentioned, results are also provided for certain special cases of the standard continuum in order to derive comparable results with key previous research. Out of the range of comparison cases labeled 1.5, case 1.5.1 is identical to the two-stage model of Claus/Thomas (2001). Case 1.5.2 is based on the Gebhardt/Lee/Swaminathan (2001) model with a fade period to the target $\tilde{r}^b$ and zero post-horizontal residual income growth as shown in F 5-52:

F 5-52
$$P_{s+d} = \left\{ B_s + \sum_{t=s+1}^{s+5} \frac{E_{s+d}\left[\tilde{E}_t - r^e \tilde{B}_{t-1}\right]}{\left(1+r^e\right)^{t-s}} + \sum_{t=s+6}^{s+11} \frac{E_{s+d}\left[\left(\tilde{r}_t^b - r^e\right)\tilde{B}_{t-1}\right]}{\left(1+r^e\right)^{t-s}} + \frac{E_{s+d}\left[\left(\tilde{r}_{s+12}^b - r^e\right)\tilde{B}_{s+11}\right]}{r^e\left(1+r^e\right)^{11}} \right\} \left(1+r^e\right)^d$$

Finally, expected MRPs are calculated for certain one-period models similar to Gode/Mohanram (2002) and Easton (2004). Note that these models are included only for comparability purposes as the general validity of these models remains doubtful through their negligence of available forecast information beyond period one. The standard model can be expressed as follows in the RIV form:

F 5-53
$$P_{s+d} = \left\{ B_s + \frac{E_{s+d}\left[\tilde{E}_{s+1} - r^e B_s\right]\left(1+g_{RI}\right)}{\left(r^e - g_{RI}\right)} \right\} \left(1+r^e\right)^d$$

The one-period models 1.5.3, 1.5.4, and 1.5.5 together with the remaining comparison cases are summarized in Table 24.

Table 24 Summary of comparison cases based on previous models

	1.5.1 Two-stage model with inflation growth	1.5.2 Three-stage model with fading period to industry average r^b and no perpetual g_{RI}	1.5.3 One-period model with adjusted short-term earnings growth	1.5.4 One-period model similar to inverted PEG ratio	1.5.5 One-period model assuming $r_T^b = r_T^e$
Comparable model	• Claus/ Thomas (2001)[748]	• Gebhardt/Lee/ Swaminathan (2001)	• Gode/ Mohanram (2002)	• Easton (2004) – PEG version	• Easton (2004) – PE version
Valuation formula	• See F 5-51	• See F 5-52	• See F 5-34 with a specification regarding two-year forward earnings growth[749]	$P_{s+d} = \left\{ \frac{E_{s+d}\left[\tilde{E}_{s+2} - \tilde{E}_{s+1}\right]}{r^{e2}} \right\} (1+r^e)^d$ with $g_{agr} = 0$ and $E_s\left[\tilde{D}_{t+1}\right] = 0$	$P_{s+d} = \left\{ \frac{E_{s+d}\left[\tilde{E}_{s+1}\right]}{r^e} \right\} (1+r^e)^d$ with $g_{agr} = 0$ and $E_s\left[agr_{t+1}\right] = 0$

---

[748] Note that the standard version of the one-period RIV model with perpetual inflation growth is only exactly equal to the Claus/Thomas version of the one period dividend growth model if the firm is in a steady state at this growth level.

[749] Two-year forward earnings growth is flattened by including the long-term earnings growth rate in the calculation of two-year ahead expected earnings:

$$E_{s+d}\left[agr_{s+1}\right] = E_{s+d}\left[\tilde{E}_{s+2} - \tilde{E}_{s+1}\right] + r^e E_{s+d}\left[\tilde{D}_{s+1} - \tilde{E}_{s+1}\right]$$

with

$$E_{s+d}\left[\tilde{E}_{s+2}\right] = E_{s+d}\left[\tilde{E}_{s+1}\right]\left(1 + \frac{E_{s+d}\left[\tilde{g}_{IBES\,E+2}\right] + E_{s+d}\left[\tilde{g}_{IBES\,LTG}\right]}{2}\right)$$

Furthermore, the regression approach is implemented to simultaneously estimate the cost of equity and perpetual growth rate for the residual income model. Due to its relation to the terminal perpetuity methodology, it is referred to as approach 1.6. For the monthly estimation procedure, the approach proposed by Daske/Gebhardt/Klein[750] with the modification of using the ex-dividend day as discounting reference date is used. Recall that the regression model is based on the following linear relationship between $P_{i,s+d}/B_{i,s+d}$ and $E_s\left[\tilde{E}^c_{i,s+d}\right]/B_{i,s+d}$:

F 5-54 $$\frac{E_s\left[\tilde{E}^c_{i,s+d}\right]}{B_{i,s+d}} = \hat{\alpha} + \hat{\beta}\frac{P_{i,s+d}}{B_{i,s+d}} + \hat{\varepsilon}_i$$

with

$$E_{s+d}\left[\tilde{E}^c_{s+d}\right] = E_{s+d}\left[\tilde{E}_{s+(1-d)} + \tilde{E}_{s+2} + \tilde{E}_{s+3} + \tilde{E}_{s+4} + \tilde{E}_{s+4+d}\right] + E_{s+d}\left[\tilde{D}_{s+1}\right]\left[\left(1+r^e\right)^{3+d} - 1\right]$$
$$+ E_{s+d}\left[\tilde{D}_{s+2}\right]\left[\left(1+r^e\right)^{2+d} - 1\right] + E_{s+d}\left[\tilde{D}_{s+3}\right]\left[\left(1+r^e\right)^{1+d} - 1\right] + E_{s+d}\left[\tilde{D}_{s+1}\right]\left[\left(1+r^e\right)^{d} - 1\right]$$
$$E_{s+d}\left[\tilde{B}_{s+d}\right] = E_{s+d}\left[B_s\left(1+\tilde{r}^b_{s+1}\right)^d\right]$$

and

$$\hat{\alpha} = \left(1+g\right)^4 - 1$$
$$\hat{\beta} = \left(1+r^e\right)^4 - \left(1+g_{RI}\right)^4$$

As shown before, the expected cost of equity and perpetual growth rate can be inferred from the estimated regression coefficients:

$$g_{RI} = \sqrt[4]{\alpha+1} - 1$$
$$r^e = \sqrt[4]{\beta + \left(1+g_{RI}\right)^4} - 1$$

After the terminal perpetuity models, the standard residual income model with a five-period explicit forecast period and a terminal multiple is introduced. The terminal multiple can be interpreted as the expected market price level at the end of the explicit forecast period. For this study, the terminal multiple is defined as the one-year forward price/earnings ratio:

F 5-55 $$m^{E+1}_s = \frac{P_s}{E_s\left[\tilde{E}_{s+1}\right]}$$

[750] See Section 5.2.4.

The RIV model using the terminal multiple technique modified for the daily discounting can now be expressed as follows:

$$\textbf{F 5-56}\quad P_{s+d} = \left\{ B_s + \sum_{t=s+1}^{s+4} \frac{E_{s+d}\left[\tilde{E}_t - r^e \tilde{B}_{t-1}\right]}{\left(1+r^e\right)^{t-s}} + \frac{E_{s+d}\left[\tilde{E}_{s+5} m_s^{E+1} - \tilde{B}_{s+4}\right]}{\left(1+r^e\right)^4} \right\} \left(1+r^e\right)^d$$

The choice of the one-year forward price/earnings ratio is based on empirical findings that earnings are the most accurate reference base when employing multiple valuation as presented by the summary of key studies in Table 25[751]. However, note that these studies did not test the accuracy of different terminal multiples but full period spot multiples.

Table 25 Summary of selected studies investigating the accuracy of reference parameters in multiple valuations

Authors	Sample data	Relevant findings on the most accurate reference parameter
LeClair (1990)	• 1,165 public US firms • 1984	• Estimation error lower when using two-year historical average earnings compared to current actual earnings as reference base
Alford (1992)	• 1,471 – 1,636 public US firms • 1978, 1982, and 1986	• No improvement in valuation accuracy through the usage of average historical and projected IBES earnings as compared to current actual earnings as reference metric
Kaplan/Ruback (1995)	• 51 LBO transactions • 1980 – 1989	• No superior reference parameter can be identified
Kim/Ritter (1999)	• 190 US IPOs • 1992 and 1993	• Usage of forecasted earnings substantially increases the valuation accuracy
Gilson/Hotchkiss/Ruback (2000)	• 63 formerly insolvent firms • 1984 – 1993	• For the usage of the entity-approach-based EBIT multiple, a substantial increase in valuation quality can be achieved by utilizing IBES estimates as reference parameter
Liu/Nissim/Thomas (2002)	• 1,100 public US firms • 1982 – 1999	• Primary focus on the valuation accuracy of different reference parameters such as historical sales, EBITDA, earnings, and book value of equity (additionally projected earnings are included in the analysis) • Forecasted earnings are identified as the most accurate reference metric followed by historical earnings, cash flows, and sales • P&L metrics are generally more reliable as balance sheet items
Herrmann (2002) and Richter/Herrmann (2003)	• 1,324 US and European firms • 1997, 1998, and 1999	• Projected earnings most accurate reference base followed by current EBIAT, book value of equity, EBIDAAT, invested capital and sales

751 See also the recommendation by Koller, T./Goedhart, M./Wessels, D. (2005), p. 366.

Authors	Sample data	Relevant findings on the most accurate reference parameter
Kelleners (2004)	• 800 US and European firms • 1991 and 2001	• Based on a selection procedure of comparable companies using projected fundamentals, actual earnings are the most accurate equity value related reference metric • Projected reference metrics in general outperform the accuracy of actual reference parameters • Valuation accuracy increases with the forecast horizon

Source: Adapted from Kelleners, A. (2004), p. 202[752].

Previous research on multiple valuation accuracy also highlights that the usage of projected reference parameters leads to lower valuation errors. This higher accuracy of multiples using forecasted reference parameters indicates that current market valuations at least partially anticipate the future short-term earnings development[753]. Therefore, the usage of the one-year forward price/earnings ratio appears to be the most appropriate approach.

Similarly to the terminal perpetuity case, the key challenge is to determine the correct terminal multiple level or—in other words—the appropriate expectation on the future price level of the equity market. Entry level equal to exit level and mean reverting terminal multiple scenarios are used as illustrated in Table 26.

Table 26 Rationale of different terminal multiple cases

2.1 Entry = Exit	2.2 Convergence to in-sample mean	2.3 Convergence to out-of-sample mean
• Assumes that the fundamental factors determining the multiple value such as cost of equity, growth, and payout ratio remain constant • This implies a constant price level of the respective market	• Assumes that relative prices are stationary and mean reverting • Includes only information available at the investment decision date • Speed of convergence is neglected in this scenario, i.e., the mean is established immediately when the terminal period is reached	• Assumes that relative prices are stationary and mean reverting • Includes also information beyond in the investment decision date • Speed of convergence is neglected in this scenario, i.e., the mean is established immediately when the terminal period is reached

This concludes the presentation of utilized equity valuation models.

---

752 See Kelleners, A. (2004), pp. 170-185 for a more comprehensive summary of previous research on the accuracy of multiple-based valuation approaches.

753 See Kelleners, A. (2004), p. 245.

5.6 Sample data

After the detailed discussion of the forward-looking models to determine the expected MRP, the focus is now shifted to the underlying data.

5.6.1 Accuracy of analysts' estimates

Since the analyzed data in this chapter is almost entirely based on analysts' consensus forecasts of firm-specific financial parameters, this section explores the general properties of analysts' estimates[754]. Most academic research in this field investigates earnings forecasts by sell-side analysts'—professionals from brokerage houses and investment banks who publish their forecasts to the investing society through public databases such as Institutional Broker's Estimate System (IBES), Value Line, First Call, or Zacks[755].

The abundant empirical and theoretical literature on analysts' forecasts can be broadly divided into two categories: (1) properties of consensus (mean or median) forecasts and (2) properties of individual estimates either in the cross-section or temporally[756]. For the purposes of this empirical study, it is most important to understand the accuracy of consensus analysts' forecasts with respect to other forecasting techniques and regarding a potential systematic bias in sell-side analyst data[757].

Overall, analysts' "earnings forecasts are more accurate than time-series models of earnings, presumably in part because they are able to incorporate more timely firm and economy news into their forecasts than time series models"[758]. Other reasons for the advantage of analysts' estimates are partly attributable to their private information acquisition activities which allow them to differentiate among permanent, transitory, and price-irrelevant shocks in earnings[759]. However, there is also some

---

[754] See also Ballwieser, W. (2005), pp. 333-334.

[755] In contrast to sell-side analysts, buy-side analysts are typically employed by asset management firms, mutual, or pension funds who publish forecasts only for internal purposes.

[756] See Kothari, S. (2001), p. 152.

[757] Additionally, there is a large body of academic literature on explaining the properties of individual analysts' forecasts and the determinants of forecast bias primarily following two directions namely economic incentives-based reasons or behavioral cognitive-bias explanations. As the findings from these study fields are of no primary importance for the discussion in this dissertation, the interested reader is referred to Kothari, S. (2001), pp. 156-160.

[758] Healy, P./Palepu, K. (2001), p. 416.

[759] See Brown, L. (1996), p. 42.

research offering conflicting evidence on the superiority of analysts' forecasts. Table 27 categorizes the key studies in favor of analysts' forecasts or time-series models.

Table 27 Key studies on the accuracy of analysts' estimates versus time-series forecasts[760]

Studies favoring analysts' estimates	Studies favoring time-series models
• Brown/Rozeff (1978) • Collins/Hopwood (1980) • Fried/Givoly (1982) • Brown et al. (1987a/1987b) • Brown (2005)	• Imhoff/Paré (1982) • O'Brien (1988)

Source: Collected from Kothari, S. (2001), p. 153 and Healy, P./Palepu, K. (2001), p. 416.

Notwithstanding the conflicting evidence, it has become common practice in recent years to assume that analysts' forecasts are better estimates for market expectations than time-series surrogates and research focus has shifted to question whether analysts' forecasts are biased.

Sell-side analysts are frequently alleged to be overly optimistic about future earnings performance due to the desire to sell securities or to protect investment banking relationships[761]. An optimistic bias in the forecasts is typically inferred from a systematic positive difference between the forecast and the actual earnings per share[762]. A large body of literature is dedicated to the question of potentially biased analysts' estimates and the bias behavior over time. Table 28 summarizes key earlier studies that find a significant positive bias in analysts' forecasts.

---

760 See Brown, L. (1993) for a comprehensive review of studies regarding the accuracy of analysts' forecasts in comparison to time-series estimates.

761 See Cragg, J./Malkiel, B. (1982).

762 See Kothari, S. (2001), p. 153.

Table 28 Summary of selected early studies on the optimism bias of analysts' estimates

Studies finding optimism bias	
• Barefield/Comiskey (1975)	• Abarbanell (1991)
• Crichfield/Dyckman/Lakonsihok (1978)	• Ali/Klein/Rosenfeld (1992)
• Fried/Givoly (1982)	• Dreman/Berry (1996)
• Brown/Foster/Noreen (1985)	• Easterwood/Nutt (1999)
• O'Brien (1988)	
• Stickel (1990)	

Source: Collected from Kothari, S. (2001), pp. 153-155 and Healy, P./Palepu, K. (2001), p. 417.

Estimates of optimism magnitude vary across studies due to differences in research design, sample construction, and examined time periods [763]. In particular, the definition of variables offers a multitude of variation possibilities:

- The error measure (actual earnings – forecasts earnings) is often deflated by different variables such as actual earnings, forecasted earnings, or even stock price
- Consensus studies use mean as well as median forecasts as input data
- Due to changing database sources for actuals (e.g., IBES, Compustat, etc.), values are often calculated using different treatments of extraordinary items
- Samples are often subjectively restricted due to the exclusion of outliers in input data as well as in resulting error measures. Note that in contrast to mean forecast errors, median error measures are largely 0 indicating the strong impact of outliers in creating optimism bias

Despite the obvious variations in research designs, more recent studies investigating the time-series behavior of optimism bias in analysts' estimates—as presented in Table 29—find that the magnitude of the bias consistently declined over time.

[763] See Kothari, S. (2001), pp. 153-154.

Table 29 Key findings of selected studies on decreasing optimism bias

Authors	Key findings
Abarbanell/Lehavy (2002)	• Mean forecast errors negative in every year for all three databases (First Call, IBES, Zacks) attributable to the presence of a relatively small number of extreme negative forecast errors in quarterly cross-sections • Percentage of positive (i.e., ex-post pessimistic) forecast errors is larger than the number of negative errors in the 1992-1998 period indicating no evidence of pervasive optimism in analysts' forecasts • Decline in the magnitude of mean forecast errors for Zacks and IBES partly due to major cleanup of the databases and procedural changes to ensure greater alignment between the forecasts of analysts and their proprietary definition of reported earnings particularly with respect to the treatment of extraordinary items from 1991 onwards
Brown (1997)	• Both mean absolute surprise (average percentage deviation from actual value) and mean signed surprise (bias) decrease significantly over time due to a substantial reduction in earnings overestimates during 1984 to 1996 • Still, mean surprise is negative and significant • Errors are smaller and after 1993 insignificant when restricting the sample to S&P 500 firms
Brown (2001)	• Significant temporal shift in median earnings surprise (actual reported quarterly earnings minus latest analyst forecast before announcement in cents per share) from small negative (1984-1990 except zero in 1988), over zero (1991-1993), to slightly positive (1994-1999, except zero in 1995)
Brown (2005)	• Strong evidence of a temporal increase in the precision of analysts' quarterly earnings forecasts measured by a decreasing median of forecast dispersion (standard deviation of forecasts as of the last consensus forecast update before quarterly announcement scaled by share price)
Matsumoto (2002)	• Percentage of observations with consensus forecasts meeting or being below reported earnings increases from 41% in 1985 to 70% in 1997 • The author suggests that for firms with certain characteristics, incentive-driven managers may use either the discretion over reported earnings or their power to guide analysts' forecasts downward to increase the probability of meeting or beating these forecasts
Richardson et al. (1999)	• Strong evidence of a switch from upward-biased to downward-biased forecasts of annual earnings as the announcement date approaches in the post-1992 period based on mean and median price-scaled forecast errors • Strongest forecast pessimism for high market-to-book firms, for large firms, and in periods when real GDP is growing

Summarizing the various findings presented in Table 29, the almost unanimous conclusion of earlier studies concerning a systematic positive difference between forecasting and reported earnings is not support by more recent empirical work[764]. All studies document a strong decline in optimism bias which according to certain studies has even converted to a pessimism bias during certain periods. Reasons for such a development range from an increase in underlying data coverage and quality, over specific management incentives, to learning effects within the analyst community. However, problems in measuring forecast errors still remain persistent

[764] Keane/Runkle even find that analysts' estimates are rational forecasts and thereby unbiased; see Keane, M./Runkle, D. (1998), p. 797.

due to uncommon definitions of accounting variables in databases, mixing of stale and recent forecasts, and the potential effects of survival bias through bankruptcies and M&A activity[765].

Drawing conclusions from the aforementioned studies for the research approach of this study is problematic with respect to the time horizon of analysts' estimates. Whereas this study relies on long-term earnings forecasts for up to five years and a long-term earnings growth rate (LTG), all discussed studies focus on the accuracy of short-term quarterly forecasts meeting next quarter reported earnings. However, studies on long-term forecasts are rare and appear more frequently within investigations of capital markets topics in finance rather than in accounting literature—four of which are discussed in the following.

La Porta (1996) determines analysts' earnings forecast errors for the current fiscal year as well as one-year forward in context of analyzing the impact of systematic errors in expectations on stock price performance throughout the period of 1982-1991. He finds that analysts' forecasts are highly accurate for companies with low expected long-term earnings growth but substantial (USD 2.5 cents to USD 3.1 cents per share) for high expected long-term earnings growth companies[766]. In a similar study, Dechow/Sloan (1997) investigate the hypothesis of naïve investor expectations—i.e., the reliance on overly optimistic analysts' forecasts—being a potential reason for the outperformance of contrarian investment strategies during 1981 to 1992. The authors find that forecast errors of long-term earnings growth rates are substantially larger for high growth firms than for companies with opposite characteristics. This result is supported by a regression analysis of realized earnings growth on forecasted earnings growth indicating that forecasts are almost three times larger than realizations[767]. In another study, Rajan/Servaes (1997) investigate the relation between IPO performance and analyst coverage. With respect to analysts' forecast errors of up to two-year forward earnings, calculated as difference between actual and forecasted earnings deflated by the stock price at estimation date, the authors document a systematic highly significant optimism bias between -3.4% (three months to fiscal year-end) up to -5.8% (12 months to fiscal year-end) of the stock price within the first year after the IPO. Interestingly, in the period of one to two years

---

[765] See Kothari, S. (2001), pp. 155-156.
[766] See La Porta, R. (1996), pp. 1730-1732.
[767] See Dechow, P./Sloan, R. (1997), pp. 6-7 and pp. 18-22.

thereafter, the accuracy of estimates does not substantially increase. Still, the reported forecast errors for matching non-IPO firms within the same industry are substantially smaller (in the range between 0.3% to -3.2% of stock price) but still mostly significant at lower levels [768]. Claus/Thomas (2001) use the earnings forecasts applied in their expected MRP study for a comparison with realized earnings. For the period from 1985 to 1997, they find that median IBES estimates consistently overestimate realized earnings. This positive bias increases with the forecast horizon but declines over the analysis period[769].

Despite the detailed discussion of existing empirical investigations on a potential optimism bias of sell-side analysts' forecasts, robust evidence on a consistent and quantifiable level of bias cannot be identified. It is therefore decided—in-line with most available benchmark studies[770]—not to adjust the IBES sample data for the determination of the expected MRP. Still, the reader is made aware of a potential bias in the underlying sample data particularly in the early years of the analysis period. This chapter continues with the detailed presentation of utilized sample data for the IRR-based expected MRP estimation models.

5.6.2 Data sources

For all six countries being analyzed, the underlying sample data for the IRR-based approaches is consistently drawn from the same databases for the entire analysis period between January 1989 and December 2006. All analysts' consensus estimates are from IBES. Reported actual financials are taken from Thomson Financial – Worldscope Fundamentals (Worldscope). Finally, economic parameters are drawn from Thomson Financial – Datastream (Datastream). Table 30 provides a detailed overview of input variables and their respective source, code, and description.

---

[768] See Rajan, R./Servaes, H. (1997), pp. 515-517.
[769] See Claus, J./Thomas, J. (2001), pp. 1657 and 1660-1661.
[770] See in particular Claus, J./Thomas, J. (2001), p. 1630, fn. 3.

Table 30 Overview of input parameter sources

Input variable	Database source	Database code	Database description[771]
Median EPS estimate t+1 to t+5	IBES	F[1-5]MD	FY[1-5] median estimate
Median long-term growth rate of EPS	IBES	LTMD	LTG median estimate
Median DPS estimate t+1 to t+4	IBES	Y[1-4]MD	FY[1-4] median estimate
Share price	IBES	IBP	Price (IBES)
Number of shares outstanding	IBES	IBNOSH	IBES no. of shares
Historical EPS[772]	Worldscope	WC05201	Earnings per share
Historical DPS[772]	Worldscope	WC05101	Dividends per share
Book value	Worldscope	WC03501	Common shareholders' equity
Total debt	Worldscope	WC03255	Total debt
Risk-free rate 10-year government bond redemption yield	Datastream		
Germany		REXA10Y(RY)	Germany: REX bond sub index current, 10-year redemption yield. Other countries: Benchmark 10-year Datastream government index redemption yield
Canada		BMCN10Y(RY)	
France		BMFR10Y(RY)	
Japan		BMJP10Y(RY)	
United Kingdom		BMUK10Y(RY)	
United States		BMUS10Y(RY)	
Ex-post inflation rate	Datastream		
Germany		BDCP7500F	Inflation rate implied by the consumer price index of the respective market
Canada		CNOCP009F	
France		FRI64...F	
Japan		JPOCP009F	
United Kingdom		UKOCP009F	
United States		USOCP009F	
Nom. GDP growth rate	Datastream		
Germany		BDGDPL..	Nominal GDP growth rate for the respective market
Canada		CNGDPL..	
France		FRGDPL..	
Japan		JPGDPL..	
United Kingdom		UKGDPL..	
United States		USGDPL..	
Ex-dividend date	Worldscope	WC0592[3-6]	Ex-dividend date quarter 1 to 4
Spot exchange rates	Datastream		
USD-EUR		USEURSP	Spot rate as provided by GTIS (except USD-EUR which is based on WMR/DS)[773]
USD-CAD		USCDNDL	
USD-GBP		BRITPUS	
USD-JPY		USJAPYN	

---

771 For a more detailed description, see Thomas Financial (2003, 2008).

772 Note that reported actual financials such as EPS and DPS are also available on IBES. Still, the DPS data file in IBES is highly incomplete before 1996 particularly for DPS which requires the consistent use of Worldscope actuals for EPS and DPS. Since both variables are only used to calculate historical dividend payout ratios, there is no issue resulting from a potential difference in the underlying number of shares outstanding or accounting standards between Worldscope and IBES as identified by Philbrick/Ricks for IBES/Value Line forecasts and Compustat actuals; see Philbrick, D./Ricks, W. (1991).

773 GTIS stand for Global Treasury Information System and WMR for WM/Reuters.

5.6.3 Sample selection approach

Similarly to the analysis of historical returns, it is the goal to create the largest possible samples of firms in order to cover the market portfolio of the respective countries as closely as possible. However, the utilized IRR-based models in this section have certain requirements regarding the data completeness. In a first step, all firms are included in the sample which are constituents of the respective all-share indices used for determining the realized MRP and described in Chapter 3. In a second step, firms qualify for the samples, if they comply with a certain set of restrictions regarding the data completeness. The following enumeration summarizes the criteria for the firm selection procedure at each monthly estimation[774] date in-between 1989 and 2006:

- IBES EPS forecasts for at least for the years $t+1$ to $t+3$ or for the years $t+1$ to $t+2$ and for the long-term EPS growth rate
  - If there are less than five future years of forecasted EPS, the remaining periods are estimates as follows:
    - Two or more future years of EPS and a long-term growth rate forecasts:
      $E_s\left[\tilde{E}_t\right] = E_s\left[\tilde{E}_{t-1}\left(1+g_{LTG}\right)\right]$ with $t = s+3, 4, 5$
    - Three or more future years of EPS but no long-term growth rate forecast:
      $E_s\left[\tilde{E}_t\right] = E_s\left[\tilde{E}_{t-1}\right] + E_s\left[\tilde{E}_{t-1} - \tilde{E}_{s+1}\right] / \left(t-s-2\right)$ with $t = s+4, 5$ [775]
- IBES DPS forecasts up to year +4 or actual Worldscope EPS and DPS of latest fiscal year-end
  - In case an explicit IBES DPS forecast is missing for the respective period, a constant historical dividend payout ratio is assumed
  - In order to prevent the usage of abnormal payout ratios if explicit dividend forecasts are missing, only companies qualify for the sample if the historical payout ratio lies between 0 and 1[776]:
    $E_s\left[\tilde{D}_t\right] = E_s\left[\tilde{E}_t\right]\theta$
    with $\theta = DPS_s / EPS_s$, $0 \leq \theta \leq 1$, and $t = s+1, 2, 3, 4$

---

[774] The precise estimation date is the last trading day of each month.

[775] In-line with Daske/Gebhardt/Klein, the absolute change is chosen in this case in order to prevent hockey-stick effects of extraordinary high growth rates; see Daske, H./Gebhardt, G./Klein, S. (2006), p. 58.

[776] Note that the value limits of the historical payout ratio differentiates the sample selection approach of this study from the German studies of Daske/Gebhardt/Klein (2006) and Reese (2005, 2007).

- IBES share price, IBES number of shares outstanding and Worldscope book value of latest fiscal year-end
- All input variables denominated in the current local currency[777]

Exhibit 37 illustrates the firm selection method for the German market on 29 December 2006[778].

Exhibit 37 Illustrative sequential sample selection for the German CDAX on 29.12.2006

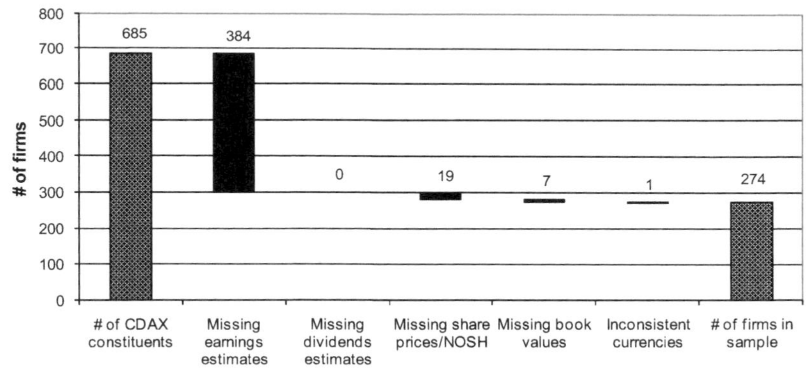

Source: IBES, Worldscope.

Finally, note that additional limitations are imposed for the implementation of the regression-based simultaneous estimation of expected return and growth. Such limitations of the independent and dependent variable impact the quality of the fitted regression line. However, the details of such additional limitations are discussed in the Section 5.8.

5.7 Methodological considerations

In addition to the sample selection procedure, it is important to discuss some further methodologies regarding data usage which are mainly related to aggregation/averaging and timing considerations.

---

[777] Problems with regards to currency denomination occur in European countries where certain items were not updated during the Euro introduction. Furthermore, there are several US-Dollar denominated stocks in the Canadian market.

[778] Note that the values of the sample selection bridge result if the selection criteria are applied in the presented sequence.

5.7.1 Averaging procedure

As it is the ultimate goal of this analysis to determine an average value of the expected MRP representative for each analyzed market for a specific time period based on different underlying models, the question arises how to technically calculate this average expected MRP for all assets in the market. The summaries of previous research approaches in Sections 5.2.4 and 5.3.3 have shown that there are two main methodologies.

Firstly, all previously discussed models can be used on an individual company basis which—as a consequence—requires an averaging procedure of the individual expected MRPs. Averages can then be calculated on an equal[779] or a value[780]-weighting basis.

Secondly, a market average expected MRP can be determined through the aggregation of all input variables so that the entire market is treated as one aggregate[781]. This approach to determine the expected market MRP is almost identical to the value-weighting technique[782] but differences still remain as market cap is not the only implicit weighting factor of the aggregation method.

Generally, aggregation or value-weighting puts more weight on large companies with lower risk and consequently lower return characteristics as opposed to equal-weighting[783]. Besides this fact, the ultimate choice of the appropriate averaging technique must be driven by the intended use of the resulting expected MRP. For asset allocation decisions the appropriate averaging approach to develop return expectations is a question of the reference portfolio construction, i.e., equally weighted, value-weighted, or other. However, for corporate investment decisions which are largely based on a CAPM-based risk-adjusted discount rates, the answer is unambiguous. The CAPM postulates that in a capital market equilibrium all investor will hold according to their level of risk aversion a certain fraction of the identical optimal risky portfolio which is—based on the CAPM assumptions—the market portfolio. “The proportion of each stock in this [market] portfolio equals the

---

779 See, e.g., Gebhardt, W./Lee, C./Swaminathan, B. (2001) or Daske, H./Gebhardt, G./Klein, S. (2006).

780 See, e.g., Reese, R. (2005, 2007).

781 See, e.g., Claus, J./Thomas, J. (2001) and the additional analysis by Reese, R. (2007), pp. 124-125. See also Damodaran, A. (2002), pp. 335-336 for a description of applying the dividend discount model to value entire markets.

782 See also Pastor, L./Sinha, M./Swaminathan, B. (2008), p. 2877.

783 See also Pastor, J./Sinha, M./Swaminathan, B. (2008), p. 2881.

market value of the stock (price per share times number of shares outstanding) divided by the sum of the market values of all stocks"[784]. This implies that the fraction of a stock in the market portfolio is determined according to its value-weight relative to the overall market. Consequently, the return expectation of the market portfolio is a value-weighted average of the return expectations of all individual stocks. Therefore, an expected MRP consistent with the CAPM can only be calculated based on a value-weighted or aggregate basis[785]. Another relevant aspect is related to the comparison of MRPs. If the expected MRP resulting from analysts' estimates is determined for a comparison with ex-post realization of returns, the same averaging procedure must be applied to both data sets.[786]

The reason for applying the market aggregate approach throughout this study is twofold. Firstly, compliance with the CAPM as well as comparability with ex-post returns which are derived from uniquely value-weighted indices[787] requires the application of a value driven method. Secondly, the aggregation method outperforms the value-weighting approach in large empirical studies due its significantly lower calculation complexity. One exception to the general aggregation method is the expected MRP estimate based on the regression approach[788].

Finally, note that the weighting approach should be taken into consideration when the results of this study are compared to other studies. As to be seen, results are strongly dependent on the averaging methodology—in particular for Germany.

5.7.2 Discounting reference date

As a consequence of the aggregation method, the input variables of firms with different fiscal year-ends are summed up to represent market aggregates. Different fiscal year-ends are an issue when determining the appropriate ex-dividend date for the entire sample as a basis for setting the appropriate monthly discounting periods as illustrated by Exhibit 38.

---

784 Bodie, Z./Kane, A./Marcus, A. (2009), p. 281.

785 See Easton, P./Sommers, G. (2007), pp. 1006-1007 and Easton, P. (2009), pp. 305-306 for a similar argument.

786 See Reese, R. (2005), pp. 18-19 and Bodie, Z./Kane, A./Marcus, A. (2009), pp. 281-282.

787 The most commonly cited equity indices—including the indices used in this study—are all calculated on a value-weighted basis worldwide.

788 Note that applying the presented regression approach to simultaneously estimate expected return and growth results in an equally weighted expected MRP estimate.

Exhibit 38 Distribution of ex-dividend-dates for the German market 2006

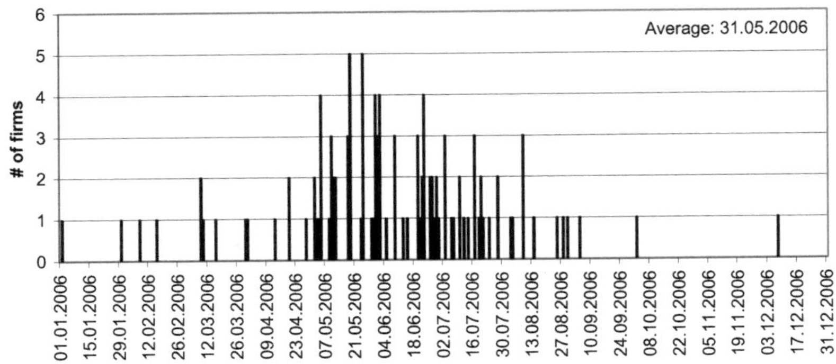

Source: Worldscope.

The ex–dividend date is therefore defined for all analyses as the annual average of the respective local market sample[789]. Since the estimation is conducted on a monthly basis, the closest month-end to the average ex-dividend date is chosen. This approach helps to average out any potential bias. Implicitly, there is a downward (upward) bias from the average (true) ex-dividend date to the true (average) ex-dividend date[790]. An alternative to prevent this source of bias would be to restrict the sample to firms with the most frequent fiscal year-end (e.g., 31 December in Germany) but this is contradictory to the general aim of this study to create a sample representative of the entire market portfolio. The development of the average ex-dividend dates over the sample period for the German CDAX is provided by Exhibit 39.

---

[789] Note that unfortunately the ex-dividend date data is not available for the selected samples. The average ex-dividend date is therefore based on all available ex-dividend dates in the database for the respective local index.

[790] The bias is related to a mismatch of implicitly assumed discounting periods and underlying market price. E.g., between the average and the true ex-dividend, the observable share price should be systematically higher due to the present value effect compared to the used discounting period based on the average date. Therefore, a too long discounting period is used resulting in a downward bias in the expected MRP.

Exhibit 39 Development of the average ex-dividend date for the German CDAX[791]

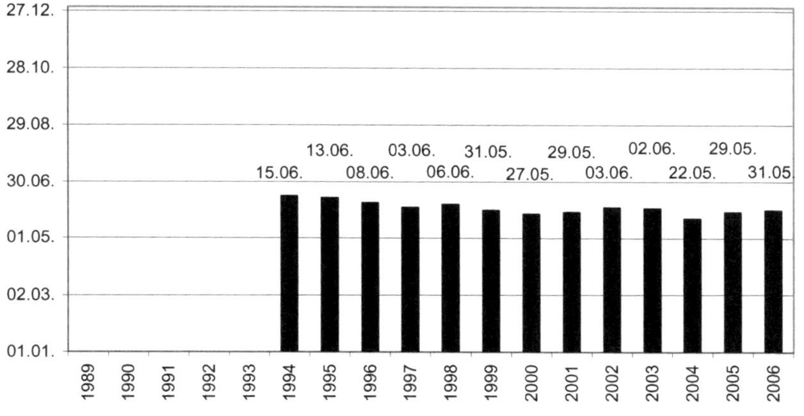

Source: Worldscope.

5.7.3 Time-matching of input variables

In addition to the aggregation methodology and its additional implications for the ex-dividend date, the time-matching of input variables requires some further discussion. The estimation of the expected MRP is conducted on a monthly basis on the last trading day of the respective month. This approach ensures that the utilized analysts' estimates were recently updated. Furthermore, the date matching of input variables is of key importance. As already discussed, a main issue in previous studies was the consistent use of currently available accounting and stock market information referring to the same point in time. This study generally follows the monthly time-matching approach introduced by Daske/Gebhardt/Klein (2006) and uses available IBES consensus forecasts as well as share prices and number of shares outstanding as of the respective estimation date each month. A remaining bias may result from the sluggishness of analyst forecasts, i.e., recent changes in market prices are potentially not yet appropriately reflected in the earnings forecasts of analysts[792]. However, arbitrarily assuming a certain time interval between the reference date of

[791] Note that there is no data on ex-dividend dates available before 1994. For the years before 1994 the average ex-dividend date is assumed to be equal to 1994.

[792] See Guay, W./Kothari, S./Shu, S. (2005), pp. 16-22 and Easton, P. (2009), p. 337.

market price and earnings estimate to allow analysts the inclusion of new information may lead to a further source of bias[793]. This issue is further explored in Section 5.14. With regards to the base date of used book value, a different concept is used compared to synthetical book value approach of Daske/Gebhardt/Klein except for the regression-based estimation[794] as already discussed[795]. The herein used model specifications allow for intra-year estimations but do not require book values based precisely on the estimation date[796]. This feature of the herein used research approach allows for the general usage of standard fiscal year-end book values.

Besides these conceptual considerations, further time-matching complications are created by the input structure of the underlying databases. Identifying the most currently available data points for analysts' earnings estimates as well as shares prices and number of shares outstanding at the estimation date is straightforward as the input structure of the IBES database guarantees continuously updated information for the next unpublished fiscal year. The IBES database entry format captures the change from one fiscal period to the next following the first database update after the announcement of prior year's financial statements resulting in estimates referring to a "past" fiscal year in the database for a certain period between beginning of the year and the earnings announcement date (e.g., a December year-end firm may announce its annual results in the second week of February. In response to the announcement, IBES forecasts for that month will be moved to the next fiscal year). This means that the database input date of the appropriate data points for the estimation procedure is always equal to the estimation date[797].

In contrast, the entry format of the underlying database for the utilized book values—Worldscope—follows precisely the fiscal year period (e.g., following the example, the announcement of results in the second week of February leads to the entry of reported financials in the database for the previous fiscal year)[798]. Therefore the precise date when book values become publicly available remains unknown. One strategy to overcome this deficiency would be to assume that the book value

[793] See Guay, W./Kothari, S./Shu, S. (2005), pp. 27-28 who use a five months interval between price observation and earnings estimate but recognize potential shortcomings of this approach.

[794] In order to implement the regression-based model, the calculation of synthetical book values for the respective estimation date is inevitable.

[795] See Section 5.5.

[796] See also Easton, P. (2009), pp. 355-356 for a similar approach.

[797] See Thomson Financial (2008).

[798] See Thomson Financial (2003).

publication date is equal to the earnings release date and to adjust the input structure of the database accordingly. However, this approach is not without error potential as earnings are often released before the entire financial statements including book value. Therefore, it is generally assumed that book values are published on average three months[799] after the fiscal year-end independent from the precise fiscal year-end and to accept a potential resulting minor mismatch between earnings release date and book value publication date implied by the three months lead time assumption[800]. Still, this approach ensures that earnings estimates and book values always relate to the appropriate fiscal years as required by the RIV model within the empirical limitations. Exhibit 40 illustrates the time-matching of input variables used throughout this study given the entry format of the respective database for an estimation of the expected MRP on 31 December in year $t=0$.

---

[799] This assumption is based on the requirement to report annual reports (10-K forms) in the US with the SEC within 90 days after fiscal year-end until 2006; see Securities and Exchange Commission (2005), p. 4. Under IFRS, the applicable reporting deadline is six months (see IAS 1.52 as of 29 September 2003; http://eur-lex.europa.eu/LexUriServ/LexUriServ.do?uri=CELEX:32003R1725:EN:NOT), but, e.g., the effective time-lag until publication of German issuers in the DAX was on average only slightly above 80 days; see Eggemann, G./Petry, M. (2002), pp. 1635-1636.

[800] A minor error resulting from the three months assumption arises when the database already contains either IBES forecasts or Worldscope book values for the next fiscal period while the other is still referring to last fiscal period. This source of error can not be eliminated and has to be taken into account when interpreting the results from this approach.

Exhibit 40 Illustrative time-matching of input variables for the RIV model for a company with 31 December fiscal year-end

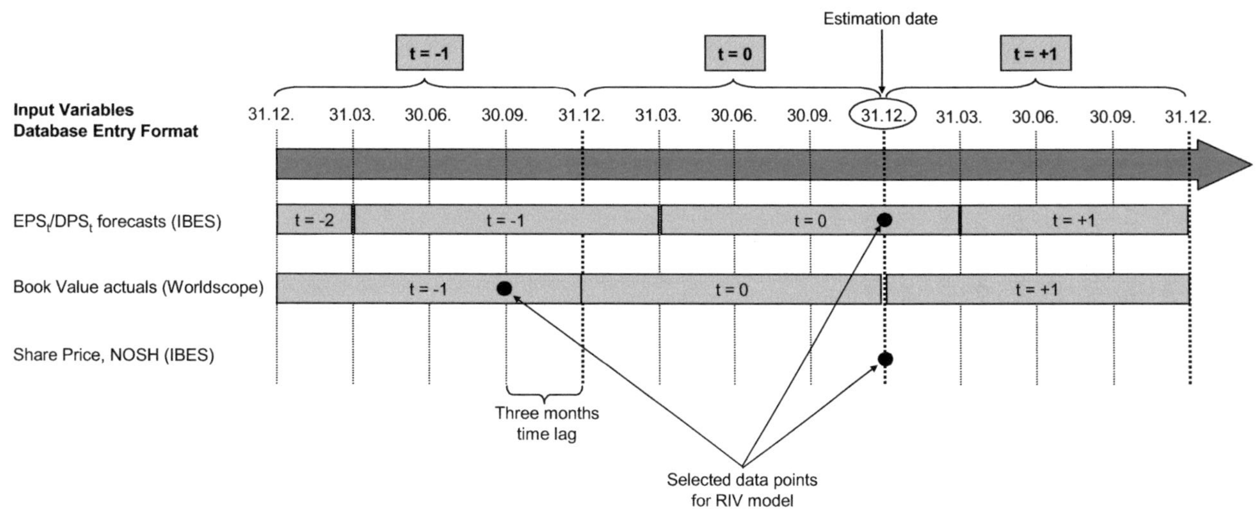

Source: IBES, Worldscope.

Another empirical timing issue is related to matching the data input structure previously discussed with the correct discounting reference date, i.e., the ex-dividend date. It is obvious that the presented time-matching approach implicitly assumes that the average sample ex-dividend date is equivalent to the date of change in forecasts from the current to the next fiscal year-end. A violation of this assumption would lead to applying an inconsistent discount period to the valuation attributes. Despite the data underlying this study does not precisely match this requirement the divergences are not substantial as illustrated by the following example. Exhibit 41 shows the distribution of fiscal year shifts in the IBES database for the German CDAX companies in 2006. The resulting average is within approximately one month to average ex-dividend date previously presented in Exhibit 38[801].

Exhibit 41 Distribution of average fiscal year shift dates in the IBES database for the German market 2006

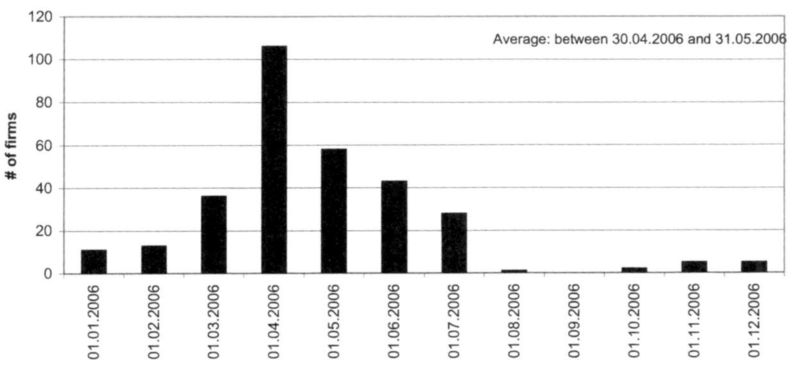

Source: IBES.

Over time the divergence is larger but never exceeds a two months difference as illustrated by Exhibit 42 with reference to Exhibit 39.

[801] Note that in contrast to the average ex-dividend date, the fiscal year shift dates in IBES are only available on a monthly as opposed to a daily basis.

Exhibit 42 Development of average fiscal year shifts in the IBES database for the German market over the analysis period

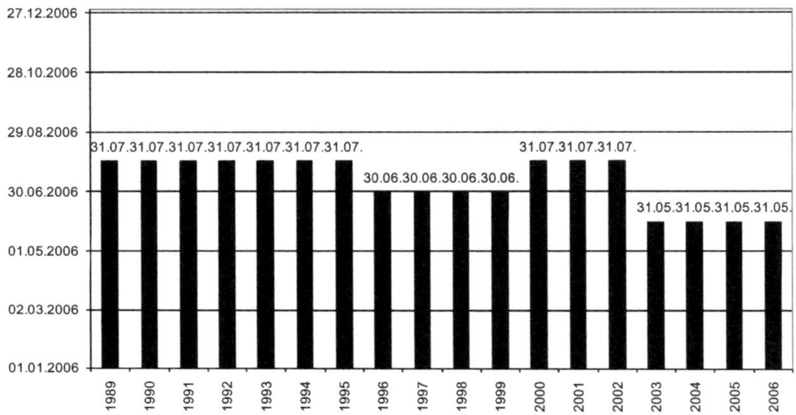

Source: IBES.

This result is similar for all analyzed countries throughout the entire analysis period. Therefore, one can conclude that there is a general match between the discounting reference date and the underlying financial parameters for the sample.

The time-matching approach in this study assures a consistent use of publicly available information at the estimation date, a correct usage of discount periods in the monthly model version of this study, and a minimum distortion from firms with different fiscal year-ends.

5.7.4 Intra-year dividend payments

A final complication in the effort to determine the appropriate discounting periods is the frequency of dividend payments. Up to now it was implicitly assumed that dividend payments are made once per fiscal year. However, dependent on the procedure of the respective country, dividends may be paid once or multiple times during the fiscal year.

Table 31 Predominant frequency of dividend payments in analyzed countries[802]

Country	Frequency
Canada	Quarterly
France	Annually
Germany	Annually
Japan	Bi-annually
United Kingdom	Bi-annually
United States	Quarterly

Source: Datastream.

In case of an annual dividend frequency, the previous specifications of intra-year expected return estimation apply. However, if the dividend payment frequency is above one, the resulting return estimates understate the true cost of equity due to the opportunity cost of sub-period dividends[803]. There are two approaches to eliminate this source of bias.

Firstly, the entire valuation model can be based on the sub-period by changing the reference period from one year to $1/f$ of a year with f being the frequency of dividends payment during the fiscal year[804]. For example, in case of four dividend payments per annum, the appropriate reference period is a quarter. This approach requires quarterly input parameters and results in quarterly expected rates of return which then have to be annualized for comparison. The following example shows the expected return estimation for a quarterly reference period illustrated by a one-year dividend discount model with four sub-periods:

F 5-57

$$\mathrm{P}_{\mathrm{s}}^{\text{ex-dividend date}} = \frac{E_s\left[\frac{1}{4}\tilde{\mathrm{D}}_{s+1}\right]}{\left(1+\mathrm{r}_{1/4}^{e}\right)} + \frac{E_s\left[\frac{1}{4}\tilde{\mathrm{D}}_{s+1}\right]}{\left(1+\mathrm{r}_{1/4}^{e}\right)^2} + \frac{E_s\left[\frac{1}{4}\tilde{\mathrm{D}}_{s+1}\right]}{\left(1+\mathrm{r}_{1/4}^{e}\right)^3} + \frac{E_s\left[\frac{1}{4}\tilde{\mathrm{D}}_{s+1}\right]}{\left(1+\mathrm{r}_{1/4}^{e}\right)^4}$$

$$+\frac{E_s\left[\frac{1}{4}\tilde{\mathrm{D}}_{s+1}\right]\left(1+\mathrm{g}_{1/4}\right)}{\left(\mathrm{r}_{1/4}^{e}-\mathrm{g}_{1/4}\right)\left(1+\mathrm{r}_{1/4}^{e}\right)^4}$$

$$\mathrm{r}^{e} = \left(1+\mathrm{r}_{1/4}^{e}\right)^4 - 1$$

802 Certain firms may have a differing dividend payment frequency from the predominant market standard.

803 See Linke, C./Zumwalt, K. (1984), pp. 15-16 and Siegel, J. (1985), pp. 47-48.

804 See Linke, C./Zumwalt, K. (1984), p. 17 and Siegel, J. (1985), p. 47.

Despite the fact that this approach eliminates the time-value of money problem associated with the annual model, it is not without additional bias. The sub-period models implicitly assume that dividends are increased on a quarterly basis rather than periodically[805]. "Thus, the quarterly dividend model correctly handles the time value of dividends but the quarterly dividend growth may cause the cost of equity capital to be understated or overstated. (...) For example, if the analysis is made immediately following the fiscal year-end, (...) the implied quarterly dividend is less than the actual dividend in three of the four quarters. However, if the analysis is made at the end of the first quarter, the implied quarterly dividend will be greater than the expected dividend in three of the four quarters. Similar discrepancies occur if the analysis is performed at the end of Q_2 or Q_3"[806].

Secondly, one may leave the full fiscal year dividends unchanged when adjusting the discounting horizon based on the weighted-average duration[807] of dividends during the year. This duration is lower than one in case of sub-period dividends. In the following, an example is provided on how to derive the correct discounting periods under the duration concept.

On the first ex-dividend date after the fiscal year-end, duration and price are estimated as follows[808] (Dur = duration and $\mathrm{m_t}$ = months to the related dividend payment):

F 5-58 $$\mathrm{Dur} = \frac{E_s\left[\tilde{\mathrm{D}}_{s+1,1}\right]\frac{\mathrm{m}_1}{12} + E_s\left[\tilde{\mathrm{D}}_{s+1,2}\right]\frac{\mathrm{m}_2}{12} + E_s\left[\tilde{\mathrm{D}}_{s+1,3}\right]\frac{\mathrm{m}_3}{12} + \ldots + E_s\left[\tilde{\mathrm{D}}_{s+1,f}\right]\frac{\mathrm{m}_f}{12}}{\sum_{t=1}^{f} E_s\left[\tilde{\mathrm{D}}_{s+1,t}\right]}$$ [809]

$$\text{with } E_s\left[\tilde{\mathrm{D}}_{s+1,1}\right] = E_s\left[\tilde{\mathrm{D}}_{s+1,2}\right] = E_s\left[\tilde{\mathrm{D}}_{s+1,3}\right] = \ldots = E_s\left[\tilde{\mathrm{D}}_{s+1,f}\right] = \frac{1}{f} E_s\left[\tilde{\mathrm{D}}_{s+1}\right]$$

---

805 Note that in practice dividend payments are generally readjusted once a year even in the case of sub-period dividend payments.

806 Linke, C./Zumwalt, K. (1984), p. 17. See also Siegel, J. (1985), pp. 48-49 for a similar discussion.

807 Duration is normally related to bonds and represents—following the Macaulay definition—"the weighted average of the times to each coupon or principal payment of the bond"; Bodie, Z./Kane, A./Marcus, A. (2009), p. 516. In the same manner, the duration concept may be applied to dividends.

808 See Morningstar Inc. (2007c), p. 68 for a similar approach.

809 $\mathrm{m_f}$ represents the outstanding months to the respective dividend payment.

F 5-59 $$\mathrm{Dur}=\frac{E_s\left[\tilde{\mathrm{D}}_{s+1,f}\right]\left[\frac{m_1}{12}+\frac{m_2}{12}+\frac{m_3}{12}+\ldots+\frac{m_f}{12}\right]}{E_s\left[\tilde{\mathrm{D}}_{s+1,f}\right]f}=\frac{\left[\frac{m_1}{12}+\frac{m_2}{12}+\frac{m_3}{12}+\ldots+\frac{m_f}{12}\right]}{f}$$

F 5-60 $$\begin{aligned}\mathrm{P}_s^{\text{ex-dividend date}}&=\left\{\frac{E_s\left[\tilde{\mathrm{D}}_{s+1}\right]}{\left(1+r^e\right)}+\frac{E_s\left[\tilde{\mathrm{D}}_{s+1}\right](1+g)}{\left(r^e-g\right)\left(1+r^e\right)}\right\}\left(1+r^e\right)^{1-\mathrm{Dur}}\\&=\frac{E_s\left[\tilde{\mathrm{D}}_{s+1}\right]}{\left(1+r^e\right)^{\mathrm{Dur}}}+\frac{E_s\left[\tilde{\mathrm{D}}_{s+1}\right](1+g)}{\left(r^e-g\right)\left(1+r^e\right)^{\mathrm{Dur}}}\end{aligned}$$

Given the availability of accumulated expected full fiscal year dividends in the utilized databases, adjusted discounting periods are based on the average duration concept of expected dividends to adjust for the present value effects of differing dividend payment frequency.

5.8 Calculation example

After the exhaustive discussion of utilized models, data, and specific empirical methodologies, this section provides a calculation example including all approaches to determine the expected MRP from analysts' consensus estimates. The estimation of the expected MRP is implemented on a monthly basis on the last trading day of the respective month. For illustrative purposes, the example is based on the German CDAX for the estimation procedure on 29.12.2006.

Firstly, Table 32 provides an overview of the underlying aggregate input data for the equity valuation models over the explicit forecast period. It also shows standard discounting periods and the adjustment according to ex-dividend date and dividend payment frequency. Table 33 and Table 34 continue to show the development of these aggregate input assumptions throughout the terminal value period and beyond as implied by the implementation of different terminal perpetuity approaches. These exhibits also show the relation between the explicit assumptions on perpetual residual income growth and the implied values for perpetual earnings growth, dividends growth, and terminal PE_{+1} multiple. It is illustrated that dividend growth is different from residual earnings growth except for the steady state case and only constant until infinity in the cases 1.1, 1.2, and 1.4. Therefore, theoretically correct implied terminal PE_{+1} multiples based on constant payout ratio, cost of equity, and perpetual dividend growth can only be calculated for these three cases. In case 1.3, the true implied terminal PE_{+1} multiple lies between the value for the first TV period and the convergence level at infinity.

Secondly, Table 35 summarizes the valuation process for all three discussed equity valuation models. In addition to the total intrinsic value per model, it also shows the net present values (NPV) of the explicit forecast period (EFP) and the terminal value (TV). The cost of equity can now be derived by determining the return that equates the implied value of the model with the currently observable market value. The determination of r^e is performed by applying a numerical estimation procedure that iteratively approaches the IRR so that:

F 5-61 $$-P_{s+d}+\left\{B_s+\sum_{t=s+1}^{s+5}\frac{E_{s+d}\left[\tilde{E}_t-r^e\tilde{B}_{t-1}\right]}{\left(1+r^e\right)^{t-s}}+\frac{E_{s+d}\left[\tilde{E}_{s+5}-r^e\tilde{B}_{s+4}\right]\left(1+g_{RI}\right)}{\left(r^e-g_{RI}\right)\left(1+r^e\right)^5}\right\}\left(1+r^e\right)^d=0$$

F 5-61 as well as all other cash flow streams used to determine IRRs within this study are regular investments, i.e., the stream of cash flows starts with a negative item, it changes sign only once, and the sum of the cash flow stream for a discount rate of zero is positive[810]. Regular investments have only one positive root and thereby a unique solution for the IRR[811]. This IRR can be manually determined using iterative procedures[812]. Since a simple algorithm is sufficient to find the appropriate stable solutions for the cost of equity, the numerical tools of Microsoft Excel are used for the estimation[813]. Table 35 further proofs the theoretically developed equivalence conditions for RIV, CAP, and DIV. Only in case 1.3 the equivalence does not hold when a terminal perpetuity approach is applied since the implied perpetual dividend growth rate is not constant.

---

810 See, e.g., Franke, G./Hax, H. (2009), p. 177 and Tietze, J. (2009), pp. 396-397.

811 See, e.g., Franke, G./Hax, H. (2009), pp. 177-178, Copeland, T./Weston, F./Shastri, K. (2004), pp. 31-33, Richter, F. (2005), p. 120, and Tietze, J. (2009), pp. 404-406. See Norstrom, C. (1972) for a general proof that regular investments have only one positive IRR. See also Botosan, C. (1997), pp. 339-440 for an empirical demonstration.

812 See Claus, J./Thomas, J. (2001), p. 1641.

813 The Goal Seek/Solver functions in Excel are applied.

Table 32 Aggregate input data for the calculation example

Calculation example	
Country	Germany (CDAX)
# of included companies	274
Estimation date	29.12.2006
Ex-dividend date	31.05.2006
in EUR million	

		Explicit forecast period (EFP)					CAGR
Period	**t=0**	**t+1**	**t+2**	**t+3**	**t+4**	**t+5**	**t+1 - t+5**
Earnings		72,409	78,597	87,080	91,294	96,302	7.4%
% Growth			*8.55%*	*10.79%*	*4.84%*	*5.49%*	
Dividends		26,534	29,701	32,629	33,874	35,732	7.7%
% Growth			*11.94%*	*9.86%*	*3.82%*	*5.49%*	
Implied payout ratio		36.64%	37.79%	37.47%	37.10%	37.10%	
Book value	508,071	553,946	602,842	657,293	714,713	775,283	8.8%
% Growth			*8.83%*	*9.03%*	*8.74%*	*8.47%*	
Implied residual income (RI) (1)		16,254	17,371	20,450	18,646	17,308	1.6%
% Growth			*6.87%*	*17.72%*	*-8.82%*	*-7.18%*	
Implied agr (1)		1,117	3,079	-1,804	-1,338	1,467	7.0%
% Growth			*175.58%*	*-158.60%*	*-25.83%*	*-209.60%*	
Implied return on book equity		*14.25%*	*14.19%*	*14.44%*	*13.89%*	*13.47%*	
Current market value (MV)	1,068,804						
One-year forward PE multiple (entry)		14.8x					
Standard discount period		1	2	3	4	5	
Discount period adjustment	0.58						

(1) Based on steady state case estimated cost of equity of 11.05%.

Table 33 Aggregate input data development based on different terminal perpetuity scenarios (I)

Calculation example	
Country	Germany (CDAX)
# of included companies	274
Estimation date	29.12.2006
Ex-dividend date	31.05.2006
in EUR million	

Steady state parameters	
RI growth rate	8.47%
payout ratio	37.10%

	1.1 Zero RI		1.2 Zero RI growth		1.3 Inflation growth		1.4 Steady state	
Period	t+6 = TV	t+7	t+6 = TV	t+7	t+6 = TV	t+7	t+6 = TV	t+7
Earnings	-25,040	-24,532	100,997	105,920	101,794	107,578	104,464	113,317
% Growth	*-126.00%*	*-2.03%*	*4.87%*	*4.87%*	*5.70%*	*5.68%*	*8.47%*	*8.47%*
Dividends	-9,291	-9,102	37,474	39,301	37,770	39,916	38,760	42,045
% Growth	*-126.00%*	*-2.03%*	*4.87%*	*4.87%*	*5.70%*	*5.68%*	*8.47%*	*8.47%*
Implied payout ratio	37.10%	37.10%	37.10%	37.10%	37.10%	37.10%	37.10%	37.10%
Book value	759,533	744,104	838,805	905,424	839,307	906,969	840,986	912,257
% Growth	*-2.03%*	*-2.03%*	*8.19%*	*7.94%*	*8.26%*	*8.06%*	*8.47%*	*8.47%*
Implied residual income (RI)	0	0	40,911	40,911	38,059	38,579	18,774	20,365
% Growth	*-100.00%*	*NM*	*0.00%*	*0.00%*	*1.37%*	*1.37%*	*8.47%*	*8.47%*
Implied agr	0	NA	0	NA	520	NA	1,591	NA
% Growth	*-100.00%*	*NA*	*-100.00%*	*NA*	*1.37%*	*NA*	*8.47%*	*NA*
Implied return on book equity	*-3.23%*	*-3.23%*	*13.03%*	*12.63%*	*13.13%*	*12.82%*	*13.47%*	*13.47%*
Convergence to (1)		*-3.23%*		*7.75%*		*8.22%*		*13.47%*
Implied one-year forward PE multiple (2)	NM	NM	12.9x	12.9x	14.7x	14.6x	14.4x	14.4x
Convergence to (3)		NM		12.9x		12.2x		14.4x

Note: Grey marked fields indicate explicit assumptions.
(1) Based on the approach to determine the post-horizontal behavior outlined in Appendix 6.
(2) Implied calculation based on current payout ratio, cost of equity, and dividend growth rate.
(3) Implied calculation based on payout ratio, cost of equity, and long-term converging dividend growth rate: $\mathrm{Max}\left[g_{\infty};r^{*}(1-\theta)\right]$ (See Appendix 6).

Table 34 Aggregate input data development based on different terminal perpetuity scenarios (II)

Calculation example

Country	Germany (CDAX)
# of included companies	274
Estimation date	29.12.2006
Ex-dividend date	31.05.2006
in EUR million	

	1.5.2 Zero RI growth after fade period to target r^b								
Period	**t+6**	**t+7**	**t+8**	**t+9**	**t+10**	**t+11**	**t+12 = TV**	**t+13**	**t+14**
Earnings	101,071	105,688	110,101	114,259	118,105	121,585	124,642	130,467	136,564
% Growth	*4.95%*	*4.57%*	*4.18%*	*3.78%*	*3.37%*	*2.95%*	*2.51%*	*4.67%*	*4.67%*
Dividends	37,502	39,215	40,852	42,395	43,822	45,113	46,248	48,409	50,671
% Growth	*4.95%*	*4.57%*	*4.18%*	*3.78%*	*3.37%*	*2.95%*	*2.51%*	*4.67%*	*4.67%*
Implied payout ratio	37.10%	37.10%	37.10%	37.10%	37.10%	37.10%	37.10%	37.10%	37.10%
Book value	838,852	905,325	974,574	1,046,438	1,120,721	1,197,193	1,275,588	1,357,646	1,443,539
% Growth	*8.20%*	*7.92%*	*7.65%*	*7.37%*	*7.10%*	*6.82%*	*6.55%*	*6.43%*	*6.33%*
Implied residual income (RI)	43,467	43,360	42,835	41,846	40,353	38,314	35,689	35,689	35,689
% Growth	*0.62%*	*-0.25%*	*-1.21%*	*-2.31%*	*-3.57%*	*-5.05%*	*-6.85%*	*0.00%*	*0.00%*
Implied agr	-2,409	-2,934	-3,497	-4,097	-4,730	-5,395	-2,840	-2,973	NA
% Growth	*NM*	*21.75%*	*19.20%*	*17.16%*	*15.47%*	*14.04%*	*-47.36%*	*4.67%*	*NA*
Implied return on book equity	*13.04%*	*12.60%*	*12.16%*	*11.72%*	*11.29%*	*10.85%*	*10.41%*	*10.23%*	*10.06%*
Convergence to (1)									*7.43%*
Implied one-year forward PE multiple (2)								13.5x	13.5x
Convergence to (3)									13.5x

Note: Grey marked fields indicate explicit assumptions.
(1) Based on the approach to determine the post-horizontal behavior outlined in Appendix 6.
(2) Implied calculation based on current payout ratio, cost of equity, and dividend growth rate.
(3) Implied calculation based on payout ratio, cost of equity, and long-term converging dividend growth rate: $\text{Max}\left[g_{m};r^{*}\left(1-\theta\right)\right]$ (See Appendix 6).

Table 35 Overview of expected MRP estimation procedures for all three equity valuation models

Terminal value techniques

	1. Terminal perpetuity				
	1.1 Zero RI	1.2 Zero RI growth	1.3 Inflation growth	1.4 Steady state	1.5.2 Zero RI growth + fade
Assumptions					
PGR RI	0.00%	0.00%	1.37%	8.47%	0.00%
Impl. PGR agr	0.00%	0.00%	1.37%	8.47%	0.00%
Impl. conv. PGR Div. (1)	-2.03%	4.87%	5.17%	8.47%	4.67%
Impl. conv. PE multiple	NM	12.9x	12.2x	14.4x	13.5x
r^b behavior	equal to r^e	conv. to r^e	conv. to r^e	const.	conv. to r^e
Valuation					
NPV EFP RIV	1,068,804	689,178	677,169	610,442	841,130
NPV EFP CAP	1,068,804	1,068,804	1,003,749	717,350	1,068,804
NPV EFP DIV	172,541	131,631	130,808	122,493	294,077
NPV TV RIV	0	379,626	391,635	458,362	227,673
NPV TV CAP	0	0	65,054	351,454	0
NPV TV DIV	896,263	937,173	937,995	946,310	774,726
P RIV	1,068,804	1,068,804	1,068,804	1,068,804	1,068,804
P CAP	1,068,804	1,068,804	1,068,804	1,068,804	1,068,804
P DIV	1,068,804	1,068,804	1,068,804	1,068,804	1,068,804
Iteration P RIV=MV	0	0	0	0	0
Iteration P CAP=MV	0	0	0	0	0
Iteration P DIV=MV	0	0	0	0	0
Implied expected returns/MRPs					
r^e RIV	-3.23%	7.75%	8.22%	11.05%	7.43%
r^e CAP	-3.23%	7.75%	8.22%	11.05%	7.43%
r^e DIV	-3.23%	7.75%	8.03%	11.05%	7.43%
r^f	3.93%	3.93%	3.93%	3.93%	3.93%
r^p RIV	-7.16%	3.82%	4.29%	7.12%	3.50%
r^p CAP	-7.16%	3.82%	4.29%	7.12%	3.50%
r^p DIV	-7.16%	3.82%	4.10%	7.12%	3.50%

	2. Terminal multiple		
	2.1 Exit = Entry	2.2 Exit = In-sample avg.	2.3 Exit = Out of sample avg.
Assumptions			
Exit P/E ratio	14.76x	19.03x	19.39x
Earnings t+5	96,302	96,302	96,302
Implied PGR Div.	9.32%	20.04%	20.66%
Valuation			
NPV EFP RIV	586,460	469,589	462,060
NPV EFP CAP	654,204	344,152	331,182
NPV EFP DIV	98,696	86,654	85,853
NPV TV RIV	482,344	599,215	606,744
NPV TV CAP	414,599	724,651	737,621
NPV TV DIV	970,108	982,150	982,951
P RIV	1,068,804	1,068,804	1,068,804
P CAP	1,068,804	1,068,804	1,068,804
P DIV	1,068,804	1,068,804	1,068,804
Iteration P RIV=MV	0	0	0
Iteration P CAP=MV	0	0	0
Iteration P DIV=MV	0	0	0
Implied expected returns/MRPs			
r^e RIV	11.83%	20.04%	20.66%
r^e CAP	11.83%	20.04%	20.66%
r^e DIV	11.83%	20.04%	20.66%
r^f	3.93%	3.93%	3.93%
r^p RIV	7.90%	16.11%	16.73%
r^p CAP	7.90%	16.11%	16.73%
r^p DIV	7.90%	16.11%	16.73%

(1) Long-term converging dividend growth rate based on $\text{Max}\left[g_{ss};r^{e}\left(1-\theta\right)\right]$ (See Appendix 6).

Finally, the implementation of the regression-based approach (1.6) to simultaneously estimate cost of equity and residual earnings growth is demonstrated. The method is implemented by an ordinary-least-squares (OLS) regression approach[814] in order to establish a linear relationship between the cum-dividend earnings/book ratio (dependent variable) and the price/book ratio (independent variable). Since the cum-dividend earnings require the cost of equity as an input parameter which itself needs to be estimated, a circular reference occurs which is resolved by the iterative procedure of Excel. Cost of equity and residual earnings growth can now be inferred from the estimated regression coefficients.

The OLS regression is highly sensitive to input data outliers of the independent and dependent variable[815]. An outlier is not a formally defined term in econometrics but can be interpreted as an observation which has a large influence on the estimation result[816]. Particularly outliers at the boarders of the observation spectrum do not only impact the standard errors of coefficients but also the parameters for the regression line itself[817] which are the basis for estimating expected return and growth. Still, the elimination of outliers by setting boarders for the allowed value range of observations may cause distortions or a loss of important information due to the subjective judgment of the researcher. It is therefore suggested to first check whether the outliers are related to errors in the data set and, if outliers remain, to estimate the regression parameters both including and excluding the outliers[818]. Alternatively, estimation methods could be used which are less sensitive to outliers such as the median regression[819]. However, the former approach is chosen for this analysis in order to maintain consistency with the OLS approach used in comparable studies[820].

In order to run regressions excluding outliers, the input value range is limited for the cum-dividend earnings/book ratio from -10 to 10 and for the price/book ratio from 0 to 10. The rationale for a lower bound of zero for the price/book ratio is that neither the market price nor the book value should be negative. The limit for the remaining

[814] See Greene, W. (2008), pp. 11-19 and Wooldridge, J. (2009), pp. 157-158 for a summary of key assumptions for the application of the classical linear regression model. See also Greene, W. (2008), pp. 20-39 and Wooldridge, J. (2009), pp. 27-36 for the basic foundations of OLS estimation.
[815] See Wooldridge, J. (2009), p. 325.
[816] See Fahrmeir, L./Kneib, T./Lang, S. (2009), p. 173 and Wooldridge, J. (2009), p. 325.
[817] See Fahrmeir, L./Kneib, T./Lang, S. (2009), p. 173.
[818] See Fahrmeir, L./Kneib, T./Lang, S. (2009), pp. 175-176.
[819] See Fahrmeir, L./Kneib, T./Lang, S. (2009), pp. 176-177.
[820] See Easton, P. et al. (2002), Easton, P. (2004), and Daske, H./Gebhardt, G./Klein, S. (2006).

boundaries is set to +/-10 to allow for sufficient standard deviations of fluctuations around the mean. The width of this range is exemplified by recognizing that the mean and the maximum standard deviation of the monthly limited samples between 1989 and 2006, e.g., for the German market are 0.66/0.91 for the cum-dividend earnings/book ratio and 2.18/2.33 for the price/book ratio.

In order to analyze the implications of eliminating outliers, the following example shows results for regressions including and excluding outliers. Again, assume the estimation of the expected MRP for the German CDAX on 29.12.2006. Exhibit 43 firstly shows the regression analysis for the unrestricted sample[821]. The regression chart illustrates that the outliers artificially inflate the coefficient of determination since the regression line is "pulled" towards the outlining observations which causes the associated residuals to be relatively small[822]. Estimating the regression coefficients including outliers also leads to unreasonable results as evidenced by a negative perpetual growth rate and a negative expected MRP[823]. Therefore, a limitation of input data appears appropriate as exemplified by Exhibit 44. The results of the limited sample size are now plausible and the undisturbed regression quality indicators still show a clear relationship between the variables as coefficients are highly significant.

The aforementioned calculation methodology is replicated for all analyzed equity markets at each monthly estimation date throughout the entire analysis period.

---

[821] As identified by Easton et al. (2002) and Easton (2004), the error terms are heteroskedastic as they show variable variances. Therefore, the Breusch/Pagan (1979) test for heteroskedasticity is applied and robust standard errors are used in assessing the significance of coefficients.

[822] See also Fahrmeir, L./Kneib, T./Lang, S. (2009), p. 173.

[823] See also Wallmeier, M. (2007), pp. 569-570 who also finds partially implausible results using the regression approach.

Exhibit 43 Linear regression analysis for the German market on 29.12.2006 using unrestricted input data for regression variables

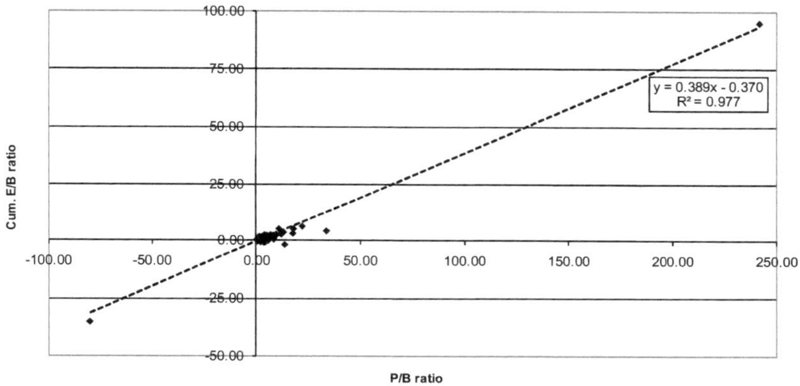

Linear regression statistics

# of firms	274	α	-0.370		**g**	**-10.92%**
df	272	se α	0.058		**r^e**	**0.45%**
		se α (1)	0.057	p-value	**r^T**	**3.93%**
R^2	97.67%	t-value α	-6.333	0.0000	**r^P**	**-3.48%**
Adj. R^2	97.66%	t-value α (1)	-6.543	0.0000		
		β	0.389			
		se β	0.004			
		se β (1)	0.008			
		t-value β	106.750	0.0000		
Test for heteroskedasticity		t-value β (1)	48.038	0.0000		
Breusch-Pagan Test						
chi²-value	51.910	F-value	11,395.532	0.0000		
p-value	0.0000	F-value (1)	2,307.330	0.0000		

(1) Based on robust standard errors.

Exhibit 44 Linear regression analysis for the German market on 29.12.2006 using restricted input data for regression variables

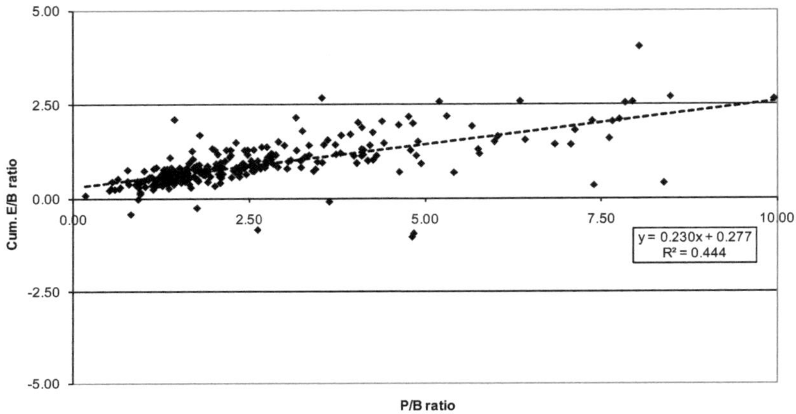

Linear regression statistics

# of firms	265	α	0.277		g	6.31%
df	263	se α	0.050		r^e	10.80%
		se α (1)	0.054	p-value	r^f	3.93%
R^2	44.42%	t-value α	5.523	0.0000	r^p	6.87%
Adj. R^2	44.21%	t-value α (1)	5.088	0.0000		
		β	0.230			
		se β	0.016			
		se β (1)	0.026			
		t-value β	14.497	0.0000		
Test for heteroskedasticity		t-value β (1)	8.996	0.0000		
Breusch-Pagan Test						
chi²-value	134.260	F-value	210.162	0.0000		
p-value	0.0000	F-value (1)	80.920	0.0000		

(1) Based on robust standard errors.

5.9 Discussion of results

The results are now presented and compared to previous studies estimating the expected MRP using forecasts of research analysts. The presentation is sequentially for each local market starting with the Germany.

5.9.1 Germany

Firstly, the expected MRP development is analyzed using the described set of terminal perpetuity approaches[824]. Exhibit 45 illustrates that for almost all terminal perpetuity assumptions the conditional expected MRP estimates increase throughout the analysis period which indicates non-stationarity. Assuming that the return on book equity equals the expected return from the terminal value period onwards appears to be a too conservative assumption. In this case, the expected MRP is with the exception of one year substantially below zero which is not consistent with the general assumption of a risk-averse investor[825]. Since this approach provides implausible results for all markets, the estimates will be continuously shown but not further discussed. Focusing on approaches using specific assumptions for the perpetual residual income growth, the rise in the expected MRP becomes more evident. The assumption of zero perpetual growth[826] in residual earnings again leads to certain periods with negative conditional MRP expectations raising doubts about the validity of this approach given the aforementioned argument. Increasing the perpetual residual earnings growth rate to the ex-post inflation rate results in an almost parallel upward shift of the expected MRP development. There are no more periods of negative conditional expected MRPs and the unconditional mean for the analysis period rises from 1.86% with no perpetual growth to 2.56% with inflation-linked perpetual growth of residual earnings as presented in Table 36. The annual expected MRP estimates derived from both approaches develop almost flat before reaching a low in 2000 after which the conditional expected MRP rises substantially to a peak level in 2003. In case of steady state perpetual residual earnings growth, the increase in the expected MRP occurs earlier and remains relatively stable after 1998. This development is driven by an almost opposite development of the implied steady state growth rate and the ex-post inflation rate as illustrated by Exhibit 46. In absolute terms, the expected MRP using the steady state terminal growth approach has an arithmetic mean of precisely 5.00% for the analysis period, almost double of the inflation-linked case. Interestingly enough, the lower—in selected cases even negative—conditional expected MRP level at the beginning of the analysis period

---

[824] The input data for the German market is summarized in Appendix 11 and Appendix 12.

[825] See, e.g., Ibbotson, R./Sinquefield, R. (1976), p. 35.

[826] It should be noted that zero perpetual growth in residual income still corresponds to implied perpetual dividend growth in the range of 3.4% to 6.7%.

coincides with high inflation rates. In particularly during these times it appears plausible to use a conditional and inflation-linked proxy as perpetual growth rate in order to derive plausible results. A final observation can be made about the implied relative price level of the terminal perpetuity growth assumptions. The forward PE_{+1} ratio implied by steady state growth is only 1.7x higher compared to no perpetual residual income growth. This illustrates the strong impact of even minor changes in the terminal multiple. It becomes also obvious that the average implied forward PE_{+1} ratios from terminal perpetuities are at a minimum 4.1x lower than the spot PE_{+1} ratios supporting the argument in Section 5.1.2.

When applying the simultaneous regression-based estimation approach for expected MRP and perpetual growth, the resulting expected MRP evolves similarly to the steady state case but is slightly lower comparing the unconditional means with an average expected MRP value of 4.12% as presented in Table 37. This result is driven by a lower average level of estimated perpetual growth in residual earnings which shows substantial fluctuations largely in-between the steady-state growth level and the ex-post inflation rate.

Exhibit 45 German expected MRP development using the standard model with various terminal perpetuity approaches

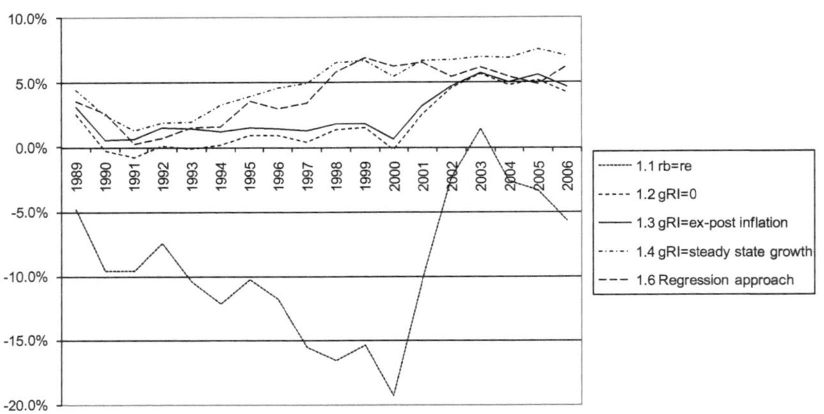

The development of other proxies for the perpetual growth rate of residual earnings is presented in Exhibit 46. The usage of the expected five-year IBES earnings CAGR[827] appears implausible as its development reaches highest level in peak market periods that are unreasonable to assume until infinity. Another popular metric—the ex-post GDP growth rate[828]—follows a path slightly higher than the ex-post inflation rate.

Exhibit 46 Development of selected perpetual growth proxies for the German market

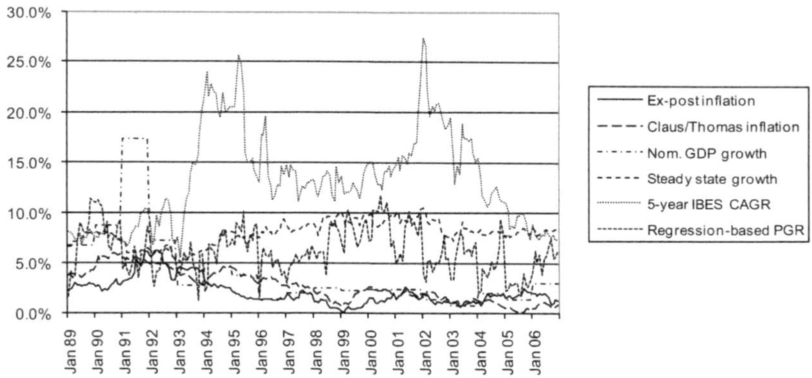

Source: IBES, Datastream.

Except for the first terminal perpetuity case, the standard deviation of the inferred premia is approximately 2% for all other approaches and thereby substantially below the volatility of ex-post MRPs. Still, this value may appear high given the absolute levels of arithmetic averages of the expected MRP but the sample for the German market substantially changed throughout the sample period as more and more firms went public and IBES coverage increased. These facts must be taken into account when interpreting the German market results and—in particular—the apparent rise of the expected MRP when inferred from valuation models using analysts' consensus estimates.

---

[827] This metric is similar to the IBES long-term earnings growth rate used in earlier studies. Here, the five-year IBES earnings CAGR is presented since the long-term earnings growth rate is not available for the entire sample.

[828] The here presented GDP growth rate is stated in nominal terms to be consistent with all other input parameters of the model. Further note that the outliers in the years 1991 and 1992 are related to the German reunification process.

The data underlying this study can also be used to calculate the expected MRP with the terminal perpetuity specifications of previous studies. Exhibit 47 summarizes the development of the expected MRP when the earlier discussed specifications of comparables studies are applied. It becomes obvious that the general development of thereby estimated expected MRPs show very similar fluctuations. Depending on the level of optimism for the terminal growth rate, the resulting expected MRP development is almost a parallel up- or downward shift. Therefore, unconditional averages of the expected MRP for the analysis period range from -0.04% to 5.29% as presented in Appendix 13. Consistent with the results in Exhibit 45, all model derivatives with non-inflation linked perpetual growth rates lead to negative conditional expected MRPs during the years 1990 to 1992.

Exhibit 47 German expected MRP development using special comparison specifications of previous studies

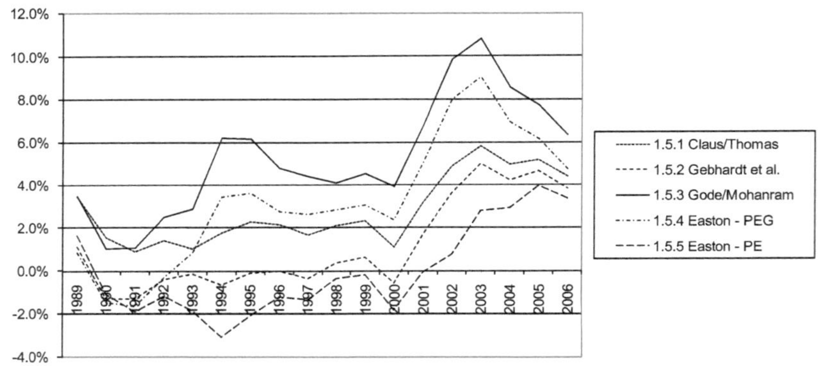

Table 36 Summary statistics of the German expected MRP estimation using the standard model with various terminal perpetuity approaches

Model (1)						1.1 $r^b=r^e$		1.2 $g_{RI}=0$					1.3 g_{RI}=ex-post inflation					1.4 g_{RI}=steady state growth			
Year	r^f (2)	θ_{TV}	$m_{P/E+1}$	N (3)	Firms (4)	r^e	r^p	r^e	r^p	$g_{RI,TV}$	$g_{D,TV}$ (5)	$m_{P/E+1,TV}$ (6)	r^e	r^p	$g_{RI,TV}$	$g_{D,TV}$ (5)	$m_{P/E+1,TV}$ (7)	r^e	r^p	$g_{RI,D,TV}$	$m_{P/E+1,TV}$ (6)
1989	6.92%	44.74%	12.2x	415	35	2.07%	-4.85%	9.44%	2.52%	0.00%	5.21%	10.6x	10.03%	3.12%	2.75%	5.54%	NA	11.41%	4.49%	7.52%	11.5x
1990	8.61%	41.13%	13.9x	491	41	-1.00%	-9.61%	8.35%	-0.25%	0.00%	4.92%	12.0x	9.16%	0.56%	2.73%	5.39%	NA	11.04%	2.43%	7.92%	13.2x
1991	8.37%	45.90%	16.0x	768	64	-1.19%	-9.56%	7.60%	-0.76%	0.00%	4.11%	13.2x	8.98%	0.61%	4.50%	4.86%	NA	9.64%	1.27%	6.42%	14.2x
1992	7.78%	45.52%	15.7x	851	71	0.30%	-7.48%	7.91%	0.13%	0.00%	4.31%	12.6x	9.29%	1.52%	5.10%	5.06%	NA	9.64%	1.87%	6.28%	13.5x
1993	6.48%	46.54%	22.8x	894	75	-3.95%	-10.42%	6.34%	-0.14%	0.00%	3.39%	15.8x	7.91%	1.43%	4.44%	4.23%	NA	8.44%	1.97%	5.71%	17.1x
1994	6.99%	46.21%	26.4x	1,021	85	-5.13%	-12.13%	7.21%	0.21%	0.00%	3.88%	13.9x	8.24%	1.24%	2.75%	4.43%	NA	10.24%	3.25%	7.29%	15.7x
1995	6.81%	43.64%	21.8x	1,112	93	-3.45%	-10.25%	7.74%	0.93%	0.00%	4.36%	12.9x	8.31%	1.51%	1.72%	4.68%	NA	10.75%	3.94%	7.73%	14.5x
1996	6.24%	38.88%	20.4x	1,245	104	-5.57%	-11.81%	7.13%	0.89%	0.00%	4.36%	14.0x	7.67%	1.43%	1.45%	4.69%	NA	10.81%	4.57%	8.38%	16.0x
1997	5.67%	38.78%	23.7x	1,409	117	-9.86%	-15.53%	6.08%	0.41%	0.00%	3.72%	16.4x	6.97%	1.31%	1.88%	4.27%	NA	10.63%	4.96%	8.62%	19.3x
1998	4.55%	40.00%	24.4x	1,606	134	-12.03%	-16.58%	5.88%	1.33%	0.00%	3.53%	17.0x	6.34%	1.79%	0.94%	3.80%	NA	11.12%	6.57%	9.17%	20.5x
1999	4.62%	37.24%	23.0x	2,072	173	-10.77%	-15.39%	6.14%	1.52%	0.00%	3.86%	16.3x	6.41%	1.79%	0.57%	4.02%	NA	11.37%	6.75%	9.46%	19.5x
2000	5.30%	34.38%	29.4x	2,947	246	-13.97%	-19.27%	5.15%	-0.15%	0.00%	3.38%	19.4x	5.93%	0.64%	1.47%	3.89%	NA	10.78%	5.49%	9.33%	23.7x
2001	4.87%	30.91%	21.5x	3,506	292	-5.36%	-10.23%	7.40%	2.53%	0.00%	5.11%	13.5x	8.11%	3.24%	1.98%	5.60%	NA	11.65%	6.78%	9.69%	15.8x
2002	4.80%	29.88%	19.3x	3,271	273	2.44%	-2.35%	9.36%	4.56%	0.00%	6.56%	10.7x	9.56%	4.77%	1.37%	6.71%	NA	11.63%	6.84%	9.05%	11.6x
2003	4.14%	31.85%	15.2x	2,464	205	5.55%	1.42%	9.80%	5.66%	0.00%	6.68%	10.2x	9.93%	5.80%	1.05%	6.77%	NA	11.21%	7.08%	8.23%	10.7x
2004	4.09%	35.20%	14.7x	2,567	214	1.46%	-2.63%	8.84%	4.75%	0.00%	5.73%	11.3x	9.17%	5.08%	1.67%	5.94%	NA	11.05%	6.97%	8.20%	12.3x
2005	3.37%	37.57%	14.1x	2,742	229	0.05%	-3.32%	8.51%	5.13%	0.00%	5.31%	11.8x	9.01%	5.64%	1.95%	5.62%	NA	11.02%	7.64%	8.11%	12.9x
2006	3.81%	36.70%	14.5x	3,122	260	-1.87%	-5.69%	8.01%	4.19%	0.00%	5.07%	12.5x	8.49%	4.68%	1.71%	5.37%	NA	10.94%	7.13%	8.31%	13.9x
Low	3.37%	29.88%	12.2x	415	35	-13.97%	-19.27%	5.15%	-0.76%	0.00%	3.38%	10.2x	5.93%	0.56%	0.57%	3.80%	NA	8.44%	1.27%	5.71%	10.7x
Arith. Mean	5.74%	39.17%	19.4x	1,806	150	-3.46%	-9.20%	7.60%	1.86%	0.00%	4.64%	13.6x	8.31%	2.56%	2.22%	5.05%	NA	10.74%	5.00%	8.08%	15.3x
Median	5.48%	38.83%	19.9x	1,508	126	-2.66%	-9.92%	7.67%	1.13%	0.00%	4.36%	13.0x	8.40%	1.65%	1.80%	4.96%	NA	10.98%	5.23%	8.22%	14.3x
High	8.61%	46.54%	29.4x	3,506	292	5.55%	1.42%	9.80%	5.66%	0.00%	6.68%	19.4x	10.03%	5.80%	5.10%	6.77%	NA	11.65%	7.64%	9.69%	23.7x
St. Dev.	1.60%	5.45%	5.0x			5.43%	5.56%	1.33%	2.12%	0.00%	1.01%	2.5x	1.24%	1.83%	1.28%	0.89%	NA	0.81%	2.12%	1.12%	3.5x

(1) All parameters are stated in nominal terms and as arithmetic average of monthly values.
(2) r^f equals redemption yield of the REX 10y subindex.
(3) Overall number of firm observations per annum.
(4) Average number of firms per annum.
(5) Implied perpetual dividend growth rate (after convergence for $0<g_{RI}<g_{RI\ steady\ state}$ cases) according to calculation approach presented in Appendix 10 - Max[$g_{RI,TV}$;$(1-\theta_{TV})r^e$].
(6) Terminal multiple implied by a calculation based on terminal period payout ratio, cost of equity, and perpetual dividend growth rate.
(7) Implied terminal multiple cannot be determined as perpetual dividend growth rate is not constant but converging.

Table 37 Summary statistics of the German expected MRP estimation using the regression-based approach

Model (1)				1.6. Regression approach					
Year	r^f (2)	N (3)	Firms (4)	r^e	r^p	$g_{RI,TV}$	$g_{D,TV}$ (5)	$m_{P/E+1,TV}$ (6)	Adj. R^2
1989	6.92%	412	34	10.50%	3.58%	7.18%	7.18%	NA	29.71%
1990	8.61%	491	41	11.20%	2.60%	9.00%	9.00%	NA	19.03%
1991	8.37%	759	63	8.62%	0.26%	5.43%	5.43%	NA	13.61%
1992	7.78%	851	71	8.48%	0.70%	5.41%	5.41%	NA	45.16%
1993	6.48%	887	74	7.95%	1.47%	4.93%	4.93%	NA	37.22%
1994	6.99%	975	81	8.60%	1.61%	6.14%	6.14%	NA	38.71%
1995	6.81%	1,067	89	10.38%	3.57%	8.06%	8.06%	NA	24.68%
1996	6.24%	1,208	101	9.19%	2.95%	4.94%	5.62%	NA	62.26%
1997	5.67%	1,362	114	9.08%	3.41%	5.37%	5.56%	NA	55.12%
1998	4.55%	1,494	125	10.39%	5.84%	6.97%	6.97%	NA	37.29%
1999	4.62%	1,812	151	11.59%	6.97%	8.24%	8.24%	NA	22.39%
2000	5.30%	2,247	187	11.58%	6.29%	9.37%	9.37%	NA	37.12%
2001	4.87%	3,302	275	11.48%	6.62%	7.88%	7.93%	NA	10.85%
2002	4.80%	3,154	263	10.27%	5.48%	5.16%	7.20%	NA	22.72%
2003	4.14%	2,405	200	10.35%	6.21%	6.08%	7.05%	NA	22.51%
2004	4.09%	2,490	208	9.56%	5.47%	5.02%	6.19%	NA	13.55%
2005	3.37%	2,634	220	8.28%	4.91%	2.80%	5.17%	NA	63.01%
2006	3.81%	2,975	248	10.09%	6.27%	5.73%	6.38%	NA	44.40%
Low	3.37%	412	34	7.95%	0.26%	2.80%	4.93%	NA	10.85%
Arith. Mean	5.74%	1,696	141	9.87%	4.12%	6.32%	6.77%	NA	33.30%
Median	5.48%	1,428	119	10.18%	4.24%	5.90%	6.68%	NA	33.41%
High	8.61%	3,302	275	11.59%	6.97%	9.37%	9.37%	NA	63.01%
St. Dev.	1.60%			1.19%	2.17%	1.70%	1.34%	NA	16.19%

(1) All parameters are stated in nominal terms and as arithmetic average of monthly values.
(2) r^f equals redemption yield of the REX 10y subindex.
(3) Overall number of firm observations per annum.
(4) Average number of firms per annum.
(5) Implied perpetual dividend growth rate after convergence according to calculation approach presented in Appendix 10 - Max[$g_{RI,TV}$;$(1-\theta_{TV})r^e$].
(6) Implied terminal multiple cannot be determined since implied perpetual dividend growth rate is not constant but converging.

Secondly, the results for the terminal multiple approach are provided. Terminal multiples were critically reviewed in Section 5.1.2 since empirical applications are only possible with spot multiples instead of theoretically required and likely lower forward multiples. This leads to the hypothesis that valuation models using spot multiples to infer the terminal value are likely to overestimate the expected MRPs.

Assuming that the terminal (exit) multiple equals the spot PE_{+1} ratio at the valuation date leads to a substantially higher expected MRP compared to even the most optimistic terminal perpetuity case. The unconditional average of the expected MRP over the analysis period is 11.97% as shown in Table 38; more than double the expected MRP in the steady state case. Calculating the perpetual dividend growth rate implied by this terminal multiple assumption shows that the expected MRP difference is attributable to much higher underlying growth level. Furthermore, Exhibit 48 illustrates a larger fluctuation of the expected MRP over time with two peak levels reached in 1994 and 2002. The higher volatility is also documented by a standard deviation of 5.17%. Given magnitude of results for the entry=exit multiple scenario, it appears questionable whether this assumption is reasonable despite its common utilization among financial practitioners.

The two alternative terminal multiple approaches assume the convergence to the in- or out-of-sample average of the historical spot PE_{+1} ratio. This assumption leads to negative correlation between current PE_{+1} multiple and the expected MRP. At the highpoint of the millennium peak, the expected MRP had been around zero whereas in down-cycle periods such as 2003 an expected MRP in excess of 25% was reached.

Exhibit 48 German expected MRP development using the standard model with various terminal multiple approaches

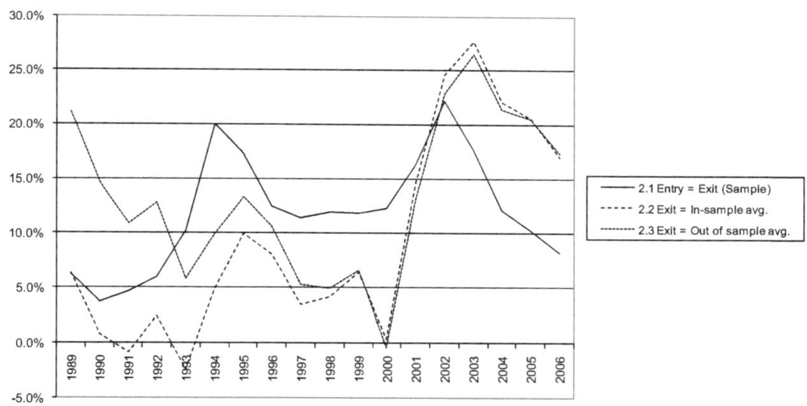

The results for the expected MRP estimation using terminal multiples show that the usage of spot multiples for terminal values calculations is not appropriate. Since the German findings are consistent with the other countries, individual results for the remaining countries in the sample are not provided.

Table 38 Summary statistics of the German expected MRP estimation using the standard model with various terminal multiple approaches

Model (1)						2.1 Entry = Exit (Sample)				2.2 Exit = In-sample avg.				2.3 Exit = Out of sample avg.			
Year	r^f (2)	θ_{TV}	$m_{P/E+1}$	N (3)	Firms (4)	r^e	r^p	$m_{P/E+1,TV}$	$g_{D,TV}$ (5)	r^e	r^p	$m_{P/E+1,TV}$	$g_{D,TV}$ (5)	r^e	r^p	$m_{P/E+1,TV}$	$g_{D,TV}$ (5)
1989	6.92%	44.74%	12.2x	415	35	13.19%	6.27%	12.2x	9.52%	13.21%	6.29%	12.2x	9.54%	28.03%	21.11%	19.4x	25.72%
1990	8.61%	41.13%	13.9x	491	41	12.39%	3.79%	13.9x	9.43%	9.41%	0.80%	12.5x	6.11%	23.23%	14.63%	19.4x	21.11%
1991	8.37%	45.90%	16.0x	768	64	13.09%	4.72%	16.0x	10.23%	7.49%	-0.88%	13.2x	4.00%	19.27%	10.90%	19.4x	16.91%
1992	7.78%	45.52%	15.7x	851	71	13.81%	6.03%	15.7x	10.91%	10.17%	2.40%	13.8x	6.88%	20.65%	12.88%	19.4x	18.31%
1993	6.48%	46.54%	22.8x	894	75	16.76%	10.28%	22.8x	14.71%	4.06%	-2.41%	14.7x	0.88%	12.25%	5.78%	19.4x	9.85%
1994	6.99%	46.21%	26.4x	1,021	85	26.99%	20.00%	26.4x	25.24%	11.95%	4.96%	16.5x	9.16%	16.93%	9.94%	19.4x	14.55%
1995	6.81%	43.64%	21.8x	1,112	93	24.03%	17.22%	21.8x	22.03%	16.76%	9.96%	17.5x	14.26%	20.17%	13.36%	19.4x	17.92%
1996	6.24%	38.88%	20.4x	1,245	104	18.77%	12.53%	20.4x	16.86%	14.26%	8.02%	17.8x	12.08%	16.89%	10.65%	19.4x	14.89%
1997	5.67%	38.78%	23.7x	1,409	117	17.15%	11.48%	23.7x	15.51%	9.16%	3.49%	18.3x	7.04%	10.92%	5.25%	19.4x	8.92%
1998	4.55%	40.00%	24.4x	1,606	134	16.54%	11.99%	24.4x	14.90%	8.69%	4.14%	18.9x	6.57%	9.52%	4.97%	19.4x	7.46%
1999	4.62%	37.24%	23.0x	2,072	173	16.51%	11.89%	23.0x	14.89%	11.00%	6.38%	19.2x	9.06%	11.25%	6.63%	19.4x	9.33%
2000	5.30%	34.38%	29.4x	2,947	246	17.63%	12.33%	29.4x	16.46%	5.61%	0.31%	19.9x	3.88%	4.87%	-0.43%	19.4x	3.10%
2001	4.87%	30.91%	21.5x	3,506	292	21.20%	16.33%	21.5x	19.76%	19.40%	14.53%	20.3x	17.87%	17.96%	13.09%	19.4x	16.37%
2002	4.80%	29.88%	19.3x	3,271	273	26.96%	22.16%	19.3x	25.41%	29.33%	24.54%	20.3x	27.86%	27.67%	22.87%	19.4x	26.13%
2003	4.14%	31.85%	15.2x	2,464	205	21.75%	17.61%	15.2x	19.66%	31.82%	27.68%	20.0x	30.23%	30.66%	26.53%	19.4x	29.02%
2004	4.09%	35.20%	14.7x	2,567	214	16.28%	12.19%	14.7x	13.88%	26.12%	22.03%	19.7x	24.34%	25.50%	21.41%	19.4x	23.68%
2005	3.37%	37.57%	14.1x	2,742	229	13.76%	10.39%	14.1x	11.10%	23.99%	20.62%	19.4x	22.05%	23.92%	20.55%	19.4x	21.98%
2006	3.81%	36.70%	14.5x	3,122	260	12.05%	8.24%	14.5x	9.52%	20.79%	16.98%	19.2x	18.87%	21.19%	17.38%	19.4x	19.30%
Low	3.37%	29.88%	12.2x	415	35	12.05%	3.79%	12.2x	9.43%	4.06%	-2.41%	12.2x	0.88%	4.87%	-0.43%	19.4x	3.10%
Arith. Mean	5.74%	39.17%	19.4x	1,806	150	17.71%	11.97%	19.4x	15.56%	15.18%	9.44%	17.4x	12.82%	18.94%	13.19%	19.4x	16.92%
Median	5.48%	38.83%	19.9x	1,508	126	16.65%	11.94%	19.9x	14.90%	12.58%	6.33%	18.6x	9.35%	19.72%	12.98%	19.4x	17.41%
High	8.61%	46.54%	29.4x	3,506	292	26.99%	22.16%	29.4x	25.41%	31.82%	27.68%	20.3x	30.23%	30.66%	26.53%	19.4x	29.02%
St. Dev.	1.60%	5.45%	5.0x			4.73%	5.17%	5.0x	5.17%	8.30%	9.35%	2.9x	8.76%	7.10%	7.32%	0.0x	7.15%

(1) All parameters are stated in nominal terms and as arithmetic average of monthly values.
(2) r^f equals redemption yield of the REX 10y subindex.
(3) Overall number of firm observations per annum.
(4) Average number of firms per annum.
(5) Implied perpetual dividend growth rate based on terminal period payout ratio, cost of equity, and terminal multiple (price/earnings ratio).

The results of this study can also be compared to several previous studies which apply a similar approach to determine the expected MRP for the German market. The conceptual details of each study have already been presented in Sections 5.2.4 and 5.3.3. Table 39 provides a first overview of the unconditional averages of all studies on the German market.

The average expected MRP estimates range depended on the selected model specifications from 1.13% to 6.78%. Differences among studies appear of minor magnitude when the same averaging approach is applied. The following section discusses key differences in results.

Firstly, the focus is on studies that use a three-stage RIV model in the Gebhardt/Lee/Swaminathan version with a fade period to a target return on book equity and a terminal perpetuity with zero growth of residual income. The key results of such studies are summarized in Appendix 14. First to publish their results were Daske/Gebhardt/Klein in a working paper already in 2004. Fluctuating around zero in the early years of the analysis period, their estimate of the conditional expected MRP rises continuously and reaches a double-digit level at the turn of the millennium. This development, consistent with the results by Lee/Ng/Swaminathan in the overlapping period, raised doubts about the validity of the used methodology. "Unklar bei dieser Studie ist allerdings, warum die [...] vorgelegten Schätzwerte für die Risikoprämie für die Jahre 1989 bis 2002 im Zeitablauf fast kontinuierlich ansteigen [...] Möglicherweise hängen diese Ergebnisse mit der Qualität der Dividenden- und Gewinnschätzungen von Analysten zusammen, für die in Deutschland noch kaum Erfahrungen vorliegen. Ohne Zweifel sollte dieses Verfahren auch für Deutschland intensiver diskutiert und regelmäßiger angewendet werden" [829]. Furthermore, Daske/Gebhardt/Klein themselves note that the continuous rise in the expected MRP is not confirmed in similar studies for the US market[830]. Despite the already identified limited validity of the German results in early years due to the restricted sample size, another important argument to explain the inconsistent results is provided by Reese.

[829] Stehle, R. (2004), p. 918.

[830] See Daske, H./Gebhardt, G./Klein, S. (2006), p. 16.

Table 39 Overview of key results of previous studies on the German market

Authors	Period	Weighting (1)	Arith. mean over analysis period (2) r^e	r^p	r^f
Claus/Thomas Model					
Claus/Thomas (2001)	1988-1998	agg	10.82%	2.23%	8.59%
Desrosiers/Lemaire/L'Her (2007) (3)	1988-2005	NA	8.34%	2.13%	6.21%
Lee/Ng/Swaminathan (2009)	1991-2000	ew	NA	4.08%	NA
Reese (2005, 2007)	1989-2004	ew	10.58%	4.56%	6.01%
Reese (2005, 2007)	1989-2004	vw	8.72%	2.70%	6.01%
Gsell (2010)	1989-2006	agg	8.53%	2.79%	5.74%
Gebhardt/Lee/Swaminathan Model					
Chen/Jorgensen/Yoo (2004)	1993-2001	NA	7.0%	1.9%	5.1%
Daske/Gebhardt/Klein (2006)	1989-2002	ew	9.95%	3.86%	6.29%
Reese (2005, 2007)	1989-2004	ew	9.85%	3.84%	6.01%
Reese (2005, 2007)	1989-2004	vw	7.74%	1.72%	6.01%
Gsell (2010)	1989-2006	agg	6.88%	1.13%	5.74%
Gode/Mohanram Model					
Chen/Jorgensen/Yoo (2004)	1993-2001	NA	12.4%	7.3%	5.1%
Reese (2005, 2007)	1989-2004	vw	10.26%	4.24%	6.01%
Reese (2005, 2007)	1989-2004	ew	11.51%	5.50%	6.01%
Lee/Ng/Swaminathan (2009)	1991-2000	ew	NA	6.78%	NA
Gsell (2010)	1989-2006	agg	11.03%	5.29%	5.74%
Easton PEG Model					
Chen/Jorgensen/Yoo (2004)	1993-2001	NA	10.6%	5.5%	5.1%
Reese (2005, 2007)	1989-2004	ew	12.48%	6.47%	6.01%
Reese (2005, 2007)	1989-2004	vw	8.93%	2.92%	6.01%
Gsell (2010)	1989-2006	agg	9.02%	3.28%	5.74%
Regression approach					
Daske/Gebhardt/Klein (2006)	1989-2002	NAp	11.25%	5.14%	6.29%
Gsell (2010)	1989-2006	NAp	9.87%	4.12%	5.74%
Other approaches					
Hail/Leuz (2006) (4)	1992-2001	NA	10.05%	NA	NA
Lee/Ng/Swaminathan (2009) (5)	1991-2000	ew	NA	4.06%	NA
Pastor/Sinha/Swaminathan (2008) (5)	1990-2002	ew	NA	4.79%	NA
Pastor/Sinha/Swaminathan (2008) (5)	1990-2002	vw	NA	1.56%	NA

(1) agg = aggregation method; ew = equal-weighted; vw = value-weighted.
(2) All parameters are stated in nominal terms.
(3) Annualized r^e based on original monthly estimate (US-Dollar denominated);
Implied r^p using own US r^f estimate;
Terminal perpetuity based on g_{RI}=ex-post inflation.
(4) Average of Claus/Thomas, Gebhardt/Lee/Swaminathan, Gode/Mohanram, and Easton-PEG model.
(5) Estimation based on dividend discount model with r^e equal to r^b after 15 years.

Source: Claus, J./Thomas, J. (2001), p. 1643, Chen, F./Jorgensen, B./Yoo, Y. (2004), p. 331, Reese, R. (2005), pp. 13 and 19, Daske, H./Gebhardt, G./Klein, S. (2006), p. 15, Hail, L./Leuz, C. (2006), pp. 494-495, Desrosiers, S./Lemaire, N./L'Her, J.-F. (2007), p. 79, Pastor, L./Sinha, M./Swaminathan, B. (2008), p. 2875, and Lee, C./Ng, D./Swaminathan, B. (2009), pp. 318 and 321.

His argument is related to the already discussed topic of the appropriate averaging or aggregation approach[831]. The Daske/Gebhardt/Klein results for the market-wide

[831] See Reese, R. (2005), pp. 18-19.

expected MRP are all equally weighted which implies that high growth/volatility firms with a small market capitalization impact the market MRP in the same magnitude as an established large cap firm with a much lower risk profile. In particular at the end of the 1990s, a large number of these high-growth firms went public creating new market segments such as the "Neuer Markt" in Germany. As firms with a high growth and volatility profile usually trade at a higher risk premium than large-cap incumbents, the equal-weighting approach should explain a substantial part of the expected MRP increase in the Daske/Gebhardt/Klein analysis. The results provided by Reese and Pastor/Sinha/Swaminathan show that the value-weighted MRPs are significantly lower—in terms of both absolute values and standard deviation—than comparable results on an equally weighted basis and thereby support the aforementioned reasoning.

Comparing the value-weighted results from Reese to the expected MRP estimates implied by the aggregation approach used in this study shows the similarity of both techniques. Variations in results are minor and mostly driven by some differences in the underlying sample and the target return on book equity definition[832].

A final point of interest is the substantially lower sample size of this study compared to Reese and Daske/Gebhardt/Klein in particular throughout the years 1989 to 2000. The reason for this divergence is primarily related to a sample selection criterion as already indicated in fn. 776. Due to missing IBES DPS forecasts, future dividends are projected by applying the payout ratio of the last historical period. In contrast to the mentioned studies, the herein accepted values for the historical payout ratio are limited to a range from zero to one. This additional restriction is appropriate as payout ratios outside this range are either unrealistic or not sustainable in the long-term[833]. The effect of the additional sample selection criterion is larger in the earlier years of the analysis period since the availability of IBES DPS forecasts increases

---

[832] Daske/Gebhardt/Klein and Reese determine the target return on book equity as the five-year average of the respective industry group of analyzed firms; see Daske, H./Gebhardt, G./Klein, S. (2006), p. 7 and Reese, R. (2005), p. 6. Since this study uses the aggregation method, individual company returns on book equity are incompatible with this approach. Instead, this study uses the five-year average return on book equity of the aggregated market values as target level. During the first five years of the analysis period (1989-1993), the out-of-sample average value is applied.

[833] Negative payout ratios implied by the database values are mostly related to negative actual EPS. Therefore, the resulting negative payout ratio cannot be used for extrapolation purposes since this leads to negative dividends. Furthermore, dividend levels above one are usually related to special dividends. In the long-term, such a payout level is not sustainable since the associated book value would become negative over time.

sharply at the end of the 1990s which in return reduces the usage of historical payout ratios.

Secondly, the studies implementing the Claus/Thomas approach can be compared. Claus/Thomas apply a two-stage RIV model with a terminal perpetuity using a perpetual growth rate equal to the expected inflation rate calculated as risk-free rate less three percent of assumed real interest. The results for such studies are provided by Appendix 15. Again, differences appear minor due to the consistency of this study to the previous research if the identical terminal value assumptions are used.

Larger differences occur in comparing the results of this study with Reese for the Gode/Mohanram version of the CAP model as presented in Appendix 16. Such differences are related to an inconsistent sample structure caused by the relaxation of one selection criterion. In the classical Gode/Mohanram version the long-term IBES earnings growth rate is used to downward adjust the short-term earnings growth rate. Since such long-term IBES earnings growth rates are only available for selected firms, the sample of Reese is substantially smaller for this estimation approach. In order to prevent a limitation of the sample, this study uses the five-year expected IBES earnings CAGR as a proxy of the long-term growth rate. Therefore, the sample size of the previous approaches can be maintained. The effect of this divergence is intuitive. The data availability for large-cap firms is higher resulting in a lower risk profile of the smaller sample of Reese. Consequently, the unconditional expected MRP average of this study is approximately one percent higher compared to the value-weighted results of the Reese analysis.

Ultimately, the results of the simultaneous estimation of expected return and perpetual growth using a linear regression model are compared to the findings of Daske/Gebhardt/Klein using the same approach in Appendix 17. The Daske/Gebhardt/Klein results are again highly volatile with a continuously increasing expected MRP and growth rate to excessive levels around the year 2000. In contrast, the findings of this study are much more stable over time. The reason for this difference is potentially related to the treatment of outliers within the regression analysis. The procedure for eliminating outliers in this study was described in Section 5.8. However, Daske/Gebhardt/Klein do not provide any further information on how they treat exceptional values in their regression analysis. Given the discrepancy, it is assumed that the authors use a less restrictive outlier treatment than employed here.

Finally, the reader should note that the main target of the previous section on the comparability with other studies on the German market was to show that the results of this analysis are consistent, i.e., if the same input data and terminal value assumptions are used, results are very similar.

5.9.2 Canada

Applying the sample selection criteria to the data available for the Canadian market results in the smallest sample for the estimation of the expected MRP[834]. The maximum number of included firms during the analysis period does not exceeding 131. Furthermore, the concentration of the resulting sample on the financial services and oil and gas industries was already discussed in 3.2.1. These special sample characteristics must be taken into account when interpreting the following results.

Similar to the non-stationary results for the German market, the expected MRP estimates from applying various terminal perpetuity approaches are upward sloping over time as shown in Exhibit 49. Whereas the spread between the expected MRP values is tight at the beginning of the analysis period, differences widen over time but during all periods the estimated MRPs are above zero. The unconditional average expected MRP estimates range from 2.89% for zero perpetual growth in residual earnings to 6.14% for a constant return on book equity to infinity. Further results are provided in Table 40. Note that again the forward PE_{+1} multiples implied by all terminal perpetuity approaches are on average at least 2.4x lower than the spot PE_{+1} multiples.

---

[834] The input data for the Canadian market is summarized in Appendix 18 and Appendix 19.

Exhibit 49 Canadian expected MRP development using the standard model with various terminal perpetuity approaches

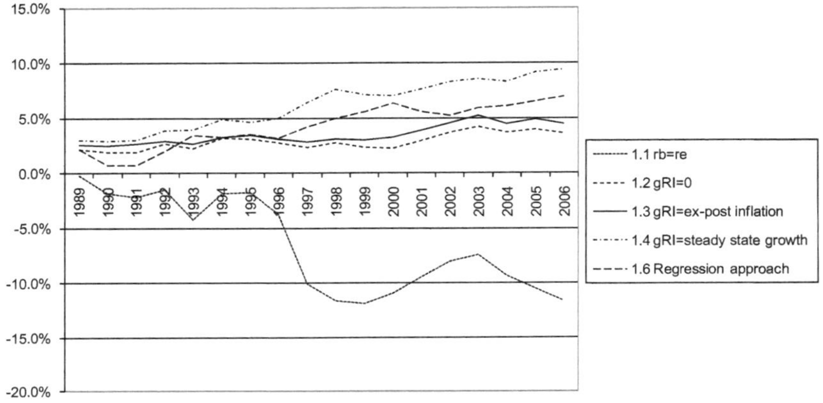

A comparison of proxies for the perpetual growth rate of residual earnings in Exhibit 50 shows that at the beginning of the analysis period all values were at closer levels explaining the proximity of early expected MRP estimates. From 1994, the nominal GDP growth rate for Canada is above the Claus/Thomas inflation estimate and the ex-post inflation rate during most periods. This may indicate that the inflation proxies are too conservative. Indeed, the regression-based estimate of the perpetual growth rate fluctuates during all periods around the level of GDP growth resulting in an expected MRP estimate of 4.26%. However, it should be noted that the implied average perpetual dividend growth rate is at 7.18%. With an average value of close to and above 10%, both the steady state growth rate as well as the five-year IBES CAGR are substantially above all other proxies. Assuming such a growth level to infinity appears unreasonable.

Exhibit 50 Development of selected perpetual growth proxies for the Canadian market

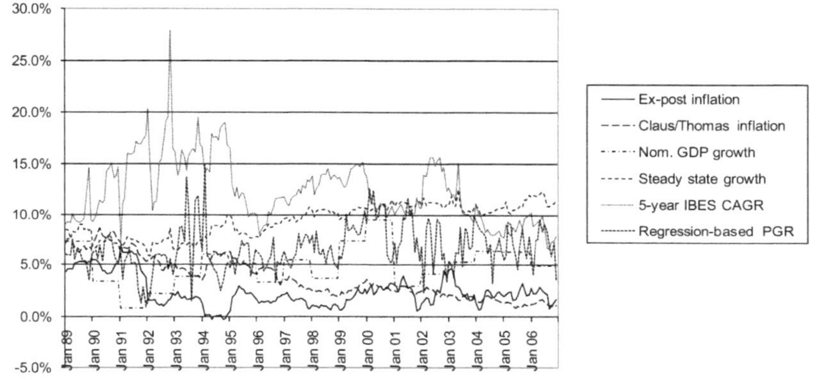

Source: IBES, Datastream.

In Exhibit 51, the expected MRP estimates using terminal perpetuity methodologies from previous studies are presented. On average, values range from 0.91% to 6.04% with the most widely recognized approaches from Claus/Thomas and Gebhardt/Lee/Swaminathan delivering unconditional averages of 3.73% and 2.59%.

Exhibit 51 Canadian expected MRP development using special comparison specifications of previous studies

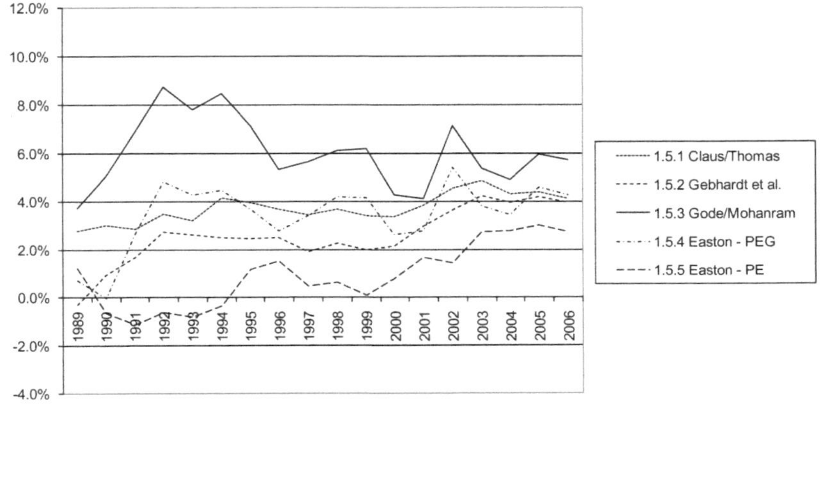

Table 40 Summary statistics of the Canadian expected MRP estimation using the standard model with various terminal perpetuity approaches

Model (1)						1.1 $r^b=r^e$		1.2 $g_{RI}=0$					1.3 g_{RI}=ex-post inflation					1.4 g_{RI}=steady state growth			
Year	r^f (2)	θ_{TV}	$m_{P/E+1}$	N (3)	Firms (4)	r^e	r^p	r^e	r^p	$g_{RI,TV}$	$g_{D,TV}$ (5)	$m_{P/E+1,TV}$ (6)	r^e	r^p	$g_{RI,TV}$	$g_{D,TV}$ (5)	$m_{P/E+1,TV}$ (7)	r^e	r^p	$g_{RI,D,TV}$	$m_{P/E+1,TV}$ (6)
1989	9.78%	37.02%	10.0x	543	45	9.50%	-0.28%	11.97%	2.19%	0.00%	7.54%	8.4x	12.42%	2.64%	4.98%	7.82%	NA	12.78%	3.00%	8.46%	8.6x
1990	10.81%	53.24%	10.7x	519	43	8.90%	-1.90%	12.72%	1.91%	0.00%	5.95%	7.9x	13.35%	2.54%	4.78%	6.24%	NA	13.71%	2.90%	7.15%	8.1x
1991	9.39%	48.14%	13.1x	477	40	7.19%	-2.21%	11.32%	1.92%	0.00%	5.87%	8.8x	12.12%	2.73%	5.64%	6.29%	NA	12.41%	3.01%	7.14%	9.1x
1992	8.08%	46.26%	14.6x	492	41	6.49%	-1.58%	10.80%	2.72%	0.00%	5.80%	9.3x	11.02%	2.94%	1.49%	5.92%	NA	11.94%	3.86%	7.13%	9.6x
1993	7.21%	46.23%	16.5x	447	37	2.94%	-4.26%	9.49%	2.28%	0.00%	5.10%	10.5x	9.89%	2.68%	1.87%	5.32%	NA	11.14%	3.93%	6.98%	11.1x
1994	8.47%	42.07%	13.2x	434	36	6.57%	-1.91%	11.69%	3.22%	0.00%	6.77%	8.6x	11.73%	3.26%	0.17%	6.80%	NA	13.30%	4.83%	8.63%	9.0x
1995	8.03%	40.92%	11.7x	492	41	6.18%	-1.84%	11.12%	3.10%	0.00%	6.57%	9.0x	11.47%	3.44%	2.15%	6.78%	NA	12.64%	4.62%	8.32%	9.5x
1996	7.19%	36.14%	12.3x	678	57	3.46%	-3.73%	10.00%	2.81%	0.00%	6.38%	10.0x	10.33%	3.14%	1.57%	6.60%	NA	12.10%	4.91%	8.71%	10.7x
1997	6.11%	36.35%	16.2x	747	62	-3.97%	-10.07%	8.42%	2.31%	0.00%	5.36%	11.9x	9.00%	2.89%	1.62%	5.73%	NA	12.52%	6.41%	9.83%	13.5x
1998	5.27%	36.24%	17.8x	791	66	-6.31%	-11.58%	8.01%	2.74%	0.00%	5.11%	12.5x	8.42%	3.15%	1.00%	5.37%	NA	12.86%	7.59%	10.37%	14.5x
1999	5.58%	35.56%	18.5x	796	66	-6.28%	-11.86%	7.89%	2.32%	0.00%	5.09%	12.7x	8.61%	3.03%	1.73%	5.55%	NA	12.67%	7.09%	10.25%	14.7x
2000	5.88%	29.89%	15.9x	806	67	-5.05%	-10.93%	8.11%	2.23%	0.00%	5.68%	12.3x	9.17%	3.29%	2.72%	6.43%	NA	12.87%	6.99%	10.78%	14.3x
2001	5.45%	27.06%	14.8x	890	74	-3.99%	-9.44%	8.39%	2.94%	0.00%	6.12%	11.9x	9.33%	3.88%	2.53%	6.81%	NA	13.09%	7.64%	11.13%	13.8x
2002	5.28%	29.87%	15.6x	972	81	-2.78%	-8.06%	9.02%	3.74%	0.00%	6.32%	11.1x	9.80%	4.52%	2.26%	6.87%	NA	13.53%	8.25%	11.17%	12.7x
2003	4.80%	31.42%	14.0x	1,157	96	-2.61%	-7.42%	9.04%	4.24%	0.00%	6.20%	11.1x	10.01%	5.21%	2.77%	6.87%	NA	13.39%	8.59%	10.91%	12.7x
2004	4.58%	33.30%	14.1x	1,263	105	-4.69%	-9.27%	8.29%	3.71%	0.00%	5.53%	12.1x	9.00%	4.42%	1.86%	6.01%	NA	12.85%	8.27%	10.45%	13.9x
2005	4.06%	33.63%	14.9x	1,442	120	-6.47%	-10.53%	8.03%	3.97%	0.00%	5.33%	12.5x	8.97%	4.91%	2.21%	5.95%	NA	13.24%	9.18%	10.94%	14.6x
2006	4.22%	30.10%	15.2x	1,570	131	-7.38%	-11.60%	7.83%	3.61%	0.00%	5.47%	12.8x	8.71%	4.49%	2.01%	6.09%	NA	13.62%	9.40%	11.65%	15.3x
Low	4.06%	27.06%	10.0x	434	36	-7.38%	-11.86%	7.83%	1.91%	0.00%	5.09%	7.9x	8.42%	2.54%	0.17%	5.32%	NA	11.14%	2.90%	6.98%	8.1x
Arith. Mean	6.68%	37.41%	14.4x	806	67	0.09%	-6.58%	9.56%	2.89%	0.00%	5.90%	10.7x	10.19%	3.51%	2.41%	6.30%	NA	12.81%	6.14%	9.44%	12.0x
Median	5.99%	36.19%	14.7x	769	64	-2.70%	-7.74%	9.03%	2.77%	0.00%	5.84%	11.1x	9.84%	3.20%	2.08%	6.26%	NA	12.86%	6.70%	10.04%	12.7x
High	10.81%	53.24%	18.5x	1,570	131	9.50%	-0.28%	12.72%	4.24%	0.00%	7.54%	12.8x	13.35%	5.21%	5.64%	7.82%	NA	13.71%	9.40%	11.65%	15.3x
St. Dev.	2.03%	7.29%	2.3x			6.11%	4.25%	1.63%	0.73%	0.00%	0.66%	1.7x	1.49%	0.84%	1.40%	0.64%	NA	0.65%	2.26%	1.63%	2.5x

(1) All parameters are stated in nominal terms and as arithmetic average of monthly values.
(2) r^f equals redemption yield of the Canadian Datastream benchmark 10y government bond index.
(3) Overall number of firm observations per annum.
(4) Average number of firms per annum.
(5) Implied perpetual dividend growth rate (after convergence for $0<g_{RI}<g_{RI\ steady\ state}$ cases) according to calculation approach presented in Appendix 10 - $Max[g_{RI,TV};(1-\theta_{TV})r^e]$.
(6) Terminal multiple implied by a calculation based on terminal period payout ratio, cost of equity, and perpetual dividend growth rate.
(7) Implied terminal multiple cannot be determined as perpetual dividend growth rate is not constant but converging.

Table 41 Summary statistics of the Canadian expected MRP estimation using the regression-based approach

Model (1)				1.6. Regression approach					
Year	r^f (2)	N (3)	Firms (4)	r^e	r^P	$g_{RI,TV}$	$g_{D,TV}$ (5)	$m_{P/E+1,TV}$ (6)	Adj. R^2
1989	9.78%	536	45	11.92%	2.14%	5.75%	7.51%	NA	54.30%
1990	10.81%	519	43	11.53%	0.72%	6.47%	6.47%	NA	30.14%
1991	9.39%	477	40	10.10%	0.71%	4.20%	5.24%	NA	45.23%
1992	8.08%	482	40	10.03%	1.96%	4.79%	5.39%	NA	67.17%
1993	7.21%	435	36	10.69%	3.49%	8.37%	8.37%	NA	37.88%
1994	8.47%	421	35	11.77%	3.30%	5.47%	6.82%	NA	40.53%
1995	8.03%	480	40	11.60%	3.58%	5.80%	6.85%	NA	41.71%
1996	7.19%	665	55	10.38%	3.19%	5.46%	6.63%	NA	53.26%
1997	6.11%	727	61	10.34%	4.23%	6.51%	6.58%	NA	60.10%
1998	5.27%	765	64	10.30%	5.02%	6.22%	6.57%	NA	50.87%
1999	5.58%	774	65	11.20%	5.62%	8.27%	8.27%	NA	42.16%
2000	5.88%	788	66	12.22%	6.35%	9.58%	9.58%	NA	28.58%
2001	5.45%	885	74	11.01%	5.55%	8.15%	8.15%	NA	14.98%
2002	5.28%	966	81	10.53%	5.25%	6.77%	7.39%	NA	25.36%
2003	4.80%	1,146	96	10.74%	5.94%	6.68%	7.36%	NA	23.51%
2004	4.58%	1,251	104	10.69%	6.11%	7.21%	7.21%	NA	23.76%
2005	4.06%	1,408	117	10.59%	6.53%	6.94%	7.03%	NA	33.86%
2006	4.22%	1,522	127	11.18%	6.96%	7.05%	7.81%	NA	24.80%
Low	4.06%	421	35	10.03%	0.71%	4.20%	5.24%	NA	14.98%
Arith. Mean	6.68%	792	66	10.93%	4.26%	6.65%	7.18%	NA	38.79%
Median	5.99%	746	62	10.72%	4.63%	6.60%	7.12%	NA	39.21%
High	10.81%	1,522	127	12.22%	6.96%	9.58%	9.58%	NA	67.17%
St. Dev.	2.03%			0.65%	1.97%	1.35%	1.05%	NA	14.40%

(1) All parameters are stated in nominal terms and as arithmetic average of monthly values.
(2) r^f equals redemption yield of the Canadian Datastream benchmark 10y government bond index.
(3) Overall number of firm observations per annum.
(4) Average number of firms per annum.
(5) Implied perpetual dividend growth rate after convergence according to calculation approach presented in Appendix 10 - $Max[g_{RI,TV};(1-\theta_{TV})r^e]$.
(6) Implied terminal multiple cannot be determined since implied perpetual dividend growth rate is not constant but converging.

The unconditional results of this study can be compared to selected other studies which apply the valuation models for the Canadian market. In their original article, Claus/Thomas themselves provide results for the period between 1985 and 1998. Their expected MRP estimate of 2.23% is lower compared to the 3.73% derived in this study and the 4.73% by Pastor/Sinha/Swaminathan for later periods. Consistent with the German market outcomes, the equally weighted results provided by Lee/Ng/Swaminathan and Pastor/Sinha/Swaminathan are substantially higher than the aggregation-based estimates. A much lower value of 1.74% is provided by Desrosiers/Lemaire/L'Her for a similar analysis period based on a US-Dollar denominated estimation with ex-post inflation as perpetual growth proxy. Unfortunately, other authors provide only limited details on the sample selection approach and further model specifications. This does not allow the full reconciliation of results. Appendix 20 summarizes the results of previous studies.

Table 42 Overview of key results of previous studies on the Canadian market

Authors	Period	Weighting (1)	Arith. mean over analysis period (2) r^e	r^p	r^f
Claus/Thomas Model					
Claus/Thomas (2001)	1985-1998	agg	10.82%	2.23%	8.59%
Desrosiers/Lemaire/L'Her (2007) (3)	1988-2005	NA	7.96%	1.74%	6.21%
Lee/Ng/Swaminathan (2009)	1991-2000	ew	NA	6.88%	NA
Gsell (2010)	1989-2006	agg	10.41%	3.73%	6.68%
Gebhardt/Lee/Swaminathan Model					
Chen/Jorgensen/Yoo (2004)	1993-2001	ew	9.0%	2.5%	6.5%
Gsell (2010)	1989-2006	agg	9.26%	2.59%	6.68%
Other approaches					
Hail/Leuz (2006) (4)	1992-2001	NA	10.53%	NA	NA
Lee/Ng/Swaminathan (2009) (5)	1991-2000	ew	NA	9.17%	NA
Pastor/Sinha/Swaminathan (2008) (5)	1990-2002	ew	NA	8.15%	NA
Pastor/Sinha/Swaminathan (2008) (5)	1990-2002	vw	NA	4.73%	NA

(1) agg = aggregation method; ew = equal-weighted; vw = value-weighted.
(2) All parameters are stated in nominal terms.
(3) Annualized r^e based on original monthly estimate (US-Dollar denominated);
Implied r^p using own US r^f estimate;
Terminal perpetuity based on g_{RI}=ex-post inflation.
(4) Average of Claus/Thomas, Gebhardt/Lee/Swaminathan, Gode/Mohanram, and Easton-PEG model.
(5) Estimation based on dividend discount model with r^e equal to r^b after 15 years.

Source: Claus, J./Thomas, J. (2001), p. 1643, Chen, F./Jorgensen, B./Yoo, Y. (2004), p. 331, Hail, L./Leuz, C. (2006), pp. 494-495, Desrosiers, S./Lemaire, N./L'Her, J.-F. (2007), p. 79, Pastor, L./Sinha, M./Swaminathan, B. (2008), p. 2875, and Lee, C./Ng, D./Swaminathan, B. (2009), pp. 318 and 321.

5.9.3 France

The results on the French market are also derived from a comparatively small sample with the maximum number of firms reaching 283 in 2006[835]. Like all previously discussed markets—i.e., Germany and Canada—the expected MRP estimates appear non-stationary and show an upward trend during the analysis period as shown in Exhibit 52. Whereas the expected MRP starts to rise after a low point in 2000 for perpetual growth estimates of zero and ex-post inflation, the steady state growth and regression-based values reached their peaks already around the same point in time. Moving almost in parallel at a small spread, the unconditional average expected MRP estimates based on zero and ex-post inflation perpetual growth are 2.29% and 2.92% respectively as presented in Table 43. The steady state growth and regression-based approach provide substantially higher values of 6.37% and 4.91% respectively. Average forward PE_{+1} multiples implied by all terminal perpetuity approaches are on average at least 3.1x lower than the spot PE_{+1} multiples.

[835] The input data for the French market is summarized in Appendix 21 and Appendix 22.

Exhibit 52 French expected MRP development using the standard model with various terminal perpetuity approaches

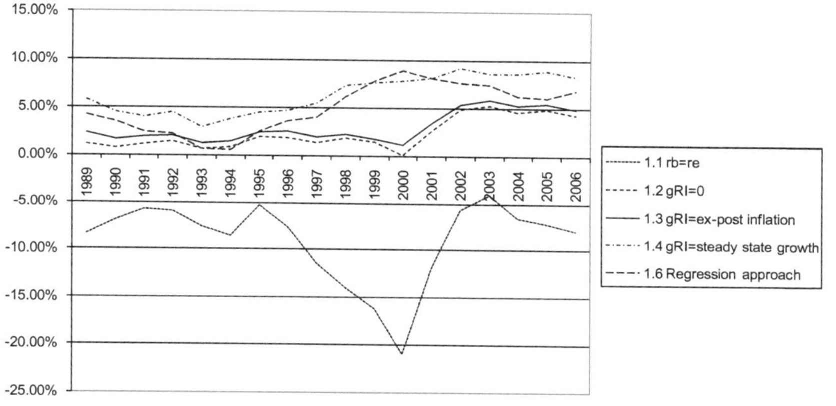

A comparison of proxies for the perpetual growth rate in Exhibit 53 shows that inflation represents the lower bound of the spectrum with nominal GDP growth exceeding the inflation level during all periods except for the recession in 1993. The perpetual growth rate implied by the regression approach develops at a similar level compared to the nominal GDP growth rate apart from the period between 1996 and 2004 during which it is on a substantially higher level. With an average value of above 10%, the steady growth level appears again overly optimistic for a perpetual growth estimate. The five-year IBES CAGR is at an even more excessive level.

Using previous approaches to calculate the expected MRP leads to a range of unconditional average expected MRPs from 0.35% to 6.68% and a similar conditional year-over-year development compared to other markets as presented in Exhibit 54 and Appendix 23. Note that for the French market, the expected MRP estimate from applying the Gebhardt et al. methodology is comparatively higher than in other countries. This is related to a substantially higher return on book equity for the French market than for all other countries in the sample.

Exhibit 53 Development of selected perpetual growth proxies for the French market

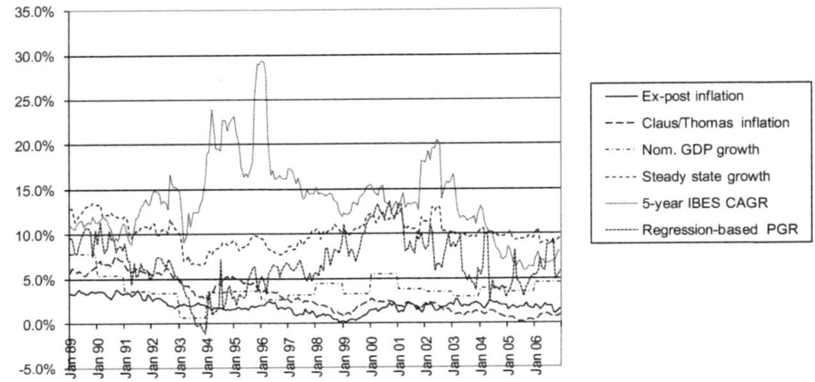

Source: IBES, Datastream.

Exhibit 54 French expected MRP development using special comparison specifications of previous studies

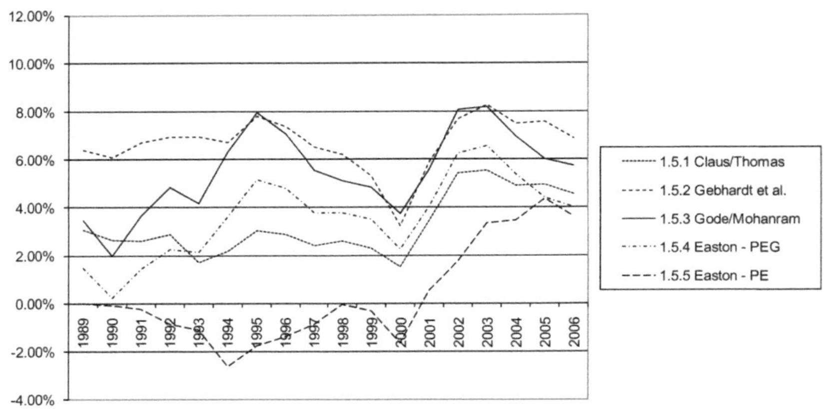

Table 43 Summary statistics of the French expected MRP estimation using the standard model with various terminal perpetuity approaches

Model (1)						1.1 $r^b=r^e$		1.2 $g_{RI}=0$					1.3 g_{RI}=ex-post inflation					1.4 g_{RI}=steady state growth			
Year	r^f (2)	θ_{TV}	$m_{P/E+1}$	N (3)	Firms (4)	r^e	r^P	r^e	r^P	$g_{RI,TV}$	$g_{D,TV}$ (5)	$m_{P/E+1,TV}$ (6)	r^e	r^P	$g_{RI,TV}$	$g_{D,TV}$ (5)	$m_{P/E+1,TV}$ (7)	r^e	r^P	$g_{RI,D,TV}$	$m_{P/E+1,TV}$ (6)
1989	8.86%	22.79%	11.7x	586	49	0.46%	-8.40%	10.07%	1.21%	0.00%	7.77%	9.9x	11.14%	2.28%	3.50%	8.60%	NA	14.66%	5.80%	12.68%	11.6x
1990	9.92%	22.32%	10.7x	693	58	2.98%	-6.94%	10.73%	0.81%	0.00%	8.33%	9.3x	11.57%	1.65%	3.38%	8.99%	NA	14.39%	4.47%	12.26%	10.5x
1991	8.97%	26.07%	12.1x	607	51	3.16%	-5.81%	10.12%	1.14%	0.00%	7.48%	9.9x	10.86%	1.89%	3.22%	8.03%	NA	12.98%	4.01%	10.59%	10.9x
1992	8.59%	27.15%	13.4x	695	58	2.58%	-6.01%	10.04%	1.45%	0.00%	7.31%	10.0x	10.62%	2.03%	2.37%	7.74%	NA	13.08%	4.49%	10.61%	11.0x
1993	6.68%	35.26%	18.8x	791	66	-1.01%	-7.69%	7.34%	0.66%	0.00%	4.75%	13.6x	7.94%	1.26%	2.09%	5.14%	NA	9.61%	2.92%	7.24%	14.9x
1994	7.29%	35.29%	22.1x	904	75	-1.30%	-8.59%	8.15%	0.86%	0.00%	5.28%	12.3x	8.66%	1.37%	1.66%	5.61%	NA	11.07%	3.78%	8.47%	13.6x
1995	7.49%	33.18%	18.2x	1,153	96	2.24%	-5.25%	9.44%	1.95%	0.00%	6.31%	10.6x	9.86%	2.38%	1.79%	6.59%	NA	11.94%	4.46%	9.07%	11.5x
1996	6.27%	37.49%	21.2x	1,208	101	-1.34%	-7.62%	8.13%	1.85%	0.00%	5.08%	12.3x	8.75%	2.47%	2.01%	5.47%	NA	10.98%	4.70%	8.22%	13.6x
1997	5.54%	32.21%	21.9x	1,703	142	-5.91%	-11.45%	6.92%	1.38%	0.00%	4.69%	14.5x	7.40%	1.86%	1.21%	5.02%	NA	11.05%	5.52%	9.12%	16.6x
1998	4.60%	31.10%	22.5x	1,851	154	-9.46%	-14.06%	6.46%	1.86%	0.00%	4.45%	15.5x	6.76%	2.16%	0.63%	4.66%	NA	11.98%	7.38%	10.31%	18.6x
1999	4.64%	31.77%	23.7x	2,320	193	-11.50%	-16.14%	6.09%	1.45%	0.00%	4.15%	16.4x	6.37%	1.73%	0.54%	4.35%	NA	12.23%	7.59%	10.66%	20.2x
2000	5.40%	33.06%	27.0x	2,730	228	-15.57%	-20.97%	5.50%	0.10%	0.00%	3.68%	18.2x	6.52%	1.12%	1.73%	4.36%	NA	13.19%	7.78%	11.78%	23.5x
2001	4.94%	32.47%	18.9x	2,997	250	-7.04%	-11.98%	7.58%	2.63%	0.00%	5.12%	13.2x	8.30%	3.35%	1.67%	5.60%	NA	13.06%	8.11%	11.00%	15.8x
2002	4.84%	31.81%	15.9x	2,930	244	-0.90%	-5.73%	9.66%	4.83%	0.00%	6.59%	10.3x	10.26%	5.42%	1.86%	7.00%	NA	14.03%	9.19%	11.37%	12.0x
2003	4.10%	34.47%	14.0x	2,778	232	-0.02%	-4.12%	9.33%	5.23%	0.00%	6.12%	10.7x	9.97%	5.87%	2.16%	6.54%	NA	12.73%	8.63%	9.86%	12.0x
2004	4.06%	34.85%	13.7x	2,789	232	-2.48%	-6.53%	8.64%	4.58%	0.00%	5.63%	11.6x	9.37%	5.31%	2.09%	6.10%	NA	12.65%	8.59%	10.02%	13.3x
2005	3.36%	38.04%	13.4x	3,198	267	-3.77%	-7.13%	8.20%	4.84%	0.00%	5.08%	12.2x	8.86%	5.50%	1.77%	5.49%	NA	12.25%	8.89%	9.53%	14.0x
2006	3.80%	40.00%	13.9x	3,396	283	-4.14%	-7.94%	8.10%	4.29%	0.00%	4.86%	12.4x	8.73%	4.93%	1.67%	5.24%	NA	12.08%	8.28%	9.26%	14.1x
Low	3.36%	22.32%	10.7x	586	49	-15.57%	-20.97%	5.50%	0.10%	0.00%	3.68%	9.3x	6.37%	1.12%	0.54%	4.35%	NA	9.61%	2.92%	7.24%	10.5x
Arith. Mean	6.07%	32.19%	17.4x	1,852	154	-2.94%	-9.02%	8.36%	2.29%	0.00%	5.70%	12.4x	9.00%	2.92%	1.96%	6.14%	NA	12.44%	6.37%	10.11%	14.3x
Median	5.47%	32.77%	17.0x	1,777	148	-1.32%	-7.65%	8.18%	1.65%	0.00%	5.20%	12.2x	8.80%	2.22%	1.83%	5.60%	NA	12.45%	6.59%	10.16%	13.6x
High	9.92%	40.00%	27.0x	3,396	283	3.16%	-4.12%	10.73%	5.23%	0.00%	8.33%	18.2x	11.57%	5.87%	3.50%	8.99%	NA	14.66%	9.19%	12.68%	23.5x
St. Dev.	2.02%	4.89%	4.8x			5.23%	4.35%	1.52%	1.68%	0.00%	1.33%	2.5x	1.59%	1.67%	0.80%	1.42%	NA	1.28%	2.09%	1.43%	3.5x

(1) All parameters are stated in nominal terms and as arithmetic average of monthly values.
(2) r^f equals redemption yield of the French Datastream benchmark 10y government bond index.
(3) Overall number of firm observations per annum.
(4) Average number of firms per annum.
(5) Implied perpetual dividend growth rate (after convergence for $0<g_{RI}<g_{RI\ steady\ state}$ cases) according to calculation approach presented in Appendix 10 - $Max[g_{RI,TV};(1-\theta_{TV})r^e]$.
(6) Terminal multiple implied by a calculation based on terminal period payout ratio, cost of equity, and perpetual dividend growth rate.
(7) Implied terminal multiple cannot be determined as perpetual dividend growth rate is not constant but converging.

Table 44 Summary statistics of the French expected MRP estimation using the regression-based approach

Model (1)				1.6. Regression approach					
Year	r^f (2)	N (3)	Firms (4)	r^e	r^p	$g_{RI,TV}$	$g_{D,TV}$ (5)	$m_{P/E+1,TV}$ (6)	Adj. R^2
1989	8.86%	563	47	13.02%	4.17%	9.41%	10.05%	NA	61.79%
1990	9.92%	675	56	13.39%	3.47%	9.04%	10.40%	NA	60.02%
1991	8.97%	598	50	11.39%	2.42%	6.20%	8.42%	NA	73.93%
1992	8.59%	688	57	10.77%	2.19%	6.41%	7.85%	NA	59.49%
1993	6.68%	781	65	7.27%	0.59%	1.53%	4.71%	NA	66.24%
1994	7.29%	889	74	7.80%	0.51%	2.63%	5.05%	NA	57.43%
1995	7.49%	1,124	94	9.93%	2.44%	4.05%	6.63%	NA	54.73%
1996	6.27%	1,196	100	9.81%	3.54%	5.67%	6.13%	NA	54.53%
1997	5.54%	1,622	135	9.53%	3.99%	5.83%	6.46%	NA	49.25%
1998	4.60%	1,713	143	10.72%	6.12%	7.23%	7.38%	NA	53.22%
1999	4.64%	2,126	177	12.44%	7.80%	9.13%	9.13%	NA	36.62%
2000	5.40%	2,155	180	14.28%	8.87%	12.41%	12.41%	NA	24.13%
2001	4.94%	2,679	223	13.02%	8.08%	9.70%	9.70%	NA	24.42%
2002	4.84%	2,795	233	12.47%	7.64%	8.15%	8.51%	NA	28.74%
2003	4.10%	2,702	225	11.55%	7.45%	6.33%	7.57%	NA	32.20%
2004	4.06%	2,685	224	10.29%	6.24%	5.06%	6.71%	NA	35.72%
2005	3.36%	3,023	252	9.41%	6.05%	4.58%	5.83%	NA	47.22%
2006	3.80%	3,228	269	10.61%	6.80%	6.82%	6.82%	NA	40.08%
Low	3.36%	563	47	7.27%	0.51%	1.53%	4.71%	NA	24.13%
Arith. Mean	6.07%	1,736	145	10.98%	4.91%	6.68%	7.76%	NA	47.76%
Median	5.47%	1,668	139	10.74%	5.11%	6.37%	7.48%	NA	51.24%
High	9.92%	3,228	269	14.28%	8.87%	12.41%	12.41%	NA	73.93%
St. Dev.	2.02%			1.90%	2.65%	2.68%	2.01%	NA	14.88%

(1) All parameters are stated in nominal terms and as arithmetic average of monthly values.
(2) r^f equals redemption yield of the French Datastream benchmark 10y government bond index.
(3) Overall number of firm observations per annum.
(4) Average number of firms per annum.
(5) Implied perpetual dividend growth rate after convergence according to calculation approach presented in Appendix 10 - $Max[g_{RI,TV};(1-\theta_{TV})r^e]$.
(6) Implied terminal multiple cannot be determined since implied perpetual dividend growth rate is not constant but converging.

In the international academic literature, several further studies analyzed the expected MRP of the French equity market using similar the IRR-based approach. Claus/Thomas and Pastor/Sinha/Swaminathan calculated a lower unconditional average expected MRP of 2.60% and 2.86% for an earlier and shorter analysis period. Desrosiers/Lemaire/L'Her cover a similar analysis period than this study but come up with an unconditional average expected MRP of 1.87% which is lower than the 3.28% unconditional estimate using data of this study. Due to the limited methodology and data discussion by other authors, the differences cannot be reconciled. Finally, one can again observe substantially higher expected MRP estimates when applying the equal-weighting approach. Table 45 summarizes the comparison of previous studies on the expected MRP in the French market.

Table 45 Overview of key results of previous studies on the French market

Authors	Period	Weighting (1)	Arith. mean over analysis period (2) r^e	r^p	r^f
Claus/Thomas Model					
Claus/Thomas (2001)	1987-1998	agg	10.34%	2.60%	7.74%
Desrosiers/Lemaire/L'Her (2007) (3)	1988-2005	NA	8.08%	1.87%	6.21%
Lee/Ng/Swaminathan (2009)	1991-2000	ew	NA	4.93%	NA
Gsell (2010)	1989-2006	agg	9.35%	3.28%	6.07%
Gebhardt/Lee/Swaminathan Model					
Chen/Jorgensen/Yoo (2004)	1993-2001	ew	8.1%	2.6%	5.5%
Gsell (2010)	1989-2006	agg	12.75%	6.68%	6.07%
Other approaches					
Hail/Leuz (2006) (4)	1992-2001	NA	10.37%	NA	NA
Lee/Ng/Swaminathan (2009) (5)	1991-2000	ew	NA	6.43%	NA
Pastor/Sinha/Swaminathan (2008) (5)	1990-2002	ew	NA	5.69%	NA
Pastor/Sinha/Swaminathan (2008) (5)	1990-2002	vw	NA	2.86%	NA

(1) agg = aggregation method; ew = equal-weighted; vw = value-weighted.
(2) All parameters are stated in nominal terms.
(3) Annualized r^e based on original monthly estimate (US-Dollar denominated);
Implied r^p using own US r^f estimate;
Terminal perpetuity based on g_{RI}=ex-post inflation.
(4) Average of Claus/Thomas, Gebhardt/Lee/Swaminathan, Gode/Mohanram, and Easton-PEG model.
(5) Estimation based on dividend discount model with r^e equal to r^b after 15 years.

Source: Claus, J./Thomas, J. (2001), p. 1643, Chen, F./Jorgensen, B./Yoo, Y. (2004), p. 331, Hail, L./Leuz, C. (2006), pp. 494-495, Desrosiers, S./Lemaire, N./L'Her, J.-F. (2007), p. 79, Pastor, L./Sinha, M./Swaminathan, B. (2008), p. 2875, and Lee, C./Ng, D./Swaminathan, B. (2009), pp. 318 and 321.

5.9.4 Japan

In contrast to Canada and France, the Japanese equity market provides a substantially larger sample of up to 806 firms meeting the selection requirements of this study[836]. Differences in the economic as well as capital markets development during the analysis period[837] compared to all Western countries in this sample raise special interest on the investigation of the Japanese equity market. During most years within the period between 1993 and 2004, the Japanese economy was in recession with deflationary sub-periods. The millennium peak which characterized all Western equity markets between 1999 and 2001 impacted the Japanese equity market only to much lower degree. Despite these differences, all expected MRP estimates for the Japanese market are also non-stationary and have an even stronger upward trend during the analysis period as shown in Exhibit 55. Starting with negative values from 1989 to 1994, the conditional expected MRP estimates based

[836] The input data for the Japanese market is summarized in Appendix 24 and Appendix 25.
[837] See Section 3.4.2.

on zero and ex-post inflation perpetual growth of residual income rise continuously until reaching the maximum level in 2003 with an unconditional average expected MRP of 2.01% and 2.28% respectively (see Table 46). In selected years, the zero perpetual residual income growth estimate exceeds the value implied by the ex-post inflation assumption since the latter is temporarily negative as a consequence of deflation. The regression-based estimates for the expected MRP are only slightly higher compared to the two former approaches at an average value of 3.30% (see Table 47) and follow a similar development over time. Applying the steady state growth assumption leads to an expected premium estimate of 4.79%. The increase in the expected MRP over time using all terminal perpetuity approaches results in a standard deviation between two and three percent. Similar to the previously discussed markets, this development may certainly be driven by changes in the sample composition particularly during the early part of the analysis. Interestingly enough, the difference between the forward PE_{+1} ratio implied by the terminal perpetuity concepts and the spot PE_{+1} ratio is largest for Japan with a minimum average discrepancy of 9.0x.

Exhibit 55 Japanese expected MRP development using the standard model with various terminal perpetuity approaches

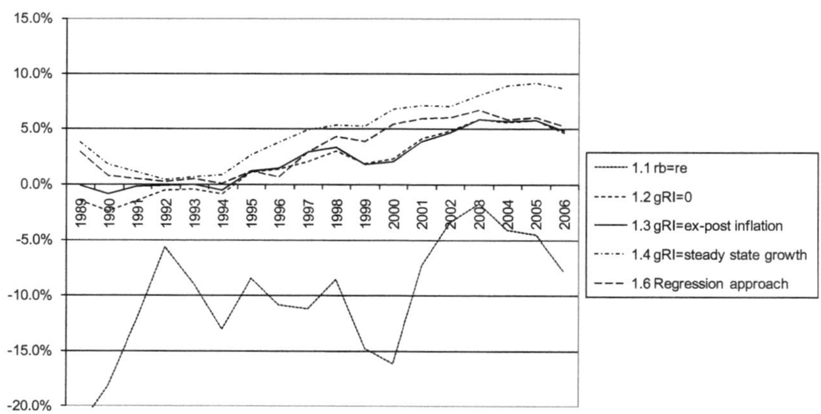

A comparison of other proxies for the perpetual growth rate of residual income in Exhibit 56 indicates that inflation rates and the nominal GDP growth rate develop at very tight spreads during most parts of the analysis period since 1992 illustrating the weak real economic performance of Japan. While the regression-based perpetual growth estimate exceeds the nominal GDP growth level during 1998 and 2004, the steady state growth level is higher than nominal GDP growth continuously since 1992. The five-year IBES CAGR develops above all proxies with large fluctuations and at unreasonable levels to be assumed until infinity.

Exhibit 56 Development of selected perpetual growth proxies for the Japanese market

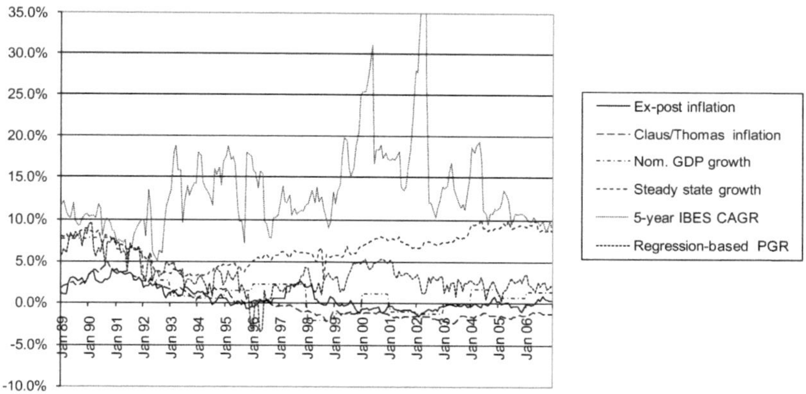

Source: IBES, Datastream.

Exhibit 57 continues to show the expected MRP estimates using previously developed terminal perpetuity assumptions (see also Appendix 26). All methods result in similarly upward sloping expected MRP estimates over time. Unconditional averages range from 0.63% to 4.81% with standard deviations at a similar magnitude as before.

Exhibit 57 Japanese expected MRP development using special comparison specifications of previous studies

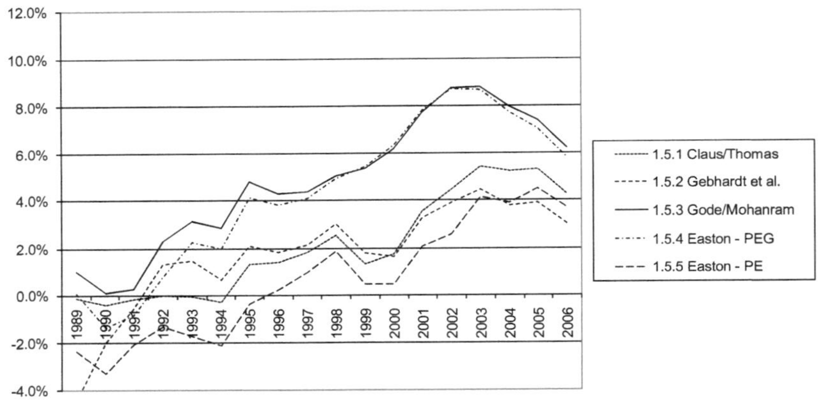

Table 46 Summary statistics of the Japanese expected MRP estimation using the standard model with various terminal perpetuity approaches

Model (1)						1.1 $r^b=r^e$		1.2 $g_{RI}=0$					1.3 g_{RI}=ex-post inflation					1.4 g_{RI}=steady state growth			
Year	r^f (2)	θ_{TV}	$m_{P/E+1}$	N (3)	Firms (4)	r^e	r^p	r^e	r^p	$g_{RI,TV}$	$g_{D,TV}$ (5)	$m_{P/E+1,TV}$ (6)	r^e	r^p	$g_{RI,TV}$	$g_{D,TV}$ (5)	$m_{P/E+1,TV}$ (7)	r^e	r^p	$g_{RI,D,TV}$	$m_{P/E+1,TV}$ (6)
1989	5.18%	20.81%	36.7x	600	50	-16.69%	-21.87%	3.74%	-1.44%	0.00%	2.96%	26.7x	5.09%	-0.09%	2.28%	4.03%	NA	8.92%	3.74%	8.26%	31.8x
1990	6.96%	19.04%	29.0x	541	45	-11.19%	-18.16%	4.61%	-2.35%	0.00%	3.73%	21.7x	6.09%	-0.88%	3.07%	4.93%	NA	8.80%	1.84%	8.04%	24.8x
1991	6.34%	20.05%	24.2x	602	50	-5.74%	-12.09%	4.95%	-1.40%	0.00%	3.95%	20.2x	6.14%	-0.20%	3.27%	4.91%	NA	7.47%	1.12%	6.55%	21.9x
1992	5.21%	27.03%	26.8x	628	52	-0.42%	-5.63%	4.75%	-0.46%	0.00%	3.47%	21.0x	5.08%	-0.13%	1.72%	3.71%	NA	5.65%	0.43%	4.42%	22.1x
1993	4.12%	36.59%	42.6x	786	66	-4.79%	-8.91%	3.73%	-0.39%	0.00%	2.37%	26.8x	4.11%	-0.01%	1.27%	2.60%	NA	4.83%	0.71%	3.52%	27.9x
1994	4.23%	37.12%	47.5x	1,534	128	-8.83%	-13.06%	3.44%	-0.80%	0.00%	2.16%	29.1x	3.71%	-0.53%	0.69%	2.33%	NA	5.11%	0.87%	3.90%	30.7x
1995	3.32%	38.12%	35.3x	1,289	107	-5.11%	-8.43%	4.51%	1.19%	0.00%	2.79%	22.2x	4.47%	1.15%	-0.12%	2.77%	NA	6.02%	2.70%	4.39%	23.3x
1996	2.99%	30.02%	32.2x	1,584	132	-7.84%	-10.83%	4.39%	1.40%	0.00%	3.07%	22.8x	4.44%	1.45%	0.13%	3.11%	NA	6.73%	3.74%	5.50%	24.5x
1997	2.31%	28.12%	31.6x	3,088	257	-8.82%	-11.13%	4.43%	2.12%	0.00%	3.19%	22.6x	5.18%	2.87%	1.77%	3.73%	NA	7.16%	4.85%	6.02%	24.7x
1998	1.49%	29.57%	30.9x	3,632	303	-7.06%	-8.56%	4.56%	3.06%	0.00%	3.21%	21.9x	4.82%	3.32%	0.67%	3.39%	NA	6.82%	5.33%	5.57%	23.6x
1999	1.76%	27.02%	47.9x	3,835	320	-13.04%	-14.80%	3.68%	1.92%	0.00%	2.69%	27.2x	3.50%	1.75%	-0.33%	2.56%	NA	6.99%	5.23%	6.10%	30.3x
2000	1.76%	27.33%	50.1x	5,316	443	-14.39%	-16.15%	4.15%	2.39%	0.00%	3.01%	24.1x	3.78%	2.02%	-0.71%	2.74%	NA	8.53%	6.77%	7.55%	27.8x
2001	1.31%	21.41%	31.1x	7,596	633	-5.90%	-7.21%	5.43%	4.12%	0.00%	4.26%	18.4x	5.17%	3.86%	-0.76%	4.06%	NA	8.39%	7.08%	7.33%	20.3x
2002	1.22%	20.67%	35.4x	7,454	621	-2.15%	-3.37%	6.09%	4.87%	0.00%	4.83%	16.4x	5.85%	4.63%	-0.90%	4.64%	NA	8.28%	7.06%	7.10%	17.6x
2003	1.00%	20.11%	20.3x	7,576	631	-0.66%	-1.67%	6.86%	5.86%	0.00%	5.48%	14.6x	6.81%	5.80%	-0.25%	5.44%	NA	9.07%	8.06%	7.78%	15.6x
2004	1.49%	18.58%	18.9x	8,878	740	-2.57%	-4.06%	7.14%	5.65%	0.00%	5.81%	14.0x	7.13%	5.64%	-0.01%	5.80%	NA	10.41%	8.92%	9.21%	15.5x
2005	1.35%	19.80%	18.0x	9,111	759	-3.10%	-4.45%	7.12%	5.77%	0.00%	5.71%	14.0x	7.03%	5.68%	-0.27%	5.64%	NA	10.53%	9.18%	9.27%	15.7x
2006	1.73%	22.51%	19.3x	9,676	806	-6.06%	-7.79%	6.41%	4.68%	0.00%	4.97%	15.6x	6.49%	4.76%	0.24%	5.03%	NA	10.36%	8.62%	9.08%	17.6x
Low	1.00%	18.58%	18.0x	541	45	-16.69%	-21.87%	3.44%	-2.35%	0.00%	2.16%	14.0x	3.50%	-0.88%	-0.90%	2.33%	NA	4.83%	0.43%	3.52%	15.5x
Arith. Mean	2.99%	25.77%	32.1x	4,096	341	-6.91%	-9.90%	5.00%	2.01%	0.00%	3.76%	21.1x	5.27%	2.28%	0.65%	3.97%	NA	7.78%	4.79%	6.64%	23.1x
Median	2.03%	24.76%	31.3x	3,360	280	-5.98%	-8.73%	4.58%	2.02%	0.00%	3.34%	21.8x	5.13%	1.88%	0.19%	3.88%	NA	7.87%	5.04%	6.83%	23.5x
High	6.96%	38.12%	50.1x	9,676	806	-0.42%	-1.67%	7.14%	5.86%	0.00%	5.81%	29.1x	7.13%	5.80%	3.27%	5.80%	NA	10.53%	9.18%	9.27%	31.8x
St. Dev.	1.91%	6.51%	10.1x			4.63%	5.43%	1.22%	2.73%	0.00%	1.16%	4.8x	1.16%	2.35%	1.29%	1.15%	NA	1.76%	3.03%	1.83%	5.3x

(1) All parameters are stated in nominal terms and as arithmetic average of monthly values.
(2) r^f equals redemption yield of the Japanese Datastream benchmark 10y government bond index.
(3) Overall number of firm observations per annum.
(4) Average number of firms per annum.
(5) Implied perpetual dividend growth rate (after convergence for $0<g_{RI}<g_{RI\ steady\ state}$ cases) according to calculation approach presented in Appendix 10 - $Max[g_{RI,TV};(1-\theta_{TV})r^e]$.
(6) Terminal multiple implied by a calculation based on terminal period payout ratio, cost of equity, and perpetual dividend growth rate.
(7) Implied terminal multiple cannot be determined as perpetual dividend growth rate is not constant but converging.

Table 47 Summary statistics of the Japanese expected MRP estimation using the regression-based approach

Model (1)				1.6. Regression approach					
Year	r^f (2)	N (3)	Firms (4)	r^e	r^p	$g_{RI,TV}$	$g_{D,TV}$ (5)	$m_{P/E+1,TV}$ (6)	Adj. R^2
1989	5.18%	590	49	8.09%	2.92%	7.55%	7.55%	NA	7.15%
1990	6.96%	528	44	7.76%	0.80%	7.09%	7.09%	NA	12.47%
1991	6.34%	599	50	6.93%	0.58%	6.10%	6.10%	NA	15.69%
1992	5.21%	628	52	5.52%	0.31%	3.86%	4.03%	NA	21.83%
1993	4.12%	785	65	4.68%	0.56%	3.27%	3.27%	NA	19.62%
1994	4.23%	1,527	127	4.35%	0.12%	2.70%	2.74%	NA	22.34%
1995	3.32%	1,285	107	4.53%	1.21%	1.86%	2.80%	NA	35.93%
1996	2.99%	1,581	132	3.73%	0.74%	-0.10%	2.61%	NA	47.00%
1997	2.31%	3,086	257	5.26%	2.95%	2.18%	3.78%	NA	52.73%
1998	1.49%	3,609	301	5.75%	4.26%	2.53%	4.05%	NA	42.44%
1999	1.76%	3,676	306	5.60%	3.84%	3.35%	4.09%	NA	40.29%
2000	1.76%	5,063	422	7.15%	5.39%	4.87%	5.19%	NA	34.44%
2001	1.31%	7,491	624	7.24%	5.94%	3.66%	5.69%	NA	37.68%
2002	1.22%	7,361	613	7.21%	5.99%	2.57%	5.72%	NA	44.67%
2003	1.00%	7,475	623	7.69%	6.68%	2.07%	6.14%	NA	53.13%
2004	1.49%	8,657	721	7.34%	5.85%	2.11%	5.98%	NA	54.11%
2005	1.35%	8,869	739	7.38%	6.03%	2.17%	5.92%	NA	65.16%
2006	1.73%	9,469	789	6.98%	5.24%	2.18%	5.41%	NA	61.86%
Low	1.00%	528	44	3.73%	0.12%	-0.10%	2.61%	NA	7.15%
Arith. Mean	2.99%	4,016	335	6.29%	3.30%	3.33%	4.90%	NA	37.14%
Median	2.03%	3,348	279	6.95%	3.40%	2.64%	5.30%	NA	38.99%
High	6.96%	9,469	789	8.09%	6.68%	7.55%	7.55%	NA	65.16%
St. Dev.	1.91%			1.36%	2.43%	1.96%	1.51%	NA	17.34%

(1) All parameters are stated in nominal terms and as arithmetic average of monthly values.
(2) r^f equals redemption yield of the Japanese Datastream benchmark 10y government bond index.
(3) Overall number of firm observations per annum.
(4) Average number of firms per annum.
(5) Implied perpetual dividend growth rate after convergence according to calculation approach presented in Appendix 10 - Max[$g_{RI,TV}$;$(1-\theta_{TV})r^e$].
(6) Implied terminal multiple cannot be determined since implied perpetual dividend growth rate is not constant but converging.

Previously, the Japanese market was analyzed by several further studies which apply valuation models to estimate the expected MRP. The Claus/Thomas study finds an average expected MRP of 0.21% for an earlier and shorter analysis period. Taking into account the upward sloping development of the expected MRP, the higher average of this study appears consistent with these results. Desrosiers/Lemaire/L'Her derive an estimate of 1.37% for a similar analysis period using US-Dollar denominated values. These values compare to a Claus/Thomas model estimate of 2.06% of this study and the estimate by Pastor/Sinha/Swaminathan of 3.12% as summarized in Table 48. Finally, the impact of equal-weighting differs among the studies by Lee/Ng/Swaminathan and Pastor/Sinha/Swaminathan.

Table 48 Overview of key results of previous studies on the Japanese market

Authors	Period	Weighting (1)	Arith. mean over analysis period (2) r^e	r^p	r^f
Claus/Thomas Model					
Claus/Thomas (2001)	1991-1998	agg	4.07%	0.21%	3.86%
Desrosiers/Lemaire/L'Her (2007) (3)	1988-2005	NA	7.57%	1.36%	6.21%
Lee/Ng/Swaminathan (2009)	1991-2000	ew	NA	3.83%	NA
Gsell (2010)	1989-2006	agg	5.05%	2.06%	2.99%
Gebhardt/Lee/Swaminathan Model					
Chen/Jorgensen/Yoo (2004)	1993-2001	ew	4.1%	2.1%	2.0%
Gsell (2010)	1989-2006	agg	4.73%	1.74%	2.99%
Other approaches					
Hail/Leuz (2006) (4)	1992-2001	NA	6.16%	NA	NA
Lee/Ng/Swaminathan (2009) (5)	1991-2000	ew	NA	2.64%	NA
Pastor/Sinha/Swaminathan (2008) (5)	1990-2002	ew	NA	5.41%	NA
Pastor/Sinha/Swaminathan (2008) (5)	1990-2002	vw	NA	3.12%	NA

(1) agg = aggregation method; ew = equal-weighted; vw = value-weighted.
(2) All parameters are stated in nominal terms.
(3) Annualized r^e based on original monthly estimate (US-Dollar denominated);
Implied r^p using own US r^f estimate;
Terminal perpetuity based on g_{RI}=ex-post inflation.
(4) Average of Claus/Thomas, Gebhardt/Lee/Swaminathan, Gode/Mohanram, and Easton-PEG model.
(5) Estimation based on dividend discount model with r^e equal to r^b after 15 years.

Source: Claus, J./Thomas, J. (2001), p. 1643, Chen, F./Jorgensen, B./Yoo, Y. (2004), p. 331, Hail, L./Leuz, C. (2006), pp. 494-495, Desrosiers, S./Lemaire, N./L'Her, J.-F. (2007), p. 79, Pastor, L./Sinha, M./Swaminathan, B. (2008), p. 2875, and Lee, C./Ng, D./Swaminathan, B. (2009), pp. 318 and 321.

5.9.5 United Kingdom

With a sample size reaching 388 in 2006, the UK equity market provides a solid data basis for investigations of the expected MRP[838]. Exhibit 58 shows the development of the expected MRP estimates using different terminal perpetuity approaches. The expected MRP curves are again upward sloping indicating non-stationarity. In addition, all estimates are positive during the entire analysis period. More specifically, expected MRP estimates based on the zero and ex-post inflation perpetual residual income growth develop flat until 2000 after which both values increase substantially. The unconditional averages over the analysis period are 2.15% and 3.03% respectively as presented in Table 49. Applying the regression-based estimation procedure results in an increasing expected MRP curve already since the early 1990s. The peak value is reached in 2000 and the expected MRP average at 3.69%. The conditional expected MRP estimates based on steady state perpetual growth start to increase at a similar point in time but reach higher values by the end of the

[838] The input data for the UK market is summarized in Appendix 27 and Appendix 28.

analysis period with an unconditional average equal to 6.10%. The upward trend in the expected MRP development leads to a standard deviation in-between 1.5% and 2.2% for the discussed terminal perpetuity approaches. Consistently with all previously analyzed countries, the implied forward PE_{+1} ratio is on average lower compared to the spot multiple.

Exhibit 58 UK expected MRP development using the standard model with various terminal perpetuity approaches

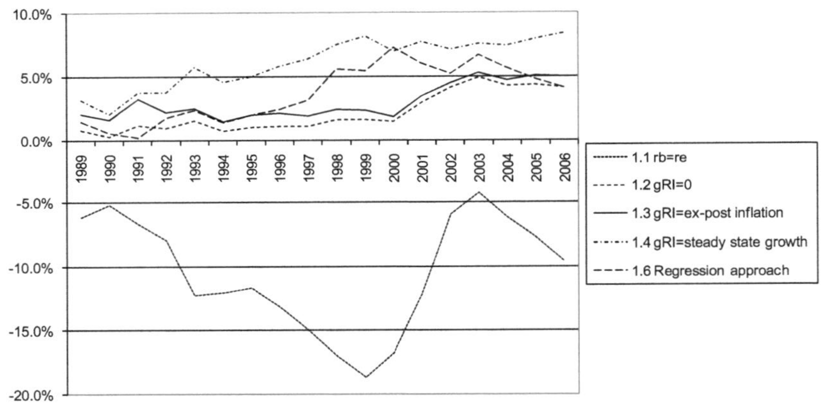

A comparison of further proxies for the perpetual growth rate of residual earnings in Exhibit 59 indicates that inflation rates are substantially below the nominal GDP growth rate after 1994 reflecting the strong performance of the UK economy. Therefore, inflation-based estimates of the expected MRP appear conservative. The nominal GDP growth rate is closely tracked by the regression-based perpetual growth estimate. Estimates of the steady state growth rate and the five-year IBES CAGR are substantially higher compared to the previously discussed proxies.

Exhibit 59 Development of selected perpetual growth proxies for the UK market

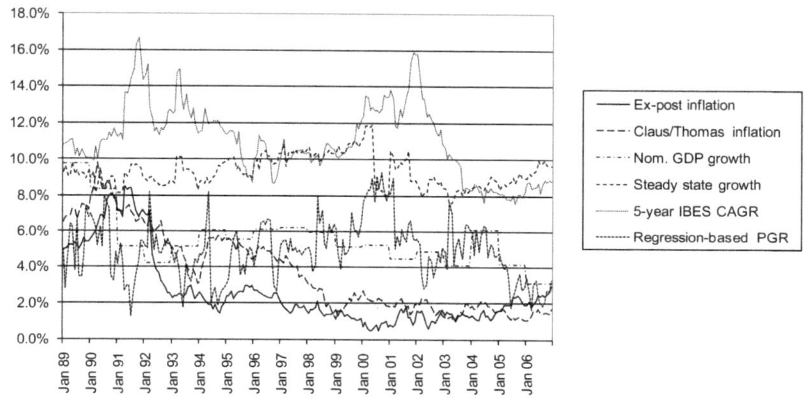

Source: IBES, Datastream.

A comparison of formerly developed approaches in Exhibit 60 results in a similar development of the conditional expected MRP curves over time (see also Appendix 29). The unconditional averages range from 0.45% to 5.09% which is consistent with the findings using the terminal value specifications proposed in this study.

Exhibit 60 UK expected MRP development using special comparison specifications of previous studies

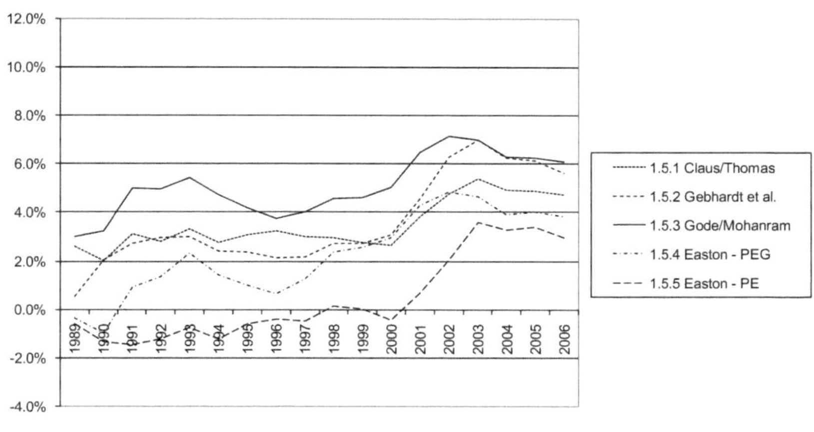

Table 49 Summary statistics of the UK expected MRP estimation using the standard model with various terminal perpetuity approaches

Model (1)						1.1 $r^b=r^e$		1.2 $g_{RI}=0$					1.3 g_{RI}=ex-post inflation					1.4 g_{RI}=steady state growth			
Year	r^f (2)	θ_{TV}	$m_{P/E+1}$	N (3)	Firms (4)	r^e	r^p	r^e	r^p	$g_{RI,TV}$	$g_{D,TV}$ (5)	$m_{P/E+1,TV}$ (6)	r^e	r^p	$g_{RI,TV}$	$g_{D,TV}$ (5)	$m_{P/E+1,TV}$ (7)	r^e	r^p	$g_{RI,D,TV}$	$m_{P/E+1,TV}$ (6)
1989	10.13%	39.89%	11.2x	645	54	4.03%	-6.10%	10.98%	0.85%	0.00%	6.60%	9.1x	12.21%	2.08%	5.23%	7.34%	NA	13.35%	3.22%	9.29%	9.8x
1990	11.57%	43.34%	10.4x	487	41	6.42%	-5.15%	11.88%	0.31%	0.00%	6.73%	8.4x	13.21%	1.64%	6.96%	7.49%	NA	13.65%	2.08%	8.78%	8.9x
1991	10.05%	45.57%	12.3x	767	64	3.38%	-6.68%	11.27%	1.21%	0.00%	6.13%	8.9x	13.33%	3.27%	7.54%	7.25%	NA	13.85%	3.79%	9.13%	9.6x
1992	9.07%	44.08%	13.4x	947	79	1.14%	-7.93%	10.06%	0.99%	0.00%	5.63%	9.9x	11.30%	2.23%	4.30%	6.32%	NA	12.82%	3.75%	8.77%	10.9x
1993	7.34%	48.21%	15.8x	1,212	101	-4.88%	-12.22%	8.87%	1.53%	0.00%	4.59%	11.3x	9.89%	2.55%	2.50%	5.12%	NA	13.08%	5.74%	9.36%	13.0x
1994	8.14%	45.95%	15.2x	1,623	135	-3.90%	-12.03%	8.89%	0.75%	0.00%	4.80%	11.3x	9.65%	1.52%	1.98%	5.22%	NA	12.76%	4.62%	9.17%	12.8x
1995	8.15%	45.80%	13.9x	2,106	176	-3.49%	-11.64%	9.18%	1.03%	0.00%	4.97%	10.9x	10.20%	2.05%	2.66%	5.53%	NA	13.19%	5.04%	9.51%	12.4x
1996	7.80%	46.62%	14.1x	2,120	177	-5.30%	-13.10%	8.96%	1.15%	0.00%	4.78%	11.2x	10.00%	2.19%	2.48%	5.34%	NA	13.63%	5.83%	10.04%	13.0x
1997	6.98%	44.64%	16.0x	2,864	239	-7.97%	-14.95%	8.09%	1.11%	0.00%	4.48%	12.4x	8.91%	1.93%	1.78%	4.93%	NA	13.44%	6.45%	10.39%	14.7x
1998	5.45%	45.91%	18.6x	3,180	265	-11.49%	-16.95%	7.11%	1.66%	0.00%	3.85%	14.1x	7.94%	2.48%	1.59%	4.29%	NA	13.02%	7.57%	10.32%	17.0x
1999	5.01%	45.68%	20.4x	3,294	275	-13.64%	-18.65%	6.65%	1.64%	0.00%	3.61%	15.0x	7.39%	2.38%	1.34%	4.01%	NA	13.19%	8.18%	10.73%	18.6x
2000	5.22%	45.02%	21.6x	3,532	294	-11.52%	-16.73%	6.72%	1.51%	0.00%	3.70%	14.9x	7.11%	1.90%	0.79%	3.91%	NA	12.24%	7.02%	9.69%	17.7x
2001	4.93%	43.82%	18.4x	3,472	289	-7.25%	-12.18%	7.90%	2.97%	0.00%	4.44%	12.7x	8.44%	3.51%	1.24%	4.74%	NA	12.67%	7.74%	9.71%	14.8x
2002	4.84%	41.89%	15.4x	3,271	273	-1.09%	-5.94%	9.00%	4.16%	0.00%	5.23%	11.1x	9.39%	4.55%	1.26%	5.46%	NA	12.03%	7.18%	8.60%	12.2x
2003	4.48%	45.14%	13.0x	3,471	289	0.26%	-4.22%	9.44%	4.95%	0.00%	5.18%	10.6x	9.82%	5.34%	1.36%	5.39%	NA	12.08%	7.60%	8.17%	11.5x
2004	4.86%	43.84%	12.9x	3,853	321	-1.29%	-6.16%	9.16%	4.30%	0.00%	5.14%	10.9x	9.59%	4.73%	1.34%	5.39%	NA	12.31%	7.45%	8.69%	12.1x
2005	4.37%	45.50%	13.5x	4,377	365	-3.34%	-7.71%	8.76%	4.40%	0.00%	4.78%	11.4x	9.52%	5.15%	2.05%	5.19%	NA	12.39%	8.02%	8.84%	12.8x
2006	4.50%	44.91%	14.1x	4,661	388	-5.00%	-9.50%	8.63%	4.12%	0.00%	4.75%	11.6x	9.57%	5.07%	2.33%	5.27%	NA	12.95%	8.44%	9.58%	13.3x
Low	4.37%	39.89%	10.4x	487	41	-13.64%	-18.65%	6.65%	0.31%	0.00%	3.61%	8.4x	7.11%	1.52%	0.79%	3.91%	NA	12.03%	2.08%	8.17%	8.9x
Arith. Mean	6.83%	44.77%	15.0x	2,549	212	-3.61%	-10.43%	8.97%	2.15%	0.00%	4.97%	11.4x	9.86%	3.03%	2.71%	5.45%	NA	12.92%	6.10%	9.38%	13.1x
Median	6.22%	45.08%	14.1x	3,022	252	-3.69%	-10.57%	8.92%	1.52%	0.00%	4.79%	11.2x	9.62%	2.43%	2.02%	5.31%	NA	12.98%	6.74%	9.32%	12.8x
High	11.57%	48.21%	21.6x	4,661	388	6.42%	-4.22%	11.88%	4.95%	0.00%	6.73%	15.0x	13.33%	5.34%	7.54%	7.49%	NA	13.85%	8.44%	10.73%	18.6x
St. Dev.	2.30%	1.84%	3.1x			5.54%	4.47%	1.44%	1.53%	0.00%	0.88%	1.9x	1.75%	1.34%	1.99%	1.04%	NA	0.56%	1.93%	0.69%	2.7x

(1) All parameters are stated in nominal terms and as arithmetic average of monthly values.
(2) r^f equals redemption yield of the UK Datastream benchmark 10y government bond index.
(3) Overall number of firm observations per annum.
(4) Average number of firms per annum.
(5) Implied perpetual dividend growth rate (after convergence for $0<g_{RI}<g_{RI\ steady\ state}$ cases) according to calculation approach presented in Appendix 10 - $Max[g_{RI,TV};(1-\theta_{TV})r^e]$.
(6) Terminal multiple implied by a calculation based on terminal period payout ratio, cost of equity, and perpetual dividend growth rate.
(7) Implied terminal multiple cannot be determined as perpetual dividend growth rate is not constant but converging.

Table 50 Summary statistics of the UK expected MRP estimation using the regression-based approach

Model (1)				1.6. Regression approach					
Year	r^f (2)	N (3)	Firms (4)	r^e	r^p	$g_{RI,TV}$	$g_{D,TV}$ (5)	$m_{P/E+1,TV}$ (6)	Adj. R^2
1989	10.13%	621	52	11.62%	1.49%	5.15%	6.99%	NA	73.58%
1990	11.57%	460	38	12.16%	0.59%	5.91%	6.89%	NA	76.27%
1991	10.05%	728	61	10.27%	0.22%	3.76%	5.59%	NA	84.64%
1992	9.07%	899	75	10.82%	1.75%	5.47%	6.05%	NA	84.30%
1993	7.34%	1,163	97	9.67%	2.33%	3.75%	5.01%	NA	77.91%
1994	8.14%	1,544	129	9.57%	1.43%	3.89%	5.17%	NA	68.07%
1995	8.15%	1,950	163	10.12%	1.97%	4.50%	5.49%	NA	67.75%
1996	7.80%	1,815	151	10.23%	2.43%	5.16%	5.46%	NA	67.06%
1997	6.98%	2,385	199	10.17%	3.18%	5.09%	5.63%	NA	71.66%
1998	5.45%	2,717	226	11.08%	5.62%	5.72%	5.99%	NA	54.63%
1999	5.01%	2,668	222	10.49%	5.48%	5.55%	5.70%	NA	56.09%
2000	5.22%	2,847	237	12.53%	7.31%	8.32%	8.32%	NA	45.24%
2001	4.93%	3,105	259	11.00%	6.07%	6.24%	6.24%	NA	50.79%
2002	4.84%	3,012	251	10.11%	5.27%	4.22%	5.88%	NA	64.79%
2003	4.48%	3,188	266	11.23%	6.75%	5.58%	6.16%	NA	54.27%
2004	4.86%	3,486	291	10.51%	5.65%	5.39%	5.90%	NA	56.16%
2005	4.37%	3,928	327	9.16%	4.79%	3.35%	4.99%	NA	62.60%
2006	4.50%	4,164	347	8.60%	4.10%	2.59%	4.74%	NA	59.09%
Low	4.37%	460	38	8.60%	0.22%	2.59%	4.74%	NA	45.24%
Arith. Mean	6.83%	2,260	188	10.52%	3.69%	4.98%	5.90%	NA	65.27%
Median	6.22%	2,527	211	10.38%	3.64%	5.16%	5.79%	NA	65.92%
High	11.57%	4,164	347	12.53%	7.31%	8.32%	8.32%	NA	84.64%
St. Dev.	2.30%			0.99%	2.23%	1.30%	0.85%	NA	11.38%

(1) All parameters are stated in nominal terms and as arithmetic average of monthly values.
(2) r^f equals redemption yield of the UK Datastream benchmark 10y government bond index.
(3) Overall number of firm observations per annum.
(4) Average number of firms per annum.
(5) Implied perpetual dividend growth rate after convergence according to calculation approach presented in Appendix 10 - $Max[g_{RI,TV};(1-\theta_{TV})r^e]$.
(6) Implied terminal multiple cannot be determined since implied perpetual dividend growth rate is not constant but converging.

The comparison of the expected MRP estimates to selected other studies in the international academic press using similar model specifications is summarized in Table 51. Claus/Thomas and Pastor/Sinha/Swaminathan calculated lower average expected MRPs of 2.81% and 2.89% for an earlier and shorter analysis period. Covering a similar analysis period than this study, Desrosiers/Lemaire/L'Her determine an average expected MRP of 0.59% which is much lower than the 3.48% estimate using data of this study. Due to the limited methodology and data discussion by other studies, the differences cannot be fully reconciled.

Table 51 Overview of key results of previous studies on the UK market

Authors	Period	Weighting (1)	Arith. mean over analysis period (2) r^e	r^p	r^f
Claus/Thomas Model					
Claus/Thomas (2001)	1985-1998	agg	11.47%	2.81%	8.66%
Desrosiers/Lemaire/L'Her (2007) (3)	1988-2005	NA	6.80%	0.59%	6.21%
Lee/Ng/Swaminathan (2009)	1991-2000	ew	NA	5.53%	NA
Gsell (2010)	1989-2006	agg	10.31%	3.48%	6.83%
Gebhardt/Lee/Swaminathan Model					
Chen/Jorgensen/Yoo (2004)	1993-2001	ew	10.9%	4.5%	6.4%
Gsell (2010)	1989-2006	agg	10.43%	3.60%	6.83%
Other approaches					
Hail/Leuz (2006) (4)	1992-2001	NA	10.64%	NA	NA
Lee/Ng/Swaminathan (2009) (5)	1991-2000	ew	NA	5.35%	NA
Pastor/Sinha/Swaminathan (2008) (5)	1990-2002	ew	NA	6.99%	NA
Pastor/Sinha/Swaminathan (2008) (5)	1990-2002	vw	NA	2.89%	NA

(1) agg = aggregation method; ew = equal-weighted; vw = value-weighted.
(2) All parameters are stated in nominal terms.
(3) Annualized r^e based on original monthly estimate (US-Dollar denominated);
Implied r^p using own US r^f estimate;
Terminal perpetuity based on g_{RI}=ex-post inflation.
(4) Average of Claus/Thomas, Gebhardt/Lee/Swaminathan, Gode/Mohanram, and Easton-PEG model.
(5) Estimation based on dividend discount model with r^e equal to r^b after 15 years.

Source: Claus, J./Thomas, J. (2001), p. 1643, Chen, F./Jorgensen, B./Yoo, Y. (2004), p. 331, Hail, L./Leuz, C. (2006), pp. 494-495, Desrosiers, S./Lemaire, N./L'Her, J.-F. (2007), p. 79, Pastor, L./Sinha, M./Swaminathan, B. (2008), p. 2875, and Lee, C./Ng, D./Swaminathan, B. (2009), pp. 318 and 321.

5.9.6 United States

The results of the US market are of particular interest since the underlying data shows the highest quality level with respect to sample size and data completeness. This is certainly one factor explaining why the US expected MRP estimates have the lowest level of volatility measured in terms of standard deviation. Furthermore, the US sample has the most balanced industry structure compared to other countries in this study as shown in Exhibit 29[839].

Unlike for previous countries, the conditional expected MRP estimates based on the terminal perpetuity scenarios with zero and ex-post inflation perpetual growth appear to be stationary over the analysis period as shown in Exhibit 61. Consistent with findings from other US studies[840], the expected MRP declines until the end of the 1990s but recovers to its level at the beginning of the analysis period. The unconditional averages for zero and ex-post inflation perpetual growth are 2.15% and

[839] The input data for the US market is summarized in Appendix 30 and Appendix 31.
[840] See also the discussion of the Fama, E./French, K. (2002) results in Section 6.3.2.6.

3.52% respectively as shown in Table 52. The steady state scenario results in an average expected MRP of 9.14% which develops inverted to the previous cases reaching its maximum level during 1998 and 2001. Applying the simultaneous regression approach yields an expected MRP of on average 5.32% (see Table 53) following a similar development compared to the steady state case. Interestingly, the coefficient of determination decreases continuously over the analysis period from around 60% to 20% as a consequence of changes in the sample structure. The general observation of lower average implied forward PE_{+1} ratios compared to their spot level at the valuation date can also be confirmed for the US market with an average decrease of at least 2.3x.

Exhibit 61 US expected MRP development using the standard model with various terminal perpetuity approaches

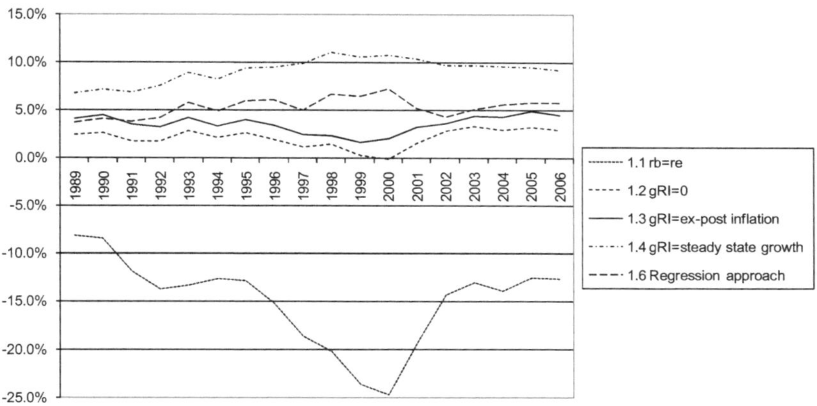

Analyzing the different proxies for the perpetual residual income growth in Exhibit 62 shows that inflation is continuously below the level of nominal GDP growth indicating that the ex-post inflation case may be too pessimistic. Nominal GDP growth itself developed in-between inflation rate and the regression-based growth estimate and tracked the latter closely from 2003 onwards. The steady state growth rate and the five-year IBES CAGR developed at a substantially higher level.

Exhibit 62 Development of selected perpetual growth proxies for the US market

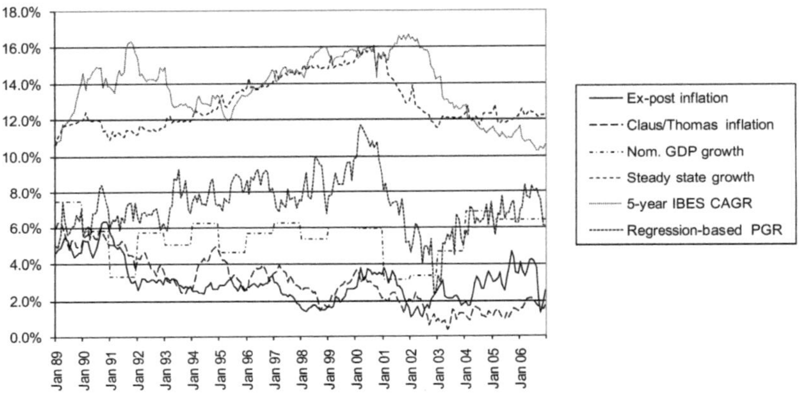

Source: IBES, Datastream.

Exhibit 63 shows the development of expected MRP estimates of previous model specifications by other authors. Models 1.5.1, 1.5.2, and 1.5.4 have on average very similar estimates of the expected MRP at around ~3.5% (see also Appendix 32) with 1.5.3 leading to an average value of 5.34%.

Exhibit 63 US expected MRP development using special comparison specifications of previous studies

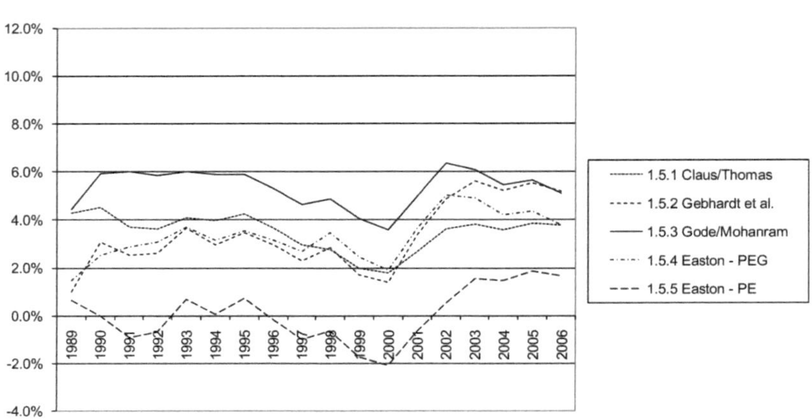

Table 52 Summary statistics of the US expected MRP estimation using the standard model with various terminal perpetuity approaches

Model (1)						1.1 $r^b=r^e$		1.2 $g_{RI}=0$					1.3 g_{RI}=ex-post inflation					1.4 g_{RI}=steady state growth			
Year	r^f (2)	θ_{TV}	$m_{P/E+1}$	N (3)	Firms (4)	r^e	r^p	r^e	r^p	$g_{RI,TV}$	$g_{D,TV}$ (5)	$m_{P/E+1,TV}$ (6)	r^e	r^p	$g_{RI,TV}$	$g_{D,TV}$ (5)	$m_{P/E+1,TV}$ (7)	r^e	r^p	$g_{RI,D,TV}$	$m_{P/E+1,TV}$ (6)
1989	8.45%	37.06%	11.8x	7,607	634	0.36%	-8.09%	10.96%	2.51%	0.00%	6.90%	9.1x	12.52%	4.07%	4.81%	7.88%	NA	15.18%	6.73%	11.61%	10.4x
1990	8.56%	38.87%	12.5x	7,802	650	0.20%	-8.36%	11.21%	2.66%	0.00%	6.86%	8.9x	13.03%	4.47%	5.39%	7.96%	NA	15.65%	7.09%	11.84%	10.2x
1991	7.79%	40.53%	15.4x	7,961	663	-4.00%	-11.80%	9.57%	1.78%	0.00%	5.69%	10.4x	11.28%	3.48%	4.27%	6.71%	NA	14.58%	6.79%	11.26%	12.2x
1992	7.02%	41.13%	16.5x	8,438	703	-6.64%	-13.67%	8.86%	1.84%	0.00%	5.22%	11.3x	10.20%	3.17%	3.02%	6.00%	NA	14.54%	7.52%	11.48%	13.5x
1993	5.84%	39.27%	16.1x	9,400	783	-7.39%	-13.24%	8.67%	2.83%	0.00%	5.27%	11.5x	10.03%	4.18%	2.97%	6.09%	NA	14.77%	8.93%	11.95%	13.9x
1994	7.13%	37.38%	14.6x	10,420	868	-5.42%	-12.56%	9.36%	2.23%	0.00%	5.86%	10.7x	10.45%	3.32%	2.59%	6.55%	NA	15.30%	8.17%	12.39%	12.8x
1995	6.49%	34.41%	14.7x	11,972	998	-6.33%	-12.82%	9.20%	2.72%	0.00%	6.04%	10.9x	10.43%	3.95%	2.82%	6.84%	NA	15.84%	9.35%	13.25%	13.3x
1996	6.46%	31.63%	16.7x	13,633	1,136	-8.67%	-15.13%	8.48%	2.02%	0.00%	5.80%	11.8x	9.87%	3.41%	2.92%	6.75%	NA	15.99%	9.53%	13.85%	14.8x
1997	6.32%	30.21%	19.6x	15,676	1,306	-12.27%	-18.59%	7.51%	1.19%	0.00%	5.24%	13.3x	8.75%	2.43%	2.35%	6.10%	NA	16.22%	9.90%	14.48%	17.3x
1998	5.21%	28.19%	22.7x	17,254	1,438	-14.96%	-20.17%	6.72%	1.51%	0.00%	4.83%	14.9x	7.60%	2.38%	1.55%	5.46%	NA	16.27%	11.06%	14.85%	19.8x
1999	5.71%	28.76%	25.9x	18,128	1,511	-17.82%	-23.53%	6.03%	0.32%	0.00%	4.29%	16.6x	7.36%	1.65%	2.17%	5.24%	NA	16.32%	10.61%	15.05%	22.6x
2000	5.98%	27.51%	26.5x	18,243	1,520	-18.66%	-24.64%	5.90%	-0.08%	0.00%	4.27%	17.0x	8.03%	2.05%	3.38%	5.82%	NA	16.79%	10.81%	15.62%	23.5x
2001	4.99%	26.85%	23.9x	19,622	1,635	-14.32%	-19.31%	6.55%	1.57%	0.00%	4.79%	15.3x	8.16%	3.17%	2.85%	5.97%	NA	15.35%	10.36%	14.00%	19.9x
2002	4.54%	28.72%	20.6x	20,614	1,718	-9.73%	-14.27%	7.42%	2.89%	0.00%	5.29%	13.5x	8.17%	3.63%	1.59%	5.82%	NA	14.22%	9.69%	12.48%	16.5x
2003	3.99%	26.98%	18.9x	21,961	1,830	-8.99%	-12.98%	7.36%	3.37%	0.00%	5.37%	13.6x	8.40%	4.41%	2.26%	6.13%	NA	13.69%	9.70%	12.05%	16.5x
2004	4.25%	27.36%	17.8x	23,815	1,985	-9.60%	-13.85%	7.25%	3.00%	0.00%	5.27%	13.8x	8.53%	4.28%	2.68%	6.20%	NA	13.82%	9.57%	12.19%	16.8x
2005	4.27%	27.26%	17.0x	26,254	2,188	-8.21%	-12.49%	7.58%	3.31%	0.00%	5.52%	13.2x	9.14%	4.87%	3.41%	6.65%	NA	13.77%	9.49%	12.05%	15.9x
2006	4.78%	26.60%	16.2x	27,182	2,265	-7.78%	-12.56%	7.78%	2.99%	0.00%	5.71%	12.9x	9.22%	4.44%	3.22%	6.77%	NA	14.01%	9.23%	12.30%	15.5x
Low	3.99%	26.60%	11.8x	7,607	634	-18.66%	-24.64%	5.90%	-0.08%	0.00%	4.27%	8.9x	7.36%	1.65%	1.55%	5.24%	NA	13.69%	6.73%	11.26%	10.2x
Arith. Mean	5.99%	32.15%	18.2x	15,888	1,324	-8.90%	-14.89%	8.14%	2.15%	0.00%	5.46%	12.7x	9.51%	3.52%	3.01%	6.39%	NA	15.13%	9.14%	12.93%	15.9x
Median	5.91%	29.48%	16.8x	16,465	1,372	-8.44%	-13.45%	7.68%	2.37%	0.00%	5.33%	13.0x	9.18%	3.56%	2.88%	6.17%	NA	15.24%	9.51%	12.35%	15.7x
High	8.56%	41.13%	26.5x	27,182	2,265	0.36%	-8.09%	11.21%	3.37%	0.00%	6.90%	17.0x	13.03%	4.87%	5.39%	7.96%	NA	16.79%	11.06%	15.62%	23.5x
St. Dev.	1.42%	5.42%	4.3x			5.28%	4.60%	1.53%	0.98%	0.00%	0.71%	2.3x	1.61%	0.92%	1.00%	0.72%	NA	0.99%	1.35%	1.36%	3.8x

(1) All parameters are stated in nominal terms and as arithmetic average of monthly values.
(2) r^f equals redemption yield of the US Datastream benchmark 10y government bond index.
(3) Overall number of firm observations per annum.
(4) Average number of firms per annum.
(5) Implied perpetual dividend growth rate (after convergence for $0<g_{RI}<g_{RI\ steady\ state}$ cases) according to calculation approach presented in Appendix 10 - $Max[g_{RI,TV};(1-\theta_{TV})r^e]$.
(6) Terminal multiple implied by a calculation based on terminal period payout ratio, cost of equity, and perpetual dividend growth rate.
(7) Implied terminal multiple cannot be determined as perpetual dividend growth rate is not constant but converging.

Table 53 Summary statistics of the US expected MRP estimation using the regression-based approach

Model (1)				1.6. Regression approach					
Year	r^f (2)	N (3)	Firms (4)	r^e	r^p	$g_{RI,TV}$	$g_{D,TV}$ (5)	$m_{P/E+1,TV}$ (6)	Adj. R^2
1989	8.45%	7,501	625	12.18%	3.73%	6.07%	7.67%	NA	63.32%
1990	8.56%	7,647	637	12.67%	4.12%	6.87%	7.75%	NA	60.95%
1991	7.79%	7,741	645	11.66%	3.87%	6.65%	6.93%	NA	67.41%
1992	7.02%	8,132	678	11.23%	4.21%	6.58%	6.61%	NA	61.39%
1993	5.84%	9,011	751	11.65%	5.81%	7.58%	7.58%	NA	40.34%
1994	7.13%	10,068	839	12.01%	4.88%	7.67%	7.67%	NA	45.27%
1995	6.49%	11,452	954	12.46%	5.97%	8.05%	8.17%	NA	51.21%
1996	6.46%	12,796	1,066	12.50%	6.04%	8.70%	8.70%	NA	47.57%
1997	6.32%	14,689	1,224	11.29%	4.98%	7.43%	7.88%	NA	39.78%
1998	5.21%	15,821	1,318	11.92%	6.70%	8.50%	8.56%	NA	27.01%
1999	5.71%	16,022	1,335	12.14%	6.43%	8.76%	8.76%	NA	29.83%
2000	5.98%	15,560	1,297	13.24%	7.26%	10.66%	10.66%	NA	19.76%
2001	4.99%	18,114	1,510	10.18%	5.19%	7.04%	7.44%	NA	18.71%
2002	4.54%	19,477	1,623	8.85%	4.32%	4.64%	6.31%	NA	25.62%
2003	3.99%	20,619	1,718	9.09%	5.10%	5.08%	6.64%	NA	25.03%
2004	4.25%	22,087	1,841	9.87%	5.62%	6.47%	7.17%	NA	26.61%
2005	4.27%	24,395	2,033	10.02%	5.75%	6.68%	7.29%	NA	23.48%
2006	4.78%	25,146	2,096	10.58%	5.80%	7.45%	7.77%	NA	21.86%
Low	3.99%	7,501	625	8.85%	3.73%	4.64%	6.31%	NA	18.71%
Arith. Mean	5.99%	14,793	1,233	11.31%	5.32%	7.27%	7.75%	NA	38.62%
Median	5.91%	15,125	1,260	11.66%	5.40%	7.23%	7.67%	NA	34.81%
High	8.56%	25,146	2,096	13.24%	7.26%	10.66%	10.66%	NA	67.41%
St. Dev.	1.42%			1.27%	1.01%	1.40%	1.01%	NA	16.65%

(1) All parameters are stated in nominal terms and as arithmetic average of monthly values.
(2) r^f equals redemption yield of the US Datastream benchmark 10y government bond index.
(3) Overall number of firm observations per annum.
(4) Average number of firms per annum.
(5) Implied perpetual dividend growth rate after convergence according to calculation approach presented in Appendix 10 - $\text{Max}[g_{RI,TV};(1-\theta_{TV})r^e]$.
(6) Implied terminal multiple cannot be determined since implied perpetual dividend growth rate is not constant but converging.

The results of this study on the US market can be compared to a number of other empirical studies using one or several equity valuation approaches to determine the expected MRP. Table 54 provides a first general comparison of the unconditional mean values classified by valuation model. The expected MRP estimates from applying the most widely used model specifications of Claus/Thomas and Gebhardt/Lee/Swaminathan range from 1.00% to 6.03%. Models using more optimistic terminal value assumptions provide estimates of up to 7.55%. It becomes further obvious that despite different analysis periods the herein calculated results are within a less than one percent range to comparable studies using the value-weighting approach.

Table 54 Overview of key results of previous studies on the US market

Authors	Period	Weighting (1)	Arith. mean over analysis period (2) r^e	r^p	r^f
Claus/Thomas Model					
Claus/Thomas (2001)	1985-1998	agg	11.04%	3.40%	7.64%
Baginski/Wahlen (2003)	1996-2004	NA	9.78%	2.74%	7.03%
Guay/Kothari/Shu (2005)	1983-2004	NA	10.3%	NA	NA
Easton/Monahan (2005)	1981-1998	NA	12.0%	NA	NA
Desrosiers/Lemaire/L'Her (2007) (3)	1988-2005	NA	8.86%	2.65%	6.21%
Esterer/Schröder (2007a)	1995-2006	ew	9.2%	NA	NA
Lee/Ng/Swaminathan (2009)	1991-2000	ew	NA	6.03%	NA
Gsell (2010)	1989-2006	agg	9.50%	3.51%	5.99%
Gebhardt/Lee/Swaminathan Model					
Gebhardt/Lee/Swaminathan (2001)	1979-1995	ew	NA	2.75%	NA
Gode/Mohanram (2003)	1984-1998	NA	NA	3.03%	7.97%
Guay/Kothari/Shu (2005)	1983-2004	NA	9.9%	NA	NA
Chen/Jorgensen/Yoo (2004)	1993-2001	NA	10.8%	5.0%	5.8%
Botosan/Plumlee (2005)	1983-1993	ew	NA	1.0%	NA
Easton/Monahan (2005)	1981-1998	NA	10.9%	NA	NA
Esterer/Schröder (2007a)	1995-2006	ew	8.16%	NA	NA
Gsell (2010)	1989-2006	agg	9.36%	3.37%	5.99%
Gode/Mohanram Model					
Gode/Mohanram (2003)	1984-1998	NA	13.49%	5.52%	7.97%
Guay/Kothari/Shu (2005)	1983-2004	NA	13.4%	NA	NA
Chen/Jorgensen/Yoo (2004)	1993-2001	NA	13.0%	7.2%	5.8%
Botosan/Plumlee (2005)	1983-1993	ew	NA	6.6%	NA
Easton/Monahan (2005)	1981-1998	NA	12.9%	NA	NA
Lee/Ng/Swaminathan (2009)	1991-2000	ew	NA	7.55%	NA
Gsell (2010)	1989-2006	agg	11.33%	5.34%	5.99%
Easton PEG Model					
Chen/Jorgensen/Yoo (2004)	1993-2001	NA	11.7%	5.9%	5.8%
Easton (2004)	1981-1999	NA	11.3%	3.18%	8.12%
Botosan/Plumlee (2005)	1983-1993	ew	NA	5.0%	NA
Easton/Monahan (2005)	1981-1998	NA	11.0%	NA	NA
Gsell (2010)	1989-2006	agg	9.33%	3.34%	5.99%
Easton PE Model					
Easton (2004)	1981-1999	NA	8.40%	0.28%	8.12%
Easton/Monahan (2005)	1981-1998	NA	8.80%	NA	NA
Gsell (2010)	1989-2006	agg	6.07%	0.08%	5.99%
Regression approach					
Easton et al. (2002)	1981-1998	NAp	13.19%	5.31%	7.89%
Easton (2004) (4)	1981-1999	NAp	13.00%	4.88%	8.12%
Easton/Monahan (2005) (4)	1981-1998	NAp	12.8%	NA	NA
Gsell (2010)	1989-2006	NAp	11.31%	5.32%	5.99%
Other approaches					
Hail/Leuz (2006) (5)	1992-2001	NA	10.24%	NA	NA
Lee/Ng/Swaminathan (2009) (6)	1991-2000	ew	NA	6.3%	NA
Pastor/Sinha/Swaminathan (2008) (6)	1990-2002	ew	NA	4.57%	NA
Pastor/Sinha/Swaminathan (2008) (6)	1990-2002	vw	NA	2.65%	NA

(1) agg = aggregation method; ew = equal-weighted; vw = value-weighted.
(2) All parameters are stated in nominal terms.
(3) Annualized value based on original monthly estimate. Terminal perpetuity based on g_{RI}=ex-post inflation.
(4) Based on CAP regression model.
(5) Average of Claus/Thomas, Gebhardt/Lee/Swaminathan, Gode/Mohanram, and Easton-PEG model.
(6) Estimation based on dividend discount model with r^e equal to r^b after 15 years.

Source: Claus, J./Thomas, J. (2001), p. 1643, Gebhardt, W./Lee, C./Swaminathan, B. (2001), p. 149, Easton, P. et al. (2002), p. 665, Baginski, S./Wahlen, J. (2003), pp. 336-337, Gode, D./Mohanram, P. (2003), pp. 410-411, Easton, P. (2004), p. 85, Botosan, C./Plumlee, M. (2005), p. 37, Easton, P./Monahan, S. (2005), p. 514, Guay, W./Kothari, S./Shu, S. (2005), p. 35, Hail, L./Leuz, C. (2006), pp. 494-495, Desrosiers, S./Lemaire, N./L'Her, J.-F. (2007), p. 79, Esterer, F./Schröder, D. (2007a), p. 29, Pastor, L./Sinha, M./Swaminathan, B. (2008), p. 2875, and Lee, C./Ng, D./Swaminathan, B. (2009), pp. 318 and 321.

A more detailed comparison of studies utilizing key comparable models on a year-by-year basis is provided in Appendix 34 and Appendix 35. While there are minor differences in the utilized risk-free rates, substantial variations exist in the sample size underlying each study. Claus/Thomas use the most comprehensive data set with up to 3,797 included firms in their sample. The authors selected all US firms with IBES forecasts meeting the outlined conditions. Authors of other studies, including myself, impose further restrictions with regards to (1) the available population, i.e., only firms being traded on a certain exchange or being included in a certain index and (2) the data completeness criteria. However, it should be noted that this study includes all firms within the Russell 3000 meeting the sample selection criteria. Taking into account that this index covers approx. 98% of the investable US equities[841], the difference in the sample size to Claus/Thomas may appear large due to the inclusion of small cap firms but has little impact on the overall result in a study using the aggregation method.

Neglecting the influence of inconsistent sample sizes and analysis periods, it becomes obvious that the variation in results when comparing studies with different averaging methodologies—i.e., aggregation method, equal-weighting, or value-weighting—is less significant than in the German market. Still, this is the main driver in explaining the differences between the Gebhardt/Lee/Swaminathan results and the herein calculated results presented in Appendix 33 as also evidenced by the Pastor/Sinha/Swaminathan study. Furthermore, Appendix 35 shows that despite a similar level of regression quality measured by the coefficient of determination, the herein calculated estimates for the expected MRP and the perpetual growth rate are lower compared to the Easton et al. study in the overlapping period. The key explanation for this divergence appears to be the larger sample size of Easton et al. who have more small caps in their sample with potentially higher associated risk and growth expectations. Whereas this effect does not become material when the aggregation method is applied, the OLS regression approach implicitly attributes equal weights to all included firms. In addition, the applied restrictions for the independent and dependent variable may cause divergences.

A final point of interest relates to the potential optimism bias in earnings forecasts. Easton/Sommers (2007) use the regression approach to quantify the impact on the

---

841 See Russell Investment Group (2006), p. 2.

expected MRP for US market data between 1992 and 2003. The authors find a bias of 2.84% calculated as difference of the expected return implied by the regression approach using earnings forecasts and actual earnings[842]. When interpreting this number, it needs to be taken into account that using actual earnings for the regression creates a mismatch of information contained in current prices and actual earnings which can cause another bias[843].

5.9.7 World (aggregation of all analyzed countries)

In the final results section, the expected MRP estimates for an aggregated world sample consisting out the six local equity markets investigated in this study are presented. In order to derive a common currency sample, all financial input data is converted into US-Dollar[844]. For the purposes of currency conversion, the respective spot exchange rate at the estimation date is used since forward exchange rates for all required horizons are not available throughout the analysis period. Exhibit 64 shows the underlying spot exchange rate development over the analysis period.

Exhibit 64 Exchange rate development over time

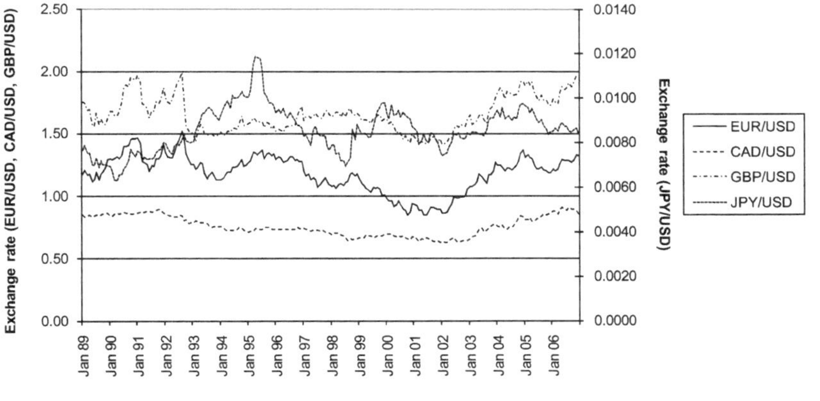

Source: Datastream.

[842] See Easton, P./Sommers, G. (2007), p. 1001.
[843] See also Easton, P. (2009), pp. 329-330.
[844] The input data for the world market is summarized in Appendix 36 and Appendix 37.

The combined sample resulting from the aggregation of all markets includes more than 4,000 firms by 2006. Within the consolidated sample, the US market represents on average approximately 64% over the entire analysis period followed by Japan 13%, the UK 9%, Germany 6%, France 6%, and Canada 2%. Exhibit 65 presents the weighting development over the analysis period.

Exhibit 65 Market capitalization weights within the World index over time

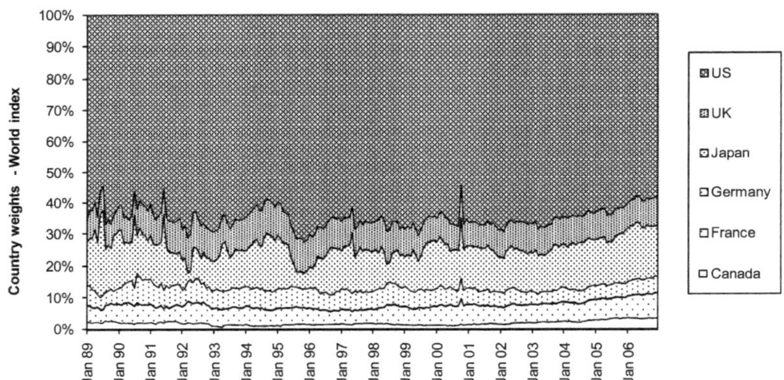

Exhibit 66 continues to show the expected MRP estimates for the world sample for the terminal perpetuity approaches. It should be noted that the regression-based estimation approach is not implemented for the world sample. The derived expected MRP curves are similar to US market with a more stationary development over time compared most other equity markets. The conditional expected MRP estimates based on zero and ex-post inflation perpetual growth develop in parallel with a temporary low in 2000 after which the estimates rise to a comparatively higher level than before the temporary low. The unconditional averages are 1.85% and 2.92% with low standard deviations of 1.13% and 1.03% respectively[845]. The expected MRP estimates based on steady state growth slightly increase over the analysis period with an arithmetic average of 7.30% and a standard deviation of 1.24%.

[845] The ex-post inflation rate applied here is a weighted-average of the local market ex-post inflation rates with market capitalization as weighting factor.

Exhibit 66 World expected MRP development using the standard model with various terminal perpetuity approaches

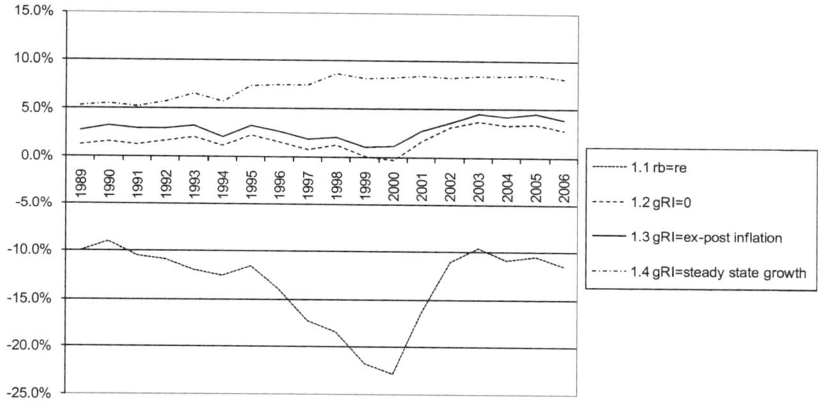

The comparison of other proxies for the perpetual growth rate in Exhibit 67 shows a large discrepancy between the weighted inflation rate/GDP growth and steady state growth/five-year IBES CAGR. Whereas the nominal GDP growth rate is only slightly above the inflation levels, the latter two proxies develop almost consistently above 10%. This explains the large difference between the ex-post inflation and steady state growth based expected MRP estimates.

Exhibit 67 Development of selected perpetual growth proxies for the World index

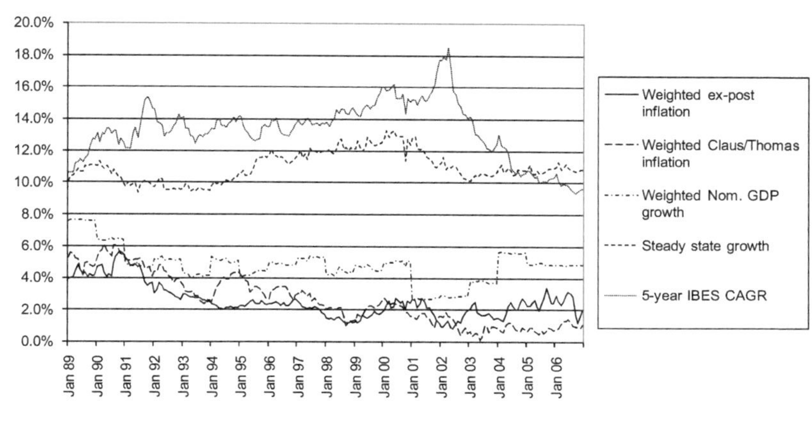

Source: IBES, Datastream.

The expected MRP curves resulting from applying formerly developed terminal perpetuity approaches are presented in Exhibit 68. Estimates based on Claus/Thomas, Gebhardt et al., and Easton (PEG) specifications move closely together with unconditional averages ranging from 2.34% to 3.15%. The Easton (PE) and Gode/Mohanram approach represent the lower and upper boundaries with arithmetic average values of -0.11% and 5.15% as shown in Appendix 38.

Exhibit 68 World expected MRP development using special comparison specifications of previous studies

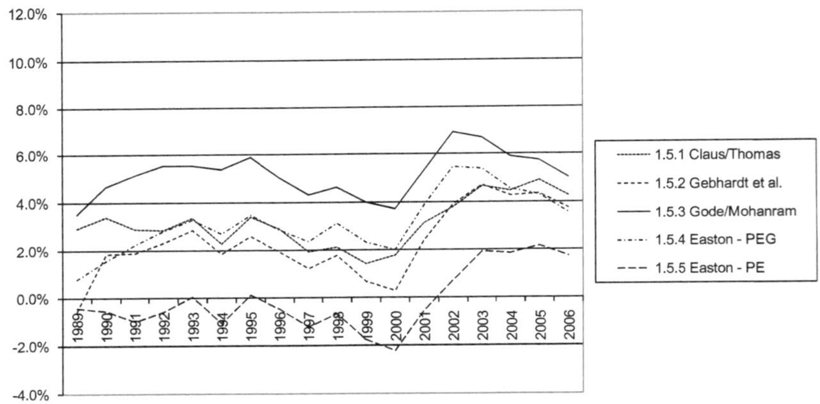

Table 55 Summary statistics of the World expected MRP estimation using the standard model with various terminal perpetuity approaches

Model (1)						1.1 $r^b=r^e$		1.2 $g_{RI}=0$					1.3 g_{RI}=ex-post inflation					1.4 g_{RI}=steady state growth			
Year	r^f (2)	θ_{TV}	$m_{P/E+1}$	N (3)	Firms (4)	r^e	r^p	r^e	r^p	$g_{RI,TV}$	$g_{D,TV}$ (5)	$m_{P/E+1,TV}$ (6)	r^e	r^p	$g_{RI,TV}$	$g_{D,TV}$ (5)	$m_{P/E+1,TV}$ (7)	r^e	r^p	$g_{RI,D,TV}$	$m_{P/E+1,TV}$ (6)
1989	8.45%	35.88%	13.2x	10,396	866	-1.50%	-9.95%	9.71%	1.26%	0.00%	6.23%	10.3x	11.18%	2.73%	4.25%	7.17%	NA	13.84%	5.39%	10.76%	11.7x
1990	8.56%	37.46%	13.3x	10,533	878	-0.44%	-9.00%	10.19%	1.63%	0.00%	6.37%	9.8x	11.79%	3.23%	4.86%	7.37%	NA	14.11%	5.55%	10.72%	11.1x
1991	7.79%	39.39%	15.5x	11,182	932	-2.66%	-10.45%	9.13%	1.34%	0.00%	5.53%	11.0x	10.74%	2.95%	4.43%	6.51%	NA	13.05%	5.26%	9.87%	12.4x
1992	7.02%	40.20%	16.3x	12,051	1,004	-3.84%	-10.86%	8.73%	1.71%	0.00%	5.22%	11.5x	9.91%	2.89%	3.11%	5.93%	NA	12.81%	5.79%	9.72%	13.0x
1993	5.84%	40.29%	17.8x	13,530	1,128	-6.15%	-11.99%	7.97%	2.12%	0.00%	4.76%	12.6x	9.12%	3.27%	2.75%	5.44%	NA	12.39%	6.55%	9.60%	14.4x
1994	7.13%	38.76%	17.2x	15,936	1,328	-5.37%	-12.50%	8.34%	1.21%	0.00%	5.11%	12.0x	9.21%	2.08%	2.17%	5.64%	NA	12.89%	5.75%	10.08%	13.8x
1995	6.49%	36.33%	15.9x	18,124	1,510	-5.08%	-11.57%	8.73%	2.25%	0.00%	5.56%	11.4x	9.69%	3.21%	2.39%	6.17%	NA	13.77%	7.29%	11.06%	13.4x
1996	6.46%	33.82%	17.5x	20,468	1,706	-7.51%	-13.97%	8.04%	1.58%	0.00%	5.32%	12.4x	9.12%	2.66%	2.42%	6.04%	NA	13.85%	7.39%	11.57%	14.9x
1997	6.32%	32.14%	20.4x	25,487	2,124	-10.91%	-17.23%	7.08%	0.76%	0.00%	4.80%	14.1x	8.14%	1.82%	2.13%	5.52%	NA	13.74%	7.43%	11.89%	17.3x
1998	5.21%	31.12%	22.9x	28,314	2,360	-13.18%	-18.39%	6.50%	1.29%	0.00%	4.48%	15.4x	7.23%	2.02%	1.37%	4.98%	NA	13.81%	8.60%	12.19%	19.2x
1999	5.71%	31.09%	26.3x	30,445	2,537	-16.01%	-21.71%	5.84%	0.14%	0.00%	4.03%	17.1x	6.77%	1.06%	1.59%	4.66%	NA	13.85%	8.14%	12.42%	21.8x
2000	5.98%	29.92%	27.5x	33,574	2,798	-16.83%	-22.82%	5.70%	-0.28%	0.00%	4.00%	17.5x	7.12%	1.14%	2.38%	4.99%	NA	14.16%	8.17%	12.84%	22.7x
2001	4.99%	28.41%	23.3x	38,083	3,174	-11.44%	-16.43%	6.66%	1.67%	0.00%	4.77%	15.0x	7.75%	2.76%	2.13%	5.55%	NA	13.37%	8.38%	11.83%	18.4x
2002	4.54%	29.56%	20.3x	38,512	3,209	-6.56%	-11.10%	7.68%	3.14%	0.00%	5.41%	13.0x	8.19%	3.65%	1.27%	5.77%	NA	12.79%	8.25%	10.84%	15.2x
2003	3.99%	29.02%	17.7x	39,407	3,284	-5.55%	-9.54%	7.75%	3.76%	0.00%	5.50%	12.9x	8.46%	4.47%	1.82%	6.00%	NA	12.43%	8.44%	10.47%	14.9x
2004	4.25%	29.03%	16.8x	43,165	3,597	-6.62%	-10.87%	7.60%	3.35%	0.00%	5.39%	13.2x	8.46%	4.21%	2.08%	6.01%	NA	12.70%	8.45%	10.81%	15.4x
2005	4.27%	29.55%	16.3x	47,124	3,927	-6.24%	-10.52%	7.73%	3.46%	0.00%	5.45%	12.9x	8.78%	4.51%	2.53%	6.19%	NA	12.75%	8.48%	10.79%	15.1x
2006	4.78%	29.58%	16.1x	49,607	4,134	-6.68%	-11.46%	7.69%	2.91%	0.00%	5.41%	13.0x	8.70%	3.92%	2.42%	6.13%	NA	12.89%	8.11%	10.95%	15.3x
Low	3.99%	28.41%	13.2x	10,396	866	-16.83%	-22.82%	5.70%	-0.28%	0.00%	4.00%	9.8x	6.77%	1.06%	1.27%	4.66%	NA	12.39%	5.26%	9.60%	11.1x
Arith. Mean	5.99%	33.42%	18.6x	26,997	2,250	-7.36%	-13.35%	7.84%	1.85%	0.00%	5.19%	13.1x	8.91%	2.92%	2.56%	5.89%	NA	13.29%	7.30%	11.02%	15.5x
Median	5.91%	31.63%	17.4x	26,901	2,242	-6.40%	-11.51%	7.74%	1.65%	0.00%	5.36%	12.9x	8.74%	2.92%	2.38%	5.97%	NA	13.21%	7.77%	10.83%	15.0x
High	8.56%	40.29%	27.5x	49,607	4,134	-0.44%	-9.00%	10.19%	3.76%	0.00%	6.37%	17.5x	11.79%	4.51%	4.86%	7.37%	NA	14.16%	8.60%	12.84%	22.7x
St. Dev.	1.42%	4.35%	4.1x			4.61%	4.19%	1.21%	1.13%	0.00%	0.64%	2.1x	1.37%	1.03%	1.01%	0.69%	NA	0.60%	1.24%	0.93%	3.2x

(1) All parameters are stated in nominal terms and as arithmetic average of monthly values.
(2) r^f equals redemption yield of the US Datastream benchmark 10y government bond index.
(3) Overall number of firm observations per annum.
(4) Average number of firms per annum.
(5) Implied perpetual dividend growth rate (after convergence for $0<g_{RI}<g_{RI\ steady\ state}$ cases) according to calculation approach presented in Appendix 10 - $Max[g_{RI,TV};(1-\theta_{TV})r^e]$.
(6) Terminal multiple implied by a calculation based on terminal period payout ratio, cost of equity, and perpetual dividend growth rate.
(7) Implied terminal multiple cannot be determined as perpetual dividend growth rate is not constant but converging.

Two further studies in the international academic press investigated the expected MRP using equity valuation models. In a comprehensive study, Desrosiers/Lemaire/L'Her provide an expected MRP estimate for a world sample comprising 19 countries. Their value-weighted unconditional average premium of 1.74% compares to an average premium of 2.92% derived from the six countries analyzed in this study on a US-Dollar denominated input data basis. Hail/Leuz only provide an estimate for the expected return which is higher in a shorter and earlier analysis period. The comparison is summarized in Table 56.

Table 56 Overview of key results of previous studies on the world sample

			Arith. mean over analysis period (2)		
Authors	Period	Weighting (1)	r^e	r^p	r^f
Terminal perpetuity with g_{RI}=ex-post inflation					
Desrosiers/Lemaire/L'Her (2007) (3)	1988-2005	NA	7.96%	1.74%	6.21%
Gsell (2010) (4)	1989-2006	agg	8.91%	2.92%	5.99%
Other approaches					
Hail/Leuz (2006) (5)	1992-2001	NA	12.97%	NA	NA

(1) agg = aggregation method; ew = equal-weighted; vw = value-weighted.
(2) All parameters are stated in nominal terms.
(3) Annualized r^e based on original monthly estimate (US-Dollar denominated);
Implied r^p using own US r^f estimate;
Terminal perpetuity based on g_{RI}=ex-post inflation. Based on a value-weighted avearge of 19 countries.
(4) US-Dollar denominated. Based on value-weighted input data for 6 countries.
(5) Average of Claus/Thomas, Gebhardt/Lee/Swaminathan, Gode/Mohanram, and Easton-PEG model.
Average of 40 countries. Standard analysis period shorter for selected countries due to data availability.

Source: Desrosiers, S./Lemaire, N./L'Her, J.-F. (2007), p. 79 and Hail, L./Leuz, C. (2006), pp. 494-495.

This concludes the presentation of results on the expected MRP estimation using equity valuation models. In the next section, the results for the six analyzed countries are compared using standard statistical tools.

5.10 Comparison of expected MRP estimates between countries

Similarly to the analysis of historical MRPs, the expected country MRPs from the IRR-based approach are tested for equivalence of means and correlation.

5.10.1 Comparison of unconditional averages

The expected MRP estimates used for the comparison are based on the terminal perpetuity approach with ex-post inflation as perpetual growth proxy. Table 57 presents the mean comparison results[846]. In contrast to the analysis of historical MRPs, a substantial number of country combinations show significant t-/Z-values at a 95% confidence level. Therefore, the null hypothesis of identical means must be rejected. One further notices that using the parametric procedure leads to a larger number of rejections than the non-parametric procedure. A particularly high probability of mean equivalence can be identified between UK/France, World/France, Japan/Germany, Canada/US, and UK/World. An unintuitive result may be the rejection of equal means between the US/World since the US is by far the largest constituent of the world aggregate. Still, the US—as well as Canada—has the highest expected MRP of all countries in addition to the lowest standard error of the estimate. Finally, one should note that the higher number of significant t-/Z-values compared to the mean historical MRP analysis is primarily due to substantially lower standard errors.

Table 57 Mean comparison tests on the expected MRP 1989-2006 between country pairs

Expected MRP 1989-2006 (g_{RI}=infl.) - Paired t-test (t-value)/Wilcoxon matched-pairs singed rank test (Z-value)

	Canada	France	Germany	Japan	UK	US	World
Canada	0.0000	2.4170	2.7220	2.2860	2.4610	0.1090	2.6350
(p-value)		(0.0156)	(0.0065)	(0.0222)	(0.0139)	(0.9133)	(0.0084)
France	2.6765	0.0000	2.5910	1.8070	-0.3700	-1.6330	0.1024
(p-value)	(0.0159)		(0.0096)	(0.0707)	(0.7112)	(0.1024)	(0.9479)
Germany	3.5546	2.9104	0.0000	0.7190	-2.3300	-2.1560	-1.0670
(p-value)	(0.0024)	(0.0097)		(0.4724)	(0.0198)	(0.0311)	(0.2860)
Japan	3.1768	2.2036	0.9426	0.0000	-1.5460	-1.3720	-1.1980
(p-value)	(0.0055)	(0.0416)	(0.3591)		(0.1221)	(0.1701)	(0.2311)
UK	2.9354	-0.7610	-2.3889	-2.2355	0.0000	-1.3720	0.6310
(p-value)	(0.0092)	(0.4571)	(0.0288)	(0.0391)		(0.1701)	(0.5277)
USA	-0.0516	-1.8363	-2.6279	-2.2338	-1.7897	0.0000	3.5930
(p-value)	(0.9595)	(0.0839)	(0.0176)	(0.0392)	(0.0913)		(0.0003)
World	3.1964	0.0027	-1.1868	-1.3161	0.5492	6.1003	0.0000
(p-value)	(0.0053)	(0.9979)	(0.2516)	(0.2056)	(0.5900)	(0.0000)	

Note: Paired t-test t-value (Wilcoxon matched-pairs singed rank test Z-value) is below (above) the diagonal. P-values at a significance level of at least 5% are highlighted in grey.

Due to the limited availability of IBES estimates in the early stage of the analysis period, it appears plausible to run the same mean comparison procedure for a time period with more satisfactory samples sizes. However, the shorter sample period implies higher standard errors of the estimates. As a consequence, this approach reduces the number of significant t-/Z-values among countries implying an increased probability of equivalence of mean expected MRP estimates as shown in Table 58. The rejection of each mean identity to the World mean is driven through the

[846] See Section 4.2 for a description of the used testing procedure.

comparatively low World mean MRP which is below all countries. This is possible through exchange rate effects from converting all local country data into dollar-denominated values and applying the comparatively high US risk-free rate to the World aggregate. If the spot exchange rate does not appropriately reflect the risk-free rate differential, distortions of the World estimates may occur.

Table 58 Mean comparison tests on the expected MRP 1998-2006 between country pairs

Expected MRP 1998-2006 (gRI=infl.) - Paired t-test (t-value)/Wilcoxon matched-pairs singed rank test (Z-value)

	Canada	France	Germany	Japan	UK	US	World
Canada	0.0000	0.4150	0.6520	-0.5330	0.7700	2.6660	2.6660
(p-value)		(0.6784)	(0.5147)	(0.5940)	(0.4413)	(0.0077)	(0.0077)
France	0.4484	0.0000	2.0730	-1.2440	0.1780	1.5990	2.5470
(p-value)	(0.6658)		(0.0382)	(0.2135)	(0.8590)	(0.1097)	(0.0109)
Germany	0.9934	2.5882	0.0000	-1.8360	-0.8890	1.1250	2.1920
(p-value)	(0.3496)	(0.0322)		(0.0663)	(0.3743)	(0.2604)	(0.0284)
Japan	-0.2150	-1.1692	-2.1399	0.0000	1.4810	2.5470	2.6660
(p-value)	(0.8352)	(0.2760)	(0.0648)		(0.1386)	(0.0109)	(0.0077)
UK	0.9604	0.1680	-0.9269	1.5467	0.0000	2.4290	2.6660
(p-value)	(0.0038)	(0.8708)	(0.3811)	(0.1605)		(0.0152)	(0.0077)
USA	4.0265	1.7705	0.9610	4.2615	3.8095	0.0000	2.3100
(p-value)	(0.0038)	(0.1146)	(0.3647)	(0.0028)	(0.0052)		(0.0209)
World	4.5781	4.4480	3.0387	12.8415	8.8020	3.3442	0.0000
(p-value)	(0.0018)	(0.0021)	(0.0161)	(0.0000)	(0.0000)	(0.0102)	

Note: Paired t-test t-value (Wilcoxon matched-pairs singed rank test Z-value) is below (above) the diagonal. P-values at a significance level of at least 5% are highlighted in grey.

The inconclusive picture on the equivalence of country mean expected MRP estimates from Table 57 remains unchanged when running the mean comparison tests on different terminal value assumptions. Table 59 shows the same test results when using the expected MRP series implied by the regression-based approach to simultaneously determine the expected return and residual earnings growth. Still, for a large number of country combinations the mean identity is rejected. Furthermore, the country pairs with statistically similar means—Germany/Canada and US/France—differ from the analysis using the terminal perpetuity-based data.

Table 59 Mean comparison tests on the regression-based expected MRP 1989-2006

Expected MRP 1998-2006 (reg.) - Paired t-test (t-value)/Wilcoxon matched-paired singed rank test (Z-value)	Canada	France	Germany	Japan	UK	US	World
Canada	0.0000	-1.3280	0.5880	2.5480	2.0250	-2.4170	NA
(p-value)		(0.1841)	(0.5566)	(0.0108)	(0.0429)	(0.0156)	NA
France	-1.5844	0.0000	2.4170	3.7240	2.9400	-0.5440	NA
(p-value)	(0.1315)		(0.0156)	(0.0002)	(0.0033)	(0.5862)	NA
Germany	0.5053	3.1734	0.0000	2.5910	1.5900	2.2430	NA
(p-value)	(0.6198)	(0.0056)		(0.0096)	(0.1119)	(0.0249)	NA
Japan	3.1672	6.0926	3.0613	0.0000	-1.4590	-2.8530	NA
(p-value)	(0.0056)	(0.0000)	(0.0071)		(0.1446)	(0.0043)	NA
UK	2.3595	4.0833	1.7544	-1.4683	0.0000	-2.8530	NA
(p-value)	(0.0305)	(0.0008)	(0.0974)	(0.1603)		(0.0043)	NA
USA	-2.9612	-0.7167	-2.7829	-3.6851	-3.8222	0.0000	NA
(p-value)	(0.0087)	(0.4833)	(0.0128)	(0.0018)	(0.0014)		NA
World	NA	NA	NA	NA	NA	NA	NA
(p-value)	NA	NA	NA	NA	NA	NA	NA

Note: Paired t-test t-value (Wilcoxon matched-pairs singed rank test Z-value) is below (above) the diagonal. P-values at a significance level of at least 5% are highlighted in grey.

5.10.2 Comparison of cross-country correlation

For the analysis of correlation between expected country MRP series, the premia estimates from the terminal perpetuity model with ex-post inflation growth are again used. It becomes obvious that all correlation coefficients are positive and significant with the exception of certain country combinations with the US market as shown in Table 60. This result is consistent with the earlier finding that the conditional expected MRP development was upward sloping for all countries except the US.

Table 60 Correlation coefficients for the expected MRP 1989-2006 between countries

Expected MRP 1989-2006 (gRI=infl.) - Pearson's/Spearman's correlation coefficient	Canada	France	Germany	Japan	UK	US	World
Canada	1.0000	0.7317	0.7234	0.8246	0.6326	0.2343	0.4819
(p-value)		(0.0006)	(0.0007)	(0.0000)	(0.0048)	(0.3495)	(0.0428)
France	0.9352	1.0000	0.8493	0.7399	0.7688	0.4881	0.6615
(p-value)	(0.0000)		(0.0000)	(0.0004)	(0.0002)	(0.0399)	(0.0028)
Germany	0.9054	0.9599	1.0000	0.8204	0.8122	0.3622	0.5666
(p-value)	(0.0000)	(0.0000)		(0.0000)	(0.0000)	(0.1396)	(0.0142)
Japan	0.8954	0.8661	0.8461	1.0000	0.7585	0.2054	0.4221
(p-value)	(0.0000)	(0.0000)	(0.0000)		(0.0003)	(0.4136)	(0.0810)
UK	0.8962	0.9416	0.9098	0.8423	1.0000	0.4365	0.6966
(p-value)	(0.0000)	(0.0000)	(0.0000)	(0.0000)		(0.0701)	(0.0013)
USA	0.4266	0.5607	0.5403	0.1941	0.5229	1.0000	0.8906
(p-value)	(0.0775)	(0.0155)	(0.0206)	(0.4402)	(0.0260)		(0.0000)
World	0.6675	0.7958	0.7395	0.4862	0.7711	0.9140	1.0000
(p-value)	(0.0025)	(0.0001)	(0.0005)	(0.0408)	(0.0002)	(0.0000)	

Note: Pearson's (Spearman's) correlation coefficient is below (above) the diagonal. P-values with a significance level of at least 5% are highlighted in grey.

However, Table 61 shows that if the analysis period is restricted to the range from 1998 to 2006 with a higher data quality, all coefficients become significant at a level of 5%. This is again consistent with previous results since the different development of the expected MRP for the US is largely attributable to the early years of the analysis period.

Table 61 Correlation coefficients for the expected MRP 1998-2006 between countries

Expected MRP 1998-2006 (gRI=infl.) - Pearson's/Spearman's correlation coefficient							
	Canada	France	Germany	Japan	UK	US	World
Canada	1.0000	0.9333	0.9000	0.9167	0.9000	0.8667	0.9000
(p-value)		(0.0002)	(0.0009)	(0.0005)	(0.0009)	(0.0025)	(0.0009)
France	0.9575	1.0000	0.9833	0.9333	0.9333	0.8333	0.9167
(p-value)	(0.0000)		(0.0000)	(0.0002)	(0.0002)	(0.0053)	(0.0005)
Germany	0.9567	0.9912	1.0000	0.9667	0.9500	0.8500	0.9500
(p-value)	(0.0001)	(0.0000)		(0.0000)	(0.0001)	(0.0037)	(0.0001)
Japan	0.9310	0.9576	0.9556	1.0000	0.9667	0.9167	0.9833
(p-value)	(0.0003)	(0.0000)	(0.0001)		(0.0000)	(0.0005)	(0.0000)
UK	0.9632	0.9844	0.9883	0.9471	1.0000	0.9333	0.9500
(p-value)	(0.0000)	(0.0000)	(0.0000)	(0.0001)		(0.0002)	(0.0001)
USA	0.9448	0.9417	0.9472	0.9640	0.9670	1.0000	0.9500
(p-value)	(0.0001)	(0.0001)	(0.0001)	(0.0000)	(0.0000)		(0.0001)
World	0.9562	0.9795	0.9779	0.9908	0.9795	0.9833	1.0000
(p-value)	(0.0001)	(0.0000)	(0.0000)	(0.0000)	(0.0000)	(0.0000)	

Note: Pearson's (Spearman's) correlation coefficient is below (above) the diagonal. P-values with a significance level of at least 5% are highlighted in grey.

Furthermore, the choice of the terminal value technique has only a marginal impact on the number of significant correlation coefficients between expected MRP series. Table 62 shows correlation coefficients when the regression-based simultaneous estimate of the expected return and residual earnings growth is used.

Table 62 Correlation coefficients for the expected regression-based MRP 1989-2006 between countries

Expected MRP 1989-2006 (reg.) - Pearson's/Spearman's correlation coefficient							
	Canada	France	Germany	Japan	UK	US	World
Canada	1.0000	0.7399	0.7998	0.8039	0.8225	0.5583	NA
(p-value)		(0.0004)	(0.0001)	(0.0001)	(0.0000)	(0.0160)	NA
France	0.7532	1.0000	0.9401	0.8473	0.8535	0.3684	NA
(p-value)	(0.0003)		(0.0000)	(0.0000)	(0.0000)	(0.1325)	NA
Germany	0.8535	0.9238	1.0000	0.7874	0.8411	0.5067	NA
(p-value)	(0.0000)	(0.0000)		(0.0001)	(0.0000)	(0.0319)	NA
Japan	0.8504	0.9063	0.8835	1.0000	0.8122	0.226	NA
(p-value)	(0.0000)	(0.0000)	(0.0000)		(0.0000)	(0.3672)	NA
UK	0.8896	0.8791	0.8879	0.8867	1.0000	0.5872	NA
(p-value)	(0.0000)	(0.0000)	(0.0000)	(0.0000)		(0.0104)	NA
USA	0.6526	0.3913	0.5467	0.3100	0.6071	1.0000	NA
(p-value)	(0.0033)	(0.1083)	(0.0189)	(0.2106)	(0.0075)		NA
World	NA	NA	NA	NA	NA	NA	NA
(p-value)	NA	NA	NA	NA	NA	NA	NA

Note: Pearson's (Spearman's) correlation coefficient is below (above) the diagonal. P-values with a significance level of at least 5% are highlighted in grey.

5.11 Comparison of expected MRP estimates between models

In the literature, the expected MRP estimates from different valuation models are also frequently compared using standard statistical models.

5.11.1 Correlation between expected MRP estimates from different models

An investigation of correlation coefficients of the expected MRP series typically shows high significance between all models[847]. This finding of previous studies was already identified in the graphical inspection of conditional expected MRP estimates over time and appears intuitive since the used valuation models primarily differ only in the assumption on the long-term growth outlook. Ultimately, highly significant correlation coefficients are also confirmed for the data set of this study as shown in Table 63. Since the results are similar for all countries, a correlation table is only provided for the German market.

Table 63 Correlation coefficients for expected MRP estimates of different valuation models

	IRR-based expected MRP models 1989-2006 - Pearson's/Spearman's correlation coefficient							
	g=ex-post infl.	g=steady state	g=reg. appr.	Claus/ Thomas	Gebhardt et al.	Gode/ Mohanram	Easton-PEG	Easton-PE
g=ex-post infl.	1.0000	0.7998	0.5377	0.8947	0.9649	0.7647	0.7915	0.8390
(p-value)		(0.0001)	(0.0214)	(0.0000)	(0.0000)	(0.0002)	(0.0001)	(0.0000)
g=steady state	0.7402	1.0000	0.7915	0.8473	0.8762	0.8184	0.8369	0.8060
(p-value)	(0.0004)		(0.0001)	(0.0000)	(0.0000)	(0.0000)	(0.0000)	(0.0001)
g=reg. appr.	0.5479	0.9247	1.0000	0.5748	0.6223	0.5397	0.5955	0.5583
(p-value)	(0.0186)	(0.0000)		(0.0126)	(0.0058)	(0.0208)	(0.0091)	(0.0160)
Claus/Thomas	0.9799	0.7695	0.5906	1.0000	0.9340	0.8514	0.8493	0.8184
(p-value)	(0.0000)	(0.0002)	(0.0099)		(0.0000)	(0.0000)	(0.0000)	(0.0000)
Gebhardt et al.	0.9920	0.7862	0.6117	0.9740	1.0000	0.7998	0.8163	0.8596
(p-value)	(0.0000)	(0.0001)	(0.0070)	(0.0000)		(0.0001)	(0.0000)	(0.0000)
Gode/Mohanram	0.8341	0.7529	0.5965	0.8621	0.8501	1.0000	0.9835	0.5315
(p-value)	(0.0000)	(0.0003)	(0.0090)	(0.0000)	(0.0000)		(0.0000)	(0.0232)
Easton-PEG	0.8345	0.8280	0.6856	0.8571	0.8633	0.9887	1.0000	0.5480
(p-value)	(0.0000)	(0.0000)	(0.0017)	(0.0000)	(0.0000)	(0.0000)		(0.0186)
Easton-PE	0.9173	0.7238	0.5659	0.8991	0.9158	0.5950	0.6240	1.0000
(p-value)	(0.0000)	(0.0000)	(0.0144)	(0.0000)	(0.0000)	(0.0092)	(0.0057)	

Note: Pearson's (Spearman's) correlation coefficient is below (above) the diagonal. P-values with a significance level of at least 5% are highlighted in grey.

Lower but still significant correlation coefficients occur in relation to the regression-based expected MRP estimates. The lower correlation coefficients between the

[847] See Gode, D./Mohanram, P. (2003), p. 413, Reese, R. (2007), p. 116, and Lee, C./Ng, D./Swaminathan, B. (2009), p. 320 for correlation analyses of expected MRP estimates. See also Chen, F./Jorgensen, B./Yoo, Y. (2004), p. 337, Easton, P. (2004), p. 86, Botosan, C./Plumlee, M. (2005), pp. 39-40, Easton, P./Monahan, P. (2005), p. 516, Guay, W./Kothari, S./Shu, S. (2005), p. 35, and Hail, L./Leuz, C. (2006), pp. 493-494 for correlation analyses on expected return estimates. See also Trombetta, M. (2004), p. 346.

Gode/Mohanram and Easton-PE estimates and the Easton-PEG and Easton-PE estimates are consistent with earlier findings[848].

5.11.2 Cross-sectional analyses of expected MRP estimates

Another issue discussed in the literature is the identification of the most accurate valuation model to estimate the expected MRP. While in this study, the evaluation of the appropriate valuation model is determined based on the plausibility of the long-term growth assumption and the implied return on book equity[849], the literature also determines the accuracy based on the association of expected MRP estimates with typical risk factors using cross-sectional firm/industry level multivariate regression analyses[850]. Such analysis are either based on the Fama/MacBeth (1973) approach of estimating cross-sectional regression parameters at all measurement dates and averaging thereafter [851] or pooled data from all measurement dates for one estimation[852]. Typically used risk factors are taken from established asset pricing models such as the CAPM-based beta factor and the additional components of the three-factor model—i.e., size and book-to-market ratio—by Fama/French (1992, 1993, and 1996)[853]. Furthermore, several other risk proxies are used like volatility of realized returns (unsystematic risk), leverage, volatility of estimates, dividend yield, PE ratio, or long-term growth rate[854]. Apart from the beta factor, none of these indicators is based on a profound theoretical framework[855]. Still, various studies use this approach to test the validity of valuation models to estimate the expected return/MRP as summarized in Table 64.

---

848 See Easton, P. (2004), p. 413 and Easton, P./Monahan, P. (2005), p. 516.

849 Similar to Claus, J./Thomas, J. (2001).

850 For a review of empirical studies see also Easton, P. (2009), pp. 312-316.

851 See Fama, E./MacBeth, J. (1973), pp. 614-617.

852 See Reese, R. (2007), p. 117, fn. 474.

853 See Esterer, F./Schröder, D. (2007a), p. 2.

854 See, e.g., Daske, H./Gebhardt, G./Klein, S. (2006), pp. 19-21, Reese, R. (2007), pp. 111-115, and Wallmeier, M. (2007), pp. 570-571. See also Fama, E./French, K. (1992) for the seminal paper on risk factor analysis.

855 See Wallmeier, M. (2007), p. 571.

Table 64 Summary of previous analyses of the correlation between expected MRP estimates and selected risk factors

Authors/ Sample	Used risk factors (expected relationship)[856]	Tested valuation models *(metric)*[857]	Highest adj.-R^2/ coeff. significance (sig)	Comments on full model
Gebhardt et al. (2001) US market (1993-2001)	• Levered beta (+) • Ln leverage (+) • Ln market cap (-) • Ln st. dev. of estimates (+) • Lt. earnings growth • Ln book-to-market (+) • Average ind. MRP (+)	• Gebhardt et al. • *(expected MRP)*	• NA	• Book-to-market ratio most important variable followed by st. dev. of estimates, lt. growth, and avg. ind. MRP • Firm size is generally insignificant • Beta insignificant after controlling for industry
Gode/ Mohanram (2003) US market (1984-1998)	• Lev. beta (+) • Unsystematic risk (+)[858] • Earnings variability (+) • Ln leverage (+) • Ln market cap (-) • Lt. earnings growth (+) • Ln book-to-market ratio (+) • Average ind. MRP (+)	• Gebhardt et al. (1) excl. neg. $\tilde{r}^b$ (2) incl. all $\tilde{r}^b$ • Gode/Mohanram • Easton-PE • *(expected MRP)*	• R^2: Gebhardt et al. (2) • Sig: NA	• Highest significance levels for avg. ind. MRP, book-to-market ratio, and lt. growth • Results similar in pooled as well as Fama/MacBeth regressions but at lower significance levels and higher R-squared • Firm size not significant using Fama-MacBeth regressions
Chen/ Jorgensen/ Yoo (2004) Seven countries (1993-2001)	• Levered beta (+) • Ln market cap (-) • Leverage (+) • St. dev. of estimates (+) • Idiosyncractic risk (+)[859]	• RIV model (two periods then g=0) • Gebhardt et al. • Gordon/Gordon • Gode/Mohanram • Easton-PEG *(expected return)*	• R^2: Gebhardt et al. for Canada, Germany, Japan, and the US; Easton-PEG for France and the UK • Sig: Gode/ Mohanram and Easton-PEG	• CAP-based model more accurate in countries with larger clean-surplus violations (e.g., France and UK) • R^2 better than significance

856 Note that the comparability of studies is limited due to different parameterization approaches for the risk factors.
857 See Sections 5.1.3, 5.2.4, and 5.3.3 for the detailed specifications of each model.
858 Measured as the variance of residuals from the regressions of beta estimation.
859 Measured as the variance of residuals from the regressions of beta estimation.

Authors/ Sample	Used risk factors (expected relationship)[856]	Tested valuation models *(metric)*[857]	Highest adj.-R^2/ coeff. significance (sig)	Comments on full model
Botosan/ Plumlee (2005) US market (1983-1993)	• Unlevered beta (+) • Leverages (+) • Information risk (+)[860] • Ln market cap (-) • Book-to-market (+) • Earnings growth (+)	• DIV model (analyst target price as terminal value) • Gebhardt et al. • Gordon/Gordon • Gode/Mohanram • Easton-PEG *(expected MRP)*	• R^2: Easton-PEG • Sig: Easton-PEG	• Significant coefficients for earnings growth, book-to-market ratio, and leverage • Unlev. beta negatively related for Gebhardt et al., Gordon/Gordon, and Gode/Mohanram models • Significance better than R^2
Easton/ Monahan (2005) US market (1981-1998)	• Levered beta (+) • St. dev. daily returns (+) • Market cap (-) • Book-to-market ratio (+) • Avg. industry MRP (+)	• Claus/Thomas • Gebhardt et al. • Easton-reg. • Gode/Mohanram • Easton-MPEG • Easton-PEG • Easton-PE • *(expected MRP)*	• R^2: Easton-PE • Sig: Easton-PEG	• Most significant coefficient for avg. industry MRP followed by book-to-market ratio (except Claus/Thomas) • Low significance level for the market cap factor
Daske/ Gebhardt/ Klein (2006) German market (1989-2002)	• Levered beta (+) • St. dev. daily returns (+) • Leverage (+) • Ln market cap (-) • Std. dev. estimates (+) • Book-to-market ratio (+) • Prior-year ind. MRP (+) • Time (count variable)	• Gebhardt et al. • *(expected MRP)*	• NA	• Strongest significance level for industry MRP coefficient followed by the book-to-market ratio • Low impact of beta, return volatility, and st. dev. of estimates on the expected MRP

[860] Measured by the width of the range of analyst price forecasts scaled by the midpoint.

Authors/ Sample	Used risk factors (expected relationship)[856]	Tested valuation models *(metric)*[857]	Highest adj.-R^2/ coeff. significance (sig)	Comments on full model
Reese (2007) German market (1989-2004)	• Volatility of returns (+) • Levered beta (+) • Leverage (+) • # of analyst forecasts (-) • Ln market cap (-) • St. dev. of estimates (+) • Book-to-market ratio (+) • Lt. growth rate (+) • Prior-year ind. MRP (+)	• Claus/Thomas • Gebhardt/Lee/ Swaminathan • Gode/Mohanram • Easton-PEG • *(expected MRP)*	• R^2: Gebhardt et al. • Sig: Easton-PEG	• Significant coefficients for st. dev. of estimates, book-to-market ratio (except Claus/Thomas), lt. growth rate, and leverage (except Gode/Mohanram) • Lev. beta negative for Claus/Thomas and Gebhardt et al.
Schröder (2007) EU market (March 2003)[861]	• Levered beta (+) • Volatility of returns (+) • Ln market cap (-) • Ln book-to-market ratio (+) • Dividend yield (+) • Ln PE ratio (-)	• Two and three stage DIV model • Two and three stage RIV model • *(expected MRP)*	• R^2: Two-stage DIV • Sig: Two-stage DIV	• Only significant coefficient for dividend yield using RIV models • Beta and PE ratio significant for DIV models • Almost identical results when using country betas

[861] Using only a single estimation date appears insufficient and limits the comparability to other studies which use monthly estimation over several years.

Authors/ Sample	**Used risk factors (expected relationship)**[856]	**Tested valuation models *(metric)***[857]	**Highest adj.-R^2/ coeff. significance (sig)**	**Comments on full model**
Lee/Ng/ Swaminathan (2009) Pooled data for G-7 countries (1990-2000)	• World market beta (+) • Local market beta (+) • Currency beta (+) • Ln market cap (-) • Ln book-to-market ratio (+) • Leverage (+) • Volatility (idiosyncratic risk) (+)	• Lee/Ng/ Swaminathan (similar to Cornell) • Claus/Thomas • Gode/Mohanram • Easton-MPEG • *(expected MRP)*	• R^2: Easton-MPEG • Sig: Marginal differences between models	• Higher significance for world market than local market beta in univariate quintile analysis • High-low quintile differences are significant for all other risk factors • Relations between risk factors and realized return almost entirely not significant in uni- and multivariate analyses • In multivariate analysis, betas as well as firm factors are significant at typical levels with higher significance for firm characteristics than for betas (selected betas only significant at 10% level); Results robust to ex-post biases in forecasts • Differences between expected return models are marginal

Table 64 shows that several studies find that the Easton-PEG model provides expected return/MRP estimates with the highest risk factor correlation. However, this finding in not unanimous with other studies coming to contrary conclusions. Furthermore, testing the accuracy of expected return/MRP models based on correlations with different risk factors is related to several issues that are individually evaluated in the following.

In a recent study, Wallmeier shows that the relation between the book-to-market ratio and the expected return is biased due to misspecifications of the regression models. He shows that the linear relationships between the book-to-market ratio and the expected return are also influenced by the inverted PE ratio for a simplified Claus/Thomas model which leads to partially insignificant coefficients for the book-to-market ratio after controlling for the inverted PE ratio[862]. Wallmeier also shows for a simplified Gebhardt/Lee/Swaminathan model that the linear relationship between the book-to-market ratio and the expected return is additionally affected by the industry average return on book equity (used for the convergence and terminal value period). However, using an industry average return on book equity is only appropriate if all firms in the industry use the same "conservative accounting", since otherwise a combination of book-to-market ratios with an average return on book equity leads to a spurious correlation between expected returns and the book-to-market ratio. These arguments can be also empirically verified[863].

Using a multivariate regression approach on risk factors, the level of model accuracy can be ranked either according the significance level of coefficients or based on the coefficient of determination[864]. Among authors, there is no agreement on the correct choice since significance levels of coefficients can be biased due to multicollinearity[865] and coefficients of determination can lead to incorrect inferences in case of endogeneity, i.e., the independent variable influences the calculation of the dependent variable[866]. Furthermore, the ranking of valuation models according to the R-squared may change when including so far omitted risk factors[867]. Finally,

---

[862] See Wallmeier, M. (2007), pp. 563-564.
[863] See Wallmeier, M. (2007), pp. 565-567.
[864] See Easton, P. (2009), pp. 313-314.
[865] See Chen, F./Jorgensen, B./Yoo, Y. (2004), p. 336.
[866] See Botosan, C./Plumlee, M. (2005), p. 48, Reese, R. (2007), p. 120, and Easton, P. (2009), pp. 314-315.
[867] See Easton, P. (2009), p. 314.

differences in R-squared may not be significant and the validity of inferences from low R-squared levels is generally questionable[868]. Reese comes therefore to the conclusion that definite inferences on the validity of one model can not be made[869].

The approach using risk factors can also be generally challenged. Firstly, the true risk factors that describe the total risk of the firm are unknown[870]. The beta factor is the only risk factor with a profound underlying theory (CAPM) but other risk factors lack this foundation. Wallmeier therefore also questions the usage of anomaly factors such as market cap (size) or book-to-market ratio in order to test the validity of the expected return estimates since no significant association with anomalies could also imply that IRR-based models are free of such phenomena. He also rejects leverage as a factor due to the endogeneity problem that high operational risk firms choose low leverage levels.[871]

Wallmeier therefore proposes to test the validity of expected return estimates from different valuation models by their ability to explain cross-sectional variations in future realized returns similarly to Guay/Kothari/Shu (2005). Table 65 summarizes the results of different studies investigating the forecasting accuracy of expected return/MRP estimates from valuation models:

---

[868] See Trombetta, M. (2004), p. 346.

[869] See Reese, R. (2007), p. 121.

[870] See Easton, P./Monahan, S. (2005), p. 503, Reese, R. (2007), p. 111, and Wallmeier, M. (2007), p. 571.

[871] See Wallmeier, M. (2007), pp. 570-571.

Table 65 Summary of studies on the forecasting accuracy of expected return/MRP estimates from various valuation models

Authors/ Sample	Tested valuation models[872]	Test design	Key findings
Gebhardt/Lee/ Swaminathan (2003) US market 1979-1995	• Gebhardt/Lee/ Swaminathan	• Quintile analysis for expected MRPs and future realized returns	• Higher expected MRPs are associated with higher future realized MRPs at the firm level • Significance of differences between quintiles increases from one-year ahead to three-year ahead realized MRPs but remains marginal • At the industry level, a regression of one-year ahead realized MRPs on expected MRPs results in a significant positive coefficient which is however highly sensitive
Guay/Kothari/ Shu (2005) US market 1983-2004	• Claus/Thomas • Gebhardt/Lee/ Swaminathan • Gordon/Gordon • Gode/Mohanram	• One-year ahead realized return regressed on expected return (Fama-MacBeth regression)	• Coefficients not significantly different from zero either at firm or industry level • Expected return estimates are systematically biased due to slow updating of analyst forecasts as response to large price changes which imparts a predictable error (forecast errors are negatively related to recent stock returns) • Eliminating firms with large recent stock price reactions leads to significant positive relations between one-year ahead realized return and expected return estimates from Claus/Thomas, Gebhardt et al., and Gordon/Gordon models (Gode/Mohanram model not significant) • Partially significant positive relations between one-year ahead realized return and expected return estimates from Claus/Thomas, Gebhardt et al., and Gordon/Gordon models also achieved by (1) specifically adjusting for the forecast error (at industry and firm level) or (2) by including a 5-months lag between price observation and analysts' forecasts (only at firm level)

[872] See Sections 5.1.3, 5.2.4, and 5.3.3 for the detail specifications of each model.

Authors/ Sample	Tested valuation models[872]	Test design	Key findings
Gode/ Mohanram (2003) US market (1984-1998)	• Gebhardt et al. (1) excl. neg. $\tilde{r}^b$ (2) incl. all $\tilde{r}^b$ • Gode/Mohanram • Easton-PE	• Quintile analysis for expected MRPs and future realized returns	• Significance of differences for Gode/Mohanram model increases with the horizon of realized future returns • Significance strong for the Gebhardt et al. (1) model for all realized returns between one-year and three-years ahead (lower results for Gebhardt et al. (2) model) • Overall, significant ability of Gode/Mohanram and Gebhardt et al. (1) models to predict future returns
Easton/ Monahan (2005) US market (1981-1998)	• Claus/Thomas • Gebhardt et al. • Easton-reg. • Gode/Mohanram • Easton-MPEG • Easton-PEG • Easton-PE	• One-year ahead realized return regressed on expected return controlling for cash flow and return news[873]	• Expected return estimates of all models have no positive relationship with realized returns • Measurement error variance of naïve estimates based on PE_{+1} ratio is never greater and often lower compared to other proxies • Reliability of estimates found to decrease with the magnitude of the long-term earnings growth rate (Claus/Thomas model estimates for low long-term growth rates found to be reliable) • With low ex-post analysts' forecasts errors, all expected return estimate are positively related to future returns
Schröder (2007) EU market[874] (March 2003)	• Two and three stage DIV model • Two and three stage RIV model	• One to four quarters ahead realized return regressed on expected return	• DIV model-based estimates have a significant positive relation to future realized returns • RIV model-based estimates have a positive relation to future realized returns which is only significant in selected cases

[873] The model is based on the linear return decomposition approach by Vuolteenaho, T. (2002).

[874] Using only a single estimation date appears insufficient and limits the comparability to other studies which use monthly estimation over several years.

Authors/ Sample	Tested valuation models[872]	Test design	Key findings
Esterer/ Schröder (2007a)[875] G-7 countries (1995-2006)[876]	• Cornell • Claus/Thomas • Mod. Gebhardt et al. (with projected payout ratios)	• One-year and two-year ahead realized returns regressed on expected return (Pooled regression)	• US expected return estimates from all models have a significant positive relation to one-year as well as two-year ahead realized returns • Significance is maintained when controlling for risk factors such as beta, book-to-market ratio, log market cap, and hist. price momentum (strongest significance for Claus/Thomas) • Significantly positive coefficients are also found for all other G-7 countries in univariate analysis of expected return estimates and future realized return • Controlling for risk factors leads to positive but insignificant coefficients for the Cornell model in Canada, France, and Italy. Claus/Thomas based estimates have significant positive coefficients except for Germany. Gebhardt et al. based estimates, however, are negatively related for Germany and Italy while significantly positive for the remaining countries
Wallmeier (2007) German market (DAX 100) (1991-2000)	• Claus/Thomas • Gebhardt/Lee/ Swaminathan • Easton et al.-reg.	• One-year ahead realized return regressed on expected return (Fama-MacBeth regression)	• All expected return estimates negatively related to realized returns (significant for Gebhardt et al.) • Book-to-market and inverted PE ratio negatively related to realized returns
Lee/Ng/ Swaminathan (2007) Pooled G-7 countries (1990-2000)	• Lee/Ng/ Swaminathan (similar to Cornell)	• Quintile analysis for expected MRPs and future realized returns	• Significant differences between lowest and highest quintile supporting positive relation between expected MRPs and one- as well as two-year ahead realized returns • Monotonic increase in realized returns across quintiles

[875] In addition, Esterer, F./Schröder, D. (2007b) show for the G-7 countries between 1995 and 2006 that trading strategies based on expected return estimates from DIV and RIV models outperform indices supporting the predictive power of the IRR-based method.

[876] The used samples sizes (only transparent for the US) appear rather small so that potentially not the entire market portfolio is covered.

Despite findings of a significant prediction ability of expected return/MRP estimates from the IRR-based approach as identified by Gebhardt/Lee/Swaminathan, Gode/Mohanram, Schröder, and Esterer/Schröder, other studies provide inconsistent results such as Easton/Monahan and Wallmeier or can only find positive relations after controlling for sluggishness in analysts' forecasts (Guay/Kothari/Shu). Issues in testing procedures are largely related to the noise in realized returns[877], a low number of years available, potentially wrong parameter assumptions, and biases in analysts' estimates[878].

Wallmeier concludes that the validity of valuation models should be tested based on the plausibility of the implied long-term development of the return on book equity[879]. This argument appears valid, in particular since all tested models are essentially identical with the exception of the optimism for the long-term growth assumption. The conclusion is also in-line with the approach of this study which argued that expected MRP estimates from models with perpetual residual income growth higher than inflation are questionable given the implied excessive perpetual dividend growth.

5.12 Time-variability of conditional expected MRPs estimates

Similar to previous studies on the expected MRP using the IRR-based method, the conditional expected MRPs estimates show considerable variation over time for all analyzed markets.

Several studies using the dividend discount model identified a highly significant negative relation between risk-free rate and expected MRP[880]. This implies that changes in the risk-free rate, e.g., caused by an increase in inflation, do not lead to a one-to-one change in the expected return. Proposed explanations of the phenomenon include the inferior hedge qualities of bonds compared to stocks against unanticipated inflation which therefore require higher liquidity premiums to

---

[877] See Pastor, L./Sinha, M./Swaminathan, B. (2008), p. 2860.

[878] See Guay, W./Kothari, S./Shu, S. (2005), p. 16.

[879] See Wallmeier, M. (2007), p. 577.

[880] See Brigham, E./Shome, D./Vinson, S. (1985), pp. 42-44, Harris, R./Marston, F. (1992), pp. 68-69, Maddox, F./Pippert, D./Sullivan, R. (1995), pp. 93-94, and Harris, R./Marston, F. (2001), pp. 13-15. Note that during certain periods of the studies, the relation can also be positive. In addition, regression analyses between the expected MRP and the risk-free rate suffer from endogeneity since the independent variable is used in the calculation of the dependent variable.

induce investors to bear the risk of inflation[881]. However, relations between the expected MRP and the risk-free rate need to be carefully interpreted due to endogeneity since the risk-free rate is directly used to calculate the expected MRP.

Another factor that was identified to be related to the expected MRP is the dividend yield. As discussed in Section 2.2.3.2, previous research found that the price-dividend ratio can predict partial variations of the future return/MRP development[882]. These findings can be generally considered as dependence on relative price parameters as indicators of the market price level[883]. Before analyzing whether the conditional expected MRP estimates of this study are price level dependent, hypotheses are derived concerning the impact of the terminal approach.

Within this study, various concepts are applied to measure the terminal value component of the valuation equation. All concepts relate to a specific future price level development implied by the assumptions on the perpetual growth rate or the terminal multiples and lead to substantially different results for the conditional expected MRP estimates. One can therefore formulate the hypothesis that expected returns are price level dependent with negative correlation when the used terminal value concept assumes a convergence from the current price level to an unconditional long-term level. In contrast, terminal value concepts assuming a persistence of the current price level until infinity are not expected to be price level dependent.

A typical metric to measure the price level dependency is the correlation coefficient between the expected MRP estimates and the PE_{+1} ratio at the valuation date[884]. Table 66 shows Pearson correlation coefficients assuming that both analyzed variables are normally distributed. It is shown that the correlation coefficient for zero and ex-post inflation perpetual growth are negative for all countries except Canada. The reason for this result appears intuitive since both perpetual growth proxies are not directly related to the current market price level, i.e. they do not show a cyclical fluctuation which is positively correlated with the price level. Therefore, a zero or inflation-based perpetual growth estimate is consistent with a convergence of the current market price level to the unconditional long-term price level implied by the

---

881 See Brigham, E./Shome, D./Vinson, S. (1985), pp. 42-43 and Maddox, F./Pippert, D./Sullivan, R. (1995), p. 90.

882 See Section 2.2.3.2.

883 See Richter, F. (2005), p. 110 who suggests price-to-book as well as price-to-cash flow (e.g. dividends) multiples to measure the market price level.

884 See, e.g., Richter, F. (2005), pp. 114-115 for an analysis using correlation coefficients.

assumed sustainable perpetual growth rate[885]. This leads to above (below) average expected MRP estimates in times of low (high) price levels. The negative correlation coefficients are significant at a 95% confidence level for Germany, Japan (ex-post inflation based perpetual growth only), the US, and for the World sample. Lowering the confidence level to 90% would also include France and Japan (at zero perpetual growth). The results for the steady state expected MRP estimates are less consistent among the analyzed countries. Still, high positive and significant correlation coefficients are found for Canada, the UK, the US, and the World sample. This result is not counterintuitive since the steady state growth rate is essentially driven by the growth in book value implied by terminal period earnings and dividends forecasts in order to maintain a stable return on book equity[886]. In times of high price levels such estimates show the strongest growth rates and therefore imply higher steady state growth rates. Analyzing the regression-based expected MRP estimates leads to the same results. This implies that both formerly mentioned terminal perpetuity approaches are based on perpetual growth rates which are positively correlated with the current price level. Even in times of low dividend yields, the expected MRP does not decline in parallel since low dividend yields are overcompensated by large expected growth rates. Obviously, this result is inconsistent with the empirically found dependence of returns and MRPs on the dividend yield and the validity of these terminal value concepts appears questionable.

Correlation coefficients for terminal multiple based premium estimates are easier to interpret since the future price level assumption in form of a multiple is made directly transparent. Despite delivering implausible absolute results for the expected MRP, the correlation coefficients are also shown for the terminal multiple approach to illustrate the impact of converging multiples. For the entry equal to exit multiple assumption, the correlation coefficients are positive and significant (at a significance level of approximately 10%) across all analyzed countries. Applying the convergence scenarios leads to the already discovered opposite effect with consistently negative correlation coefficients. Again all coefficients are at least significant at a level of ~10%.

---

[885] However, it should be noted that the herein modeled convergence of the price level is only driven by the growth rate since the other main price level driver, expected returns, must be constant in the IRR-based approach. As to be seen in Chapter 6, this is inconsistent with empirical evidence of time-variable expected returns.

[886] See also F 5-47.

Table 66 Pearson correlation coefficients for various expected MRP estimates and the current one-year forward PE ratio

	Expected MRP 1989-2006 - Pearson's correlation coefficient						
	Canada	France	Germany	Japan	UK	US	World
1.2 g_{RI}=0	0.0911	-0.4141	-0.4783	-0.4327	-0.0304	-0.6746	-0.5114
(p-value)	(0.7192)	(0.0876)	(0.0447)	(0.0729)	(0.9046)	(0.0021)	(0.0301)
1.3 g_{RI}=ex-post inflation	0.1626	-0.4621	-0.5197	-0.5299	-0.1930	-0.7229	-0.6428
(p-value)	(0.5192)	(0.0535)	(0.0271)	(0.0237)	(0.4429)	(0.0007)	(0.0040)
1.4 g_{RI}=steady state growth	0.5658	-0.0035	-0.0174	-0.4045	0.5817	0.8349	0.5903
(p-value)	(0.0144)	(0.9890)	(0.9455)	(0.0959)	(0.0113)	(0.0000)	(0.0099)
1.6. Regression approach	0.5931	0.1757	0.1193	-0.3051	0.6315	0.6227	NA
(p-value)	(0.0095)	(0.4855)	(0.6372)	(0.2184)	(0.0049)	(0.0058)	NA
2.1 Entry = Exit (Sample)	0.3859	0.6019	0.4717	0.4470	0.6341	0.6534	0.6823
(p-value)	(0.1137)	(0.0082)	(0.0482)	(0.0629)	(0.0047)	(0.0033)	(0.0018)
2.2 Exit = In-sample avg.	-0.4628	-0.4401	-0.3976	-0.7173	-0.6146	-0.6812	-0.6252
(p-value)	(0.0531)	(0.0676)	(0.1023)	(0.0008)	(0.0066)	(0.0019)	(0.0055)
2.3 Exit = Out of sample avg	-0.8366	-0.8999	-0.7951	-0.7647	-0.9464	-0.9650	-0.9685
(p-value)	(0.0000)	(0.0000)	(0.0001)	(0.0002)	(0.0000)	(0.0000)	(0.0000)

Note: P-values with a significance level of at least 5% are highlighted in grey.

Relaxing the normal distribution assumption, Table 67 provides the non-parametric correlation coefficients according to Spearman. With respect to the sign of the correlation coefficient the results are almost entirely consistent with the Pearson results. However, the significance levels are lower from a general perspective.

Table 67 Spearman correlation coefficients for various expected MRP estimates and the current one-year forward PE ratio

	Expected MRP 1989-2006 - Spearman's correlation coefficient						
	Canada	France	Germany	Japan	UK	US	World
1.2 g_{RI}=0	0.0836	-0.1682	-0.3664	-0.4056	0.1889	-0.3870	-0.3189
(p-value)	(0.7416)	(0.5046)	(0.1348)	(0.0950)	(0.4529)	(0.1126)	(0.1971)
1.3 g_{RI}=ex-post inflation	0.1662	-0.3437	-0.4097	-0.4345	-0.1311	-0.5501	-0.4799
(p-value)	(0.5100)	(0.1626)	(0.0913)	(0.0716)	(0.6042)	(0.0180)	(0.0439)
1.4 g_{RI}=steady state growth	0.4675	-0.0052	-0.1868	-0.4241	0.4881	0.9319	0.5666
(p-value)	(0.0504)	(0.9838)	(0.4580)	(0.0794)	(0.0399)	(0.0000)	(0.0142)
1.6. Regression approach	0.5253	0.3086	0.1166	-0.3313	0.5397	0.5521	NA
(p-value)	(0.0252)	(0.2128)	(0.6449)	(0.1793)	(0.0208)	(0.0175)	NA
2.1 Entry = Exit (Sample)	0.3457	0.7007	0.4654	0.4427	0.5170	0.6656	0.8163
(p-value)	(0.1600)	(0.0012)	(0.0516)	(0.0658)	(0.0280)	(0.0026)	(0.0000)
2.2 Exit = In-sample avg.	-0.5728	-0.4014	-0.3560	-0.6491	-0.6471	-0.4489	-0.4386
(p-value)	(0.0130)	(0.0987)	(0.1470)	(0.0036)	(0.0037)	(0.0617)	(0.0686)
2.3 Exit = Out of sample avg	-0.8700	-0.8452	-0.8101	-0.7957	-0.9505	-0.9752	-0.8658
(p-value)	(0.0000)	(0.0000)	(0.0000)	(0.0001)	(0.0000)	(0.0000)	(0.0000)

Note: P-values with a significance level of at least 5% are highlighted in grey.

5.13 Unconditional versus conditional expected MRP estimates for corporate valuations

Recognizing the price level dependence of expected MRPs, the consequences for valuation analyses need to be further discussed. For the determination of risk-adjusted discount rates, expected MRP estimates from the IRR-based approach are available in two forms: (1) as conditional value at the valuation date or (2) as unconditional average of the analysis period.

When the distributions of MRPs are assumed to be independent, the unconditional average of historical expected MRPs needs to be used for valuation. Regarding a potential bias in the mean estimator, the same issues apply as for historical realized MRPs discussed in Chapter 4. Still, the discussion in Section 2.2.3.2 together with the results of the preceding section has shown that there is evidence for expected returns/MRPs being dependent on the current price level of the market. Under such circumstances, the conditional estimate of the expected MRP is the appropriate premium to determine the cost of capital. Similarly to the risk-free rate, the expected MRP is then solely based on the market expectations at the valuation date[887]. Finally note that if the market were to price asset using converging expected MRPs, then the conditional observation, despite being constant, would—similarly to a spot rate of the risk-free rate—be a consolidation of the market forward curve in one value[888].

In summary, assuming that the expected MRP is dependent on the market price level, conditional estimates of the expected MRP are appropriate for valuations since they adequately reflect the instantaneous market opportunity return at the valuation date. Given the consensus in the literature to use realizable market spot rates at the valuation date as proxy for the risk-free rate based on the "cut-off date principle"[889], it appears surprising that a similar approach is not applied for the expected MRP. An argument against the application of the expected MRPs based on the IRR method relates the assumption of i.i.d. return distributions which is obviously violated in case the market price level affects returns. Still, this only implies that the IRR is not equal to the expected return as discussed in Section 2.3.1 but when the IRR is applied for the valuation of identical or proportionate cash flows, it is the correct discount rate[890].

---

[887] See Damodaran, A. (2002), pp. 173-174 and Richter, F. (2005), p. 103.

[888] See also Lambert, R. (2009), p. 267.

[889] See Section 2.4.1.

[890] See Richter, F. (2006a), p. 18.

5.14 Conditional expected MRP estimates during the financial crisis

In times of high market volatility such as the financial crisis starting 2008, the application of time-conditional expected MRP estimates is particularly important. Exhibit 69 presents the expected MRP development for the German market since 2007. Following the market peak of the CDAX in October 2007, the expected MRP estimate increased from 6.07% to 9.52% at year-end 2008. During the market recovery in 2009, the expected MRP declined to 6.66% at the end of September 2009.

Exhibit 69 Monthly conditional expected MRP forecast for Germany from January 2007 to September 2009

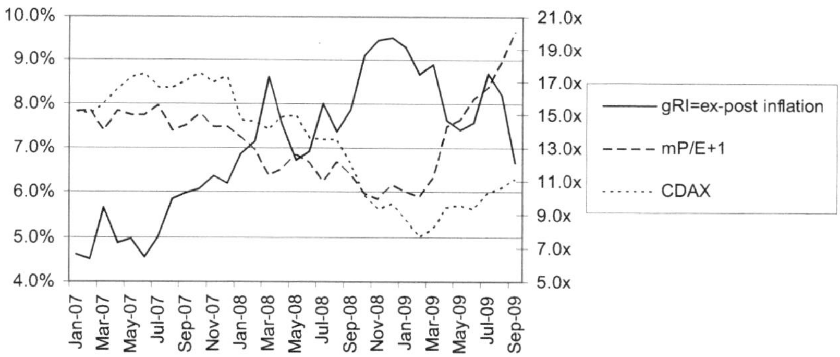

Source CDAX: Datastream (code: CDAXGEN(RI)).

Given this development, it is not surprising that the correlation coefficient between the expected MRP and the one-year forward PE multiple is significantly negative during this period (see Table 68) supporting the hypothesis of price level dependence when using a terminal value concept with price level convergence. The correlation coefficient is even higher and significant with the market index itself.

Table 68 Correlation coefficients for the monthly expected MRP and price level indicators for Germany from January 2007 to September 2009

Pearson's correlation coefficient			
	g_{RI}=ex-post infl.	g_{RI}=ex-post infl. lagged	g_{RI}=swap infl.
CDAX	-0.8131	-0.8062	-0.8578
(p-value)	(0.0000)	(0.0000)	(0.0000)
$m_{P/E+1}$	-0.5509	-0.4955	-0.4710
(p-value)	(0.0009)	(0.0054)	(0.0057)

Spearman's correlation coefficient			
	g_{RI}=ex-post infl.	g_{RI}=ex-post infl. lagged	g_{RI}=swap infl.
CDAX	-0.8392	-0.7967	-0.8559
(p-value)	(0.0000)	(0.0000)	(0.0000)
$m_{P/E+1}$	-0.6090	-0.5261	-0.5498
(p-value)	(0.0002)	(0.0028)	(0.0009)

Note: P-values with a significance level of at least 5% are highlighted in grey.

As discussed at the end of Section 5.11.2, expected MRP estimates are distorted by lagging updates of analyst forecasts[891]. This bias is particularly important in times of substantial forecast revisions such as 2008 and 2009. Despite the fact that a precise lag cannot be determined, it is illustratively assumed that estimates lag the reflection of new information in market prices by three months. Moving the underlying forecasts three months backward and assuring consistent samples for forecast and price data results in the expected MRP estimate shown in Exhibit 70. The development is similarly upward sloping but with a lower maximum expected MRP level during the relevant period. A potential explanation is that a higher expected return is required to equate the present value of residual earnings plus initial book value with the current market capitalization when only prices but not forecasts have declined. Still, since the precise date when the analyst develops his forecast—and thereby the available information set—remains unknown, this approach cannot entirely eliminate the potential bias[892].

[891] See also Easton, P. (2009), pp. 336-337.
[892] See also Easton, P. (2009), p. 337.

Exhibit 70 Alternative monthly estimates for the conditional expected MRP for Germany from January 2007 to September 2009

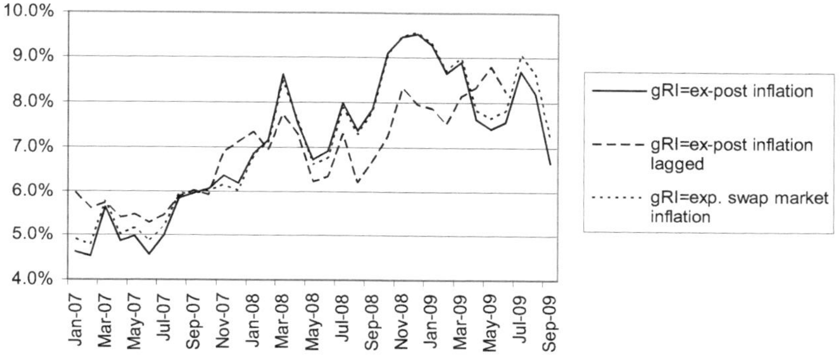

Exhibit 70 also provides expected MRP estimates using a long-term expected inflation rate observed in the swap market for the Eurozone instead of the historical inflation rate as proxy for the perpetual growth rate[893]. Since such direct[894] inflation expectations have only recently become available, they were not used for the core analysis period 1989 to 2006. The maximum difference between both estimates of 58 basis points is reached in July 2009 with actual inflation at -0.28% and a long-term inflation forecast from the swap market of 2.55%. Table 69 summarizes the data set of this section.

[893] Inflation rate swaps are traded OTC and are quoted as zero courpon spot rates for different maturities. The long-term inflation rate used is calculated based on the 30-year spot quote from which the last annual expected forward rate is calculated by linear interpolation of the one year prior spot rate based on the 20-year spot quote. 20 and 30-year expected inflation quotes for the Euorzone are available from Bloomberg (codes: EUSWI20 and EUSWI30). Individual quotes for Germany have only become available since mid-2009. Note that expected inflation rates based on swap market quotes are not distorted by surcharges for counterparty risk since it is compensated separately as part of transaction costs.

[894] Direct market expectations should not be confused indirect estimates derived from inflation-indexed bonds.

Table 69 Summary statistics for the monthly expected MRP estimation for Germany from January 2007 to September 2009

Model (1)						g_{RI}=ex-post inflation					g_{RI}=exp. swap market inflation			
Date	CDAX	r^f (2)	θ_{TV}	$m_{P/E+1}$	Firms (3)	r^e	r^p	r^p lagged	$g_{RI,TV}$	$g_{D,TV}$ (4)	r^e	r^p	$g_{RI,TV}$	$g_{D,TV}$ (4)
31-Jan-07	419.9	4.10%	36.58%	15.2x	300	8.70%	4.60%	5.97%	1.69%	5.52%	9.01%	4.91%	2.51%	5.71%
28-Feb-07	416.3	3.93%	38.44%	15.3x	302	8.45%	4.51%	5.61%	1.78%	5.20%	8.70%	4.77%	2.43%	5.36%
30-Mar-07	431.5	4.04%	38.28%	14.0x	314	9.68%	5.64%	5.74%	1.98%	5.98%	9.82%	5.78%	2.38%	6.06%
30-Apr-07	456.4	4.20%	36.89%	15.3x	306	9.07%	4.87%	5.41%	2.07%	5.72%	9.21%	5.01%	2.46%	5.82%
31-May-07	476.8	4.36%	35.00%	15.0x	304	9.33%	4.97%	5.47%	2.07%	6.07%	9.52%	5.15%	2.56%	6.19%
29-Jun-07	482.5	4.54%	33.86%	15.0x	304	9.10%	4.56%	5.27%	1.87%	6.02%	9.39%	4.85%	2.63%	6.21%
31-Jul-07	459.7	4.35%	33.83%	15.5x	312	9.35%	5.00%	5.46%	2.06%	6.19%	9.55%	5.19%	2.55%	6.32%
31-Aug-07	459.4	4.28%	33.80%	14.1x	317	10.13%	5.84%	5.88%	2.16%	6.70%	10.26%	5.97%	2.53%	6.79%
28-Sep-07	471.6	4.40%	33.72%	14.4x	328	10.37%	5.98%	6.02%	2.66%	6.87%	10.34%	5.94%	2.57%	6.85%
31-Oct-07	484.5	4.19%	33.62%	15.1x	327	10.26%	6.07%	5.94%	2.75%	6.81%	10.22%	6.03%	2.64%	6.78%
30-Nov-07	469.6	4.01%	33.57%	14.3x	330	10.37%	6.36%	6.91%	3.24%	6.89%	10.16%	6.15%	2.67%	6.75%
31-Dec-07	478.7	4.39%	34.56%	14.3x	340	10.59%	6.19%	7.12%	3.13%	6.93%	10.41%	6.02%	2.66%	6.81%
31-Jan-08	406.9	4.01%	34.47%	13.7x	341	10.86%	6.86%	7.34%	2.83%	7.12%	10.81%	6.80%	2.67%	7.08%
29-Feb-08	403.5	3.95%	33.44%	12.8x	342	11.11%	7.16%	6.94%	2.82%	7.40%	11.07%	7.12%	2.68%	7.37%
31-Mar-08	391.1	3.70%	34.21%	11.3x	346	12.31%	8.61%	7.74%	3.10%	8.10%	12.17%	8.47%	2.60%	8.01%
30-Apr-08	411.1	3.87%	34.49%	11.7x	341	11.42%	7.55%	7.31%	2.41%	7.48%	11.47%	7.60%	2.59%	7.51%
30-May-08	414.2	4.27%	36.04%	12.6x	340	10.99%	6.72%	6.23%	2.99%	7.03%	10.90%	6.63%	2.69%	6.97%
30-Jun-08	375.8	4.40%	35.63%	12.1x	335	11.31%	6.92%	6.35%	3.28%	7.28%	11.16%	6.76%	2.72%	7.18%
31-Jul-08	374.5	4.40%	36.10%	10.9x	336	12.39%	7.99%	7.31%	3.26%	7.92%	12.28%	7.88%	2.77%	7.85%
29-Aug-08	373.6	4.03%	37.70%	12.1x	335	11.40%	7.37%	6.20%	3.07%	7.11%	11.33%	7.29%	2.77%	7.06%
30-Sep-08	332.1	4.04%	37.19%	11.4x	339	11.90%	7.86%	6.69%	2.88%	7.48%	11.84%	7.80%	2.56%	7.44%
31-Oct-08	279.5	3.97%	37.16%	10.3x	340	13.07%	9.10%	7.25%	2.39%	8.21%	13.04%	9.07%	2.15%	8.19%
28-Nov-08	257.3	3.50%	38.87%	9.9x	347	12.96%	9.46%	8.32%	1.43%	7.92%	12.98%	9.48%	1.74%	7.93%
31-Dec-08	266.3	3.30%	38.61%	10.8x	351	12.82%	9.52%	7.96%	1.14%	7.87%	12.86%	9.57%	1.78%	7.90%
30-Jan-09	239.6	3.61%	39.88%	10.3x	337	12.89%	9.28%	7.87%	0.95%	7.75%	12.92%	9.31%	1.90%	7.77%
27-Feb-09	212.8	3.36%	39.71%	10.0x	344	12.02%	8.66%	7.52%	1.04%	7.25%	12.06%	8.70%	1.73%	7.27%
31-Mar-09	224.9	3.19%	40.04%	11.2x	336	12.08%	8.89%	8.14%	0.47%	7.24%	12.18%	9.00%	1.74%	7.31%
30-Apr-09	260.3	3.33%	40.56%	14.3x	343	10.96%	7.62%	8.33%	0.66%	6.51%	11.17%	7.83%	2.13%	6.64%
29-May-09	263.7	3.71%	40.74%	14.7x	349	11.12%	7.41%	8.79%	0.00%	6.59%	11.38%	7.67%	2.39%	6.74%
30-Jun-09	257.7	3.47%	40.31%	16.0x	344	11.03%	7.57%	8.24%	0.09%	6.59%	11.29%	7.82%	2.42%	6.74%
31-Jul-09	283.8	3.59%	39.49%	16.6x	342	12.29%	8.70%	NA	-0.46%	7.44%	12.66%	9.07%	2.47%	7.66%
31-Aug-09	293.7	3.44%	39.22%	18.3x	344	11.62%	8.19%	NA	0.00%	7.07%	12.06%	8.63%	2.52%	7.33%
30-Sep-09	306.9	3.43%	40.50%	20.1x	329	10.09%	6.66%	NA	-0.28%	6.01%	10.67%	7.24%	2.55%	6.35%
Low	212.8	3.19%	33.44%	9.9x	300	8.45%	4.51%	5.27%	-0.46%	5.20%	8.70%	4.77%	1.73%	5.36%
Arith. Mean	367.8	3.92%	36.86%	13.6x	332	10.97%	7.05%	6.84%	1.86%	6.92%	11.06%	7.14%	2.43%	6.97%
Median	391.1	4.01%	36.89%	14.1x	337	11.03%	7.16%	6.92%	2.07%	7.03%	11.16%	7.24%	2.55%	6.97%
High	484.5	4.54%	40.74%	20.1x	351	13.07%	9.52%	8.79%	3.28%	8.21%	13.04%	9.57%	2.77%	8.19%
St. Dev.	89.6	0.39%	2.54%	2.4x		1.29%	1.53%	1.04%	1.15%	0.77%	1.24%	1.51%	0.31%	0.71%

(1) All parameters are stated in nominal terms and as arithmetic average of monthly values.

(2) r^f equals redemption yield of the REX 10y subindex.

(3) Number of firms per month.

(4) Implied perpetual dividend growth rate (after convergence for $0<g_{RI}<g_{RI\ steady\ state}$ cases) according to calculation approach presented in Appendix 10 - $Max[g_{RI,TV};(1-\theta_{TV})r^e]$.

5.15 Conclusions

The IRR approach to determine the expected MRP using analysts' forecasts has become a popular methodology within the academic community as a reference point for the magnitude of the expected MRP. In this context, a several valuation models can be used to calculate the IRR.

- In previous research, DIV, RIV, and CAP models were predominantly used to estimate the expected MRP using forecasts from analysts. It was formally and practically shown that all three models deliver isomorphic results if a consistent set of input data is used. Therefore, the results of this study are almost exclusively derived on the basis of the RIV model since calculating expected MRPs on identical models is redundant. With most models differing essentially only regarding the level of optimism about perpetual growth, future research should rather focus on the appropriate post-horizontal behavior of the valuation attribute instead of developing ever new structural model derivatives.
- Despite their equivalence, it was shown that the valuation attribute of the DIV model (dividends) and the RIV/CAP models (residual income/agr) grow at different rates unless the valuation object is in a steady state. This is important when evaluating the results from the RIV/CAP model since, e.g., zero perpetual growth in residual earnings does not necessarily imply perpetual dividend growth of zero[895].
- In order to facilitate the evaluation of different terminal value assumptions, a concept was presented to determine the impact of different perpetual growth assumptions on the post-horizontal development of the return on book equity. This concept was used to define the lower and upper boundaries for the expected MRP estimate. While the return on book equity immediately converges to the cost of capital for the lower bound, it is assumed to remain constant for the upper bound.
- The discussion of terminal value approaches also included an evaluation of using terminal multiples. It was formally shown that forward multiples need to be used which may differ from the observables spot multiples dependent on the expected return and growth during the explicit forecast period.

---

[895] When perpetual residual income growth is zero, dividend growth is only also equal to zero if the payout ratio is one.

- In contrast to previous research, this study uses a consistent framework to allow for intra-year estimation and dividend payments. In particular, the ex-dividend date is chosen as valuation reference date.
- It was shown that either the aggregation or value-weighting approach need to be utilized to determine expected MRP estimates in compliance with CAPM since otherwise the market portfolio is not correctly reflected.

In addition to conceptual advances, this study provides a comprehensive empirical analysis of the magnitude of IRR-based expected MRPs for all six countries in the sample individually and in aggregate.

- The results of this study confirm the findings by earlier research that the unconditional average of the expected MRP estimates using the IRR-based approach with conservative terminal value assumptions is substantially lower than the unconditional average of realized MRPs. As shown by Table 70, the average results range from 2% to 9% for terminal perpetuities. The unconditional average expected MRPs for the widely recognized terminal perpetuity approach with inflation-based growth (1.3) are within a narrow band of 2.28% to 3.52% implying a range of less than 1.24%. Interestingly enough, the estimate for Germany of 2.56% is the lowest among Western countries.
- The usage of expected perpetual growth rates of residual income higher than inflation-based proxies appears unreasonable. Firstly, perpetual residual income growth at a level higher than inflation implies perpetual dividend growth substantially above the growth rates of mature Western economies. Secondly, the implied return on book equity converges to the cost of capital at this growth level which is consistent with competition theory suggesting that returns above the cost of capital are not sustainable in the long-term[896].
- The calculated expected MRP series have a much lower standard deviation compared to historical MRPs indicating an increase in measurement accuracy when inferring expected MRP estimates from the IRR approach[897].
- It was further shown that terminal multiples based on spot multiples lead to implausible (too high) results using the IRR approach. Implied forward terminal multiples by the post-horizontal development of drivers are substantially lower. As

---

[896] See Koller, T./Goedhart, M./Wessels, D. (2005), p. 279 and Richter, F. (2006a), pp. 14-15.
[897] See also Lee, C./Ng, D./Swaminathan, B. (2009), p. 320.

a consequence, the application of the popular assumption of entry multiple equal to exit multiple in discounted cash flow valuations leads to inflated valuation results.

Table 70 Summary of unconditional expected MRP averages from equity valuation models using analysts' estimates for the period 1989-2006

	Unconditional mean expected MRP (1)						
Terminal value approach	Canada	France	Germany	Japan	UK	US	World
1.2 g_{RI}=0	2.89%	2.29%	1.86%	2.01%	2.15%	2.15%	1.85%
1.3 g_{RI}=ex-post inflation	3.51%	2.92%	2.56%	2.28%	3.03%	3.52%	2.92%
1.4 g_{RI}=steady state growth	6.14%	6.37%	5.00%	4.79%	6.10%	9.14%	7.30%
1.6 Regression approach	4.26%	4.91%	4.12%	3.30%	3.69%	5.32%	NA
2.1 Entry = Exit (Sample)	12.53%	12.17%	11.97%	14.52%	10.61%	13.85%	13.26%

(1) All values are stated in nominal terms.

- The development of conditional expected MRPs over time was found to be non-stationary and upward sloping for all countries except the US[898]. Increasing expected MRPs over time are potentially explained by increasing sample sizes due to analyst coverage expanding to smaller and higher risk firms. An important finding is the reversal of the expected MRP decline for the US around 2000. This explains significant correlation coefficients between all countries except the US.
- The results of this study provide evidence that negative expected MRPs for the German market during 1990 and 1992 are related to model specifications that do not appropriately reflect conditional inflation expectations during this period.
- In order to more formally analyze the equivalence of unconditional averages of expected MRP estimates across countries matched-pair tests were used. The analysis has shown that for several country combinations the null hypothesis of equal means is rejected.
- A statistical comparison of the conditional expected MRP estimates by model shows highly significant correlation coefficients between all model estimates which underlines that the key difference among the models relates to the absolute level of the expected MRP but not to the development of conditional estimates over time.
- An important property of the expected MRP from IRR-based models is time-variability. In the previous literature, the variability of the expected MRP was primarily attributed to changes in the risk-free rate[899]. Consistent with the general relationship between returns/MRPs and relative price measures, variations in the

[898] See also Pastor, L./Sinha, M./Swaminathan, B. (2008), p. 2877.
[899] See also Pastor, L./Sinha, M./Swaminathan, B. (2008), p. 2877.

conditional expected MRP estimates were found to be significantly correlated with the spot PE_{+1} multiple when using terminal value concepts with converging perpetual growth rates or multiples. This supports the hypothesis that the current market price level is related to the expected MRP.

- The time-variability of conditional expected MRP estimates is most substantial during times of extraordinary market movements such as the recent financial crisis. An extended expected MRP series for the German market until September 2009 shows fluctuations between 4.51% and 9.52% for the period since 2007. Unsurprisingly, the correlation coefficient between the expected MRP estimates and the spot PE_{+1} multiples are negative and highly significant for this period.

When interpreting the results of the IRR approach, several methodological issues need to be addressed.

- The return distribution assumption of the IRR approach is inconsistent with empirical evidence[900]. While returns need to follow an i.i.d. distribution so that the IRR of the valuation formula equals the expected one-period return, empirical evidence suggests that return distributions could be dependent[901]. Hughes/Liu/Liu (2009) developed a conceptual model for IRR-based expected return/MRP estimates with stochastic log expected returns capturing correlations between expected returns and cash flows, cash flow growth, and leverage. Taking assumptions on the volatilities of expected returns and cash flows, cash flow growth, and the correlation between cash flow news and expected returns, their model suggests that IRR-based estimates are between 1.2% and 3% downward biased estimates of the expected MRP, however assuming a substantially larger standard deviation of expected returns compared the herein analyzed data[902].
- Ballwieser argues that the current market capitalization is not the appropriate value measure since in takeover situations substantially higher prices are paid[903]. However, it is plausible to use market capitalization as value measure since analysts' estimates do not include any merger benefits. When using takeover prices in the equation to estimate the expected MRP, then any merger benefits must be also reflected in the numerator.

---

[900] See Richter, F. (2006a), p. 18.
[901] See Section 2.2.3 for a review.
[902] See Hughes, J./Liu, J./Liu, J. (2009), pp. 249-255. For a discussion of the Hughes/Liu/Liu (2009) model, see Lambert, R. (2009).
[903] See Ballwieser, W. (2005), pp. 320-330. See also Hachmeister, D./Wiese, J. (2009), p. 59.

- Another issue is related to other distribution mechanisms such as share repurchases[904]. Since the herein presented valuation models only measure expected dividend payments, the resulting expected MRP estimates are downward biased if there are firms in the market portfolio that distribute cash to shareholders on a recurring basis outside the regular dividend streams.
- Low sample sizes for non-US countries in the early years of the analysis period may distort the results[905]. Distortions may also occur due to the time-matching assumptions for input parameters and the mix of fiscal year-ends through the aggregation method. Furthermore, a potential bias or time-delay in analyst forecasts may influence the expected MRP estimates[906].
- The IRR-based estimation procedure only allows to determine constant expected MRPs. However, the fluctuating conditional expected MRP estimates show that the premium is likely not constant over time[907]. While it is possible to model variations of the price level driven by growth rates, a time-variable expected return cannot be determined based on the IRR approach[908].

Despite its limitations, the IRR approach is a useful tool to calculate the conditional expected MRP to be used for valuation purposes assuming that it correctly reflects the future development[909]. Based on the "cut-off date principle", the cost of capital can then be constructed out of two forward-looking measures that incorporate the current price level on the equity and debt markets and thereby the instantaneous opportunity return: the conditional expected MRP and the long-term spot rate of the risk-free asset. The importance for such conditional estimates is exemplified by the high fluctuations of the expected MRP during the recent financial crisis. Still, in order to use the least restrictive valuation formula F 2-28, a time-variable expected rate of return would be required; an issue that will be approached in the next section.

---

904 See also Fama, E./French, K. (2002), pp. 653-654.
905 See also Esterer, F./Schröder, D. (2007), p. 21.
906 See Ballwieser, W. (2005), p. 333, Richter, F. (2005), p. 127, Easton, P. (2009), pp. 324-325, and Hachmeister, D./Wiese, J. (2009), p. 58.
907 See also Pastor, L./Sinha, M./Swaminathan, B. (2008), p. 2861.
908 See Richter, F. (2005), p. 122 and Richter, F. (2006a), p. 18.
909 See also Richter, F. (2006a), p. 17.

6 Expected MRP estimation based on the return decomposition approach

In the previous chapters, two methods to estimate the expected MRP were presented based on ex-post and ex-ante data. Despite relying on fundamentally different input data both methods have in common that they provide a constant estimate for the expected MRP. Still, the empirical results presented in Section 5.9 which are consistent with previous research indicate that the expected MRP is variable over time and not constant[910].

In this chapter an approach is presented to determine a time-variable expected MRP based on the approach presented by Richter (2006a)[911]. This approach makes use of the widely recognized fact that certain variations in expected returns can be explained through the price-dividend ratio[912]. As a starting point, a formula is derived that decomposes the return into its constituents. It is not only applied in various studies using ex-post as well as ex-ante data to estimate the expected MRP[913] but also provides the basis for the time-variable expected MRP estimation. Following the conceptual sections, the resulting expected MRP estimates from the decomposition approach are discussed for all analyzed countries.

6.1 Models and assumptions

6.1.1 Base model

The cornerstone of this section is an expected return formula that makes the impact of a changing price-dividend ratio transparent[914]. Applying trite manipulations to the standard total return expression, the components of the total return can be divided into dividend yield, dividend growth, and change in price-dividend ratio[915]:

---

[910] See Richter, F. (2006a), pp. 18-19 and 30.

[911] See Richter, F. (2006a), pp. 22-29.

[912] See Section 2.2.3.1 incl. fn. 98. See also Richter, F. (2005), pp. 106-107.

[913] See, e.g., Fama, E./French, K. (2001), Arnott, R./Ryan, R. (2001), Arnott, R./Bernstein, P. (2002), Ibbotson, R./Chen, P. (2003), Richter, F. (2005), Richter, F. (2006a), and Dimson, E./Marsh, P./Staunton, M. (2008).

[914] See also Campbell, J./Shiller, R. (1988a,b), Campbell, J./Lo, A./MacKinlay, C. (1997), p. 261, and Cochrane, J. (2005), pp. 404-410 for a more sophisticated linearized expected return model driven by the log price-dividend ratio.

[915] See for similar approaches, e.g., Arnott, R./Ryan, R. (2001), pp. 62-63, Arnott, R./Bernstein, P. (2002), pp. 71-72, Ibbotson, R./Chen, P. (2003), pp. 90-91 (Ibbotson/Chen call this approach also the supply-side method), and Dimson, E./Marsh, P./Staunton, M. (2008), pp. 505-506. Some of these studies further decompose returns according to factors such as inflation, exchange rates, etc. In addition, one can alternatively use earnings instead of dividends for the manipulation of the total return expression.

$$\tilde{r}_t = \frac{\tilde{D}_t}{\tilde{P}_{t-1}} + \frac{\tilde{P}_t}{\tilde{P}_{t-1}} - 1$$

F 6-1

$$= \frac{\tilde{D}_t}{\tilde{P}_{t-1}} + \frac{\tilde{P}_t}{\tilde{P}_{t-1}} \frac{\tilde{D}_t}{\tilde{D}_{t-1}} \frac{\tilde{D}_{t-1}}{\tilde{D}_t} - 1 = \frac{\tilde{D}_t}{\tilde{P}_{t-1}} + \frac{\frac{\tilde{P}_t}{\tilde{D}_t}}{\frac{\tilde{P}_{t-1}}{\tilde{D}_{t-1}}} \frac{\tilde{D}_t}{\tilde{D}_{t-1}} - 1 = \frac{\tilde{D}_t}{\tilde{P}_{t-1}} + \frac{m_t^D}{m_{t-1}^D} \frac{\tilde{D}_t}{\tilde{D}_{t-1}} - 1$$

$$= \frac{\tilde{D}_t}{\tilde{P}_{t-1}} + \left(1 + \tilde{g}_t^{m^D}\right)\left(1 + \tilde{g}_t^D\right) - 1 = \frac{\tilde{D}_t}{\tilde{P}_{t-1}} + \tilde{g}_t^{m^D} + \tilde{g}_t^D + \tilde{g}_t^{m^D} \tilde{g}_t^D$$

When expressing F 6-1 in a forward-looking format using expected values, the equation resembles to the constant growth version of the dividend discount model presented in Section 5.1[916]:

F 6-2

$$E_t\left[\tilde{r}_{t+1}\right] = \frac{E_t\left[\tilde{D}_{t+1}\right]}{\tilde{P}_t} + E_t\left[\left(1 + \tilde{g}_{t+1}^{m^D}\right)\left(1 + \tilde{g}_{t+1}^D\right)\right] - 1$$

$$= \frac{E_t\left[\tilde{D}_{t+1}\right]}{\tilde{P}_t} + E_t\left[\tilde{g}_{t+1}^{m^D}\right] + E_t\left[\tilde{g}_{t+1}^D\right] + E_t\left[\tilde{g}_{t+1}^{m^D} \tilde{g}_{t+1}^D\right]$$

assuming $\tilde{g}_{t+1}^{m^D}$ and $\tilde{g}_{t+1}^D$ to be independent

$$= \frac{E_t\left[\tilde{D}_{t+1}\right]}{\tilde{P}_t} + E_t\left[\tilde{g}_{t+1}^{m^D}\right] + E_t\left[\tilde{g}_{t+1}^D\right] + E_t\left[\tilde{g}_{t+1}^{m^D}\right] E_t\left[\tilde{g}_{t+1}^D\right]$$

However, the key difference is related to the term measuring the expected growth in the price-dividend ratio or, stated differently, the expected change in the market price level during a specific period.

6.1.2 Unconditional expected MRP estimates

For the moment, the issue of identifying a conditional time-variable estimate for the expected MRP is put aside, since F 6-1 is so far primarily used in empirical research to estimate the unconditional expected MRP. In a widely recognized article, Fama/French (2002) estimate the unconditional expected MRP from historical data under the assumption that the dividend yield is stationary and mean reverting over time, i.e., it has a constant unconditional mean. In this case, the price return element of the total stock return (capital gain) is equivalent to growth in dividends. This can be also seen by assuming that there is no price-dividend ratio expansion ($\tilde{g}_t^{m^D} = 0$) in F 6-1 because the dividend yield distribution is assumed to have a constant mean

---

[916] Note that this expression with conditional expected values requires growth of dividends and the price-dividend ratio to be indepedent.

over time. Furthermore, Fama/French assume that the earnings yield is stationary so that the price return is also equal to the earnings growth rate[917]:

F 6-3 $$\tilde{r}_t = \frac{\tilde{D}_t}{\tilde{P}_{t-1}} + \frac{\tilde{P}_t - \tilde{P}_{t-1}}{\tilde{P}_{t-1}} = \frac{\tilde{D}_t}{\tilde{P}_{t-1}} + \tilde{g}_t^P$$

$$\text{with } \frac{\tilde{D}_t}{\tilde{P}_{t-1}} \text{ and } \frac{\tilde{E}_t}{\tilde{P}_{t-1}} \text{ being stationary } \tilde{g}_t^P = \tilde{g}_t^D = \tilde{g}_t^E$$

F 6-4 $$\begin{aligned}\tilde{r}_t &= \frac{\tilde{D}_t}{\tilde{P}_{t-1}} + \frac{\tilde{P}_t - \tilde{P}_{t-1}}{\tilde{P}_{t-1}} = \frac{\tilde{D}_t}{\tilde{P}_{t-1}} + \frac{\tilde{D}_t - \tilde{D}_{t-1}}{\tilde{D}_{t-1}} = \frac{\tilde{D}_t}{\tilde{P}_{t-1}} + \tilde{g}_t^D \\ &= \frac{\tilde{D}_t}{\tilde{P}_{t-1}} + \frac{\tilde{P}_t - \tilde{P}_{t-1}}{\tilde{P}_{t-1}} = \frac{\tilde{D}_t}{\tilde{P}_{t-1}} + \frac{\tilde{E}_t - \tilde{E}_{t-1}}{\tilde{E}_{t-1}} = \frac{\tilde{D}_t}{\tilde{P}_{t-1}} + \tilde{g}_t^E\end{aligned}$$

Averaging the values of F 6-4 over all available historical periods leads to the unconditional estimate of the expected return. Any variations of dividends and earnings yield over time are consistent with this approach due to the assumption of mean reversion to the unconditional mean. The expected MRP is then calculated by deducting the average historical risk-free rate from the expected return estimate[918]. It provides an estimate for the unconditional mean to which it is supposed to converge to[919].

The authors claim that their approach is more precise than standard estimates of the unconditional expected MRP from historical return averages since the standard error is substantially lower and the Sharpe ratio[920] is more stable over time implying stable risk aversion[921]. Despite its advantages, the model produces biased estimates of the expected return due to the different volatilities in dividend growth, earnings growth and capital gains[922]. Note that this procedure has the same averaging and survivorship bias issues as unconditional means of ex-post returns[923].

Richter (2005) uses a similar approach to determine the unconditional expected stock return that can also be aligned with the return decomposition framework despite a different formal derivation. He uses a version of the total return expression

---

[917] See Fama, E./French, K. (2002), pp. 637-638.
[918] See Fama, E./French, K. (2002), pp. 637-638.
[919] See Richter, F. (2006a), p. 21.
[920] The Sharpe ratio is defined as the MRP divided by the standard deviation of return.
[921] See Fama, E./French, K. (2002), pp. 639 and 644.
[922] See Fama, E./French, K. (2002), p. 654. The bias can be measured as one half of the difference in variances.
[923] See Fama, E./French, K. (2002), p. 646.

that makes the current price level transparent through price-dividend multiples[924]. As shown in the following, this approach is another presentation of F 6-1:

$$\tilde{r}_t = \frac{\tilde{D}_t}{\tilde{P}_{t-1}} + \frac{\tilde{P}_t - \tilde{P}_{t-1}}{\tilde{P}_{t-1}} = \frac{\tilde{D}_t + \tilde{P}_t}{\tilde{P}_{t-1}} - 1$$

with $\tilde{P}_t = m_t^D \tilde{D}_t$ and $\tilde{D}_t = \tilde{D}_{t-1}\left(1+\tilde{g}_t^D\right)$

$$\tilde{r}_t = \frac{\tilde{D}_{t-1}\left(1+\tilde{g}_t^D\right) + m_t^D \tilde{D}_{t-1}\left(1+\tilde{g}_t^D\right)}{m_{t-1}^D \tilde{D}_{t-1}} - 1 = \left(1+\tilde{g}_t^D\right)\frac{1+m_t^D}{m_{t-1}^D} - 1 \quad \text{(Richter expression)}$$

F 6-5

$$= \left(1+\tilde{g}_t^D\right)\left(\frac{1}{m_{t-1}^D} + \frac{m_t^D}{m_{t-1}^D}\right) - 1 = \left(1+\tilde{g}_t^D\right)\left(\frac{\tilde{D}_{t-1}}{\tilde{P}_{t-1}} + \left(1+\tilde{g}_t^{m^D}\right)\right) - 1$$

$$= \frac{\tilde{D}_t}{\tilde{P}_{t-1}} + \left(1+\tilde{g}_t^D\right)\left(1+\tilde{g}_t^{m^D}\right) - 1 = \frac{\tilde{D}_t}{\tilde{P}_{t-1}} + \tilde{g}_t^D + \tilde{g}_t^{m^D} + \tilde{g}_t^D \tilde{g}_t^{m^D}$$

For the empirical determination of expected returns, Richter assumes m_t^D to be constant so that F 6-5 reduces to the Fama/French expression of dividend yield plus dividend growth[925].

As discussed, the decomposition approach using ex-post data provides an unconditional mean estimate to which the expected MRP is supposed to converge to. This concept is based on the assumption of a stationary dividend yield which practically implies that from an unconditional perspective there is no impact of changes in the price level on the ex-post return[926]. Even if the expected MRP is determined for a period with a non-stationary development of the divided yield, the decomposition approach by Fama/French or Richter provides an unbiased estimate of the unconditional expected MRP like the IRR approach but unlike the unconditional average of realized MRPs—an issue of average ex-post MRPs already raised at the end of Section 4.4.

The following example (presented in Table 71) shall illustrate the impact of a non-stationary expected MRP on the average of realized MRPs. The required relationship can be established by assuming that market prices are determined by the dividend discount model with constant perpetual growth[927]. It becomes obvious that theoretically the annual realized and expected MRP are equal if there is no change in

---

[924] See Richter, F. (2005), pp. 114-119.

[925] See Richter, F. (2005), pp. 130-131 and Richter, F. (2006a), pp. 19-21.

[926] This is essentially the same argument why only income return is used for the historical risk-free rate; see also Section 2.4.4.

[927] See also Section 5.1.

the market price level measured by the price-dividend ratio. Any negative (positive) change in the expected MRP leads ceteris paribus (i.e., no change in the expected perpetual growth rate) to a change in the market price level and thereby to a higher (lower) ex-post MRP. This basic example shows that using average ex-post MRPs to estimate the expected MRP overestimates (underestimates) results when the expected MRP is non-stationary during the periods 1-12 and 13-23. However, if the expected MRP is mean reverting, the unconditional average of the realized MRPs is almost equal to the unconditional average of the expected MRP[928]. The example also shows that using the decomposition approach proposed by Fama/French, i.e., calculating the expected MRP as the sum of the unconditional averages of ex-post dividend yield and dividend growth is equal to the direct estimate of the unconditional expected MRP. Therefore, the essence of the unconditional decomposition approach is to eliminate the impact of price level changes on ex-post MRPs.

---

[928] See also Cornell, B. (1999), pp. 55-59, Richter, F. (2005), p. 130, and Brealey, R./Myers, S./Allen, F. (2008), pp. 178-180.

Table 71 Relationship between ex-post and expected MRP

	Period	Ex-ante analysis: Expected MRP	Ex-ante analysis: Risk-free rate	Ex-ante analysis: Expected return	Dividend discount model: Expected dividend growth	Dividend discount model: Dividends	Dividend discount model: Implied price (end-of-period)	Dividend discount model: Price growth	Dividend discount model: Price/dividend ratio	Ex-post total return components: Lagged dividend yield	Implied ex-post price return: Dividend growth	Implied ex-post price return: Expected return (decomp. appr.)	Implied ex-post price return: Price/dividend ratio expansion	Implied ex-post price return: Exp. div. growth * div./price ratio growth	Ex-post analysis: Ex-post total return	Ex-post analysis: Risk-free rate	Ex-post analysis: Ex-post MRP
	0	7.0%	5.0%	12.0%	5.0%	10.0	150.0	NA	15.0x	NA	NA	NA	NA	NA	NA	5.0%	NA
	1	7.0%	5.0%	12.0%	5.0%	10.5	157.5	5.0%	15.0x	7.0%	5.0%	12.0%	0.0%	0.0%	12.0%	5.0%	7.0%
Mean reversion	2	7.0%	5.0%	12.0%	5.0%	11.0	170.2	8.1%	15.4x	7.0%	5.0%	12.0%	2.9%	0.1%	15.1%	5.0%	10.1%
Non-stationarity	3	6.8%	5.0%	11.8%	5.0%	11.6	184.2	8.2%	15.9x	6.8%	5.0%	11.8%	3.0%	0.2%	15.0%	5.0%	10.0%
	4	6.6%	5.0%	11.6%	5.0%	12.2	199.4	8.3%	16.4x	6.6%	5.0%	11.6%	3.1%	0.2%	14.9%	5.0%	9.9%
	5	6.4%	5.0%	11.4%	5.0%	12.8	216.1	8.4%	16.9x	6.4%	5.0%	11.4%	3.2%	0.2%	14.8%	5.0%	9.8%
	6	6.2%	5.0%	11.2%	5.0%	13.4	234.5	8.5%	17.5x	6.2%	5.0%	11.2%	3.3%	0.2%	14.7%	5.0%	9.7%
	7	6.0%	5.0%	11.0%	5.0%	14.1	254.7	8.6%	18.1x	6.0%	5.0%	11.0%	3.4%	0.2%	14.6%	5.0%	9.6%
	8	5.8%	5.0%	10.8%	5.0%	14.8	277.0	8.8%	18.8x	5.8%	5.0%	10.8%	3.6%	0.2%	14.6%	5.0%	9.5%
	9	5.6%	5.0%	10.6%	5.0%	15.5	301.6	8.9%	19.4x	5.6%	5.0%	10.6%	3.7%	0.2%	14.5%	5.0%	9.5%
	10	5.4%	5.0%	10.4%	5.0%	16.3	328.9	9.0%	20.2x	5.4%	5.0%	10.4%	3.8%	0.2%	14.4%	5.0%	9.4%
	11	5.2%	5.0%	10.2%	5.0%	17.1	359.2	9.2%	21.0x	5.2%	5.0%	10.2%	4.0%	0.2%	14.4%	5.0%	9.4%
	12	5.0%	5.0%	10.0%	5.0%	18.0	377.1	5.0%	21.0x	5.0%	5.0%	10.0%	0.0%	0.0%	10.0%	5.0%	5.0%
	13	5.0%	5.0%	10.0%	5.0%	18.9	380.8	1.0%	20.2x	5.0%	5.0%	10.0%	-3.8%	-0.2%	6.0%	5.0%	1.0%
Non-stationarity	14	5.2%	5.0%	10.2%	5.0%	19.8	385.0	1.1%	19.4x	5.2%	5.0%	10.2%	-3.7%	-0.2%	6.3%	5.0%	1.3%
	15	5.4%	5.0%	10.4%	5.0%	20.8	389.8	1.3%	18.8x	5.4%	5.0%	10.4%	-3.6%	-0.2%	6.6%	5.0%	1.6%
	16	5.6%	5.0%	10.6%	5.0%	21.8	395.2	1.4%	18.1x	5.6%	5.0%	10.6%	-3.4%	-0.2%	7.0%	5.0%	2.0%
	17	5.8%	5.0%	10.8%	5.0%	22.9	401.1	1.5%	17.5x	5.8%	5.0%	10.8%	-3.3%	-0.2%	7.3%	5.0%	2.3%
	18	6.0%	5.0%	11.0%	5.0%	24.1	407.6	1.6%	16.9x	6.0%	5.0%	11.0%	-3.2%	-0.2%	7.6%	5.0%	2.6%
	19	6.2%	5.0%	11.2%	5.0%	25.3	414.6	1.7%	16.4x	6.2%	5.0%	11.2%	-3.1%	-0.2%	7.9%	5.0%	2.9%
	20	6.4%	5.0%	11.4%	5.0%	26.5	422.1	1.8%	15.9x	6.4%	5.0%	11.4%	-3.0%	-0.2%	8.2%	5.0%	3.2%
	21	6.6%	5.0%	11.6%	5.0%	27.9	430.2	1.9%	15.4x	6.6%	5.0%	11.6%	-2.9%	-0.1%	8.5%	5.0%	3.5%
	22	6.8%	5.0%	11.8%	5.0%	29.3	438.8	2.0%	15.0x	6.8%	5.0%	11.8%	-2.9%	-0.1%	8.8%	5.0%	3.8%
	23	7.0%	5.0%	12.0%	5.0%	30.7	460.7	5.0%	15.0x	7.0%	5.0%	12.0%	0.0%	0.0%	12.0%	5.0%	7.0%
	24	7.0%	5.0%	12.0%	5.0%	32.3	NA	NA	NA	7.0%	5.0%	12.0%	NA	NA	NA	NA	NA
	Arith. mean																
	2-12	6.0%	5.0%	11.0%	5.0%	NM	NM	8.3%	18.2x	6.0%	5.0%	11.0%	3.1%	0.2%	14.3%	5.0%	9.3%
	13-23	6.0%	5.0%	11.0%	5.0%	NM	NM	1.8%	17.2x	6.0%	5.0%	11.0%	-3.0%	-0.2%	7.8%	5.0%	2.8%
	2-23	6.0%	5.0%	11.0%	5.0%	NM	NM	5.1%	17.7x	6.0%	5.0%	11.0%	0.1%	0.0%	11.1%	5.0%	6.1%

Note: All numbers for illustrative purposes only.

6.1.3 Conditional time-variable expected MRP estimates

In a working paper, Richter revisits the determination of the expected MRP based on the return decomposition approach and suggests a concept to determine conditional and time-variable expected MRP estimates[929]. His key argument is related to the problem that the unconditional average MRP based on individual values according to F 6-4 is only a value to which the MRP is expected to converge to. When valuing future cash flows, this unconditional expected MRP estimate may be helpful to determine the appropriate discount rate for a terminal value in the distant future. However, the appropriate discount rate for the short-term cash flows should rely on a different, time-varying expected MRP estimate taking into account the expected convergence of the price level.[930]

In order to provide a conditional expected MRP estimate reflecting the prevailing price level at a specific point in time, Richter (2006a) proposes to use the forward-looking version F 6-2 with expected dividend growth and a specific assumption on the expected price-dividend ratio development. It is assumed that the price-dividend ratio is mean reverting[931] and develops according to the following convergence model[932]:

F 6-6 $m_t^D = \eta m_{t-1}^D + (1-\eta)\overline{m}^D + \varepsilon_t$

The convergence factor can be estimated based on the following regression equation:

F 6-7 $m_t^D - \overline{m}^D = \alpha + \eta\left(m_{t-1}^D - \overline{m}^D\right) + \varepsilon_t$

For the period 1954 to 2002, Richter estimates the convergence factor based on data for the German DAX index to be ~0.768 implying slow convergence over time. Still, the precision of price-dividend ratio forecasts based on this procedure is limited as shown by Richter[933]. Cochrane determines a higher convergence factor for the US market of ~0.9 which is, however, the first-order autocorrelation coefficient of the

---

929 See also Blanchard, O. (1993) for a more complex approach to model the conditional expected MRP development.

930 See Richter, F. (2006a), p. 21.

931 See, e.g., Fama, E./French, F. (2002), pp. 638 and 642. For formal evidence, see also Fama, E./French, F. (1988b), Cochrane, J. (1994), and Lamont, O. (1998).

932 See Richter, F. (2006a), p. 21. See also Richter, F. (2005), p. 107. See also Pastor, L./Sinha, M./Swaminathen (2008), p. 2891 who propose to use the dividend yield to capture time-variation in expected returns.

933 See Richter, F. (2006a), pp. 21-22. See also Richter, F. (2005), p. 107 where a similar convergence factor of 0.816 is estimated for the period 1954-2002.

price-dividend ratio and therefore not directly comparable with the convergence factor calculated by Richter[934].

Based the on convergence approach for the price-dividend ratio by Richter, a conditional and time-variable expected forward return estimate can be determined using F 6-2 for each of the future periods with a consistent set of expected dividend yield, annual dividend growth, and annual price-dividend ratio growth. In order to derive the conditional expected forward MRP estimate, the consistent risk-free forward rate needs to be deducted.

6.2 Methodological considerations

In order to derive the necessary data to apply the decomposition approach for empirical analyses, some methodological aspects need to be further discussed. The dividend yield is a core element of the return decomposition approach. It can be defined as dividends relative to either current or historical prices. In its standard form as calculated by data providers, the dividend yield is measured based on current prices[935]. However, for return purposes the dividend yield must be based on the one-year prior price. This requires the transformation of current price dividend yields into price-lagged (or lagged) dividend yields which can be achieved by the following relationships which deliver identical results:

F 6-8
$$\frac{\tilde{D}_t}{\tilde{P}_{t-1}} = \frac{\tilde{D}_{t-1}\left(1+\tilde{g}_t^D\right)}{\tilde{P}_{t-1}} = \tilde{\delta}_{t-1}\left(1+\tilde{g}_t^D\right)$$
$$\frac{\tilde{D}_t}{\tilde{P}_{t-1}} = \frac{\tilde{D}_t}{\tilde{P}_t/\left(1+\tilde{g}_t^P\right)} = \tilde{\delta}_t\left(1+\tilde{g}_t^P\right)$$

These relationships are of relevance not only for the historical return decomposition but also for the derivation of conditional and time-variable expected MRP estimates.

Another critical element of the historical decomposition analysis is the one period ex-post dividend growth rate of the underlying index. Its precise determination poses several challenges to the empirical researcher. The quality of direct historical dividend growth data in Datastream with respect to completeness and comparability is limited. Furthermore, the replication of the weighted index dividend growth using identical weights compared to the price index is impractical. Therefore, the historical dividend growth rates required for the ex-post return decomposition analysis in this

---

934 See Cochrane, J. (2005), pp. 394, 406, and 408.

935 See, e.g., the Datastream definition of the dividend yield.

study are inferred from the development in the respective index dividend yield. Using the available dividend yield and price return information for the index, the implied index dividend growth can be calculated. Formally, the historical dividend growth can be expressed as follows:

F 6-9
$$\frac{\tilde{D}_t}{\tilde{P}_t} = \frac{\tilde{D}_{t-1}\left(1+\tilde{g}_t^D\right)}{\tilde{P}_{t-1}\left(1+\tilde{g}_t^P\right)}$$
$$\tilde{g}_t^D = \frac{\tilde{D}_t}{\tilde{P}_t}\frac{\tilde{P}_{t-1}}{\tilde{D}_{t-1}}\left(1+\tilde{g}_t^P\right)-1 = \frac{\tilde{\delta}_t}{\tilde{\delta}_{t-1}}\left(1+\tilde{g}_t^P\right)-1$$

A last aspect is related to the risk-free rate. Since the decomposition approach is used with both ex-post as well as ex-ante data, different proxies for the risk-free rate are required. While the historical income return is applied for historical data, the redemption yield is used for ex-ante data. These methodological preparations are the basis for following discussion of results.

6.3 Discussion of results

This section shows the results of applying the previously discussed return decomposition approaches to determine the unconditional and conditional expected MRP estimates. Before the findings of this study are discussed, results from other authors are summarized. This is important as other analyses use longer analysis periods which may increase the data precision. The presented results of this study are based on the same equity indices and risk-free rates as presented in Chapter 3 and are consistent with the ex-post and ex-ante expected MRP data shown in chapters 4 and 5.

6.3.1 Summary of previous studies on unconditional expected MRPs

Previous studies mainly provide estimates for the unconditional expected MRP in the US. The seminal paper by Fama/French (2002) is centered around one key finding: their unconditional expected real MRP estimates based on F 6-4 for dividend and earnings growth of 2.55% (annual 3.83%/long-term 2.55% [936]) and 4.32% (4.78%/3.50%) for the period 1951-2000 is substantially lower than the arithmetic mean of the realized MRP for the same period of 7.43% (7.43%/6.16%)[937] consistent

[936] Adjusted for the bias of 1.28% (0.46%) due to the difference in variances between dividend (earnings) growth estimates and capital gains; see Fama, E./French, K. (2002), p. 654.

[937] See Fama, E./French, K. (2002), p. 641.

with the results from the IRR method. Table 72 summarizes the results of studies providing unconditional expected MRP estimates using a similar return decomposition approach. The finding of a comparatively low and declining expected MRP estimates is generally confirmed. Note that selected studies provide conditional expected MRP estimates using equation F 6-4 assuming market efficiency so that price level changes are zero in expectation[938].

[938] See, e.g., Arnott, R./Ryan, R. (2001), p. 62 and Arnott, R./Bernstein, P. (2002), pp. 65 and 71.

Table 72 **Summary of MRP studies using the decomposition approach with ex-post data**

Authors	Description	Period (denomination)	$E[\tilde{r}]$	r^f	$E[\tilde{r}^p]$
Arnott/Ryan (2001)[939]	• Component approach estimating the unconditional and conditional expected real stock return as the sum of average dividend yield plus expected dividend growth • Simple MRP calculation based on arithmetic averages • r^f equal to the income yield of primarily 10-year government bonds • Ex-post real return benchmark: 8.4% arithmetic mean	1926-1999 Jan 2000 (real values)	6.4% 3.2%	3.7% 4.1%	2.7% -0.9%
Arnott/ Bernstein (2002)[940]	• Component approach estimating the expected real stock return as the average sum of dividend yield plus expected dividend growth • Simple MRP calculation based on arithmetic averages • r^f equal to the income yield of primarily 10-year government bonds • Ex-post real return benchmarks: ~8% arithmetic mean	1810-2001 (real values)	6.1%	3.7%	2.4%
Dimson/ Marsh/ Staunton (2006)[941]	• Component approach estimating the expected real stock return as the sum of average dividend yield plus average historical dividend growth or earnings growth • Geometric MRP calculation based on geometric averages • r^f equal to the yield of government bills • Ex-post return benchmarks: 10.7% geometric/12.6% arithmetic mean	1900-2005 US World (USD) (real values)	 5.7% 5.1%	 1.0% 1.0%	 4.7% 4.1%
Fama/French (2002)[942]	• Component approach estimating the expected real stock return as the sum of average dividend yield plus average historical dividend growth or earnings growth • Based on S&P 500 (results similar for CRSP value-weight portfolio of NYSE, AMEX, and Nasdaq stocks) • Simple MRP calculation based on arithmetic averages • r^f equal to the yield of 3- to 6-months commercial papers • Ex-post real return benchmarks: 8.8% arithmetic mean (MRP 5.6%)	1872-2000 (g^D) 1872-1950 (g^D) 1951-2000 (g^D) 1951-2000 (g^E) (real values)	6.8% 8.1% 4.7% 6.5%	3.2% 3.9% 2.2% 2.2%	3.5% 4.2% 2.6% 4.3%

939 See Arnott, R./Ryan, R. (2001), pp. 62-67.
940 See Arnott, R./Bernstein, P. (2002), pp. 65-78.
941 See Dimson, E./Marsh, P./Staunton, M. (2006), pp. 23-28.
942 See Fama, E./French, K. (2002), pp. 638-643.

Authors	Description	Period (denomination)	$E[\tilde{r}]$	r^f	$E[\tilde{r}^p]$
Ibbotson/ Chen (2003)[943]	• Several component approaches to estimate the expected nominal stock return: e.g., sum of average dividend yield plus average nominal earnings growth • Geometric MRP calculation based on geometric averages • r^f equal to the income yield of long-term government bonds • Ex-post stock return benchmarks: 10.7% geometric/12.6% arithmetic mean	1926-2000 (nominal values)	9.4%	5.2%	4.0%
Jagannathan/ McGrattan/ Scherbina (2000)[944]	• Component approach estimating the unconditional expected real return as the sum of the average historical dividend yield plus expected dividend growth (historical average 5.19%) • Based on S&P 500 • Simple MRP calculation based on arithmetic averages • r^f equal to the income yield of 5-year government bond	1926-1999 (nominal)	9.7%	NA	5.9%
Richter (2005)[945]	• Component approach estimating the expected return as average historical dividend yield and average historical dividend growth • Average historical dividend growth using in-sample concept from 1962-2002 and out-of-sample concept for 1954-2002 (5.24%) • Based on German DAX	1962-2002 In-sample Out-of-sample (nominal values)	 10.6% 8.4%	 NA NA	 NA NA
Siegel (1999)[946]	• Component approach estimating the conditional expected real stock return in 1999 as the sum of current dividend yield plus expected dividend growth (historical average) • Based on S&P 500 • Simple MRP calculation based on arithmetic averages • r^f equal to the income yield of primarily 10 and 30-year treasury inflation-protected securities (TIPS) • Ex-post real stock return benchmark: ~7% geometric mean (1802-1998)	1999 (1871-1998 avg. g^D) 1999 (1946-1998 avg. g^D) (real values)	2.5% 3.3%	~ 4%	-1.5% -0.7%

[943] See Ibbotson, R./Cheng, P. (2003), pp. 94-95.
[944] See Jagannathan, R./McGrattan, E./Scherbina, A. (2000), pp. 4-7, chart 4 and 5, table 2 and 4.
[945] See Richter, F. (2005), p. 131.
[946] See Siegel, J. (1999), pp. 13-14.

In addition to the summary table, some findings of Fama/French (2002) are discussed in further detail. The authors regard their decomposition based expected MRP estimates as more reliable and plausible since an average book-to-price ratio over their analysis period of 0.66 implies a cost of equity below the return on book equity which is not the case for the expected MRP estimates based on ex-post MRP averages. Furthermore, the standard error of the estimate is lower and the Sharpe ratio of the period 1951-2000 is stable compared to a previous sample period from 1872-1950 while the Sharpe ratio for realized MRPs increases in the second period thereby showing an implausible increase in risk aversion[947]. The superior out-of-sample MRP prediction performance of decomposition-based estimates compared to historical MRP averages is also verified in the empirical study by Campbell/Thompson (2008) due to smaller mean-squared prediction errors[948].

In the remainder of their paper, Fama/French investigate the reasons for the divergence in expected MRP estimates from F 6-4 and realized MRP averages. Obviously, the approximation of capital gains through dividends and earnings growth due to the assumed stationarity of the dividend yield and the consequent assumption of no expected price level changes (i.e., $\tilde{g}_t^{m^D} = 0$) is the root of the difference. Therefore, unexpected (i.e., not measured by F 6-4) capital gains due to changes in the dividend yield (or market price level) lead to a divergence in expected MRP estimates[949]. Indeed, the authors find the dividend and earnings yield to decline within the period 1951-2000 from above average levels at the beginning of the period to below average levels at the end[950].

As already discussed, changes in the dividend yield can be related to changes in return and growth expectations. The dividend yield can be expressed as follows when a constant growth dividend discount model is used[951]:

F 6-10 $$\delta_t = \frac{D_t}{P_t} = \frac{r^e - g_D}{1 + g_D}$$

[947] See Fama, E./French, K. (2002), pp. 650-651.

[948] See Campbell, J./Thompson, S. (2008), pp. 1514 and 1517-1521.

[949] See also Arnott, R./Bernstein, P. (2002), p. 66.

[950] See Fama, E./French, K. (2002), pp. 651-652. See also Siegel, J. (1999), pp. 14-15, Jagannathan, R./McGrattan, E./Scherbina, A. (2000), chart 2, Arnott, R./Ryan, R. (2001), p. 62, Arnott, R./Bernstein, P. (2002), pp. 64 and 72-73, and Dimson, E./Marsh, P./Staunton, M. (2006), p. 23.

[951] See also Fama, E./French, F. (1988b), p. 5, Siegel, J. (1999), p. 14, Fama, E./French, F. (2002), pp. 640, 645, and 651, and Richter, F. (2005), p. 130.

When the price level fluctuates over time, this behavior is consequently driven by changes in the expected return (cost of equity) and perpetual growth. If the expected return is assumed to be constant, then changes in the price level would be fully attributable to revisions of the perpetual growth estimates [952]. However, since Fama/French as well as other authors view the long-term dividend (and also earnings) growth as unpredictable, they see no evidence that unexpected changes in long-term dividends or earnings growth explain the unexpected capital gains. Therefore, the authors conclude that the unexpected capital gains resulting from dividend yield contraction are largely attributable to a decline in the expected return[953]. These results are consistent with the findings of Richter for the German market [954]. Ultimately, Fama/French argue that some of the expected return decline may have been expected since the dividend yield was above its unconditional out-of-sample average at the beginning of the analysis period[955].

The Fama/French findings underline that the determination of conditional and time-variable expected returns is important in order to reflect expected price level changes. The introduced Richter concept allows to capture such expected price level changes in the expected return using the forward-looking version F 6-2 as to be demonstrated for the German market in Section 6.3.2.1.

6.3.2 Results for the data set of this study

In the following section, the results of the empirical investigations of this study are presented and discussed. Despite the shorter analysis period, the goal is to verify the key finding of Fama/French (2002) that the lower expected MRP from fundamental models compared to realized MRP averages is related to an increasing price-dividend ratios in the late 1990s[956]. In addition, the presented approach to determine conditional and time-variable expected MRP estimates is illustrated. Since the analysis is identical for all countries, an example for the application is only provided for the German market.

---

952 See Blanchard, O. (1993), p. 82 and Fama, E./French, F. (2002), p. 642.

953 See also Fama, E./French, F. (2002), pp. 640 and 650-653. See also Campbell, J. (1991), Cochrane, J. (1991, 1994), Campbell, J./Shiller, R. (1998), Campbell, J./Thompson, S. (2008), p. 1519, and Cochrane, J. (2008), pp. 1533-1534. For the period 1978 to 1992, Blanchard, O. (1993), p. 83 finds that dividend growth rates do not compensate for a decrease in the dividend yield based on US market data.

954 See Richter, F. (2005), p. 131.

955 See Fama, E./French, K. (2002), pp. 651-652.

956 See Fama, E./French, K. (2002), p. 652.

6.3.2.1 Germany

In a first step to develop an estimate for the unconditional expected MRP, the historical total return of the CDAX is decomposed into its elements dividend yield, dividend growth, and price-dividend ratio expansion according to F 6-1 based on historical data. Table 73 summarizes the decomposition results for the period 1989 to 2006[957]. Out of the historical arithmetic mean return of 11.21%, 2.45% are related to changes in the price-dividend ratio. During the analysis period there is no evidence of a monotonic increase in the market price level. In contrast, the peak of the price-dividend ratio is reached in 1999 and declines thereafter. The average of the ex-post one-period dividend growth rate with 6.74% is above the 5.24% estimate of Richter for the DAX during 1954-2002[958]. Note that an increase of the price-dividend ratio is consistent with negative dividend growth in the same period (e.g., 1993 and 2003). This is plausible since the herein used dividend growth rate is for a historical period only and does not provide any estimate for the long-term dividend growth which influences the price-dividend ratio.

Table 74 continues to compare the unconditional expected MRP estimates resulting from the ex-post and ex-ante decomposition models benchmarked against the arithmetic mean MRP of 5.52% from ex-post returns. Eliminating the impact of the price level on the historical MRPs leads to a lower unconditional expected MRP estimate of 3.07%. The associated unconditional expected return equals 8.77% and compares to Richter's out-of-sample estimate of 8.4% for the period 1962-2002[959]. When using expected dividend growth—dividend growth rate implied by ex-post inflation-based residual income growth—in contrast to the ex-post one-period

---

[957] The decomposition is mainly driven by the lagged dividend yield and price return of the underlying index. Since most index providers offer total as well as price return indices, it would appear most intuitive to derive the price return based on the price index and the dividend yield as difference between total return and price return. However, the calculated lagged dividend yield using this approach is volatile and implies even more volatile and implausible dividend growth rates. Appendix 40 shows the decomposition results using a lagged dividend yield calculated as the difference between the total return and price return on the CDAX. The implausible results for the lagged dividend yield and dividend growth rate are immediately obvious. Due to this issue, lagged dividend yields are used which are implied by directly calculated dividend yields as provided by Datastream and only the price return is used based on the official CDAX index. This leads to a much smoother development of the lagged dividend yield and the dividend growth rate as shown in Table 73. The resulting total returns for the index differ on average only marginally from the official total return of the CDAX performance index. Since the issue is similar for all countries within the sample, the same methodology of using directly calculated dividend yields is used.

[958] See Richter, F. (2005), p. 131.

[959] See Richter, F. (2005), p. 131.

dividend growth, the expected MRP estimate declines further to 1.33%[960]. Note that the ex-ante model should provide similar results to the expected MRP estimates from residual income models due to their origin in the dividend discount model. However, the decomposition-based estimates neglect to reflect the high growth during the explicit forecast period which explains the lower result. In summary, changes in the price level lead to a higher unconditional expected MRP estimate from realized returns compared to models eliminating this effect.

[960] A discussion of the negative conditional expected MRP estimates in the early years of the analysis period is provided in Section 5.9.1 and mainly focused on the potential inconsistent reflection of expected inflation in the nominal risk-free rate and the expected long-term dividends growth rate.

Table 73 Ex-post total return decomposition for Germany 1989-2006

	Ex-post total return			Price-dividend ratios		Ex-post total return components				Ex-post MRP		
							Price return					
Year	Dividend yield (D_t/P_{t-1}) (1)	Price return ($[P_t-P_{t-1}]/P_{t-1}$) (2)	Ex-post return (r_t) (3)	Price-dividend ratio (P_{t-1}/D_t) (4)	Price-dividend ratio (P_t/D_t) (5)	Dividend yield (D_t/P_{t-1})	Dividend growth ($g_{D,t}$)	Price-div. ratio expansion ($g_{m,t}$)	$g_{D,t}*g_{m,t}$	Ex-post return	Risk-free rate (6)	Ex-post MRP
1989	2.40%	34.80%	37.20%	41.68x	56.18x	2.40%	8.08%	24.72%	2.00%	37.20%	7.15%	30.05%
1990	1.91%	-16.72%	-14.82%	52.44x	43.67x	1.91%	7.14%	-22.27%	-1.59%	-14.82%	9.00%	-23.82%
1991	2.34%	2.18%	4.52%	42.74x	43.67x	2.34%	2.18%	0.00%	0.00%	4.52%	8.15%	-3.63%
1992	2.17%	-8.94%	-6.77%	46.14x	42.02x	2.17%	-5.36%	-3.78%	0.20%	-6.77%	7.22%	-13.99%
1993	2.31%	41.66%	43.97%	43.31x	61.35x	2.31%	-2.98%	46.01%	-1.37%	43.97%	5.87%	38.10%
1994	1.66%	-7.46%	-5.80%	60.37x	55.87x	1.66%	1.62%	-8.94%	-0.15%	-5.80%	7.58%	-13.38%
1995	1.97%	2.60%	4.57%	50.76x	52.08x	1.97%	10.05%	-6.77%	-0.68%	4.57%	6.29%	-1.72%
1996	2.05%	19.84%	21.89%	48.80x	58.48x	2.05%	6.73%	12.28%	0.83%	21.89%	6.05%	15.84%
1997	1.97%	38.63%	40.59%	50.80x	70.42x	1.97%	15.12%	20.42%	3.09%	40.59%	5.71%	34.88%
1998	1.63%	13.99%	15.62%	61.35x	69.93x	1.63%	14.79%	-0.70%	-0.10%	15.62%	4.45%	11.17%
1999	1.75%	29.77%	31.52%	57.08x	74.07x	1.75%	22.51%	5.93%	1.33%	31.52%	5.36%	26.16%
2000	1.38%	-11.07%	-9.69%	72.55x	64.52x	1.38%	2.11%	-12.90%	-0.27%	-9.69%	5.09%	-14.78%
2001	1.63%	-19.47%	-17.84%	61.47x	49.50x	1.63%	4.95%	-23.27%	-1.15%	-17.84%	4.98%	-22.82%
2002	1.74%	-40.99%	-39.25%	57.45x	33.90x	1.74%	-13.82%	-31.53%	4.36%	-39.25%	4.71%	-43.96%
2003	2.57%	33.97%	36.54%	38.88x	52.08x	2.57%	-12.81%	53.65%	-6.87%	36.54%	3.90%	32.64%
2004	1.98%	6.27%	8.25%	50.59x	53.76x	1.98%	2.95%	3.23%	0.10%	8.25%	3.73%	4.52%
2005	2.48%	25.07%	27.55%	40.38x	50.51x	2.48%	33.14%	-6.06%	-2.01%	27.55%	3.44%	24.10%
2006	2.48%	21.33%	23.80%	40.40x	49.02x	2.48%	25.00%	-2.94%	-0.74%	23.80%	3.81%	19.99%
Arith. mean	2.02%	9.19%	11.21%	50.95x	54.50x	2.02%	6.74%	2.62%	-0.17%	11.21%	5.69%	5.52%
Geo. mean	2.02%	6.59%	8.62%			2.02%	6.09%	0.47%		8.62%	5.68%	2.68%
St. Dev.	0.35%	23.36%	23.57%	9.28x	10.68x	0.35%	12.27%	22.33%	2.33%	23.57%	1.62%	23.98%

(1) Implied by lagged Datastream CDAX dividend yield.
(2) Based on official CDAX price return.
(3) Implied ex-post total return by adding lagged Datastream dividend yield and official CDAX price return. Differs marginally from official CDAX ex-post total return.
(4) Calculated as Datastream CDAX price-dividend ratio divided by one plus official CDAX price return.
(5) Based on CDAX dividend yield provided by Datastream.
(6) Year-end income return of 10-year government bonds.

Note: All values are stated in nominal terms.

Table 74 Decomposition-based unconditional expected MRP estimates for Germany

	Ex-ante analysis					Adj. ex-post analysis				Ex-post analysis				
Year	**Ex-ante MRP**	Risk-free rate (1)	**Implied cost of equity**	Expected dividend growth (2)	**Dividend yield (D_t/P_{t-1})**	Hist. dividend growth ($g_{D,t}$)	**Ex-post total return adj.**	Risk-free rate (3)	**Implied ex-post adj. MRP**	Price-div. ratio expansion ($g_{m,t}$)	$g_{D,t}{}^*g_{m,t}$	**Ex-post total return**	Risk-free rate (3)	**Implied ex-post MRP**
1989	**1.03%**	6.92%	**7.94%**	5.54%	**2.40%**	8.08%	**10.48%**	7.15%	**3.33%**	24.72%	2.00%	**37.20%**	7.15%	**30.05%**
1990	**-1.31%**	8.61%	**7.30%**	5.39%	**1.91%**	7.14%	**9.04%**	9.00%	**0.04%**	-22.27%	-1.59%	**-14.82%**	9.00%	**-23.82%**
1991	**-1.17%**	8.37%	**7.20%**	4.86%	**2.34%**	2.18%	**4.52%**	8.15%	**-3.63%**	0.00%	0.00%	**4.52%**	8.15%	**-3.63%**
1992	**-0.55%**	7.78%	**7.23%**	5.06%	**2.17%**	-5.36%	**-3.19%**	7.22%	**-10.41%**	-3.78%	0.20%	**-6.77%**	7.22%	**-13.99%**
1993	**0.06%**	6.48%	**6.54%**	4.23%	**2.31%**	-2.98%	**-0.67%**	5.87%	**-6.54%**	46.01%	-1.37%	**43.97%**	5.87%	**38.10%**
1994	**-0.91%**	6.99%	**6.09%**	4.43%	**1.66%**	1.62%	**3.28%**	7.58%	**-4.30%**	-8.94%	-0.15%	**-5.80%**	7.58%	**-13.38%**
1995	**-0.15%**	6.81%	**6.65%**	4.68%	**1.97%**	10.05%	**12.02%**	6.29%	**5.73%**	-6.77%	-0.68%	**4.57%**	6.29%	**-1.72%**
1996	**0.50%**	6.24%	**6.74%**	4.69%	**2.05%**	6.73%	**8.78%**	6.05%	**2.73%**	12.28%	0.83%	**21.89%**	6.05%	**15.84%**
1997	**0.57%**	5.67%	**6.24%**	4.27%	**1.97%**	15.12%	**17.08%**	5.71%	**11.37%**	20.42%	3.09%	**40.59%**	5.71%	**34.88%**
1998	**0.89%**	4.55%	**5.43%**	3.80%	**1.63%**	14.79%	**16.42%**	4.45%	**11.97%**	-0.70%	-0.10%	**15.62%**	4.45%	**11.17%**
1999	**1.15%**	4.62%	**5.77%**	4.02%	**1.75%**	22.51%	**24.26%**	5.36%	**18.90%**	5.93%	1.33%	**31.52%**	5.36%	**26.16%**
2000	**-0.02%**	5.30%	**5.27%**	3.89%	**1.38%**	2.11%	**3.48%**	5.09%	**-1.61%**	-12.90%	-0.27%	**-9.69%**	5.09%	**-14.78%**
2001	**2.36%**	4.87%	**7.23%**	5.60%	**1.63%**	4.95%	**6.58%**	4.98%	**1.60%**	-23.27%	-1.15%	**-17.84%**	4.98%	**-22.82%**
2002	**3.65%**	4.80%	**8.45%**	6.71%	**1.74%**	-13.82%	**-12.08%**	4.71%	**-16.79%**	-31.53%	4.36%	**-39.25%**	4.71%	**-43.96%**
2003	**5.21%**	4.14%	**9.34%**	6.77%	**2.57%**	-12.81%	**-10.23%**	3.90%	**-14.14%**	53.65%	-6.87%	**36.54%**	3.90%	**32.64%**
2004	**3.83%**	4.09%	**7.92%**	5.94%	**1.98%**	2.95%	**4.93%**	3.73%	**1.20%**	3.23%	0.10%	**8.25%**	3.73%	**4.52%**
2005	**4.73%**	3.37%	**8.10%**	5.62%	**2.48%**	33.14%	**35.62%**	3.44%	**32.17%**	-6.06%	-2.01%	**27.55%**	3.44%	**24.10%**
2006	**4.03%**	3.81%	**7.85%**	5.37%	**2.48%**	25.00%	**27.48%**	3.81%	**23.67%**	-2.94%	-0.74%	**23.80%**	3.81%	**19.99%**
Arith. mean	**1.33%**	5.74%	**7.07%**	5.05%	**2.02%**	6.74%	**8.77%**	5.69%	**3.07%**	2.62%	-0.17%	**11.21%**	5.69%	**5.52%**

(1) Year-average redemption yield of 10-year government bonds.
(2) Implied year-average dividend growth rate assuming ex-post inflation based residual income growth.
(3) Year-end income return of 10-year government bonds.

Note: All values are stated in nominal terms.

As already indicated, the previously presented approach to estimate a conditional and time-variable expected MRP shall be illustratively applied for the German data set. The following example does not intend to provide expected forward MRPs that can be generally used for valuation purposes at all times. Due to the assumed dependence on the current price level of the market, the conditional expected forward MRPs need to be calculated individually for each valuation date and the following example only shows an illustrative expected forward curve of the MRP for historical valuation dates.

The previous paragraphs show that the estimate for the unconditional expected MRP in a flat price level environment is between 1.33% and 3.07% dependent on the used dividend growth rate. However, these levels can only be used as expected MRP estimates if MRPs are assumed to be independent from each other. When the expected MRPs are assumed to be dependent on the market price level measured by a mean-reverting price-dividend ratio, then the unconditional estimate provides only an indication to which level the expected MRP should converge to. In Section 6.1.3, a framework was developed to model the behavior of the expected MRP over time using the return decomposition methodology. The cornerstone of this approach is the assumed convergence of the price-dividend ratio to its unconditional in-sample mean over time. Datastream provides price-dividend ratios for the CDAX since 1973 allowing for in-sample averages from 1973 to the respective estimation date[961].

Table 75 shows the illustrative calculations of the conditional expected forward MRPs for the example years 2000 and 2002 and a forecast period of 10 years. The input parameters are the current and forecasted price-dividend ratio based on the in-sample convergence factor and the expected dividend growth rates based on IBES dividend growth until period +3 and implied perpetual dividend growth thereafter[962]. In order to be consistent with the IRR approach, the perpetual dividend growth rate is based on the rate implied by ex-post inflation-based perpetual residual earnings growth. Applying the return decomposition formula F 6-2 results in the conditional

---

[961] In-sample means that only occurances are included that are observable at the valuation date, e.g., for the estimation in the year 2000, the in-sample average includes observations from 1973 to 2000.

[962] Note that the IBES dividend growth rate for period +1 cannot be determined since IBES does not provide data for period 0 with a consistent definition. Therefore, the growth rate +1 is assumed to be equal to the growth rate +2. Since IBES dividend growth rates for the periods +4 and +5 are very volatile due to insufficient explicit dividend forecasts, the implied perpetual dividend growth rate is already applied from period +4 onwards. The underlying IBES dividend data is identical to the data used in Chapter 5 which is summarized in Appendix 11 and Appendix 12.

expected forward return. The conditional expected MRP can now be derived by deducting the risk-free forward rate implied by the term structure curve of risk-free spot rates. The example calculation for 2002 (2000) shows the impact of the price level convergence on the expected forward MRP from a below (above) average conditional starting level. Thereby, the impact of the anticipated price level change can be reflected in the MRP expectation already at the valuation date resulting in higher (lower) estimates during the convergence period compared to a constant unconditional average. The final column "steady" of Table 75 shows the expected target MRP level after completing the convergence to the unconditional average price-dividend ratio. The table also provides the spot rates implied by the calculated expected forward MRP curve.

In order to analyze the sensitivity of the conditional expected MRP estimates to the persistence of the price-dividend ratio, Table 76 shows expected MRP estimates at various convergence factors between zero and one for the year 2000. Thereby, a zero convergence factor implies immediate price level convergence to the unconditional average. A convergence factor of one is consistent with the efficient markets hypothesis implying no predictability and an expected change in the price level of zero. It is obvious that a lower convergence factor accelerates the convergence to the expected MRP implied by the unconditional average price-dividend ratio. This analysis also shows that the conditional expected MRP is time-variable even when there is no change in the price level due to the fluctuating dividend growth rates until period +3[963].

[963] See also Richter, F. (2006a), p. 24.

Table 75 Calculation of conditional/time-variable expected MRP estimates

Year		0	+1	+2	+3	+4	+5	+6	+7	+8	+9	+10	Steady
Example 2000	**Price-div. ratio (P_t/D_t)**	**64.52x**	**61.48x**	**58.90x**	**56.71x**	**54.84x**	**53.26x**	**51.91x**	**50.76x**	**49.79x**	**48.96x**	**48.26x**	**44.25x**
	Convergence factor	**0.850**											
	Exp. dividend yield (D_t/P_{t-1})		1.65%	1.73%	1.85%	1.84%	1.91%	1.96%	2.01%	2.06%	2.10%	2.14%	2.36%
	Exp. dividend growth ($g_{D,t}$)		6.15%	6.15%	8.92%	4.57%	4.57%	4.57%	4.57%	4.57%	4.57%	4.57%	4.57%
	Exp. price-div. ratio expansion ($g_{m,t}$)		-4.70%	-4.20%	-3.72%	-3.29%	-2.89%	-2.53%	-2.21%	-1.92%	-1.66%	-1.44%	0.00%
	Exp. $g_{D,t}$*$g_{m,t}$		-0.29%	-0.26%	-0.33%	-0.15%	-0.13%	-0.12%	-0.10%	-0.09%	-0.08%	-0.07%	0.00%
	Expected return (r_t) forward		**2.80%**	**3.42%**	**6.71%**	**2.98%**	**3.46%**	**3.89%**	**4.28%**	**4.62%**	**4.93%**	**5.20%**	**6.94%**
	Expected return (r_t) spot		**2.80%**	**3.11%**	**4.30%**	**3.97%**	**3.86%**	**3.87%**	**3.93%**	**4.01%**	**4.12%**	**4.22%**	
	Risk-free rate (r_t^f) forward (3)		4.65%	4.46%	4.55%	4.72%	4.92%	5.11%	5.25%	5.30%	5.24%	5.03%	5.03%
	Risk-free rate (r_t^f) spot (3)		4.65%	4.56%	4.56%	4.60%	4.66%	4.74%	4.81%	4.87%	4.91%	4.92%	
	Expected MRP (r_t^P) forward		**-1.85%**	**-1.04%**	**2.16%**	**-1.74%**	**-1.46%**	**-1.23%**	**-0.97%**	**-0.67%**	**-0.30%**	**0.17%**	**1.90%**
	Expected MRP (r_t^P) spot		**-1.85%**	**-1.44%**	**-0.26%**	**-0.63%**	**-0.80%**	**-0.87%**	**-0.89%**	**-0.86%**	**-0.80%**	**-0.70%**	
	Discount factor forward-based (1)		0.972735	0.940551	0.881410	0.855919	0.827323	0.796352	0.763681	0.729922	0.695611	0.661204	
	Discount factor spot-based (2)		0.972735	0.940558	0.881433	0.855959	0.827380	0.796418	0.763747	0.729980	0.695655	0.661241	
Example 2002	**Price-div. ratio (P_t/D_t)**	**33.90x**	**35.94x**	**37.57x**	**38.88x**	**39.92x**	**40.76x**	**41.42x**	**41.96x**	**42.38x**	**42.72x**	**43.00x**	**44.08x**
	Convergence factor	**0.799**											
	Exp. dividend yield (D_t/P_{t-1})		3.24%	3.06%	2.94%	2.70%	2.63%	2.57%	2.53%	2.50%	2.47%	2.45%	2.38%
	Exp. dividend growth ($g_{D,t}$)		9.87%	9.87%	10.59%	4.80%	4.80%	4.80%	4.80%	4.80%	4.80%	4.80%	4.80%
	Exp. price-div. ratio expansion ($g_{m,t}$)		6.03%	4.54%	3.47%	2.68%	2.09%	1.64%	1.29%	1.02%	0.80%	0.64%	0.00%
	Exp. $g_{D,t}$*$g_{m,t}$		0.59%	0.45%	0.37%	0.13%	0.10%	0.08%	0.06%	0.05%	0.04%	0.03%	0.00%
	Expected return (r_t) forward		**19.73%**	**17.91%**	**17.37%**	**10.31%**	**9.61%**	**9.09%**	**8.68%**	**8.36%**	**8.11%**	**7.92%**	**7.18%**
	Expected return (r_t) spot		**19.73%**	**18.82%**	**18.33%**	**16.27%**	**14.91%**	**13.92%**	**13.15%**	**12.54%**	**12.04%**	**11.62%**	
	Risk-free rate (r_t^f) forward (3)		2.64%	2.92%	3.51%	4.03%	4.44%	4.75%	4.96%	5.11%	5.19%	5.24%	5.24%
	Risk-free rate (r_t^f) spot (3)		2.64%	2.78%	3.02%	3.27%	3.51%	3.71%	3.89%	4.04%	4.17%	4.28%	
	Expected MRP (r_t^P) forward		**17.08%**	**15.00%**	**13.86%**	**6.28%**	**5.17%**	**4.34%**	**3.72%**	**3.25%**	**2.92%**	**2.68%**	**1.93%**
	Expected MRP (r_t^P) spot		**17.08%**	**16.03%**	**15.31%**	**12.98%**	**11.37%**	**10.17%**	**9.22%**	**8.46%**	**7.83%**	**7.30%**	
	Discount factor forward-based (1)		0.835238	0.708348	0.603501	0.547108	0.499121	0.457552	0.421016	0.388529	0.359369	0.332995	
	Discount factor spot-based (2)		0.835238	0.708364	0.603563	0.547490	0.499790	0.458459	0.422111	0.389762	0.360694	0.334375	

(1) $\left(1 + r^f_{t,t+1} + r^P_{t,t+1}\right)\left(1 + r^f_{t+1,t+2} + r^P_{t+1,t+2}\right)\ldots\left(1 + r^f_{T-1,T} + r^P_{T-1,T}\right)$.

(2) $\left(1 + r^f_{t,T} + r^P_{t,T}\right)^T$.

(3) Based on year-end risk-free rates.

Table 76 Conditional/time-variable expected MRP estimates at various convergence factors

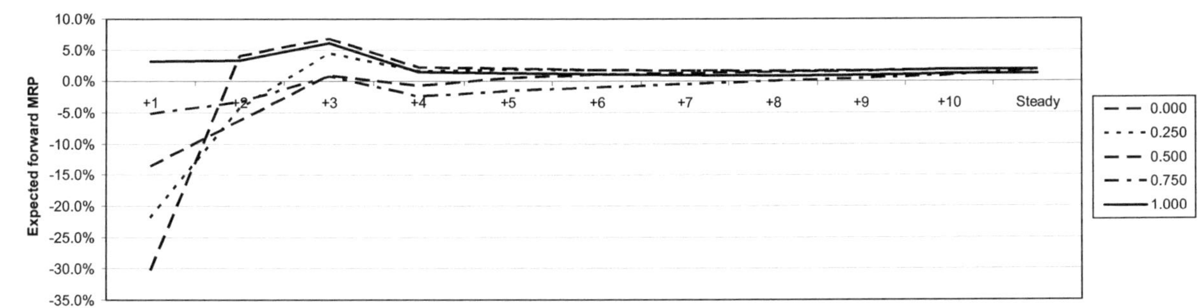

Year	Sensitivities	Conv. Factor	+1	+2	+3	+4	+5	+6	+7	+8	+9	+10	Steady
Example	Exp. price-dividend ratio (P_t/D_t)	0.000	44.25x	44.25x	44.25x	44.25x	44.25x	44.25x	44.25x	44.25x	44.25x	44.25x	44.25x
2000	Exp. dividend yield (D_t/P_{t-1})		1.65%	2.40%	2.46%	2.36%	2.36%	2.36%	2.36%	2.36%	2.36%	2.36%	2.36%
	Expected MRP (r_t^P) forward		-30.19%	4.08%	6.82%	2.21%	2.02%	1.82%	1.69%	1.64%	1.70%	1.90%	1.90%
	Expected MRP (r_t^P) spot		-30.19%	-14.76%	-8.10%	-5.62%	-4.14%	-3.17%	-2.49%	-1.99%	-1.58%	-1.24%	
	Exp. price-dividend ratio (P_t/D_t)	0.250	49.32x	45.52x	44.57x	44.33x	44.27x	44.26x	44.25x	44.25x	44.25x	44.25x	44.25x
	Exp. dividend yield (D_t/P_{t-1})		1.65%	2.15%	2.39%	2.35%	2.36%	2.36%	2.36%	2.36%	2.36%	2.36%	2.36%
	Expected MRP (r_t^P) forward		-21.86%	-4.34%	4.48%	1.64%	1.87%	1.79%	1.68%	1.64%	1.70%	1.90%	1.90%
	Expected MRP (r_t^P) spot		-21.86%	-13.54%	-7.91%	-5.61%	-4.16%	-3.19%	-2.51%	-2.00%	-1.60%	-1.25%	
	Exp. price-dividend ratio (P_t/D_t)	0.500	54.38x	49.32x	46.79x	45.52x	44.89x	44.57x	44.41x	44.33x	44.29x	44.27x	44.25x
	Exp. dividend yield (D_t/P_{t-1})		1.65%	1.95%	2.21%	2.24%	2.30%	2.33%	2.35%	2.35%	2.36%	2.36%	2.36%
	Expected MRP (r_t^P) forward		-13.52%	-6.25%	0.98%	-0.74%	0.49%	1.05%	1.30%	1.45%	1.60%	1.86%	1.90%
	Expected MRP (r_t^P) spot		-13.52%	-9.96%	-6.45%	-5.06%	-3.97%	-3.15%	-2.53%	-2.04%	-1.64%	-1.30%	
	Exp. price-dividend ratio (P_t/D_t)	0.750	59.45x	55.65x	52.80x	50.66x	49.06x	47.86x	46.96x	46.28x	45.77x	45.39x	44.25x
	Exp. dividend yield (D_t/P_{t-1})		1.65%	1.79%	1.96%	1.98%	2.06%	2.13%	2.19%	2.23%	2.26%	2.28%	2.36%
	Expected MRP (r_t^P) forward		-5.19%	-3.31%	0.74%	-2.40%	-1.59%	-0.97%	-0.46%	0.00%	0.45%	0.96%	1.90%
	Expected MRP (r_t^P) spot		-5.19%	-4.26%	-2.62%	-2.56%	-2.37%	-2.14%	-1.90%	-1.67%	-1.43%	-1.20%	
	Exp. price-dividend ratio (P_t/D_t)	1.000	64.52x	64.52x	64.52x	64.52x	64.52x	64.52x	64.52x	64.52x	64.52x	64.52x	64.52x
	Exp. dividend yield (D_t/P_{t-1})		1.65%	1.65%	1.69%	1.62%	1.62%	1.62%	1.62%	1.62%	1.62%	1.62%	1.62%
	Expected MRP (r_t^P) forward		3.15%	3.33%	6.05%	1.47%	1.27%	1.08%	0.94%	0.90%	0.96%	1.16%	1.16%
	Expected MRP (r_t^P) spot		3.15%	3.24%	4.17%	3.49%	3.04%	2.71%	2.46%	2.26%	2.11%	2.02%	

Table 77 continues to show conditional expected MRP estimates over time to their steady state price-dividend ratio level for all year-ends analyzed within this study. Since the current price-dividend ratio is larger than the in-sample average for all years except 2002, the assumed convergence of the price-dividend ratio has mostly a negative impact on the conditional expected forward MRP. Furthermore, until the year 2000, the expected forward MRPs are mostly negative throughout the ten-year forecast horizon (only 1993 and 1996 have a positive expected spot MRP over the ten year horizon) [964]. Long-term expected forward MRPs after completing the convergence to the in-sample average price-dividend ratio are all positive as shown in column "steady". Despite positive long-term MRPs, these results imply that investors, in particular with short-term investment horizons, used a different model or a convergence factor closer to one in order to develop expectations of the price-dividend ratio development since negative expected forward MRPs are inconsistent with the general assumption of risk-averse investors[965].

In summary, the Richter approach to derive time-variable expected forward MRPs can be easily applied for empirical purposes. Still, the underlying model for the price-dividend ratio convergence is inconsistent with the assumption of risk-averse investors during selected periods as evidenced by negative expected forward MRPs.

---

[964] See also Richter, F. (2006a), p. 28 who also identified negative expected forward MRPs in several years.

[965] However, it may also be possible that investors had different expectations of perpetual dividend growth or the risk-free rate; see Richter, F. (2006a), p. 25.

Table 77 Conditional/time-variable expected MRP estimates for Germany

Assumptions	
Starting year for in-sample averages - P_t/D_t and conv. factor	1973
Starting year for in-sample average - g^D	1989

						Expected MRP											
						Forward rates											
						IBES dividend growth rates			Implied perpetual dividend growth rate								
Year	Forward r^f +10	In-sample avg. exp. perp. g^D	**Current P_t/D_t**	In-sample avg. P_t/D_t	**In-sample conv. factor (1)**	+1	+2	+3	+4	+5	+6	+7	+8	+9	+10	**Steady (2)**	Spot rate +10 (3)
1989	5.65%	5.54%	**56.18x**	35.47x	**0.784**	-6.42%	-4.83%	-5.35%	-4.86%	-3.87%	-2.94%	-2.01%	-1.01%	0.07%	1.29%	**2.87%**	-3.02%
1990	7.87%	5.47%	**43.67x**	35.93x	**0.692**	-8.87%	-7.07%	-2.05%	-3.18%	-2.55%	-2.02%	-1.53%	-1.02%	-0.42%	0.25%	**0.53%**	-2.89%
1991	7.53%	5.26%	**43.67x**	36.33x	**0.697**	-6.41%	-4.51%	6.91%	-2.18%	-1.31%	-0.71%	-0.30%	-0.06%	0.21%	0.36%	**0.63%**	-0.85%
1992	7.86%	5.21%	**42.02x**	36.62x	**0.696**	-5.53%	-3.52%	0.40%	-0.34%	-0.04%	0.05%	0.06%	0.04%	0.03%	0.03%	**0.23%**	-0.90%
1993	6.10%	5.02%	**61.35x**	37.79x	**0.743**	14.11%	17.14%	17.12%	-3.42%	-2.56%	-1.95%	-1.48%	-1.01%	-0.39%	0.48%	**1.70%**	3.50%
1994	7.59%	4.92%	**55.87x**	38.62x	**0.735**	-4.17%	-3.53%	3.91%	-4.97%	-4.01%	-3.20%	-2.49%	-1.86%	-1.31%	-0.79%	**0.04%**	-2.27%
1995	6.31%	4.89%	**52.08x**	39.20x	**0.733**	-2.22%	-1.07%	2.36%	-1.90%	-1.74%	-1.54%	-1.26%	-0.83%	-0.20%	0.65%	**1.25%**	-0.78%
1996	6.20%	4.86%	**58.48x**	40.01x	**0.766**	9.98%	10.98%	2.21%	-2.91%	-2.65%	-2.36%	-1.97%	-1.44%	-0.73%	0.19%	**1.28%**	1.02%
1997	6.16%	4.80%	**70.42x**	41.22x	**0.839**	-1.65%	-1.43%	0.03%	-3.74%	-3.29%	-2.82%	-2.35%	-1.90%	-1.55%	-1.30%	**1.18%**	-2.00%
1998	3.67%	4.70%	**69.93x**	42.33x	**0.855**	0.38%	0.91%	1.82%	-1.63%	-1.42%	-1.22%	-0.96%	-0.54%	0.11%	1.08%	**3.50%**	-0.15%
1999	6.10%	4.63%	**74.07x**	43.50x	**0.888**	0.26%	-0.27%	0.92%	-3.06%	-2.87%	-2.66%	-2.43%	-2.20%	-1.98%	-1.80%	**0.95%**	-1.62%
2000	5.03%	4.57%	**64.52x**	44.25x	**0.850**	-1.85%	-1.04%	2.16%	-1.74%	-1.46%	-1.23%	-0.97%	-0.67%	-0.30%	0.17%	**1.90%**	-0.70%
2001	5.67%	4.65%	**49.50x**	44.43x	**0.811**	4.30%	3.98%	8.56%	0.71%	0.68%	0.72%	0.80%	0.88%	0.95%	0.96%	**1.33%**	2.22%
2002	5.24%	4.80%	**33.90x**	44.08x	**0.799**	17.08%	15.00%	13.86%	6.28%	5.17%	4.34%	3.72%	3.25%	2.92%	2.68%	**1.93%**	7.30%
2003	5.47%	4.93%	**52.08x**	44.34x	**0.776**	19.47%	19.53%	6.81%	1.07%	1.16%	1.29%	1.43%	1.52%	1.52%	1.37%	**1.83%**	5.29%
2004	4.51%	4.99%	**53.76x**	44.63x	**0.779**	9.68%	10.11%	8.18%	1.60%	1.78%	1.92%	2.03%	2.12%	2.21%	2.30%	**2.84%**	4.14%
2005	3.57%	5.03%	**50.51x**	44.81x	**0.777**	9.33%	9.72%	7.85%	2.70%	2.93%	3.08%	3.19%	3.29%	3.38%	3.50%	**3.81%**	4.86%
2006	3.87%	5.05%	**49.02x**	44.94x	**0.776**	8.21%	8.65%	6.97%	2.41%	2.63%	2.79%	2.91%	3.02%	3.15%	3.29%	**3.52%**	4.38%
Arith. mean	5.80%	4.96%	**54.50x**	41.03x	**0.778**	3.09%	3.82%	4.59%	-1.06%	-0.75%	-0.47%	-0.20%	0.09%	0.43%	0.82%	**1.74%**	0.97%

(1) Based on OLS regressions.
(2) Implied expected MRPs after completed convergence to in-sample average.
(3) Implied spot rate by the ten individual forward MRPs.

6.3.2.2 Canada

The historical return decomposition for the Canadian market presented in Table 78 shows a 2.15% price level impact on the arithmetic average return of 11.08%. This is a consequence of the end-of-period price-dividend ratios remaining above the price level before the peak in 2000. Interestingly, from 2004 to 2006 the price-dividend ratio declines despite high returns of the price index implying over proportionate dividend growth during this period. The average historical dividend growth rate of 6.60% is on a very similar level compared to the previously discussed results for Germany. Eliminating the price level effect reduces the unconditional expected MRP estimate from realized returns of 4.51% to 2.36% based on historical dividend growth. When using expected dividend growth, the premium estimate is at 1.96%. Similarly to the IRR-based results, an upward trend can be identified in the conditional expected MRP estimate over time (see Appendix 42).

6.3.2.3 France

The analysis of the price-dividend ratio development for the French market presented in Table 78 shows a mean-reverting behavior with similar levels reached both before and after the peak in 1999/2000. Consequently, the impact of price level changes on the ex-post total return of 12.78% is minimal. Compared to the previous countries, the historical dividend growth rate is at a substantially higher level with an average of 9.80%. With respect to the unconditional expected MRP estimates, there is only a slight difference between the ex-post average MRP (6.73%) and the adjusted ex-post average MRP neglecting the impact of price level changes (6.92%). Due to the lower expected dividend growth rates compared to the comparatively high historical rates, the unconditional expected MRP estimate of the ex-ante analysis is at 3.23%. Again, an increasing trend in the conditional expected MRP estimates can be observed over time with an obvious negative relationship to the risk-free rate (see Appendix 44).

6.3.2.4 Japan

The extraordinary characteristics of Japan within the country sample of this study become again obvious when analyzing the return decomposition results in Table 78[966]. Despite a similar peak of the price-dividend ratio in 1999 compared to other

---

[966] Other aspects such as the comparatively low interest environment were already discussed in Section 3.4.

countries, higher levels were achieved not at the end but at the beginning of the analysis period. This explains that in case of Japan the change in price level does not have an expansionary effect on the arithmetic average of realized returns in the amount of 1.82% but rather contracts the return by 2.11%. The observed dividend growth of 3.06% is comparatively low. Eliminating the negative effects of price level changes results in a low positive unconditional expected MRP estimate of 0.94% compared to the negative average historical premium of -1.17%. Higher expected dividend growth rates result in an unconditional ex-ante MRP estimate of 1.85%.

6.3.2.5 United Kingdom

The historical return decomposition for the UK market, as shown in Table 78, again reveals the impact of an, on average, increasing price level. While the price-dividend ratio declines post the peak in 1999, it remains on a higher level compared to the pre-peak period. This development may indicate that there is a permanent shift in the average price-dividend ratio implying non-stationarity during the period. The price level impact of 3.83% on the ex-post total return of 12.07% is therefore substantial. This results in a high discrepancy of the unconditional expected MRP between the historical average of 5.30% and price level adjusted average of 1.47%. With slightly higher expected dividend growth, the unconditional expected MRP estimate increases to 2.36%.

6.3.2.6 United States

The historical return decomposition for the US market, as presented in Table 78, shows an even stronger impact of the change in price-dividend ratio compared to the UK market. These findings confirm the trend to decreasing dividend yields indentified by Fama/French (2002). With price level related components of the total average ex-post return in the amount of 4.70%, there is an indication of non-stationarity of the price-dividend ratio during the analysis period. Similarly to the UK, the price-dividend ratio before the peak in 2000 is consistently lower than thereafter. The unconditional average US price-dividend ratio of 21.55x for the period 1872-2000 estimated by Fama/French[967] compared to the average of the analysis period of 51.35x is a further

[967] See Fama, E./French, K. (2002), p. 651. The authors provide an average dividend yield of 4.64% for 1872-2000. See also Cochrane, J. (2005), p. 408 who uses an unconditional average dividend yield of 4%.

indication that the average price-dividend ratio may have shifted upwards. Even in the post peak period, the price-dividend ratio was consistently above 50x. As a consequence, the unconditional expected MRP neglecting price level effects of 2.70% is substantially below the average historical MRP of 7.40%. Due to almost identical historical and expected dividend growth rates, the ex-ante and ex-post expected MRP estimates are very similar. These findings appear consistent with the results of comparable studies summarized in Section 6.3.1.

Table 78 **Decomposition based unconditional expected MRP estimates and price-dividend ratio development for all countries**

Arithmetic means (1989-2006)

	Ex-ante analysis					Adj. ex-post analysis				Ex-post analysis					
Country	**Ex-ante MRP**	Risk-free rate (1)	**Implied cost of equity**	Expected dividend growth (2)	**Dividend yield (D_t/P_{t-1})**	Hist. dividend growth ($g_{D,t}$)	**Ex-post total return adj.**	Risk-free rate (3)	**Implied ex-post adj. MRP**	Price-div. ratio expansion ($g_{m,t}$)	$g_{D,t}*g_{m,t}$	**Ex-post total return**	Risk-free rate (3)	**Implied ex-post MRP**	Impact of price-div. ratio
Canada	**1.96%**	6.68%	**8.63%**	6.30%	**2.33%**	6.60%	**8.93%**	6.57%	**2.36%**	3.12%	-0.96%	**11.08%**	6.57%	**4.51%**	2.15%
France	**3.23%**	6.07%	**9.30%**	6.14%	**3.16%**	9.80%	**12.96%**	6.05%	**6.92%**	0.25%	-0.43%	**12.78%**	6.05%	**6.73%**	-0.19%
Germany	**1.33%**	5.74%	**7.07%**	5.05%	**2.02%**	6.74%	**8.77%**	5.69%	**3.07%**	2.62%	-0.17%	**11.21%**	5.69%	**5.52%**	2.45%
Japan	**1.85%**	2.99%	**4.83%**	3.97%	**0.87%**	3.06%	**3.93%**	2.99%	**0.94%**	-1.67%	-0.44%	**1.82%**	2.99%	**-1.17%**	-2.11%
UK	**2.36%**	6.83%	**9.19%**	5.45%	**3.73%**	4.51%	**8.25%**	6.77%	**1.47%**	3.97%	-0.14%	**12.07%**	6.77%	**5.30%**	3.83%
US	**2.74%**	5.99%	**8.73%**	6.39%	**2.34%**	6.17%	**8.51%**	5.81%	**2.70%**	4.29%	0.41%	**13.20%**	5.81%	**7.40%**	4.70%

(1) Year-average redemption yield of 10-year government bonds.
(2) Implied year-average dividend growth rate assuming ex-post inflation based residual income growth.
(3) Year-end income return of 10-year government bonds.

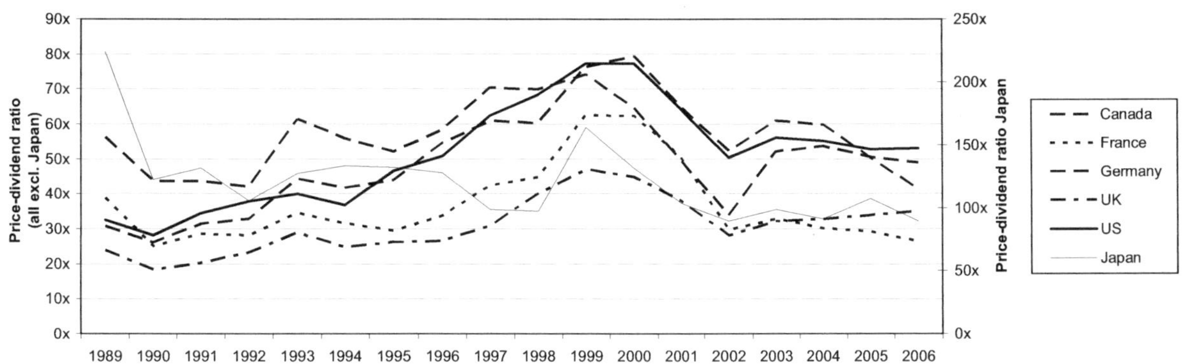

Note: See Appendix 41 to Appendix 50 for the underlying data tables.

6.4 Conclusions

The role of the market price level for the estimation of the expected MRP is an often neglected topic in the recently published literature on the expected MRP[968]. It was shown how price level changes lead to a distortion of unconditional ex-post MRP averages and how to eliminate the bias using the return decomposition approach using ex-post as well as ex-ante data. Ultimately, a practicable concept to estimate conditional and time-variable expected MRPs was presented.

- During 1989 to 2006, decreases in dividend yields have inflated the unconditional averages of realized MRPs in all countries except Japan. The strongest impact can be observed for the US market with 4.70% out of an average realized MRP of 7.40% being related to changes in the price-dividend ratio. The influence for the German market was lower but still considerable with 2.45% out of a realized MRP average of 5.52% being attributable to changes in the price level.
- Consequently, the adjusted unconditional expected MRP estimates using the return decomposition approach are, similarly to the IRR-based estimates, lower than the realized ex-post averages. Depending on whether using ex-post or ex-ante dividend growth, the expected MRP estimates range between 1.33% and 3.07% for Germany and between 2.70% and 2.74% for the US. The estimates for the remaining countries are summarized in the following table:

Table 79 Summary of decomposition based unconditional expected MRP estimates

	Unconditional mean expected MRP (1)					
Dividend growth rate	Canada	France	Germany	Japan	UK	US
Ex-post dividend growth	2.36%	6.92%	3.07%	0.94%	1.47%	2.70%
Ex-ante dividend growth (2)	1.96%	3.23%	1.33%	1.85%	2.36%	2.74%

(1) All values are stated in nominal terms.
(2) Implied average expected dividend growth rate assuming ex-post inflation-based residual income growth.

- The distortion of realized MRP estimates during periods of non-stationary price-dividend ratios is related to unexpected capital gains that increase/decrease the initially expected MRP. Such capital gains are unexpected if markets are assumed to follow random walks implying independent MRPs.

Empirical evidence suggests that expected returns are being dependent on the current market price level. In order to reflect expected price level changes in the

[968] See, e.g., Daske, H./Gebhardt, G./Klein, S. (2006), Daske, H./Gebhardt, G. (2006), and Reese, R. (2007).

expected MRP estimate, Richter (2006a) proposed a practicable approach with the following key characteristics:

- The approach is based on a forward-looking version of the return decomposition formula and uses an integrated set of input parameters consisting of expected dividend yield, dividend growth, and change in price-dividend ratio as well as the forward risk-free rate.
- The price-dividend ratio is assumed to converge to its unconditional in-sample mean at an empirically determined convergence rate which is low due to the persistence of the price-dividend ratio. The low precision of the convergence factor needs to be refined in further research.
- A further issue of the approach is related to empirical evidence that for selected historical estimation dates, the estimated expected forward MRPs were negative during the ten year forecast period. Since negative expected MRPs are inconsistent with the assumption of risk-averse investors, the general validity of the price-dividend convergence model is questionable.

Besides the Richter approach to determine time-variable expected MRPs, the IRR-based concept also provides conditional but constant expected MRP estimates. When assuming that market prices include a convergence from abnormally high or low price levels, then, despite being constant, the IRR-based expected MRP incorporates the MRP convergence in one weighted-average rate[969] which can be interpreted as an infinite spot rate. However, price level dependent expected returns violate the assumption of i.i.d. returns so that the estimated IRR equals the expected return. On the contrary, the Richter approach allows to explicitly model the forward development of the conditional expected MRP. Still, the empirical results have shown that the underlying model for the convergence of the price-dividend ratio needs to be developed further in order to increase the precision of expected MRP estimates.

[969] See Lambert, R. (2009), p. 267.

7 Summarizing theses

The expected MRP is a crucial parameter in financial decision making in particular for corporate valuations using risk-adjusted discount rates. Despite its importance, there is no consensus on the correct measurement of the expected MRP due to the restrictive assumptions on distributional as well as time-series properties required for different approaches. Consequently, leading textbooks differ in their recommendation which methodology to use in order to determine the expected MRP. So far, different measurement approaches have been primarily discussed in isolation neglecting the interdependences with other methodologies. In contrast, this dissertation covers several frequently used measurement methodologies and classifies them according to the criteria unconditional vs. conditional estimates and ex-post vs. ex-ante data. In addition to a conceptual review of these key methodologies, empirical evidence is provided for applying each methodology using data from key global equity markets. A special focus is thereby put on expected MRP estimates that are conditional on the current market price level. Ultimately, the implications of each methodology for corporate valuations are discussed.

Selecting the appropriate methodology is crucial to determine estimates for the expected MRP. For the three approaches discussed in this study, assumptions are required with respect to the dependence, stationarity, and time-variability of MRPs. Firstly, using unconditional averages of ex-post MRPs assumes independence and stationarity of MRPs and a constant expected MRP. Secondly, the IRR-based methodology can be applied under independence and constancy by calculating the unconditional average of ex-post expected MRPs while stationarity is not required. However, it also allows for conditional estimates which are constant but dependent on the current market price level. Thirdly, the return decomposition approach can be applied for independent as well as dependent MRP distributions. Furthermore, when the expected MRP is assumed to be dependent on the market price level, this methodology can be used to determine time-variable expected MRP estimates.

In addition to the underlying assumptions, further findings on conceptual as well as empirical aspects for all three estimation procedures are important when using expected MRP estimates for valuation purposes.

- The results from studies measuring the expected MRP as an average of ex-post MRPs assuming independence, stationarity, and constancy are non-uniform due to several measurement issues primarily with regards to averaging methodology and measurement period.

- The arithmetic mean is the correct unbiased estimator when (log) return/MRP distributions are i.i.d. normal and if there is certainty about the return/MRP distribution parameters. Under parameter uncertainty, an unbiased estimator for compounding is provided by the arithmetic mean, if the horizon is only one period, or by the geometric mean, if the horizon equals the number of observations. In all other multi-period compounding scenarios or generally for discounting neither the arithmetic nor the geometric average are unbiased estimators of the true result. Unbiased estimators can be derived through a combination of both averages which have, however, only plausible values at long compounding/discounting horizons for i.i.d. normal log-returns/MRPs.
- For practical purposes, the consideration of estimation errors for the MRP determination appears questionable since similar errors for other components of the cost of capital or cash flows are typically not recognized and since the multi-period usage of the CAPM requires a deterministic expected MRP which is inconsistent with measurement errors due to uncertain distribution parameters.
- Based on the assumption of i.i.d. normal (log) return and MRP distributions, the longest possible measurement period should be used in order to minimize the standard error of the mean estimator. Any adjustments to the measurement period, apart from insufficient data quality, appear arbitrary.

- Using the IRR approach to determine the expected MRP has seen a rapid proliferation within the academic community since it is said to overcome several issues associated with averages of realized MRPs and provides new insights on the magnitude of the expected MRP. Despite the meanwhile accepted finding that direct estimates of the expected MRP are on average below estimates from realized MRPs until 2006 and variable over time, the restrictive assumptions underlying these results are often overlooked. Still, the IRR-based method provides an important reference point when determining the expected MRP particularly due to the possibility to calculate conditional estimates.
  - The IRR-based method to estimate the expected MRP relies on cash flow valuation models with risk-adjusted discount rates. When such risk-adjusted discount rates are determined as constant IRRs, the estimate equals the expected return when returns have an i.i.d. distribution implying deterministic conditional and constant unconditional expected returns. The expected MRP can then be determined as the difference between the expected market return

and the deterministic risk-free rate whereby the expected market return is based on the constant IRR that equates the net present value of the infinite stream of expected market cash flows with the current market value of all traded assets. A capital market model such as the CAPM is not required to hold for this estimation approach of the expected MRP. However, the assumption of an i.i.d. return distribution is inconsistent with empirical evidence.

- In previous studies, a multitude of valuation models have been developed that all originate from the DIV model which mainly differ in their assumption on the post-horizontal growth behavior. It is often neglected that all models deliver isomorphic results, also in empirical applications, when an integrated set of input financials is used. The focus should therefore be put on the appropriate post-horizontal value estimation rather than developing ever new model derivatives. For each model, it is most important to make the consequences of the terminal growth assumption on the infinite development of the return on book equity transparent.
- In order to ensure consistent estimates for the expected MRP, several conceptual aspects need to be reflected in the model structure and the estimation procedure. Firstly, the reference date for the intra-year estimation must be the ex-dividend date and not the fiscal year-end as almost uniformly implemented in previous research. Secondly, the present value effect of intra-year dividend payments in selected countries needs to be captured in the model. Thirdly, compliance with the CAPM requires to either use aggregated market input data for the model or value-weighted expected MRPs. The often proposed equal-weighting of expected MRPs is not consistent with the market portfolio which leads to an overweighting of small firms and typically results in inflated expected MRPs.
- It is common among financial practitioners to use current or average spot multiples as terminal multiples. Firstly, it can be analytically shown that terminal multiples should be based on forward multiples which differ from spot multiples depending on the expected return and the foregone growth of the explicit forecast period. Secondly, it can be empirically shown that at expected return levels implied by the terminal perpetuity approach, forward multiples are consistently below spot multiples. When determining continuing values based on terminal multiples which are equal to the entry multiple, the implied

expected MRP estimates are substantially above terminal perpetuity-based estimates. In other words, when using terminal multiples based on the entry=exit assumption for valuation purposes, one would consequently have to use a substantially higher expected MRP estimate in order to prevent inflated valuation levels.

- The accuracy of the IRR-based expected MRP estimates is limited due to irresolvable empirical issues. Firstly, small sample sizes in non-US countries in the early years of the analysis period as well as the changing sample structure over time limit the estimation quality. Other sources of bias relate to the time-matching procedure of input parameters, the inclusion of firms in the aggregation with different fiscal year-ends, neglected share repurchases as recurring distribution mechanism, as well as the accuracy and time-delay of analysts' forecasts.
- Using inflation-based perpetual residual earnings growth, the unconditional average expected MRP estimates for all countries are substantially below the unconditional averages of realized MRPs. The implied standard deviations of the expected MRP series are lower than the volatility of realized MRPs. Inflation was found to be the best proxy for perpetual growth for three reasons. Firstly, inflation-based residual income growth is related to reasonable implied growth rates for dividends. Secondly, the implied return on book equity converges to the expected return which is consistent with competition theory suggesting that profits above cost of capital are not sustainable. Thirdly, inflation is a core component of the nominal risk-free rate. Using inflation-based perpetual growth ensures that the inflation expectation in the risk-free rate is at least similar to the inflation assumption for the infinite cash flow stream. Inconsistencies occur when non-inflation based perpetual growth proxies are used resulting in implausible negative expected MRP estimates.
- Statistically comparing the expected MRP estimates for all countries in the sample leads to significant positive correlations except for combinations with the US. This finding is explained by the continuous non-stationary rise in the expected MRP level for all non-US countries while the expected US MRP develops stationary. Earlier findings for the US market that the expected MRP declined towards the end of the 1990s appear to be reversed after the peak market levels around 2000. Despite significant correlations among most

countries, the unconditional means of the expected MRP distributions are not identical at typical significance levels.

- Confirming the results of previous research, the expected MRP estimates are variable over time. The variation of the expected MRP over time is found to be correlated to the current market price level when terminal value concepts are used assuming a converging market price level. This finding underlines the importance of expected MRP estimates conditional on the current market price level.
- During times of extraordinary market movements such as the recent financial crisis, the time-variability of conditional expected MRP estimates is most substantial. An analysis for the German capital market from January 2007 to September 2009 shows expected MRP fluctuations in a corridor of up to 5% and significant negative correlation coefficients between expected MRP estimates and the spot PE_{+1} multiple as well as the market index. Adjusting for a potential lag in the revision of forecasts by analysts results in lower fluctuations likely due to a shorter lag between the incorporation of new information in market prices and financial forecasts.

• The impact of the market price level, measured by indicators such as the dividend-price ratio, on unconditional averages of realized MRPs as well as IRR-based conditional expected MRP estimates is material. Against this background, the decomposition approach is an important tool to separate the effect of price level changes from the other return components.
  - Separating the return into its components lagged dividend yield, dividend growth, and change in price-dividend ratio allows for the identification and elimination of changes in the market price level. Since such changes lead to unexpected capital gains, they may not be recognized when determining the expected MRP unless certain variations in the price-dividend ratio are expected, e.g., through a convergence to the unconditional historical average.
  - Assuming the price-dividend ratio to be stationary over time implies that the long-term expected return will converge to the sum of expected dividend yield and expected dividend growth. When using realized MRPs to determine this unconditional expected MRP, it is therefore required to eliminate the impact of historical changes in the price-dividend ratio using the decomposition approach. Empirical evidence for all countries except Japan shows that capital

gains related to changes in the price-dividend ratio made up a substantial part of the average realized MRPs during the analysis period. However, if the price-dividend ratio was perfectly stationary and mean reverting, capital gains/losses during periods of increasing/decreasing price-dividend ratios would compensate each other so that the result is identical to the standard unconditional average of ex-post MRPs.

- A forward-looking application of the return decomposition formula allows to determine conditional and time-variable expected MRP estimates until the unconditional level is reached. Cornerstone of this methodology is an assumed mean-reversion model for the price-dividend ratio which determines the annual expected capital gain that affects expected return and MRP. Apart from determining the empirical convergence rate of the price-dividend ratio, the application is simple since the integrated set of input parameters can be fully compiled from market data. However, calculations for historical valuation dates show that the applied convergence model for the price-dividend ratio leads to negative expected forward MRPs during selected periods which contradicts with the assumption of risk-averse investors.

• The findings of this study have several important implications for corporate valuations. Foremost, the usage of conditional as opposed to unconditional expected MRP estimates is supported to capture time-variations in the expected MRP. This is in-line with the widely accepted "cut-off date principle" applied when determining the risk-free rate. Conditional expected MRPs are available either in form of constant or time-variable estimates. Firstly, time-variable estimates are in compliance with the CAPM in a multi-period context which requires the usage of variable forward expected returns for each future period. Conditional and time-variable estimates for the forward expected MRP are provided by the decomposition approach. Secondly, in empirical as well as practical valuation analyses, the assumption of constant expected returns is predominant. Accepting this simplification, constant conditional expected MRPs from the IRR-based method can be applied which consolidate the market expectation about the future MRP development in one "spot rate". Still, the constant IRR-based estimate may be biased due to a violation of the assumed i.i.d. return distribution. Under both approaches, it is important to maintain consistency between the maturity of the risk-free rate used for the valuation analysis and the maturity of the risk-free rate used to determine the expected MRP in order to prevent valuation errors.

After a comprehensive conceptual as well as empirical review of key contemporary methodologies to estimate the expected MRP, an appropriate question to ask is: What have we learnt to make us reconsider the widely recognized practitioner's rule of the "magic 5%" as expected MRP estimate? This number was and directionally still is supported by the mid-point between the arithmetic and geometric mean ex-post MRP of long-horizon studies for the US market based on data from Shiller, Siegel, or Morningstar Inc.[970]. The core argument against this approach relates to the conclusion that the expected MRP should be estimated conditionally on the current market environment at the valuation date due to a dependence of expected MRP on relative price measures as confirmed by the empirical results of this study. This implies a general rejection of unconditional averages of ex-post MRPs and ex-post expected MRPs. However, an unanswered question is whether to use a constant or time-variable conditional expected MRP estimate. The former approach suffers from the inconsistency of the i.i.d. return distribution assumption and the latter from the absence of a more precise model to predict the development of the price-dividend ratio. From a practitioner's perspective, the IRR-based estimate is convenient since it is consistent with the widely-used valuation framework using constant expected returns. In order to provide more precise estimates from the IRR method, models are currently developed to allow for not only i.i.d. but also dependent return distributions. This should be a focus of future research[971].

In the meantime, the author hopes that conditional estimates of the expected MRP will find a stronger proliferation especially among practitioners. While current estimates may be biased, they still appear superior to unconditional averages of realized returns. The German IRR-based expected MRP reached almost 10% during the recent financial crisis while the historical average remained at ~6% until 2007. An opposite situation was observable during the millennium bubble when expected MRPs were substantially below the historical average. These examples illustrate the necessity of using conditional estimates for valuation purposes. Unsophisticated current estimates are already now available from financial data providers and research departments of banks[972].

---

[970] See also Richter, F. (2006a), p. 9.

[971] See also Lambert, R. (2009), pp. 260-261 and 268.

[972] See, e.g., the expected country MRPs provided by Bloomberg under the code "CRP" or the "Global Economics Weekly" from Goldman Sachs Global Economics, Commodities and Strategy Research. See also Goldman Sachs Global Economics, Commodities and Strategy Research (2009).

References

Abarbanell, Jeffery (1991), Do analysts' earnings forecasts incorporate information in prior stock price changes?, Journal of Accounting and Economics, 14, 147-165.

Abarbanell, Jeffery/Bernard, Victor (2000), Is the U.S. stock market myopic?, Journal of Accounting Research, 38, 221-242.

Abarbanell, Jeffery/Lehavy, Reuven (2002), Differences in commercial database reported earnings: Implications for empirical research, Working Paper, June 2002, University of North Carolina.

Adler, Michael/Dumas, Bernard (1983), International portfolio choice and corporation finance: A synthesis, Journal of Finance, 38, 925-984.

Alford, Andrew W. (1992), The effect of the set of comparable firms on the accuracy of the price-earnings valuation method, Journal of Accounting Research, 30, 94-108.

Ali, Ashiq/Hwang, Lee-Seok/Trombley, Mark A. (2003), Residual-income-based valuation predicts future stock returns: Evidence on mispricing vs. risk explanations, Accounting Review, 78, 377-396.

Ali, Ashiq/Klein, April/Rosenfeld, James (1992), Analysts' use of information about permanent and transitory earnings components in forecasting annual EPS, Accounting Review, 67, 183-198.

Ang, Andrew/Bekaert, Geert (2007), Stock Return Predictability: Is it There?, Review of Financial Studies, 20, 651-707.

Ang, Andrew/Liu, Jun (2004), How to discount cashflows with time-varying expected returns, Journal of Finance, 59, 2745-2783.

Arnott, Robert D./Bernstein, Peter L. (2002), What risk premium is „normal"?, Financial Analysts Journal, 58 (2), 64-85.

Arnott, Robert D./Ryan, Ronald J. (2001), The death of the risk premium, Journal of Portfolio Management, 27 (3), 61-74.

Auerbach, Alan J. (1983), Taxation, corporate financial policy and the cost of capital, Journal of Economic Literature, 21, 905-940.

Baginski, Stephen P./Wahlen, James M. (2003), Residual income risk, intrinsic value, and share prices, Accounting Review, 78, 327-352.

Baetge, Jörg/Krause, Clemens (1994), Die Berücksichtigung des Risikos bei der Unternehmensbewertung, Betriebswirtschaftliche Forschung und Praxis, 46, 433-456.

Baetge, Jörg/Niemeyer, Kai/Kümmel, Jens (2005), Darstellung der Discounted Cash Flow-Verfahren (DCF-Verfahren) mit Beispiel, in: Peemöller, Volker (ed.), Praxishandbuch der Unternehmensbewertung, 3rd ed., Herne/Berlin, 265-362.

Ballwieser, Wolfgang (1988), Unternehmensbewertung bei unsicherer Geldentwertung, Zeitschrift für betriebswirtschaftliche Forschung, 40, 798-812.

Ballwieser, Wolfgang (1995), Unternehmensbewertung und Steuern, in: Elschen, Rainer/Siegel, Theodor/Wagner, Franz W. (eds.), Unternehmenstheorie und Besteuerung, Festschrift Schneider, Wiesbaden, 15-38.

Ballwieser, Wolfgang (2002), Der Kalkulationszinsfuß in der Unternehmensbewertung, Die Wirtschaftsprüfung, 55, 736-743.

Ballwieser, Wolfgang (2005), Die Ermittlung impliziter Eigenkapitalkosten aus Gewinnschätzungen und Aktienkursen: Ansatz und Probleme, in: Schneider, Dieter/Rückle, Dieter/Küpper, Hans-Ulrich/Wagner Franz W. (eds.), Kritisches zur Rechnungslegung und Unternehmensbewertung, Festschrift Siegel, Berlin, 321-337.

Ballwieser, Wolfgang (2007), Unternehmensbewertung, 2nd ed., Stuttgart.

Ballwieser, Wolfgang/Kruschwitz, Lutz/Löffler, Andreas (2007), Einkommensteuer und Unternehmensbewertung – Probleme mit der Steuerreform 2008, Die Wirtschaftsprüfung, 60, 765-769.

Bamberg, Günter/Dorfleitner, Gregor/Krapp, Michael (2004), Zur Bewertung risikobehafteter Zahlungsströme mit intertemporaler Abhängigkeitsstruktur, Betriebswirtschaftliche Forschung und Praxis, 56, 101-118.

Bamberg, Günter/Dorfleitner, Gregor/Krapp, Michael (2006), Unternehmensbewertung unter Unsicherheit: Zur entscheidungstheoretischen Fundierung der Risikoanalyse, Zeitschrift für Betriebswirtschaft, 76, 287-307.

Bank of International Settlement (2005), Zero-coupon yield curves: Technical documentation, BIS-Papers, No. 25, I-37.

Barefield, Russell M./Comiskey, Eugene E. (1975), The accuracy of analysts' forecasts of earnings per share, Journal of Business Research, 3, 241-252.

Beaver, William/Morse, Dale (1978), What determines price-earnings ratios?, Financial Analysts Journal, 34 (4), 65-76.

Beyer, Sven (2008), Unternehmensbewertung, Wachstum und Abgeltungssteuer, Finanz Betrieb, 10, 256-267.

Bimberg, Lothar H. (1993), Langfristige Renditeberechnung zur Ermittlung von Risikoprämien, 2nd ed., Frankfurt.

Blanchard, Olivier J. (1993), Movements in the equity premium, Brookings Papers of Economic Activity, 2, 75-138.

Blanchard, Olivier J. (2009), Macroeconomics, 5th ed., Upper Saddle River.

Blume, Marshall E. (1974), Unbiased estimators of long-run expected rates of return, Journal of the American Statistical Association, 69, 634-638.

Bodie, Zvi (1976), Common stocks as a hedge against inflation, Journal of Finance, 31, 459-470.

Bodie, Zvi/Kane, Alex/Marcus, Alan J. (2009), Investments, 8th ed., New York.

Botosan, Christine A. (1997), Disclosure level and the cost of equity capital, Accounting Review, 72, 323-349.

Botosan, Christine A./Plumlee, Marlene A. (2002), A re-examination of disclosure levels and expected cost of equity capital, Journal of Accounting Research, 40, 21-40.

Botosan, Christine A./Plumlee, Marlene A. (2005), Assessing alternative proxies for the expected risk premium, Accounting Review, 80, 21-53.

Boudoukh, Jacob/Richardson, Matthew (1993), Stock returns and inflation: A long-horizon perspective, American Economic Review, 83, 1346-1355.

Boudoukh, Jacob/Richardson, Matthew/Whitelaw, Robert F. (2008), The myth of long-horizon predictability, Review of Financial Studies, 21, 1577-1605.

Bradley, Michael H./Jarrell, Gregg A. (2008), Expected inflation and the constant-growth valuation model, Journal of Applied Corporate Finance, 20 (2), 66-78.

Brav, Alon/Lehavy, Reuven/Michaely, Roni (2005), Using expectations to test asset pricing models, Financial Management, 34 (3), 31-64.

Brealey, Richard A./Myers, Steward C./Allen, Franklin (2008), Principles of corporate finance, 9th ed., Boston et al.

Brennan, Michael J. (1970), Taxes, market valuation and corporate financial policy, National Tax Journal, 23, 417-427.

Brennan, Michael J. (1997), The term structure of discount rates, Journal of Financial Management, 26 (1), 81-90.

Brennan, Michael J. (2003), Corporate investment policy, in: Constantinides, George M./Harris, Milton/Stulz, Rene M. (eds.), Handbook of the economics of finance, Vol. 1A, Amsterdam et al., 167-214.

Breuer, Wolfgang/Fucks, Daniel/Mark, Klaus (2009), Estimating cost of capital in firm valuations with arithmetic or geometric mean – or better use the Cooper estimator?, Working Paper, March 2009, RWTH Aachen.

Breusch, Trevor S./Pagan, Adrian R. (1979), A simple test for heteroskedasticity and random coefficient variation, Econometrica, 47, 1287-1294.

Brief, Richard P. (1996), The accounting component of discounted residual earnings: Some theoretical and empirical evidence, Working Paper, March 1996, New York University.

Brief, Richard P./Lawson, Raef A. (1992), The role of the accounting rate of return in financial statement analysis, Accounting Review, 67, 411-426.

Brief, Richard P./O'Hanlon, John/Peasnell, Kenneth V. (2005), Error in constant growth accounting valuation models, Working Paper, November 2005, New York University.

Brigham, Eugene F./Shome, Dilip K./Vinson, Steve R. (1985), Risk premium approach to measuring a utility's cost of capital, Financial Management, 14 (1), 33-45.

Brown, Stephen J./Goetzmann, William N./Ross, Stephen A. (1995), Survival, Journal of Finance, 50, 353-373.

Brown, Lawrence D. (1993), Earnings forecasting research: Its implications for capital markets research, International Journal of Forecasting, 9, 295-320.

Brown, Lawrence D. (1996), Analyst forecasting errors and their implications for security analysis: An alternative perspective, Financial Analysts Journal, 52 (1), 40-47.

Brown, Lawrence D. (1997), Analyst forecasting errors: Additional evidence, Financial Analysts Journal, 53 (6), 81-88.

Brown, Lawrence D. (2001), A temporal analysis of earnings surprises: Profits versus losses, Journal of Accounting Research, 39, 221-241.

Brown, Lawrence D. (2005), A temporal analysis of quarterly earnings thresholds: Propensities and valuation consequences, Accounting Review, 80, 423-440.

Brown, Lawrence D./Hagerman, Robert L./Griffin, Paul A./Zmijewski, Mark E. (1987a), Security analyst superiority relative to univariate time-series models in forecasting quarterly earnings, Journal of Accounting and Economics, 9, 61-87.

Brown, Lawrence D./Hagerman, Robert L./Griffin, Paul A./Zmijewski, Mark E. (1987b), An evaluation of alternative proxies for the market's expectation of earnings, Journal of Accounting and Economics, 9, 159-193.

Brown, Lawrence D./Rozeff, Michael S. (1978), The superiority of analyst forecasts as measures of expectations: Evidence from earnings, Journal of Finance, 33, 1-16.

Brown, Philip/Foster, George/Noreen, Eric (1985), Security analyst multi-year earnings forecasts and the capital market, American Accounting Association, Sarasota, Florida/USA.

Bruner, Robert F./Eades, Kenneth M./Harris, Robert S./Higgins, Robert C. (1998), Best practices in estimating the cost of capital: Survey and synthesis, Financial Practice & Education, 8, 13-28.

Bundesnetzagentur (2008), Beschlusskammer 4, BK4-08-068, Beschluss (...) hinsichtlich der Festlegung von Eigenkapitalzinssätzen für Alt- und Neuanlagen für Betreiber von Elektrizitätsversorgungsnetzen und für Betreiber von Gasversorgungsnetzen für die erste Regulierungsperiode in der Anreizregulierung, July 2008, Bonn.

Butler, J.S./Schachter, Barry (1989), The investment decision: Estimation risk and risk adjusted discount rates, Financial Management, 18 (4), 13-22.

Campbell, John Y. (1991), A variance decomposition of stock returns, Economic Journal, 101, 157-179.

Campbell, John Y./Lo, Andrew W./MacKinlay, A. Craig (1997), The econometrics of financial markets, Princeton.

Campbell, John Y./Shiller, Robert J. (1988a), The dividend-price ratio and expectations of future dividends and discount factors, Review of Financial Studies, 1, 195-227.

Campbell, John Y./Shiller, Robert J. (1988b), Stock prices, earnings, and expected dividends, Journal of Finance, 43, 661-676.

Campbell, John Y./Shiller, Robert J. (1998), Valuation ratios and the long-run stock market outlook, Journal of Portfolio Management, 24 (2), 11-26.

Campbell, John Y./Thompson, Samuel B. (2008), Predicting excess stock returns out of sample: Can anything beat the historical average?, Review of Financial Studies, 21, 1509-1531.

Campbell, John Y./Yogo, Motohiro (2006), Efficient tests of stock return predictability, Journal of Financial Economics, 81, 27-60.

Cavanagh, Christopher L./Elliott, Graham/Stock, James H. (1995), Inference in models with nearly integrated regressors, Econometric Theory, 11, 1131-1147.

Chan, K.C./Karolyi, U. Andrew/Stulz, Rene M. (1992), Global financial markets and the risk premium on U.S. equity, Journal of Financial Economics, 32, 137-167.

Chen, Feng/Jorgensen, Bjorn N./Yoo, Yong K. (2004), Implied cost of equity capital in earnings-based valuation: International evidence, Accounting & Business Research, 34, 323-348.

Claus, James/Thomas, Jacob (2001), Equity premia as low as three percent? Evidence from analysts' earnings forecasts for domestic and international stock markets, Journal of Finance, 56, 1629-1666.

Cochrane, John H. (1991), Volatility tests and efficient markets: A review essay, Journal of Monetary Economics, 27, 463-487.

Cochrane, John H. (1994), Permanent and transitory components of GNP and stock prices, Quarterly Journal of Economics, 109, 241-265.

Cochrane, John H. (1997), Where is the market going? Uncertain facts and novel theories, Economic Perspectives, Federal Reserve Bank of Chicago, 21 (6), 3-37.

Cochrane, John H. (2005), Asset pricing, Rev. ed., Princeton/Oxford.

Cochrane, John H. (2008), The dog that did not bark: A defense of return predictability, Review of Financial Studies, 21, 1533-1575.

Collins, William A./Hopwood, William S. (1980), A multivariate analysis of annual earnings generated from quarterly forecasts of financial analysts and univariate time-series models, Journal of Accounting Research, 18, 390-406.

Conen, Ralf/Väth, Hubertus (1993), Risikoprämien am deutschen Kapitalmarkt, Die Bank, 33, 642-647.

Cooper, Ian (1996), Arithmetic versus geometric mean estimators: Setting discount rates for capital budgeting, European Financial Management, 2, 157-167.

Cooray, Arusha (2003), The Fisher effect: A survey, Singapore Economic Review, 48, 135-150.

Copeland, Thomas E./Weston, J. Fred/Shastri, Kuldeep (2005), Financial theory and corporate policy, 4th ed., Boston et al.

Cornell, Bradford (1993), Corporate valuation: Tools for effective appraisal and decision making, New York.

Cornell, Bradford (1999), The equity risk premium: The long-run future of the stock market, New York et al.

Cornell, Bradford/Hirshleifer, John I./James, Elizabeth P. (1997), Estimating the cost of equity capital, Contemporary Finance Digest, 1, 5-26.

Courteau, Lucie/Kao, Jennifer L./Richardson, Gordon D. (2001), Equity valuation employing the ideal versus ad hoc terminal value expressions, Contemporary Accounting Research, 18, 625-661.

Cox, John C./Ross, Stephan A./Rubinstein, Mark (1979), Option pricing: A simplified approach, Journal of Financial Economics, 7, 229-263.

Cragg, John G./Malkiel, Burton G. (1982), Expectations and the structure of stock prices, Chicago.

Crichfield, Timothy/Dyckman, Thomas/Lakonishok, Josef (1978), An evaluation of security analysts' forecasts, Accounting Review, 53, 651-668.

Dhaliwal, Dan/Krull, Linda/Li, Oliver Z. (2007), Did the 2003 tax act reduce the cost of equity capital?, Journal of Accounting and Economics, 43, 121-150.

Dhaliwal, Dan/Krull, Linda/Li, Oliver Z./Moser, William (2005), Dividend taxes and implied cost of equity capital, Journal of Accounting Research, 43, 675-708.

Damodaran, Aswath (2002), Investment valuation, 2nd ed., New York.

Daske, Holger (2006), Economic benefits of adopting IFRS or US-GAAP – Have the expected cost of capital really decreased?, Journal of Business Finance & Accounting, 33, 329-373.

Daske, Holger/Wiesenbach, Kai (2005), Praktische Probleme der zukunftsorientierten Schätzung von Eigenkapitalkosten am deutschen Kapitalmarkt, Finanz Betrieb, 7, 407-419.

Daske, Holger/Gebhardt, Günther/Klein, Stefan (2006), Estimating the expected cost of equity capital using analysts' consensus forecasts, Schmalenbach Business Review, 58, 2-36.

Daske, Holger/Gebhardt, Günther (2006), Zukunftsorientierte Bestimmung von Risikoprämien und Eigenkapitalkosten für die Unternehmensbewertung, Zeitschrift für betriebswirtschaftliche Forschung, 58, 530-551.

Daske, Holger/Hail, Luzi/Leuz, Christian/Versi, Rodrigo (2008), Mandatory IFRS reporting around the world: Early evidence on the economic consequences, Journal of Accounting Research, 46, 1085-1142.

Dausend, Florian/Lenz, Hansrudi (2006), Unternehmensbewertung mit dem Residualeinkommensmodell unter Einschluss persönlicher Steuern, Die Wirtschaftsprüfung, 59, 719-729.

Dausend, Florian/Schmitt, Dirk (2006a), Implizite Schätzung der Marktrisikoprämie nach Steuern für den deutschen Kapitalmarkt, Working Paper, November 2006, University of Würzburg.

Dausend, Florian/Schmitt, Dirk (2006b), Erste empirische Befunde zum Tax CAPM, Finanz Betrieb, 8, 153-161.

Dausend, Florian/Schmitt, Dirk (2007), Abgeltungssteuern und die Zukunft des IDW S1 – Konsequenzen der Unternehmenssteuerreform 2008 für die Unternehmensbewertung, Finanz Betrieb, 9, 287-292.

Dechow, Patricia M./Hutton, Amy P./Sloan, Richard G. (1999), An empirical assessment of the residual income valuation model, Journal of Accounting and Economics, 26, 1-34.

Dechow, Patricia M./Sloan, Richard G. (1997), Returns to contrarian investment strategies: Tests of naïve expectations hypotheses, Journal of Financial Economics, 43, 3-27.

Deller, Dominic (2002), Auswirkungen von Dirty Surplus Accounting auf Investitionspolitik und Unternehmenskennzahlen, Lohmar.

De Santis, Giorgio/Gerard, Bruno (1998), How big is the premium for currency risk?, Journal of Financial Economics, 49, 375-412.

Desrosiers, Stephanie/Lemaire, Natacha/L'Her, Jean-Francois (2007), Residual income approach to equity country selection, Financial Analysts Journal, 63 (2), 76-89.

Deutsche Börse AG (2003), Europe's premier listing platform: Standards, transparency, liquidity, March 2003, Frankfurt.

Deutsche Börse AG (2007a), Guide to the equity indices of Deutsche Börse, Version 6.2, March 2007, Frankfurt.

Deutsche Börse AG (2007b), Act on facts: The index world of Deutsche Börse, February 2007, Frankfurt.

Deutsche Bundesbank (1997), Monatsbericht Oktober, Frankfurt.

Dimson, Elroy/Marsh, Paul/Staunton, Mike (2002), Triumph of the optimists, Princeton.

Dimson, Elroy/Marsh, Paul/Staunton, Mike (2003), Global evidence on the equity risk premium, Journal of Applied Corporate Finance, 15, 1-15.

Dimson, Elroy/Marsh, Paul/Staunton, Mike (2008), The worldwide equity premium: A smaller puzzle, in: Mehra, Rajnish (ed.), Handbook of the equity risk premium, Amsterdam et al., 467-514.

Dirrigl, Hans (1988), Die Bewertung von Beteiligungen an Kapitalgesellschaften – Betriebswirtschaftliche Methoden und steuerlicher Einfluss, Hamburg.

Dixit, Avinash K./Pindyck, Robert S. (1993), Investment under uncertainty, Princeton.

Dow Jones & Company Inc./Wilshire Associates Inc. (2007), Dow Jones Wilshire 5000 composite index: Fact sheet, New York.

Dreman, David N./Berry, Michael A. (1995), Analyst forecasting errors and their implications for security analysis, Financial Analysts Journal, 51 (3), 30-41.

Drobetz, Wolfgang (2000), Wie hoch ist die Risikoprämie am Schweizer Aktienmarkt?, Finanzmarkt und Portfolio Management, 14, 364-386.

Drobetz, Wolfgang (2003a), Wie hoch ist die Markrisikoprämie?, Working Paper, April 2003, University of Basel.

Drobetz, Wolfgang (2003b), Statistische Eigenschaften von Finanzmarktzeitreihen, Working Paper, May 2003, University of Basel.

Drukarczyk, Jochen/Schüler, Andreas (2009), Unternehmensbewertung, 6th ed., Munich.

Dumas, Bernard/Solnik, Bruno (1995), The world price of foreign exchange risk, Journal of Finance, 50, 445-479.

Easterwood, John C./Nutt, Stacey R. (1999), Inefficiency in analysts' earnings forecasts: Systematic misreaction or systematic optimism, Journal of Finance, 54, 1777-1797.

Easton, Peter D. (2004), PE ratios, PEG ratios, and estimating the implied expected rate of return on equity capital, Accounting Review, 79, 73-95.

Easton, Peter D. (2006), Use of forecasts of earnings to estimate and compare cost of capital across regimes, Journal of Business Finance & Accounting, 33, 374-394.

Easton, Peter D. (2009), Estimating the cost of capital implied by market prices and accounting data, Foundations and Trends in Accounting, 2, 241-364.

Easton, Peter D./Harris, Trevor S./Ohlson, James A. (1992), Aggregate accounting earnings can explain most of security returns, Journal of Accounting and Economics, 15, 119-142.

Easton, Peter D./Monahan, Steven J. (2005), An evaluation of accounting-based measures of expected returns, Accounting Review, 80, 501-538.

Easton, Peter D./Sommers, Gregory A. (2007), Effect of analysts' optimism on estimates of the expected rate of return implied by earnings forecasts, Journal of Accounting Research, 45, 983-1015.

Easton, Peter D./Taylor, Gary/Shroff, Pervin/Sougiannis, Theodore (2002), Using forecasts of earnings to simultaneously estimate growth and the rate of return on equity investment, Journal of Accounting Research, 40, 657-676.

Edwards, Edgar O./Bell, Philip W. (1961), The theory of measurement of business income, Berkeley.

Eggemann, Gerd/Petry, Martin (2002), Fast Close – Verkürzung von Aufstellungs- und Veröffentlichungszeiten für Jahres- und Konzernabschlüsse, Betriebs-Berater, 57, 1635-1639.

Elton, Edwin J. (1999), Expected return, realized return, and asset pricing tests, Journal of Finance, 54, 1199-1220.

Elton, Edwin J./Gruber, Martin J. (1974), On the maximization of the geometric mean with lognormal return distribution, Management Science, 21, 483-488.

Erb, Claude B./Harvey, Campbell R./Viskanta, Tadas E. (1996), Expected returns and volatility in 135 countries, Journal of Portfolio Management, 22 (3), 46-58.

Esterer, Florian/Schröder, David (2007a), Predicting equity returns with the implied cost of capital, Working Paper, November 2007, Bonn Graduate School of Economics.

Esterer, Florian/Schröder, David (2007b), Implied cost of capital based investment strategies – Evidence from international stock markets, Working Paper, November 2007, Bonn Graduate School of Economics.

Euronext NV (2005), Guide to Euronext's French market indices, December 2005, Paris.

Ewert, Ralf/Wagenhofer, Alfred (2008), Interne Unternehmensrechnung, 7th ed., Berlin/Heidelberg.

Fabozzi, Frank J. (2005), The structure of interest rates, in: Frank J./Mann, Steven V. (eds.), The handbook of fixed income securities, 7th ed., New York et al., 135-157.

Fabozzi, Frank J./Buetow, Gerald W. Jr./Johnson, Robert R. (2005), Measuring interest-rate risk, in: Fabozzi, Frank J./Mann, Steven V. (eds.), The handbook of fixed income securities, 7th ed., New York et al., 183-226.

Fabozzi, Frank J./Flemming, Michael J. (2005), U.S. treasury and agency securities, in: Fabozzi, Frank J./Mann, Steven V. (eds.), The handbook of fixed income securities, 7th ed., New York et al., 229-250.

Fabozzi, Frank J./Mann, Steven V./Choudhry, Moorad (2005), Interest rate swaps and swaptions, in: Fabozzi, Frank J./Mann, Steven V. (eds.), The handbook of fixed income securities, 7th ed., New York et al., 1249-1281.

Fahrmeir, Ludwig/Kneib, Thomas/Lang, Stefan (2009), Regression, 2nd ed., Berlin/Heidelberg.

Fairfield, Patricia M. (1994), P/E, P/B and the present value of future dividends, Financial Analysts Journal, 50 (4), 23-31.

Fama, Eugene F. (1970a), Multiperiod consumption-investment decisions, American Economics Review, 60, 163-174.

Fama, Eugene F. (1970b), Efficient capital markets: A review of theory and empirical work, Journal of Finance, 25, 383-417.

Fama, Eugene F. (1977), Risk-adjusted discount rates and capital budgeting under uncertainty, Journal of Financial Economics, 5, 3-24.

Fama, Eugene F. (1981), Stock returns, real activity, inflation, and money, American Economic Review, 71, 545-565.

Fama, Eugene F. (1991), Efficient capital markets: II, Journal of Finance, 46, 1575-617.

Fama, Eugene F. (1996), Discounting under uncertainty, Journal of Business, 69, 415-428.

Fama, Eugene F. (1998), Market efficiency, long-term returns, and behavioral finance, Journal of Financial Economics, 49, 283-306.

Fama, Eugene F./French, Kenneth R. (1988a), Permanent and temporary components of stock prices, Journal of Political Economy, 96, 246-273.

Fama, Eugene F./French, Kenneth R. (1988b), Dividend yields and expected stock returns, Journal of Financial Economics, 22, 3-27.

Fama, Eugene F./French, Kenneth R. (1989), Business conditions and expected returns on stocks and bonds, Journal of Financial Economics, 25, 23-49.

Fama, Eugene F./French, Kenneth R. (1992), On the cross-section of expected stock returns, Journal of Finance, 47, 427-466.

Fama, Eugene F./French, Kenneth R. (1993), Common risk factors in returns on stocks and bonds, Journal of Financial Economics, 33, 3-56.

Fama, Eugene F./French, Kenneth R. (1996), Multifactor explanations of asset pricing anomalies, Journal of Finance, 51, 55-84.

Fama, Eugene F./French, Kenneth R. (1998), Taxes, financing decisions, and firm value, Journal of Finance, 53, 819-843.

Fama, Eugene F./French, Kenneth R. (1999), The corporate cost of capital and the return on corporate investment, Journal of Finance, 54, 1939-1967.

Fama, Eugene F./French, Kenneth R. (2002), The equity premium, Journal of Finance, 57, 637-659.

Fama, Eugene F./French, Kenneth R. (2004), The capital asset pricing model, Theory and evidence, Journal of Economic Perspectives, 18, 25-46.

Fama, Eugene F./MacBeth, James D. (1974), Tests of the multiperiod two-parameter model, Journal of Financial Economics, 1, 43-66.

Fama, Eugene F./Schwert, G. William (1977), Asset returns and inflation, Journal of Financial Economics, 5, 115-146.

Feldstein, Martin (1980), Inflation and the stock market, American Economic Review, 70, 839-847.

Feltham, Gerald A./Ohlson, James A. (1995), Valuation and clean surplus accounting for operating and financial activities, Contemporary Accounting Review, 11, 689-731.

Fernandez, Pablo (2006), The equity premium in finance and valuation textbooks, Working Paper, October 2006, IESE Business School.

Fernandez, Pablo (2008), The equity premium in 100 textbooks, Working Paper, December 2008, IESE Business School.

Ferson, Wayne E./Harvey, Campbell R. (1993), The risk and predictability of international equity markets, Review of Financial Studies, 6, 527-566.

Ferson, Wayne E./Harvey, Campbell R. (1994), Sources of risk and expected returns in global equity markets, Journal of Banking and Finance, 18, 775-803.

Finnerty, John D./Leistikow, Dean (1993), The behavior of equity and debt risk premiums: Are they mean reverting and downward trending?, Journal of Portfolio Management, 19 (4), 73-84.

Finnerty, John D./Leistikow, Dean (1994), The behavior of equity and debt risk premiums: Reply to comment, Journal of Portfolio Management, 20 (4), 101-102.

Fisher, Irving (1930), The theory of interest, reprint of the 1930 edition 1977, Philadelphia.

Francis, Jennifer/Olsson, Per/Oswald, Dennis R. (2000), Comparing the accuracy and explainability of dividend, free cash flow, and abnormal earnings equity estimates, Journal of Accounting Research, 38, 45-70.

Franke, Günther/Hax, Herbert (2009), Finanzwirtschaft des Unternehmens am Kapitalmarkt, 6th ed., Berlin/Heidelberg/New York.

Frankel, Richard/Lee, Charles M. C. (1998), Accounting valuation, market expectation, and cross-sectional stock returns, Journal of Accounting and Economics, 25, 283-319.

Frankel, Richard/Lee, Charles M. C. (1999), Accounting diversity and international valuation, Working Paper, May 1999, University of Michigan.

Fried, Dov/Givoly, Dan (1982), Financial analysts' forecasts of earnings: A better surrogate for market expectations, Journal of Accounting and Economics, 4, 85-107.

Friedl, Gunther/Schwetzler, Bernhard (2009a), Inflation, Wachstum und Unternehmensbewertung, Die Wirtschaftsprüfung, 62, 152-158.

Friedl, Gunther/Schwetzler, Bernhard (2009b), Terminal Value, Inflation und Wachstum, Working Paper, June 2009, HHL Leipzig/TU Munich.

Frontier Economics Ltd. (2008), Ermittlung des Zuschlags zur Abdeckung netzbetriebsspezifischer Wagnisse im Bereich Strom und Gas, Gutachten im Auftrag der Bundesnetzagentur, June 2008, London.

FTSE International Limited (2005), Guide to calculation methods for the UK series of the FTSE actuaries share indices, Version 4.0, May 2005, London.

FTSE International Limited (2007a), FTSE products, London.

FTSE International Limited (2007b), Ground rules for the management of the UK series of the FTSE actuaries share indices, Version 9.9, January 2007, London.

Gebhardt, Günther/Daske, Holger (2005), Kapitalmarktorientierte Bestimmung von risikofreien Zinssätzen für die Unternehmensbewertung, Die Wirtschaftsprüfung, 58, 649-655.

Gebhardt, William R./Lee, Charles M. C./Swaminathan, Bhaskaran (2001), Toward an implied cost of capital, Journal of Accounting Research, 39, 135-176.

Geske, Robert/Roll, Richard (1983), The fiscal and monetary linkage between stock returns and inflation, Journal of Finance, 38, 1-33.

Gielen, Gregor (1994), Können Aktienkurse noch steigen? Langfristige Trendanalyse des deutschen Aktienmarktes, Wiesbaden.

Gilson, Stuart C./Hotchkiss, Edith S./Ruback, Richard S. (2000), Valuation of bankrupt firms, Review of Financial Studies, 13, 43-74.

Gode, Dan/Mohanram, Partha (2003), Inferring the cost of capital using the Ohlson-Juettner model, Review of Accounting Studies, 8, 399-431.

Goetzmann, William N./Ibbotson, Roger G. (2006), The equity risk premium: Essays and explorations, New York.

Goetzmann, William N./Ibbotson, Roger G. (2008), History and the equity risk premium, in: Mehra, Rajnish (ed.), Handbook of the equity risk premium, Amsterdam et al., 515-529.

Goetzmann, William N./Jorion, Philippe (1993), Testing the predictive power of dividend yields, Journal of Finance, 48, 663-679.

Goetzmann, William N./Jorion, Philippe (1995), A longer look at dividend yields, Journal of Business, 68, 483-508.

Goldman Sachs Global Economics, Commodities and Strategy Research, Global economics weekly, weekly publication.

Goldman Sachs Global Economics, Commodities and Strategy Research (2009), Portfolio Strategy, Finding 'fair value' in global equities; part I, 6 February 2009.

Gordon, Joseph R./Gordon, Myron J. (1997), The finite horizon expected return model, Financial Analysts Journal, 53 (3), 52-61.

Gordon, Myron J./Shapiro, Eli (1956), Capital equipment analysis: The required rate of profit, Management Science, 3, 102-110.

Gordon, Myron J. (1962), The investment, financing and valuation of the corporation, Homewood.

Gordon, Myron J. (1974), The cost of capital to a public utility, MSU Public Utilities Studies, East Lansing.

Goyal, Amit/Welch, Ivo (2003), Predicting the equity premium with dividend ratios, Management Science, 49, 639-654.

Goyal, Amit/Welch, Ivo (2008), A comprehensive look at the empirical performance of equity risk premium prediction, Review of Financial Studies, 21, 1455-1508.

Graham, John R./Harvey, Campbell R. (2008), The equity risk premium in 2008: Evidence from the global CFO outlook survey, Working Paper, Duke University.

Grauer, Frederick L. A./Litzenberger, Robert H./Stehle, Richard E. (1976), Sharing rules and equilibrium in an international market under uncertainty, Journal of Financial Economics, 3, 233-256.

Greene, William H. (2008), Econometric analysis, 6th ed., Upper Saddle River.

Griffin, John M. (2002), Are the Fama and French factors global or country specific?, Review of Financial Studies, 15, 783-803.

Grinblatt, Mark/Longstaff, Francis A. (2000), Financial innovation and the role of derivatives: An empirical analysis of the treasury strips program, Journal of Finance, 55, 1415-1436.

Grinblatt, Mark/Titman, Sheridan (2002), Financial Markets and Corporate Strategy, 2nd ed., Boston et al.

Guay, Wayne/Kothari, S.P./Shu, Susan (2005), Properties of the implied cost of capital using analysts' forecasts, Working Paper, July 2005, MIT Sloan School of Management.

Gruber, Walter/Overbeck, Ludger (1998), „Nie mehr Bootstrapping", Finanzmarkt und Portfolio Management, 12, 59-73.

Gujarati, Damodar N./Porter, Dawn C. (2009), Basic econometrics, 5th ed., New York.

Hachmeister, Dirk (2000), Der Discounted Cash Flow als Maß der Unternehmenswertsteigerung, 4th ed., Frankfurt.

Hachmeister, Dirk (2006), Diskontierung unsicherer Zahlungsströme: Methodische Anmerkungen zur Bestimmung risikoangepasster Kapitalkosten, Controlling & Management, 50, 143-149.

Hachmeister, Dirk/Wiese, Jörg (2009), Der Zinsfuß in der Unternehmensbewertung: Aktuelle Probleme und Rechtssprechung, Die Wirtschaftsprüfung, 62, 54-65.

Hail, Luzi/Leuz, Christian (2006), International differences in the cost of equity capital: Do legal institutions and securities regulation matter?, 44, 485-531.

Hail, Luzi/Leuz, Christian (2009), Cost of capital effects and changes in growth expectations around U.S. cross-listings, Journal of Financial Economics, 93, 428-454.

Harris, Robert S./Marston, Felicia C. (1992), Estimating shareholder risk premia using analyst's growth forecasts, Financial Management, 21 (2), 63-70.

Harris, Robert S./Marston, Felicia C. (2001), The market risk premium: Expectational estimates using analysts' forecasts, Journal of Applied Finance, 11, 6-16.

Harris, Trevor S./Kemsley, Deen (1999), Dividend taxation in firm valuation: New evidence, Journal of Accounting Research, 37, 275-291.

Harrison, Michael J./Kreps, David M. (1979), Martingales and arbitrage in multiperiod securities markets, Journal of Economic Theory, 20, 381-401.

Hartung, Joachim/Elpelt, Bärbel/Klösener, Karl-Heinz (2009), Statistik, 15th ed., Munich.

Harvey, Campbell R. (1991), The world price of covariance risk, Journal of Finance, 46, 111-157.

Harvey, Campbell R. (1995), Predictable risk and returns in emerging markets, Review of Financial Studies, 8, 773-816.

Harvey, Campbell R. (2000), Drivers of expected returns in international markets, Emerging Market Quarterly, 4, 3-49.

Healy, Paul M./Palepu, Krishna G. (2001), Information asymmetry, corporate disclosure, and the capital markets: A review of the empirical disclosure literature, Journal of Accounting and Economics, 31, 405-440.

Heintzen, Markus/Kruschwitz, Lutz/Löffler, Andreas/Maiterth, Ralf (2008), Die typisierende Berücksichtigung der persönlichen Steuerbelastung des Anteilseigners beim Squeeze-out, Zeitschrift für Betriebswirtschaft, 78, 1-14.

Herrmann, Volker (2002), Schätzung potentieller Marktpreise von Unternehmen mit kontrollierten Multiplikatoren, Lohmar/Köln.

Hetzel, Heiko (1988), Stichtagszins oder zukünftiger Zins zur Ertragswertermittlung im Rahmen der Unternehmensbewertung, Betriebs-Berater, 43, 725-728.

Hodrick, Robert J. (1992), Dividend yields and expected stock returns: Alternative procedures for inference and measurement, Review of Financial Studies, 5, 357-386.

Hower, Sascha (2008), Unternehmensbewertung mit dem Tax-CAPM: Fortschritt oder nicht pragmatische Komplexitätssteigerung, Aachen.

Hribar, Paul/Jenkins, Nicole Thorne (2004), The effect of accounting restatements on earnings revisions and the estimated cost of capital, Review of Accounting Studies, 9, 337-356.

Hughes, John/Liu, Jing/Liu, Jun (2009), On the relation between expected returns and implied cost of capital, Review of Accounting Studies, 14, 246-259.

Ibbotson, Roger G./Chen, Peng (2003), Long-run stock returns: Participating in the real economy, Financial Analysts Journal, 59 (1), 88-98.

Ibbotson, Roger G./Lummer, Scott L. (1994), The behavior of equity and debt premiums: Comment, Journal of Portfolio Management, 20 (4), 98-100.

Ibbotson, Roger G./Sinquefield, Rex A. (1976), Stocks, bonds, bills, and inflation: Year-by-year historical returns (1926-1974), Journal of Business, 49, 11-47.

IDW (2000), IDW Standard: Grundsätze zur Durchführung von Unternehmensbewertungen (IDW S 1), Die Wirtschaftsprüfung, 53, 825-842.

IDW (2005), IDW Standard: Grundsätze zur Durchführung von Unternehmensbewertungen (IDW S 1), Die Wirtschaftsprüfung, 58, 1303-1327.

IDW (2008a), IDW Standard: Grundsätze zur Durchführung von Unternehmensbewertungen (IDW S 1 i.d.F. 2008), Die Wirtschaftsprüfung, 61, Supplement 3, 68-89.

IDW (2008b), Ergänzende Hinweise des FAUB zur Bestimmung des Basiszinssatzes im Rahmen objektivierter Unternehmensbewertungen, FN-IDW, 490-491.

Ilmanen, Antti (2005), Overview of forward rate analysis, in: Fabozzi, Frank J./Mann, Steven V. (eds.), The handbook of fixed income securities, 7th ed., New York et al., 159-181.

Imhoff, Eugene A./Pare, Paul V. (1982), Analysis and comparison of earnings forecast agents, Journal of Accounting Research, 20, 429-439.

Indro, Daniel C./Lee, Wayne Y. (1997), Biases in arithmetic and geometric averages as estimates for long-run expected returns and risk premia, Financial Management, 26 (4), 81-90.

Isidro, Hellen/O'Hanlon, John/Young, Steve (2004), Dirty surplus accounting flows: International evidence, Accounting and Business Research, 34, 383-410.

Jacquier, Eric/Kane, Alex/Marcus, Alan J. (2003), Geometric or arithmetic mean: A reconsideration, Financial Analysts Journal, 59 (6), 46-53.

Jacquier, Eric/Kane, Alex/Marcus, Alan J. (2005), Optimal estimation of the risk premium for the long run and asset allocation: A case of compounded estimation risk, Journal of Financial Econometrics, 3, 37-55.

Jagannathan, Ravi/McGrattan, Ellen R./Scherbina, Anna (2000), The declining U.S. equity premium, Federal Reserve Bank of Minneapolis Quarterly Review, 24 (4), 3-19.

Jansson, Michael/Moreira, Marcelo J. (2006), Optimal inference in regression models with nearly integrated regressors, Econometrica, 74, 681-714.

Johnson, L. Todd/Reither, Cheri L./Swieringa, Robert J. (1995), Toward reporting comprehensive income: A commentary, Accounting Horizon, 9, 128-137.

Jonas, Martin/Löffler, Andreas/Wiese, Jörg (2004), Das CAPM mit deutscher Einkommenssteuer, Die Wirtschaftsprüfung, 57, 898-906.

Jonas, Martin/Wieland-Blöse, Heike/Schiffarth, Stefanie (2005), Basiszinssatz in der Unternehmensbewertung, Finanz Betrieb, 7, 647-653.

Jorion, Philippe (2003), The long-term risks of global stock markets, Financial Management, 32 (4), 5-26.

Jorion, Philippe/Goetzmann, William M. (1999), Global stock markets in the twentieth century, Journal of Finance, 54, 953-980.

Jüttner-Nauroth, Beate (2006), Unternehmensbewertung mit Hilfe von Rechnungswesengrößen: Ein Überblick, in: Mika, Werner (ed.), Die Fachhochschule der Bundesbank, Festschrift Schönwitz, Frankfurt, 125-148.

Kaplan, Steven N./Ruback, Richard S. (1995), The valuation of cash flow forecasts: An empirical analysis, Journal of Finance, 50, 1059-1093.

Karolyi, G. Andrew/Stulz, Rene M. (2003), Are financial assets priced locally or globally, in: Constantinides, George M./Harris, Milton/Stulz, Rene M. (eds.), Handbook of the economics of finance, Vol. 1B, Amsterdam et al., 975-1020.

Kaul, Gautam (1987), Stock returns and inflation: The role of the monetary sector, Journal of Financial Economics, 18, 253-276.

Käfer, Karl (1946), Zur Bewertung des Unternehmens als Ganzes, Rechnungsführung in Unternehmung und Staatsverwaltung, Festschrift Juzi, 71-98, reprint in: Helbling, Carl (1996) (ed.), Käfer Karl: Zur Bewertung der Unternehmung, Zurich, 15-42.

Keane, Michael P./Runkle, David E. (1998), Are financial analysts' forecasts of corporate profits rational?, Journal of Political Economy, 106, 768-805.

Kelleners, Andre (2004), Risikoneutrale Unternehmensbewertung und Multiplikatoren, Wiesbaden.

Khorana, Ajay/Moyer, R. Charles/Patel, Ajay (1997), An examination of equity risk premium forecasts in G-6 countries, Working Paper, November 1997, Wake Forest University.

Kim, Moonchul/Ritter, Jay R. (1999), Valuing IPOs, Journal of Financial Economics, 53, 409-437.

Kim, Myung J./Nelson, Charles R./Startz, Richard (1991), Mean reversion in stock prices: Evidence and implications, Review of Economic Studies, 58, 515-528.

Knoll, Leonhard/Deininger, Claus (2004), Der Basiszinssatz der Unternehmensbewertung zwischen theoretisch Wünschenswertem und praktisch Machbarem, Zeitschrift für Bankrecht und Bankwirtschaft, 16, 371-381.

Knoll, Leonhard (2006), Basiszins und Zinsstruktur, Anmerkungen zu einer methodischen Neuausrichtung des IDW, Wirtschaftswissenschaftliches Studium, 35, 525-528.

Knoll, Leonhard/Rasinger, Wilhelm/Wala, Thomas (2006), Bewertungsstandards, Anteilseignersteuern und die Entschädigung von Minderheitsaktionären, Ecolex (Skript), 17, 1-8.

KPMG International (2006), KPMG's corporate tax rate survey: An international analysis of corporate tax rates from 1993 to 2006, Switzerland.

Koch, Joachim (2005), Rechnungswesenbasierte Verfahren der Aktienbewertung, Wiesbaden.

Koller, Tim/Goedhart, Marc/Wessels, David (2005), Valuation, 4th ed., Hoboken.

Kothari, S.P. (2001), Capital markets research in accounting, Journal of Accounting and Economics, 31, 105-231.

Kothari, S.P./Shanken, Jay (1997), Book-to-market, dividend yield, and expected market returns: A time-series analysis, Journal of Financial Economics, 44, 169-203.

Kritzman, Mark (1994), What practitioners need to know about future value, Financial Analysts Journal, 50 (2), 12-15.

Krotter, Simon (2007), Zur Relevanz von Kongruenzdurchbrechungen für die Bewertung und Performance-Messung mit Residualgewinnen, Die Betriebswirtschaft, 67, 692-718.

Kruschwitz, Lutz (2009), Investitionsrechnung, 12th ed., Munich.

Kruschwitz, Lutz/Löffler, Andreas (2005), Discounted cash flow – A theory of the valuation of firms, Chichester.

Kruschwitz, Lutz/Löffler, Andreas (2008), Kapitalkosten aus theoretischer und praktischer Perspektive, Die Wirtschaftsprüfung, 61, 803-810.

Kürsten, Wolfgang (2002), "Unternehmensbewertung unter Unsicherheit", oder: Theoriedefizit einer künstlichen Diskussion über Sicherheitsäquivalent- und Risikozuschlagsmethode, Zeitschrift für betriebswirtschaftliche Forschung, 54, 128-144.

Lachnit, Laurenz/Müller, Stefan (2005), Other comprehensive income nach HGB, IFRS und US-GAAP – Konzeption und Nutzung im Rahmen der Jahresabschlussanalyse, Der Betrieb, 58, 1637-1645.

Laitenberger, Jörg (2006), Rendite und Kapitalkosten, Zeitschrift für Betriebswirtschaft, 76, 79-101.

Laitenberger, Jörg/Löffler, Andreas (2006), The structure of the distributions of cash flows and discount rates in multiperiod valuation problems, OR Spectrum, 28, 289-299.

Laitenberger, Jörg/Tschöpel, Andreas (2003), Vollausschüttung und Halbeinkünfteverfahren, Die Wirtschaftsprüfung, 56, 1357-1367.

Lambert, Richard A. (2009), Discussion of „On the relation between expected returns and implied cost of capital“, Review of Accounting Studies, 14, 260-268.

Lampenius, Niklas/Obermaier, Robert/Schüler, Andreas (2008), Der Einfluss stichtags- und laufzeitequivalenter Basiszinssätze auf den Unternehmenswert: Eine empirische Untersuchung, Zeitschrift für Bankrecht und Bankwirtschaft, 20, 245-254.

Lamont, Owen (1998), Earnings and expected returns, Journal of Finance, 53, 1563-1587.

La Porta, Rafael (1996), Expectations and the cross-section of stock returns, Journal of Finance, 51, 1715-1742.

LeClair, Mark S. (1990), Valuing the closely held corporation: The validity and performance of established valuation procedures, Accounting Horizons, 4 (3), 31-42.

Lee, Charles M. C. (1999), Accounting-based valuation: Impact on business practices and research, Accounting horizons, 13, 413-425.

Lee, Charles M. C./Myers, James/Swaminathan, Bhaskaran (1999), What is the intrinsic value of the Dow?, Journal of Finance, 54, 1693-1741.

Lee, Charles M. C./Ng, David/Swaminathan, Bhaskaran (2009), Testing international asset pricing models using implied costs of capital, Journal of Financial and Quantitative Analysis, 44, 307-335.

Lettau, Martin/Ludvigson, Sydney (2001), Consumption, aggregate wealth, and expected stock returns, Journal of Finance, 56, 815-849.

Lettau, Martin/Nieuwerburgh, Stijn van (2008), Reconciling the return predictability evidence, Review of Financial Studies, 21, 1607-1652.

Leuthier, Rainer (1988a), Zur Berücksichtigung der Besteuerung bei der Unternehmensbewertung, Betriebswirtschaftliche Forschung und Praxis, 40, 505-521.

Leuthier, Rainer (1988b), Das Interdependenzproblem in der Unternehmensbewertung, Frankfurt.

Levy, Haim/Gunthorpe, Deborah (1993), Optimal investment proportions in senior securities and equities under alternative holding periods, Journal of Portfolio Management, 19 (4), 30-36.

Levy, Haim/Sarnat, Marshall (1994), Capital investment and financial decisions, 5th ed., New York et al.

Lewellen, Jonathan (2004), Predicting returns with financial ratios, Journal of Financial Economics, 74, 209-235.

Linke, Charles M./Zumwalt, Kenton J. (1984), Estimation bias in discounted cash flow analyses of equity cost of capital in rate regulation, Financial Management, 13 (3), 15-21.

Lintner, John (1965), The valuation of risk assets and the selection of risky investments in stock portfolios and capital budgets, Review of Economics and Statistics, 47, 13-37.

Lintner, John (1975), Inflation and security returns, Journal of Finance, 30, 259-280.

Litzenberger, Robert H./Ramaswamy, Krishna (1979), The effect of personal taxes and dividends on capital asset prices, Journal of Financial Economics, 7, 163-195.

Liu, Jing/Nissim, Doron/Thomas, Jacob (2002), Equity valuation using multiples, Journal of Accounting Research, 40, 135-172.

Liu, Jing/Thomas, Jacob (2000), Stock returns and accounting earnings, Journal of Accounting Research, 38, 71-101.

Lo, Andrew W./MacKinlay, A. Craig (1988), Stock market prices do not follow random walks: Evidence from a simple specification test, Review of Financial Studies, 1, 41-66.

Lo, Kin/Lys, Thomas (2000), The Ohlson model: Contribution to valuation theory, limitations, and empirical applications, Journal of Accounting, Auditing and Finance, 15, 337-367.

Lobe, Sebastian (2006), Unternehmensbewertung und Terminal Value, Frankfurt.

Löffler, Andreas/Schneider, Dirk (2002), Martingales, taxes, and neutrality, Working Paper, University of Hannover.

Long, John B. (1974), Stock prices, inflation, and the term structure of interest rates, Journal of Financial Economics, 1, 131-170.

Long, John B. (1977), Efficient portfolio selection choice with differential taxation of dividends and capital gains, Journal of Financial Economics, 5, 25-53.

Lücke, Wolfgang (1955), Investitionsrechnung auf der Basis von Ausgaben oder Kosten?, Zeitschrift für handelswissenschaftliche Forschung, 7, 310-324.

Lundholm, Russell/O'Keefe, Terry (2001a), Reconciling value estimates from the discounted cash flow model and the residual income model, Contemporary Accounting Review, 18, 311-335.

Lundholm, Russell/O'Keefe, Terry (2001b), On comparing residual income and discounted cash flow models of equity valuation: A response to Penman 2001, Contemporary Accounting Review, 18, 693-696.

Maddox, Farris M./Pippert, Donna T./Sullivan, Rodney N. (1995), An empirical study of ex ante risk premiums for the electric utility industry, Financial Management, 24 (3), 89-95.

Mai, Jan M. (2006), Mehrperiodige Bewertung mit dem Tax-CAPM und Kapitalkostenkonzept, Zeitschrift für Betriebswirtschaft, 76, 1225-1253.

Malkiel, Burton G. (1979), The capital formation problem in the United States, Journal of Finance, 34, 291-306.

Malkiel, Burton G. (1992), Efficient market hypothesis, in: Newman, Peter/Milgate, Murray/Eatwell, John (eds.), The new Palgrave dictionary of money and finance, Vol. 1, London.

Mandelbrot, Benoit (1963), The variation of certain speculative prices, Journal of Business, 36, 394-419.

Mankiw, N. Gregory (2007), Macroeconomics, 6th ed., New York.

Marten, Kai-Uwe/Müller, Stefan (2005), Squeeze-out-Prüfung, in: Crezelius, Georg/Hirte, Heribert/Vieweg, Klaus (eds.), Gesellschaftsrecht – Rechnungslegung – Sportrecht, Festschrift Röhricht, Köln, 963-986.

Marten, Kai-Uwe/Quick, Reiner/Ruhnke, Klaus (2007), Wirtschaftsprüfung, 3rd. ed., Stuttgart.

Matschke, Manfred J. (1979), Funktionale Unternehmensbewertung, Vol. 2, Wiesbaden.

Matsumoto, Dawn A. (2002), Management's incentives to avoid negative earnings surprises, Accounting Review, 77, 483-514.

Mehra, Rajnish (2003), The equity premium: Why is it a puzzle?, Financial Analysts Journal, 59 (1), 54-69.

Mehra, Rajnish/Prescott, Edward C. (2003), The equity premium in retrospect, in: Constantinides, George M./Harris, Milton/Stulz, Rene M. (eds.), Handbook of the economics of finance, Vol. 1B, Amsterdam et al., 889-938.

Mehra, Rajnish/Prescott, Edward C. (2008), The equity premium: ABCs, in: Mehra, Rajnish (ed.), Handbook of the equity risk premium, Amsterdam et al., 2-36.

Merton, Robert C. (1973), An intertemporal asset pricing model, Econometrica, 41, 867-888.

Miller, Merton H./Modigliani, Franco (1961), Dividend policy, growth, and the valuation of shares, Journal of Business, 34, 411-433.

Mills, Terence C./Markellos, Raphael N. (2008), The econometric modeling of financial time series, 3rd ed., Cambridge et al.

Missiakoulis, Spyros/Vasiliou, Dimitrios/Eriotis, Nikolaos (2008), Arithmetic mean: A bellwether for unbiased forecasting of portfolio performance, Working Paper, Hellenic Open University.

Morawietz, Markus (1994), Rentabilität und Risiko deutscher Aktien- und Rentenanlagen seit 1870, Wiesbaden.

Markowitz, Harry (1952), Portfolio selection, Journal of Finance, 7, 77-99.

Modigliani, Franco/Cohn, Richard A. (1979), Inflation and the stock market, Financial Analysts Journal, 35 (2), 24-44.

Modigliani, Franco/Miller, Merton H. (1958), The cost of capital, corporation finance, and the theory of investment, American Economic Review, 48, 261-297.

Modigliani, Franco/Miller, Merton H. (1963), Corporate taxes and the cost of capital: A correction, American Economic Review, 53, 433-443.

Molodovsky, Nicholas (1953), A theory of price-earnings ratios, Financial Analysts Journal, 9 (2), 65-80.

Morningstar Inc. (2007a), International equity risk premia report 2007, Chicago.

Morningstar Inc. (2007b), Risk premia over time report: 2007, Chicago.

Morningstar Inc. (2007c), Stocks, bonds, bills, and inflation 2007 – Valuation edition yearbook, Chicago.

Mossin, Jan (1966), Equilibrium in a capital asset market, Econometrica, 34, 768-783.

Moxter, Adolf (1983), Grundsätze ordnungsgemäßer Unternehmensbewertung, 2nd ed., Wiesbaden.

Nelson, Charles R./Kim, Myung J. (1993), Predictable stock returns: The role of small sample bias, Journal of Finance, 48, 641-661.

Nelson, Charles R./Siegel, Andrew F. (1987), Parsimonious modeling of yield curves, Journal of Business, 60, 473-489.

Neumann, John von/Morgenstern, Oskar (1967), Spieltheorie und wirtschaftliches Verhalten, 2nd ed., Würzburg.

Nicholson, S. Francis (1960), Price-earnings ratios, Financial Analysts Journal, 16 (4), 43-45.

Norstrom, Carl J. (1972), A sufficient condition for a unique nonnegative internal rate of return, Journal of Financial and Quantitative Analysis, 7, 1835-1839.

O'Brien, Patricia C. (1988), Analysts' forecasts as earnings expectations, Journal of Accounting and Economics, 10, 53-83.

O'Hanlon, John/Steele, Anthony (2000), Estimating the equity risk premium using accounting fundamentals, Journal of Business Finance & Accounting, 27, 1051-1083.

Obermaier, Robert (2005), Unternehmensbewertung, Basiszinssatz und Zinsstruktur, Working Paper, November 2005, University of Regensburg.

Obermaier, Robert (2006), Marktzinsorientierte Bestimmung des Basiszinssatzes in der Unternehmensbewertung, Finanz Betrieb, 8, 472-479.

Obermaier, Robert (2008), Die kapitalmarktorientierte Bestimmung des Basiszinssatzes für die Unternehmensbewertung: The Good, the Bad and the Ugly, Finanz Betrieb, 10, 493-507.

Ohlson, James A. (1990), A synthesis of security valuation theory and the role of dividends, cash flows, and earnings, Contemporary Accounting Review, 6, 648-676.

Ohlson, James A. (1995), Earnings, book values, and dividends in equity valuation, Contemporary Accounting Review, 11, 661-687.

Ohlson, James A. (2005), On accounting-based valuation formulae, Review of Accounting Studies, 10, 323-347.

Ohlson, James A./Goa, Zhan (2006), Earnings, earnings growth, and value, Foundations and Trends in Accounting, 1, 1-70.

Ohlson, James A./Jüttner-Nauroth, Beate (2005), Expected EPS and EPS growth as determinants of value, Review of Accounting Studies, 10, 349-365.

Ollmann, Michael/Richter, Frank (1999), Kapitalmarktorientierte Unternehmensbewertung und Einkommenssteuer – Eine deutsche Perspektive im Kontext internationaler Praxis, in: Kleineidam, Hans-Jochen (ed.), Unternehmenspolitik und internationale Besteuerung, Festschrift Fischer, Berlin, 159-178.

Olsson, Rickard (2005), Implications of constant growth of abnormal earnings in perpetuity for equity premia, discount rates, earnings, dividends, book values, and key financial ratios – An extension of Claus and Thomas, Working Paper, May 2005, Umea School of Business and Economics.

Ordelheide, Dieter (1998), Bedeutung und Wahrnehmung des Kongruenzprinzips ("Clean Surplus") im internationalen Rechnungswesen, in: Matschke, Manfred J./Schildbach, Thomas (eds.), Unternehmensberatung und Wirtschaftsprüfung, Festschrift Sieben, Stuttgart, 515-530.

Palepu, Krishna G./Healy, Paul M./Bernard, Victor L. (2000), Business analysis and valuation, 2nd ed., Cincinnati.

Pastor, Lubos/Sinha, Meenakshi/Swaminathan, Bhaskaran (2008), Estimating the intertemporal risk-return tradeoff using implied cost of capital, Journal of Finance, 63, 2859-2897.

Peasnell, Kenneth V. (1982), Some formal connections between economic values and yields and accounting numbers, Journal of Business Finance & Accounting, 9, 361-381.

Penman, Stephen H. (1998), A synthesis of equity valuation techniques and the terminal value calculation for the dividend discount model, Review of Accounting Studies, 4, 303-323.

Penman, Stephen H. (2001), On comparing cash flow and accrual accounting models for use in equity valuation: A response to Lundholm and O'Keefe, Contemporary Accounting Review, 18 (4), 681-692.

Penman, Stephen H. (2010), Financial statement analysis and security valuation, 4th ed., New York.

Penman, Stephen H./Sougiannis, Theodore (1998), A comparison of dividend, cash flow, and earnings approaches to equity valuation, Contemporary Accounting Research, 15, 343-383.

Pesaran, M. Hashem (2006), Market efficiency today, Medium For Econometric Applications, 14, 47-54.

Philbrick, Donna R./Ricks, William E. (1991), Using Value Line and IBES analyst forecasts in accounting research, Journal of Accounting Research, 29, 397-417.

Poddig, Thorsten/Dichtl, Hubert/Petersmeier, Kerstin (2008), Statistik, Ökonometrie, Optimierung – Methoden und praktische Anwendungen in Finanzanalyse und Portfoliomanagement, 4th ed., Bad Soden.

Polk, Christopher/Thompson, Samuel B./Vuolteenaho, Tuojmo (2006), Cross-sectional forecasts of the equity premium, Journal of Financial Economics, 81, 101-147.

Poterba, James M./Summers, Lawrence H. (1988), Mean reversion in stock prices, Journal of Financial Economics, 22, 27-59.

Preinreich, Gabriel A. D. (1937), Valuation and amortization, Accounting Review, 12, 209-226.

Preinreich, Gabriel A. D. (1938), Annual survey of economics theory: The theory of depreciation, Econometrica, 6, 219-241.

Prokop, Jörg (2003), Die Bewertung zukünftiger Unternehmenserfolge, Wiesbaden.

Rajan, Raghuram/Servaes, Henri (1997), Analyst following of initial public offerings, Journal of Finance, 52, 507-529.

Rapp, Marc S. (2004), Arbitragefreie Bewertung von Investitionsprojekten: Ein Brückenschlag zwischen No-Arbitrage-Theorie und DCF-Verfahren mittels stochastischer Diskontierungssätze, Working Paper, July 2004, HHL Leipzig.

Rapp, Marc S. (2006), Die arbitragefreie Adjustierung von Diskontierungssätzen bei einfacher Gewinnsteuer, Zeitschrift für betriebswirtschaftliche Forschung, 58, 771-806.

Reese, Raimo (2005), Alternative Modelle zur Schätzung der erwarteten Eigenkapitalkosten – Eine empirische Untersuchung für den deutschen Aktienmarkt, Working Paper, December 2005, LMU Munich.

Reese, Raimo (2007), Schätzung von Eigenkapitalkosten für die Unternehmensbewertung, Frankfurt.

Reese, Raimo/Wiese, Jörg (2007), Die kapitalmarktorientierte Ermittlung des Basiszinses für die Unternehmensbewertung, Zeitschrift für Bankrecht und Bankwirtschaft, 19, 38-52.

Reichert, Jörg (2007), Das Residual-Income-Model: Eine kritische Analyse, Frankfurt.

Richardson, Matthew/Stock, James H. (1989), Drawing inferences from statistics based on multiyear asset returns, Journal of Financial Economics, 25, 323-348.

Richter, Frank (1999), Konzeption eines marktwertorientierten Steuerungs- und Monitoringsystems, 2nd ed., Frankfurt.

Richter, Frank (2001), Simplified discounting rules in binomial models, Schmalenbach Business Review, 53, 175-196.

Richter, Frank (2002a), Kapitalmarktorientierte Unternehmensbewertung, Frankfurt.

Richter, Frank (2002b), On the relevance and irrelevance of personal income taxes for the valuation of equity investments, Working Paper, January 2002, University Witten/Herdecke.

Richer, Frank (2002c), Simplified discounting rules, variable growth, and leverage, Schmalenbach Business Review, 54, 136-147.

Richter, Frank (2003), Relativer Unternehmenswert und Einkommensteuer oder: Was ist paradox am Steuerparadoxon?, in: Richter, Frank/Schüler, Andreas/Schwetzler, Bernhard (eds.), Kapitalgeberansprüche, Marktwertorientierung und Unternehmenswert, Festschrift Drukarczyk, Munich, 307-329.

Richter, Frank (2004), Valuation with or without personal income taxes, Schmalenbach Business Review, 56, 20-45.

Richter, Frank (2005), Mergers & acquisitions, Munich.

Richter, Frank (2006a), Market risk premium and cash flow valuation: Three funerals and a wedding, Working Paper, August 2006, Ulm University.

Richter, Frank (2006b), Zwei Klarstellungen zu den "Bemerkungen über Kapitalkosten vor und nach Steuer" von Lutz Kruschwitz und Andreas Löffler, Zeitschrift für Betriebswirtschaft, 76, 103-110.

Richter, Frank (2007a), Steuerparadoxon 2.0? – Zur Bestimmung und Kommunizierbarkeit von Unternehmensbewertungen unter Berücksichtigung der zukünftigen Abgeltungssteuer, Working Paper, June 2007, Ulm University.

Richter, Frank (2007b), Unternehmenswert in Abhängigkeit von der Haltedauer? – Zur Berücksichtigung der Einkommensteuer bei der Unternehmensbewertung nach der Steuerreform 2008, Working Paper, November 2007, Ulm University.

Richter, Frank/Herrmann, Volker (2003), Pricing with performance-controlled multiples, Schmalenbach Business Review, 55, 194-219.

Richter, Frank/Honold, Dirk (2000), Das Schöne, das Unattraktive und das Hässliche an EVA & Co., Finanz Betrieb, 2, 265-274.

Roberts, Harry V. (1967), Statistical versus clinical prediction of the stock market, Unpublished Manuscript.

Röder, Klaus/Müller, Sarah (2001), Mehrperiodige Anwendung des CAPM im Rahmen von DCF-Verfahren, Finanz Betrieb, 3, 225-233.

Roll, Richard (1992), Industrial structure and the comparative behavior of international stock market indices, Journal of Finance, 47, 3-41.

Rosarius, Stephan (2007), Bewertung von Leveraged Buyouts, Frankfurt.

Ross, Stephan A. (1978), A simple approach to the valuation of risky income streams, Journal of Business, 51, 453-475.

Ross, Stephen A./Westerfield, Randolph W./Jaffe, Jeffrey F. (2008), Corporate finance, 8th ed., Boston et al.

Rozeff, Michael S. (1984), Dividend yields are equity risk premiums, Journal of Portfolio Management, 11 (1), 68-75.

Russell Investment Group (2006), Russell U.S. market indexes: Understanding managers creates better indexes, Washington.

Russell Investment Group (2007), Russell U.S. equity indexes: Construction and methodology, April 2007, Washington.

Sack, Brian (2000), Using treasury strips to measure the yield curve, Finance and Economics Discussion Series (FEDS) Working Paper, No. 42, October 2000, The Federal Reserve Board, Washington.

Samuelson, Paul A. (1964), Tax deductibility of economic depreciation to insure invariant valuations, Journal of Political Economy, 72, 604-606.

Samuelson, Paul A. (1965), Proof that properly anticipated prices fluctuate randomly, Industrial Management Review, 6, 41-49.

Schildbach, Thomas (1999), Externe Rechnungslegung und Kongruenz – Ursache für die Unterlegenheit deutscher verglichen mit angelsächsischer Bilanzierung?, Der Betrieb, 52, 1813-1820.

Schmitt, Dirk/Dausend, Florian (2006), Unternehmensbewertung mit dem Tax-CAPM, Finanz Betrieb, 8, 233-242.

Schneeweiß, Hans (1967), Entscheidungskriterien bei Risiko, Berlin et al.

Schneider, Dieter (1992), Investition, Finanzierung und Besteuerung, 7th ed., Wiesbaden.

Schröder, David (2007), The implied equity risk premium – An evaluation of empirical methods, Kredit und Kapital, 40, 583-613.

Schwetzler, Bernhard (1996), Zinsänderungsrisiko und Unternehmensbewertung: Das Basisfuß-Problem bei der Ertragswertermittlung, Zeitschrift für Betriebswirtschaft, 66, 1081-1101.

Schwetzler, Bernhard (2000), Unternehmensbewertung unter Unsicherheit – Sicherheitsäquivalent- oder Risikozuschlagsmethode, Zeitschrift für betriebswirtschaftliche Forschung, 52, 469-486.

Schwetzler, Bernhard (2002), Das Ende des Ertragswertverfahrens?, Zeitschrift für betriebswirtschaftliche Forschung, 54, 145-158.

Schwetzler, Bernhard (2005), Halbeinkünfteverfahren und Ausschüttungsequivalenz – die „Übertypisierung" der Ertragswertbestimmung, Die Wirtschaftsprüfung, 58, 601-617.

Schwetzler, Bernhard (2007), „Nebeneinander" von organischem und thesaurierungsbedingtem Wachstum in der Unternehmensbewertung, BewertungsPraktiker, April 2007, 2-6.

Securities and Exchange Commission (2005), Revisions to accelerated filer definition and accelerated deadlines for filing periodic reports, Release number 33-8644.

Sercu, Piet (1980), A generalization of the international asset pricing model, Revue de l'Association Frangaise de Finance, 1, 91-135.

Shackelford, Douglas A./Shevlin, Terry (2001), Empirical tax research in accounting, Journal of Accounting and Economics, 31, 321-387.

Sharpe, Steven A. (2002), Reexamining stock valuation and inflation: The implication of analysts' earnings forecasts, Review of Economics & Statistics, 84, 632-648.

Sharpe, William F. (1964), Capital asset prices: A theory of market equilibrium under conditions of risk, Journal of Finance, 19, 425-442.

Shiller, Robert J. (1984), Stock prices and social dynamics, Brookings Papers on Economic Activity, 2, 457-498.

Shiller, Robert J. (1993), Market volatility, 4th ed., Cambridge.

Shiller, Robert J. (2005), Irrational exuberance, 2nd ed., Princeton/Oxford.

Sick, Gordon (1990), Tax-adjusted discount rates, Management Science, 36, 1432-1450.

Siegel, Jeremy J. (1985), The application of the DCF methodology for determining the cost of equity capital, Financial Management, 14 (1), 46-53.

Siegel, Jeremy J. (1992), The equity premium: Stock and bond returns since 1802, Financial Analysts Journal, 48 (1), 28-38.

Siegel, Jeremy J. (1999), The shrinking equity premium, Journal of Portfolio Management, 26 (1), 10-17.

Siegel, Jeremy J. (2008), Stocks for the long-run, 4th ed., New York.

Solnik, Bruno H. (1974a), The international pricing of risk: An empirical investigation of the world capital market structure, Journal of Finance, 29, 365-378.

Solnik, Bruno H. (1974b), Why not diversify internationally rather than domestically?, Financial Analysts Journal, 30 (4), 48-54.

Solnik, Bruno H. (1974c), An equilibrium model of the international capital market, Journal of Economic Theory, 8, 500-524.

Solnik, Bruno H. (1974d), An international market model of security price behavior, Journal of Financial and Quantitative Analysis, 9, 537-554.

Solnik, Bruno H. (1977), Testing international asset pricing: Some pessimistic views, Journal of Finance, 32, 503-512.

Solnik, Bruno H./McLeavey, Dennis W. (2008), Global investments, 6th ed., Boston.

Spremann, Klaus (2002), Finanzanalyse und Unternehmensbewertung, Munich.

Spremann, Klaus (2004), Valuation, Munich.

Stambaugh, Robert F. (1999), Predictive regressions, Journal of Financial Economics, 54, 375-421.

Standard & Poor's (2006), S&P/TSX Canadian indices methodology, August 2006, New York.

Standard & Poor's (2007), S&P U.S. indices: Index methodologies, July 2007, New York.

Stehle, Richard (1977), An empirical test of the alternative hypotheses of national and international pricing of risky assets, Journal of Finance, 32, 493-502.

Stehle, Richard (1999), Renditevergleich von Aktien und festverzinslichen Wertpapieren auf Basis des DAX und des REXP, Working Paper, April 1999, Humboldt University Berlin.

Stehle, Richard (2004), Die Festlegung der Risikoprämie von Aktien im Rahmen der Schätzung des Wertes von börsennotierten Kapitalgesellschaften, Die Wirtschaftsprüfung, 57, 906-927.

Stehle, Richard/Hartmond, Anette (1991), Durchschnittsrenditen deutscher Aktien 1954-1988, Kredit und Kapital, 24, 371-411.

Stehle, Richard/Hausladen, Julie (2004), Die Schätzung der US-amerikanischen Risikoprämie auf Basis der historischen Renditezeitreihe, Die Wirtschaftsprüfung, 57, 928-936.

Stehle, Richard/Huber, Rainer/Maier, Jürgen (1996), Rückberechnung des DAX für die Jahre 1955 bis 1987, Kredit und Kapital, 29, 277-304.

Stehle, Richard/Wulff, Christian/Richter, Yvett (1999), Die Rendite deutscher Blue-Chip-Aktien in der Nachkriegszeit – Rückberechnung des DAX für die Jahre 1948-1954, Working Paper, July 1999, Humboldt University Berlin.

Steiner, Peter/Uhlir, Helmut (2001), Wertpapieranalyse, 4th ed., Heidelberg/Wien.

Stickel, Scott E. (1990), Predicting individual analyst earnings forecasts, Journal of Accounting Research, 28, 409-417.

Stulz, Rene M. (1981), A model of international asset pricing, Journal of Financial Economics, 9, 383-406.

Stulz, Rene M. (1995a), Globalization of capital markets and the cost of capital: The case of Nestle, Journal of Applied Corporate Finance, 8, 30-38.

Stulz, Rene M. (1995b), The cost of capital in internationally integrated markets: The case of Nestle, European Financial Management, 1, 11-22.

Stulz, Rene M./Wasserfallen, Walter (1995), Foreign equity investment restrictions, capital flight, and shareholder wealth maximization: Theory and evidence, Review of Financial Studies, 8, 1019-1057.

Svensson, Lars E. O. (1994), Estimating and interpreting forward interest rates: Sweden 1992-1994, IMF Working Paper 94/114, September 1994.

Thomson Financial (2003), Worldscope database, datatype definitions guide.

Thomson Financial (2008), Estimates glossary, A guide to understanding the terms and conventions of the First Call and I/B/E/S estimates databases.

Tietze, Jürgen (2009), Einführung in die Finanzmathematik, 9th ed., Wiesbaden.

Tobin, James (1958), Liquidity preference as behavior towards risk, Review of Economic Studies, 65-86.

Tokyo Stock Exchange Inc. (2007), Factbook 2007, Tokyo.

Torous, Walter/Valkanov, Rossen/Yan, Shu (2004), On Predicting stock returns with nearly integrated explanatory variables, Journal of Business, 77, 937-966.

Treynor, Jack L. (1961), Toward a theory of market value of risky assets, unpublished manuscript, subsequently in: Korajczyk, Robert A. (ed.), Asset pricing and portfolio performance: Models, strategy and performance metrics, London 1999, 15-22.

Trombetta, Marco (2004), Discussion of 'Implied cost of equity capital in earnings-based valuation: International evidence', Accounting & Business Research, 34, 345-348.

Tsay, Ruey S. (2005), Analysis of financial time series, 2nd ed., Hoboken.

Varian, Hal R. (2006), Intermediate microeconomics, 7th ed., New York/London.

Vasicek, Oldrich A. (1977), An equilibrium characterization of the term structure, Journal of Financial Economics, 5, 178-198.

Vuolteenaho, Tuomo (2002), What drives firm-level stock returns?, Journal of Finance, 57, 233-264.

Wagner, Wolfgang/Jonas, Martin/Ballwieser, Wolfgang/Tschöpel, Andreas (2004), Weiterentwicklung der Grundsätze zur Durchführung von Unternehmensbewertungen (IDW S 1), Die Wirtschaftsprüfung, 57, 889-898.

Wagner, Wolfgang/Jonas, Martin/Ballwieser, Wolfgang/Tschöpel, Andreas (2006), Unternehmensbewertung in der Praxis – Empfehlungen und Hinweise zur Anwendung von IDW S 1, Die Wirtschaftsprüfung, 59, 1005-1028.

Wagner, Wolfgang/Saur, Gerhard/Willershausen, Timo (2008), Zur Anwendung der Neuerungen der Unternehmensbewertungsgrundsätze des IDW S 1 i.d.F. 2008 in der Praxis, Die Wirtschaftsprüfung, 61, 731-747.

Wallmeier, Martin (1997), Prognose von Aktienrenditen und -risiken mit Mehrfaktorenmodellen – Eine empirische Untersuchung von erwarteten Renditen und Renditekorrelationen in Deutschland unter besonderer Berücksichtigung von Bilanzinformationen und Renditeanomalien, Bad Soden.

Wallmeier, Martin (2007), Implizite Kapitalkostensätze und der Fortführungswert im Residualgewinnmodell, Betriebswirtschaftliche Forschung und Praxis, 59, 558-579.

Welch, Ivo (2000), Views of financial economists on the equity premium and on professional controversies, Journal of Business, 73, 501-537.

Welch, Ivo (2001), The equity premium consensus forecast revisited, Cowles Foundation Discussion Paper, September 2001, Yale University.

Wenger, Ekkehard (2003), Der unerwünscht niedrige Basiszins als Störfaktor bei der Ausbootung von Minderheiten, in: Richter, Frank/Schüler, Andreas/Schwetzler, Bernhard (eds.), Kapitalgeberansprüche, Marktorientierung und Unternehmenswert, Festschrift Drukarczyk, Stuttgart, 475-495.

Wilhelm, Jochen/Brüning, Lars (1992), Die Fristigkeitsstruktur der Zinssätze: Theoretisches Konstrukt und empirische Evaluierung, Kredit und Kapital, 25, 259-294.

Williams, John B. (1938), The theory of investment value, Cambridge.

Widmann, Bernd/Schieszl, Sven/Jeromin, Axel (2003), Der Kapitalisierungszinssatz in der praktischen Unternehmensbewertung, Finanz Betrieb, 5, 800-810.

Wiese, Jörg (2006a), Komponenten des Zinsfußes in Unternehmensbewertungskalkülen, Frankfurt.

Wiese, Jörg (2006b), Das Nachsteuer-CAPM im Mehrperiodenkontext, Finanz Betrieb, 8, 242-248.

Wiese, Jörg (2006c), Unternehmensbewertung mit dem Nachsteuer-CAPM?, Working Paper, July 2006, LMU Munich.

Wiese, Jörg (2007a), Unternehmensbewertung und Abgeltungssteuer, Die Wirtschaftsprüfung, 60, 368-375.

Wiese, Jörg (2007b), Unternehmensbewertung unter neuen steuerlichen Rahmenbedingungen, Working Paper, February 2007, LMU Munich.

Wiese, Jörg (2007c), Steuerinduziertes und / oder inflationsbedingtes Wachstum in der Unternehmensbewertung? – Zur konsistenten Anwendung des Gordon/Shapiro-Modells bei Inflation und persönlicher Besteuerung, Working Paper, December 2007, LMU Munich.

Wong, Ka-Fu/Wu, Hai-Jun (2003), Testing Fisher hypothesis in long horizons for G7 and eight Asian countries, Applied Economics Letters, 10, 917-923.

Wooldridge, Jeffery M. (2008), Introductory econometrics, 4th ed., Boston.

Zeidler, Gernot W./Schöninger, Stefan/Tschöpel, Andreas (2008), Auswirkungen der Unternehmensteuerreform 2008 auf Unternehmensbewertungskalküle, Finanz Betrieb, 10, 276-288.

Zhang, Xiaoyan (2006), Specification tests of international asset pricing models, Journal of International Money and Finance, 25, 275-307.

Zimmermann, Jochen/Prokop, Jörg (2003), Rechnungswesenorientierte Unternehmensbewertung und Clean Surplus Accounting, Zeitschrift für internationale und kapitalmarktorientierte Rechnungslegung, 3, 134-142.

Appendix

Appendix 1 Results from the quarterly CFO survey on the expected MRP by Graham/Harvey

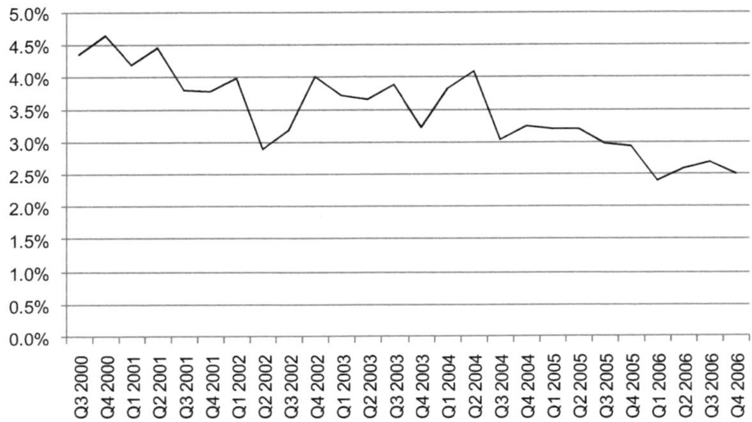

Source: Graham, J./Harvey, C. (2008), p. 5.

Appendix 2 Derivation of real vs. nominal MRP relationship for the standard valuation formula

$$V^r_{M,t} = \frac{C^r_{M,t+1}}{r^e_{M,r} - g^r_M} = \frac{C^r_{M,t+1}}{r^f_r + r^p_r - g^r_M}$$

$$V^r_{M,t} = V^n_{M,t}$$

$$\frac{C^r_{M,t+1}}{r^f_r + r^p_r - g^r_M} = \frac{C^n_{M,t+1}}{r^f_n + r^p_n - g^n_M} = \frac{C^r_{M,t+1}(1+\pi)}{\left[(1+r^f_r)(1+\pi)-1\right] + r^p_n - \left[(1+g^r_M)(1+\pi)-1\right]}$$

$$\left[(1+r^f_r)(1+\pi)-1\right] + r^p_n - \left[(1+g^r_M)(1+\pi)-1\right] = (1+\pi)(r^f_r + r^p_r - g^r_M)$$

$$1 + r^f_r + \pi + \pi r^f_r - 1 + r^p_n - 1 - g^r_M - \pi - \pi g^r_M + 1 = r^f_r + r^p_r - g^r_M + \pi r^f_r + \pi r^p_r - \pi g^r_M$$

$$r^p_n = r^p_r + \pi r^p_r$$

$$r^p_n = r^p_r(1+\pi)$$

Note: Expectation operators and random variable symbols are intentionally neglected.

Appendix 3 Bias of mean estimators in discrete return simulations

The following tables illustrate the bias in the arithmetic and geometric mean using a MRP simulation for compounding/discounting an amount of EUR 1 over an increasing horizon. For the purposes of the simulation, 1,000 samples of discrete normally distributed MRPs are generated using the parameters of Stehle's German CDAX data set for the period 1955 to 2006 with $\mu_R = 6.10\%,\ \text{std}\left[\tilde{R}\right] = 24.87\%, n = 52$.

Compounding estimators:

Holding period	True exp. value	True exp. return	Arith. mean estimator	Implied return	Geo. mean estimator	Implied return	Blume estimator	Implied return
1	1.0610	6.10%	1.0610	6.10%	1.0301	3.01%	1.0610	6.10%
2	1.1257	6.10%	1.1270	6.16%	1.0624	3.07%	1.1257	6.10%
5	1.3445	6.10%	1.3589	6.33%	1.1744	3.27%	1.3444	6.10%
10	1.8078	6.10%	1.8947	6.60%	1.4222	3.59%	1.8114	6.12%
15	2.4307	6.10%	2.7093	6.87%	1.7744	3.90%	2.4527	6.16%
20	3.2682	6.10%	3.9705	7.14%	2.2777	4.20%	3.3398	6.22%
25	4.3942	6.10%	5.9586	7.40%	3.0043	4.50%	4.5683	6.27%
30	5.9083	6.10%	9.1494	7.66%	4.0654	4.79%	6.2585	6.30%
35	7.9440	6.10%	14.3600	7.91%	5.6351	5.06%	8.5434	6.32%
40	10.6811	6.10%	23.0116	8.16%	7.9874	5.33%	11.5225	6.30%
45	14.3613	6.10%	37.6052	8.39%	11.5580	5.59%	15.1331	6.22%
50	19.3094	6.10%	62.5901	8.63%	17.0453	5.84%	18.8313	6.05%
60	34.9078	6.10%	182.2256	9.06%	38.9901	6.30%	16.5218	4.79%
70	63.1069	6.10%	562.0086	9.47%	94.4469	6.71%	-70.5749	NM
80	114.0856	6.10%	1,818.5395	9.84%	239.7576	7.09%	-627.0247	NM
90	206.2455	6.10%	6,122.6038	10.17%	632.4131	7.43%	-3,458.3173	NM
100	372.8536	6.10%	21,301.6545	10.48%	1,721.6316	7.74%	-16,706.6253	NM

Discounting estimators:

Holding period	True exp. value	True exp. return	Arith. mean estimator	Implied return	Geo. mean estimator	Implied return	Cooper estimator	Implied return
1	0.9425	6.10%	0.9435	5.99%	0.9720	2.88%	0.9423	6.12%
2	0.8883	6.10%	0.8911	5.94%	0.9460	2.81%	0.8878	6.13%
5	0.7437	6.10%	0.7555	5.77%	0.8788	2.62%	0.7409	6.18%
10	0.5532	6.10%	0.5861	5.49%	0.7975	2.29%	0.5405	6.35%
15	0.4114	6.10%	0.4670	5.21%	0.7475	1.96%	0.3790	6.68%
20	0.3060	6.10%	0.3823	4.93%	0.7236	1.63%	0.2417	7.36%
25	0.2276	6.10%	0.3214	4.64%	0.7231	1.31%	0.1166	8.98%
30	0.1693	6.10%	0.2775	4.37%	0.7454	0.98%	-0.0070	NM
35	0.1259	6.10%	0.2458	4.09%	0.7917	0.67%	-0.1395	NM
40	0.0936	6.10%	0.2233	3.82%	0.8652	0.36%	-0.2926	NM
45	0.0696	6.10%	0.2079	3.55%	0.9714	0.06%	-0.4808	NM
50	0.0518	6.10%	0.1980	3.29%	1.1186	-0.22%	-0.7226	NM
60	0.0286	6.10%	0.1915	2.79%	1.5890	-0.77%	-1.4801	NM
70	0.0158	6.10%	0.1996	2.33%	2.4460	-1.27%	-2.9277	NM
80	0.0088	6.10%	0.2215	1.90%	4.0276	-1.73%	-5.8235	NM
90	0.0048	6.10%	0.2586	1.51%	7.0146	-2.14%	-11.7962	NM
100	0.0027	6.10%	0.3145	1.16%	12.7977	-2.52%	-24.4071	NM

This simulation confirms the directional bias of both mean estimators formally derived in Section 4.3.1.2 and the implausible results of the Blume and Cooper estimator for long-term analyses.

Appendix 4 Bias of mean estimators in continuous return simulations

The following tables illustrate the bias in the arithmetic and geometric mean using a MRP simulation for compounding/discounting an amount of EUR 1 over an increasing horizon. For the purposes of the simulation, 1,000 samples of continuous normally distributed MRPs are generated using the parameters of Stehle's German CDAX data set for the period 1955 to 2006 with $\mu_r = 3.16\%$, $\text{std}[\tilde{r}] = 24.03\%$, $n = 52$.

Compounding estimators:

Holding period	True exp. value	True exp. return	Arith. mean estimator	Implied return	Geo. mean estimator	Implied return	JKM estimator	Implied return
1	1.0623	6.23%	1.0627	6.27%	1.0326	3.26%	1.0621	6.21%
2	1.1286	6.23%	1.1305	6.33%	1.0674	3.32%	1.1280	6.21%
5	1.3530	6.23%	1.3704	6.50%	1.1869	3.49%	1.3516	6.21%
10	1.8307	6.23%	1.9311	6.80%	1.4479	3.77%	1.8270	6.21%
15	2.4771	6.23%	2.7978	7.10%	1.8150	4.05%	2.4695	6.21%
20	3.3516	6.23%	4.1668	7.40%	2.3372	4.34%	3.3360	6.21%
25	4.5349	6.23%	6.3766	7.69%	3.0898	4.62%	4.5010	6.20%
30	6.1359	6.23%	10.0217	7.99%	4.1902	4.89%	6.0598	6.19%
35	8.3022	6.23%	16.1636	8.28%	5.8233	5.16%	8.1305	6.17%
40	11.2333	6.23%	26.7285	8.56%	8.2837	5.43%	10.8549	6.14%
45	15.1992	6.23%	45.2636	8.84%	12.0447	5.69%	14.3944	6.11%
50	20.5652	6.23%	78.3967	9.12%	17.8749	5.94%	18.9207	6.06%
60	37.6496	6.23%	250.1805	9.64%	41.5947	6.41%	31.5616	5.92%
70	68.9267	6.23%	858.6596	10.13%	103.0945	6.85%	49.4961	5.73%
80	126.1868	6.23%	3,135.3017	10.59%	269.1121	7.24%	71.7376	5.49%
90	231.0153	6.23%	12,066.2422	11.01%	732.8324	7.61%	94.6182	5.19%
100	422.9291	6.23%	48,570.4324	11.39%	2,066.0699	7.93%	112.0462	4.83%

Discounting estimators:

Holding period	True exp. value	True exp. return	Arith. mean estimator	Implied return	Geo. mean estimator	Implied return	JKM estimator	Implied return
1	0.9413	6.23%	0.9421	6.15%	0.9695	3.14%	0.9416	6.21%
2	0.8861	6.23%	0.8885	6.09%	0.9410	3.09%	0.8866	6.21%
5	0.7391	6.23%	0.7504	5.91%	0.8660	2.92%	0.7402	6.20%
10	0.5462	6.23%	0.5791	5.61%	0.7709	2.64%	0.5482	6.20%
15	0.4037	6.23%	0.4596	5.32%	0.7051	2.36%	0.4062	6.19%
20	0.2984	6.23%	0.3750	5.03%	0.6625	2.08%	0.3013	6.18%
25	0.2205	6.23%	0.3146	4.73%	0.6391	1.81%	0.2237	6.17%
30	0.1630	6.23%	0.2711	4.45%	0.6326	1.54%	0.1663	6.16%
35	0.1204	6.23%	0.2400	4.16%	0.6420	1.27%	0.1237	6.15%
40	0.0890	6.23%	0.2179	3.88%	0.6674	1.02%	0.0921	6.14%
45	0.0658	6.23%	0.2029	3.61%	0.7099	0.76%	0.0687	6.13%
50	0.0486	6.23%	0.1935	3.34%	0.7716	0.52%	0.0512	6.13%
60	0.0266	6.23%	0.1877	2.83%	0.9679	0.05%	0.0283	6.12%
70	0.0145	6.23%	0.1969	2.35%	1.3030	-0.38%	0.0155	6.14%
80	0.0079	6.23%	0.2204	1.91%	1.8615	-0.77%	0.0083	6.18%
90	0.0043	6.23%	0.2603	1.51%	2.7924	-1.13%	0.0043	6.25%
100	0.0024	6.23%	0.3210	1.14%	4.3575	-1.46%	0.0021	6.35%

This simulation confirms the directional bias of both mean estimators formally derived in Section 4.3.1.3 and the higher accuracy of unbiased (JKM) estimators when using continuous returns.

Appendix 5 Relationship between book value, earnings, and dividends growth

The relationship between earnings growth and retention rate $(1-\theta)$ times the return on book equity $r_t^b = E_t / B_{t-1}$ is derived in the following[973].

Firstly, the growth rate of book value is established:

$$g_t^B = \frac{B_t}{B_{t-1}} - 1 = \frac{B_{t-1} + E_t - D_t}{B_{t-1}} - 1 = \frac{E_t - D_t}{B_{t-1}} = \frac{E_t - E_t \theta_t}{B_{t-1}} = (1-\theta_t) r_t^b$$

Using this relationship, the standard earnings/dividend growth expressions can be derived:

$$g_{t+1}^E = \frac{E_t}{E_{t-1}} - 1 = \frac{D_t + (B_t - B_{t-1})}{D_{t-1} + (B_{t-1} - B_{t-2})} - 1 = \frac{D_t + g_t^B B_{t-1}}{D_{t-1} + g_{t-1}^B B_{t-2}} - 1$$

with $g_t^B = (1-\theta_t) r_t^b$ and $D_t = r_t^b B_{t-1} \theta_t$

$$g_t^E = \frac{r_t^b B_{t-1} \theta_t + (1-\theta_t) r_t^b B_{t-1}}{r_{t-1}^b B_{t-2} \theta_{t-1} + (1-\theta_{t-1}) r_{t-1}^b B_{t-2}} - 1 = \frac{r_t^b B_{t-1}}{r_{t-1}^b B_{t-2}} - 1 = \frac{r_t^b}{r_{t-1}^b} \left[1 + (1-\theta_{t-1}) r_{t-1}^b\right] - 1$$

with $r^b, \theta = \text{const.}$

$$g_E = (1-\theta) r^b = g_B$$

$$g_t^D = \frac{D_t}{D_{t-1}} - 1 = \frac{E_t - (B_t - B_{t-1})}{E_{t-1} - (B_{t-1} - B_{t-2})} - 1 = \frac{E_t - g_t^B B_{t-1}}{E_{t-1} - g_{t-1}^B B_{t-2}} - 1$$

with $g_t^B = (1-\theta_t) r_t^b$ and $E_t = r_t^b B_{t-1}$

$$g_t^D = \frac{r_t^b B_{t-1} - (1-\theta_t) r_t^b B_{t-1}}{r_{t-1}^b B_{t-2} - (1-\theta_{t-1}) r_{t-1}^b B_{t-2}} - 1 = \frac{r_t^b \theta_t B_{t-1}}{r_{t-1}^b \theta_{t-1} B_{t-2}} - 1 = \frac{r_t^b \theta_t}{r_{t-1}^b \theta_{t-1}} \left[1 + (1-\theta_{t-1}) r_{t-1}^b\right] - 1$$

with $r^b, \theta = \text{const.}$

$$g_D = (1-\theta) r^b = g_B = g_E$$

Note: Expectation operators and random variable symbols are intentionally neglected.

---

[973] See also Damodaran, A. (2002), p. 284 and Ross, S./Westerfield, R./Jaffe, J. (2008), pp. 141-142.

Appendix 6 Post-horizontal behavior of key value indicators under the RIV model – Olsson (2005) framework

Olsson (2005)[974] derives explicit formulas for the post-horizontal and asymptotic behavior of dividends, earnings, book values, return on book equity, price/book, and price/earnings ratios. His analysis is based on the following assumptions:

Cost of equity: r^e = positive and constant

Payout ratio: $0 < \theta \leq 1$ and constant

Growth of residual income: $-1 < g_{RI} < r_e$ and constant

Starting point for the derivation is the residual income definition and the clean-surplus relation:

$$RI_{t+1} = E_{t+1} - r^e B_t = (1+g_{RI})(E_t - r^e B_{t-1})$$
$$B_{t+1} = B_t + E_{t+1} - E_{t+1}\theta$$

The solution for this homogeneous equation system for E_t and B_t can be expressed in terms of E_1 and B_0:

$$E_t = \frac{g_{RI}(1+g_{RI})^{t-1}(E_1 - r^e B_0) + (g_{RI} B_0 + E_1(\theta-1)) r^e (1+r^e-\theta r^e)^{t-1}}{g_{RI} - (r^e - \theta r^e)}$$
$$B_t = \frac{-(1+g_{RI})^t(\theta-1)(E_1 - r^e B_0) + (g_{RI} B_0 + E_1(\theta-1))(1+r^e-\theta r^e)^t}{g_{RI} - (r^e - \theta r^e)}$$

with $g_{RI} \neq (r^e - \theta r^e)$

Based on both equations, one can extrapolate the development of all future parameters as mentioned above. Interesting general observations can now be drawn on the growth of earnings and book value as well as on the future r^b development.

First, the "inspection of (...) [both equations] reveals that the respective asymptotic growth rates of E_t and B_t converge to either the retention rate $r^e(1-\theta)$ or g_{RI} depending on what term is larger"[975]. Formally, this can be expressed as follows $\lim_{t\to\infty} g_E$ and $g_B = \text{Max}\left[g_{RI}; r^e(1-\theta)\right]$. The same expression is also applicable for dividend growth if the payout ratio is constant.

---

[974] See Olsson, R. (2005) for the entire appendix.

[975] Olsson, R. (2005), p. 8. Note that symbols are adapted to the standard format of this dissertation.

With respect to the implied future development of r^b Olsson derives the following expression

$$\lim_{t\to\infty}\frac{E_t}{B_{t-1}}=\lim_{t\to\infty}r^b=\frac{\dfrac{g_{RI}\left(1+g_{RI}\right)^{t-1}\left(E_1-r^eB_0\right)+\left(g_{RI}B_0+E_1\left(\theta-1\right)\right)r^e\left(1+r^e-\theta r^e\right)^{t-1}}{g_{RI}-\left(r^e-\theta r^e\right)}}{\dfrac{-\left(1+g_{RI}\right)^{t-1}\left(\theta-1\right)\left(E_1-r^eB_0\right)+\left(g_{RI}B_0+E_1\left(\theta-1\right)\right)\left(1+r^e-\theta r^e\right)^{t-1}}{g_{RI}-\left(r^e-\theta r^e\right)}}$$

$$=\frac{g_{RI}\left(1+g_{RI}\right)^{t-1}\left(E_1-r^eB_0\right)+\left(g_{RI}B_0+E_1\left(\theta-1\right)\right)r^e\left(1+r^e-\theta r^e\right)^{t-1}}{-\left(1+g_{RI}\right)^{t-1}\left(\theta-1\right)\left(E_1-r^eB_0\right)+\left(g_{RI}B_0+E_1\left(\theta-1\right)\right)\left(1+r^e-\theta r^e\right)^{t-1}}$$

$$=\begin{cases} r^e & \text{for } r^e\left(1-\theta\right)>g_{RI} \\ \dfrac{g_{RI}}{\left(1-\theta\right)} & \text{for } r^e\left(1-\theta\right)<g_{RI} \end{cases}$$

The additional prediction of market value related ratios such as PE or PB requires a model for the post-horizontal price behavior.

$$P_t=P_0=B_0+\frac{E_1-r^eB_0}{r^e-g_{RI}}=\frac{E_1-g_{RI}B_0}{r^e-g_{RI}}$$

$$P_t=\frac{g_{RI}\left(1+g_{RI}\right)^t\theta\left(E_1-r^eB_0\right)+\left(g_{RI}B_0+E_1\left(\theta-1\right)\right)\left(r^e-g_{RI}\right)\left(1+r^e\left(1-\theta\right)\right)^t}{\left(r^e-g_{RI}\right)\left(g_{RI}+r^e\left(\theta-1\right)\right)}$$

$$\text{Asymptotic } P_t/E_t \text{ ratio }=\begin{cases} 1-\theta+\dfrac{1}{r^e} & \text{for } r^e\left(1-\theta\right)>g_{RI} \\ \dfrac{\theta\left(1+g_{RI}\right)}{\left(r^e-g_{RI}\right)} & \text{for } r^e\left(1-\theta\right)<g_{RI} \end{cases}$$

$$\text{Asymptotic } P_t/B_t \text{ ratio }=\begin{cases} 1 & \text{for } r^e\left(1-\theta\right)>g_{RI} \\ \dfrac{\theta g_{RI}}{\left(1-\theta\right)\left(r^e-g_{RI}\right)} & \text{for } r^e\left(1-\theta\right)<g_{RI} \end{cases}$$

Finally note that the results derived by Olssen were verified using a tabulated procedure.[976]

Note: Expectation operators and random variable symbols are intentionally neglected.

[976] See also the summary by Reese, R. (2007), pp. 85-89.

Appendix 7 Illustrative derivation of two-period aggregated residual earnings

$$\sum_{t=s+1}^{s+2}\frac{E_t - r^e B_{t-1}}{\left(1+r^e\right)^{t-s}} = \frac{E_{s+1}-r^e B_s}{\left(1+r^e\right)} + \frac{E_{s+2}-r^e B_{s+1}}{\left(1+r^e\right)^2}$$

$$= \frac{\left(1+r^e\right)\left(E_{s+1}-r^e B_s\right)+E_{s+2}-r^e\left(B_s+E_{s+1}-D_{s+1}\right)}{\left(1+r^e\right)^2}$$

$$= \frac{1}{\left(1+r^e\right)^2}\left\{E_{s+1}-r^e B_s + r^e E_{s+1} - r^{e2}B_s + E_{s+2} - r^e B_s + r^e E_{s+1} - r^e D_{s+1}\right\}$$

$$= \frac{1}{\left(1+r^e\right)^2}\left\{\sum_{t=s+1}^{s+2} E_t - r^e B_s - r^{e2} B_s - r^e B_s + r^e D_{s+1}\right\}$$

$$= \frac{1}{\left(1+r^e\right)^2}\left\{\sum_{t=s+1}^{s+2} E_t + r^e D_{s+1} + D_{s+1} - D_{s+1} - \left(r^{e2}+2r^e+1-1\right)B_s\right\}$$

$$= \frac{1}{\left(1+r^e\right)^2}\left\{\sum_{t=s+1}^{s+2} E_t + \left[\left(1+r^e\right)-1\right]D_{s+1} - \left[\left(1+r^e\right)^2-1\right]B_s\right\}$$

Note: For simplification, the derivation of the two-period aggregation case is demonstrated. Expectation operators and random variable signs are intentionally neglected.

Appendix 8 Derivation of the CAP model

$$\mathrm{P_s} = \frac{E_s\left[\tilde{\mathrm{E}}_{s+1}\right]}{\mathrm{r^e}} + \sum_{t=s+1}^{\infty} \frac{E_s\left[\tilde{\mathrm{D}}_t\right] + \frac{E_s\left[\tilde{\mathrm{E}}_{t+1}\right]}{\mathrm{r^e}} - \left(1+\mathrm{r^e}\right)\frac{E_s\left[\tilde{\mathrm{E}}_t\right]}{\mathrm{r^e}}}{\left(1+\mathrm{r^e}\right)^{t-s}}$$

$$= \frac{E_s\left[\tilde{\mathrm{E}}_{s+1}\right]}{\mathrm{r^e}} + \sum_{t=s+1}^{\infty} \frac{E_s\left[\tilde{\mathrm{D}}_t\right] + \frac{E_s\left[\tilde{\mathrm{E}}_{t+1}\right]}{\mathrm{r^e}} - \frac{E_s\left[\tilde{\mathrm{E}}_t\right]}{\mathrm{r^e}} - E_s\left[\tilde{\mathrm{E}}_t\right]}{\left(1+\mathrm{r^e}\right)^{t-s}}$$

$$= \frac{E_s\left[\tilde{\mathrm{E}}_{s+1}\right]}{\mathrm{r^e}} + \sum_{t=s+1}^{\infty} \frac{\frac{1}{\mathrm{r^e}}\left(\mathrm{r^e}E_s\left[\tilde{\mathrm{D}}_t\right] + E_s\left[\tilde{\mathrm{E}}_{t+1}\right] - E_s\left[\tilde{\mathrm{E}}_t\right] - \mathrm{r^e}E_s\left[\tilde{\mathrm{E}}_t\right]\right)}{\left(1+\mathrm{r^e}\right)^{t-s}}$$

$$= \frac{E_s\left[\tilde{\mathrm{E}}_{s+1}\right]}{\mathrm{r^e}} + \sum_{t=s+1}^{\infty} \frac{\frac{1}{\mathrm{r^e}}\left(E_s\left[\tilde{\mathrm{E}}_{t+1}\right] + \mathrm{r^e}E_s\left[\tilde{\mathrm{D}}_t\right] - \left(1+\mathrm{r^e}\right)E_s\left[\tilde{\mathrm{E}}_t\right]\right)}{\left(1+\mathrm{r^e}\right)^{t-s}}$$

$$= \frac{E_s\left[\tilde{\mathrm{E}}_{s+1}\right]}{\mathrm{r^e}} + \sum_{t=s+1}^{\infty} \frac{\left(E_s\left[\tilde{\mathrm{E}}_{t+1}\right] + \mathrm{r^e}E_s\left[\tilde{\mathrm{D}}_t\right] - \left(1+\mathrm{r^e}\right)E_s\left[\tilde{\mathrm{E}}_t\right]\right)}{\mathrm{r^e}\left(1+\mathrm{r^e}\right)^{t-s}}$$

$$= \frac{E_s\left[\tilde{\mathrm{E}}_{s+1}\right]}{\mathrm{r^e}} + \sum_{t=s+1}^{\infty} \frac{E_s\left[\mathrm{agr}_t\right]}{\mathrm{r^e}\left(1+\mathrm{r^e}\right)^{t-s}}$$

Appendix 9 Derivation of steady state book value and agr growth

Book value development with steady state from TV-2 onwards:
(steady state TV-1 case identical by moving all parameters one period forward)

$$\begin{aligned}
B_{TV-1} &= B_{TV-2} + E_{TV-1} - D_{TV-1} \\
&= B_{TV-2} + \left(RI_{TV-1} + r^e B_{TV-2}\right)(1-\theta) \\
&= B_{TV-2} + RI_{TV-1} + r^e B_{TV-2} - RI_{TV-1}\theta - r^e B_{TV-2}\theta \\
&= B_{TV-2} + \left(r^b - r^e\right) B_{TV-2} + r^e B_{TV-2} - \left(r^b - r^e\right) B_{TV-2}\theta - r^e B_{TV-2}\theta \\
&= B_{TV-2} + r^b B_{TV-2} - r^e B_{TV-2} + r^e B_{TV-2} - r^b B_{TV-2}\theta + r^e B_{TV-2}\theta - r^e B_{TV-2}\theta \\
&= B_{TV-2}\left(1 + r^b - r^b\theta\right) \\
&= B_{TV-2}\left(1 + r^b(1-\theta)\right) \\
&= B_{TV-2}(1+g)
\end{aligned}$$

with $RI_{TV-1} = \left(r^b - r^e\right) B_{TV-2}$, $r^b = \text{const.}$ in steady state, $g = r^b(1-\theta)$ in steady state

agr development with steady state from TV-2 or TV-1 onwards:

$$\begin{aligned}
agr_{TV-1} &= E_{TV} - E_{TV-1} + r^e\left(D_{TV-1} - E_{TV-1}\right) \\
&= (1+g) RI_{TV-1} + r^e B_{TV-1} - RI_{TV-1} - r^e B_{TV-2} + r^e\left(\left(RI_{TV-1} + r^e B_{TV-2}\right)\theta_{TV-1} - RI_{TV-1} - r^e B_{TV-2}\right) \\
&= RI_{TV-1}\left(g - r^e\right) + r^e\left(B_{TV-1} + \theta_{TV-1}\left(RI_{TV-1} + r^e B_{TV-2}\right) - B_{TV-2}\left(1 + r^e\right)\right) \\
&= RI_{TV-1}\left(g - r^e\right) + r^e\left(B_{TV-1} + \frac{B_{TV-2} - B_{TV-1} + RI_{TV-1} + r^e B_{TV-2}}{RI_{TV-1} + r^e B_{TV-2}}\left(RI_{TV-1} + r^e B_{TV-2}\right) - B_{TV-2}\left(1 + r^e\right)\right) \\
&= RI_{TV-1}\left(g - r^e\right) + r^e\left(RI_{TV-1} + B_{TV-1} - B_{TV-1} + B_{TV-2}\left(1 + r^e\right) - B_{TV-2}\left(1 + r^e\right)\right) \\
&= RI_{TV-1}g - RI_{TV-1}r^e + r^e RI_{TV-1} \\
&= RI_{TV-1}g
\end{aligned}$$

with $\theta_{TV-1} = \frac{D_{TV-1}}{E_{TV-1}} = \frac{B_{TV-2} - B_{TV-1} + E_{TV-1}}{E_{TV-1}} = \frac{B_{TV-2} - B_{TV-1} + RI_{TV-1} + r^e B_{TV-2}}{RI_{TV-1} + r^e B_{TV-2}}$

Note: Expectation operators and random variable symbols are neglected.

Appendix 10 Equality between daily RIV model and simple compounding of full-year RIV model

$$P_s^{\text{daily RIV}} = E_s\left[\tilde{B}_s\right] + \frac{E_s\left[\tilde{E}_{1-s} - \left[\left(1+r^e\right)^{1-s} - 1\right]\tilde{B}_s\right]}{\left(1+r^e\right)^{1-s}} + \frac{E_s\left[\tilde{E}_2 - r^e\tilde{B}_1\right]}{\left(1+r^e\right)^{2-s}} + \frac{E_s\left[\tilde{E}_3 - r^e\tilde{B}_2\right]}{\left(r^e - g_{RI}\right)\left(1+r^e\right)^{2-s}}$$

$$P_s^{\text{full-year RIV}} = \left\{B_0 + \frac{E_s\left[\tilde{E}_1 - r^eB_0\right]}{\left(1+r^e\right)} + \frac{E_s\left[\tilde{E}_2 - r^e\tilde{B}_1\right]}{\left(1+r^e\right)^2} + \frac{E_s\left[\tilde{E}_3 - r^e\tilde{B}_2\right]}{\left(r^e - g_{RI}\right)\left(1+r^e\right)^2}\right\}\left(1+r^e\right)^s$$

generally assume $s \in \left[0;1\right]$ representing the fraction of the year already past

$$\begin{aligned}
P_s^{\text{full-year RIV}} &= \left\{B_0 + \frac{E_s\left[\tilde{E}_1 - r^eB_0\right]}{\left(1+r^e\right)} + \frac{E_s\left[\tilde{E}_2 - r^e\tilde{B}_1\right]}{\left(1+r^e\right)^2} + \frac{E_s\left[\tilde{E}_3 - r^e\tilde{B}_2\right]}{\left(r^e - g_{RI}\right)\left(1+r^e\right)^2}\right\}\left(1+r^e\right)^s \\
&= B_0\left(1+r^e\right)^s + \frac{E_s\left[\tilde{E}_1 - r^eB_0\right]}{\left(1+r^e\right)^{1-s}} + \frac{E_s\left[\tilde{E}_2 - r^e\tilde{B}_1\right]}{\left(1+r^e\right)^{2-s}} + \frac{E_s\left[\tilde{E}_3 - r^e\tilde{B}_2\right]}{\left(r^e - g_{RI}\right)\left(1+r^e\right)^{2-s}} \\
&= E_s\left[B_0\left(1+r^b\right)^s\right] - E_s\left[B_0\left(1+r^b\right)^s\right] + B_0\left(1+r^e\right)^s + \frac{E_s\left[\tilde{E}_1 - r^eB_0\right]}{\left(1+r^e\right)^{1-s}} + \frac{E_s\left[\tilde{E}_2 - r^e\tilde{B}_1\right]}{\left(1+r^e\right)^{2-s}} \\
&\quad + \frac{E_s\left[\tilde{E}_3 - r^e\tilde{B}_2\right]}{\left(r^e - g_{RI}\right)\left(1+r^e\right)^{2-s}} \\
&= E_s\left[B_0\left(1+r^b\right)^s\right] + \frac{E_s\left[\tilde{E}_1 - r^eB_0 - B_0\left(1+r^e\right)^{1-s}\left(1+r_1^b\right)^s + B_0\left(1+r^e\right)\right]}{\left(1+r^e\right)^{1-s}} \\
&\quad + \frac{E_s\left[\tilde{E}_2 - r^e\tilde{B}_1\right]}{\left(1+r^e\right)^{2-s}} + \frac{E_s\left[\tilde{E}_3 - r^e\tilde{B}_2\right]}{\left(r^e - g_{RI}\right)\left(1+r^e\right)^{2-s}} \\
&= E_s\left[B_0\left(1+r^b\right)^s\right] + \frac{E_s\left[\tilde{E}_1 - r^eB_0 - B_0\left(1+r^e\right)^{1-s}\left(1+r_1^b\right)^s + \tilde{B}_0\left(1+r^e\right) + B_0\left(1+r_1^b\right)^s - B_0\left(1+r_1^b\right)^s\right]}{\left(1+r^e\right)^{1-s}} \\
&\quad + \frac{E_s\left[\tilde{E}_2 - r^e\tilde{B}_1\right]}{\left(1+r^e\right)^{2-s}} + \frac{E_s\left[\tilde{E}_3 - r^e\tilde{B}_2\right]}{\left(r^e - g_{RI}\right)\left(1+r^e\right)^{2-s}} \\
&= E_s\left[B_0\left(1+r^b\right)^s\right] + \frac{E_s\left[\tilde{E}_1 - B_0\left(1+r_1^b\right)^s + B_0 - \left[\left(1+r^e\right)^{1-s} - 1\right]B_0\left(1+r_1^b\right)^s\right]}{\left(1+r^e\right)^{1-s}} \\
&\quad + \frac{E_s\left[\tilde{E}_2 - r^e\tilde{B}_1\right]}{\left(1+r^e\right)^{2-s}} + \frac{E_s\left[\tilde{E}_3 - r^e\tilde{B}_2\right]}{\left(r^e - g_{RI}\right)\left(1+r^e\right)^{2-s}} \\
&= E_s\left[\tilde{B}_s\right] + \frac{E_s\left[\tilde{E}_{1-s} - \left[\left(1+r^e\right)^{1-s} - 1\right]\tilde{B}_s\right]}{\left(1+r^e\right)^{1-s}} + \frac{E_s\left[\tilde{E}_2 - r^e\tilde{B}_1\right]}{\left(1+r^e\right)^{2-s}} + \frac{E_s\left[\tilde{E}_3 - r^e\tilde{B}_2\right]}{\left(r^e - g_{RI}\right)\left(1+r^e\right)^{2-s}} \\
&= P_s^{\text{daily RIV}}
\end{aligned}$$

with $E_s\left[B_0\left(1+r^b\right)^s\right] = E_s\left[\tilde{B}_s\right]$ and $E_s\left[\tilde{E}_1 - B_0\left(1+r_1^b\right)^s + B_0\right] = E_s\left[\tilde{E}_1 - B_0\left(\left(1+r_1^b\right)^s - 1\right)\right] = E_s\left[\tilde{E}_{1-s}\right]$

Appendix 11 Summary of German input data for the expected MRP estimation based on analysts' consensus estimates 1989-1997

	29.12.1989	31.12.1990	31.12.1991	31.12.1992	31.12.1993	30.12.1994	29.12.1995	31.12.1996	31.12.1997
Sample size									
Sum companies included	21	57	57	69	73	80	87	108	119
LTM average of included companies	35	41	64	71	75	85	93	104	117
LTM number of observations	415	491	768	851	894	1021	1112	1245	1409
Input variables (EUR million)									
Sum earnings +1 (IBES)	7,926	9,468	8,842	8,658	6,942	8,667	12,997	16,608	21,237
Sum earnings +2 (IBES)	8,568	9,751	9,394	8,947	8,973	11,424	14,814	19,606	24,477
Sum earnings +3 (IBES)	9,156	10,612	11,028	9,455	11,128	13,834	16,703	21,993	27,153
Sum earnings +4 (IBES)	9,901	11,541	12,037	10,369	13,278	16,237	19,010	24,429	30,517
Sum earnings +5 (IBES)	10,708	12,538	13,144	11,315	14,534	18,247	21,626	27,779	35,001
Implied earnings CAGR (IBES)	*7.8%*	*7.3%*	*10.4%*	*6.9%*	*20.3%*	*20.5%*	*13.6%*	*13.7%*	*13.3%*
Sum dividends +1 (IBES/WS ratio)	3,484	3,885	4,150	4,012	3,243	3,828	4,856	6,164	8,001
Sum dividends +2 (IBES/WS ratio)	3,763	4,021	4,386	4,157	4,219	4,164	5,166	7,398	8,632
Sum dividends +3 (IBES/WS ratio)	3,995	4,320	5,068	4,429	5,394	4,797	5,654	8,170	9,418
Sum dividends +4 (IBES/WS ratio)	4,314	4,684	5,528	4,844	6,581	6,723	8,388	8,169	12,120
Sum dividends +5 (IBES/WS ratio)	4,665	5,089	6,037	5,285	7,204	7,555	9,541	9,289	13,901
Implied dividends CAGR (IBES/WS ratio)	*7.6%*	*7.0%*	*9.8%*	*7.1%*	*22.1%*	*18.5%*	*18.4%*	*10.8%*	*14.8%*
Implied payout ratio +1	44.0%	41.0%	46.9%	46.3%	46.7%	44.2%	37.4%	37.1%	37.7%
Implied payout ratio +2	43.9%	41.2%	46.7%	46.5%	47.0%	36.5%	34.9%	37.7%	35.3%
Implied payout ratio +3	43.6%	40.7%	46.0%	46.8%	48.5%	34.7%	33.9%	37.1%	34.7%
Implied payout ratio +4	43.6%	40.6%	45.9%	46.7%	49.6%	41.4%	44.1%	33.4%	39.7%
Implied payout ratio +5	43.6%	40.6%	45.9%	46.7%	49.6%	41.4%	44.1%	33.4%	39.7%
Sum book value 0 (Worldscope)	54,881	75,988	84,824	89,103	94,743	99,409	114,192	143,202	166,016
Sum implied book value +1	59,323	81,572	89,516	93,749	98,442	104,247	122,333	153,646	179,252
Sum implied book value +2	64,127	87,302	94,525	98,538	103,196	111,507	131,982	165,854	195,096
Sum implied book value +3	69,288	93,594	100,484	103,564	108,929	120,544	143,030	179,678	212,831
Sum implied book value +4	74,875	100,451	106,993	109,089	115,626	130,059	153,653	195,938	231,228
Sum implied book value +5	80,918	107,900	114,100	115,119	122,956	140,751	165,738	214,427	252,328
Sum market capitalization (IBES)	93,614	133,138	138,814	138,356	205,229	186,025	244,792	339,822	487,972

Note: The large change in payout ratios in the years 1994 to 1997 from +3 to +4 is due to the discrepancy between current and historical average payout ratios. Note that the used methodology implies that when no direct dividends forecasts are available, historical payout ratios are to be used.

Source: Datastream, IBES, Worldscope (WS).

Appendix 12 Summary of German input data for the expected MRP estimation based on analysts' consensus estimates 1998-2006

	31.12.1998	31.12.1999	29.12.2000	31.12.2001	31.12.2002	31.12.2003	31.12.2004	30.12.2005	29.12.2006
Sample size									
Sum companies included	146	201	280	303	238	205	235	263	274
LTM average of included companies	134	173	246	292	273	205	214	229	260
LTM number of observations	1606	2072	2947	3506	3271	2464	2567	2742	3122
Input variables (EUR million)									
Sum earnings +1 (IBES)	25,919	32,869	38,245	35,422	32,874	35,796	45,521	58,182	72,409
Sum earnings +2 (IBES)	28,891	38,462	43,065	48,864	43,749	47,039	53,520	65,930	78,597
Sum earnings +3 (IBES)	32,835	44,229	49,329	61,191	52,660	55,849	59,919	72,401	87,080
Sum earnings +4 (IBES)	36,085	49,218	58,120	69,455	58,861	57,937	65,156	73,542	91,294
Sum earnings +5 (IBES)	42,320	56,724	65,516	82,068	65,358	62,766	69,510	77,543	96,302
Implied earnings CAGR (IBES)	*13.0%*	*14.6%*	*14.4%*	*23.4%*	*18.7%*	*15.1%*	*11.2%*	*7.4%*	*7.4%*
Sum dividends +1 (IBES/WS ratio)	9,422	13,486	14,812	16,197	13,936	12,317	16,457	21,035	26,534
Sum dividends +2 (IBES/WS ratio)	10,186	14,515	15,723	17,417	15,311	15,204	18,780	23,725	29,701
Sum dividends +3 (IBES/WS ratio)	11,060	15,798	17,125	19,561	16,932	16,828	21,001	26,209	32,629
Sum dividends +4 (IBES/WS ratio)	12,796	17,604	19,561	20,782	18,248	18,418	23,920	27,788	33,874
Sum dividends +5 (IBES/WS ratio)	15,007	20,289	22,051	24,556	20,262	19,953	25,518	29,300	35,732
Implied dividends CAGR (IBES/WS ratio)	*12.3%*	*10.7%*	*10.5%*	*11.0%*	*9.8%*	*12.8%*	*11.6%*	*8.6%*	*7.7%*
Implied payout ratio +1	36.4%	41.0%	38.7%	45.7%	42.4%	34.4%	36.2%	36.2%	36.6%
Implied payout ratio +2	35.3%	37.7%	36.5%	35.6%	35.0%	32.3%	35.1%	36.0%	37.8%
Implied payout ratio +3	33.7%	35.7%	34.7%	32.0%	32.2%	30.1%	35.0%	36.2%	37.5%
Implied payout ratio +4	35.5%	35.8%	33.7%	29.9%	31.0%	31.8%	36.7%	37.8%	37.1%
Implied payout ratio +5	35.5%	35.8%	33.7%	29.9%	31.0%	31.8%	36.7%	37.8%	37.1%
Sum book value 0 (Worldscope)	194,746	267,426	333,205	410,531	458,200	391,702	391,264	431,825	508,071
Sum implied book value +1	211,243	286,809	356,637	429,757	477,138	415,180	420,328	468,972	553,946
Sum implied book value +2	229,947	310,756	383,979	461,203	505,576	447,016	455,068	511,178	602,842
Sum implied book value +3	251,723	339,187	416,182	502,833	541,303	486,036	493,986	557,370	657,293
Sum implied book value +4	275,012	370,800	454,741	551,507	581,917	525,555	535,223	603,123	714,713
Sum implied book value +5	302,326	407,235	498,207	609,019	627,012	568,368	579,215	651,366	775,283
Sum market capitalization (IBES)	574,127	879,840	1,006,981	828,560	508,922	626,148	663,891	857,159	1,068,804

Source: Datastream, IBES, Worldscope (WS).

Appendix 13 Summary statistics of the German expected MRP estimation using special comparison specifications of previous studies

Model (1)						1.5.1 Claus/Thomas			1.5.2 Gebhardt et al.			1.5.3 Gode/Mohanram			1.5.4 Easton - PEG		1.5.5 Easton - PE	
Year	r^f (2)	θ_{TV}	$m_{P/E+1}$	N (3)	Firms (4)	r^e	r^P	$g_{RI,TV}$	r^e	r^P	Target r^b	r^e	r^P	$g_{agr,TV}$	r^e	r^P	r^e	r^P
1989	6.92%	44.74%	12.2x	415	35	10.34%	3.43%	3.92%	8.03%	1.11%	9.35%	10.39%	3.48%	3.92%	7.76%	0.85%	8.54%	1.62%
1990	8.61%	41.13%	13.9x	491	41	10.16%	1.55%	5.61%	7.30%	-1.30%	9.35%	9.64%	1.03%	5.61%	7.14%	-1.47%	7.51%	-1.09%
1991	8.37%	45.90%	16.0x	768	64	9.27%	0.90%	5.37%	7.05%	-1.32%	9.35%	9.43%	1.06%	5.37%	6.74%	-1.63%	6.47%	-1.90%
1992	7.78%	45.52%	15.7x	851	71	9.18%	1.40%	4.78%	7.38%	-0.39%	9.35%	10.27%	2.49%	4.78%	7.49%	-0.29%	6.62%	-1.16%
1993	6.48%	46.54%	22.8x	894	75	7.52%	1.05%	3.48%	6.34%	-0.14%	9.35%	9.39%	2.91%	3.48%	7.33%	0.85%	4.62%	-1.86%
1994	6.99%	46.21%	26.4x	1,021	85	8.75%	1.76%	3.99%	6.33%	-0.66%	9.37%	13.19%	6.19%	3.99%	10.46%	3.46%	3.93%	-3.06%
1995	6.81%	43.64%	21.8x	1,112	93	9.10%	2.29%	3.81%	6.72%	-0.08%	9.30%	12.96%	6.15%	3.81%	10.45%	3.64%	4.75%	-2.06%
1996	6.24%	38.88%	20.4x	1,245	104	8.42%	2.18%	3.24%	6.22%	-0.02%	9.11%	11.03%	4.79%	3.24%	9.00%	2.76%	5.02%	-1.21%
1997	5.67%	38.78%	23.7x	1,409	117	7.36%	1.69%	2.67%	5.30%	-0.37%	8.99%	10.06%	4.39%	2.67%	8.31%	2.64%	4.31%	-1.35%
1998	4.55%	40.00%	24.4x	1,606	134	6.66%	2.12%	1.55%	4.93%	0.38%	8.97%	8.66%	4.11%	1.55%	7.38%	2.83%	4.21%	-0.34%
1999	4.62%	37.24%	23.0x	2,072	173	6.94%	2.32%	1.62%	5.24%	0.62%	9.05%	9.14%	4.52%	1.62%	7.70%	3.08%	4.46%	-0.17%
2000	5.30%	34.38%	29.4x	2,947	246	6.41%	1.11%	2.30%	4.70%	-0.59%	9.24%	9.22%	3.92%	2.30%	7.65%	2.36%	3.48%	-1.82%
2001	4.87%	30.91%	21.5x	3,506	292	8.07%	3.20%	1.87%	6.61%	1.74%	9.49%	11.63%	6.76%	1.87%	9.93%	5.06%	4.82%	-0.05%
2002	4.80%	29.88%	19.3x	3,271	273	9.66%	4.87%	1.80%	8.45%	3.65%	9.76%	14.66%	9.86%	1.80%	12.75%	7.95%	5.58%	0.79%
2003	4.14%	31.85%	15.2x	2,464	205	9.96%	5.82%	1.14%	9.17%	5.03%	10.00%	14.97%	10.84%	1.14%	13.14%	9.01%	6.94%	2.80%
2004	4.09%	35.20%	14.7x	2,567	214	9.03%	4.94%	1.09%	8.33%	4.24%	10.19%	12.64%	8.55%	1.09%	11.02%	6.93%	6.99%	2.90%
2005	3.37%	37.57%	14.1x	2,742	229	8.56%	5.18%	0.37%	8.05%	4.67%	10.31%	11.11%	7.74%	0.37%	9.55%	6.18%	7.33%	3.96%
2006	3.81%	36.70%	14.5x	3,122	260	8.20%	4.38%	0.81%	7.66%	3.84%	10.39%	10.16%	6.35%	0.81%	8.55%	4.73%	7.15%	3.33%
Low	3.37%	29.88%	12.2x	415	35	6.41%	0.90%	0.37%	4.70%	-1.32%	8.97%	8.66%	1.03%	0.37%	6.74%	-1.63%	3.48%	-3.06%
Arith. Mean	5.74%	39.17%	19.4x	1,806	150	8.53%	2.79%	2.74%	6.88%	1.13%	9.50%	11.03%	5.29%	2.74%	9.02%	3.28%	5.71%	-0.04%
Median	5.48%	38.83%	19.9x	1,508	126	8.65%	2.24%	2.48%	6.89%	0.18%	9.35%	10.33%	4.66%	2.48%	8.43%	2.96%	5.30%	-0.72%
High	8.61%	46.54%	29.4x	3,506	292	10.34%	5.82%	5.61%	9.17%	5.03%	10.39%	14.97%	10.84%	5.61%	13.14%	9.01%	8.54%	3.96%
St. Dev.	1.60%	5.45%	5.0x			1.19%	1.60%	1.60%	1.29%	2.16%	0.44%	1.92%	2.77%	1.60%	1.92%	3.02%	1.49%	2.12%

(1) All parameters are stated in nominal terms and as arithmetic average of monthly values.
(2) r^f equals redemption yield of the REX 10y subindex.
(3) Overall number of firm observations per annum.
(4) Average number of firms per annum.

Appendix 14 Comparison of studies using the Gebhardt/Lee/Swaminathan version of the RIV model to determine the expected MRP for the German market

Model (1)	Gebhardt/Lee/Swaminathan Model																	
Study	Gsell (2010)					Reese (2005, 2007)						Daske/Gebhardt/Klein (2006)				Lee et al. (2009) (5)	
Year	N	Companies	agg(2) - r^e	agg - r^p	r^f	N	ew(3) - r^e	ew - r^p	vw(4) - r^e	vw - r^p	r^f	N	ew - r^e	ew - r^p	r^f	Companies	ew-r^p
1989	415	35	8.03%	1.11%	6.92%	613	7.93%	1.04%	8.68%	1.79%	6.89%	581	7.9%	0.9%	6.9%	NA	NA
1990	491	41	7.30%	-1.30%	8.61%	719	7.25%	-1.36%	7.79%	-0.82%	8.61%	826	7.4%	-1.5%	8.6%	NA	NA
1991	768	64	7.05%	-1.32%	8.37%	1,102	7.60%	-0.78%	7.88%	-0.50%	8.38%	1,125	7.8%	-0.8%	8.4%	19	1.0%
1992	851	71	7.38%	-0.39%	7.78%	1,290	8.14%	0.37%	7.91%	0.14%	7.77%	1,530	8.2%	0.2%	7.8%	40	0.5%
1993	894	75	6.34%	-0.14%	6.48%	1,404	7.87%	1.36%	6.82%	0.31%	6.51%	1,588	7.8%	1.5%	6.5%	50	2.9%
1994	1,021	85	6.33%	-0.66%	6.99%	1,581	7.74%	0.77%	6.84%	-0.13%	6.97%	1,618	7.6%	1.1%	6.9%	69	3.2%
1995	1,112	93	6.72%	-0.08%	6.81%	1,695	8.62%	1.80%	7.17%	0.35%	6.82%	1,862	8.4%	2.0%	6.8%	73	4.3%
1996	1,245	104	6.22%	-0.02%	6.24%	1,826	9.31%	3.07%	6.92%	0.68%	6.24%	2,038	9.1%	3.5%	6.3%	75	4.4%
1997	1,409	117	5.30%	-0.37%	5.67%	2,151	8.42%	2.74%	6.12%	0.44%	5.68%	2,220	8.9%	3.8%	5.7%	86	3.8%
1998	1,606	134	4.93%	0.38%	4.55%	2,442	8.89%	4.32%	5.82%	1.25%	4.57%	2,576	9.9%	5.6%	4.6%	84	5.0%
1999	2,072	173	5.24%	0.62%	4.62%	2,818	10.34%	5.77%	6.27%	1.70%	4.57%	3,021	11.6%	7.4%	4.6%	94	6.7%
2000	2,947	246	4.70%	-0.59%	5.30%	3,470	10.62%	5.31%	6.25%	0.94%	5.31%	3,219	11.6%	6.4%	5.3%	131	8.7%
2001	3,506	292	6.61%	1.74%	4.87%	3,754	14.71%	9.83%	8.53%	3.65%	4.88%	3,306	15.6%	11.0%	4.9%	NA	NA
2002	3,271	273	8.45%	3.65%	4.80%	3,434	16.35%	11.53%	10.39%	5.57%	4.82%	3,383	17.5%	13.0%	4.8%	NA	NA
2003	2,464	205	9.17%	5.03%	4.14%	2,611	13.57%	9.44%	10.79%	6.66%	4.13%	NA	NA	NA	NA	NA	NA
2004	2,567	214	8.33%	4.24%	4.09%	2,659	10.24%	6.16%	9.60%	5.52%	4.08%	NA	NA	NA	NA	NA	NA
2005	2,742	229	8.05%	4.67%	3.37%	NA	NA	NA	NA	NA	NA	NA	NA	NA	NA	NA	NA
2006	3,122	260	7.66%	3.84%	3.81%	NA	NA	NA	NA	NA	NA	NA	NA	NA	NA	NA	NA
Low	415	35	4.70%	-1.32%	3.37%	613	7.25%	-1.36%	5.82%	-0.82%	4.08%	581	7.40%	-1.50%	4.60%	19	0.5%
Arith. Mean	1,806	150	6.88%	1.13%	5.74%	2,098	9.85%	3.84%	7.74%	1.72%	6.01%	2,064	9.95%	3.86%	6.29%	72	4.1%
Median	1,508	126	6.89%	0.18%	5.48%	1,989	8.76%	2.91%	7.48%	0.81%	5.96%	1,950	8.65%	2.75%	6.40%	74	4.1%
High	3,506	292	9.17%	5.03%	8.61%	3,754	16.35%	11.53%	10.79%	6.66%	8.61%	3,383	17.50%	13.00%	8.60%	131	8.7%
St. Dev.			1.29%	2.16%	1.60%		2.74%	3.90%	1.52%	2.34%	1.48%		3.13%	4.35%	1.37%		2.4%

(1) All parameters are stated in nominal terms.
(2) Aggregation method.
(3) Equal-weighted.
(4) Value-weighted.
(5) Estimation based on dividend discount model with r^e equal to r^b after 15 years. This assumption should be more conservative compared to the Gebhardt/Lee/Swaminathan model with constant RI post the horizon.

Source: Reese, R. (2005), pp. 13 and 19, Daske, H./Gebhardt, G./Klein, S. (2006), p. 15, and Lee, C./Ng, D./Swaminathan, B. (2009), p. 318.

Appendix 15 Comparison of studies using the Claus/Thomas version of the RIV model to determine the expected MRP for the German market

Model (1)	Claus/Thomas Model																	
Study	Gsell (2010)					Reese (2005, 2007)								Claus/Thomas (2001)				
Year	N	Companies	agg(2) - r^e	agg - r^p	r^f	N	Companies	ew(3) - r^e	ew - r^p	vw(4) - r^e	vw - r^p	r^f	N	Companies	agg - r^e	agg - r^p	r^f
1988	NA	NA	NA	NA	NA	NA	NA	NA	NA	NA	NA	NA	NA	NA	10.2%	3.43%	6.78%
1989	415	35	10.34%	3.43%	6.92%	613	NA	9.98%	3.09%	10.81%	3.92%	6.89%	NA	NA	10.7%	3.87%	6.83%
1990	491	41	10.16%	1.55%	8.61%	719	NA	10.30%	1.69%	10.59%	1.98%	8.61%	NA	NA	10.1%	1.10%	8.99%
1991	768	64	9.27%	0.90%	8.37%	1,102	NA	9.66%	1.28%	9.99%	1.61%	8.38%	NA	NA	9.5%	1.03%	8.42%
1992	851	71	9.18%	1.40%	7.78%	1,290	NA	9.58%	1.81%	9.68%	1.91%	7.77%	NA	NA	10.1%	2.16%	7.89%
1993	894	75	7.52%	1.05%	6.48%	1,404	NA	8.68%	2.17%	8.00%	1.49%	6.51%	NA	NA	6.8%	0.70%	6.14%
1994	1,021	85	8.75%	1.76%	6.99%	1,581	NA	9.50%	2.53%	9.20%	2.23%	6.97%	NA	NA	8.6%	1.30%	7.26%
1995	1,112	93	9.10%	2.29%	6.81%	1,695	NA	10.48%	3.66%	9.76%	2.94%	6.82%	NA	NA	8.9%	2.22%	6.70%
1996	1,245	104	8.42%	2.18%	6.24%	1,826	NA	10.04%	3.80%	8.79%	2.55%	6.24%	NA	NA	8.6%	2.14%	6.41%
1997	1,409	117	7.36%	1.69%	5.67%	2,151	NA	9.04%	3.36%	7.66%	1.98%	5.68%	NA	NA	8.0%	2.28%	5.68%
1998	1,606	134	6.66%	2.12%	4.55%	2,442	NA	9.00%	4.43%	6.83%	2.26%	4.57%	NA	NA	NA	NA	NA
1999	2,072	173	6.94%	2.32%	4.62%	2,818	NA	10.27%	5.70%	6.68%	2.11%	4.57%	NA	NA	NA	NA	NA
2000	2,947	246	6.41%	1.11%	5.30%	3,470	NA	9.88%	4.57%	6.52%	1.21%	5.31%	NA	NA	NA	NA	NA
2001	3,506	292	8.07%	3.20%	4.87%	3,754	NA	14.62%	9.74%	7.92%	3.04%	4.88%	NA	NA	NA	NA	NA
2002	3,271	273	9.66%	4.87%	4.80%	3,434	NA	15.88%	11.06%	9.22%	4.40%	4.82%	NA	NA	NA	NA	NA
2003	2,464	205	9.96%	5.82%	4.14%	2,611	NA	12.70%	8.57%	9.33%	5.20%	4.13%	NA	NA	NA	NA	NA
2004	2,567	214	9.03%	4.94%	4.09%	2,659	NA	9.65%	5.57%	8.48%	4.40%	4.08%	NA	NA	NA	NA	NA
2005	2,742	229	8.56%	5.18%	3.37%	NA	NA	NA	NA	NA	NA	NA	NA	NA	NA	NA	NA
2006	3,122	260	8.20%	4.38%	3.81%	NA	NA	NA	NA	NA	NA	NA	NA	NA	NA	NA	NA
Low	415	35	6.41%	0.90%	3.37%	613	NA	8.68%	1.28%	6.52%	1.21%	4.08%	NA	NA	6.84%	0.70%	5.68%
Arith. Mean	1,806	150	8.53%	2.79%	5.74%	2,098	NA	10.58%	4.56%	8.72%	2.70%	6.01%	NA	NA	9.13%	2.02%	7.11%
Median	1,508	126	8.65%	2.24%	5.48%	1,989	NA	9.93%	3.73%	9.00%	2.25%	5.96%	NA	NA	9.19%	2.15%	6.81%
High	3,506	292	10.34%	5.82%	8.61%	3,754	NA	15.88%	11.06%	10.81%	5.20%	8.61%	NA	NA	10.70%	3.87%	8.99%
St. Dev.			1.19%	1.60%	1.60%			2.04%	2.93%	1.35%	1.18%	1.48%			1.20%	0.96%	1.09%

(1) All parameters are stated in nominal terms.
(2) Aggregation method.
(3) Equal-weighted.
(4) Value-weighted.

Source: Reese, R. (2005), pp. 13 and 19 and Claus, J./Thomas, J. (2001), p. 1649.

Appendix 16 Comparison of studies using the Gode/Mohanram version of the CAP (Ohlson/Jüttner-Nauroth) model to determine the expected MRP for the German market

Model (1)	Ohlson/Juettner-Nauroth Model										
Study	Gsell (2010)					Reese (2005, 2007)					
Year	N	Companies	agg(2) - r^e	agg - r^p	r^f	N	ew(3) - r^e	ew - r^e	vw(4) - r^e	vw - r^p	r^f
1989	415	35	10.39%	3.48%	6.92%	524	10.32%	3.43%	10.75%	3.86%	6.89%
1990	491	41	9.64%	1.03%	8.61%	589	10.47%	1.86%	10.35%	1.74%	8.61%
1991	768	64	9.43%	1.06%	8.37%	939	10.46%	2.08%	10.05%	1.67%	8.38%
1992	851	71	10.27%	2.49%	7.78%	982	10.73%	2.96%	10.41%	2.64%	7.77%
1993	894	75	9.39%	2.91%	6.48%	916	9.79%	3.28%	9.60%	3.09%	6.51%
1994	1,021	85	13.19%	6.19%	6.99%	987	10.83%	3.86%	11.15%	4.18%	6.97%
1995	1,112	93	12.96%	6.15%	6.81%	1,015	11.62%	4.80%	11.61%	4.79%	6.82%
1996	1,245	104	11.03%	4.79%	6.24%	914	11.41%	5.17%	9.67%	3.43%	6.24%
1997	1,409	117	10.06%	4.39%	5.67%	1,233	10.52%	4.84%	9.46%	3.78%	5.68%
1998	1,606	134	8.66%	4.11%	4.55%	1,277	10.55%	5.98%	8.64%	4.07%	4.57%
1999	2,072	173	9.14%	4.52%	4.62%	1,048	11.06%	6.49%	8.41%	3.84%	4.57%
2000	2,947	246	9.22%	3.92%	5.30%	839	11.46%	6.15%	8.31%	3.00%	5.31%
2001	3,506	292	11.63%	6.76%	4.87%	857	13.50%	8.62%	10.23%	5.35%	4.88%
2002	3,271	273	14.66%	9.86%	4.80%	1,206	14.83%	10.01%	11.94%	7.12%	4.82%
2003	2,464	205	14.97%	10.84%	4.14%	1,524	14.25%	10.12%	12.42%	8.29%	4.13%
2004	2,567	214	12.64%	8.55%	4.09%	1,526	12.41%	8.33%	11.14%	7.06%	4.08%
2005	2,742	229	11.11%	7.74%	3.37%	NA	NA	NA	NA	NA	NA
2006	3,122	260	10.16%	6.35%	3.81%	NA	NA	NA	NA	NA	NA
Low	415	35	8.66%	1.03%	3.37%	524	9.79%	1.86%	8.31%	1.67%	4.08%
Arith. Mean	1,806	150	11.03%	5.29%	5.74%	1,024	11.51%	5.50%	10.26%	4.24%	6.01%
Median	1,508	126	10.33%	4.66%	5.48%	985	10.95%	5.01%	10.29%	3.85%	5.96%
High	3,506	292	14.97%	10.84%	8.61%	1,526	14.83%	10.12%	12.42%	8.29%	8.61%
St. Dev.			1.92%	2.77%	1.60%		1.48%	2.65%	1.22%	1.89%	1.48%

(1) All parameters are stated in nominal terms.
(2) Aggregation method.
(3) Equal-weighted.
(4) Value-weighted.

Source: Reese, R. (2005), pp. 13 and 19.

Appendix 17 Comparison of studies using the regression-based estimation approach to determine the expected MRP for the German market

Model (1)	Regression-based estimation approach										
Study	Gsell (2010)						Daske/Gebhardt/Klein (2006)				
Year	N	Companies	r^e	g	r^p	r^f	N	r^e	g	r^p	r^f
1989	412	34	10.50%	7.18%	3.58%	6.92%	541	10.70%	7.30%	3.60%	6.9%
1990	491	41	11.20%	9.00%	2.60%	8.61%	772	10.50%	8.20%	1.60%	8.6%
1991	759	63	8.62%	5.43%	0.26%	8.37%	1,065	8.20%	5.10%	-0.40%	8.4%
1992	851	71	8.48%	5.41%	0.70%	7.78%	1,453	8.30%	4.20%	0.30%	7.8%
1993	887	74	7.95%	4.93%	1.47%	6.48%	1,499	7.90%	4.50%	1.60%	6.5%
1994	975	81	8.60%	6.14%	1.61%	6.99%	1,549	8.10%	4.00%	1.50%	6.9%
1995	1,067	89	10.38%	8.06%	3.57%	6.81%	1,779	9.30%	4.40%	2.90%	6.8%
1996	1,208	101	9.19%	4.94%	2.95%	6.24%	1,954	9.00%	3.80%	3.40%	6.3%
1997	1,362	114	9.08%	5.37%	3.41%	5.67%	2,135	9.00%	5.20%	3.90%	5.7%
1998	1,494	125	10.39%	6.97%	5.84%	4.55%	2,488	11.70%	9.20%	7.30%	4.6%
1999	1,812	151	11.59%	8.24%	6.97%	4.62%	2,915	15.60%	13.90%	11.40%	4.6%
2000	2,247	187	11.58%	9.37%	6.29%	5.30%	3,089	22.10%	21.20%	16.80%	5.3%
2001	3,302	275	11.48%	7.88%	6.62%	4.87%	3,166	14.80%	12.10%	10.20%	4.9%
2002	3,154	263	10.27%	5.16%	5.48%	4.80%	3,231	12.30%	8.00%	7.90%	4.8%
2003	2,405	200	10.35%	6.08%	6.21%	4.14%	NA	NA	NA	NA	NA
2004	2,490	208	9.56%	5.02%	5.47%	4.09%	NA	NA	NA	NA	NA
2005	2,634	220	8.28%	2.80%	4.91%	3.37%	NA	NA	NA	NA	NA
2006	2,975	248	10.09%	5.73%	6.27%	3.81%	NA	NA	NA	NA	NA
Low	412	34	7.95%	2.80%	0.26%	3.37%	541	7.90%	3.80%	-0.40%	4.60%
Arith. Mean	1,696	141	9.87%	6.32%	4.12%	5.74%	1,974	11.25%	7.94%	5.14%	6.29%
Median	1,428	119	10.18%	5.90%	4.24%	5.48%	1,867	9.90%	6.25%	3.50%	6.40%
High	3,302	275	11.59%	9.37%	6.97%	8.61%	3,231	22.10%	21.20%	16.80%	8.60%
St. Dev.			1.19%	1.70%	2.17%	1.60%		3.97%	4.94%	4.94%	1.37%

(1) All parameters are stated in nominal terms.

Source: Daske, H./Gebhardt, G./Klein, S. (2006), p. 15.

Appendix 18 Summary of Canadian input data for the expected MRP estimation based on analysts' consensus estimates 1989-1997

	29.12.1989	31.12.1990	31.12.1991	31.12.1992	31.12.1993	30.12.1994	29.12.1995	31.12.1996	31.12.1997
Sample size									
Sum companies included	47	43	41	39	39	42	45	64	69
LTM average of included companies	45	43	40	41	37	36	41	57	62
LTM number of observations	543	519	477	492	447	434	492	678	747
Input variables (C$ million)									
Sum earnings +1 (IBES)	7,431	5,042	4,718	2,634	3,844	5,572	9,790	11,582	15,552
Sum earnings +2 (IBES)	7,964	5,801	6,092	3,149	4,819	6,737	11,193	13,351	17,984
Sum earnings +3 (IBES)	8,855	7,132	7,286	3,910	5,621	7,958	12,405	14,736	20,319
Sum earnings +4 (IBES)	9,716	8,160	8,126	4,384	6,417	9,155	13,303	16,303	22,917
Sum earnings +5 (IBES)	10,680	8,716	9,076	4,847	7,176	10,397	14,448	18,090	25,638
Implied earnings CAGR (IBES)	*9.5%*	*14.7%*	*17.8%*	*16.5%*	*16.9%*	*16.9%*	*10.2%*	*11.8%*	*13.3%*
Sum dividends +1 (IBES/WS ratio)	2,807	2,795	2,359	1,551	1,939	2,342	4,178	4,230	6,044
Sum dividends +2 (IBES/WS ratio)	3,034	3,244	3,006	1,700	2,281	2,691	4,709	4,786	6,796
Sum dividends +3 (IBES/WS ratio)	3,365	3,908	3,555	1,925	2,572	3,047	5,403	5,101	7,508
Sum dividends +4 (IBES/WS ratio)	3,677	4,399	3,929	2,047	2,801	3,413	5,891	5,602	8,257
Sum dividends +5 (IBES/WS ratio)	4,042	4,698	4,388	2,264	3,133	3,876	6,398	6,216	9,238
Implied dividends CAGR (IBES/WS ratio)	*9.5%*	*13.9%*	*16.8%*	*9.9%*	*12.7%*	*13.4%*	*11.2%*	*10.1%*	*11.2%*
Implied payout ratio +1	37.8%	55.4%	50.0%	58.9%	50.4%	42.0%	42.7%	36.5%	38.9%
Implied payout ratio +2	38.1%	55.9%	49.4%	54.0%	47.3%	39.9%	42.1%	35.8%	37.8%
Implied payout ratio +3	38.0%	54.8%	48.8%	49.2%	45.8%	38.3%	43.6%	34.6%	37.0%
Implied payout ratio +4	37.8%	53.9%	48.3%	46.7%	43.7%	37.3%	44.3%	34.4%	36.0%
Implied payout ratio +5	37.8%	53.9%	48.3%	46.7%	43.7%	37.3%	44.3%	34.4%	36.0%
Sum book value 0 (Worldscope)	56,703	45,429	57,271	32,364	43,330	47,485	77,610	88,498	103,146
Sum implied book value +1	61,327	47,676	59,629	33,447	45,235	50,714	83,222	95,850	112,654
Sum implied book value +2	66,257	50,233	62,714	34,896	47,774	54,761	89,705	104,416	123,842
Sum implied book value +3	71,748	53,456	66,446	36,881	50,823	59,671	96,707	114,052	136,653
Sum implied book value +4	77,787	57,218	70,643	39,217	54,438	65,413	104,120	124,752	151,313
Sum implied book value +5	84,425	61,235	75,331	41,801	58,482	71,934	112,170	136,626	167,713
Sum market capitalization (IBES)	75,719	58,824	73,018	43,878	66,126	65,041	115,469	157,851	274,171

Source: Datastream, IBES, Worldscope (WS).

Appendix 19 Summary of Canadian input data for the expected MRP estimation based on analysts' consensus estimates 1998-2006

	31.12.1998	31.12.1999	29.12.2000	31.12.2001	31.12.2002	31.12.2003	31.12.2004	30.12.2005	29.12.2006
Sample size									
Sum companies included	71	66	79	88	88	112	123	137	145
LTM average of included companies	66	66	67	74	81	96	105	120	131
LTM number of observations	791	796	806	890	972	1157	1263	1442	1570
Input variables (C$ million)									
Sum earnings +1 (IBES)	14,739	17,638	26,656	26,134	29,414	35,984	48,198	61,041	68,841
Sum earnings +2 (IBES)	17,099	21,044	28,912	26,376	33,433	37,728	53,167	69,630	76,992
Sum earnings +3 (IBES)	19,494	23,819	32,656	30,249	37,057	41,524	55,437	73,786	82,399
Sum earnings +4 (IBES)	21,902	26,796	36,005	34,857	41,485	46,373	59,466	77,684	87,233
Sum earnings +5 (IBES)	24,502	29,889	40,432	39,376	46,969	51,309	65,455	89,688	93,507
Implied earnings CAGR (IBES)	*13.5%*	*14.1%*	*11.0%*	*10.8%*	*12.4%*	*9.3%*	*8.0%*	*10.1%*	*8.0%*
Sum dividends +1 (IBES/WS ratio)	6,276	6,053	7,768	6,482	9,208	11,309	15,262	19,097	24,358
Sum dividends +2 (IBES/WS ratio)	7,057	6,905	8,312	6,499	10,665	12,467	17,066	21,819	26,617
Sum dividends +3 (IBES/WS ratio)	6,945	7,610	9,504	7,487	11,471	14,136	18,096	24,687	28,172
Sum dividends +4 (IBES/WS ratio)	7,742	9,224	10,284	8,632	12,850	15,030	18,900	25,218	27,269
Sum dividends +5 (IBES/WS ratio)	8,661	10,289	11,548	9,752	14,549	16,630	20,803	29,115	29,230
Implied dividends CAGR (IBES/WS ratio)	*8.4%*	*14.2%*	*10.4%*	*10.7%*	*12.1%*	*10.1%*	*8.1%*	*11.1%*	*4.7%*
Implied payout ratio +1	42.6%	34.3%	29.1%	24.8%	31.3%	31.4%	31.7%	31.3%	35.4%
Implied payout ratio +2	41.3%	32.8%	28.8%	24.6%	31.9%	33.0%	32.1%	31.3%	34.6%
Implied payout ratio +3	35.6%	31.9%	29.1%	24.8%	31.0%	34.0%	32.6%	33.5%	34.2%
Implied payout ratio +4	35.3%	34.4%	28.6%	24.8%	31.0%	32.4%	31.8%	32.5%	31.3%
Implied payout ratio +5	35.3%	34.4%	28.6%	24.8%	31.0%	32.4%	31.8%	32.5%	31.3%
Sum book value 0 (Worldscope)	109,468	122,962	161,420	171,544	195,709	215,416	268,647	314,670	348,504
Sum implied book value +1	117,931	134,546	180,307	191,196	215,916	240,091	301,583	356,614	392,988
Sum implied book value +2	127,974	148,685	200,906	211,073	238,684	265,353	337,683	404,425	443,363
Sum implied book value +3	140,523	164,894	224,058	233,835	264,271	292,741	375,025	453,523	497,590
Sum implied book value +4	154,683	182,466	249,780	260,059	292,906	324,083	415,591	505,989	557,554
Sum implied book value +5	170,524	202,067	278,664	289,683	325,326	358,762	460,243	566,563	621,832
Sum market capitalization (IBES)	257,065	322,519	400,742	404,698	424,232	522,176	704,918	943,626	1,086,669

Source: Datastream, IBES, Worldscope (WS).

Appendix 20 Summary statistics of the Canadian expected MRP estimation using special comparison specifications of previous studies

Model (1)						1.5.1 Claus/Thomas			1.5.2 Gebhardt et al.			1.5.3 Gode/Mohanram			1.5.4 Easton - PEG		1.5.5 Easton - PE	
Year	r^f (2)	θ_{TV}	$m_{P/E+1}$	N (3)	Firms (4)	r^e	r^p	$g_{RI,TV}$	r^e	r^p	Target r^b	r^e	r^p	$g_{agr,TV}$	r^e	r^p	r^e	r^p
1989	9.78%	37.02%	10.0x	543	45	12.56%	2.78%	6.78%	9.48%	-0.30%	11.35%	13.52%	3.74%	6.78%	10.48%	0.70%	10.97%	1.19%
1990	10.81%	53.24%	10.7x	519	43	13.81%	3.01%	7.81%	11.77%	0.97%	12.38%	15.89%	5.09%	7.81%	10.77%	-0.04%	10.11%	-0.70%
1991	9.39%	48.14%	13.1x	477	40	12.26%	2.87%	6.39%	11.09%	1.70%	12.38%	16.29%	6.89%	6.39%	12.08%	2.68%	8.24%	-1.15%
1992	8.08%	46.26%	14.6x	492	41	11.57%	3.50%	5.08%	10.84%	2.76%	12.38%	16.81%	8.74%	5.08%	12.89%	4.82%	7.42%	-0.65%
1993	7.21%	46.23%	16.5x	447	37	10.42%	3.22%	4.21%	9.84%	2.63%	12.38%	15.00%	7.79%	4.21%	11.48%	4.28%	6.38%	-0.83%
1994	8.47%	42.07%	13.2x	434	36	12.63%	4.16%	5.47%	10.98%	2.50%	12.10%	16.92%	8.45%	5.47%	12.95%	4.47%	8.10%	-0.37%
1995	8.03%	40.92%	11.7x	492	41	11.98%	3.95%	5.03%	10.50%	2.47%	11.61%	15.17%	7.14%	5.03%	11.72%	3.70%	9.17%	1.14%
1996	7.19%	36.14%	12.3x	678	57	10.89%	3.70%	4.19%	9.68%	2.49%	11.43%	12.53%	5.34%	4.19%	9.98%	2.79%	8.71%	1.52%
1997	6.11%	36.35%	16.2x	747	62	9.56%	3.45%	3.11%	8.02%	1.92%	11.35%	11.74%	5.63%	3.11%	9.53%	3.43%	6.56%	0.45%
1998	5.27%	36.24%	17.8x	791	66	8.97%	3.69%	2.27%	7.55%	2.28%	11.32%	11.40%	6.13%	2.27%	9.48%	4.21%	5.87%	0.60%
1999	5.58%	35.56%	18.5x	796	66	8.97%	3.39%	2.58%	7.58%	2.00%	11.42%	11.77%	6.19%	2.58%	9.75%	4.17%	5.65%	0.08%
2000	5.88%	29.89%	15.9x	806	67	9.24%	3.37%	2.88%	8.03%	2.15%	11.64%	10.18%	4.30%	2.88%	8.50%	2.63%	6.65%	0.77%
2001	5.45%	27.06%	14.8x	890	74	9.30%	3.85%	2.45%	8.45%	2.99%	11.91%	9.60%	4.15%	2.45%	8.25%	2.79%	7.14%	1.69%
2002	5.28%	29.87%	15.6x	972	81	9.82%	4.54%	2.28%	8.90%	3.62%	12.20%	12.42%	7.14%	2.28%	10.69%	5.41%	6.72%	1.44%
2003	4.80%	31.42%	14.0x	1,157	96	9.67%	4.86%	1.80%	9.03%	4.23%	12.46%	10.17%	5.37%	1.80%	8.61%	3.81%	7.54%	2.73%
2004	4.58%	33.30%	14.1x	1,263	105	8.89%	4.31%	1.58%	8.54%	3.96%	12.65%	9.51%	4.93%	1.58%	8.01%	3.43%	7.36%	2.78%
2005	4.06%	33.63%	14.9x	1,442	120	8.47%	4.41%	1.06%	8.26%	4.20%	12.81%	10.03%	5.97%	1.06%	8.64%	4.58%	7.06%	3.00%
2006	4.22%	30.10%	15.2x	1,570	131	8.35%	4.13%	1.22%	8.19%	3.97%	12.94%	9.95%	5.73%	1.22%	8.49%	4.27%	6.95%	2.73%
Low	4.06%	27.06%	10.0x	434	36	8.35%	2.78%	1.06%	7.55%	-0.30%	11.32%	9.51%	3.74%	1.06%	8.01%	-0.04%	5.65%	-1.15%
Arith. Mean	6.68%	37.41%	14.4x	806	67	10.41%	3.73%	3.68%	9.26%	2.59%	12.04%	12.72%	6.04%	3.68%	10.13%	3.45%	7.59%	0.91%
Median	5.99%	36.19%	14.7x	769	64	9.74%	3.70%	2.99%	8.96%	2.50%	12.15%	12.09%	5.85%	2.99%	9.86%	3.75%	7.25%	0.96%
High	10.81%	53.24%	18.5x	1,570	131	13.81%	4.86%	7.81%	11.77%	4.23%	12.94%	16.92%	8.74%	7.81%	12.95%	5.41%	10.97%	3.00%
St. Dev.	2.03%	7.29%	2.3x			1.67%	0.59%	2.03%	1.32%	1.17%	0.54%	2.66%	1.43%	2.03%	1.60%	1.38%	1.42%	1.35%

(1) All parameters are stated in nominal terms and as arithmetic average of monthly values.
(2) r^f equals redemption yield of the Canadian Datastream benchmark 10y government bond index.
(3) Overall number of firm observations per annum.
(4) Average number of firms per annum.

Appendix 21 Summary of French input data for the expected MRP estimation based on analysts' consensus estimates 1989-1997

	29.12.1989	31.12.1990	31.12.1991	31.12.1992	31.12.1993	30.12.1994	29.12.1995	31.12.1996	31.12.1997
Sample size									
Sum companies included	56	60	45	64	63	74	102	111	151
LTM average of included companies	49	58	51	58	66	75	96	101	142
LTM number of observations	586	693	607	695	791	904	1153	1208	1703
Input variables (EUR million)									
Sum earnings +1 (IBES)	9,672	9,578	9,078	9,625	6,993	8,087	8,271	10,987	19,900
Sum earnings +2 (IBES)	11,018	10,404	10,900	10,660	8,567	10,917	13,756	13,056	23,225
Sum earnings +3 (IBES)	12,233	12,064	12,106	12,147	10,290	14,048	16,928	15,283	26,604
Sum earnings +4 (IBES)	13,502	13,293	13,446	14,140	11,406	16,220	20,019	17,513	30,161
Sum earnings +5 (IBES)	14,919	14,674	14,955	16,956	12,656	18,479	22,848	20,054	34,178
Implied earnings CAGR (IBES)	*11.4%*	*11.3%*	*13.3%*	*15.2%*	*16.0%*	*22.9%*	*28.9%*	*16.2%*	*14.5%*
Sum dividends +1 (IBES/WS ratio)	2,106	2,180	2,466	2,785	2,700	3,130	4,093	4,160	6,933
Sum dividends +2 (IBES/WS ratio)	2,407	2,399	2,801	3,077	3,218	3,614	4,660	4,525	7,870
Sum dividends +3 (IBES/WS ratio)	2,693	2,735	3,094	3,407	3,855	4,082	5,217	5,072	8,732
Sum dividends +4 (IBES/WS ratio)	2,989	3,031	3,453	3,790	4,290	5,382	6,231	6,503	9,416
Sum dividends +5 (IBES/WS ratio)	3,302	3,346	3,840	4,544	4,760	6,132	7,112	7,447	10,671
Implied dividends CAGR (IBES/WS ratio)	*11.9%*	*11.3%*	*11.7%*	*13.0%*	*15.2%*	*18.3%*	*14.8%*	*15.7%*	*11.4%*
Implied payout ratio +1	21.8%	22.8%	27.2%	28.9%	38.6%	38.7%	49.5%	37.9%	34.8%
Implied payout ratio +2	21.8%	23.1%	25.7%	28.9%	37.6%	33.1%	33.9%	34.7%	33.9%
Implied payout ratio +3	22.0%	22.7%	25.6%	28.1%	37.5%	29.1%	30.8%	33.2%	32.8%
Implied payout ratio +4	22.1%	22.8%	25.7%	26.8%	37.6%	33.2%	31.1%	37.1%	31.2%
Implied payout ratio +5	22.1%	22.8%	25.7%	26.8%	37.6%	33.2%	31.1%	37.1%	31.2%
Sum book value 0 (Worldscope)	50,741	60,707	71,317	85,506	93,378	101,854	127,937	121,027	163,484
Sum implied book value +1	58,308	68,105	77,929	92,346	97,672	106,811	132,115	127,855	176,452
Sum implied book value +2	66,918	76,110	86,029	99,930	103,021	114,115	141,211	136,386	191,806
Sum implied book value +3	76,458	85,439	95,041	108,669	109,456	124,080	152,922	146,598	209,678
Sum implied book value +4	86,972	95,701	105,035	119,019	116,572	134,917	166,709	157,608	230,423
Sum implied book value +5	98,589	107,028	116,150	131,430	124,468	147,264	182,446	170,215	253,930
Sum market capitalization (IBES)	112,912	93,805	114,114	131,981	170,502	159,148	194,335	225,040	392,347

Source: Datastream, IBES, Worldscope (WS).

Appendix 22 Summary of French input data for the expected MRP estimation based on analysts' consensus estimates 1998-2006

	31.12.1998	31.12.1999	29.12.2000	31.12.2001	31.12.2002	31.12.2003	31.12.2004	30.12.2005	29.12.2006
Sample size									
Sum companies included	177	224	238	251	250	248	247	286	284
LTM average of included companies	154	193	228	250	244	232	232	267	283
LTM number of observations	1851	2320	2730	2997	2930	2778	2789	3198	3396
Input variables (EUR million)									
Sum earnings +1 (IBES)	24,890	36,040	51,603	51,107	47,402	52,631	70,404	88,937	109,234
Sum earnings +2 (IBES)	28,563	43,026	59,573	57,938	57,555	62,333	78,952	96,957	118,619
Sum earnings +3 (IBES)	32,908	49,801	69,336	66,161	66,584	70,417	86,304	104,234	129,478
Sum earnings +4 (IBES)	36,002	56,498	73,500	75,201	73,949	76,660	88,325	107,213	141,400
Sum earnings +5 (IBES)	39,159	64,100	86,143	99,526	85,580	83,832	93,702	113,548	148,795
Implied earnings CAGR (IBES)	*12.0%*	*15.5%*	*13.7%*	*18.1%*	*15.9%*	*12.3%*	*7.4%*	*6.3%*	*8.0%*
Sum dividends +1 (IBES/WS ratio)	8,897	12,494	16,525	18,354	17,452	17,703	22,934	32,003	43,603
Sum dividends +2 (IBES/WS ratio)	9,947	14,236	18,746	20,045	18,527	20,164	25,944	35,517	47,684
Sum dividends +3 (IBES/WS ratio)	11,112	16,167	21,352	22,020	20,734	22,637	29,232	39,100	52,362
Sum dividends +4 (IBES/WS ratio)	9,998	18,433	23,929	25,263	23,203	25,858	31,981	42,161	57,253
Sum dividends +5 (IBES/WS ratio)	10,875	20,914	28,044	33,435	26,853	28,277	33,928	44,652	60,247
Implied dividends CAGR (IBES/WS ratio)	*5.1%*	*13.7%*	*14.1%*	*16.2%*	*11.4%*	*12.4%*	*10.3%*	*8.7%*	*8.4%*
Implied payout ratio +1	35.7%	34.7%	32.0%	35.9%	36.8%	33.6%	32.6%	36.0%	39.9%
Implied payout ratio +2	34.8%	33.1%	31.5%	34.6%	32.2%	32.3%	32.9%	36.6%	40.2%
Implied payout ratio +3	33.8%	32.5%	30.8%	33.3%	31.1%	32.1%	33.9%	37.5%	40.4%
Implied payout ratio +4	27.8%	32.6%	32.6%	33.6%	31.4%	33.7%	36.2%	39.3%	40.5%
Implied payout ratio +5	27.8%	32.6%	32.6%	33.6%	31.4%	33.7%	36.2%	39.3%	40.5%
Sum book value 0 (Worldscope)	196,958	232,381	298,828	415,312	413,479	375,918	396,162	475,803	634,017
Sum implied book value +1	212,951	255,926	333,905	448,065	443,428	410,846	443,632	532,736	699,648
Sum implied book value +2	231,567	284,717	374,733	485,958	482,455	453,014	496,639	594,176	770,583
Sum implied book value +3	253,363	318,350	422,717	530,099	528,306	500,795	553,711	659,309	847,699
Sum implied book value +4	279,367	356,415	472,289	580,037	579,052	551,597	610,055	724,361	931,846
Sum implied book value +5	307,651	399,601	530,387	646,127	637,779	607,151	669,829	793,257	1,020,393
Sum market capitalization (IBES)	548,332	1,001,904	1,225,585	935,722	683,336	817,131	938,205	1,233,141	1,593,011

Source: Datastream, IBES, Worldscope (WS).

Appendix 23 Summary statistics of the French expected MRP estimation using special comparison specifications of previous studies

Model (1)						1.5.1 Claus/Thomas			1.5.2 Gebhardt et al.			1.5.3 Gode/Mohanram			1.5.4 Easton - PEG		1.5.5 Easton - PE	
Year	r^f (2)	θ_{TV}	$m_{P/E+1}$	N (3)	Firms (4)	r^e	r^p	$g_{RI,TV}$	r^e	r^p	Target r^b	r^e	r^p	$g_{agr,TV}$	r^e	r^p	r^e	r^p
1989	8.86%	22.79%	11.7x	586	49	11.93%	3.08%	5.86%	15.26%	6.40%	24.99%	12.31%	3.45%	5.86%	10.31%	1.46%	8.87%	0.01%
1990	9.92%	22.32%	10.7x	693	58	12.57%	2.65%	6.92%	16.00%	6.08%	24.99%	11.89%	1.97%	6.92%	10.14%	0.22%	9.83%	-0.09%
1991	8.97%	26.07%	12.1x	607	51	11.58%	2.61%	5.97%	15.70%	6.73%	24.99%	12.65%	3.67%	5.97%	10.41%	1.44%	8.74%	-0.24%
1992	8.59%	27.15%	13.4x	695	58	11.48%	2.90%	5.59%	15.53%	6.95%	24.99%	13.43%	4.85%	5.59%	10.86%	2.27%	7.74%	-0.84%
1993	6.68%	35.26%	18.8x	791	66	8.40%	1.72%	3.68%	13.66%	6.98%	24.99%	10.86%	4.18%	3.68%	8.81%	2.13%	5.60%	-1.08%
1994	7.29%	35.29%	22.1x	904	75	9.50%	2.21%	4.29%	14.01%	6.72%	25.53%	13.60%	6.31%	4.29%	10.93%	3.64%	4.68%	-2.61%
1995	7.49%	33.18%	18.2x	1,153	96	10.56%	3.07%	4.49%	15.32%	7.83%	25.68%	15.47%	7.98%	4.49%	12.64%	5.15%	5.75%	-1.74%
1996	6.27%	37.49%	21.2x	1,208	101	9.16%	2.89%	3.27%	13.66%	7.39%	24.80%	13.35%	7.08%	3.27%	11.09%	4.81%	4.92%	-1.36%
1997	5.54%	32.21%	21.9x	1,703	142	7.95%	2.41%	2.54%	12.06%	6.53%	23.65%	11.09%	5.55%	2.54%	9.32%	3.79%	4.69%	-0.84%
1998	4.60%	31.10%	22.5x	1,851	154	7.23%	2.63%	1.60%	10.82%	6.22%	22.52%	9.72%	5.12%	1.60%	8.37%	3.77%	4.56%	-0.04%
1999	4.64%	31.77%	23.7x	2,320	193	6.95%	2.31%	1.64%	9.96%	5.32%	21.61%	9.46%	4.82%	1.64%	8.14%	3.49%	4.32%	-0.32%
2000	5.40%	33.06%	27.0x	2,730	228	6.93%	1.53%	2.40%	8.64%	3.24%	20.82%	9.14%	3.74%	2.40%	7.66%	2.26%	3.78%	-1.62%
2001	4.94%	32.47%	18.9x	2,997	250	8.43%	3.48%	1.94%	10.83%	5.88%	20.20%	10.53%	5.59%	1.94%	8.99%	4.05%	5.48%	0.54%
2002	4.84%	31.81%	15.9x	2,930	244	10.28%	5.44%	1.84%	12.56%	7.72%	19.78%	12.95%	8.11%	1.84%	11.09%	6.25%	6.59%	1.75%
2003	4.10%	34.47%	14.0x	2,778	232	9.66%	5.56%	1.10%	12.40%	8.29%	19.46%	12.31%	8.21%	1.10%	10.67%	6.57%	7.45%	3.35%
2004	4.06%	34.85%	13.7x	2,789	232	9.00%	4.94%	1.06%	11.55%	7.50%	19.12%	11.00%	6.94%	1.06%	9.43%	5.38%	7.51%	3.45%
2005	3.36%	38.04%	13.4x	3,198	267	8.33%	4.97%	0.36%	10.94%	7.58%	18.80%	9.36%	6.00%	0.36%	7.78%	4.42%	7.72%	4.36%
2006	3.80%	40.00%	13.9x	3,396	283	8.39%	4.59%	0.80%	10.68%	6.88%	18.55%	9.55%	5.75%	0.80%	7.83%	4.03%	7.43%	3.62%
Low	3.36%	22.32%	10.7x	586	49	6.93%	1.53%	0.36%	8.64%	3.24%	18.55%	9.14%	1.97%	0.36%	7.66%	0.22%	3.78%	-2.61%
Arith. Mean	6.07%	32.19%	17.4x	1,852	154	9.35%	3.28%	3.07%	12.75%	6.68%	22.52%	11.59%	5.52%	3.07%	9.69%	3.62%	6.43%	0.35%
Median	5.47%	32.77%	17.0x	1,777	148	9.08%	2.89%	2.47%	12.48%	6.80%	23.09%	11.49%	5.57%	2.47%	9.78%	3.78%	6.17%	-0.16%
High	9.92%	40.00%	27.0x	3,396	283	12.57%	5.56%	6.92%	16.00%	8.29%	25.68%	15.47%	8.21%	6.92%	12.64%	6.57%	9.83%	4.36%
St. Dev.	2.02%	4.89%	4.8x			1.73%	1.27%	2.02%	2.23%	1.14%	2.69%	1.80%	1.74%	2.02%	1.42%	1.72%	1.80%	2.08%

(1) All parameters are stated in nominal terms and as arithmetic average of monthly values.
(2) r^f equals redemption yield of the French Datastream benchmark 10y government bond index.
(3) Overall number of firm observations per annum.
(4) Average number of firms per annum.

Appendix 24 Summary of Japanese input data for the expected MRP estimation based on analysts' consensus estimates 1989-1997

	29.12.1989	31.12.1990	31.12.1991	31.12.1992	31.12.1993	30.12.1994	29.12.1995	31.12.1996	31.12.1997
Sample size									
Sum companies included	38	37	34	62	69	197	31	225	313
LTM average of included companies	50	45	50	52	66	128	107	132	257
LTM number of observations	600	541	602	628	786	1534	1289	1584	3088
Input variables (Yen million)									
Sum earnings +1 (IBES)	1,882,995	1,840,984	1,503,261	1,036,324	987,599	1,367,635	820,730	3,408,721	5,379,787
Sum earnings +2 (IBES)	2,033,957	1,947,936	1,691,000	1,221,179	1,185,790	1,655,448	1,153,079	3,767,964	6,141,755
Sum earnings +3 (IBES)	2,285,213	2,178,730	1,861,734	1,498,594	1,418,083	1,975,948	1,274,236	4,178,050	6,863,998
Sum earnings +4 (IBES)	2,550,033	2,360,939	2,032,283	1,583,811	1,547,975	2,260,069	1,411,034	4,605,476	7,603,902
Sum earnings +5 (IBES)	2,822,254	2,559,317	2,198,419	1,669,681	1,684,546	2,555,874	1,565,446	5,081,767	8,360,680
Implied earnings CAGR (IBES)	*10.6%*	*8.6%*	*10.0%*	*12.7%*	*14.3%*	*16.9%*	*17.5%*	*10.5%*	*11.7%*
Sum dividends +1 (IBES/WS ratio)	358,098	342,078	339,904	309,216	363,408	473,071	260,412	848,760	1,341,038
Sum dividends +2 (IBES/WS ratio)	389,259	357,414	385,329	380,002	440,354	484,947	262,029	860,662	1,345,536
Sum dividends +3 (IBES/WS ratio)	435,735	395,359	433,962	498,086	563,114	739,712	454,558	1,092,648	1,506,721
Sum dividends +4 (IBES/WS ratio)	486,152	430,902	478,683	528,637	615,723	838,918	510,124	1,284,038	2,065,333
Sum dividends +5 (IBES/WS ratio)	538,050	467,108	517,814	557,298	670,046	948,718	565,947	1,416,831	2,270,886
Implied dividends CAGR (IBES/WS ratio)	*10.7%*	*8.1%*	*11.1%*	*15.9%*	*16.5%*	*19.0%*	*21.4%*	*13.7%*	*14.1%*
Implied payout ratio +1	19.0%	18.6%	22.6%	29.8%	36.8%	34.6%	31.7%	24.9%	24.9%
Implied payout ratio +2	19.1%	18.3%	22.8%	31.1%	37.1%	29.3%	22.7%	22.8%	21.9%
Implied payout ratio +3	19.1%	18.1%	23.3%	33.2%	39.7%	37.4%	35.7%	26.2%	22.0%
Implied payout ratio +4	19.1%	18.3%	23.6%	33.4%	39.8%	37.1%	36.2%	27.9%	27.2%
Implied payout ratio +5	19.1%	18.3%	23.6%	33.4%	39.8%	37.1%	36.2%	27.9%	27.2%
Sum book value 0 (Worldscope)	18,613,871	21,551,179	23,095,161	27,048,906	27,548,972	29,590,961	17,476,338	51,228,604	80,914,768
Sum implied book value +1	20,138,768	23,050,085	24,258,518	27,776,014	28,173,163	30,485,525	18,036,656	53,788,565	84,953,517
Sum implied book value +2	21,783,467	24,640,607	25,564,189	28,617,191	28,918,598	31,656,026	18,927,706	56,695,868	89,749,737
Sum implied book value +3	23,632,944	26,423,978	26,991,961	29,617,699	29,773,567	32,892,262	19,747,383	59,781,270	95,107,014
Sum implied book value +4	25,696,826	28,354,016	28,545,562	30,672,873	30,705,819	34,313,413	20,648,294	63,102,708	100,645,582
Sum implied book value +5	27,981,030	30,446,225	30,226,166	31,785,255	31,720,319	35,920,569	21,647,792	66,767,644	106,735,377
Sum market capitalization (IBES)	64,045,207	38,600,560	36,730,664	36,482,799	43,956,758	58,434,987	29,746,860	105,253,428	156,421,617

Source: Datastream, IBES, Worldscope (WS).

Appendix 25 Summary of Japanese input data for the expected MRP estimation based on analysts' consensus estimates 1998-2006

	31.12.1998	31.12.1999	29.12.2000	31.12.2001	31.12.2002	31.12.2003	31.12.2004	30.12.2005	29.12.2006
Sample size									
Sum companies included	293	418	623	653	616	677	753	790	835
LTM average of included companies	303	320	443	633	621	631	740	759	806
LTM number of observations	3632	3835	5316	7596	7454	7576	8878	9111	9676
Input variables (Yen million)									
Sum earnings +1 (IBES)	4,106,647	4,119,921	7,955,476	5,379,980	8,924,060	11,410,400	16,989,599	21,142,798	25,008,129
Sum earnings +2 (IBES)	4,704,152	6,584,722	10,315,995	9,265,698	10,953,630	14,080,951	19,176,336	23,333,747	28,646,054
Sum earnings +3 (IBES)	5,386,300	7,661,413	11,709,687	11,093,030	12,429,193	15,553,884	21,100,978	25,607,439	31,032,984
Sum earnings +4 (IBES)	6,071,802	8,655,277	13,391,222	13,078,728	13,488,696	18,084,232	23,384,728	28,661,568	32,396,993
Sum earnings +5 (IBES)	6,767,859	10,046,712	15,040,208	14,464,112	15,027,251	20,033,307	25,952,214	31,570,160	35,467,380
Implied earnings CAGR (IBES)	*13.3%*	*25.0%*	*17.3%*	*28.0%*	*13.9%*	*15.1%*	*11.2%*	*10.5%*	*9.1%*
Sum dividends +1 (IBES/WS ratio)	1,137,049	1,380,547	1,816,741	2,126,422	1,971,611	2,415,480	3,286,999	4,424,671	5,554,436
Sum dividends +2 (IBES/WS ratio)	1,147,958	1,415,047	1,879,660	2,147,016	2,088,432	2,485,361	3,366,180	4,636,775	5,893,104
Sum dividends +3 (IBES/WS ratio)	1,311,969	1,708,932	2,427,395	2,387,344	2,280,532	2,621,041	3,617,589	5,086,233	6,441,808
Sum dividends +4 (IBES/WS ratio)	1,508,843	2,443,908	3,529,493	2,649,310	2,750,530	3,411,108	4,316,350	6,356,807	7,277,538
Sum dividends +5 (IBES/WS ratio)	1,681,813	2,836,794	3,964,113	2,929,942	3,064,262	3,778,749	4,790,257	7,001,899	7,967,258
Implied dividends CAGR (IBES/WS ratio)	*10.3%*	*19.7%*	*21.5%*	*8.3%*	*11.7%*	*11.8%*	*9.9%*	*12.2%*	*9.4%*
Implied payout ratio +1	27.7%	33.5%	22.8%	39.5%	22.1%	21.2%	19.3%	20.9%	22.2%
Implied payout ratio +2	24.4%	21.5%	18.2%	23.2%	19.1%	17.7%	17.6%	19.9%	20.6%
Implied payout ratio +3	24.4%	22.3%	20.7%	21.5%	18.3%	16.9%	17.1%	19.9%	20.8%
Implied payout ratio +4	24.9%	28.2%	26.4%	20.3%	20.4%	18.9%	18.5%	22.2%	22.5%
Implied payout ratio +5	24.9%	28.2%	26.4%	20.3%	20.4%	18.9%	18.5%	22.2%	22.5%
Sum book value 0 (Worldscope)	72,395,310	85,332,450	113,175,639	141,011,807	126,050,296	134,730,616	169,292,206	186,292,198	226,421,263
Sum implied book value +1	75,364,907	88,071,825	119,314,374	144,265,366	133,002,745	143,725,536	182,994,805	203,010,326	245,874,956
Sum implied book value +2	78,921,101	93,241,500	127,750,709	151,384,047	141,867,942	155,321,125	198,804,961	221,707,298	268,627,906
Sum implied book value +3	82,995,432	99,193,981	137,033,001	160,089,734	152,016,604	168,253,969	216,288,349	242,228,504	293,219,082
Sum implied book value +4	87,558,391	105,405,350	146,894,729	170,519,152	162,754,770	182,927,093	235,356,727	264,533,265	318,338,537
Sum implied book value +5	92,644,437	112,615,268	157,970,824	182,053,322	174,717,759	199,181,651	256,518,684	289,101,526	345,838,659
Sum market capitalization (IBES)	133,757,613	258,721,256	269,480,911	222,159,739	180,275,029	234,200,768	287,004,110	445,979,491	483,450,652

Source: Datastream, IBES, Worldscope (WS).

Appendix 26 Summary statistics of the Japanese expected MRP estimation using special comparison specifications of previous studies

Model						1.5.1 Claus/Thomas			1.5.2 Gebhardt et al.			1.5.3 Gode/Mohanram			1.5.4 Easton - PEG		1.5.5 Easton - PE	
Year	r^f (2)	θ_{TV}	$m_{P/E+1}$	N (3)	Firms (4)	r^e	r^p	$g_{RI,TV}$	r^e	r^p	Target r^b	r^e	r^p	$g_{agr,TV}$	r^e	r^p	r^e	r^p
1989	5.18%	20.81%	36.7x	600	50	5.02%	-0.16%	2.18%	0.76%	-4.42%	7.94%	6.17%	1.00%	2.18%	5.21%	0.03%	2.82%	-2.36%
1990	6.96%	19.04%	29.0x	541	45	6.54%	-0.42%	3.96%	5.00%	-1.96%	8.66%	7.05%	0.09%	3.96%	5.59%	-1.37%	3.68%	-3.28%
1991	6.34%	20.05%	24.2x	602	50	6.18%	-0.17%	3.34%	5.79%	-0.55%	8.66%	6.59%	0.25%	3.34%	5.50%	-0.84%	4.28%	-2.06%
1992	5.21%	27.03%	26.8x	628	52	5.18%	-0.03%	2.21%	6.53%	1.31%	8.66%	7.50%	2.28%	2.21%	5.98%	0.77%	3.90%	-1.31%
1993	4.12%	36.59%	42.6x	786	66	4.06%	-0.06%	1.12%	5.60%	1.49%	8.66%	7.25%	3.13%	1.12%	6.38%	2.26%	2.40%	-1.72%
1994	4.23%	37.12%	47.5x	1,534	128	3.95%	-0.28%	1.23%	4.90%	0.66%	8.57%	7.10%	2.86%	1.23%	6.21%	1.97%	2.15%	-2.09%
1995	3.32%	38.12%	35.3x	1,289	107	4.63%	1.31%	0.32%	5.44%	2.12%	8.20%	8.10%	4.78%	0.32%	7.45%	4.13%	2.93%	-0.39%
1996	2.99%	30.02%	32.2x	1,584	132	4.38%	1.39%	-0.01%	4.83%	1.84%	7.70%	7.26%	4.27%	-0.01%	6.80%	3.81%	3.19%	0.20%
1997	2.31%	28.12%	31.6x	3,088	257	4.16%	1.84%	-0.69%	4.48%	2.17%	7.20%	6.65%	4.34%	-0.69%	6.40%	4.09%	3.25%	0.94%
1998	1.49%	29.57%	30.9x	3,632	303	4.02%	2.52%	-1.51%	4.50%	3.01%	6.80%	6.52%	5.02%	-1.51%	6.42%	4.92%	3.34%	1.84%
1999	1.76%	27.02%	47.9x	3,835	320	3.07%	1.31%	-1.24%	3.54%	1.79%	6.53%	7.08%	5.33%	-1.24%	7.16%	5.40%	2.19%	0.44%
2000	1.76%	27.33%	50.1x	5,316	443	3.50%	1.74%	-1.24%	3.40%	1.64%	6.37%	7.98%	6.22%	-1.24%	8.13%	6.37%	2.21%	0.45%
2001	1.31%	21.41%	31.1x	7,596	633	4.84%	3.54%	-1.69%	4.57%	3.26%	6.29%	9.05%	7.74%	-1.69%	9.13%	7.82%	3.35%	2.04%
2002	1.22%	20.67%	35.4x	7,454	621	5.64%	4.42%	-1.78%	5.11%	3.89%	6.26%	9.98%	8.76%	-1.78%	9.95%	8.73%	3.79%	2.57%
2003	1.00%	20.11%	20.3x	7,576	631	6.42%	5.41%	-2.00%	5.44%	4.44%	6.24%	9.82%	8.81%	-2.00%	9.71%	8.71%	5.10%	4.10%
2004	1.49%	18.58%	18.9x	8,878	740	6.70%	5.21%	-1.51%	5.26%	3.77%	6.25%	9.47%	7.98%	-1.51%	9.22%	7.73%	5.36%	3.87%
2005	1.35%	19.80%	18.0x	9,111	759	6.63%	5.27%	-1.65%	5.22%	3.87%	6.28%	8.80%	7.44%	-1.65%	8.43%	7.08%	5.81%	4.45%
2006	1.73%	22.51%	19.3x	9,676	806	5.94%	4.21%	-1.27%	4.77%	3.04%	6.36%	7.97%	6.24%	-1.27%	7.57%	5.83%	5.40%	3.66%
Low	1.00%	18.58%	18.0x	541	45	3.07%	-0.42%	-2.00%	0.76%	-4.42%	6.24%	6.17%	0.09%	-2.00%	5.21%	-1.37%	2.15%	-3.28%
Arith. Mean	2.99%	25.77%	32.1x	4,096	341	5.05%	2.06%	-0.01%	4.73%	1.74%	7.31%	7.80%	4.81%	-0.01%	7.29%	4.30%	3.62%	0.63%
Median	2.03%	24.76%	31.3x	3,360	280	4.93%	1.57%	-0.97%	4.95%	1.98%	7.00%	7.38%	4.90%	-0.97%	6.98%	4.52%	3.34%	0.44%
High	6.96%	38.12%	50.1x	9,676	806	6.70%	5.41%	3.96%	6.53%	4.44%	8.66%	9.98%	8.81%	3.96%	9.95%	8.73%	5.81%	4.45%
St. Dev.	1.91%	6.51%	10.1x			1.16%	2.12%	1.91%	1.24%	2.23%	1.04%	1.18%	2.79%	1.91%	1.50%	3.24%	1.16%	2.46%

(1) All parameters are stated in nominal terms; all values represent monthly arithmetic averages.
(2) r^f equals redemption yield of the Japanese Datastream benchmark 10y government bond index.
(3) Overall number of firm observations per annum.
(4) Average number of firms per annum.

Appendix 27 Summary of UK input data for the expected MRP estimation based on analysts' consensus estimates 1989-1997

	29.12.1989	31.12.1990	31.12.1991	31.12.1992	31.12.1993	30.12.1994	29.12.1995	31.12.1996	31.12.1997
Sample size									
Sum companies included	41	36	88	77	112	148	178	209	263
LTM average of included companies	54	41	64	79	101	135	176	177	239
LTM number of observations	645	487	767	947	1212	1623	2106	2120	2864
Input variables (GBP million)									
Sum earnings +1 (IBES)	10,605	10,910	13,265	12,639	13,814	19,524	22,453	27,026	29,726
Sum earnings +2 (IBES)	11,467	12,145	15,862	14,392	15,774	22,050	24,644	29,196	33,005
Sum earnings +3 (IBES)	12,670	13,507	17,986	16,387	17,327	24,490	26,537	32,094	36,744
Sum earnings +4 (IBES)	14,045	15,059	20,177	18,253	19,164	27,012	28,878	35,550	40,010
Sum earnings +5 (IBES)	15,584	16,793	22,643	20,419	21,292	30,120	31,366	39,189	44,052
Implied earnings CAGR (IBES)	*10.1%*	*11.4%*	*14.3%*	*12.7%*	*11.4%*	*11.4%*	*8.7%*	*9.7%*	*10.3%*
Sum dividends +1 (IBES/WS ratio)	4,186	4,982	5,670	5,331	6,998	8,651	10,307	12,751	13,929
Sum dividends +2 (IBES/WS ratio)	4,565	5,582	6,980	6,136	7,538	9,420	11,258	13,509	15,309
Sum dividends +3 (IBES/WS ratio)	5,061	6,183	7,919	7,089	8,492	10,365	12,331	14,711	16,860
Sum dividends +4 (IBES/WS ratio)	5,617	6,874	8,888	7,902	10,245	11,417	14,027	16,093	17,997
Sum dividends +5 (IBES/WS ratio)	6,232	7,666	9,974	8,839	11,382	12,730	15,235	17,741	19,815
Implied dividends CAGR (IBES/WS ratio)	*10.5%*	*11.4%*	*15.2%*	*13.5%*	*12.9%*	*10.1%*	*10.3%*	*8.6%*	*9.2%*
Implied payout ratio +1	39.5%	45.7%	42.7%	42.2%	50.7%	44.3%	45.9%	47.2%	46.9%
Implied payout ratio +2	39.8%	46.0%	44.0%	42.6%	47.8%	42.7%	45.7%	46.3%	46.4%
Implied payout ratio +3	39.9%	45.8%	44.0%	43.3%	49.0%	42.3%	46.5%	45.8%	45.9%
Implied payout ratio +4	40.0%	45.7%	44.1%	43.3%	53.5%	42.3%	48.6%	45.3%	45.0%
Implied payout ratio +5	40.0%	45.7%	44.1%	43.3%	53.5%	42.3%	48.6%	45.3%	45.0%
Sum book value 0 (Worldscope)	70,639	80,866	102,136	95,236	86,013	122,669	124,694	140,770	154,878
Sum implied book value +1	77,058	86,794	109,730	102,544	92,829	133,542	136,840	155,045	170,674
Sum implied book value +2	83,959	93,357	118,612	110,800	101,065	146,172	150,226	170,731	188,370
Sum implied book value +3	91,568	100,682	128,680	120,098	109,900	160,297	164,432	188,114	208,254
Sum implied book value +4	99,996	108,866	139,968	130,450	118,819	175,893	179,284	207,570	230,268
Sum implied book value +5	109,348	117,992	152,637	142,030	128,728	193,282	195,415	229,019	254,505
Sum market capitalization (IBES)	117,705	117,866	165,437	183,418	235,854	258,474	320,334	382,318	518,844

Source: Datastream, IBES, Worldscope (WS).

Appendix 28 Summary of UK input data for the expected MRP estimation based on analysts' consensus estimates 1998-2006

	31.12.1998	31.12.1999	29.12.2000	31.12.2001	31.12.2002	31.12.2003	31.12.2004	30.12.2005	29.12.2006
Sample size									
Sum companies included	272	291	295	291	270	312	330	375	419
LTM average of included companies	265	275	294	289	273	289	321	365	388
LTM number of observations	3180	3294	3532	3472	3271	3471	3853	4377	4661
Input variables (GBP million)									
Sum earnings +1 (IBES)	30,758	36,278	44,549	47,591	52,678	59,360	64,562	73,296	83,488
Sum earnings +2 (IBES)	34,156	41,244	51,346	54,875	59,543	65,543	71,333	80,229	91,666
Sum earnings +3 (IBES)	37,873	46,795	58,163	62,264	65,987	71,643	77,232	87,365	99,922
Sum earnings +4 (IBES)	41,980	51,990	67,777	73,675	72,613	77,271	82,929	94,602	107,859
Sum earnings +5 (IBES)	45,899	57,468	73,819	85,531	79,609	81,828	88,550	100,570	116,895
Implied earnings CAGR (IBES)	*10.5%*	*12.2%*	*13.5%*	*15.8%*	*10.9%*	*8.4%*	*8.2%*	*8.2%*	*8.8%*
Sum dividends +1 (IBES/WS ratio)	15,751	18,294	23,171	23,026	24,427	26,241	29,191	33,488	39,248
Sum dividends +2 (IBES/WS ratio)	17,231	19,888	24,990	25,116	26,096	28,401	31,376	36,427	42,306
Sum dividends +3 (IBES/WS ratio)	18,765	21,667	26,755	26,942	28,018	30,605	33,714	39,294	45,866
Sum dividends +4 (IBES/WS ratio)	19,247	23,959	29,391	29,577	31,155	34,013	36,427	43,393	49,054
Sum dividends +5 (IBES/WS ratio)	21,043	26,483	32,011	34,337	34,157	36,019	38,896	46,130	53,164
Implied dividends CAGR (IBES/WS ratio)	*7.5%*	*9.7%*	*8.4%*	*10.5%*	*8.7%*	*8.2%*	*7.4%*	*8.3%*	*7.9%*
Implied payout ratio +1	51.2%	50.4%	52.0%	48.4%	46.4%	44.2%	45.2%	45.7%	47.0%
Implied payout ratio +2	50.4%	48.2%	48.7%	45.8%	43.8%	43.3%	44.0%	45.4%	46.2%
Implied payout ratio +3	49.5%	46.3%	46.0%	43.3%	42.5%	42.7%	43.7%	45.0%	45.9%
Implied payout ratio +4	45.8%	46.1%	43.4%	40.1%	42.9%	44.0%	43.9%	45.9%	45.5%
Implied payout ratio +5	45.8%	46.1%	43.4%	40.1%	42.9%	44.0%	43.9%	45.9%	45.5%
Sum book value 0 (Worldscope)	165,933	186,905	404,576	442,936	393,200	394,376	400,206	421,702	451,501
Sum implied book value +1	180,940	204,888	425,955	467,501	421,451	427,495	435,578	461,510	495,741
Sum implied book value +2	197,865	226,244	452,311	497,261	454,898	464,637	475,535	505,312	545,101
Sum implied book value +3	216,974	251,372	483,718	532,583	492,867	505,675	519,053	553,383	599,158
Sum implied book value +4	239,707	279,403	522,104	576,680	534,324	548,933	565,555	604,592	657,962
Sum implied book value +5	264,564	310,388	563,912	627,874	579,776	594,742	615,209	659,032	721,694
Sum market capitalization (IBES)	568,833	783,499	1,004,230	893,365	678,197	780,266	859,156	1,021,046	1,234,739

Source: Datastream, IBES, Worldscope (WS).

Appendix 29 Summary statistics of the UK expected MRP estimation using special comparison specifications of previous studies

Model (1)						1.5.1 Claus/Thomas			1.5.2 Gebhardt et al.			1.5.3 Gode/Mohanram			1.5.4 Easton - PEG		1.5.5 Easton - PE	
Year	r^f (2)	θ_{TV}	$m_{P/E+1}$	N (3)	Firms (4)	r^e	r^p	$g_{RI,TV}$	r^e	r^p	Target r^b	r^e	r^p	$g_{agr,TV}$	r^e	r^p	r^e	r^p
1989	10.13%	39.89%	11.2x	645	54	12.72%	2.59%	7.13%	10.68%	0.55%	16.29%	13.12%	2.99%	7.13%	9.76%	-0.37%	9.55%	-0.58%
1990	11.57%	43.34%	10.4x	487	41	13.59%	2.02%	8.57%	13.64%	2.07%	17.77%	14.79%	3.21%	8.57%	10.59%	-0.98%	10.26%	-1.32%
1991	10.05%	45.57%	12.3x	767	64	13.17%	3.11%	7.05%	12.79%	2.74%	17.77%	15.04%	4.98%	7.05%	10.98%	0.93%	8.62%	-1.43%
1992	9.07%	44.08%	13.4x	947	79	11.88%	2.80%	6.07%	12.03%	2.96%	17.77%	14.00%	4.93%	6.07%	10.44%	1.37%	7.89%	-1.18%
1993	7.34%	48.21%	15.8x	1,212	101	10.67%	3.33%	4.34%	10.35%	3.01%	17.77%	12.77%	5.44%	4.34%	9.69%	2.35%	6.60%	-0.74%
1994	8.14%	45.95%	15.2x	1,623	135	10.90%	2.76%	5.14%	10.56%	2.42%	17.58%	12.84%	4.71%	5.14%	9.58%	1.44%	6.92%	-1.21%
1995	8.15%	45.80%	13.9x	2,106	176	11.21%	3.06%	5.15%	10.53%	2.38%	17.09%	12.31%	4.16%	5.15%	9.15%	1.00%	7.58%	-0.57%
1996	7.80%	46.62%	14.1x	2,120	177	11.03%	3.23%	4.80%	9.93%	2.13%	16.68%	11.54%	3.74%	4.80%	8.48%	0.68%	7.43%	-0.38%
1997	6.98%	44.64%	16.0x	2,864	239	9.97%	2.98%	3.98%	9.16%	2.18%	16.49%	10.99%	4.01%	3.98%	8.25%	1.27%	6.53%	-0.46%
1998	5.45%	45.91%	18.6x	3,180	265	8.40%	2.95%	2.45%	8.20%	2.74%	16.51%	10.01%	4.56%	2.45%	7.81%	2.36%	5.60%	0.15%
1999	5.01%	45.68%	20.4x	3,294	275	7.77%	2.76%	2.01%	7.73%	2.72%	16.65%	9.62%	4.61%	2.01%	7.57%	2.56%	5.08%	0.07%
2000	5.22%	45.02%	21.6x	3,532	294	7.86%	2.65%	2.22%	8.29%	3.07%	16.83%	10.25%	5.03%	2.22%	8.17%	2.95%	4.78%	-0.44%
2001	4.93%	43.82%	18.4x	3,472	289	8.75%	3.82%	1.93%	9.48%	4.55%	17.05%	11.42%	6.49%	1.93%	9.21%	4.28%	5.66%	0.73%
2002	4.84%	41.89%	15.4x	3,271	273	9.59%	4.75%	1.84%	11.13%	6.29%	17.25%	11.98%	7.14%	1.84%	9.67%	4.83%	6.94%	2.10%
2003	4.48%	45.14%	13.0x	3,471	289	9.87%	5.39%	1.48%	11.46%	6.98%	17.32%	11.47%	6.99%	1.48%	9.11%	4.62%	8.09%	3.60%
2004	4.86%	43.84%	12.9x	3,853	321	9.76%	4.90%	1.86%	11.09%	6.23%	17.30%	11.13%	6.27%	1.86%	8.76%	3.90%	8.16%	3.30%
2005	4.37%	45.50%	13.5x	4,377	365	9.26%	4.89%	1.37%	10.50%	6.14%	17.24%	10.62%	6.26%	1.37%	8.36%	4.00%	7.80%	3.43%
2006	4.50%	44.91%	14.1x	4,661	388	9.23%	4.72%	1.50%	10.13%	5.63%	17.18%	10.57%	6.06%	1.50%	8.32%	3.81%	7.47%	2.97%
Low	4.37%	39.89%	10.4x	487	41	7.77%	2.02%	1.37%	7.73%	0.55%	16.29%	9.62%	2.99%	1.37%	7.57%	-0.98%	4.78%	-1.43%
Arith. Mean	6.83%	44.77%	15.0x	2,549	212	10.31%	3.48%	3.83%	10.43%	3.60%	17.14%	11.92%	5.09%	3.83%	9.10%	2.28%	7.27%	0.45%
Median	6.22%	45.08%	14.1x	3,022	252	9.92%	3.09%	3.22%	10.51%	2.85%	17.21%	11.51%	4.96%	3.22%	9.13%	2.35%	7.45%	-0.41%
High	11.57%	48.21%	21.6x	4,661	388	13.59%	5.39%	8.57%	13.64%	6.98%	17.77%	15.04%	7.14%	8.57%	10.98%	4.83%	10.26%	3.60%
St. Dev.	2.30%	1.84%	3.1x			1.73%	1.00%	2.30%	1.54%	1.86%	0.48%	1.59%	1.24%	2.30%	0.98%	1.73%	1.45%	1.79%

(1) All parameters are stated in nominal terms and as arithmetic average of monthly values.
(2) r^f equals redemption yield of the UK Datastream benchmark 10y government bond index.
(3) Overall number of firm observations per annum.
(4) Average number of firms per annum.

Appendix 30 Summary of US input data for the expected MRP estimation based on analysts' consensus estimates 1989-1997

	29.12.1989	31.12.1990	31.12.1991	31.12.1992	31.12.1993	30.12.1994	29.12.1995	31.12.1996	31.12.1997
Sample size									
Sum companies included	661	659	668	718	804	888	1057	1198	1365
LTM average of included companies	634	650	663	703	783	868	998	1136	1306
LTM number of observations	7607	7802	7961	8438	9400	10420	11972	13633	15676
Input variables (US$ million)									
Sum earnings +1 (IBES)	120,181	112,966	112,274	120,005	138,493	164,846	223,936	241,523	297,813
Sum earnings +2 (IBES)	135,529	128,244	134,421	140,330	157,172	192,423	257,708	280,831	342,157
Sum earnings +3 (IBES)	151,076	150,774	155,847	161,697	178,319	220,359	291,843	324,458	393,702
Sum earnings +4 (IBES)	172,873	169,766	179,565	183,695	200,060	244,929	326,174	368,424	449,690
Sum earnings +5 (IBES)	202,939	189,838	201,395	207,830	223,833	272,232	369,080	418,783	512,712
Implied earnings CAGR (IBES)	*14.0%*	*13.9%*	*15.7%*	*14.7%*	*12.8%*	*13.4%*	*13.3%*	*14.8%*	*14.5%*
Sum dividends +1 (IBES/WS ratio)	45,189	47,201	47,555	50,956	56,444	64,037	81,015	80,506	95,966
Sum dividends +2 (IBES/WS ratio)	50,290	52,335	55,504	58,685	62,092	73,189	90,840	90,776	107,686
Sum dividends +3 (IBES/WS ratio)	55,466	60,525	63,560	66,715	69,225	82,609	99,915	102,514	121,288
Sum dividends +4 (IBES/WS ratio)	62,800	67,094	72,120	75,120	76,859	90,461	108,876	113,644	135,134
Sum dividends +5 (IBES/WS ratio)	73,722	75,027	80,887	84,990	85,993	100,545	123,198	129,178	154,072
Implied dividends CAGR (IBES/WS ratio)	*13.0%*	*12.3%*	*14.2%*	*13.6%*	*11.1%*	*11.9%*	*11.0%*	*12.5%*	*12.6%*
Implied payout ratio +1	37.6%	41.8%	42.4%	42.5%	40.8%	38.8%	36.2%	33.3%	32.2%
Implied payout ratio +2	37.1%	40.8%	41.3%	41.8%	39.5%	38.0%	35.2%	32.3%	31.5%
Implied payout ratio +3	36.7%	40.1%	40.8%	41.3%	38.8%	37.5%	34.2%	31.6%	30.8%
Implied payout ratio +4	36.3%	39.5%	40.2%	40.9%	38.4%	36.9%	33.4%	30.8%	30.1%
Implied payout ratio +5	36.3%	39.5%	40.2%	40.9%	38.4%	36.9%	33.4%	30.8%	30.1%
Sum book value 0 (Worldscope)	714,876	703,317	734,059	710,869	746,259	845,462	1,092,214	1,239,671	1,450,493
Sum implied book value +1	789,868	769,082	798,778	779,918	828,307	946,271	1,235,135	1,400,687	1,652,339
Sum implied book value +2	875,107	844,991	877,695	861,563	923,387	1,065,504	1,402,002	1,590,741	1,886,810
Sum implied book value +3	970,717	935,240	969,983	956,544	1,032,482	1,203,254	1,593,930	1,812,685	2,159,223
Sum implied book value +4	1,080,790	1,037,912	1,077,428	1,065,119	1,155,682	1,357,722	1,811,229	2,067,465	2,473,779
Sum implied book value +5	1,210,006	1,152,723	1,197,936	1,187,959	1,293,523	1,529,408	2,057,111	2,357,070	2,832,419
Sum market capitalization (IBES)	1,598,913	1,487,035	1,897,160	2,097,394	2,258,335	2,317,653	3,687,560	4,422,203	6,336,553

Source: Datastream, IBES, Worldscope (WS).

Appendix 31 Summary of US input data for the expected MRP estimation based on analysts' consensus estimates 1998-2006

	31.12.1998	31.12.1999	29.12.2000	31.12.2001	31.12.2002	31.12.2003	31.12.2004	30.12.2005	29.12.2006
Sample size									
Sum companies included	1500	1560	1665	1738	1782	1911	2093	2279	2346
LTM average of included companies	1438	1511	1520	1635	1718	1830	1985	2188	2265
LTM number of observations	17254	18128	18243	19622	20614	21961	23815	26254	27182
Input variables (US$ million)									
Sum earnings +1 (IBES)	302,960	373,493	459,195	403,133	432,293	523,680	665,688	779,842	901,120
Sum earnings +2 (IBES)	356,889	437,649	521,703	478,271	500,849	599,488	751,567	892,699	997,735
Sum earnings +3 (IBES)	416,019	509,143	604,436	573,994	575,271	680,868	830,561	982,703	1,105,627
Sum earnings +4 (IBES)	479,523	583,311	701,360	655,867	652,773	757,586	926,386	1,083,063	1,212,509
Sum earnings +5 (IBES)	549,178	672,044	813,552	747,292	735,654	845,428	1,028,668	1,202,309	1,348,340
Implied earnings CAGR (IBES)	*16.0%*	*15.8%*	*15.4%*	*16.7%*	*14.2%*	*12.7%*	*11.5%*	*11.4%*	*10.6%*
Sum dividends +1 (IBES/WS ratio)	89,099	117,322	136,865	124,663	134,659	155,009	220,980	216,423	248,566
Sum dividends +2 (IBES/WS ratio)	101,756	133,724	149,422	139,923	141,064	169,299	202,439	232,007	262,929
Sum dividends +3 (IBES/WS ratio)	116,016	150,924	166,242	160,691	163,002	178,672	220,091	252,098	282,273
Sum dividends +4 (IBES/WS ratio)	130,853	167,718	185,427	179,807	185,431	204,198	245,986	288,018	321,554
Sum dividends +5 (IBES/WS ratio)	149,861	193,231	215,088	204,871	208,975	227,875	273,145	319,729	357,576
Implied dividends CAGR (IBES/WS ratio)	*13.9%*	*13.3%*	*12.0%*	*13.2%*	*11.6%*	*10.1%*	*5.4%*	*10.2%*	*9.5%*
Implied payout ratio +1	29.4%	31.4%	29.8%	30.9%	31.1%	29.6%	33.2%	27.8%	27.6%
Implied payout ratio +2	28.5%	30.6%	28.6%	29.3%	28.2%	28.2%	26.9%	26.0%	26.4%
Implied payout ratio +3	27.9%	29.6%	27.5%	28.0%	28.3%	26.2%	26.5%	25.7%	25.5%
Implied payout ratio +4	27.3%	28.8%	26.4%	27.4%	28.4%	27.0%	26.6%	26.6%	26.5%
Implied payout ratio +5	27.3%	28.8%	26.4%	27.4%	28.4%	27.0%	26.6%	26.6%	26.5%
Sum book value 0 (Worldscope)	1,577,778	1,836,500	2,252,383	2,675,283	2,997,085	3,225,039	3,833,904	4,500,606	4,951,645
Sum implied book value +1	1,791,639	2,092,671	2,574,714	2,953,752	3,294,719	3,593,709	4,278,612	5,064,024	5,604,198
Sum implied book value +2	2,046,772	2,396,595	2,946,995	3,292,101	3,654,505	4,023,898	4,827,740	5,724,717	6,339,004
Sum implied book value +3	2,346,775	2,754,814	3,385,189	3,705,404	4,066,774	4,526,094	5,438,210	6,455,322	7,162,358
Sum implied book value +4	2,695,445	3,170,407	3,901,123	4,181,465	4,534,116	5,079,482	6,118,611	7,250,367	8,053,313
Sum implied book value +5	3,094,761	3,649,221	4,499,586	4,723,886	5,060,795	5,697,035	6,874,134	8,132,947	9,044,077
Sum market capitalization (IBES)	7,591,747	10,629,528	11,681,526	10,477,306	8,189,042	10,635,862	12,515,858	13,723,348	15,321,865

Source: Datastream, IBES, Worldscope (WS).

Appendix 32 Summary statistics of the US expected MRP estimation using special comparison specifications of previous studies

Model (1)						1.5.1 Claus/Thomas			1.5.2 Gebhardt et al.			1.5.3 Gode/Mohanram			1.5.4 Easton - PEG		1.5.5 Easton - PE	
Year	r^f (2)	θ_{TV}	$m_{P/E+1}$	N (3)	Firms (4)	r^e	r^p	$g_{RI,TV}$	r^e	r^p	Target r^b	r^e	r^p	$g_{agr,TV}$	r^e	r^p	r^e	r^p
1989	8.45%	37.06%	11.8x	7,607	634	12.74%	4.29%	5.45%	9.48%	1.03%	14.71%	12.89%	4.44%	5.45%	9.95%	1.49%	9.11%	0.66%
1990	8.56%	38.87%	12.5x	7,802	650	13.09%	4.54%	5.56%	11.66%	3.10%	16.05%	14.49%	5.93%	5.56%	11.10%	2.54%	8.55%	0.00%
1991	7.79%	40.53%	15.4x	7,961	663	11.51%	3.72%	4.79%	10.35%	2.56%	16.05%	13.80%	6.01%	4.79%	10.69%	2.90%	6.87%	-0.92%
1992	7.02%	41.13%	16.5x	8,438	703	10.67%	3.64%	4.02%	9.65%	2.62%	16.05%	12.87%	5.85%	4.02%	10.10%	3.08%	6.35%	-0.67%
1993	5.84%	39.27%	16.1x	9,400	783	9.97%	4.12%	2.84%	9.52%	3.68%	16.05%	11.84%	6.00%	2.84%	9.54%	3.70%	6.52%	0.67%
1994	7.13%	37.38%	14.6x	10,420	868	11.13%	4.00%	4.13%	10.12%	2.99%	16.02%	13.01%	5.88%	4.13%	10.30%	3.16%	7.22%	0.08%
1995	6.49%	34.41%	14.7x	11,972	998	10.73%	4.24%	3.49%	9.96%	3.47%	15.89%	12.39%	5.90%	3.49%	10.03%	3.54%	7.21%	0.72%
1996	6.46%	31.63%	16.7x	13,633	1,136	10.13%	3.67%	3.46%	9.42%	2.96%	15.86%	11.76%	5.30%	3.46%	9.64%	3.18%	6.31%	-0.15%
1997	6.32%	30.21%	19.6x	15,676	1,306	9.28%	2.96%	3.32%	8.62%	2.30%	15.95%	10.97%	4.65%	3.32%	9.03%	2.71%	5.34%	-0.98%
1998	5.21%	28.19%	22.7x	17,254	1,438	7.98%	2.77%	2.21%	8.07%	2.86%	16.13%	10.11%	4.90%	2.21%	8.67%	3.46%	4.57%	-0.65%
1999	5.71%	28.76%	25.9x	18,128	1,511	7.70%	1.99%	2.71%	7.45%	1.74%	16.35%	9.76%	4.05%	2.71%	8.15%	2.45%	3.99%	-1.72%
2000	5.98%	27.51%	26.5x	18,243	1,520	7.78%	1.79%	2.98%	7.41%	1.43%	16.58%	9.58%	3.60%	2.98%	7.92%	1.93%	3.89%	-2.09%
2001	4.99%	26.85%	23.9x	19,622	1,635	7.67%	2.68%	1.99%	8.39%	3.40%	16.81%	10.00%	5.01%	1.99%	8.66%	3.67%	4.34%	-0.65%
2002	4.54%	28.72%	20.6x	20,614	1,718	8.18%	3.64%	1.54%	9.43%	4.89%	17.00%	10.90%	6.36%	1.54%	9.56%	5.02%	5.09%	0.55%
2003	3.99%	26.98%	18.9x	21,961	1,830	7.81%	3.82%	0.99%	9.62%	5.64%	17.13%	10.07%	6.08%	0.99%	8.91%	4.93%	5.53%	1.54%
2004	4.25%	27.36%	17.8x	23,815	1,985	7.84%	3.59%	1.25%	9.49%	5.24%	17.18%	9.71%	5.46%	1.25%	8.47%	4.22%	5.71%	1.46%
2005	4.27%	27.26%	17.0x	26,254	2,188	8.15%	3.88%	1.27%	9.84%	5.57%	17.18%	9.94%	5.66%	1.27%	8.63%	4.36%	6.14%	1.87%
2006	4.78%	26.60%	16.2x	27,182	2,265	8.56%	3.78%	1.78%	9.98%	5.20%	17.14%	9.89%	5.10%	1.78%	8.56%	3.78%	6.47%	1.68%
Low	3.99%	26.60%	11.8x	7,607	634	7.67%	1.79%	0.99%	7.41%	1.03%	14.71%	9.58%	3.60%	0.99%	7.92%	1.49%	3.89%	-2.09%
Arith. Mean	5.99%	32.15%	18.2x	15,888	1,324	9.50%	3.51%	2.99%	9.36%	3.37%	16.34%	11.33%	5.34%	2.99%	9.33%	3.34%	6.07%	0.08%
Median	5.91%	29.48%	16.8x	16,465	1,372	8.92%	3.70%	2.91%	9.51%	3.04%	16.09%	10.93%	5.56%	2.91%	9.29%	3.32%	6.22%	0.04%
High	8.56%	41.13%	26.5x	27,182	2,265	13.09%	4.54%	5.56%	11.66%	5.64%	17.18%	14.49%	6.36%	5.56%	11.10%	5.02%	9.11%	1.87%
St. Dev.	1.42%	5.42%	4.3x			1.81%	0.77%	1.42%	1.05%	1.42%	0.65%	1.58%	0.77%	1.42%	0.91%	0.94%	1.44%	1.16%

(1) All parameters are stated in nominal terms and as arithmetic average of monthly values.
(2) r^f equals redemption yield of the US Datastream benchmark 10y government bond index.
(3) Overall number of firm observations per annum.
(4) Average number of firms per annum.

Appendix 33 Comparison of studies using the Gebhardt/Lee/Swaminathan version of the RIV model to determine the expected MRP for the US market

Model (1)	Gebhardt/Lee/Swaminathan Model															
Study	Gsell (2010)				Gebhardt/Lee/Swaminathan (2001)				Gode/Mohanram (2003)				Guay/Kothari/Shu (2005)		Lee et al. (2009) (4)	
Year	Companies	agg(2) - r^e	agg - r^p	r^f	Companies	ew(3) - r^e	ew - r^p	r^f	Companies	r^e	r^p	r^f	Companies	r^e	Companies	ew-r^p
1979	NA	NA	NA	NA	1,044	NA	5.20%	NA	NA	NA	NA	NA	NA	NA	NA	NA
1980	NA	NA	NA	NA	1,040	NA	4.10%	NA	NA	NA	NA	NA	NA	NA	NA	NA
1981	NA	NA	NA	NA	1,044	NA	0.20%	NA	NA	NA	NA	NA	NA	NA	NA	NA
1982	NA	NA	NA	NA	1,054	NA	1.90%	NA	NA	NA	NA	NA	NA	NA	NA	NA
1983	NA	NA	NA	NA	1,056	NA	0.60%	NA	NA	NA	NA	NA	1,230	10.6%	NA	NA
1984	NA	NA	NA	NA	1,060	NA	-0.20%	NA	711	NA	0.20%	13.60%	1,491	12.6%	NA	NA
1985	NA	NA	NA	NA	1,038	NA	1.60%	NA	794	NA	1.90%	10.20%	1,518	11.4%	NA	NA
1986	NA	NA	NA	NA	1,018	NA	2.60%	NA	807	NA	2.80%	7.80%	1,540	9.8%	NA	NA
1987	NA	NA	NA	NA	1,025	NA	1.70%	NA	857	NA	1.90%	8.40%	1,739	9.9%	NA	NA
1988	NA	NA	NA	NA	1,019	NA	2.80%	NA	839	NA	2.60%	8.90%	1,623	11.1%	1,262	6.2%
1989	634	9.48%	1.03%	8.45%	1,049	NA	3.80%	NA	876	NA	2.90%	8.30%	1,678	10.7%	1,438	7.0%
1990	650	11.66%	3.10%	8.56%	1,092	NA	3.30%	NA	941	NA	3.00%	8.50%	1,713	10.8%	1,636	7.4%
1991	663	10.35%	2.56%	7.79%	1,091	NA	3.10%	NA	1,044	NA	2.80%	8.30%	1,787	10.4%	1,837	6.2%
1992	703	9.65%	2.62%	7.02%	1,150	NA	3.40%	NA	1,092	NA	3.50%	7.30%	1,996	10.2%	2,047	7.0%
1993	783	9.52%	3.68%	5.84%	1,230	NA	4.40%	NA	1,086	NA	4.40%	6.00%	2,247	9.6%	2,061	6.1%
1994	868	10.12%	2.99%	7.13%	1,269	NA	3.60%	NA	1,200	NA	3.30%	7.10%	2,639	9.9%	2,105	5.3%
1995	998	9.96%	3.47%	6.49%	1,333	NA	4.60%	NA	1,219	NA	4.30%	6.20%	2,765	9.9%	1,832	5.8%
1996	1,136	9.42%	2.96%	6.46%	NA	NA	NA	NA	1,344	NA	3.50%	6.90%	3,049	9.2%	1,718	6.5%
1997	1,306	8.62%	2.30%	6.32%	NA	NA	NA	NA	1,423	NA	3.70%	6.50%	3,354	9.0%	1,474	5.6%
1998	1,438	8.07%	2.86%	5.21%	NA	NA	NA	NA	1,352	NA	4.70%	5.50%	3,378	8.9%	NA	NA
1999	1,511	7.45%	1.74%	5.71%	NA	NA	NA	NA	NA	NA	NA	NA	3,079	9.5%	NA	NA
2000	1,520	7.41%	1.43%	5.98%	NA	NA	NA	NA	NA	NA	NA	NA	2,710	9.7%	NA	NA
2001	1,635	8.39%	3.40%	4.99%	NA	NA	NA	NA	NA	NA	NA	NA	2,237	8.9%	NA	NA
2002	1,718	9.43%	4.89%	4.54%	NA	NA	NA	NA	NA	NA	NA	NA	2,259	8.9%	NA	NA
2003	1,830	9.62%	5.64%	3.99%	NA	NA	NA	NA	NA	NA	NA	NA	2,365	8.9%	NA	NA
2004	1,985	9.49%	5.24%	4.25%	NA	NA	NA	NA	NA	NA	NA	NA	2,437	8.4%	NA	NA
2005	2,188	9.84%	5.57%	4.27%	NA	NA	NA	NA	NA	NA	NA	NA	NA	NA	NA	NA
2006	2,265	9.98%	5.20%	4.78%	NA	NA	NA	NA	NA	NA	NA	NA	NA	NA	NA	NA
Low	634	7.41%	1.03%	3.99%	1,018	NA	-0.20%	NA	711	NA	0.20%	5.50%	1,230	8.4%	1,262	5.3%
Arith. Mean	1,324	9.36%	3.37%	5.99%	1,095	NA	2.75%	NA	1,039	NA	3.03%	7.97%	2,220	9.9%	1,741	6.3%
Median	1,372	9.51%	3.04%	5.91%	1,054	NA	3.10%	NA	1,044	NA	3.00%	7.80%	2,242	9.9%	1,775	6.2%
High	2,265	11.66%	5.64%	8.56%	1,333	NA	5.20%	NA	1,423	NA	4.70%	13.60%	3,378	12.6%	2,105	7.4%
St. Dev.		1.05%	1.42%	1.42%		NA	1.57%	NA		NA	1.14%	NA		1.0%		0.7%

(1) All parameters are stated in nominal terms.
(2) Aggregation method.
(3) Equal-weighted.
(4) Estimation based on dividend discount model with r^e equal to r^b after 15 years. This assumption should be more conservative compared to the Gebhardt/Lee/Swaminathan model with constant RI post the horizon.

Source: Gebhardt, W./Lee, C./Swaminathan, B. (2001), p. 149, Gode, D./Mohanram, P. (2003), pp. 410-411, Guay, W./Kothari, S./Shu, S. (2005), p. 35, and Lee, C./Ng, D./Swaminathan, B. (2009), p. 318.

Appendix 34 Comparison of studies using the Claus/Thomas version of the RIV model to determine the expected MRP for the US market

Model (1)	Claus/Thomas Model														
Study	Gsell (2010)				Claus/Thomas (2001)				Baginski/Wahlen (2003)				Guay/Kothari/Shu (2005)		
Year	Companies	agg(2) - r^e	agg - r^p	r^f	Companies	agg - r^e	agg - r^p	r^f	Companies	r^e	r^p	r^f	Companies	r^e
1983	NA	NA	NA	NA	NA	NA	NA	NA	NA	NA	NA	NA	1,230	12.7%
1984	NA	NA	NA	NA	NA	NA	NA	NA	NA	NA	NA	NA	1,491	15.5%
1985	NA	NA	NA	NA	1,559	14.38%	2.95%	11.43%	NA	NA	NA	NA	1,518	12.9%
1986	NA	NA	NA	NA	1,613	11.28%	3.98%	7.30%	NA	NA	NA	NA	1,540	10.2%
1987	NA	NA	NA	NA	1,774	11.12%	3.10%	8.02%	NA	NA	NA	NA	1,739	10.5%
1988	NA	NA	NA	NA	1,735	12.15%	3.43%	8.72%	NA	NA	NA	NA	1,623	11.8%
1989	634	12.74%	4.29%	8.45%	1,809	12.75%	3.57%	9.18%	NA	NA	NA	NA	1,678	11.1%
1990	650	13.09%	4.54%	8.56%	1,889	12.33%	3.54%	8.79%	NA	NA	NA	NA	1,713	11.5%
1991	663	11.51%	3.72%	7.79%	1,939	11.05%	3.01%	8.04%	NA	NA	NA	NA	1,787	10.9%
1992	703	10.67%	3.64%	7.02%	2,106	10.57%	3.09%	7.48%	NA	NA	NA	NA	1,996	10.5%
1993	783	9.97%	4.12%	5.84%	2,386	9.62%	3.65%	5.97%	NA	NA	NA	NA	2,247	9.5%
1994	868	11.13%	4.00%	7.13%	2,784	10.03%	4.06%	5.97%	NA	NA	NA	NA	2,639	10.2%
1995	998	10.73%	4.24%	6.49%	2,965	11.03%	3.97%	7.06%	NA	NA	NA	NA	2,765	9.9%
1996	1,136	10.13%	3.67%	6.46%	3,360	9.96%	3.45%	6.51%	665	10.80%	2.00%	8.80%	3,049	9.5%
1997	1,306	9.28%	2.96%	6.32%	3,797	10.12%	3.23%	6.89%	773	9.70%	1.70%	8.00%	3,354	9.2%
1998	1,438	7.98%	2.77%	5.21%	3,673	8.15%	2.51%	5.64%	802	9.60%	2.10%	7.50%	3,378	8.8%
1999	1,511	7.70%	1.99%	5.71%	NA	NA	NA	NA	822	9.30%	3.30%	6.00%	3,079	9.6%
2000	1,520	7.78%	1.79%	5.98%	NA	NA	NA	NA	908	9.80%	2.80%	7.00%	2,710	10.5%
2001	1,635	7.67%	2.68%	4.99%	NA	NA	NA	NA	898	10.30%	3.30%	7.00%	2,237	8.7%
2002	1,718	8.18%	3.64%	4.54%	NA	NA	NA	NA	966	9.70%	3.20%	6.50%	2,259	8.4%
2003	1,830	7.81%	3.82%	3.99%	NA	NA	NA	NA	1,060	10.00%	3.10%	6.90%	2,365	7.5%
2004	1,985	7.84%	3.59%	4.25%	NA	NA	NA	NA	1,073	8.80%	3.20%	5.60%	2,437	7.5%
2005	2,188	8.15%	3.88%	4.27%	NA	NA	NA	NA	NA	NA	NA	NA	NA	NA
2006	2,265	8.56%	3.78%	4.78%	NA	NA	NA	NA	NA	NA	NA	NA	NA	NA
Low	634	7.67%	1.79%	3.99%	1,559	8.15%	2.51%	5.64%	665	8.80%	1.70%	5.60%	1,230	7.5%
Arith. Mean	1,324	9.50%	3.51%	5.99%	2,385	11.04%	3.40%	7.64%	885	9.78%	2.74%	7.03%	2,220	10.3%
Median	1,372	8.92%	3.70%	5.91%	2,023	11.04%	3.44%	7.39%	898	9.70%	3.10%	7.00%	2,242	10.2%
High	2,265	13.09%	4.54%	8.56%	3,797	14.38%	4.06%	11.43%	1,073	10.80%	3.30%	8.80%	3,378	15.5%
St. Dev.		1.81%	0.77%	1.42%		1.54%	0.44%	1.55%		0.57%	0.63%	0.98%		1.8%

(1) All parameters are stated in nominal terms.
(2) Aggregation method.

Source: Baginski, S./Wahlen, J. (2003), pp. 336-337, Claus, J./Thomas, J. (2001), p. 1643, and Guay, W./Kothari, S./Shu, S. (2005), p. 35.

Appendix 35 Comparison of studies using the regression-based estimation approach to determine the expected MRP for the US market

Model (1)	Regression-based estimation approach											
Study	Gsell (2010)						Easton et al. (2002)					
Year	Companies	r^e	r^P	r^f	g_{RI}	R^2	Companies	r^e	r^P	r^f	g_{RI}	R^2
1981	NA	NA	NA	NA	NA	NA	756	16.20%	2.20%	14.00%	11.50%	54.00%
1982	NA	NA	NA	NA	NA	NA	986	13.80%	3.90%	9.90%	9.20%	54.00%
1983	NA	NA	NA	NA	NA	NA	1,098	13.90%	2.50%	11.40%	9.60%	47.00%
1984	NA	NA	NA	NA	NA	NA	1,158	14.60%	3.60%	11.00%	9.00%	57.00%
1985	NA	NA	NA	NA	NA	NA	1,137	12.70%	4.10%	8.60%	8.30%	48.00%
1986	NA	NA	NA	NA	NA	NA	1,150	12.40%	5.50%	6.90%	8.20%	50.00%
1987	NA	NA	NA	NA	NA	NA	1,153	14.20%	5.90%	8.30%	10.20%	36.00%
1988	NA	NA	NA	NA	NA	NA	1,173	13.50%	4.30%	9.20%	8.40%	49.00%
1989	625	12.18%	3.73%	8.45%	6.07%	63.33%	1,221	13.20%	5.30%	7.90%	9.10%	44.00%
1990	637	12.67%	4.12%	8.56%	6.87%	60.95%	1,168	13.60%	5.90%	7.70%	9.50%	42.00%
1991	645	11.66%	3.87%	7.79%	6.65%	67.41%	1,284	12.20%	6.20%	6.00%	9.10%	49.00%
1992	678	11.23%	4.21%	7.02%	6.58%	61.39%	1,460	11.30%	5.20%	6.10%	7.00%	59.00%
1993	751	11.65%	5.81%	5.84%	7.58%	40.34%	1,717	11.60%	6.40%	5.20%	7.50%	53.00%
1994	839	12.01%	4.88%	7.13%	7.67%	45.28%	1,907	13.50%	5.70%	7.80%	9.80%	43.00%
1995	954	12.46%	5.97%	6.49%	8.05%	51.21%	2,042	13.20%	7.80%	5.40%	10.00%	43.00%
1996	1,066	12.50%	6.04%	6.46%	8.70%	47.57%	2,402	12.40%	6.20%	6.20%	9.20%	44.00%
1997	1,224	11.29%	4.98%	6.32%	7.43%	39.79%	2,508	12.20%	6.50%	5.70%	9.10%	42.00%
1998	1,318	11.92%	6.70%	5.21%	8.50%	27.02%	2,241	13.00%	8.30%	4.70%	10.30%	39.00%
1999	1,335	12.14%	6.43%	5.71%	8.76%	29.84%	NA	NA	NA	NA	NA	NA
2000	1,297	13.24%	7.26%	5.98%	10.66%	19.77%	NA	NA	NA	NA	NA	NA
2001	1,510	10.18%	5.19%	4.99%	7.04%	18.71%	NA	NA	NA	NA	NA	NA
2002	1,623	8.85%	4.32%	4.54%	4.64%	25.62%	NA	NA	NA	NA	NA	NA
2003	1,718	9.09%	5.10%	3.99%	5.08%	25.04%	NA	NA	NA	NA	NA	NA
2004	1,841	9.87%	5.62%	4.25%	6.47%	26.61%	NA	NA	NA	NA	NA	NA
2005	2,033	10.02%	5.75%	4.27%	6.68%	23.49%	NA	NA	NA	NA	NA	NA
2006	2,096	10.58%	5.80%	4.78%	7.45%	21.86%	NA	NA	NA	NA	NA	NA
Low	625	8.85%	3.73%	3.99%	4.64%	18.71%	756	11.30%	2.20%	4.70%	7.00%	36.00%
Arith. Mean	1,233	11.31%	5.32%	5.99%	7.27%	38.62%	1,476	13.19%	5.31%	7.89%	9.17%	47.39%
Median	1,260	11.66%	5.40%	5.91%	7.23%	34.81%	1,197	13.20%	5.60%	7.75%	9.15%	47.50%
High	2,096	13.24%	7.26%	8.56%	10.66%	67.41%	2,508	16.20%	8.30%	14.00%	11.50%	59.00%
St. Dev.		1.27%	1.01%	1.42%	1.40%	16.65%		1.16%	1.63%	2.48%	1.06%	6.32%

(1) All parameters are stated in nominal terms.

Source: Easton, P. et al. (2002), p. 665.

Appendix 36 Summary of World input data for the expected MRP estimation based on analysts' consensus estimates 1989-1997

	29.12.89	31.12.90	31.12.91	31.12.92	31.12.93	30.12.94	29.12.95	31.12.96	31.12.97
Sample size									
Sum companies included	864	892	933	1029	1160	1429	1500	1915	2280
LTM average of included companies	866	878	932	1004	1128	1328	1510	1706	2124
LTM number of observations	10396	10533	11182	12051	13530	15936	18124	20468	25487
Exchange rates (spot)									
EUR/USD	1.28303	1.45366	1.41099	1.24837	1.12509	1.24112	1.33139	1.27112	1.09073
CAD/USD	0.86356	0.86207	0.86543	0.78653	0.75540	0.71291	0.73292	0.72966	0.69915
JPY/USD	0.00696	0.00736	0.00801	0.00801	0.00896	0.01004	0.00967	0.00863	0.00766
GBP/USD	1.61400	1.93000	1.86950	1.51450	1.47950	1.56500	1.55300	1.71250	1.65080
Input variables (US$ million)									
Sum earnings +1 (IBES)	179,393	179,612	178,485	172,346	186,362	233,898	302,231	360,756	443,828
Sum earnings +2 (IBES)	200,192	200,329	211,531	198,864	214,510	276,083	353,370	414,613	508,283
Sum earnings +3 (IBES)	222,512	231,999	243,338	228,563	245,003	318,803	399,243	473,619	579,769
Sum earnings +4 (IBES)	251,699	259,351	276,559	258,073	274,901	356,704	446,378	534,266	656,180
Sum earnings +5 (IBES)	289,828	288,164	308,843	291,237	306,441	398,024	502,729	603,760	742,846
Implied earnings CAGR (IBES)	*12.7%*	*12.5%*	*14.7%*	*14.0%*	*13.2%*	*14.2%*	*13.6%*	*13.7%*	*13.7%*
Sum dividends +1 (IBES/WS ratio)	64,032	70,561	72,256	71,213	78,204	92,632	114,517	125,877	149,745
Sum dividends +2 (IBES/WS ratio)	70,903	77,871	84,382	81,391	87,281	104,371	127,389	139,988	166,015
Sum dividends +3 (IBES/WS ratio)	78,153	88,994	96,435	92,739	99,182	119,449	141,894	157,692	185,706
Sum dividends +4 (IBES/WS ratio)	87,792	98,543	108,644	103,711	111,880	134,209	159,372	175,025	209,924
Sum dividends +5 (IBES/WS ratio)	101,091	109,491	121,326	117,038	124,716	149,755	179,491	197,791	237,650
Implied dividends CAGR (IBES/WS ratio)	*12.1%*	*11.6%*	*13.8%*	*13.2%*	*12.4%*	*12.8%*	*11.9%*	*12.0%*	*12.2%*
Implied payout ratio +1	35.7%	39.3%	40.5%	41.3%	42.0%	39.6%	37.9%	34.9%	33.7%
Implied payout ratio +2	35.4%	38.9%	39.9%	40.9%	40.7%	37.8%	36.0%	33.8%	32.7%
Implied payout ratio +3	35.1%	38.4%	39.6%	40.6%	40.5%	37.5%	35.5%	33.3%	32.0%
Implied payout ratio +4	34.9%	38.0%	39.3%	40.2%	40.7%	37.6%	35.7%	32.8%	32.0%
Implied payout ratio +5	34.9%	38.0%	39.3%	40.2%	40.7%	37.6%	35.7%	32.8%	32.0%
Sum book value 0 (Worldscope)	1,142,857	1,255,958	1,379,937	1,315,239	1,364,731	1,618,180	1,834,082	2,323,377	2,757,380
Sum implied book value +1	1,258,218	1,365,009	1,486,166	1,416,372	1,472,889	1,759,447	2,021,797	2,558,255	3,051,463
Sum implied book value +2	1,387,507	1,487,467	1,613,316	1,533,845	1,600,117	1,931,158	2,247,777	2,832,880	3,393,730
Sum implied book value +3	1,531,866	1,630,472	1,760,219	1,669,669	1,745,938	2,130,512	2,505,125	3,148,807	3,787,793
Sum implied book value +4	1,695,773	1,791,279	1,928,135	1,824,031	1,908,959	2,353,007	2,792,131	3,508,047	4,234,049
Sum implied book value +5	1,884,510	1,969,953	2,115,652	1,998,230	2,090,683	2,601,276	3,115,369	3,914,016	4,739,244
Sum market capitalization (IBES)	2,564,787	2,379,372	2,920,831	3,039,457	3,473,806	3,783,631	5,141,921	6,818,640	9,542,928

Source: Datastream, IBES, Worldscope (WS).

Appendix 37 Summary of World input data for the expected MRP estimation based on analysts' consensus estimates 1998-2006

	31.12.98	31.12.99	29.12.00	31.12.01	31.12.02	31.12.03	31.12.04	30.12.05	29.12.06
Sample size									
Sum companies included	2459	2760	3180	3324	3244	3465	3781	4130	4303
LTM average of included companies	2360	2537	2798	3174	3209	3284	3597	3927	4134
LTM number of observations	28314	30445	33574	38083	38512	39407	43165	47124	49607
Exchange rates (spot)									
EUR/USD	1.17430	1.00240	0.93890	0.89040	1.04940	1.26135	1.35925	1.17955	1.31865
CAD/USD	0.65347	0.69242	0.66713	0.62657	0.63621	0.77337	0.83222	0.86022	0.85807
JPY/USD	0.00881	0.00979	0.00874	0.00763	0.00842	0.00933	0.00975	0.00848	0.00840
GBP/USD	1.65950	1.61530	1.49600	1.45565	1.60965	1.78555	1.91855	1.72295	1.95890
Input variables (US$ million)									
Sum earnings +1 (IBES)	459,496	553,723	697,544	606,900	695,175	875,466	1,152,852	1,311,550	1,573,369
Sum earnings +2 (IBES)	533,676	665,005	804,374	740,507	816,493	1,014,992	1,299,664	1,480,929	1,744,094
Sum earnings +3 (IBES)	616,288	770,503	927,036	881,659	934,843	1,145,247	1,429,316	1,622,310	1,918,361
Sum earnings +4 (IBES)	701,673	876,569	1,067,446	1,013,595	1,048,983	1,269,876	1,571,552	1,769,264	2,077,674
Sum earnings +5 (IBES)	796,695	1,005,064	1,224,862	1,168,576	1,178,592	1,402,988	1,727,856	1,945,988	2,278,742
Implied earnings CAGR (IBES)	*14.7%*	*16.1%*	*15.1%*	*17.8%*	*14.1%*	*12.5%*	*10.6%*	*10.4%*	*9.7%*
Sum dividends +1 (IBES/WS ratio)	150,872	190,626	222,019	209,239	229,374	271,006	375,270	390,649	485,501
Sum dividends +2 (IBES/WS ratio)	168,723	213,307	241,151	230,302	242,948	297,445	370,444	422,756	520,196
Sum dividends +3 (IBES/WS ratio)	189,294	239,968	269,959	259,850	274,126	318,479	403,376	461,224	562,488
Sum dividends +4 (IBES/WS ratio)	207,919	272,861	307,951	289,492	310,411	364,219	449,660	520,915	622,352
Sum dividends +5 (IBES/WS ratio)	236,076	312,859	353,364	333,756	348,765	402,398	494,382	572,947	682,580
Implied dividends CAGR (IBES/WS ratio)	*11.8%*	*13.2%*	*12.3%*	*12.4%*	*11.0%*	*10.4%*	*7.1%*	*10.0%*	*8.9%*
Implied payout ratio +1	32.8%	34.4%	31.8%	34.5%	33.0%	31.0%	32.6%	29.8%	30.9%
Implied payout ratio +2	31.6%	32.1%	30.0%	31.1%	29.8%	29.3%	28.5%	28.5%	29.8%
Implied payout ratio +3	30.7%	31.1%	29.1%	29.5%	29.3%	27.8%	28.2%	28.4%	29.3%
Implied payout ratio +4	29.6%	31.1%	28.8%	28.6%	29.6%	28.7%	28.6%	29.4%	30.0%
Implied payout ratio +5	29.6%	31.1%	28.8%	28.6%	29.6%	28.7%	28.6%	29.4%	30.0%
Sum book value 0 (Worldscope)	3,022,780	3,560,165	4,548,334	5,239,324	5,730,504	6,320,747	7,545,866	8,149,009	9,543,446
Sum implied book value +1	3,331,405	3,923,263	5,023,859	5,636,984	6,196,305	6,925,207	8,323,448	9,069,910	10,631,313
Sum implied book value +2	3,696,358	4,374,960	5,587,082	6,147,190	6,769,850	7,642,755	9,252,668	10,128,083	11,855,211
Sum implied book value +3	4,123,352	4,905,495	6,244,159	6,768,999	7,430,567	8,469,523	10,278,608	11,289,169	13,211,083
Sum implied book value +4	4,617,106	5,509,203	7,003,653	7,493,102	8,169,139	9,375,180	11,400,500	12,537,518	14,666,405
Sum implied book value +5	5,177,725	6,201,408	7,875,151	8,327,921	8,998,966	10,375,771	12,633,974	13,910,559	16,262,567
Sum market capitalization (IBES)	11,200,814	16,538,198	17,903,682	15,298,160	12,319,546	16,437,882	19,726,211	22,543,710	26,244,797

Source: Datastream, IBES, Worldscope (WS).

Appendix 38 Summary statistics of the World expected MRP estimation using special comparison specifications of previous studies

Model (1)						1.5.1 Claus/Thomas			1.5.2 Gebhardt et al.			1.5.3 Gode/Mohanram			1.5.4 Easton - PEG		1.5.5 Easton - PE	
Year	r^f (2)	θ_{TV}	$m_{P/E+1}$	N (3)	Firms (4)	r^e	r^p	$g_{RI,TV}$	r^e	r^p	Target r^b	r^e	r^p	$g_{agr,TV}$	r^e	r^p	r^e	r^p
1989	8.45%	35.88%	13.2x	10,396	866	11.39%	2.94%	5.00%	7.89%	-0.56%	12.98%	11.97%	3.51%	5.00%	9.23%	0.78%	8.03%	-0.43%
1990	8.56%	37.46%	13.3x	10,533	878	11.98%	3.42%	5.72%	10.41%	1.85%	14.16%	13.21%	4.65%	5.72%	10.13%	1.58%	8.02%	-0.54%
1991	7.79%	39.39%	15.5x	11,182	932	10.67%	2.88%	4.96%	9.68%	1.89%	14.16%	12.93%	5.14%	4.96%	10.03%	2.24%	6.80%	-0.99%
1992	7.02%	40.20%	16.3x	12,051	1,004	9.88%	2.85%	4.25%	9.34%	2.31%	14.16%	12.54%	5.51%	4.25%	9.85%	2.83%	6.43%	-0.59%
1993	5.84%	40.29%	17.8x	13,530	1,128	9.21%	3.37%	2.88%	8.72%	2.88%	14.16%	11.35%	5.51%	2.88%	9.15%	3.30%	5.87%	0.03%
1994	7.13%	38.76%	17.2x	15,936	1,328	9.39%	2.25%	3.82%	8.97%	1.83%	14.09%	12.50%	5.36%	3.82%	9.83%	2.70%	6.08%	-1.05%
1995	6.49%	36.33%	15.9x	18,124	1,510	9.87%	3.38%	3.44%	9.06%	2.58%	13.79%	12.37%	5.88%	3.44%	9.99%	3.50%	6.60%	0.12%
1996	6.46%	33.82%	17.5x	20,468	1,706	9.35%	2.89%	3.18%	8.38%	1.93%	13.46%	11.47%	5.01%	3.18%	9.32%	2.87%	5.98%	-0.48%
1997	6.32%	32.14%	20.4x	25,487	2,124	8.25%	1.93%	2.76%	7.51%	1.20%	13.22%	10.61%	4.29%	2.76%	8.65%	2.34%	5.09%	-1.23%
1998	5.21%	31.12%	22.9x	28,314	2,360	7.33%	2.12%	1.78%	6.97%	1.76%	13.09%	9.83%	4.61%	1.78%	8.33%	3.11%	4.54%	-0.68%
1999	5.71%	31.09%	26.3x	30,445	2,537	7.11%	1.41%	2.03%	6.36%	0.65%	13.07%	9.69%	3.98%	2.03%	8.02%	2.31%	3.92%	-1.79%
2000	5.98%	29.92%	27.5x	33,574	2,798	7.74%	1.76%	2.26%	6.26%	0.27%	13.12%	9.71%	3.72%	2.26%	7.98%	1.99%	3.74%	-2.24%
2001	4.99%	28.41%	23.3x	38,083	3,174	8.13%	3.14%	1.50%	7.40%	2.41%	13.23%	10.30%	5.31%	1.50%	8.87%	3.88%	4.46%	-0.53%
2002	4.54%	29.56%	20.3x	38,512	3,209	8.32%	3.78%	1.20%	8.48%	3.94%	13.36%	11.44%	6.90%	1.20%	9.99%	5.45%	5.24%	0.70%
2003	3.99%	29.02%	17.7x	39,407	3,284	8.64%	4.65%	0.68%	8.71%	4.72%	13.46%	10.65%	6.66%	0.68%	9.37%	5.39%	5.92%	1.93%
2004	4.25%	29.03%	16.8x	43,165	3,597	8.72%	4.47%	0.89%	8.52%	4.27%	13.52%	10.14%	5.89%	0.89%	8.82%	4.56%	6.10%	1.84%
2005	4.27%	29.55%	16.3x	47,124	3,927	9.16%	4.89%	0.74%	8.63%	4.35%	13.56%	9.98%	5.71%	0.74%	8.60%	4.32%	6.44%	2.17%
2006	4.78%	29.58%	16.1x	49,607	4,134	9.06%	4.28%	1.11%	8.55%	3.77%	13.59%	9.78%	5.00%	1.11%	8.35%	3.57%	6.53%	1.75%
Low	3.99%	28.41%	13.2x	10,396	866	7.11%	1.41%	0.68%	6.26%	-0.56%	12.98%	9.69%	3.51%	0.68%	7.98%	0.78%	3.74%	-2.24%
Arith. Mean	5.99%	33.42%	18.6x	26,997	2,250	9.12%	3.13%	2.68%	8.33%	2.34%	13.57%	11.14%	5.15%	2.68%	9.14%	3.15%	5.88%	-0.11%
Median	5.91%	31.63%	17.4x	26,901	2,242	9.11%	3.04%	2.51%	8.54%	2.12%	13.49%	11.00%	5.23%	2.51%	9.19%	2.99%	6.03%	-0.51%
High	8.56%	40.29%	27.5x	49,607	4,134	11.98%	4.89%	5.72%	10.41%	4.72%	14.16%	13.21%	6.90%	5.72%	10.13%	5.45%	8.03%	2.17%
St. Dev.	1.42%	4.35%	4.1x			1.30%	1.01%	1.59%	1.09%	1.46%	0.43%	1.21%	0.92%	1.59%	0.72%	1.25%	1.21%	1.30%

(1) All parameters are stated in nominal terms and as arithmetic average of monthly values.
(2) r^f equals redemption yield of the US Datastream benchmark 10y government bond index.
(3) Overall number of firm observations per annum.
(4) Average number of firms per annum.

Appendix 39 Summary of German input data for the expected MRP estimation based on analysts' consensus estimates from January 2007 to September 2009

	31.01.2007	29.06.2007	30.11.2007	30.04.2008	30.05.2008	31.10.2008	31.03.2009	30.04.2009	30.09.2009
Sample size									
Sum companies included	300	304	330	341	340	340	336	343	329
Input variables (EUR million)									
Sum earnings +1 (IBES)	71,257	81,247	85,308	88,783	86,991	78,581	52,370	45,623	38,897
Sum earnings +2 (IBES)	77,438	91,654	96,706	102,231	100,805	92,311	63,215	61,641	58,225
Sum earnings +3 (IBES)	85,988	101,972	108,563	113,951	112,390	102,917	72,829	72,226	72,738
Sum earnings +4 (IBES)	93,477	111,449	118,733	125,382	121,761	113,038	82,082	80,491	82,942
Sum earnings +5 (IBES)	99,751	123,387	132,929	144,412	139,008	127,935	92,311	89,930	96,219
Implied earnings CAGR (IBES)	*8.8%*	*11.0%*	*11.7%*	*12.9%*	*12.4%*	*13.0%*	*15.2%*	*18.5%*	*25.4%*
Sum dividends +1 (IBES/WS ratio)	26,366	30,993	31,691	35,712	35,876	35,460	25,989	24,730	23,983
Sum dividends +2 (IBES/WS ratio)	29,430	34,157	35,421	39,283	39,285	38,739	28,255	27,240	25,896
Sum dividends +3 (IBES/WS ratio)	32,450	37,744	39,267	42,860	42,950	42,058	30,468	29,785	29,461
Sum dividends +4 (IBES/WS ratio)	34,190	37,736	39,853	43,245	43,888	42,010	32,865	32,647	33,595
Sum dividends +5 (IBES/WS ratio)	36,485	41,778	44,619	49,809	50,105	47,546	36,961	36,475	38,973
Implied dividends CAGR (IBES/WS ratio)	*8.5%*	*7.8%*	*8.9%*	*8.7%*	*8.7%*	*7.6%*	*9.2%*	*10.2%*	*12.9%*
Implied payout ratio +1	37.0%	38.1%	37.1%	40.2%	41.2%	45.1%	49.6%	54.2%	61.7%
Implied payout ratio +2	38.0%	37.3%	36.6%	38.4%	39.0%	42.0%	44.7%	44.2%	44.5%
Implied payout ratio +3	37.7%	37.0%	36.2%	37.6%	38.2%	40.9%	41.8%	41.2%	40.5%
Implied payout ratio +4	36.6%	33.9%	33.6%	34.5%	36.0%	37.2%	40.0%	40.6%	40.5%
Implied payout ratio +5	36.6%	33.9%	33.6%	34.5%	36.0%	37.2%	40.0%	40.6%	40.5%
Sum book value 0 (Worldscope)	498,237	552,207	557,298	605,715	605,952	604,199	605,312	527,695	562,350
Sum implied book value +1	542,629	601,176	609,577	659,102	659,022	648,334	640,165	554,076	577,642
Sum implied book value +2	590,245	657,891	669,482	722,428	721,971	704,302	675,400	589,036	609,749
Sum implied book value +3	643,557	721,079	737,102	793,810	793,061	768,728	722,073	631,397	652,579
Sum implied book value +4	700,326	793,322	815,946	876,291	875,198	840,576	775,376	680,614	704,190
Sum implied book value +5	761,686	874,588	908,973	977,473	969,802	920,263	835,966	735,964	768,840
Sum market capitalization (IBES)	1,037,032	1,193,699	1,263,807	1,002,866	1,038,409	913,086	634,238	585,526	719,067

Source: Datastream, IBES, Worldscope (WS).
Note: Only selected months shown.

Appendix 40 Ex-post total return decomposition for Germany between 1989 and 2006 using implied dividend yields

	Ex-post total return			Price-dividend ratios		Ex-post total return components				Ex-post MRP		
							Price return					
Year	Dividend yield (D_t/P_{t-1}) (1)	Price return ($[P_t-P_{t-1}]/P_{t-1}$) (2)	Ex-post return (r_t) (3)	Price-dividend ratio (P_{t-1}/D_t) (4)	Price-dividend ratio (P_t/D_t) (5)	Dividend yield (D_t/P_{t-1})	Dividend growth ($g_{D,t}$)	Price-div. ratio expansion ($g_{m,t}$)	$g_{D,t}*g_{m,t}$	Ex-post return	Risk-free rate (6)	Ex-post MRP
1989	2.32%	34.80%	37.11%	43.19x	58.22x	2.32%	9.94%	22.61%	2.25%	37.11%	7.15%	29.96%
1990	2.03%	-16.72%	-14.69%	49.22x	40.99x	2.03%	18.29%	-29.60%	-5.41%	-14.69%	9.00%	-23.69%
1991	2.57%	2.18%	4.74%	38.98x	39.83x	2.57%	5.17%	-2.84%	-0.15%	4.74%	8.15%	-3.41%
1992	2.54%	-8.94%	-6.39%	39.31x	35.80x	2.54%	1.30%	-10.11%	-0.13%	-6.39%	7.22%	-13.62%
1993	2.90%	41.66%	44.56%	34.51x	48.89x	2.90%	3.73%	36.57%	1.36%	44.56%	5.87%	38.69%
1994	1.63%	-7.46%	-5.83%	61.18x	56.62x	1.63%	-20.08%	15.79%	-3.17%	-5.83%	7.58%	-13.40%
1995	2.15%	2.60%	4.75%	46.54x	47.75x	2.15%	21.65%	-15.66%	-3.39%	4.75%	6.29%	-1.54%
1996	2.30%	19.84%	22.14%	43.41x	52.02x	2.30%	10.01%	8.93%	0.89%	22.14%	6.05%	16.09%
1997	2.20%	38.63%	40.83%	45.46x	63.01x	2.20%	14.43%	21.14%	3.05%	40.83%	5.71%	35.11%
1998	1.55%	13.99%	15.54%	64.62x	73.66x	1.55%	-2.49%	16.90%	-0.42%	15.54%	4.45%	11.09%
1999	1.90%	29.77%	31.68%	52.55x	68.19x	1.90%	40.18%	-7.43%	-2.98%	31.68%	5.36%	26.31%
2000	1.16%	-11.07%	-9.91%	86.50x	76.93x	1.16%	-21.17%	12.81%	-2.71%	-9.91%	5.09%	-15.01%
2001	1.55%	-19.47%	-17.91%	64.32x	51.80x	1.55%	19.60%	-32.66%	-6.40%	-17.91%	4.98%	-22.89%
2002	1.05%	-40.99%	-39.94%	95.07x	56.10x	1.05%	-45.52%	8.30%	-3.78%	-39.94%	4.71%	-44.65%
2003	3.61%	33.97%	37.58%	27.73x	37.15x	3.61%	102.31%	-33.78%	-34.56%	37.58%	3.90%	33.67%
2004	2.19%	6.27%	8.47%	45.61x	48.47x	2.19%	-18.54%	30.46%	-5.65%	8.47%	3.73%	4.74%
2005	3.13%	25.07%	28.20%	31.94x	39.95x	3.13%	51.75%	-17.58%	-9.10%	28.20%	3.44%	24.76%
2006	2.76%	21.33%	24.09%	36.22x	43.95x	2.76%	10.28%	10.02%	1.03%	24.09%	3.81%	20.28%
Arith. mean	2.20%	9.19%	11.39%	50.35x	52.19x	2.20%	11.16%	1.88%	-3.85%	11.39%	5.69%	5.69%
Geo. mean	2.19%	6.59%	8.73%			2.19%	7.05%	-0.43%		8.73%	5.68%	2.79%
St. Dev.	0.67%	23.36%	23.81%	18.06x	12.25x	0.67%	32.12%	21.57%	8.34%	23.81%	1.62%	24.23%

(1) Implied by the difference between CDAX total and price return.
(2) Based on official CDAX price return.
(3) Based on official CDAX total return.
(4) Inverted difference between CDAX total and price return.
(5) Lagged dividend yield times one plus the price return.
(6) Year-end income return of 10-year government bonds.

Note: All values are stated in nominal terms.

Appendix 41 Ex-post total return decomposition for Canada between 1989 and 2006

	Ex-post total return			Price-dividend ratios		Ex-post total return components				Ex-post MRP		
							Price return					
Year	Dividend yield (D_t/P_{t-1}) (1)	Price return $([P_t-P_{t-1}]/P_{t-1})$ (2)	Ex-post return (r_t) (3)	Price-dividend ratio (P_{t-1}/D_t) (4)	Price-dividend ratio (P_t/D_t) (5)	Dividend yield (D_t/P_{t-1})	Dividend growth $(g_{D,t})$	Price-div. ratio expansion $(g_{m,t})$	$g_{D,t}*g_{m,t}$	Ex-post return	Risk-free rate (6)	Ex-post MRP
1989	3.81%	17.10%	20.91%	26.28x	30.77x	3.81%	13.27%	3.38%	0.45%	20.91%	9.42%	11.49%
1990	3.14%	-17.96%	-14.82%	31.83x	26.11x	3.14%	-3.32%	-15.14%	0.50%	-14.82%	10.79%	-25.61%
1991	3.43%	7.85%	11.28%	29.16x	31.45x	3.43%	-10.46%	20.44%	-2.14%	11.28%	8.86%	2.42%
1992	2.91%	-4.61%	-1.70%	34.37x	32.79x	2.91%	-8.51%	4.26%	-0.36%	-1.70%	7.58%	-9.28%
1993	2.91%	28.98%	31.90%	34.31x	44.25x	2.91%	-4.43%	34.96%	-1.55%	31.90%	7.05%	24.84%
1994	2.33%	-2.49%	-0.16%	42.91x	41.84x	2.33%	3.11%	-5.44%	-0.17%	-0.16%	7.77%	-7.93%
1995	2.54%	11.86%	14.40%	39.38x	44.05x	2.54%	6.25%	5.29%	0.33%	14.40%	7.83%	6.58%
1996	2.30%	25.75%	28.05%	43.46x	54.64x	2.30%	1.37%	24.04%	0.33%	28.05%	6.71%	21.34%
1997	1.85%	13.03%	14.89%	53.95x	60.98x	1.85%	1.30%	11.59%	0.15%	14.89%	6.48%	8.40%
1998	1.61%	-3.19%	-1.58%	62.22x	60.24x	1.61%	-2.01%	-1.20%	0.02%	-1.58%	5.54%	-7.12%
1999	1.70%	29.72%	31.42%	58.85x	76.34x	1.70%	2.37%	26.72%	0.63%	31.42%	5.81%	25.62%
2000	1.34%	6.18%	7.52%	74.75x	79.37x	1.34%	2.13%	3.97%	0.08%	7.52%	5.46%	2.06%
2001	1.33%	-13.94%	-12.61%	75.45x	64.94x	1.33%	5.19%	-18.18%	-0.94%	-12.61%	5.73%	-18.34%
2002	1.64%	-13.97%	-12.32%	60.86x	52.36x	1.64%	6.70%	-19.37%	-1.30%	-12.32%	5.08%	-17.40%
2003	2.04%	24.29%	26.32%	49.06x	60.98x	2.04%	6.72%	16.46%	1.11%	26.32%	5.03%	21.30%
2004	1.88%	12.48%	14.36%	53.24x	59.88x	1.88%	14.53%	-1.80%	-0.26%	14.36%	4.75%	9.61%
2005	2.43%	21.91%	24.33%	41.22x	50.25x	2.43%	45.27%	-16.08%	-7.28%	24.33%	4.32%	20.01%
2006	2.77%	14.51%	17.29%	36.08x	41.32x	2.77%	39.26%	-17.77%	-6.98%	17.29%	4.03%	13.26%
Arith. mean	2.33%	8.75%	11.08%	47.08x	50.70x	2.33%	6.60%	3.12%	-0.96%	11.08%	6.57%	4.51%
Geo. mean	2.33%	7.71%	10.05%			2.33%	5.76%	1.84%		10.05%	6.55%	3.33%
St. Dev.	0.72%	15.14%	15.26%	14.90x	15.40x	0.72%	14.53%	16.77%	2.39%	15.26%	1.86%	15.78%

(1) Implied by lagged direct S&P/TSX Comp. dividend yield.
(2) Based on official S&P/TSX Comp. price return.
(3) Implied ex-post total return by adding lagged direct S&P/TSX Comp. dividend yield and official S&P/TSX Comp. price return. Differs marginally from official S&P/TSX Comp. ex-post total return.
(4) Calculated as Datastream direct S&P/TSX Comp. price-dividend ratio divided by one plus official S&P/TSX Comp. price return.
(5) Based on direct S&P/TSX Comp. dividend yield.
(6) Year-end income return of 10-year government bonds.

Note: All values are stated in nominal terms.

Appendix 42 Decomposition-based unconditional expected MRP estimates for Canada

Year	Ex-ante analysis: Ex-ante MRP	Risk-free rate (1)	Implied cost of equity	Expected dividend growth (2)	Dividend yield (D_t/P_{t-1})	Adj. ex-post analysis: Hist. dividend growth ($g_{D,t}$)	Ex-post total return adj.	Risk-free rate (3)	Implied ex-post adj. MRP	Ex-post analysis: Price-div. ratio expansion ($g_{m,t}$)	$g_{D,t}*g_{m,t}$	Ex-post total return	Risk-free rate (3)	Implied ex-post MRP
1989	**1.85%**	9.78%	**11.63%**	7.82%	**3.81%**	13.27%	**17.08%**	9.42%	**7.65%**	3.38%	0.45%	**20.91%**	9.42%	**11.49%**
1990	**-1.42%**	10.81%	**9.38%**	6.24%	**3.14%**	-3.32%	**-0.18%**	10.79%	**-10.97%**	-15.14%	0.50%	**-14.82%**	10.79%	**-25.61%**
1991	**0.32%**	9.39%	**9.72%**	6.29%	**3.43%**	-10.46%	**-7.03%**	8.86%	**-15.89%**	20.44%	-2.14%	**11.28%**	8.86%	**2.42%**
1992	**0.75%**	8.08%	**8.83%**	5.92%	**2.91%**	-8.51%	**-5.60%**	7.58%	**-13.18%**	4.26%	-0.36%	**-1.70%**	7.58%	**-9.28%**
1993	**1.03%**	7.21%	**8.23%**	5.32%	**2.91%**	-4.43%	**-1.51%**	7.05%	**-8.56%**	34.96%	-1.55%	**31.90%**	7.05%	**24.84%**
1994	**0.65%**	8.47%	**9.13%**	6.80%	**2.33%**	3.11%	**5.44%**	7.77%	**-2.33%**	-5.44%	-0.17%	**-0.16%**	7.77%	**-7.93%**
1995	**1.29%**	8.03%	**9.32%**	6.78%	**2.54%**	6.25%	**8.79%**	7.83%	**0.96%**	5.29%	0.33%	**14.40%**	7.83%	**6.58%**
1996	**1.71%**	7.19%	**8.90%**	6.60%	**2.30%**	1.37%	**3.67%**	6.71%	**-3.03%**	24.04%	0.33%	**28.05%**	6.71%	**21.34%**
1997	**1.47%**	6.11%	**7.58%**	5.73%	**1.85%**	1.30%	**3.15%**	6.48%	**-3.33%**	11.59%	0.15%	**14.89%**	6.48%	**8.40%**
1998	**1.70%**	5.27%	**6.98%**	5.37%	**1.61%**	-2.01%	**-0.40%**	5.54%	**-5.94%**	-1.20%	0.02%	**-1.58%**	5.54%	**-7.12%**
1999	**1.67%**	5.58%	**7.25%**	5.55%	**1.70%**	2.37%	**4.07%**	5.81%	**-1.73%**	26.72%	0.63%	**31.42%**	5.81%	**25.62%**
2000	**1.89%**	5.88%	**7.77%**	6.43%	**1.34%**	2.13%	**3.46%**	5.46%	**-1.99%**	3.97%	0.08%	**7.52%**	5.46%	**2.06%**
2001	**2.68%**	5.45%	**8.13%**	6.81%	**1.33%**	5.19%	**6.51%**	5.73%	**0.78%**	-18.18%	-0.94%	**-12.61%**	5.73%	**-18.34%**
2002	**3.24%**	5.28%	**8.52%**	6.87%	**1.64%**	6.70%	**8.35%**	5.08%	**3.27%**	-19.37%	-1.30%	**-12.32%**	5.08%	**-17.40%**
2003	**4.10%**	4.80%	**8.90%**	6.87%	**2.04%**	6.72%	**8.75%**	5.03%	**3.73%**	16.46%	1.11%	**26.32%**	5.03%	**21.30%**
2004	**3.30%**	4.58%	**7.88%**	6.01%	**1.88%**	14.53%	**16.41%**	4.75%	**11.67%**	-1.80%	-0.26%	**14.36%**	4.75%	**9.61%**
2005	**4.32%**	4.06%	**8.38%**	5.95%	**2.43%**	45.27%	**47.69%**	4.32%	**43.37%**	-16.08%	-7.28%	**24.33%**	4.32%	**20.01%**
2006	**4.64%**	4.22%	**8.86%**	6.09%	**2.77%**	39.26%	**42.03%**	4.03%	**38.00%**	-17.77%	-6.98%	**17.29%**	4.03%	**13.26%**
Arith. mean	**1.96%**	6.68%	**8.63%**	6.30%	**2.33%**	6.60%	**8.93%**	6.57%	**2.36%**	3.12%	-0.96%	**11.08%**	6.57%	**4.51%**

(1) Year-average redemption yield of 10-year government bonds.
(2) Implied year-average dividend growth rate assuming ex-post inflation based residual income growth.
(3) Year-end income return of 10-year government bonds.

Note: All values are stated in nominal terms.

Appendix 43 Ex-post total return decomposition for France 1989-2006

Year	Ex-post total return			Price-dividend ratios		Ex-post total return components				Ex-post MRP		
							Price return					
	Dividend yield (D_t/P_{t-1}) (1)	Price return ($[P_t-P_{t-1}]/P_{t-1}$) (2)	Ex-post return (r_t) (3)	Price-dividend ratio (P_{t-1}/D_t) (4)	Price-dividend ratio (P_t/D_t) (5)	Dividend yield (D_t/P_{t-1})	Dividend growth ($g_{D,t}$)	Price-div. ratio expansion ($g_{m,t}$)	$g_{D,t}*g_{m,t}$	Ex-post return	Risk-free rate (6)	Ex-post MRP
1989	3.28%	27.14%	30.42%	30.46x	38.73x	3.28%	21.31%	4.80%	1.02%	30.42%	8.78%	21.64%
1990	3.04%	-24.14%	-21.10%	32.84x	24.91x	3.04%	17.93%	-35.68%	-6.40%	-21.10%	9.32%	-30.42%
1991	4.06%	16.32%	20.38%	24.62x	28.64x	4.06%	1.19%	14.95%	0.18%	20.38%	8.99%	11.40%
1992	3.73%	5.22%	8.95%	26.79x	28.19x	3.73%	6.87%	-1.55%	-0.11%	8.95%	8.25%	0.70%
1993	3.53%	22.09%	25.63%	28.31x	34.57x	3.53%	-0.42%	22.61%	-0.09%	25.63%	6.22%	19.40%
1994	2.63%	-17.06%	-14.44%	38.06x	31.57x	2.63%	-9.18%	-8.68%	0.80%	-14.44%	7.50%	-21.93%
1995	3.38%	-0.49%	2.89%	29.63x	29.48x	3.38%	6.55%	-6.60%	-0.43%	2.89%	7.20%	-4.31%
1996	3.67%	23.71%	27.38%	27.24x	33.69x	3.67%	8.24%	14.29%	1.18%	27.38%	6.20%	21.18%
1997	3.05%	29.50%	32.55%	32.79x	42.46x	3.05%	2.75%	26.03%	0.72%	32.55%	5.43%	27.12%
1998	2.94%	31.47%	34.41%	34.03x	44.74x	2.94%	24.77%	5.37%	1.33%	34.41%	6.21%	28.20%
1999	2.42%	51.12%	53.54%	41.38x	62.54x	2.42%	8.12%	39.77%	3.23%	53.54%	4.49%	49.05%
2000	1.59%	-0.54%	1.06%	62.76x	62.42x	1.59%	-0.35%	-0.19%	0.00%	1.06%	5.30%	-4.24%
2001	1.55%	-21.97%	-20.42%	64.53x	50.35x	1.55%	-3.26%	-19.34%	0.63%	-20.42%	5.86%	-26.27%
2002	2.24%	-33.75%	-31.51%	44.74x	29.64x	2.24%	12.56%	-41.14%	-5.17%	-31.51%	4.57%	-36.09%
2003	3.54%	16.12%	19.66%	28.27x	32.83x	3.54%	4.83%	10.77%	0.52%	19.66%	4.08%	15.58%
2004	3.57%	7.40%	10.96%	28.05x	30.12x	3.57%	17.06%	-8.25%	-1.41%	10.96%	3.90%	7.07%
2005	4.23%	23.40%	27.62%	23.66x	29.20x	4.23%	27.30%	-3.07%	-0.84%	27.62%	3.08%	24.55%
2006	4.46%	17.53%	21.99%	22.44x	26.37x	4.46%	30.12%	-9.68%	-2.92%	21.99%	3.44%	18.54%
Arith. mean	3.16%	9.62%	12.78%	34.48x	36.69x	3.16%	9.80%	0.25%	-0.43%	12.78%	6.05%	6.73%
Geo. mean	3.16%	7.24%	10.39%			3.16%	9.27%	-1.86%		10.39%	6.03%	4.08%
St. Dev.	0.88%	26.50%	26.99%	12.62x	11.70x	0.88%	9.28%	22.01%	2.45%	24.62%	1.70%	24.93%

(1) Implied by lagged IBES CAC 40 dividend yield.
(2) Based on official CAC 40 price return.
(3) Implied ex-post total return by adding lagged IBES CAC 40 dividend yield and official CAC 40 price return. Differs marginally from official CAC 40 ex-post total return.
(4) Calculated as IBES CAC 40 price-dividend ratio divided by one plus official CAC 40 price return.
(5) Based on IBES CAC 40 dividend yield.
(6) Year-end income return of 10-year government bonds.

Note: All values are stated in nominal terms.

Appendix 44 Decomposition-based unconditional expected MRP estimates for France

	Ex-ante analysis					Adj. ex-post analysis				Ex-post analysis				
Year	**Ex-ante MRP**	Risk-free rate (1)	**Implied cost of equity**	Expected dividend growth (2)	**Dividend yield (D_t/P_{t-1})**	Hist. dividend growth ($g_{D,t}$)	**Ex-post total return adj.**	Risk-free rate (3)	**Implied ex-post adj. MRP**	Price-div. ratio expansion ($g_{m,t}$)	$g_{D,t}*g_{m,t}$	**Ex-post total return**	Risk-free rate (3)	**Implied ex-post MRP**
1989	**3.02%**	8.86%	**11.88%**	8.60%	**3.28%**	21.31%	**24.59%**	8.78%	**15.81%**	4.80%	1.02%	**30.42%**	8.78%	**21.64%**
1990	**2.11%**	9.92%	**12.03%**	8.99%	**3.04%**	17.93%	**20.97%**	9.32%	**11.65%**	-35.68%	-6.40%	**-21.10%**	9.32%	**-30.42%**
1991	**3.12%**	8.97%	**12.09%**	8.03%	**4.06%**	1.19%	**5.26%**	8.99%	**-3.73%**	14.95%	0.18%	**20.38%**	8.99%	**11.40%**
1992	**2.88%**	8.59%	**11.47%**	7.74%	**3.73%**	6.87%	**10.61%**	8.25%	**2.35%**	-1.55%	-0.11%	**8.95%**	8.25%	**0.70%**
1993	**1.99%**	6.68%	**8.67%**	5.14%	**3.53%**	-0.42%	**3.11%**	6.22%	**-3.11%**	22.61%	-0.09%	**25.63%**	6.22%	**19.40%**
1994	**0.94%**	7.29%	**8.23%**	5.61%	**2.63%**	-9.18%	**-6.55%**	7.50%	**-14.05%**	-8.68%	0.80%	**-14.44%**	7.50%	**-21.93%**
1995	**2.48%**	7.49%	**9.97%**	6.59%	**3.38%**	6.55%	**9.92%**	7.20%	**2.73%**	-6.60%	-0.43%	**2.89%**	7.20%	**-4.31%**
1996	**2.87%**	6.27%	**9.14%**	5.47%	**3.67%**	8.24%	**11.91%**	6.20%	**5.72%**	14.29%	1.18%	**27.38%**	6.20%	**21.18%**
1997	**2.53%**	5.54%	**8.07%**	5.02%	**3.05%**	2.75%	**5.80%**	5.43%	**0.37%**	26.03%	0.72%	**32.55%**	5.43%	**27.12%**
1998	**3.00%**	4.60%	**7.60%**	4.66%	**2.94%**	24.77%	**27.71%**	6.21%	**21.50%**	5.37%	1.33%	**34.41%**	6.21%	**28.20%**
1999	**2.12%**	4.64%	**6.76%**	4.35%	**2.42%**	8.12%	**10.54%**	4.49%	**6.04%**	39.77%	3.23%	**53.54%**	4.49%	**49.05%**
2000	**0.55%**	5.40%	**5.96%**	4.36%	**1.59%**	-0.35%	**1.24%**	5.30%	**-4.05%**	-0.19%	0.00%	**1.06%**	5.30%	**-4.24%**
2001	**2.21%**	4.94%	**7.15%**	5.60%	**1.55%**	-3.26%	**-1.71%**	5.86%	**-7.57%**	-19.34%	0.63%	**-20.42%**	5.86%	**-26.27%**
2002	**4.40%**	4.84%	**9.23%**	7.00%	**2.24%**	12.56%	**14.79%**	4.57%	**10.22%**	-41.14%	-5.17%	**-31.51%**	4.57%	**-36.09%**
2003	**5.97%**	4.10%	**10.07%**	6.54%	**3.54%**	4.83%	**8.37%**	4.08%	**4.29%**	10.77%	0.52%	**19.66%**	4.08%	**15.58%**
2004	**5.61%**	4.06%	**9.67%**	6.10%	**3.57%**	17.06%	**20.63%**	3.90%	**16.73%**	-8.25%	-1.41%	**10.96%**	3.90%	**7.07%**
2005	**6.36%**	3.36%	**9.72%**	5.49%	**4.23%**	27.30%	**31.53%**	3.08%	**28.45%**	-3.07%	-0.84%	**27.62%**	3.08%	**24.55%**
2006	**5.89%**	3.80%	**9.69%**	5.24%	**4.46%**	30.12%	**34.58%**	3.44%	**31.14%**	-9.68%	-2.92%	**21.99%**	3.44%	**18.54%**
Arith. mean	**3.23%**	6.07%	**9.30%**	6.14%	**3.16%**	9.80%	**12.96%**	6.05%	**6.92%**	0.25%	-0.43%	**12.78%**	6.05%	**6.73%**

(1) Year-average redemption yield of 10-year government bonds.
(2) Implied year-average dividend growth rate assuming ex-post inflation based residual income growth.
(3) Year-end income return of 10-year government bonds.

Note: All values are stated in nominal terms.

Appendix 45 Ex-post total return decomposition for Japan 1989-2006

	Ex-post total return			Price-dividend ratios		Ex-post total return components				Ex-post MRP		
							Price return					
Year	Dividend yield (D_t/P_{t-1}) (1)	Price return ($[P_t-P_{t-1}]/P_{t-1}$) (2)	Ex-post return (r_t) (3)	Price-dividend ratio (P_{t-1}/D_t) (4)	Price-dividend ratio (P_t/D_t) (5)	Dividend yield (D_t/P_{t-1})	Dividend growth ($g_{D,t}$)	Price-div. ratio expansion ($g_{m,t}$)	$g_{D,t}*g_{m,t}$	Ex-post return	Risk-free rate (6)	Ex-post MRP
1989	0.55%	22.25%	22.79%	183.41x	224.22x	0.55%	8.18%	13.00%	1.06%	22.79%	4.92%	17.87%
1990	0.49%	-39.83%	-39.34%	203.66x	122.55x	0.49%	10.09%	-45.34%	-4.58%	-39.34%	5.47%	-44.80%
1991	0.75%	-1.10%	-0.35%	133.40x	131.93x	0.75%	-8.13%	7.65%	-0.62%	-0.35%	6.23%	-6.58%
1992	0.72%	-23.74%	-23.01%	138.32x	105.49x	0.72%	-4.62%	-20.04%	0.93%	-23.01%	5.17%	-28.18%
1993	0.86%	10.07%	10.93%	115.74x	127.39x	0.86%	-8.86%	20.76%	-1.84%	10.93%	4.06%	6.87%
1994	0.81%	8.32%	9.13%	123.42x	133.69x	0.81%	3.22%	4.95%	0.16%	9.13%	4.23%	4.90%
1995	0.77%	1.19%	1.96%	130.54x	132.10x	0.77%	2.41%	-1.19%	-0.03%	1.96%	4.12%	-2.16%
1996	0.73%	-6.77%	-6.04%	137.33x	128.04x	0.73%	-3.81%	-3.07%	0.12%	-6.04%	2.91%	-8.95%
1997	0.81%	-20.12%	-19.31%	123.45x	98.62x	0.81%	3.71%	-22.98%	-0.85%	-19.31%	2.45%	-21.76%
1998	0.95%	-7.49%	-6.54%	105.36x	97.47x	0.95%	-6.40%	-1.17%	0.07%	-6.54%	1.81%	-8.36%
1999	0.97%	58.44%	59.40%	103.47x	163.93x	0.97%	-5.80%	68.20%	-3.96%	59.40%	1.78%	57.62%
2000	0.56%	-25.46%	-24.90%	176.99x	131.93x	0.56%	-7.38%	-19.53%	1.44%	-24.90%	1.86%	-26.76%
2001	0.78%	-19.59%	-18.82%	129.01x	103.73x	0.78%	2.26%	-21.37%	-0.48%	-18.82%	1.39%	-20.21%
2002	0.91%	-18.30%	-17.38%	109.57x	89.53x	0.91%	-5.33%	-13.70%	0.73%	-17.38%	1.25%	-18.64%
2003	1.26%	23.76%	25.02%	79.60x	98.52x	1.26%	12.46%	10.05%	1.25%	25.02%	1.39%	23.63%
2004	1.21%	10.15%	11.36%	82.61x	90.99x	1.21%	19.27%	-7.64%	-1.47%	11.36%	1.57%	9.79%
2005	1.33%	43.50%	44.84%	74.93x	107.53x	1.33%	21.44%	18.17%	3.90%	44.84%	1.50%	43.34%
2006	1.14%	1.90%	3.04%	87.86x	89.53x	1.14%	22.39%	-16.74%	-3.75%	3.04%	1.70%	1.34%
Arith. mean	0.87%	0.95%	1.82%	124.37x	120.95x	0.87%	3.06%	-1.67%	-0.44%	1.82%	2.99%	-1.17%
Geo. mean	0.87%	-1.86%	-1.00%			0.87%	2.58%	-4.32%		-1.00%	2.98%	-4.20%
St. Dev.	0.24%	25.03%	25.18%	35.70x	32.79x	0.24%	10.46%	24.35%	2.11%	25.18%	1.67%	25.63%

(1) Implied by lagged IBES Japan index dividend yield.
(2) Based on official TOPIX price return.
(3) Implied ex-post total return by adding lagged IBES Japan index dividend yield and official TOPIX price return. Differs marginally from official TOPIX ex-post total return.
(4) Calculated as IBES Japan index price-dividend ratio divided by one plus official TOPIX price return.
(5) Based on IBES Japan index dividend yield.
(6) Year-end income return of 10-year government bonds.

Note: All values are stated in nominal terms.

Appendix 46 Decomposition-based unconditional expected MRP estimates for Japan

	Ex-ante analysis					Adj. ex-post analysis				Ex-post analysis				
Year	**Ex-ante MRP**	Risk-free rate (1)	**Implied cost of equity**	Expected dividend growth (2)	**Dividend yield (D_t/P_{t-1})**	Hist. dividend growth ($g_{D,t}$)	**Ex-post total return adj.**	Risk-free rate (3)	**Implied ex-post adj. MRP**	Price-div. ratio expansion ($g_{m,t}$)	$g_{D,t}$*$g_{m,t}$	**Ex-post total return**	Risk-free rate (3)	**Implied ex-post MRP**
1989	**-0.60%**	5.18%	**4.58%**	4.03%	**0.55%**	8.18%	**8.72%**	4.92%	**3.81%**	13.00%	1.06%	**22.79%**	4.92%	**17.87%**
1990	**-1.54%**	6.96%	**5.42%**	4.93%	**0.49%**	10.09%	**10.58%**	5.47%	**5.12%**	-45.34%	-4.58%	**-39.34%**	5.47%	**-44.80%**
1991	**-0.68%**	6.34%	**5.66%**	4.91%	**0.75%**	-8.13%	**-7.38%**	6.23%	**-13.61%**	7.65%	-0.62%	**-0.35%**	6.23%	**-6.58%**
1992	**-0.78%**	5.21%	**4.43%**	3.71%	**0.72%**	-4.62%	**-3.90%**	5.17%	**-9.07%**	-20.04%	0.93%	**-23.01%**	5.17%	**-28.18%**
1993	**-0.65%**	4.12%	**3.47%**	2.60%	**0.86%**	-8.86%	**-7.99%**	4.06%	**-12.06%**	20.76%	-1.84%	**10.93%**	4.06%	**6.87%**
1994	**-1.09%**	4.23%	**3.14%**	2.33%	**0.81%**	3.22%	**4.03%**	4.23%	**-0.20%**	4.95%	0.16%	**9.13%**	4.23%	**4.90%**
1995	**0.21%**	3.32%	**3.53%**	2.77%	**0.77%**	2.41%	**3.18%**	4.12%	**-0.94%**	-1.19%	-0.03%	**1.96%**	4.12%	**-2.16%**
1996	**0.85%**	2.99%	**3.84%**	3.11%	**0.73%**	-3.81%	**-3.08%**	2.91%	**-5.99%**	-3.07%	0.12%	**-6.04%**	2.91%	**-8.95%**
1997	**2.23%**	2.31%	**4.54%**	3.73%	**0.81%**	3.71%	**4.52%**	2.45%	**2.08%**	-22.98%	-0.85%	**-19.31%**	2.45%	**-21.76%**
1998	**2.85%**	1.49%	**4.34%**	3.39%	**0.95%**	-6.40%	**-5.45%**	1.81%	**-7.26%**	-1.17%	0.07%	**-6.54%**	1.81%	**-8.36%**
1999	**1.77%**	1.76%	**3.52%**	2.56%	**0.97%**	-5.80%	**-4.84%**	1.78%	**-6.62%**	68.20%	-3.96%	**59.40%**	1.78%	**57.62%**
2000	**1.55%**	1.76%	**3.31%**	2.74%	**0.56%**	-7.38%	**-6.81%**	1.86%	**-8.67%**	-19.53%	1.44%	**-24.90%**	1.86%	**-26.76%**
2001	**3.53%**	1.31%	**4.84%**	4.06%	**0.78%**	2.26%	**3.03%**	1.39%	**1.64%**	-21.37%	-0.48%	**-18.82%**	1.39%	**-20.21%**
2002	**4.33%**	1.22%	**5.55%**	4.64%	**0.91%**	-5.33%	**-4.42%**	1.25%	**-5.67%**	-13.70%	0.73%	**-17.38%**	1.25%	**-18.64%**
2003	**5.69%**	1.00%	**6.69%**	5.44%	**1.26%**	12.46%	**13.72%**	1.39%	**12.33%**	10.05%	1.25%	**25.02%**	1.39%	**23.63%**
2004	**5.52%**	1.49%	**7.01%**	5.80%	**1.21%**	19.27%	**20.48%**	1.57%	**18.90%**	-7.64%	-1.47%	**11.36%**	1.57%	**9.79%**
2005	**5.62%**	1.35%	**6.97%**	5.64%	**1.33%**	21.44%	**22.77%**	1.50%	**21.27%**	18.17%	3.90%	**44.84%**	1.50%	**43.34%**
2006	**4.43%**	1.73%	**6.17%**	5.03%	**1.14%**	22.39%	**23.53%**	1.70%	**21.83%**	-16.74%	-3.75%	**3.04%**	1.70%	**1.34%**
Arith. mean	**1.85%**	2.99%	**4.83%**	3.97%	**0.87%**	3.06%	**3.93%**	2.99%	**0.94%**	-1.67%	-0.44%	**1.82%**	2.99%	**-1.17%**

(1) Year-average redemption yield of 10-year government bonds.
(2) Implied year-average dividend growth rate assuming ex-post inflation based residual income growth.
(3) Year-end income return of 10-year government bonds.

Note: All values are stated in nominal terms.

Appendix 47 Ex-post total return decomposition for the UK 1989-2006

	Ex-post total return			Price-dividend ratios		Ex-post total return components				Ex-post MRP		
							Price return					
Year	Dividend yield (D_t/P_{t-1}) (1)	Price return ($[P_t-P_{t-1}]/P_{t-1}$) (2)	Ex-post return (r_t) (3)	Price-dividend ratio (P_{t-1}/D_t) (4)	Price-dividend ratio (P_t/D_t) (5)	Dividend yield (D_t/P_{t-1})	Dividend growth ($g_{D,t}$)	Price-div. ratio expansion ($g_{m,t}$)	$g_{D,t}*g_{m,t}$	Ex-post return	Risk-free rate (6)	Ex-post MRP
1989	5.45%	30.01%	35.46%	18.36x	23.87x	5.45%	16.15%	11.93%	1.93%	35.46%	9.76%	25.70%
1990	4.68%	-14.31%	-9.64%	21.37x	18.32x	4.68%	11.66%	-23.26%	-2.71%	-9.64%	10.61%	-20.25%
1991	5.67%	15.06%	20.73%	17.63x	20.28x	5.67%	3.89%	10.75%	0.42%	20.73%	9.74%	10.99%
1992	4.95%	14.83%	19.78%	20.21x	23.20x	4.95%	0.39%	14.39%	0.06%	19.78%	8.88%	10.89%
1993	4.27%	23.35%	27.61%	23.43x	28.90x	4.27%	-0.98%	24.57%	-0.24%	27.61%	7.05%	20.56%
1994	3.64%	-9.55%	-5.92%	27.50x	24.88x	3.64%	5.08%	-13.93%	-0.71%	-5.92%	7.74%	-13.66%
1995	4.53%	18.51%	23.04%	22.09x	26.18x	4.53%	12.62%	5.24%	0.66%	23.04%	7.91%	15.13%
1996	4.20%	11.68%	15.88%	23.81x	26.60x	4.20%	9.92%	1.60%	0.16%	15.88%	7.51%	8.37%
1997	3.87%	19.73%	23.60%	25.86x	30.96x	3.87%	2.86%	16.41%	0.47%	23.60%	6.78%	16.82%
1998	2.77%	10.91%	13.68%	36.07x	40.00x	2.77%	-14.16%	29.20%	-4.13%	13.68%	6.59%	7.09%
1999	2.57%	21.25%	23.82%	38.90x	47.17x	2.57%	2.82%	17.92%	0.51%	23.82%	5.64%	18.18%
2000	2.05%	-7.97%	-5.91%	48.72x	44.84x	2.05%	-3.19%	-4.93%	0.16%	-5.91%	5.41%	-11.33%
2001	2.22%	-15.41%	-13.19%	44.95x	38.02x	2.22%	-0.24%	-15.21%	0.04%	-13.19%	5.02%	-18.21%
2002	2.66%	-24.97%	-22.30%	37.54x	28.17x	2.66%	1.28%	-25.92%	-0.33%	-22.30%	4.78%	-27.08%
2003	3.61%	16.56%	20.18%	27.67x	32.26x	3.61%	1.79%	14.52%	0.26%	20.18%	4.92%	15.26%
2004	3.33%	9.21%	12.54%	30.02x	32.79x	3.33%	7.45%	1.64%	0.12%	12.54%	4.84%	7.70%
2005	3.48%	18.10%	21.58%	28.70x	33.90x	3.48%	14.22%	3.39%	0.48%	21.58%	4.52%	17.06%
2006	3.24%	13.15%	16.39%	30.90x	34.97x	3.24%	9.70%	3.15%	0.31%	16.39%	4.24%	12.15%
Arith. mean	3.73%	8.34%	12.07%	29.10x	30.85x	3.73%	4.51%	3.97%	-0.14%	12.07%	6.77%	5.30%
Geo. mean	3.73%	7.17%	10.87%			3.73%	4.26%	2.79%		10.87%	6.76%	4.05%
St. Dev.	1.06%	15.64%	16.17%	8.97x	8.01x	1.06%	7.33%	15.63%	1.33%	16.17%	2.01%	15.91%

(1) Implied by lagged direct FTSE All-Share dividend yield.
(2) Based on official FTSE All-Share price return.
(3) Implied ex-post total return by adding lagged direct dividend yield and official FTSE All-Share price return. Differs marginally from official FTSE All-Share ex-post total return.
(4) Calculated as direct FTSE All-Share price-dividend ratio divided by one plus official FTSE All-Share price return.
(5) Based on direct FTSE All-Share dividend yield.
(6) Year-end income return of 10-year government bonds.

Note: All values are stated in nominal terms.

Appendix 48 Decomposition-based unconditional expected MRP estimates for the UK

	Ex-ante analysis					Adj. ex-post analysis				Ex-post analysis				
Year	**Ex-ante MRP**	Risk-free rate (1)	**Implied cost of equity**	Expected dividend growth (2)	**Dividend yield (D_t/P_{t-1})**	Hist. dividend growth ($g_{D,t}$)	**Ex-post total return adj.**	Risk-free rate (3)	**Implied ex-post adj. MRP**	Price-div. ratio expansion ($g_{m,t}$)	$g_{D,t}*g_{m,t}$	**Ex-post total return**	Risk-free rate (3)	**Implied ex-post MRP**
1989	**2.66%**	10.13%	**12.79%**	7.34%	**5.45%**	16.15%	**21.60%**	9.76%	**11.84%**	11.93%	1.93%	**35.46%**	9.76%	**25.70%**
1990	**0.59%**	11.57%	**12.16%**	7.49%	**4.68%**	11.66%	**16.34%**	10.61%	**5.72%**	-23.26%	-2.71%	**-9.64%**	10.61%	**-20.25%**
1991	**2.87%**	10.05%	**12.93%**	7.25%	**5.67%**	3.89%	**9.56%**	9.74%	**-0.18%**	10.75%	0.42%	**20.73%**	9.74%	**10.99%**
1992	**2.20%**	9.07%	**11.27%**	6.32%	**4.95%**	0.39%	**5.33%**	8.88%	**-3.55%**	14.39%	0.06%	**19.78%**	8.88%	**10.89%**
1993	**2.05%**	7.34%	**9.39%**	5.12%	**4.27%**	-0.98%	**3.29%**	7.05%	**-3.76%**	24.57%	-0.24%	**27.61%**	7.05%	**20.56%**
1994	**0.72%**	8.14%	**8.85%**	5.22%	**3.64%**	5.08%	**8.72%**	7.74%	**0.98%**	-13.93%	-0.71%	**-5.92%**	7.74%	**-13.66%**
1995	**1.90%**	8.15%	**10.05%**	5.53%	**4.53%**	12.62%	**17.14%**	7.91%	**9.23%**	5.24%	0.66%	**23.04%**	7.91%	**15.13%**
1996	**1.73%**	7.80%	**9.53%**	5.34%	**4.20%**	9.92%	**14.12%**	7.51%	**6.62%**	1.60%	0.16%	**15.88%**	7.51%	**8.37%**
1997	**1.82%**	6.98%	**8.80%**	4.93%	**3.87%**	2.86%	**6.72%**	6.78%	**-0.05%**	16.41%	0.47%	**23.60%**	6.78%	**16.82%**
1998	**1.61%**	5.45%	**7.07%**	4.29%	**2.77%**	-14.16%	**-11.39%**	6.59%	**-17.97%**	29.20%	-4.13%	**13.68%**	6.59%	**7.09%**
1999	**1.57%**	5.01%	**6.58%**	4.01%	**2.57%**	2.82%	**5.39%**	5.64%	**-0.25%**	17.92%	0.51%	**23.82%**	5.64%	**18.18%**
2000	**0.75%**	5.22%	**5.96%**	3.91%	**2.05%**	-3.19%	**-1.14%**	5.41%	**-6.55%**	-4.93%	0.16%	**-5.91%**	5.41%	**-11.33%**
2001	**2.03%**	4.93%	**6.96%**	4.74%	**2.22%**	-0.24%	**1.98%**	5.02%	**-3.04%**	-15.21%	0.04%	**-13.19%**	5.02%	**-18.21%**
2002	**3.28%**	4.84%	**8.12%**	5.46%	**2.66%**	1.28%	**3.94%**	4.78%	**-0.84%**	-25.92%	-0.33%	**-22.30%**	4.78%	**-27.08%**
2003	**4.52%**	4.48%	**9.00%**	5.39%	**3.61%**	1.79%	**5.40%**	4.92%	**0.49%**	14.52%	0.26%	**20.18%**	4.92%	**15.26%**
2004	**3.86%**	4.86%	**8.72%**	5.39%	**3.33%**	7.45%	**10.78%**	4.84%	**5.94%**	1.64%	0.12%	**12.54%**	4.84%	**7.70%**
2005	**4.30%**	4.37%	**8.67%**	5.19%	**3.48%**	14.22%	**17.71%**	4.52%	**13.19%**	3.39%	0.48%	**21.58%**	4.52%	**17.06%**
2006	**4.01%**	4.50%	**8.51%**	5.27%	**3.24%**	9.70%	**12.93%**	4.24%	**8.69%**	3.15%	0.31%	**16.39%**	4.24%	**12.15%**
Arith. mean	**2.36%**	6.83%	**9.19%**	5.45%	**3.73%**	4.51%	**8.25%**	6.77%	**1.47%**	3.97%	-0.14%	**12.07%**	6.77%	**5.30%**

(1) Year-average redemption yield of 10-year government bonds.
(2) Implied year-average dividend growth rate assuming ex-post inflation based residual income growth.
(3) Year-end income return of 10-year government bonds.

Note: All values are stated in nominal terms.

Appendix 49 Ex-post total return decomposition for the US 1989-2006

	Ex-post total return			Price-dividend ratios		Ex-post total return components				Ex-post MRP		
								Price return				
Year	Dividend yield (D_t/P_{t-1}) (1)	Price return ($[P_t-P_{t-1}]/P_{t-1}$) (2)	Ex-post return (r_t) (3)	Price-dividend ratio (P_{t-1}/D_t) (4)	Price-dividend ratio (P_t/D_t) (5)	Dividend yield (D_t/P_{t-1})	Dividend growth ($g_{D,t}$)	Price-div. ratio expansion ($g_{m,t}$)	$g_{D,t}*g_{m,t}$	Ex-post return	Risk-free rate (6)	Ex-post MRP
1989	3.84%	25.23%	29.08%	26.02x	32.58x	3.84%	11.66%	12.15%	1.42%	29.08%	7.90%	21.17%
1990	3.26%	-8.36%	-5.11%	30.69x	28.12x	3.26%	6.18%	-13.70%	-0.85%	-5.11%	8.26%	-13.37%
1991	3.77%	29.54%	33.30%	26.54x	34.38x	3.77%	5.97%	22.24%	1.33%	33.30%	7.09%	26.21%
1992	2.81%	6.54%	9.35%	35.57x	37.89x	2.81%	-3.35%	10.23%	-0.34%	9.35%	6.52%	2.83%
1993	2.71%	8.06%	10.77%	36.96x	39.94x	2.71%	2.53%	5.39%	0.14%	10.77%	5.77%	5.00%
1994	2.66%	-2.43%	0.23%	37.61x	36.70x	2.66%	6.18%	-8.11%	-0.50%	0.23%	7.85%	-7.62%
1995	2.86%	33.56%	36.42%	34.95x	46.69x	2.86%	4.99%	27.22%	1.36%	36.42%	5.75%	30.68%
1996	2.35%	19.34%	21.69%	42.62x	50.86x	2.35%	9.53%	8.95%	0.85%	21.69%	6.46%	15.22%
1997	2.08%	29.58%	31.66%	48.11x	62.34x	2.08%	5.72%	22.57%	1.29%	31.66%	5.96%	25.70%
1998	1.79%	22.34%	24.13%	55.91x	68.40x	1.79%	11.51%	9.71%	1.12%	24.13%	4.71%	19.41%
1999	1.54%	19.36%	20.91%	64.79x	77.34x	1.54%	5.57%	13.07%	0.73%	20.91%	6.19%	14.72%
2000	1.18%	-8.53%	-7.35%	84.42x	77.22x	1.18%	-8.39%	-0.15%	0.01%	-7.35%	5.48%	-12.83%
2001	1.36%	-12.63%	-11.27%	73.47x	64.18x	1.36%	5.11%	-16.88%	-0.86%	-11.27%	5.02%	-16.29%
2002	1.53%	-22.81%	-21.28%	65.30x	50.40x	1.53%	-1.71%	-21.47%	0.37%	-21.28%	3.95%	-25.22%
2003	2.29%	28.74%	31.03%	43.59x	56.12x	2.29%	15.63%	11.34%	1.77%	31.03%	4.26%	26.78%
2004	2.00%	10.08%	12.07%	50.11x	55.16x	2.00%	11.99%	-1.71%	-0.21%	12.07%	4.24%	7.83%
2005	1.98%	4.28%	6.25%	50.63x	52.80x	1.98%	8.94%	-4.28%	-0.38%	6.25%	4.46%	1.79%
2006	2.14%	13.66%	15.80%	46.75x	53.13x	2.14%	12.94%	0.64%	0.08%	15.80%	4.66%	11.15%
Arith. mean	2.34%	10.86%	13.20%	47.45x	51.35x	2.34%	6.17%	4.29%	0.41%	13.20%	5.81%	7.40%
Geo. mean	2.34%	9.61%	11.93%			2.34%	6.00%	3.41%		11.93%	5.80%	6.08%
St. Dev.	0.77%	16.63%	16.97%	16.22x	14.74x	0.77%	6.08%	13.70%	0.84%	16.97%	1.35%	16.84%

(1) Implied by lagged IBES USA index dividend yield.
(2) Based on official Russell 3000 price return.
(3) Implied ex-post total return by adding lagged IBES USA index dividend yield and official Russell 3000 price return. Differs marginally from official Russell 3000 ex-post total return.
(4) Calculated as IBES USA index price-dividend ratio divided by one plus official Russell 3000 price return.
(5) Based on IBES USA index dividend yield.
(6) Year-end income return of 10-year government bonds.

Note: All values are stated in nominal terms.

Appendix 50 Decomposition-based unconditional expected MRP estimates for the US

	Ex-ante analysis					Adj. ex-post analysis				Ex-post analysis				
Year	**Ex-ante MRP**	Risk-free rate (1)	**Implied cost of equity**	Expected dividend growth (2)	**Dividend yield (D_t/P_{t-1})**	Hist. dividend growth ($g_{D,t}$)	**Ex-post total return adj.**	Risk-free rate (3)	**Implied ex-post adj. MRP**	Price-div. ratio expansion ($g_{m,t}$)	$g_{D,t}$*$g_{m,t}$	**Ex-post total return**	Risk-free rate (3)	**Implied ex-post MRP**
1989	**3.27%**	8.45%	**11.72%**	7.88%	**3.84%**	11.66%	**15.51%**	7.90%	**7.60%**	12.15%	1.42%	**29.08%**	7.90%	**21.17%**
1990	**2.66%**	8.56%	**11.22%**	7.96%	**3.26%**	6.18%	**9.44%**	8.26%	**1.17%**	-13.70%	-0.85%	**-5.11%**	8.26%	**-13.37%**
1991	**2.68%**	7.79%	**10.47%**	6.71%	**3.77%**	5.97%	**9.74%**	7.09%	**2.64%**	22.24%	1.33%	**33.30%**	7.09%	**26.21%**
1992	**1.79%**	7.02%	**8.81%**	6.00%	**2.81%**	-3.35%	**-0.54%**	6.52%	**-7.06%**	10.23%	-0.34%	**9.35%**	6.52%	**2.83%**
1993	**2.95%**	5.84%	**8.79%**	6.09%	**2.71%**	2.53%	**5.24%**	5.77%	**-0.53%**	5.39%	0.14%	**10.77%**	5.77%	**5.00%**
1994	**2.07%**	7.13%	**9.20%**	6.55%	**2.66%**	6.18%	**8.84%**	7.85%	**0.99%**	-8.11%	-0.50%	**0.23%**	7.85%	**-7.62%**
1995	**3.22%**	6.49%	**9.70%**	6.84%	**2.86%**	4.99%	**7.85%**	5.75%	**2.10%**	27.22%	1.36%	**36.42%**	5.75%	**30.68%**
1996	**2.64%**	6.46%	**9.09%**	6.75%	**2.35%**	9.53%	**11.88%**	6.46%	**5.42%**	8.95%	0.85%	**21.69%**	6.46%	**15.22%**
1997	**1.86%**	6.32%	**8.18%**	6.10%	**2.08%**	5.72%	**7.80%**	5.96%	**1.84%**	22.57%	1.29%	**31.66%**	5.96%	**25.70%**
1998	**2.03%**	5.21%	**7.24%**	5.46%	**1.79%**	11.51%	**13.29%**	4.71%	**8.58%**	9.71%	1.12%	**24.13%**	4.71%	**19.41%**
1999	**1.08%**	5.71%	**6.79%**	5.24%	**1.54%**	5.57%	**7.11%**	6.19%	**0.92%**	13.07%	0.73%	**20.91%**	6.19%	**14.72%**
2000	**1.02%**	5.98%	**7.00%**	5.82%	**1.18%**	-8.39%	**-7.20%**	5.48%	**-12.69%**	-0.15%	0.01%	**-7.35%**	5.48%	**-12.83%**
2001	**2.34%**	4.99%	**7.33%**	5.97%	**1.36%**	5.11%	**6.47%**	5.02%	**1.45%**	-16.88%	-0.86%	**-11.27%**	5.02%	**-16.29%**
2002	**2.81%**	4.54%	**7.35%**	5.82%	**1.53%**	-1.71%	**-0.17%**	3.95%	**-4.12%**	-21.47%	0.37%	**-21.28%**	3.95%	**-25.22%**
2003	**4.44%**	3.99%	**8.43%**	6.13%	**2.29%**	15.63%	**17.92%**	4.26%	**13.67%**	11.34%	1.77%	**31.03%**	4.26%	**26.78%**
2004	**3.94%**	4.25%	**8.19%**	6.20%	**2.00%**	11.99%	**13.99%**	4.24%	**9.75%**	-1.71%	-0.21%	**12.07%**	4.24%	**7.83%**
2005	**4.35%**	4.27%	**8.63%**	6.65%	**1.98%**	8.94%	**10.91%**	4.46%	**6.45%**	-4.28%	-0.38%	**6.25%**	4.46%	**1.79%**
2006	**4.13%**	4.78%	**8.91%**	6.77%	**2.14%**	12.94%	**15.08%**	4.66%	**10.43%**	0.64%	0.08%	**15.80%**	4.66%	**11.15%**
Arith. mean	**2.74%**	5.99%	**8.73%**	6.39%	**2.34%**	6.17%	**8.51%**	5.81%	**2.70%**	4.29%	0.41%	**13.20%**	5.81%	**7.40%**

(1) Year-average redemption yield of 10-year government bonds.
(2) Implied year-average dividend growth rate assuming ex-post inflation based residual income growth.
(3) Year-end income return of 10-year government bonds.

Note: All values are stated in nominal terms.

Deutsche Zusammenfassung

Die vorliegende Arbeit beschäftigt sich sowohl aus konzeptioneller als auch aus empirischer Sicht mit der Schätzung der erwarteten Marktrisikoprämie für die Unternehmensbewertung. Ein besonderer Fokus liegt auf der Analyse der Preisniveauabhängigkeit von erwarteten Marktrisikoprämien. Für die empirische Schätzung in Deutschland sowie in fünf weiteren Ländern (Frankreich, Großbritannien, Japan, Kanada und USA) von 1989 bis 2006 werden drei verschiedene Methoden angewendet, die auf unterschiedlichen Annahmengerüsten hinsichtlich der stochastischen Eigenschaften von Renditen bzw. Prämien beruhen.

Erstens werden Durchschnitte historischer Beobachtungen unter der Annahme unabhängiger und identisch verteilter Marktrisikoprämien ermittelt und Probleme historischer Durchschnitte wie die Unabhängigkeit vom aktuellen Preisniveau und die Verzerrung durch Schätzfehler bei unsicheren Verteilungsparametern diskutiert.

Zweitens werden stichtagsbezogene erwartete Marktrisikoprämien aus dem internen Zinsfuß abgeleitet, der zu einer Identität von aktueller Marktkapitalisierung und dem Barwert aggregierter Markt-Cash-Flow-Ströme führt. Hierzu wird primär das Residualeinkommensmodell angewendet, wobei die erforderlichen Parameter auf Prognosen von Analysten und einer Endwertannahme beruhen. Ferner werden unabhängige und identisch verteilte Renditen unterstellt, sodass der interne Zinsfuß der erwarteten Rendite entspricht. Die Arbeit beschäftigt sich in diesem Abschnitt auch mit der exakten Berücksichtigung von Dividendenzahltag und unterjährigen Dividenden, der korrekten Aggregations- bzw. Gewichtungsmethode, der Identität des Residualeinkommensmodells mit weiteren Bewertungsmodellen wie dem Dividendendiskontierungs- und Gewinnkapitalisierungsmodell sowie dem Einfluss verschiedener Endwertannahmen auf Basis der ewigen Rente und Multiplikatoren. Die stichtagsbezogenen Prämienschätzungen variieren über die Zeit und weisen eine signifikante Korrelation mit dem Preisniveau am Kapitalmarkt auf. Besonders deutliche Schwankungen sind während der aktuellen Finanzkrise zu beobachten. So zeigt eine erweiterte Analyse für den deutschen Markt, dass die aus dem internen Zinsfuß abgeleitete erwartete Marktrisikoprämie von Januar 2007 bis September 2009 zwischen einem Minimalwert von 4,5% und einem Maximalwert von 9,5% verlief.

Drittens wird eine Renditezerlegungsmethode angewendet, die zum einen eine Isolierung des Preisniveaueinflusses auf historische Durchschnittsprämien erlaubt und zum anderen mittels eines Konvergenzmodells für den Preis-Dividenden-Multiplikator eine zeitvariable Schätzung der erwarteten Marktrisikoprämie ermöglicht. Die Analysen zeigen einen teils substantiellen Einfluss des Preisniveaus auf historische Prämien. Die Präzision des Konvergenzmodells zur Schätzung zeitvariabler erwarteter Marktrisikoprämien erscheint fraglich, da für verschiedene Perioden negative Prämien resultieren.

Die vorliegende Arbeit verdeutlicht durch die Abhängigkeit der erwarteten Marktrisikoprämie vom Preisniveau am Kapitalmarkt die Notwendigkeit zur Verwendung stichtagsbezogener erwarteter Marktrisikoprämien bei der Bestimmung von Eigenkapitalkosten für die Unternehmensbewertung ähnlich dem derzeitigen Vorgehen zur Bestimmung des Basiszinssatzes.

Schriften zur quantitativen Wirtschaftswissenschaft

Herausgegeben von Gunter Löffler, Frank Richter und Paul Wentges

Band 1 Tobias Eichner: Restructuring and Turnaround of Distressed Manusfacturing Firms. An International Empirical Study. 2010.

Band 2 Christina Wargitsch: Management Control in Familienunternehmen. 2010.

Band 3 Fabian Stich: Listed Private Equity: Performance, Einflussfaktoren und Portfolioeffekte. Eine empirische Analyse. 2011.

Band 4 Hannes Gsell: Estimation of the Expected Market Risk Premium for Corporate Valuations. Methodologies and Empirical Evidence for Equity Markets in Key Countries. 2011.

www.peterlang.de

Bernhard Christian Kübler

Risk Classification by Means of Clustering

Frankfurt am Main, Berlin, Bern, Bruxelles, New York, Oxford, Wien, 2010.
IV, 195 pp., num tab. and graph.
Schriften zum Controlling, Finanz- und Risikomanagement.
Editor in charge: Andreas Brieden. Vol. 4
ISBN 978-3-631-59759-0 · hardback € 44,80*

Determining risk-adequate insurance premiums is a core issue in actuarial mathematics. This study is specifically concerned with identifying convenient partitions of (general) insurance collectives such that the resulting tariff classes are homogeneous to a maximum extent and – on the other hand – yet large enough to allow for the occurrence of the group balance concept and to end up with reliable estimates of the moments of the claim size distributions. Therefore, the author develops an innovative classification algorithm utilizing a multidimensional cluster approach combined with credibility-theoretical implications. Its construction stems from involving the entire claim information of risks simultaneously and in a suitable manner, and particulary from obtaining optimality regarding the cluster criterions. Under certain conditions, commonly used cross classification schemes are shown to be a particular case of the new approach. Besides desirable theoretical benefits like its generalizing established cross classification systems, an empirical investigation also suggests the practical superiority of the new algorithm.

Content: Application of Cluster Analysis in Actuarial Mathematics · Cross Classification Systems · Development of a New Classification System in order to Partition Insurance Collectives · Empirical Investigation: Comparison of the New Classification Algorithm and Cross Classification